THE ART OF
URBAN
SKETCHING

GABRIEL CAMPANARIO

Drawing on location around the world

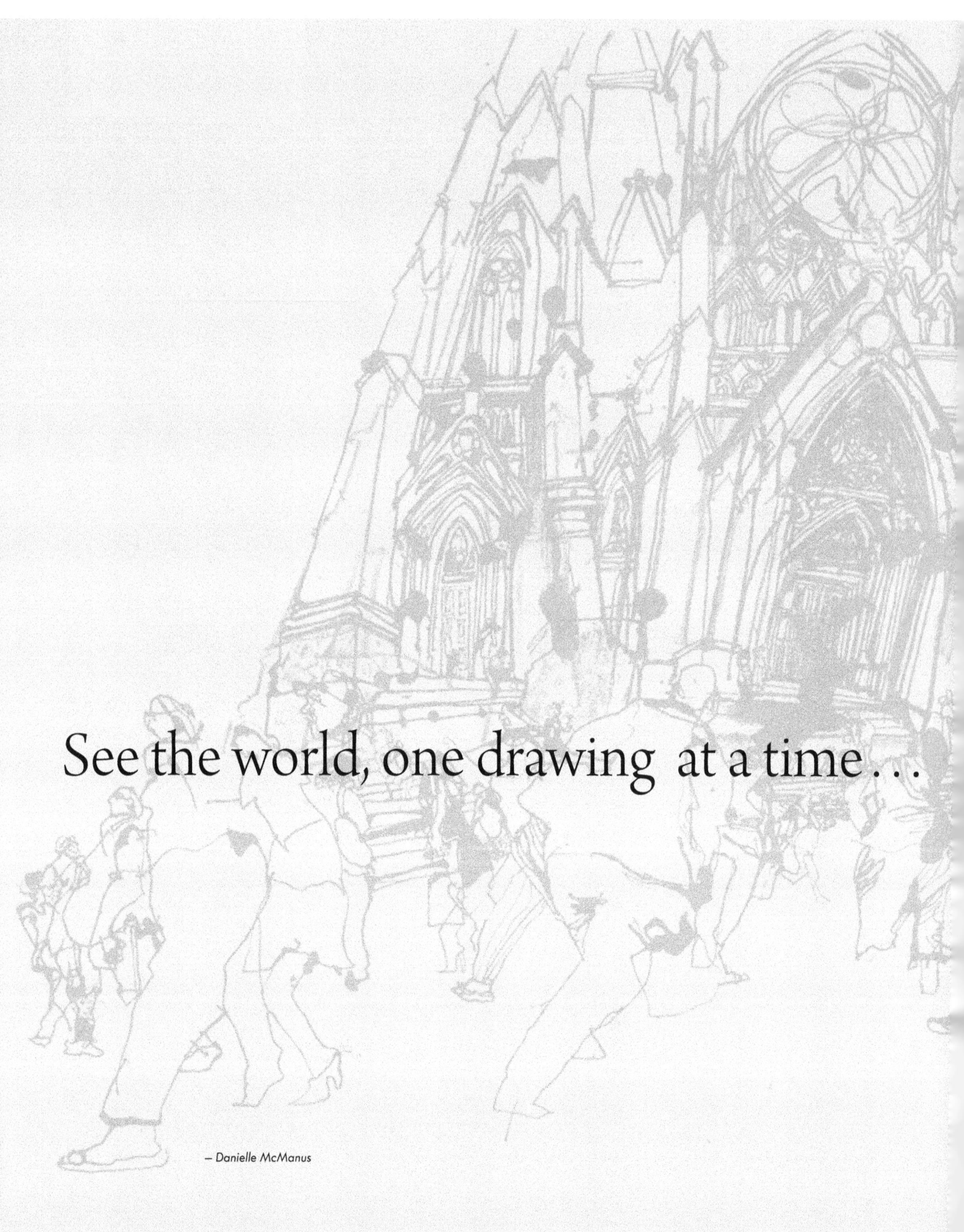

See the world, one drawing at a time . . .

— Danielle McManus

THE ART OF
URBAN
GABRIEL CAMPANARIO
SKETCHING

Drawing on location around the world

QUARRY

Inspiring | Educating | Creating | Entertaining

Brimming with creative inspiration, how-to projects, and useful information to enrich your everyday life, Quarto Knows is a favorite destination for those pursuing their interests and passions. Visit our site and dig deeper with our books into your area of interest: Quarto Creates, Quarto Cooks, Quarto Homes, Quarto Lives, Quarto Drives, Quarto Explores, Quarto Gifts, or Quarto Kids.

First published in 2012 by Quarry Books,
an imprint of The Quarto Group,
100 Cummings Center, Suite 265-D,
Beverly, MA 01915, USA.
T (978) 282-9590 F (978) 283-2742
QuartoKnows.com

Quarry Books titles are also available at discount for retail, wholesale, promotional, and bulk purchase. For details, contact the Special Sales Manager by email at specialsales@quarto.com or by mail at The Quarto Group, Attn: Special Sales Manager, 100 Cummings Center, Suite 265-D, Beverly, MA 01915, USA.

ISBN: 978-1-59253-725-9

Digital edition published in 2012
eISBN: 978-16105-896-7

Library of Congress Cataloging-in-Publication Data available
Campanario, Gabriel.
The art of urban sketching : drawing on location around the world / Gabriel Campanario.
    p. cm.
ISBN-13: 978-1-59253-725-9
ISBN-10: 1-59253-725-1
ISBN-10: (invalid) 978161058967 (digital ed.)
1. Cities and towns in art. 2. City and town life in art. 3. Drawing–Technique. I. Title. II. Title: Drawing on location around the world.
NC825.C57C36 2012
704.9'44–dc23

2011040889

Design: www.studioink.co.uk
Cover illustrations: Ch'ng Kiah Kiean, (front, top);
Paul Heaston, (front, bottom); Jana Bouc, (spine);
Walt Taylor, (back, top); Nathalie Ramírez, (back, bottom)

Map on pages 7–9 by Martin von Wyss, vW Maps

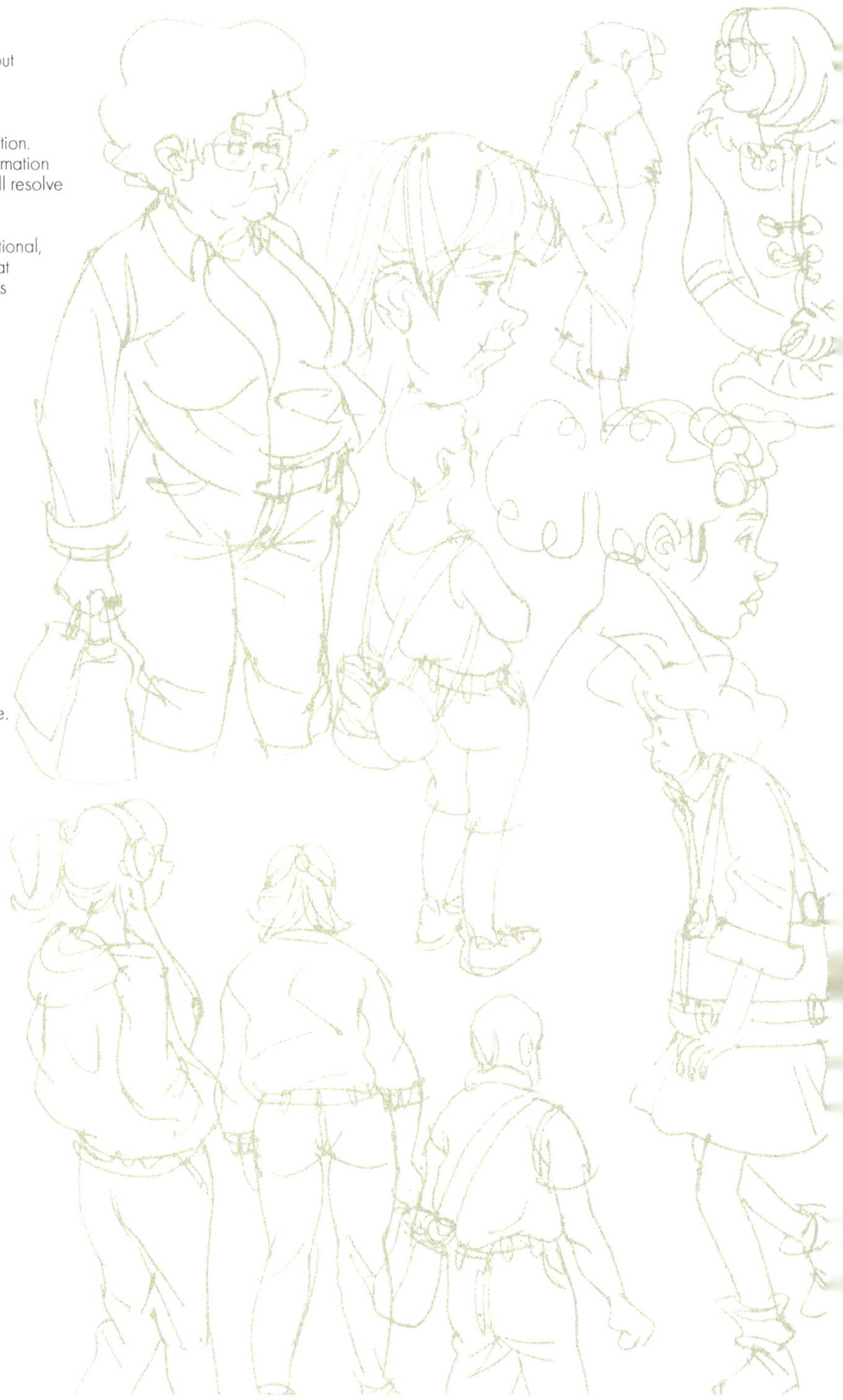

To my family, Michelle, Alex, and Olivia, and to all my fellow urban sketchers

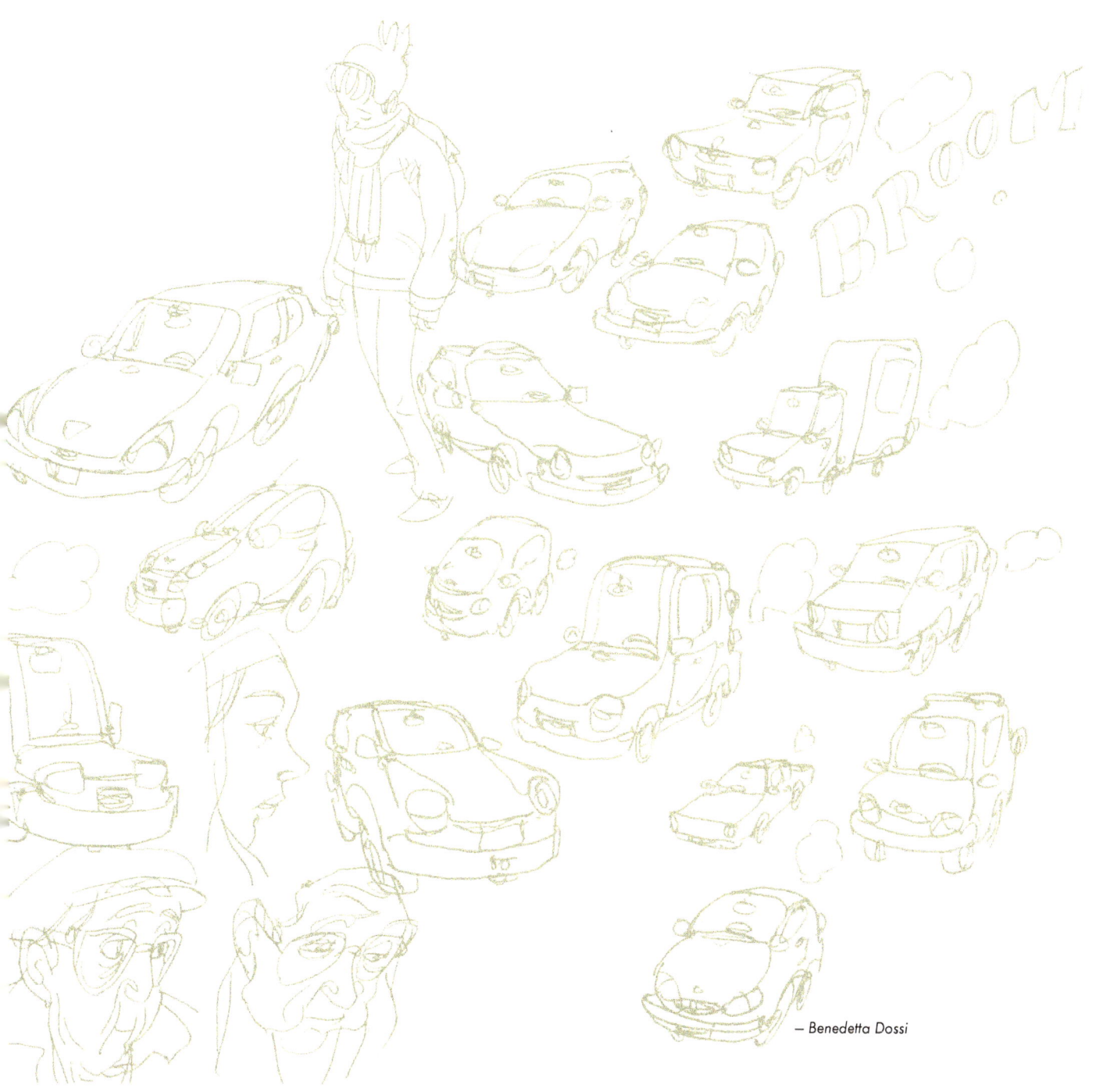

— *Benedetta Dossi*

CONTENTS

SECTION I: BECOMING AN URBAN SKETCHER

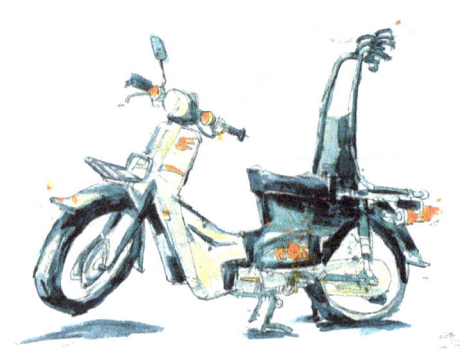

— Lok Jansen

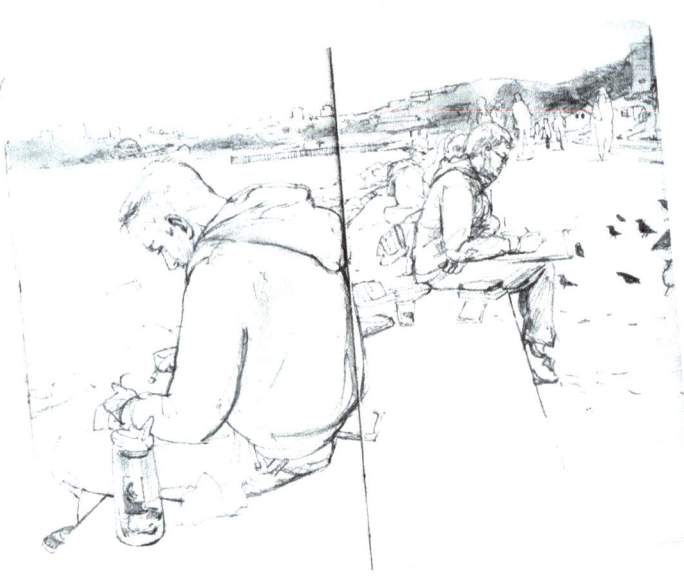

— Gary Amaro

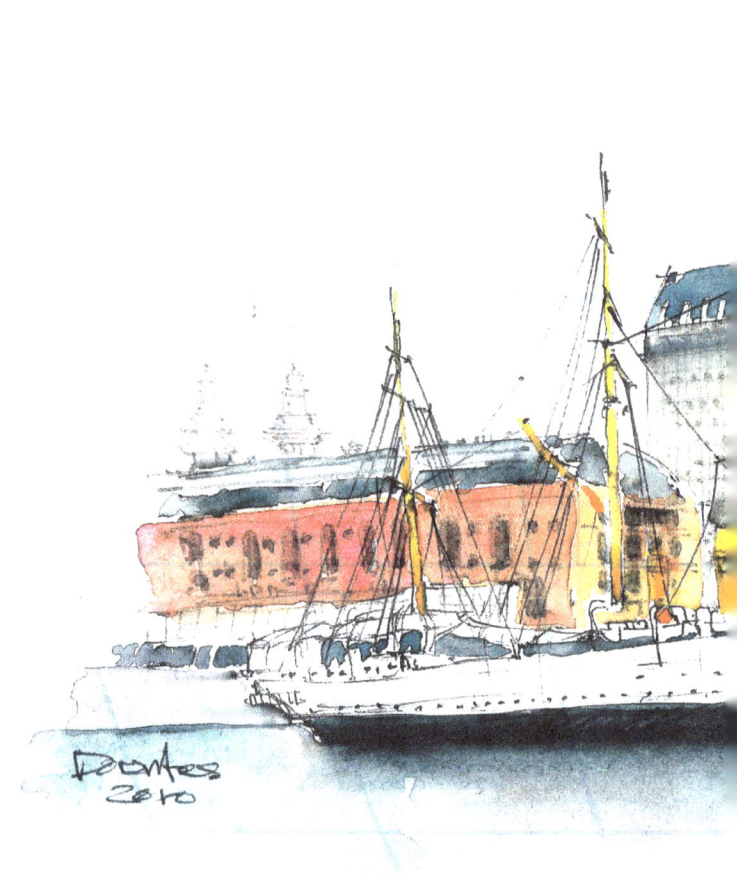

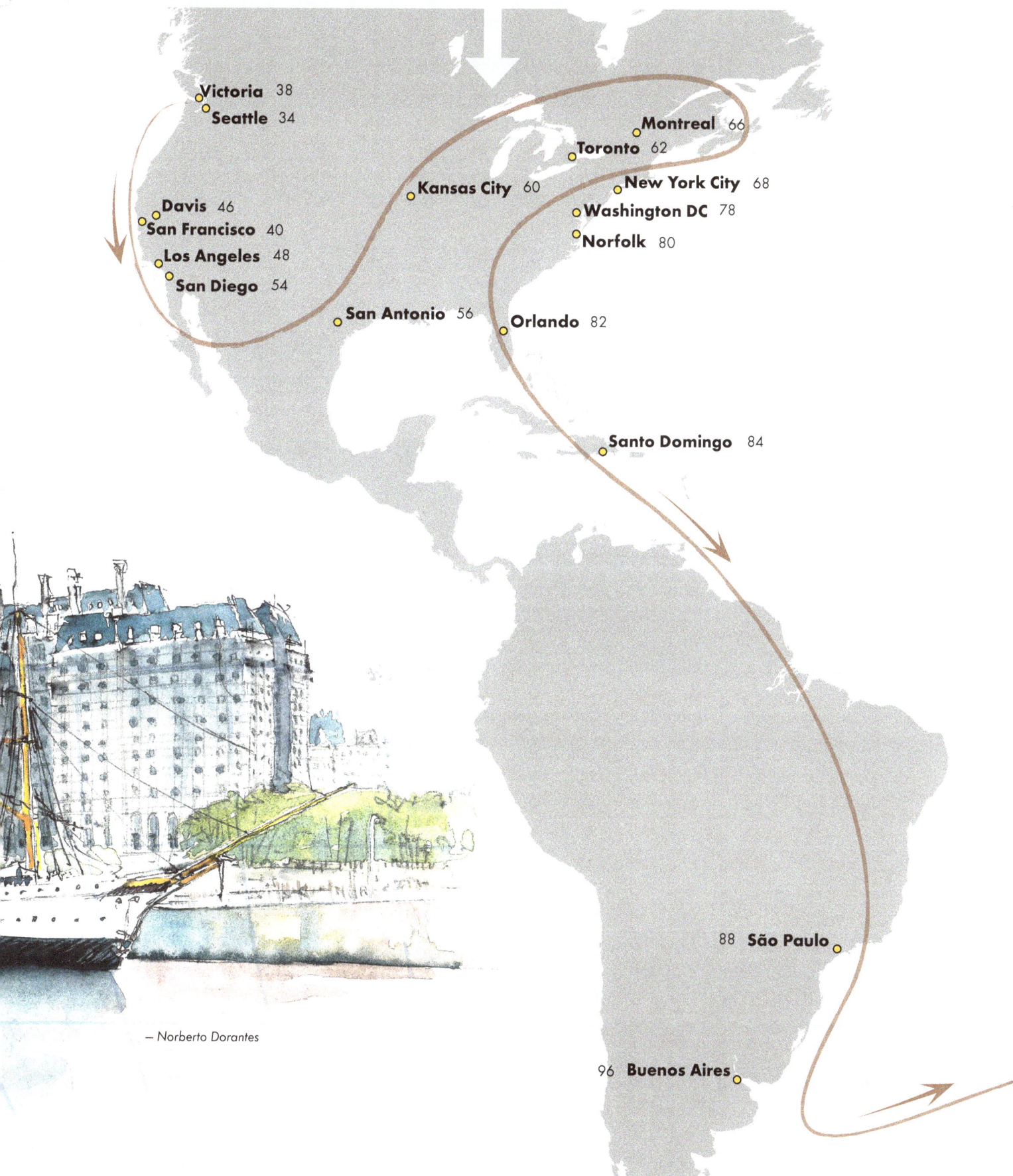

Victoria 38
Seattle 34
Montreal 66
Toronto 62
Kansas City 60
New York City 68
Washington DC 78
Norfolk 80
Davis 46
San Francisco 40
Los Angeles 48
San Diego 54
San Antonio 56
Orlando 82
Santo Domingo 84
88 São Paulo
96 Buenos Aires

— Norberto Dorantes

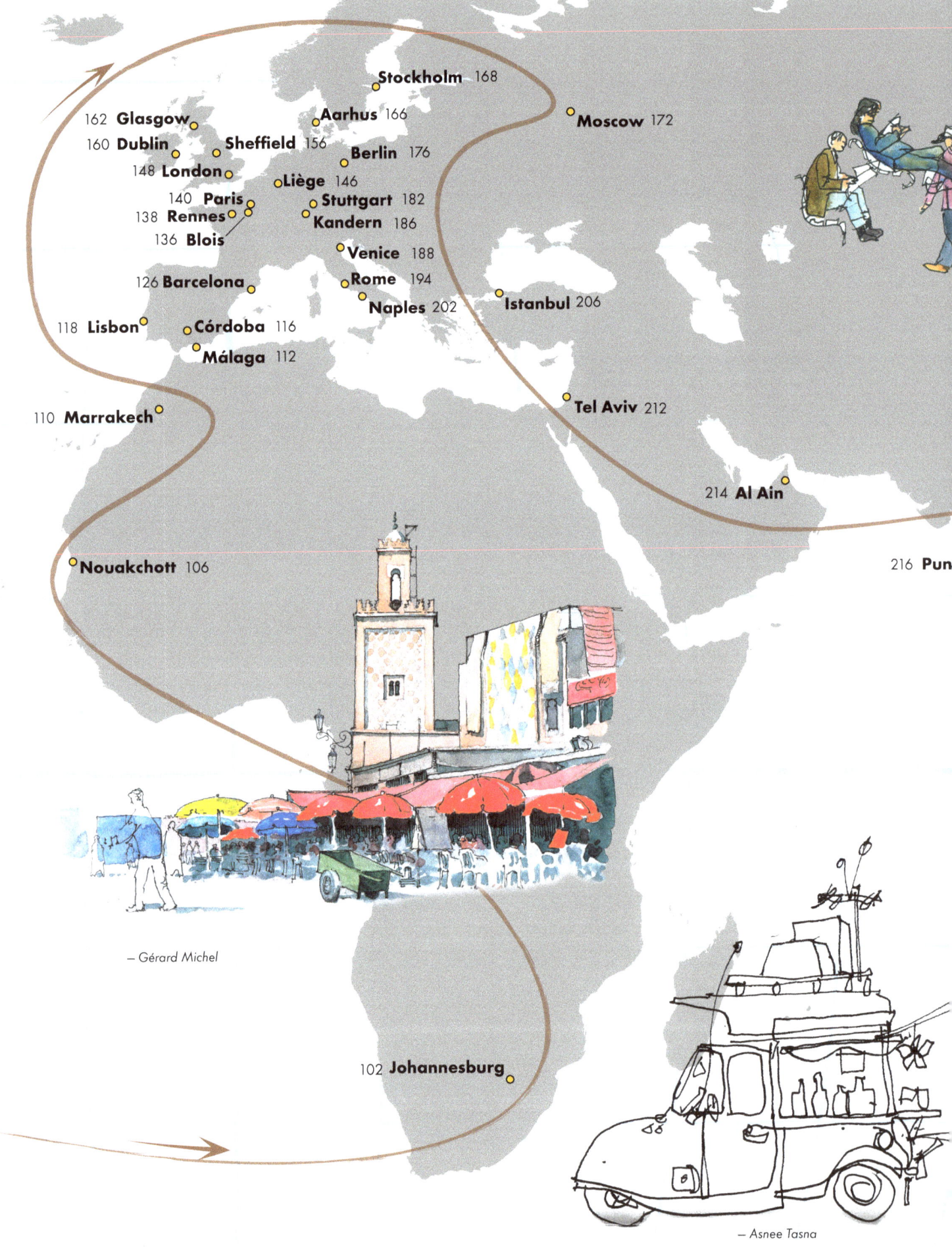

— Gérard Michel

— Asnee Tasna

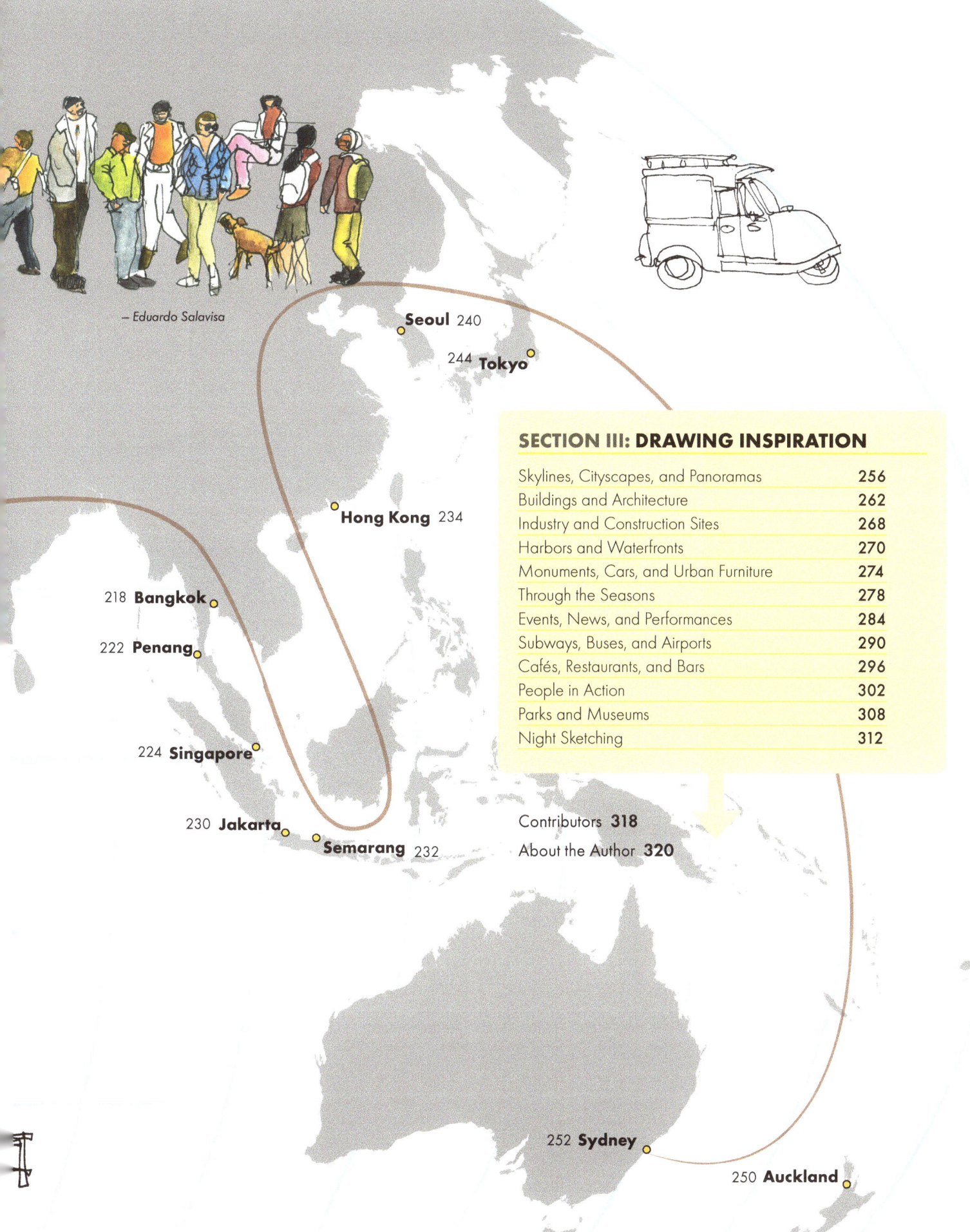

– Eduardo Salavisa

SECTION III: DRAWING INSPIRATION

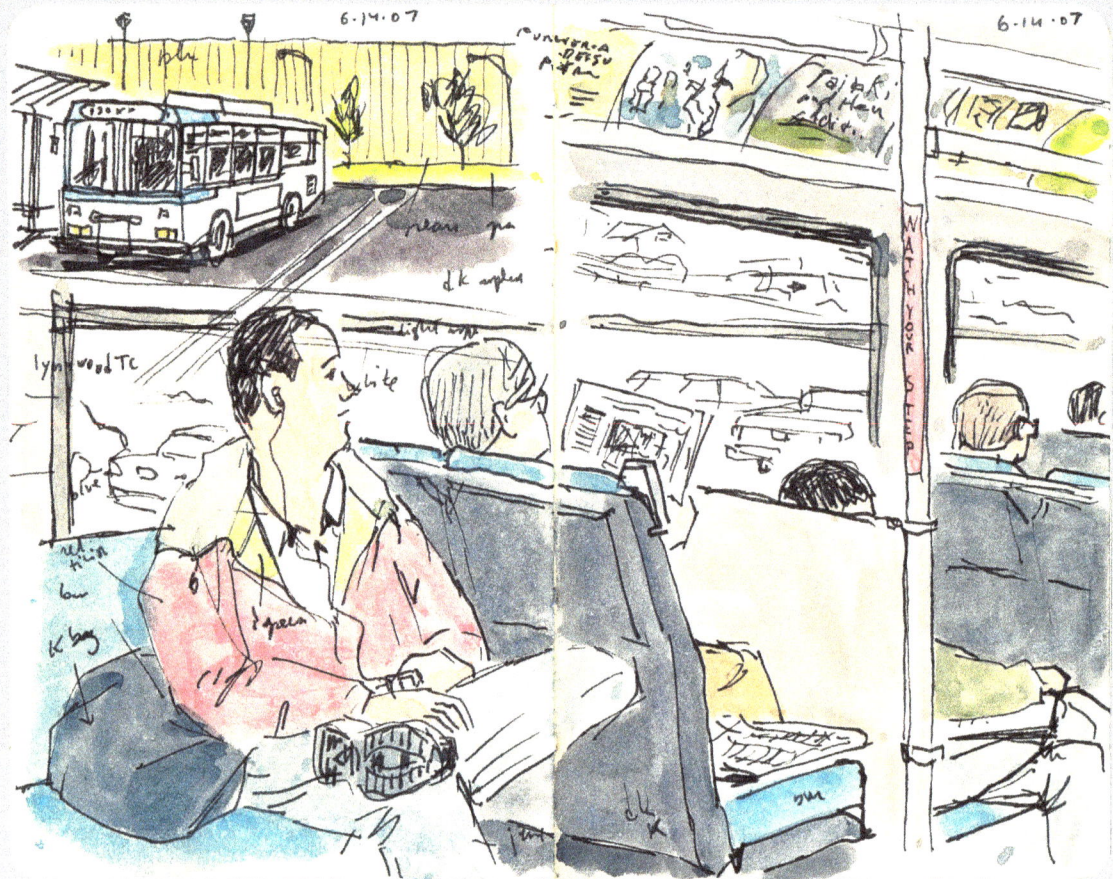

⌒ I got hooked on urban sketching when I started drawing during my bus commute.

PREFACE

Moving to a new city can be intimidating. I have done it many times since I left my hometown of Barcelona in 1987 to attend college in Pamplona. I've also called Reno, Palm Springs, and Washington D.C. home, but it was only when I settled in Seattle in 2006 that I discovered a new way to deal with the stress of landing in unknown territory. I picked up a notebook and started drawing what I saw.

I sketched my new street and marveled at the height of the fir trees up the hill. I drew bus commuters lost in their own thoughts, bent over their laptops, working on a crossword puzzle, or sipping tall cups of coffee. I sketched the snowcapped mountains around Puget Sound as my kids played on the beach.

Most days, you can still find me drawing around Seattle, gaining new appreciation for the city with every sketch I make, no matter how fast or accurately rendered. With every piece, my skills are sharpened and my connection with the community becomes stronger.

I wish my pen and sketchbook had been my companions more often, as I was growing up in Barcelona. Sketching such a beautiful place might have kept me grounded. But you never know—without leaving, I might never have encountered the art of urban sketching.

–Gabriel Campanario
Seattle, March 31, 2011

INTRODUCTION

You might have seen us at the coffee shop, on the subway, or in the park. Pen and paper in hand, we are drawing the world around us. Our open sketchbooks show lively streetscapes, soaring architecture, and intriguing faces, all quickly rendered on the spot—sometimes furtively, sometimes before a gathering crowd. In watercolor, ink, or graphite, urban sketchers draw scenes from their daily lives on location or on vacation, in cities around the globe.

In London, the shadows cast by a sunlit tree on Abbey Street stop Adebanji Alade in his tracks, and he sits on the curb to draw.

In a neighborhood of São Paulo in Brazil, João Pinheiro draws a skyline of new apartment buildings rising where older houses used to be.

In Stockholm, Nina Johansson enjoys a sunny summer day sketching boats by the water. "Drawing a city is not just capturing it on paper," she says. "It's about getting to know it, to feel it, to make it your own."

Sketching is our way of discovering our communities. We are tourists in our own cities, replicating in our own personal styles awe-inspiring landmarks or just the mundane moments of our commute. We are historians who document the changing urban landscape—like Cathy Johnson, who draws the demolition of a historic bridge.

We are also reporters, telling the stories of our travels. In Marrakech, Stuart Kerr squats drawing in the street, having conversations in bad French with cigarette vendors, while Moroccan kids lean up against him. "Sketching was an effective way to meet locals properly," he says.

In Paris, Julien Fassel, a.k.a. Lapin, braves freezing temperatures to do a sketch of Notre Dame Cathedral. It is so cold his watercolors freeze.

In Venice, Veronica Lawlor sketches a view of the Grand Canal from the Rialto bridge, Florian Afflerbach draws at San

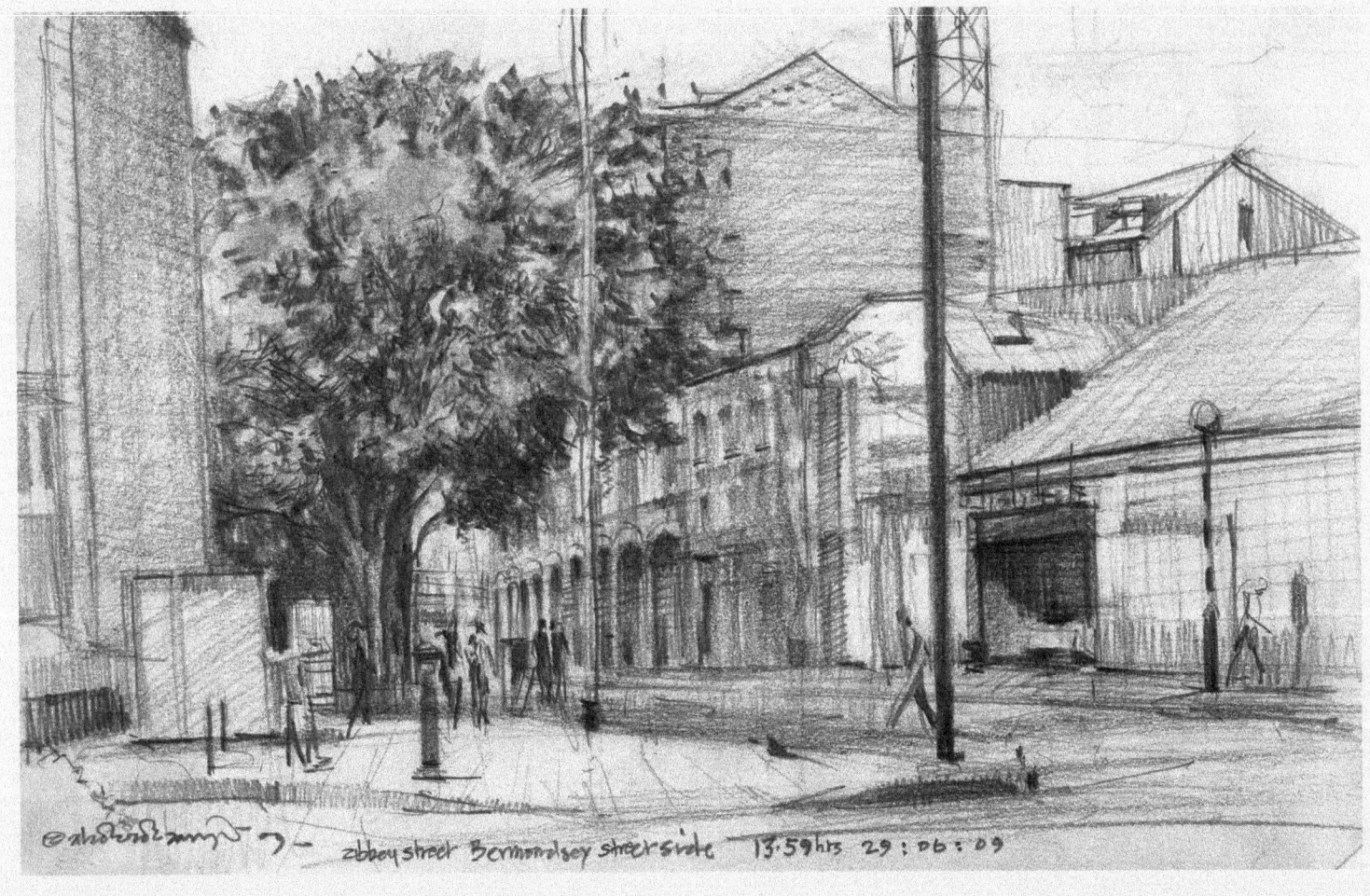

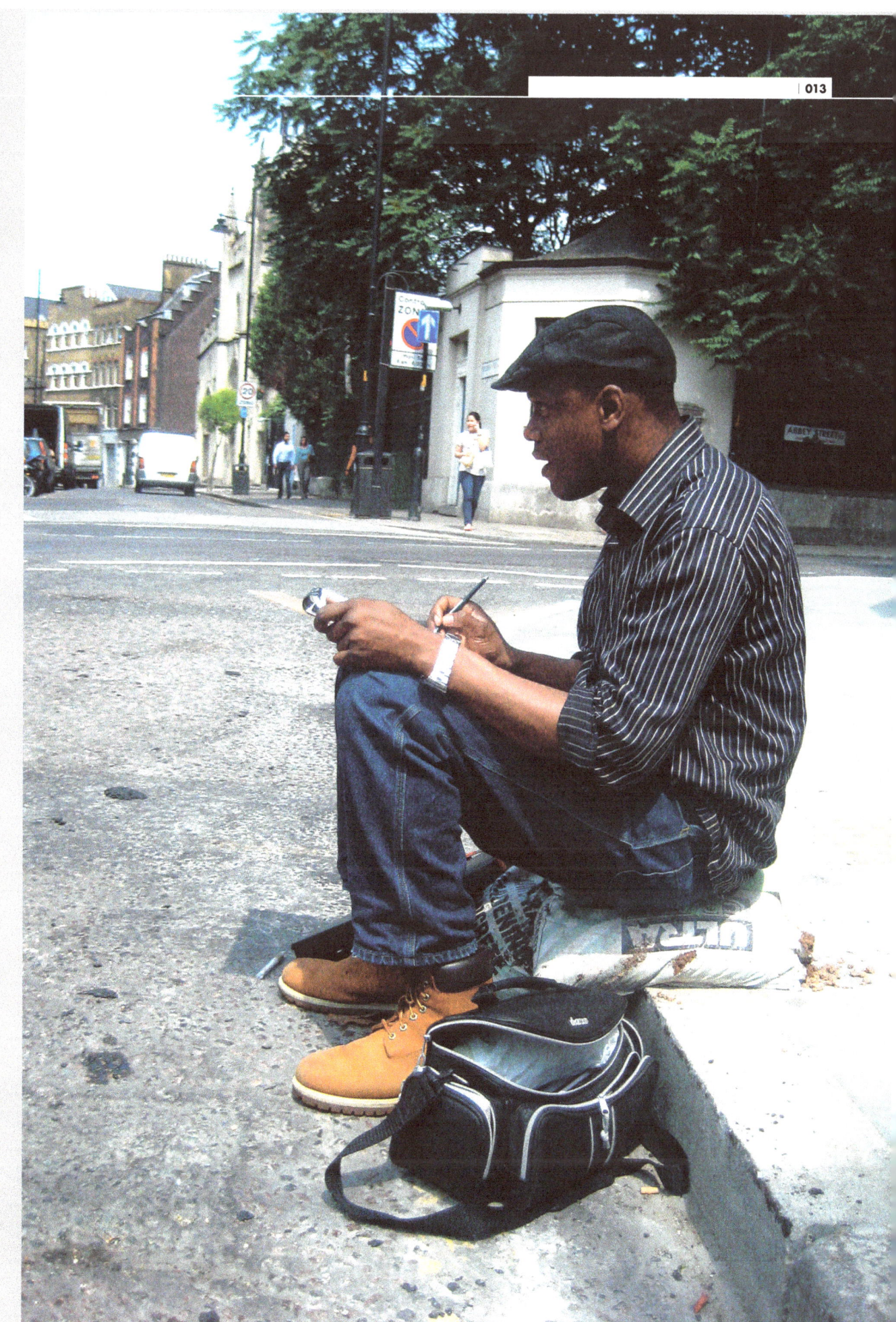

➲ **London** Adebanji Alade sits on a sack of cement to draw.

Giorgio Maggiore, and Tia Boon Sim inks a view of Piazza San Marco. The American, German, and Singaporean sketchers each visited the city of canals on different trips and are discovering each other—and each other's unique point of view—at Urban Sketchers, a site I launched with fellow sketchers in 2008 as a global sketching showcase. One hundred correspondents from five continents post their vivid sketches on the website, often adding equally colorful stories from behind the scenes. The site serves as the inspiration for this book and has launched an urban-sketching movement and created a supportive sketching community.

But the Web is a fast-paced environment, and there's little time to relish a sketch. That's why I'm really excited about *The Art of Urban Sketching*, the first compilation of our work in book form. Now, to travel vicariously through more than 500 urban sketches, you can stop clicking and start leisurely browsing. Admire a view of Manhattan's skyline drawn from a roof in Brooklyn. Take in a driver's view of Bangkok traffic or the atmosphere of a flea market in Mauritania. Sketches of crowded streets, quiet parks, and lively performances show the world, one drawing at a time. We share what it was like to capture these views and what we learned with each stroke.

We hope you'll join us with your sketchbook the next time you see us.

➲ **Paris** Lapin's watercolors froze in Paris during a winter outing.

↻ **São Paulo** João Pinheiro's skyline sketched from a window.

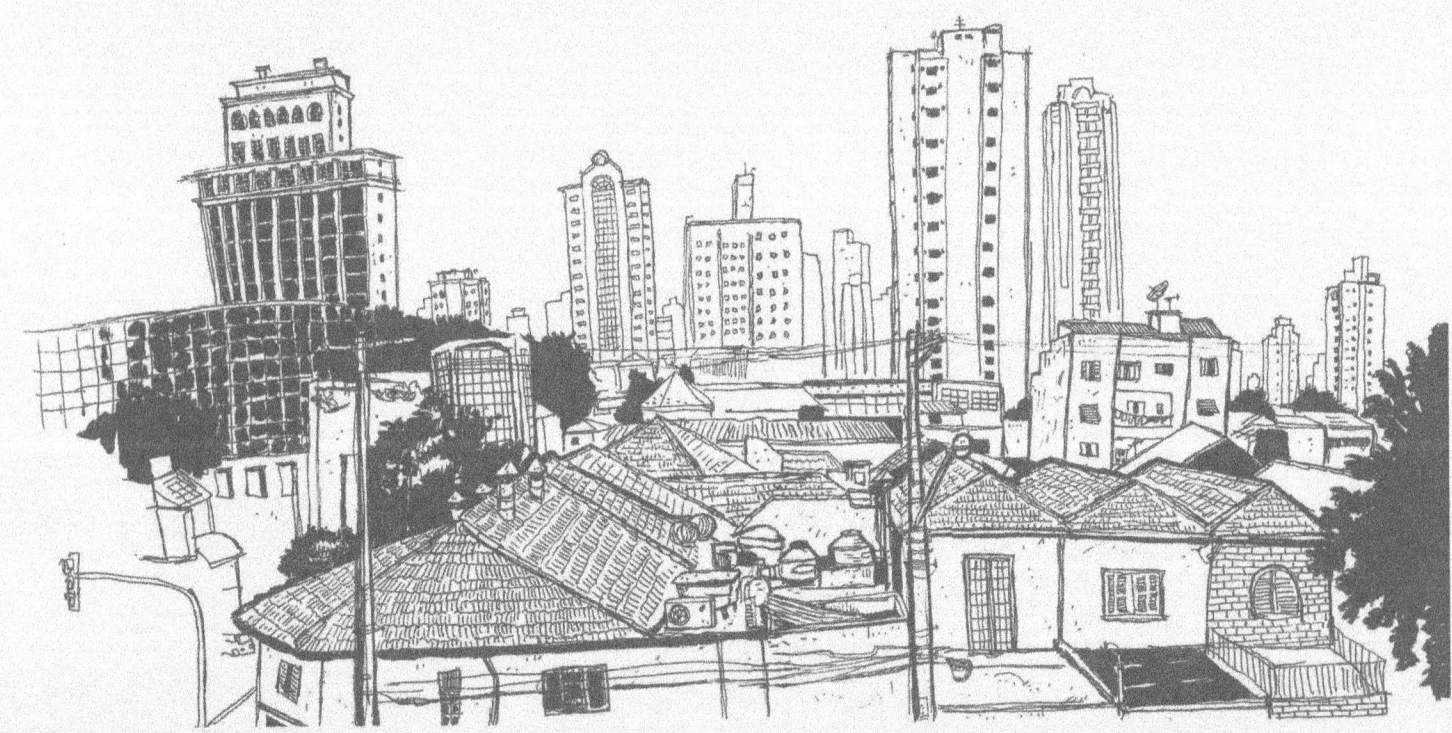

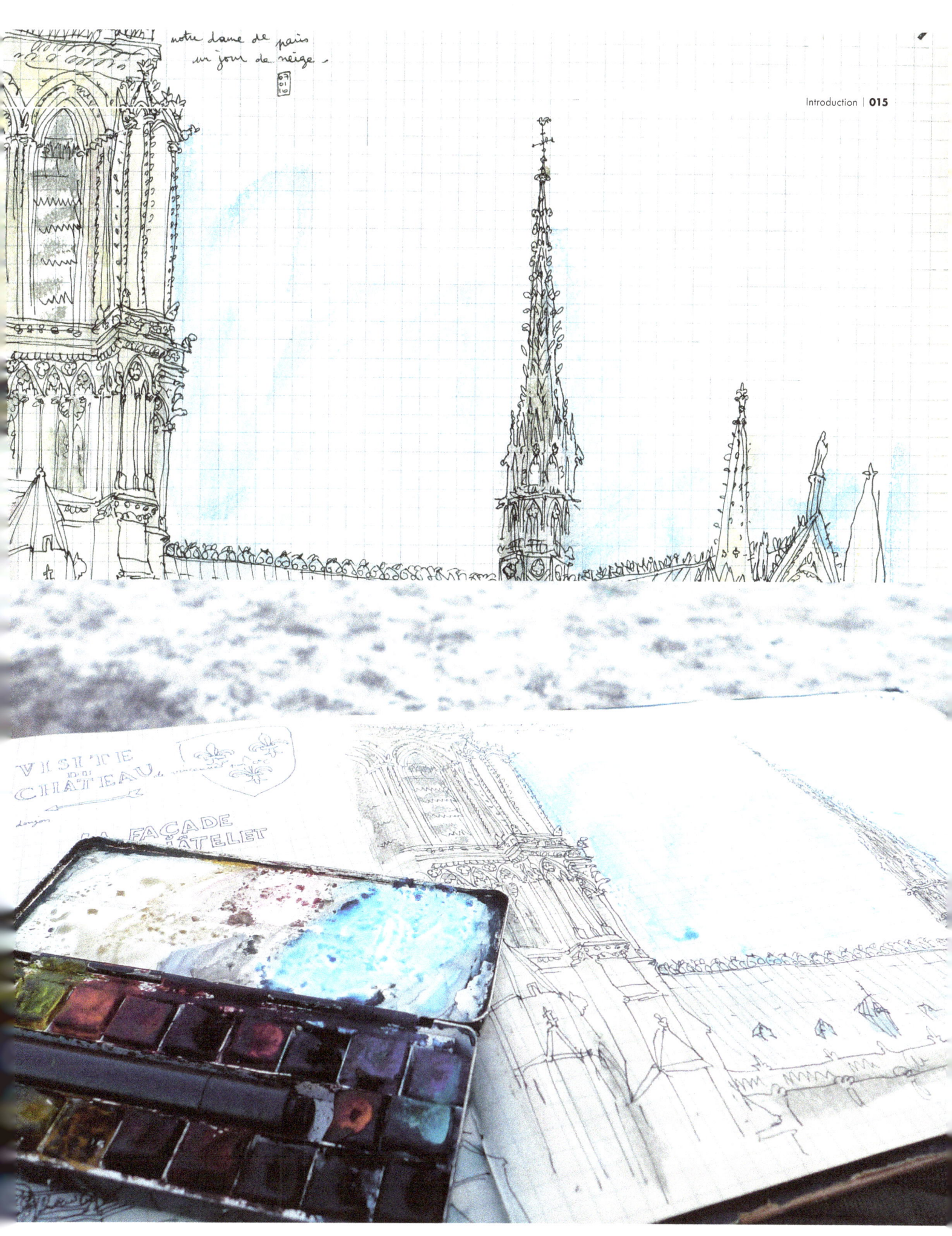

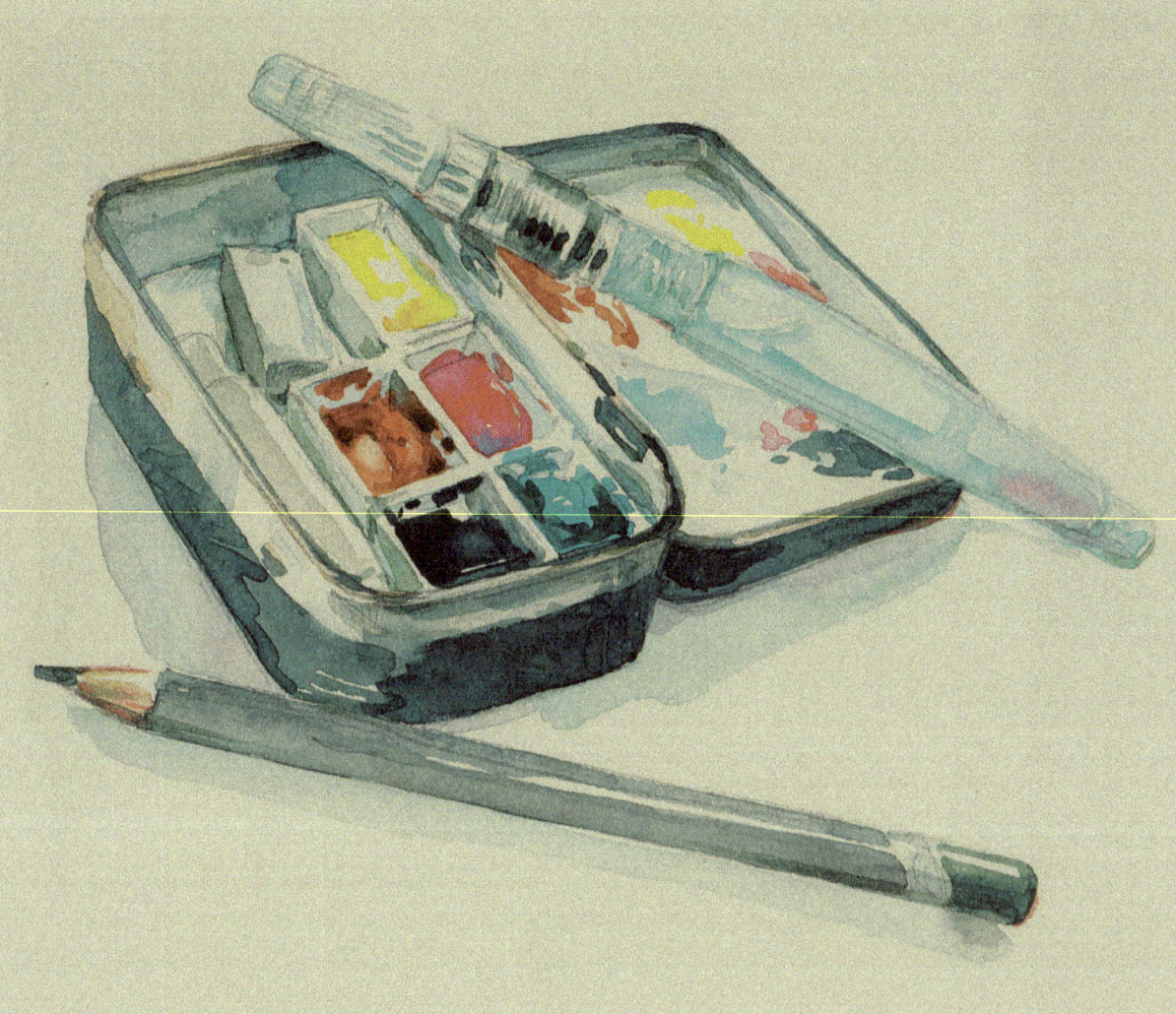

— Cathy Johnson

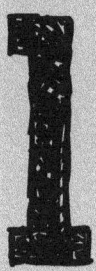

BECOMING AN URBAN SKETCHER

No extravagant tools or formal artistic training is needed to draw on location. Let your hand interpret what your eyes see, as you explore your city, making marks on paper.

WHAT IS URBAN SKETCHING?

As hobbies go, urban sketching gives you a lot of bang for your buck. With nothing more than a piece of paper and a pencil, you are equipped to start drawing your city or village, the people who live there, and the things that are happening in it.

The beauty of sketching is that, almost by definition, a sketch can be completed as simply and quickly as you like. It can involve making a fifteen-minute sketch of the view from your window or whipping out a collapsible sketching stool and spending an hour or two capturing the way the light hits that beautiful old church. In either case, sketching stops the clock and lets your mind turn off all the noise.

Although many creative professionals use field sketching in their work, urban sketching is purely for fun—a chance to step away from the computer and just draw for the sheer joy of it, without deadlines or objectives. It has the power to turn a moment of boredom into a creative pastime. In a sense, urban sketching can be more about the experience than the result.

If you make urban sketching part of your routine and continue with it in your travels, you not only end up with a work of art in your hands, you create a de facto journal of your life—from the mundane (fellow bus commuters, the view from your office window) to the exciting (a day at a ballgame or a once-in-a-lifetime overseas trip). The sketches bring back memories in a way photos don't, evoking the sounds, smells, and recollections of the places in which you created them.

You'll notice, too, that your skills will be sharper, and you'll gain a new appreciation for your surroundings. Drawing something forces you to look at it, really look at it. When sketching far from home, you are immersed in the local culture, your sketchbook sparking interactions when it draws curiosity.

Although sketching is a solitary activity, it becomes social when you share your drawings online and meet other people to draw together. The Urban Sketchers website has connected a truly global web of sketching enthusiasts. A site correspondent from the United States travels to Barcelona for the first time and has a built-in sketching companion and guide—how cool is that?

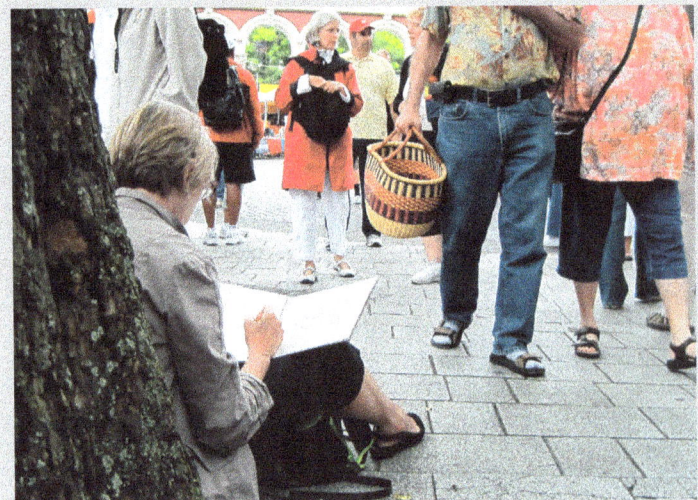

THE URBAN SKETCHERS' MANIFESTO

1. We draw on location, indoors or outdoors, capturing what we see from direct observation.

Urban sketching is a raw and pure form of art that requires drawing from life, rather than from photographs or the imagination. In most cases, urban sketching is practiced on the street. Some sketchers lean up against a tree or the corner of a building or sit on a stair or bench. Others bring along a folding stool. In daylight or at night, whether it's hot or cold, in rain or sunshine, urban sketchers draw what they witness.

2. Our drawings tell the story of our surroundings, the places we live, and where we travel.

Sketching the urban environment produces more than a hand-drawn representation of a given place. Behind each drawing is a story of what was happening before our eyes: a building being torn down, a business closing its doors, or an encounter with a stranger in the subway. Sketches become first-person accounts of life as it happens.

⊙ Laura Frankstone is oblivious to passersby as she sketches in downtown Portland, Oregon.

⊃ Kansas City's Cathy Johnson documents the demolition of a historic bridge.

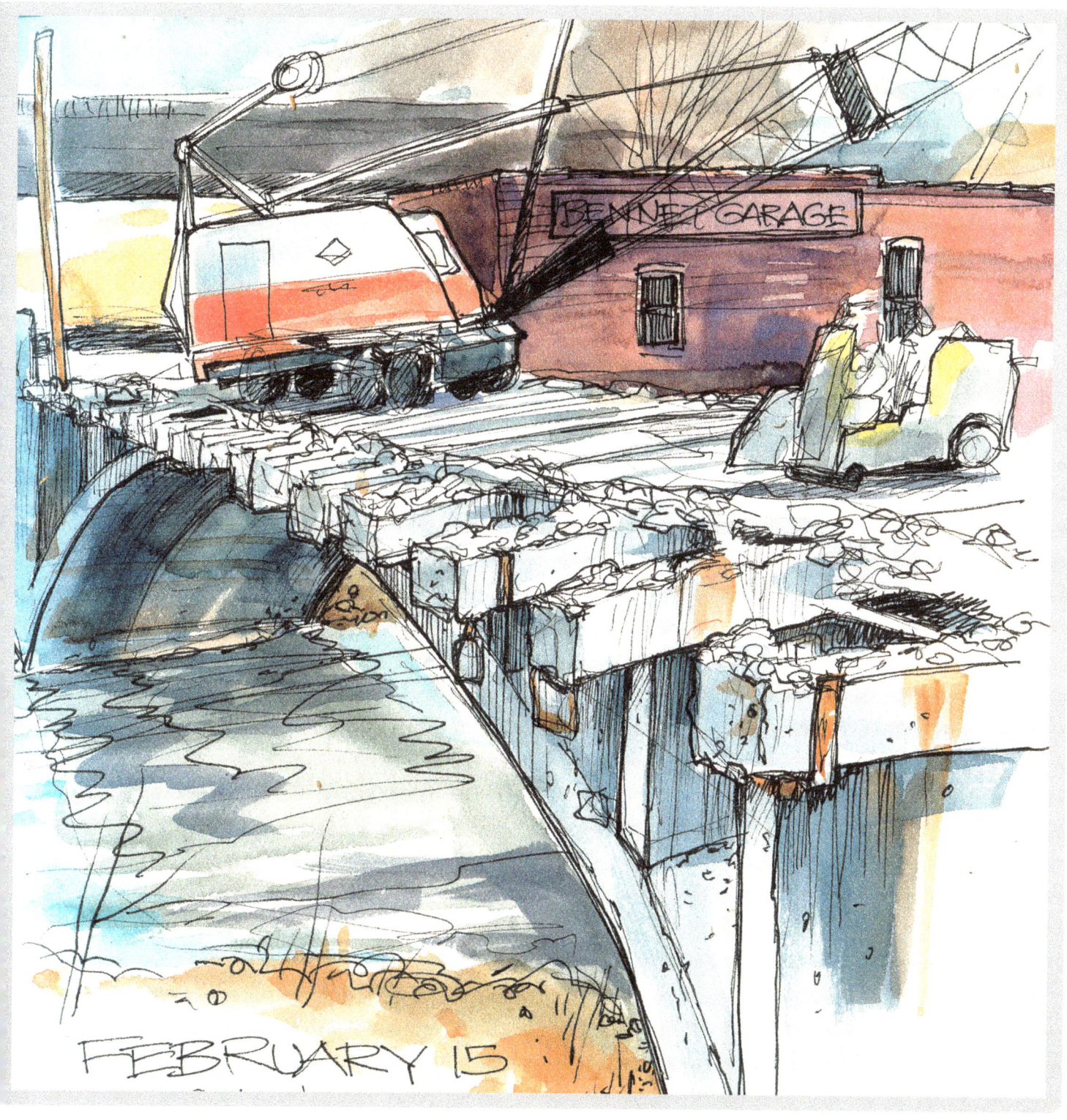

Bar Brasile

Orario di apertura
07.00 – 04.00

31
07
10

PÒ PIAZZA
VENEZIA

3. Our drawings are a record of a time and place.

In the same way a diarist dates a journal entry, urban sketchers often date their drawings, sometimes going as far as to write down the exact hour and minute at which they were completed. It's a way to prove that we've "been there, drawn that."

A sketch captures a moment, a unique experience that can't be repeated. And because we took the time to create it, instead of snapping a photo in an instant, the sketch has the power to bring back much sharper memories.

◖ Danish sketcher Ea Ejersbo sketches Rome during a summer vacation.

⬈ Benedetta Dossi sketches the aftermath of a powerful earthquake in the central Italian village of L'Aquila.

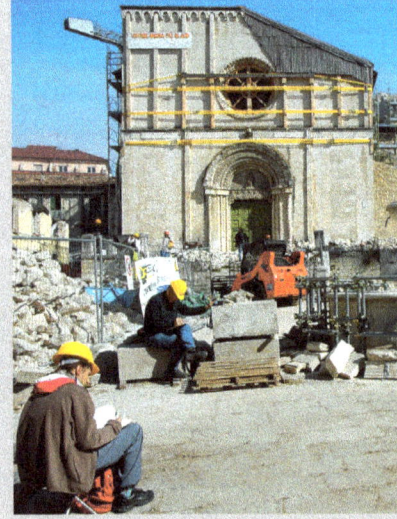

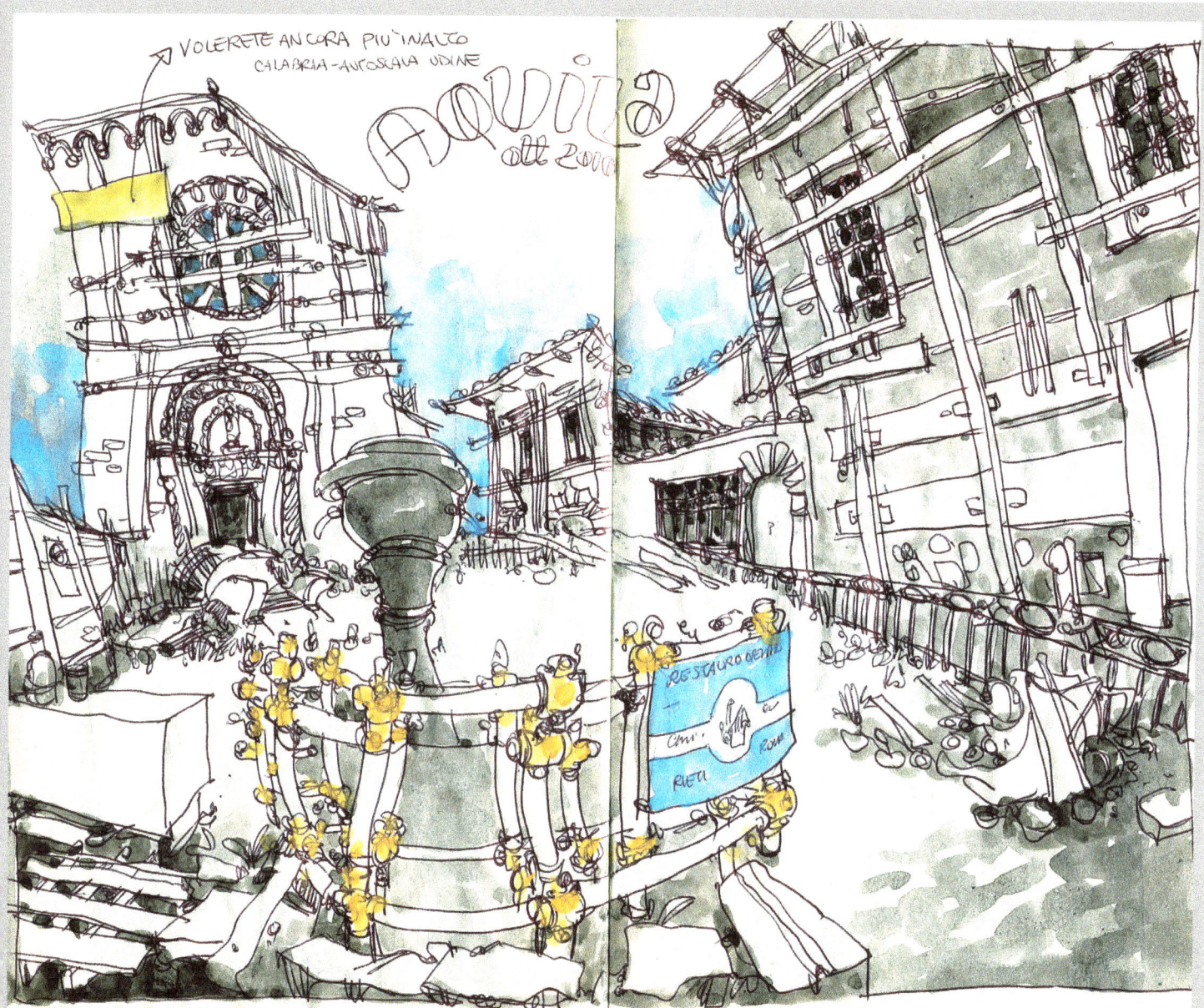

4. We are truthful to the scenes we witness.

Artists who practice urban sketching interpret the reality before them through their own points of view. Being truthful doesn't mean drawing every window in a building or keeping lines straight. Each artist is free to infuse each sketch with his or her personality, while keeping the essence of what he or she sees. Some sketchers like detailed work, spending hours in front of their subjects; others synthesize the essence of a streetscape in a few simple strokes.

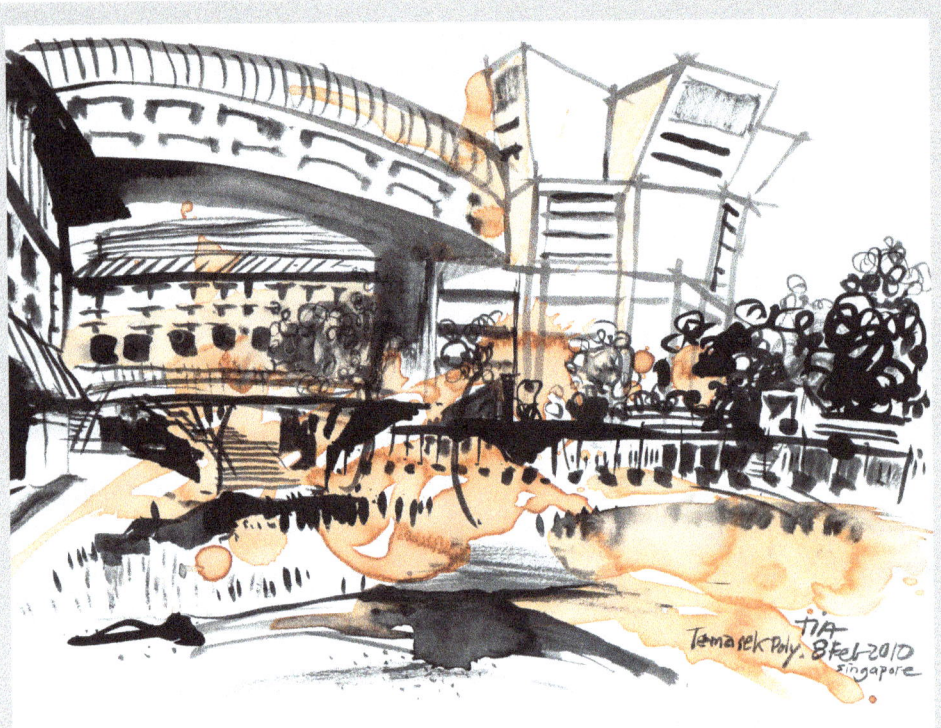

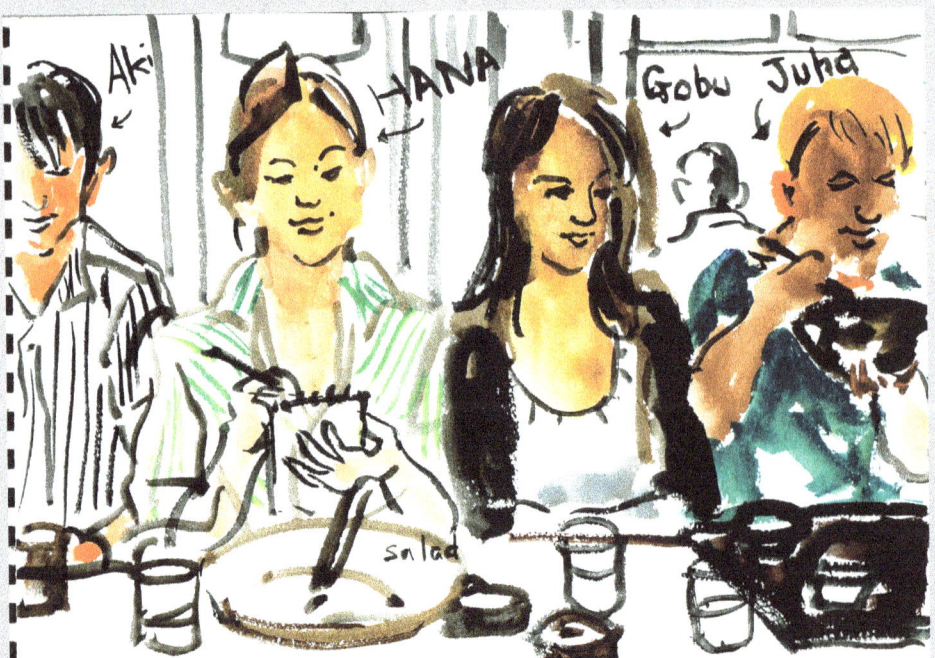

◖ Singapore art educator Tia Boon Sim encourages her students to pour coffee on their sketches as an exercise to draw without fear.

◗ Kumi Matsukawa draws her sketch pals during a sketchcrawl in Tokyo.

5. We use any kind of media and cherish our individual styles.

Pencils, pens, fountain pens, markers, colored pencils, crayons: the media urban sketchers use are endless, as are the possibilities, when you combine them to draw on any kind of paper, whether bound in sketchbooks or in single sheets. But the media doesn't define the art. All that urban sketching requires is making marks on paper to draw what we see.

6. We support each other and draw together.

The Internet has helped urban sketchers find each other; as a result, more meet to draw together than ever in the past.

Taking inspiration from pub crawls, in which friends travel from bar to bar, Italian artist Enrico Casarosa started inviting people in San Francisco to meet for a sketchcrawl, a day of communal sketching around the city. World Wide Sketchcrawl days, announced on Casarosa's SketchCrawl website, have been adopted by urban sketchers as drawing holidays. The term is also commonly used to refer to any kind of group sketch outing.

For people too nervous to draw alone or who want to overcome a fear of drawing in public, getting together with like-minded artists provides a supportive network and endless motivation. After a few hours of drawing, passing around the results from the session over a meal or drink is an extra payoff.

7. We share our drawings online.

If not for the Internet, the global urban sketching community would remain a disconnected group of artists. Using blogs and image-sharing sites, like-minded artists are calling attention to the benefits of sketching on location, opening a window onto the world, and motivating each other to draw.

➲ James Hobbs sketches while waiting to pick up his child from a friend's house.

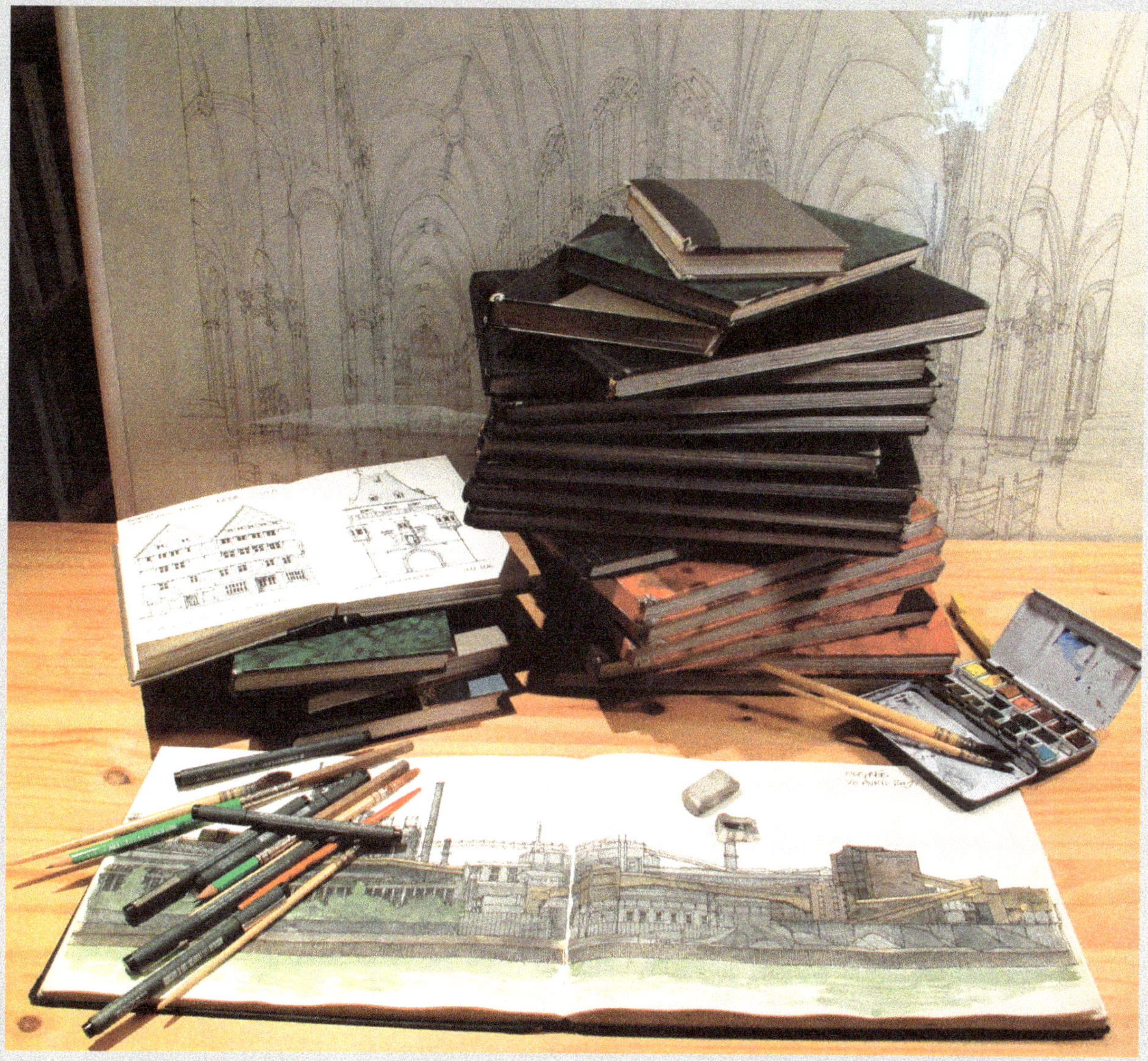

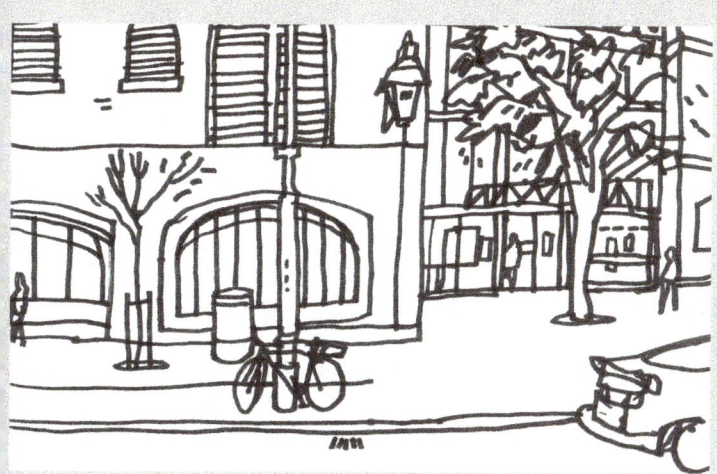

↺ Belgian architect Gérard Michel has shared more than 4,000 sketches from his finished sketchbooks online.

8. We show the world, one drawing at a time.

The urban sketcher's quest to draw the world is not limited to city landmarks or historic locations. Any scene, no matter how mundane, is worth drawing. A sketch has the ability to elevate the least picturesque location into something worth looking at and reflecting upon.

TOOLS FOR YOUR PORTABLE STUDIO

Urban sketching in public might require some courage, but it doesn't require sophisticated tools. The complexity of your urban sketching kit depends on the situations in which you like to draw and the type of sketches you want to make. A small notebook and a pencil are enough to draw quick portraits of commuters on the subway, but if you're going to spend a couple of hours drawing at your neighborhood park, you might need a bigger sketchbook and some colors. Whatever way you go, you'll want to keep your kit as portable as possible.

Paul Heaston's Sketching Tools

San Antonio artist Paul Heaston keeps a portable, yet fully loaded, sketching bag. He also brings a folding stool on long sketch outings, when he can spend one or two hours on a single drawing.

- **Pens and pencils:** waterproof pigment liners will not smear when you add watercolor
- **Sketchbooks:** landscape formats are fun to work with for panoramic drawings, a pocket sketchbook is handy for quick sketches
- **Drawing pads:** they are good if you plan to tear the sketch out
- **Mechanical pencils:** you don't have to sharpen them
- **Clips:** handy to keep sketchbook pages from flipping
- **Waterbrushes:** they can be refilled with water for easy use of watercolors on the go
- **Watercolor kit:** a limited color palette is better for quick sketches

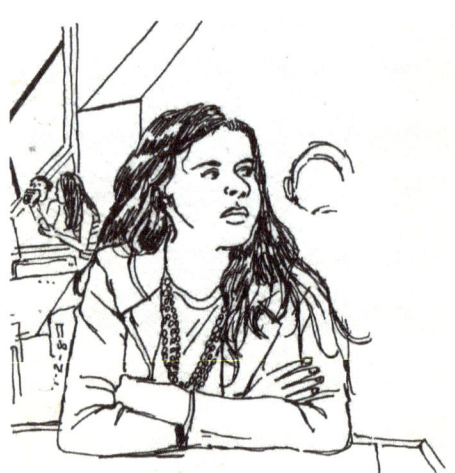

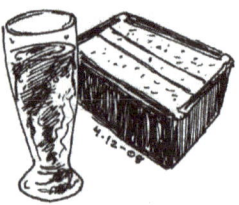

🎧 São Paulo illustrator João Pinheiro says even a cocktail napkin sketch can be full of expression.

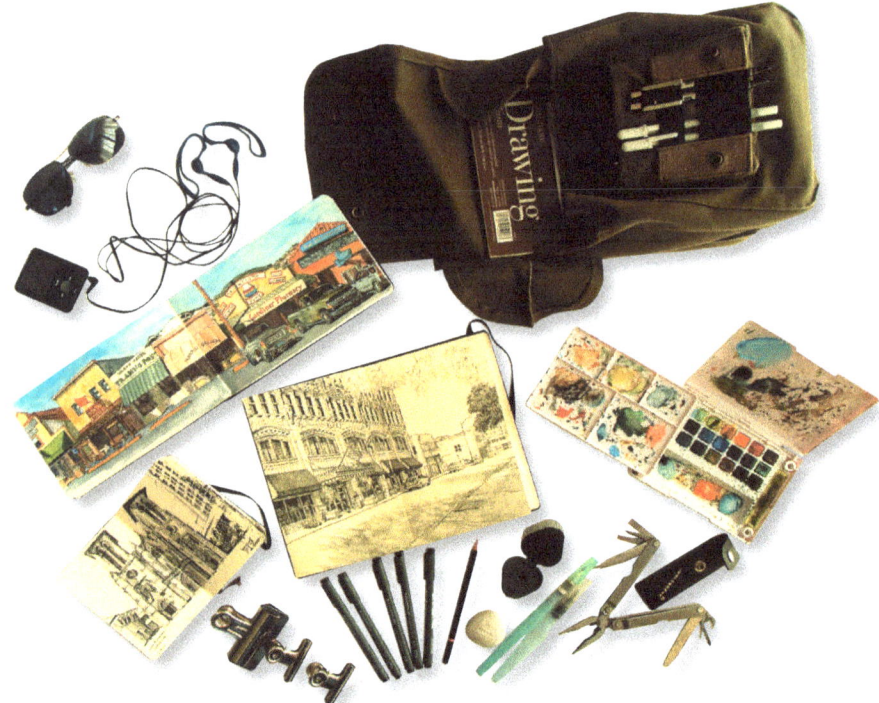

Roger O'Reilly's Sketching Tools

Irish illustrator Roger O'Reilly's tools of choice are a brush pen, a small selection of pencils, and a much-used traveling watercolor set. Also in his bag:

- **Pentel brush pen with cartridges:** instant dense blacks. This is still the best cartridge-based brush pen I've come across, O'Reilly says. Behaves exactly like a brush, though it can lay too much ink on the paper if you're not careful.

- **Staedtler liner pens:** ideal for laying down quick lines. With four sizes (01–07), you can vary line thicknesses easily, though I tend to mostly use the 03 and just go back and forth over the line.

- **Various pencils:** well-worn 2Bs and 3Bs and a mechanical pencil (2B, No. 5), which is good for occasions when you want to ghost in pencil lines and don't want them to be too visible in the finished drawing

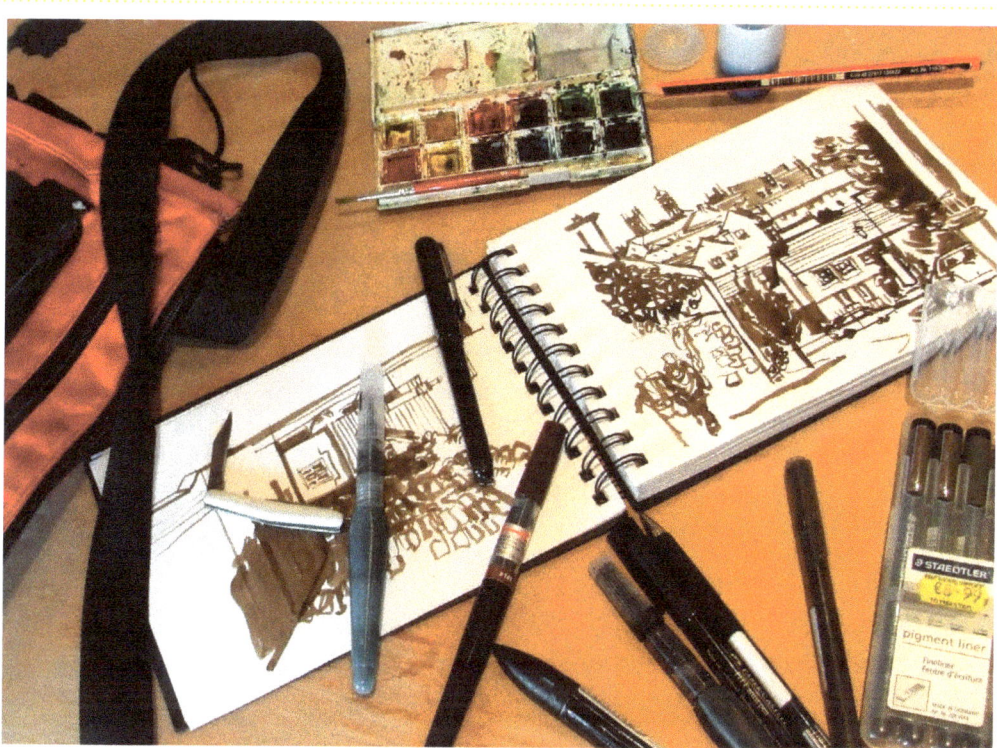

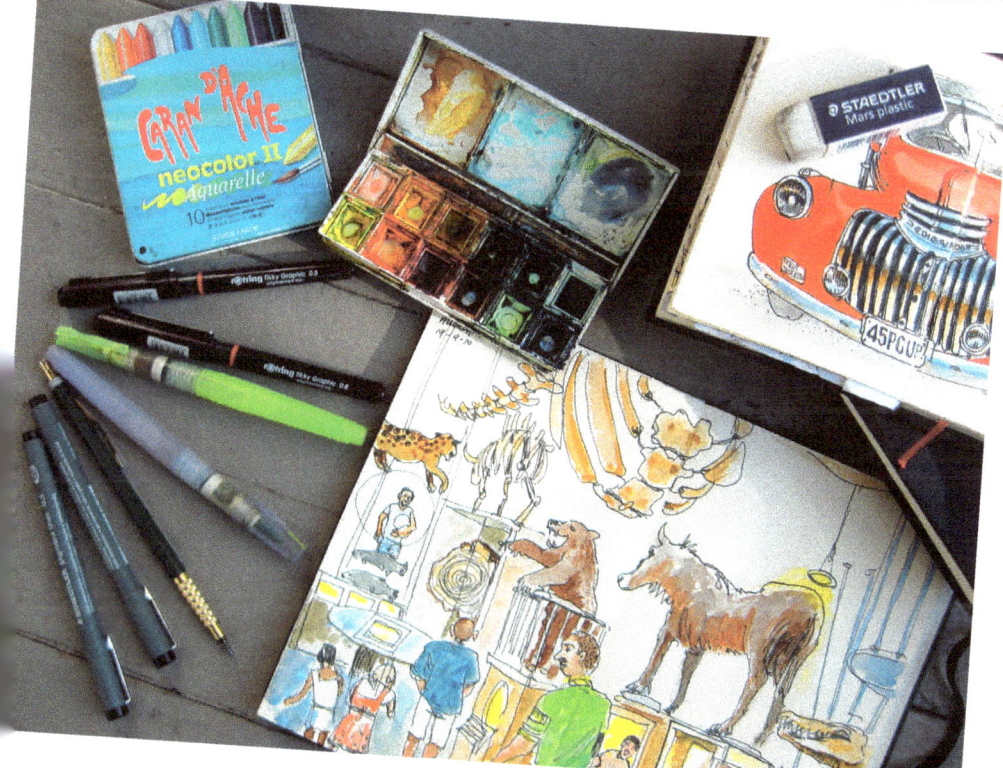

Murray Dewhurst's Sketching Tools

New Zealander Murray Dewhurst carries A6 and A5 Hahnemühle sketchbooks, which he uses depending on how much time he has to sketch. His drawing tools include the following:

- **Winsor & Newton Cotman Sketchers' Pocket Box:** small, easy to carry—the easiest way to get color into your work onsite

- **Kuretake waterbrushes:** fantastic for getting color down quickly

- **Pens:** Rotring Tikky Graphic pens or Staedtler pigment liners, .3 and .5: both brands are good and are permanent, to help avoid bleeding when watercolor is added

- **Pencils:** Faber-Castell 2 mm clutch pencil: this old mechanical pencil doubles as a sharpener, which saves packing a separate one

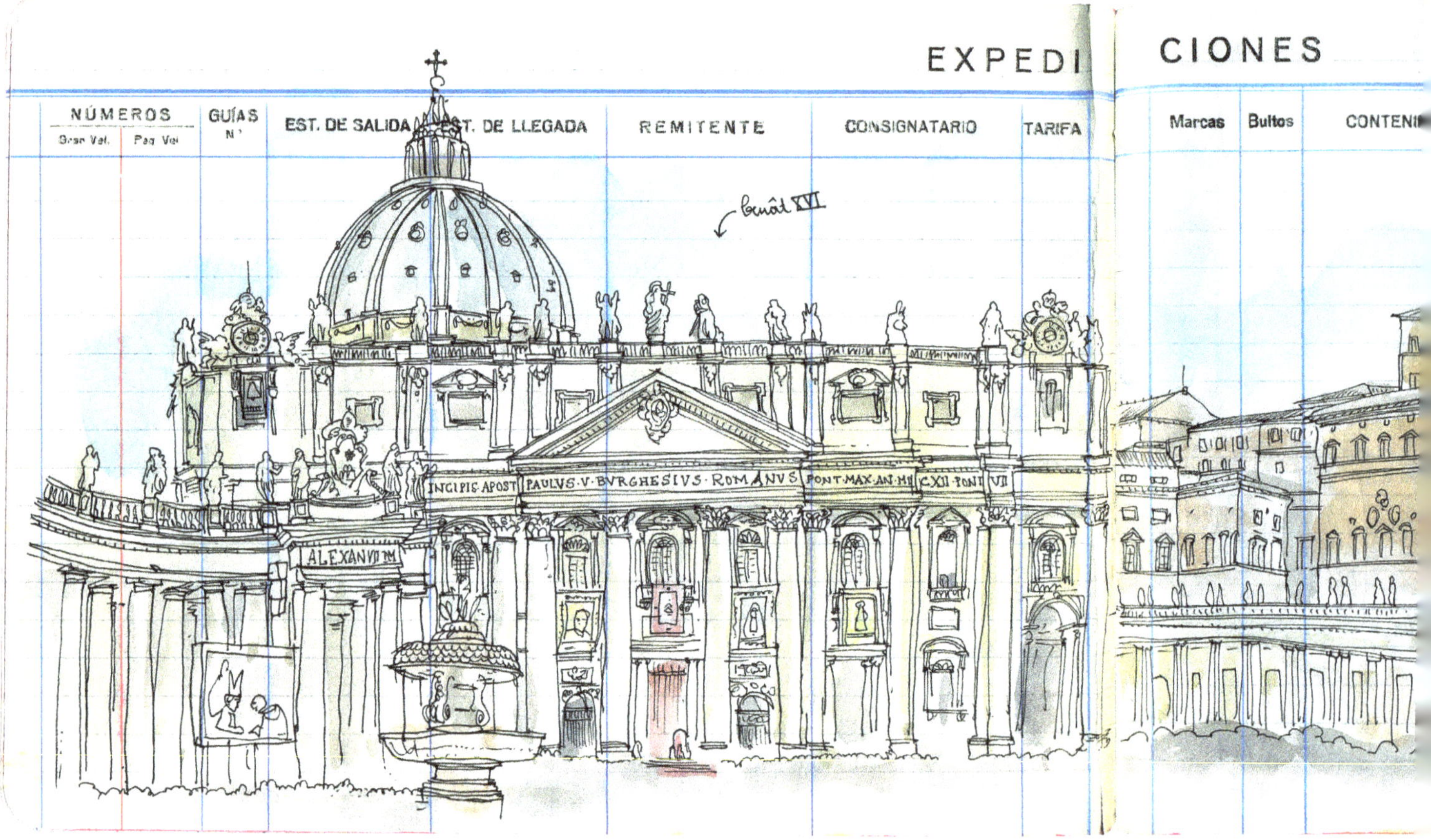

EXPEDI CIONES

NÚMEROS		GUÍAS N.°	EST. DE SALIDA	EST. DE LLEGADA	REMITENTE	CONSIGNATARIO	TARIFA	Marcas	Bultos	CONTENI
Gran Vel.	Peq Vel.									

Recycled Notebooks

French illustrator Lapin draws on old accounting ledgers he finds at flea markets. "I like the layering that this lined paper gives; it adds something that goes well with my washed watercolors," Lapin says. "I'm confused only when I want to sketch an oblique element in all those vertical lines, but what I especially like about these old papers is the quality. Even though the sheets are very fine, ink pen and watercolors do not bleed through.

It seems that after the '80s, the quality of the paper turned poor, and nowadays it's expensive to buy sketchbooks of that quality."

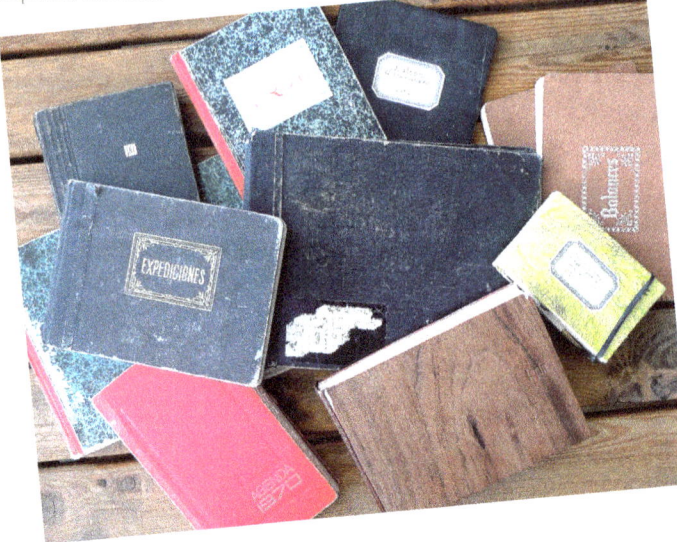

HOW TO BECOME PART OF THE ONLINE SKETCHING COMMUNITY

1. **Convert your sketches into digital files.** Take a photo of your sketch with your digital camera, or use a flatbed scanner to digitize your drawing. Scan it at full resolution (300 dots per inch), in case you'll want to print it, and then save a smaller, web-friendly low-resolution version (72 dots per inch.)

2. **Share the sketches online.** Many sketchers use blogs to share their sketches. Blogger and Wordpress are two popular platforms. Or you can share your drawings on image-sharing sites like Flickr, social-networking sites like Facebook, or post your sketches on the Urban Sketchers Facebook page.

3. **Have fun interacting with fellow artists.** Once you have shared your drawings online, you'll start attracting feedback from visitors to your blog or the social-media outlet where you shared the sketch. Their comments will be encouraging and will motivate you to keep drawing.

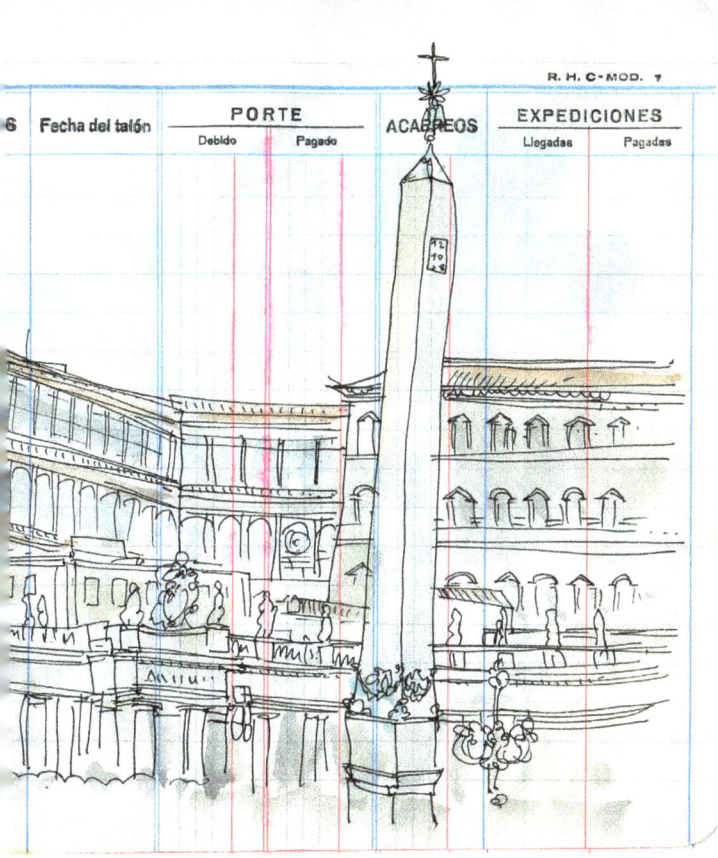

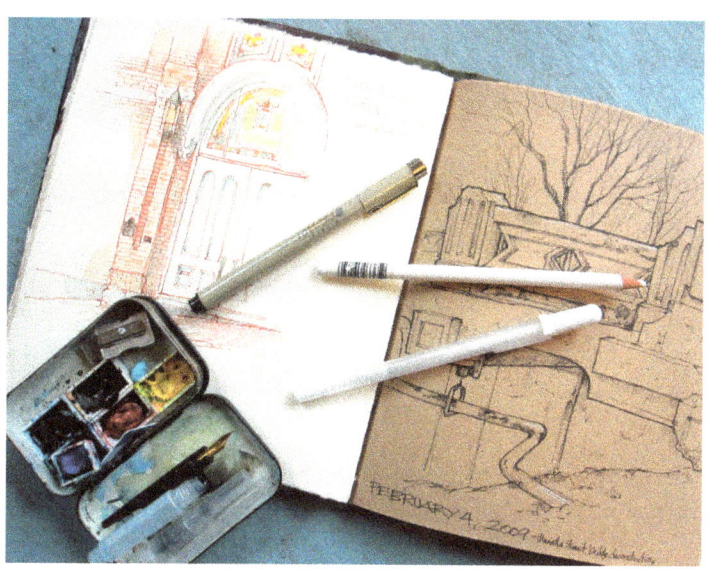

Customized Kit

Cathy Johnson devised a minimal sketching kit out of a candy tin. "I cleaned it out well and let it dry thoroughly then painted the inside white with spray paint and the outside with shiny black . . . . . I really don't need more than this," she says. It includes cadmium yellow medium, quinacridone red, phthalo blue, burnt sienna, and Payne's Gray watercolors, a Derwent Graphitint Steel Blue watercolor pencil, and a Pentel Aquash waterbrush.

For papers, Johnson likes to combine different colored papers in her own handmade sketchbooks. "It challenges me to try different approaches and mediums," she says.

Train Sketching Kit

Sheffield illustrator Lynne Chapman has a specific set of tools to sketch during her train commute. "Traveling light means I can be ready to draw at a moment's notice, pretty much anywhere," she says. In her kit:

* **A6 or A5 hardback sketchbook:** durable and small enough to hold in one hand, plus easier to conceal if I'm trying not to be spotted

* **Pencil case:** with approximately ten presharpened 3B pencils

* **Craft knife:** for emergency sharpening.

* **Mini-hairspray:** for fixing pencil (especially handy when I've drawn across both sides of the spread)

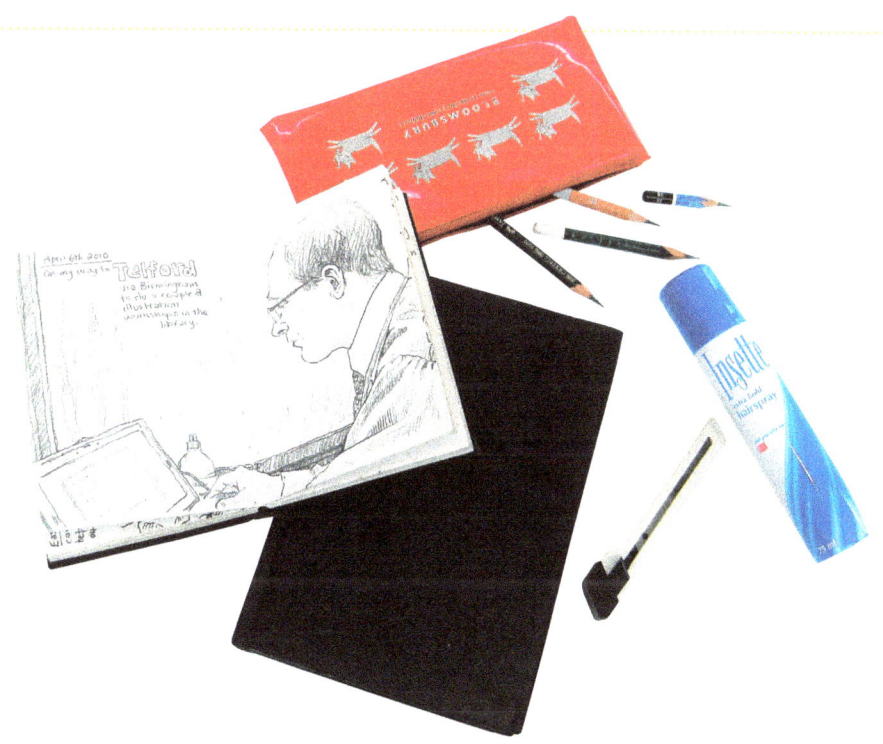

STYLE AND TECHNIQUE

There are many ways to sketch. Which one is yours? Finding the tools that are right for you is the first step toward developing your own style.

Some sketchers are loyal to a single type of pen. Others change tools according to the situation. Graphite works well with quick, gestural drawings. Watercolor applied methodically in layers can add depth to a sketch. The methods and processes used vary as well. Some compose a sketch with light pencil lines before applying ink; others swear by direct-to-paper ink sketching to create vivid, lively images. Some never go back to the sketch after leaving the spot; others add touches of color later.

Whatever tools and techniques you use, your personality will come through in your sketches and a style will develop over time.

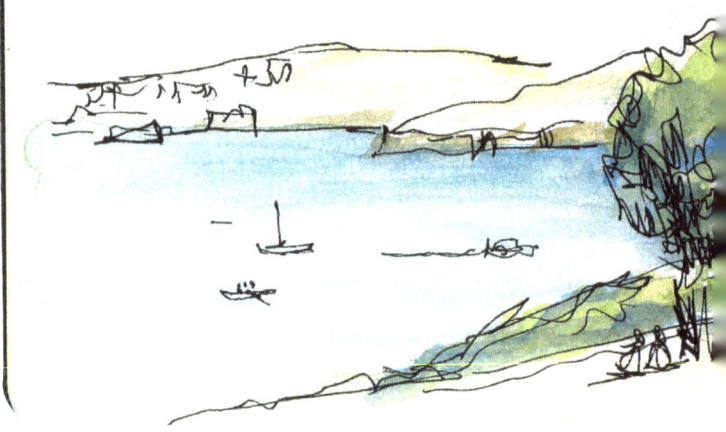

BOXING DAY PICNIC @ Q STATION

➲ "I mostly start with a very loose pencil outline to establish overall shapes, size, and composition on the page. With complicated buildings, I also setup grid lines for the major architectural elements. Then I start sketching with ink, without worrying too much about my initial pencil outline—this allows my ink lines to still be loose." — *Liz Steel (Sydney)*

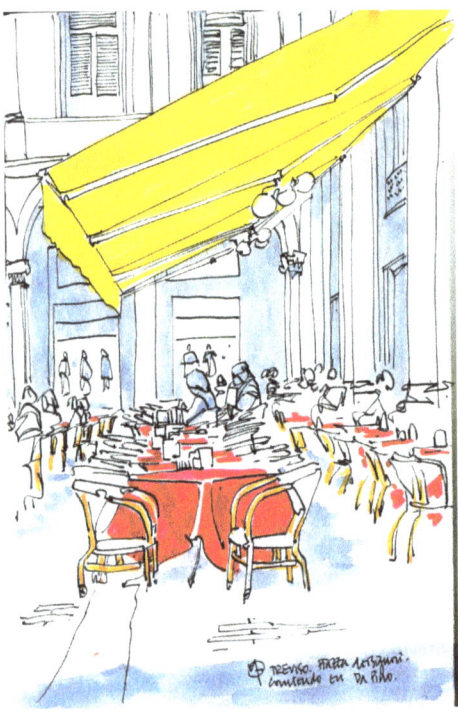

➲ "I always draw straight with ink. I only use the pencil for pencil sketches, not as a basis for an ink sketch. I start always from the point that catches my attention and try to draw as slowly as I can. I always do all the linework from life. The only postproduction I allow myself is coloring (when I can't do it from life) and writing. I never design a layout in advance for the pages." — *Miguel Herranz (Barcelona)*

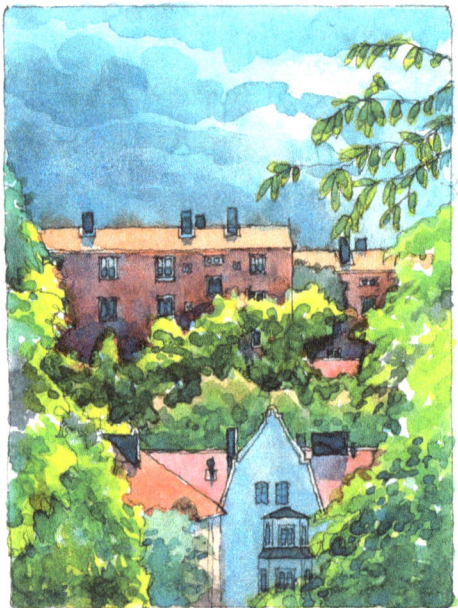

➲ "I like to draw directly in ink, because that makes me look harder and concentrate more on placing my lines on the paper. I don't mind mistakes; I just draw over them and try to incorporate them into the drawing. Then I either color my drawings with watercolors or use crosshatching to get some shading and texture." — *Nina Johansson (Stockholm)*

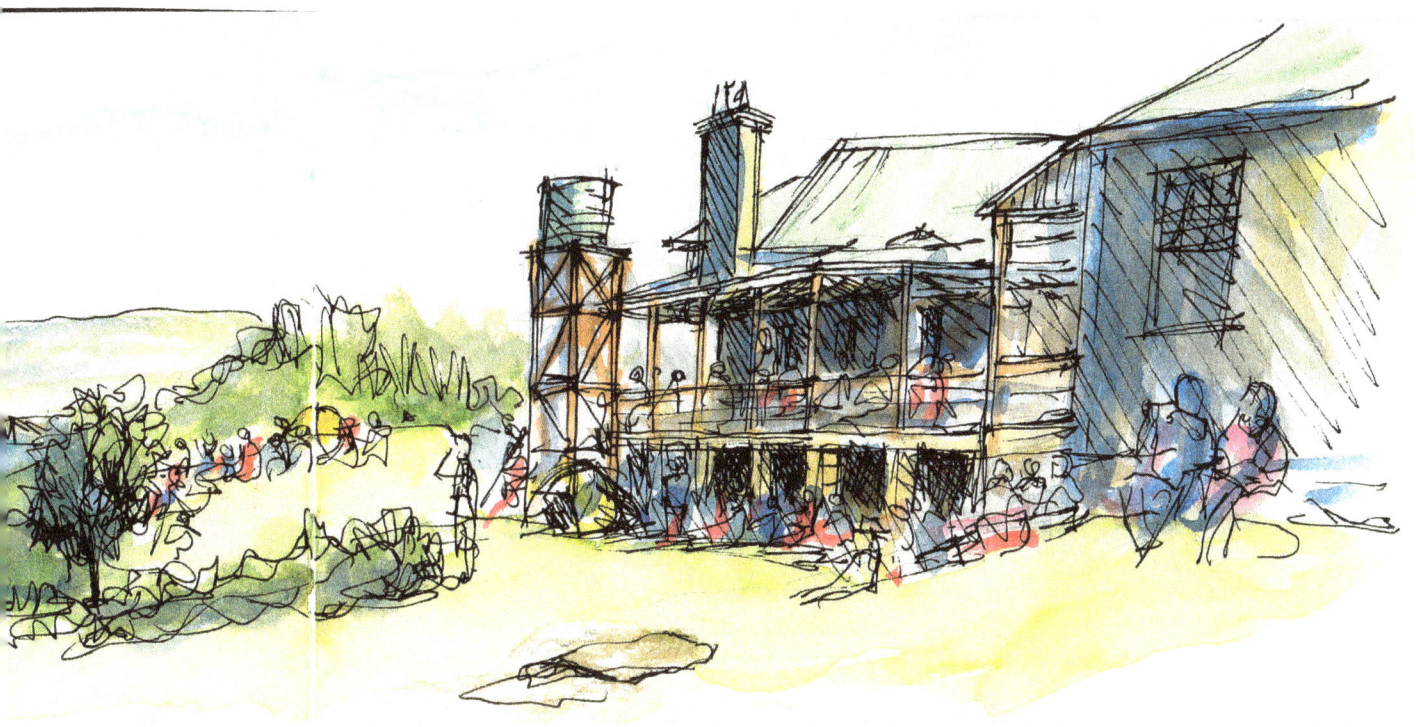

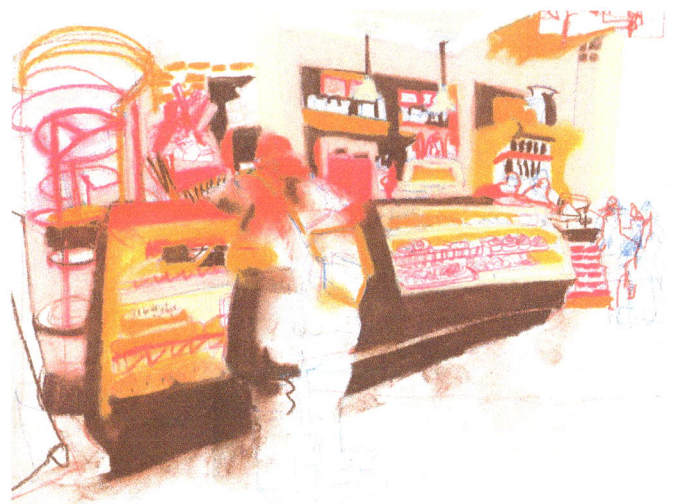

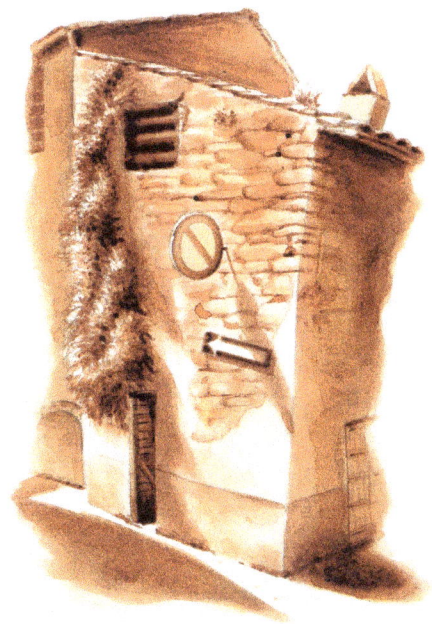

↻ "I start all my sketches the same way, with a light gestural drawing in pencil, making every effort to create with a mood, impression, or story in my head. Next come details, again in pencil, with more attention to specifics. Finally, I lay in ink washes, working from broad areas to specific details. Layers upon layers of ink lead to rich darks, which I feel add depth to my drawings. Of utmost importance to me is finishing the drawing without losing that crucial first impression—the point of the drawing."
— Fred Lynch (Boston)

∩ My technique is to experiment and mix all my materials together when I draw. I would say pastels are my favorite things to use—the softness of them, the intense colors, and the ability to blend colors. Yes, it is messy, but that is part of the fun. The best thing to do is to go out and try something different each time." — Danielle C. McManus (New York City)

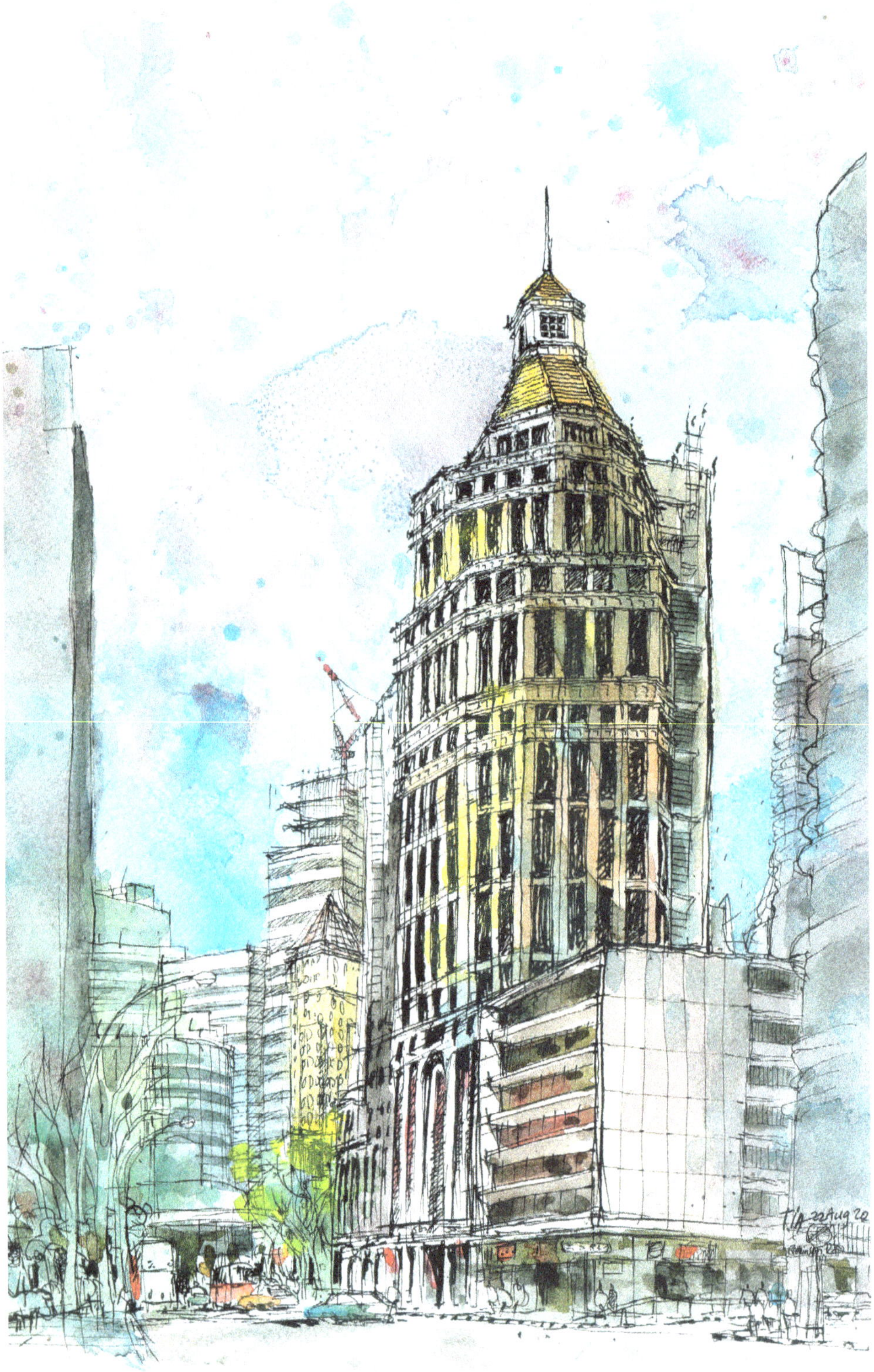

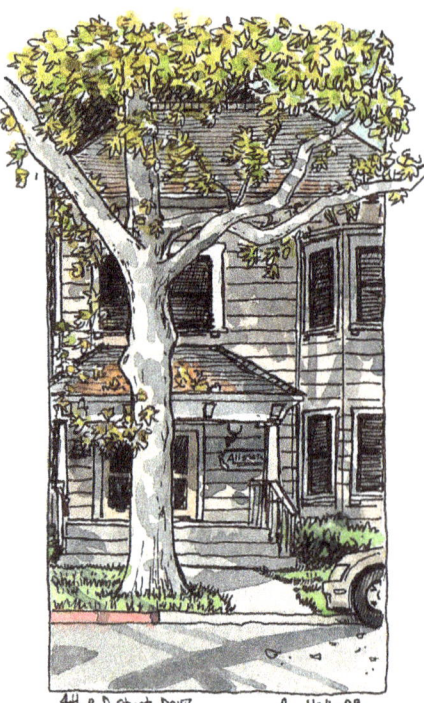

4th & D Street, Davis   P. 11-4-09

◐ "First, I choose a place to sit. I need shade, and I need to be sure that a car isn't going to park in front of me five minutes into the sketch. I usually make a few faint guidelines in H2 pencil to work out composition then do all the hard work in black pen, usually a Micron Pigma 0.1. I color onsite, using watercolors. I usually take as much time as I have—such as my lunch hour—and if there are details to fill in later, I will write notes on the sketch. I often draw a frame around my sketches to limit my composition but rather enjoy letting objects pop out of the frame."
— Pete Scully (Davis, California)

◑ "I used to do a lot of black-and-white, quick, double-spread sketches in Moleskine pocket sketchbooks. However, I find myself creating more and more ink and watercolor sketches in a bigger format. This allows me to experiment with different techniques. I find splashing the sky with blue, red, orange, and purple before adding salt for special effect a very liberating process. I am not restricting myself to a coloring exercise; I am experimenting and have no fear in seeing splashes of colors all over the paper. Depending on the splashes, I will work around them, so some of the lines and shapes are distorted or exaggerated. It provides an interesting dimension to the final product." — Tia Boon Sim (Singapore)

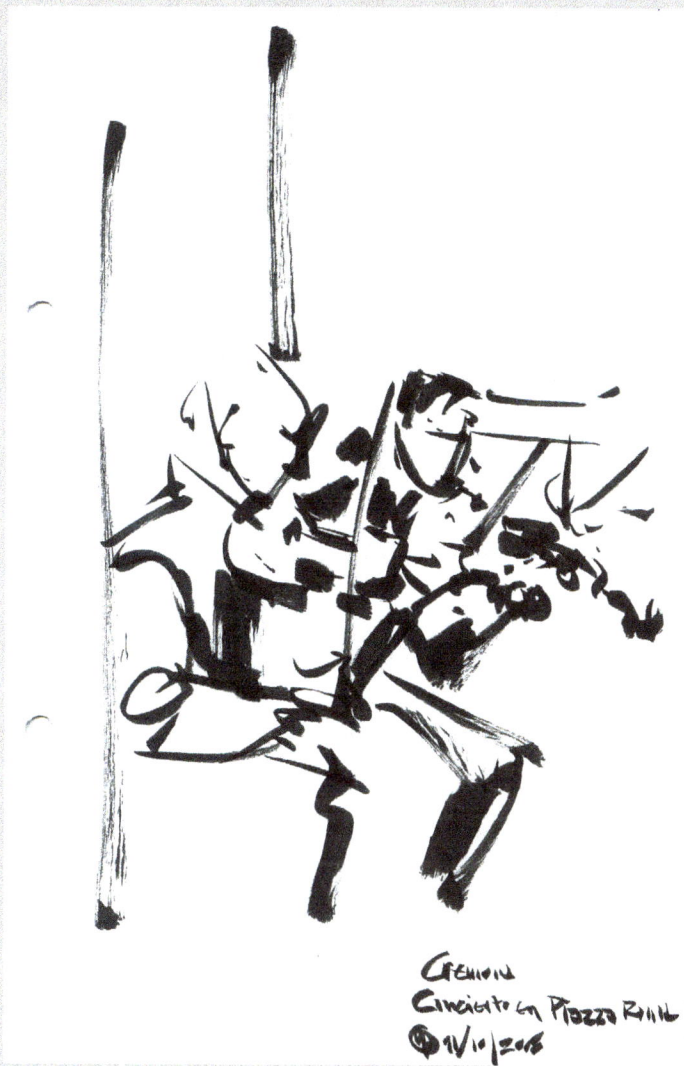

⌂ Street concert in Cremona by Miguel Herranz

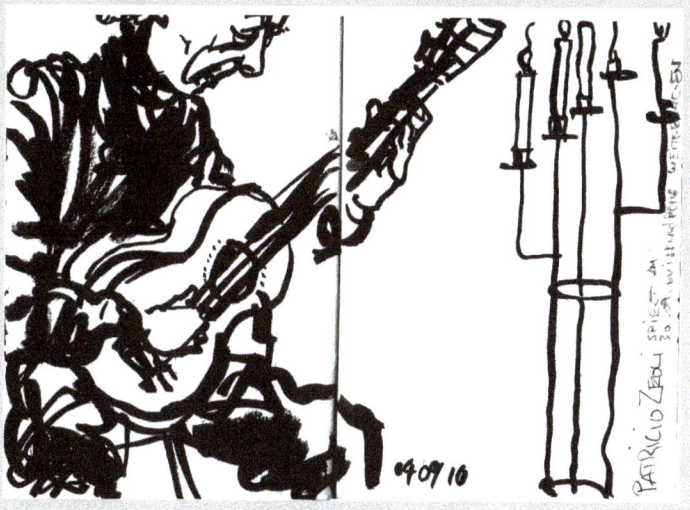

⌂ Renaissance guitar concert in Berlin by Rolf Schroeter

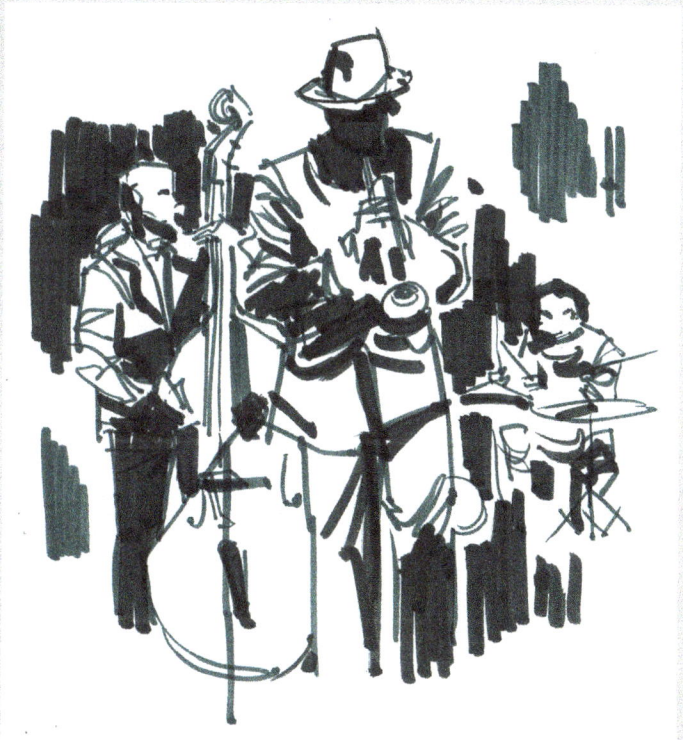

⌂ Jazz at the Set, Kilkenny by Roger O'Reilly, Ireland

STYLE AND TECHNIQUE

A Brush with Music

Even using the same tool, a Pentel brush pen, the individual style of these artists comes through in these sketches of similar subject matter. Miguel Herranz's street concert has a calligraphic quality; Roger O'Reilly's jazz quartet is bold with contrast; and Rolf Schroeter's guitar player has sensuous linework.

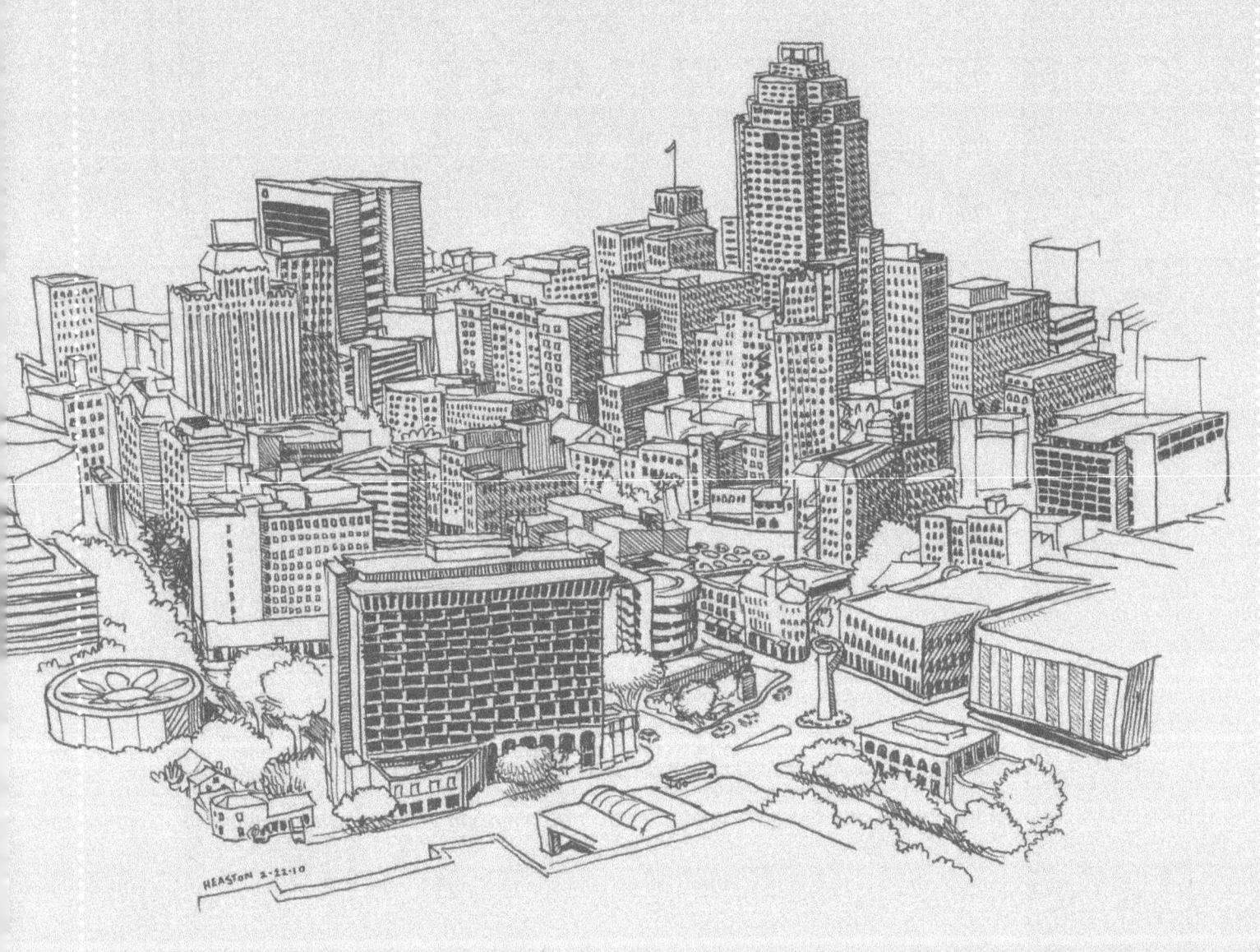

– Paul Heaston

2

SEE THE WORLD, ONE DRAWING AT A TIME

In more than 500 drawings that span every continent, urban sketchers share their experiences of drawing in cities around the world, from well-known metropolises, such as London and Seoul, to small towns, such as Davis, California, and Kandern, Germany. Discover the story behind each impression and gain valuable insight from the artists who captured them.

SEATTLE

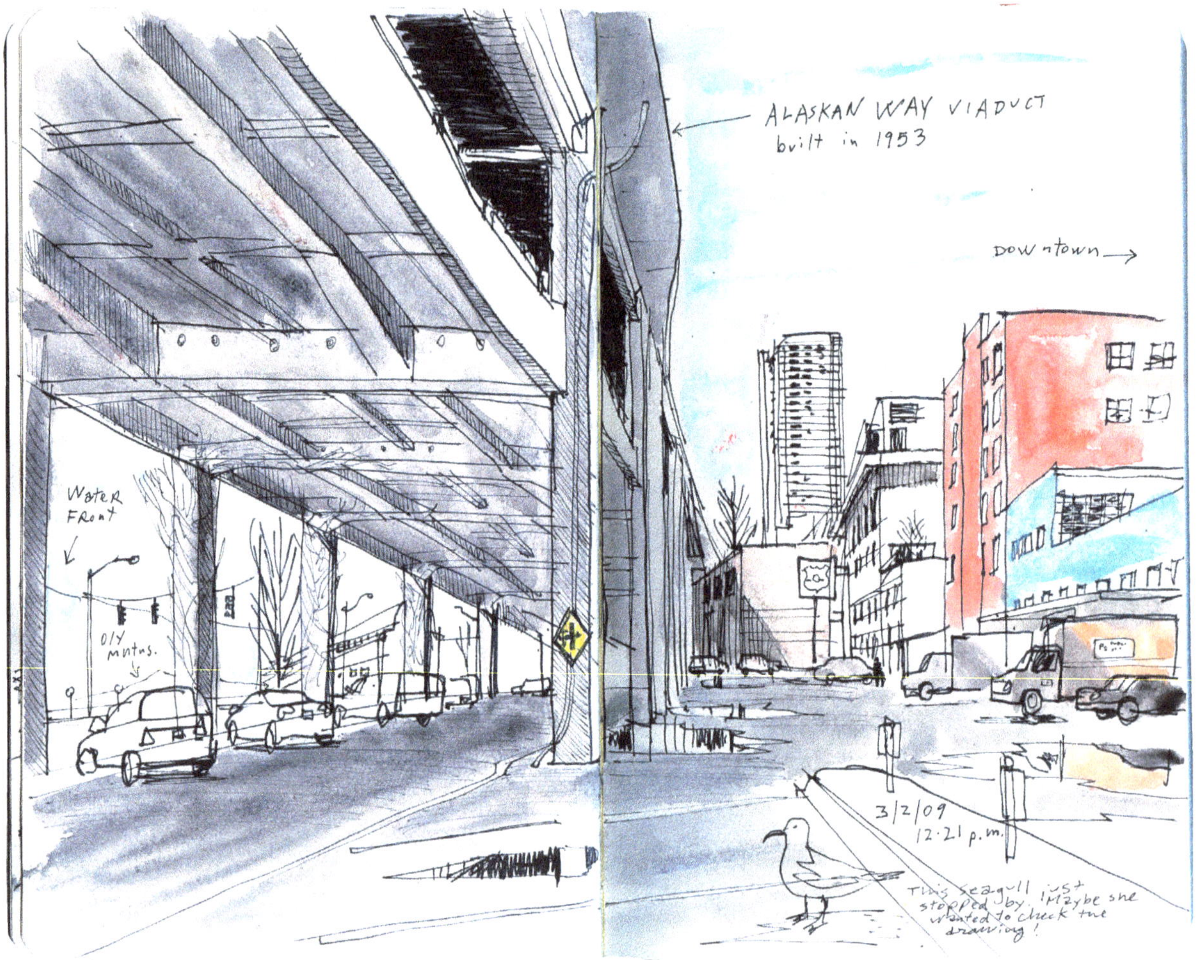

Sandwiched between a bay and a lake, life in Seattle revolves around water. Ferries taking commuters across Puget Sound, cargo ships coming from Asia, fishing boats en route to Alaska: water-related themes abound here, providing plenty of opportunities for local sketchers to draw.

"Urban sketching gives me a sense of belonging to the city where I live now. It helps me set roots."

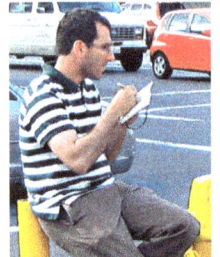

ARTIST PROFILE
Gabriel Campanario

Some of my best memories of growing up in Spain are of summers sketching in my parent's hometown of Montemolín. When I was a teenager, I would sit in the middle of the street during siesta time and draw the ruins of a medieval castle sitting atop the highest hill in a 20-mile (32 km) radius.

For the next two decades, the demands of adulthood got in the way of practicing my favorite sport, drawing in the street. But moving to Seattle was the excuse I needed to begin again, drawing every day. I started drawing in a pocket sketchbook as a way to record my experiences and get acquainted with my new city. From sketching on the bus to drawing during weekend excursions, daily sketching became a habit and a way to improve my illustration skills. Now, it's just part of who I am: an urban sketcher.

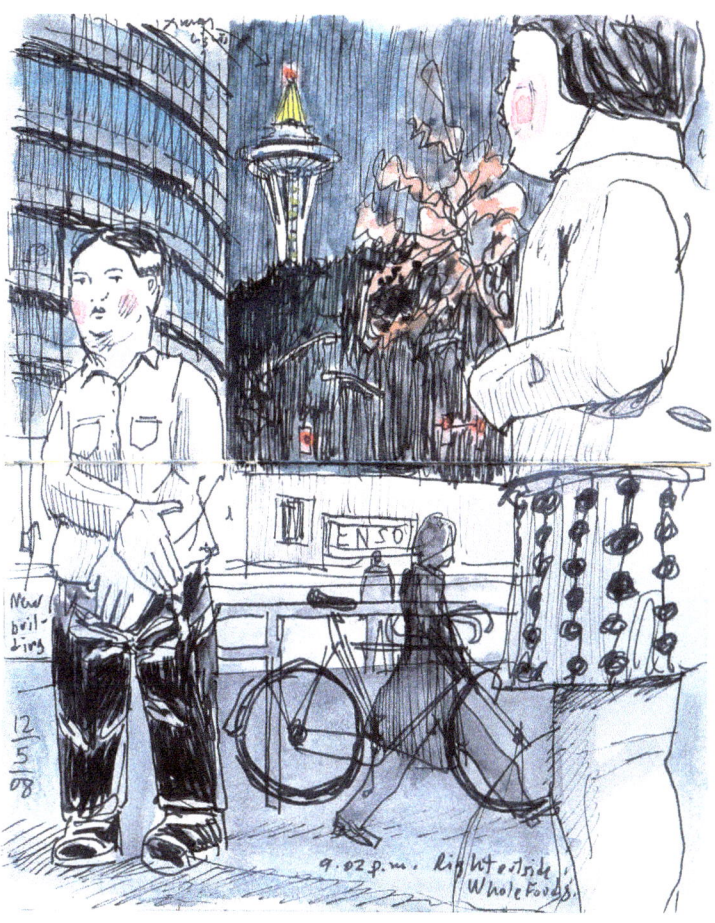

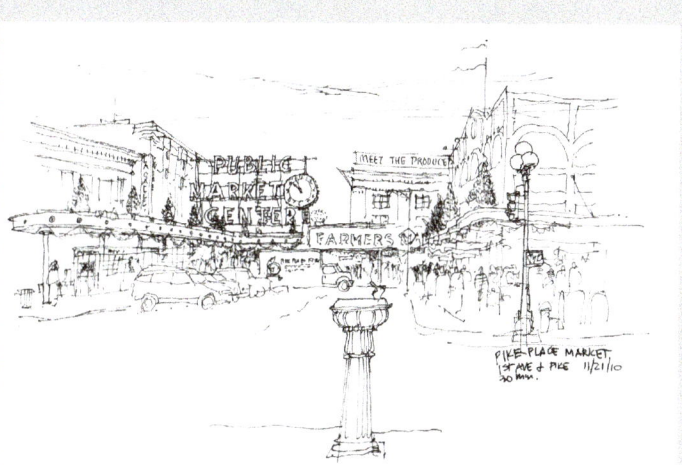

VIEW POINTS

Pike Place Market

"I started by drawing the Public Market Center sign and clock, sizing and positioning it to ensure there was enough room on the page for the side buildings that define the street space. Then, to establish the foreground, where I was sitting, I used a sidewalk water fountain. This separation between the viewer and the viewed is something I always try to convey in composing a scene." — *Frank Ching*

4" x 7" | 10 x 18 cm; Lamy fountain pen on Piccadilly sketchbook; 30 minutes

"People stopped to comment on the progress of my sketch, as I tuned out the flurry of activity around me and concentrated on my lines. All the remarks were encouraging, which is one of the things that make sketching in the street such a rewarding experience. The main challenge was to get as much of the wide scene into the somewhat square-ish format of the sketchbook spread. I placed the center of my composition on the center of the sketchbook and went from there."
— *Gabriel Campanario*

10.5" x 8.25" | 26.5 x 21 cm; Moleskine large sketchbook, Micron 08 pen, and gouache; 45 minutes

↻ **Space Needle** Giant fiberglass sculptures dominate the foreground in this night sketch, but Campanario says he was mostly drawn to the red and yellow Christmas lights atop the Space Needle.

Tip "I made sure to capture a person walking by to give a sense of scale and an indication of how large the sculptures are." — *Gabriel Campanario*

7" x 5.5" | 18 x 14 cm; Moleskine pocket sketchbook, Micron 08 pen, and gouache; about 30 minutes

↻ **Viaduct** Plans are in place to replace this double-decker elevated freeway along Seattle's waterfront with a deep-bore tunnel. "The viaduct is like a giant centipede of concrete, not a beautiful sight but a sketch-worthy subject matter nonetheless," says Campanario.

Tip "Urban sketching is not just about finding the picture-perfect postcard scene. A dark alley or seemingly uncharacteristic street can prove even more interesting to draw." — *Gabriel Campanario*

10.5" x 8.25" | 26.5 x 21 cm; Moleskine large sketchbook, Micron 08 pen, and gouache

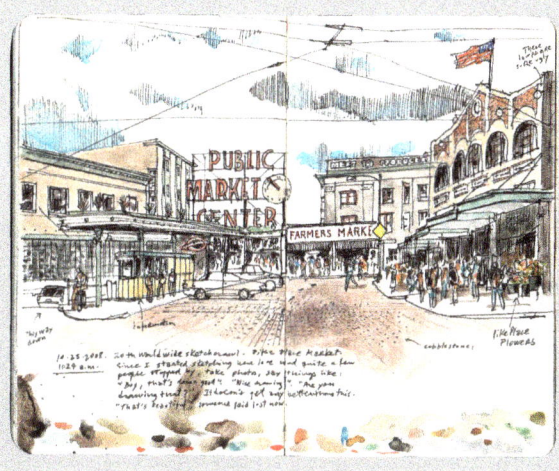

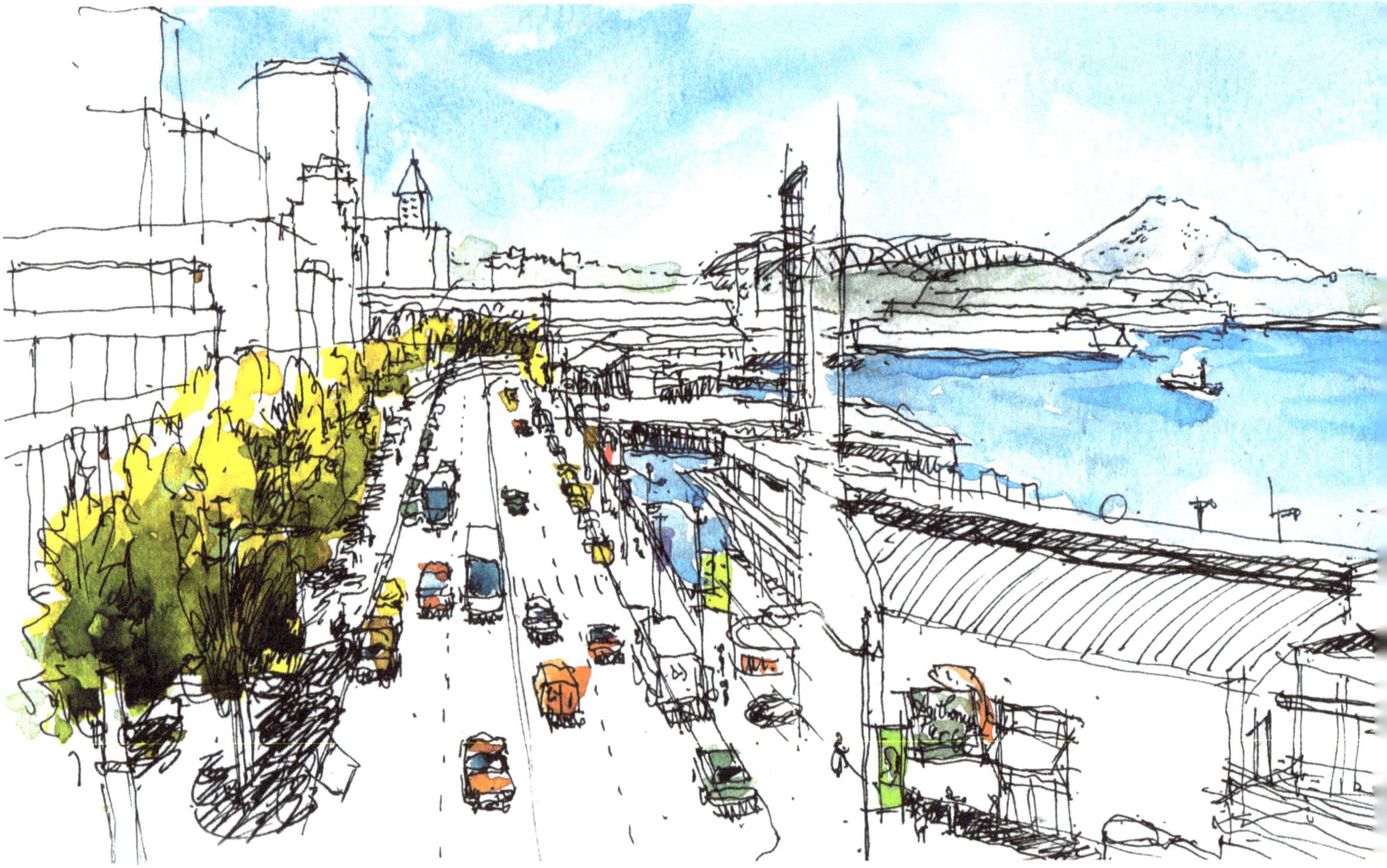

◯ Elliot Bay This panoramic view of the Seattle waterfront shows Mt. Rainier in the distance. Gail Wong says a docked cruise ship was blocking the view of the water from street level, but she found a good angle from a skybridge.

Tip "I set the horizon line high on the page so I could get the foreground of Alaskan Way, the street below, on the lower half of the page." — *Gail L. Wong*

13" x 5" | 33 x 12.5 cm; Lamy ink pen with ink converter (extra-fine nib), Noodler's Bulletproof Black ink, Daniel Smith tube paints on Moleskine watercolor notebook; 1 hour, 20 minutes

⟲ Seattle Public Library OMA/Koolhaas won an international design competition for this iconic building in Seattle, distinguished by its faceted, gridded glass form enclosing soaring interior spaces.

Tip "Normally, I think irregular forms are easier to draw, because it is more difficult to see errors in geometry, scale, and proportion. But in this case, proportion does matter. Beneath the gridded facets, you might be able to see my initial attempts at roughing out the forms, which were not broad enough, given the building's height. I kept increasing the width as the drawing developed." — *Frank Ching*

7" x 7" | 18 x 18 cm; Lamy fountain pen, Piccadilly sketchbook; 45 minutes

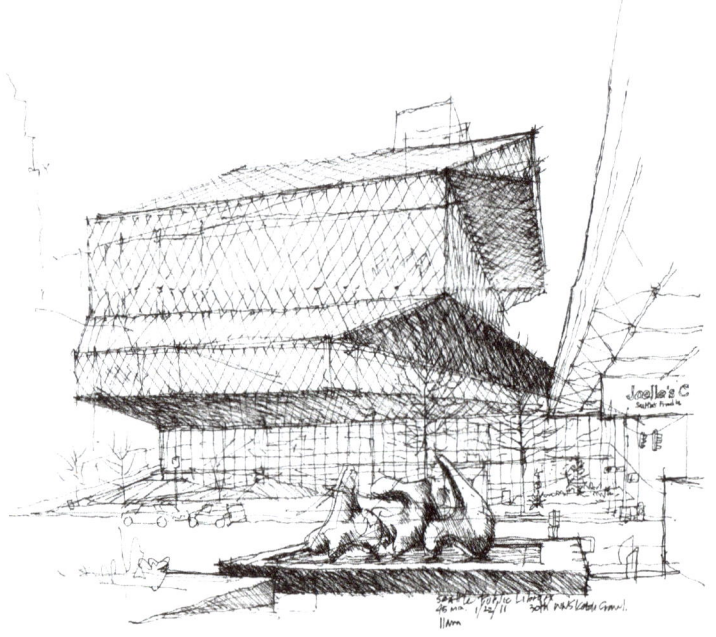

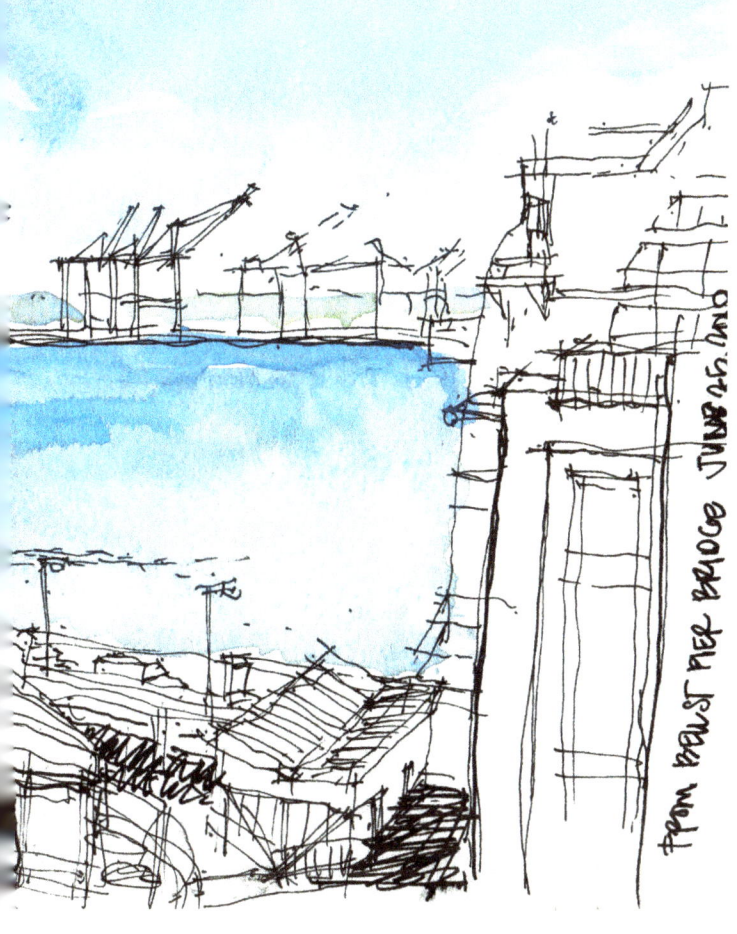

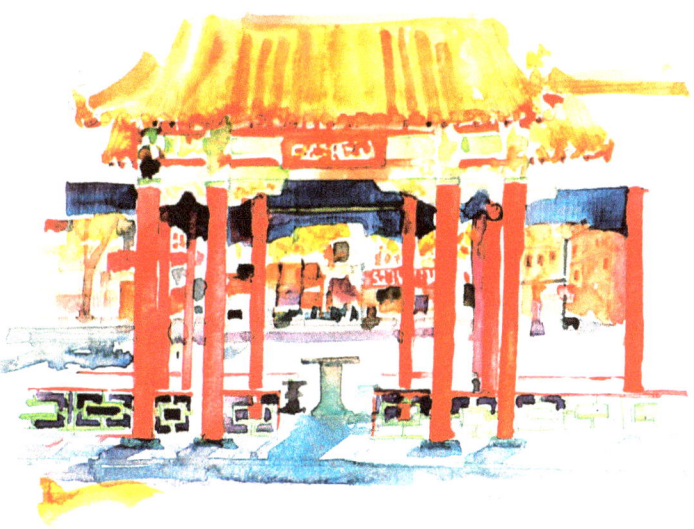

🎧 **Hing Hay Park** In the heart of the city's China-town/International District, Susan K. Miller found two elderly men practicing Qigong with taped music by the colorful Grand Pavilion.

Tip "I am a lazy urban sketcher. We are the ones who find a comfortable, shaded place to sit and then see what can be sketched from there. I kept jumping up to sketch the perspective and shadows that were most interesting and then returned to my bench to paint the sketch." — *Susan K. Miller*

11" x 8.5" | 28 x 21.6 cm; Derwent 2B pencil and Daniel Smith watercolors on Bee Paper Pen Sketcher's pad; about 50 minutes

FIRST PERSON

My Street

by Gabriel Campanario

I don't have to go very far to find sketching opportunities. My street is a stage of entertaining performances. Kids play outdoors all day long during the summer, and snow usually makes an appearance in the winter, although not as much as the year I did this winter sketch.

Left: 10.5" x 8.25" | 26.5 x 21 cm; Micron 0.8 pen and gouache on Moleskine large sketchbook spread

Right: 7" x 5.5" | 18 x 14 cm; Micron 0.8 pen and gouache on Moleskine pocket sketchbook spread

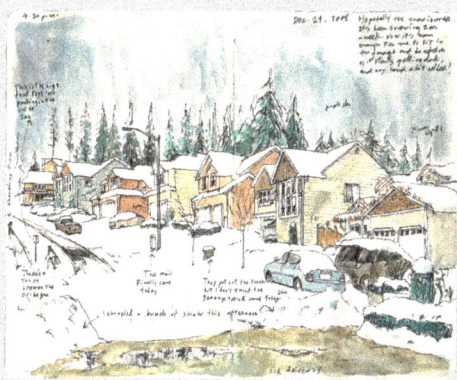

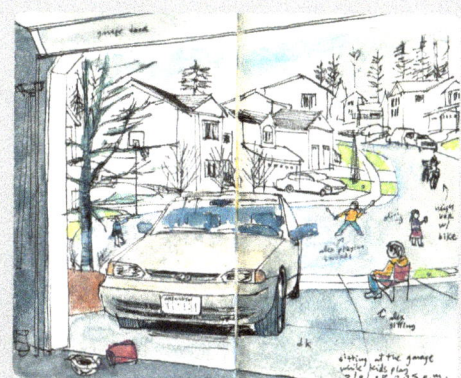

VICTORIA

For local architect Matthew Cencich, Victoria's Chinatown neighborhood and downtown ornate architecture are favorite sketching subjects. The climate in the western Canadian city is relatively mild, but it's often wet and chilly, so sketching outdoors can be a challenge. Still, Cencich says he has done some of his best sketches in winter, often making it back to a coffee shop chilled to the bone and vowing not to return until spring.

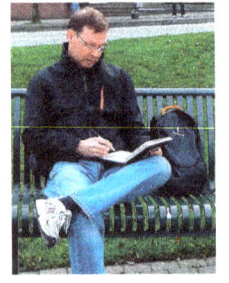

ARTIST PROFILE
Matthew Cencich

My work in the architectural field requires amazing patience before a project is actually realized. With onsite sketching, there is a much more immediate payback; the intense effort of seeing and scratching lines onto paper gives great and immediate satisfaction— sometimes!

Urban sketching, to me, is a way of capturing a place in a sketch, most often pursued while traveling but also in my own town. I started by sketching architecture that I admire and continue to find architecture—and urban design—my favorite subjects. The online urban sketchers community has inspired me to expand my range. It has been a real motivator to include the surrounding context in my sketches.

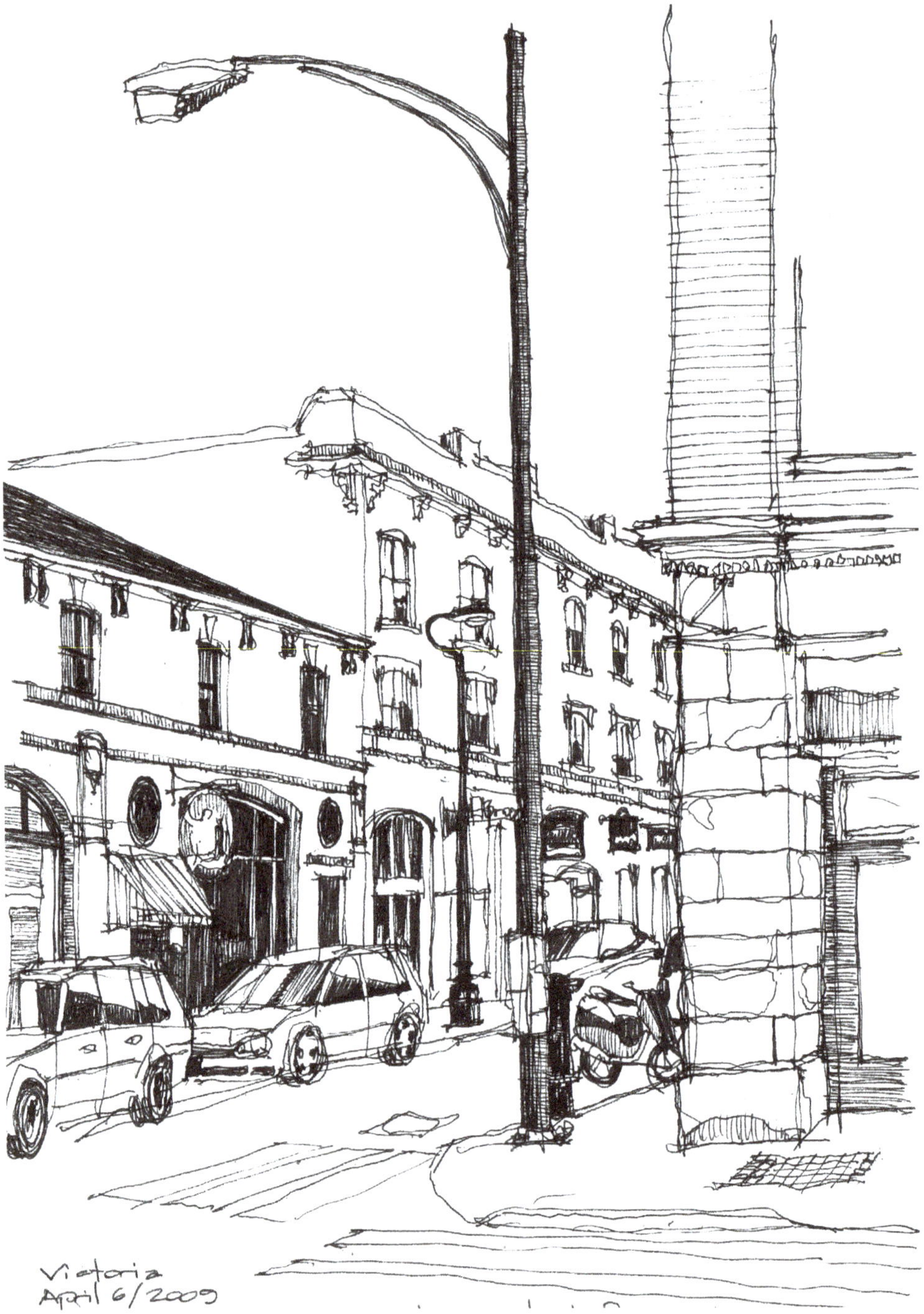

Victoria
April 6/2009

∩ **Looking into Broad Street** Cencich calls the old part of downtown Victoria Hoppertown, because the streets look like they could have a starring role in a Hopper painting.

Tip "There is something mysterious about looking into a street and not seeing the end."— *Matthew Cencich*

8.75" x 12" | 22 x 30.5 cm; black Sharpie fine-point marker on Canson sketchbook (heavyweight paper suitable for watercolor); 1 hour

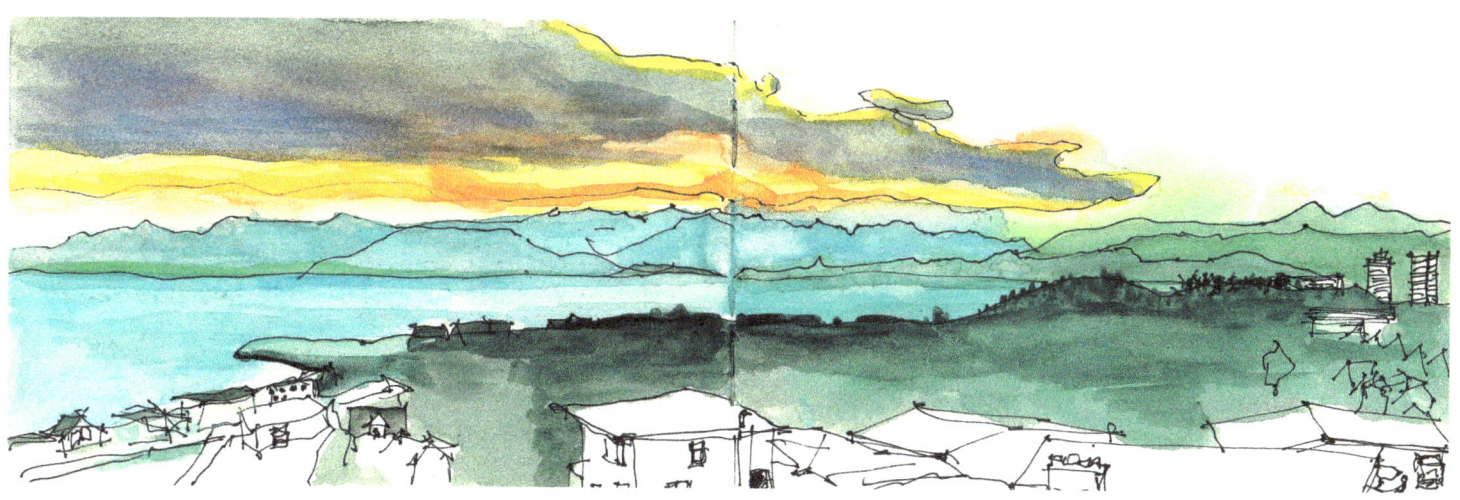

↻ Looking Over the Strait of Juan de Fuca from Moss Hill Park The strait between Vancouver Island and the Olympic mountains of Washington State shows the wild nature of Victoria's setting.

Tip "It was bitterly cold, so this drawing was done very quickly, with a loose pen sketch and the watercolors applied very wet. The sketch didn't dry out until I got it home!" — *Matthew Cencich*

5.25" x 16.5" | 13 x 42 cm; Sharpie fine-point marker, child's watercolor set on Hand-Book Travelogue Journal; about 1 hour

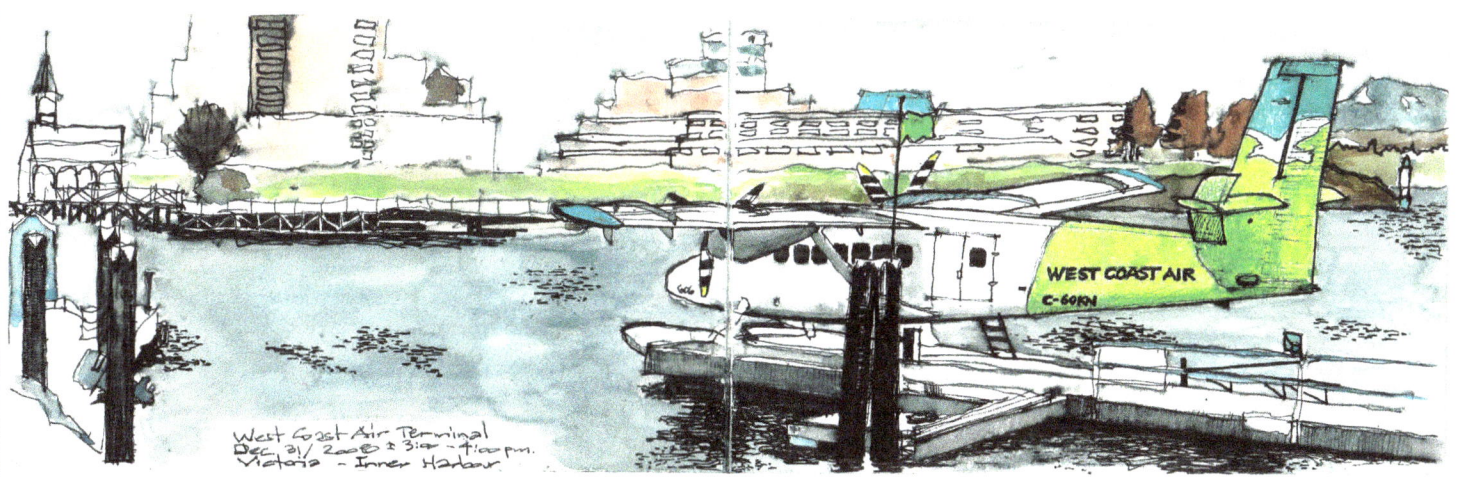

↻ West Coast Air Terminal at Inner Harbour This particular seaplane service flies to Seattle, but there's another that goes to Vancouver.

Tip "This sketch taught me that not all markers are waterproof! I now try to use waterproof markers when I think I will be using watercolor paints." — *Matthew Cencich*

5" x 16.25" | 12.5 x 41 cm; black, nonwaterproof, fine-point marker, watercolors, and Prismacolor colored pencils on Moleskine watercolor book; about 1 hour

"Drawing is a Zen experience, somehow, in that time is lost and real insight is made into an object or scene by observing it closely enough to draw it."

SAN FRANCISCO

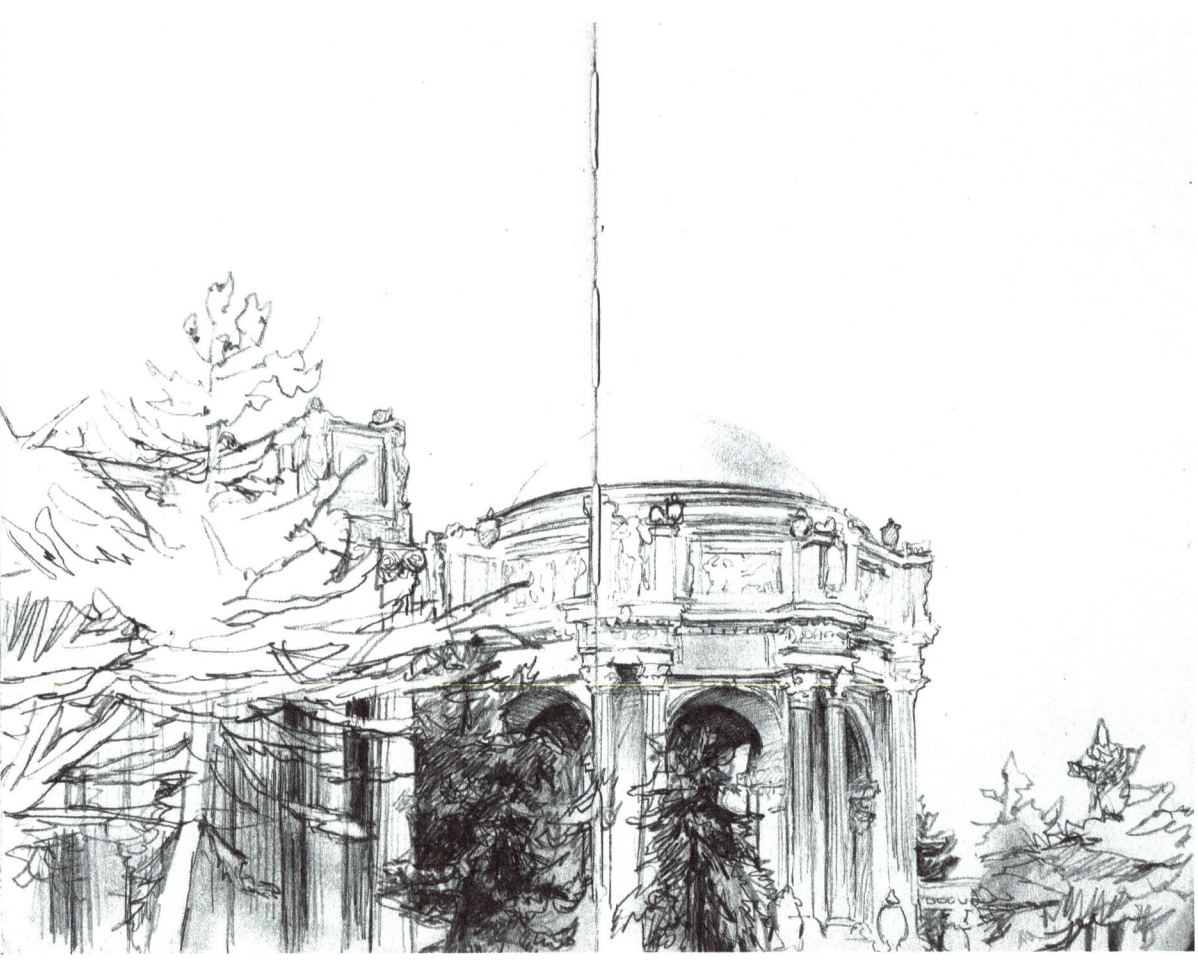

⟲ Palace of Fine Arts The Palace of Fine Arts was designed by Bernard Maybeck for the 1915 Panama-Pacific Exposition. A tourist watching Amaro sketch asked how long he'd been drawing. He told her: it's not when he started, it's that he never stopped.

Tip "The foreground trees are indicated rather than rendered, to help pull the focus past them."
— *Gary Amaro*

10.5" x 8.25" | 26.5 x 21 cm; Staedtler 2B and HB pencils, .05 HB mechanical pencil, kneaded eraser on Moleskine sketchbook; 30 minutes

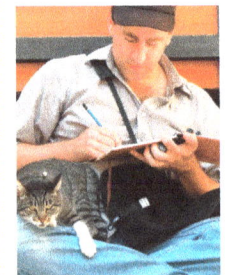

ARTIST PROFILE
Gary Amaro

I carry a sketchbook and a handful of pencils and brushes with me wherever I go, which is not to say that I can always make time to draw what catches my eye, but at least I'm prepared. Observational drawing is a constant practice and a kind of meditation.

I live on the east side of San Francisco Bay, working as a concept and storyboard artist in the video game industry and teaching sequential art at the Academy of Art University. Urban sketching sharpens my observational skills, adds to my visual vocabulary, and, especially when I get going at speed, takes me to the heart of markmaking.

"All of my sketches have a narrative quality to them. They are fragments of stories."

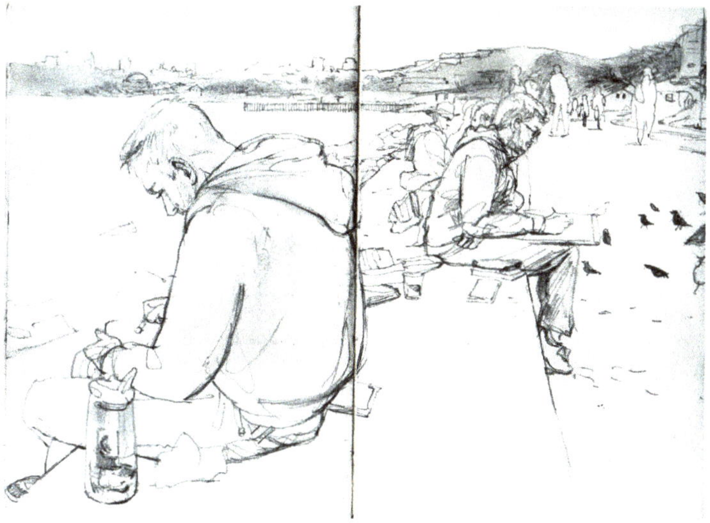

Sketchers at Crissy Field Amaro drew fellow sketchers on the waterfront near the Warming Hut at Crissy Field, overlooking the Bay.

Tip "I draw people quickly, because I never know when they are going to move. Still, I try to get a specific sense of character. They should feel like they're breathing and thinking." – *Gary Amaro*

10.5" x 8.25" | 26.5 x 21 cm; pencils, Moleskine large sketchbook; about 30 minutes

Haight Street A homeless man and a double exposure of buildings across Haight Street.

Tip "I wouldn't advise attempting something like this without a sketching buddy. Know your neighborhood. When I finished the sketch, we tucked some money into one of the man's bags." – *Gary Amaro*

10.5" x 8.25" | 26.5 x 21 cm; pencils, Moleskine large sketchbook; about 40 minutes

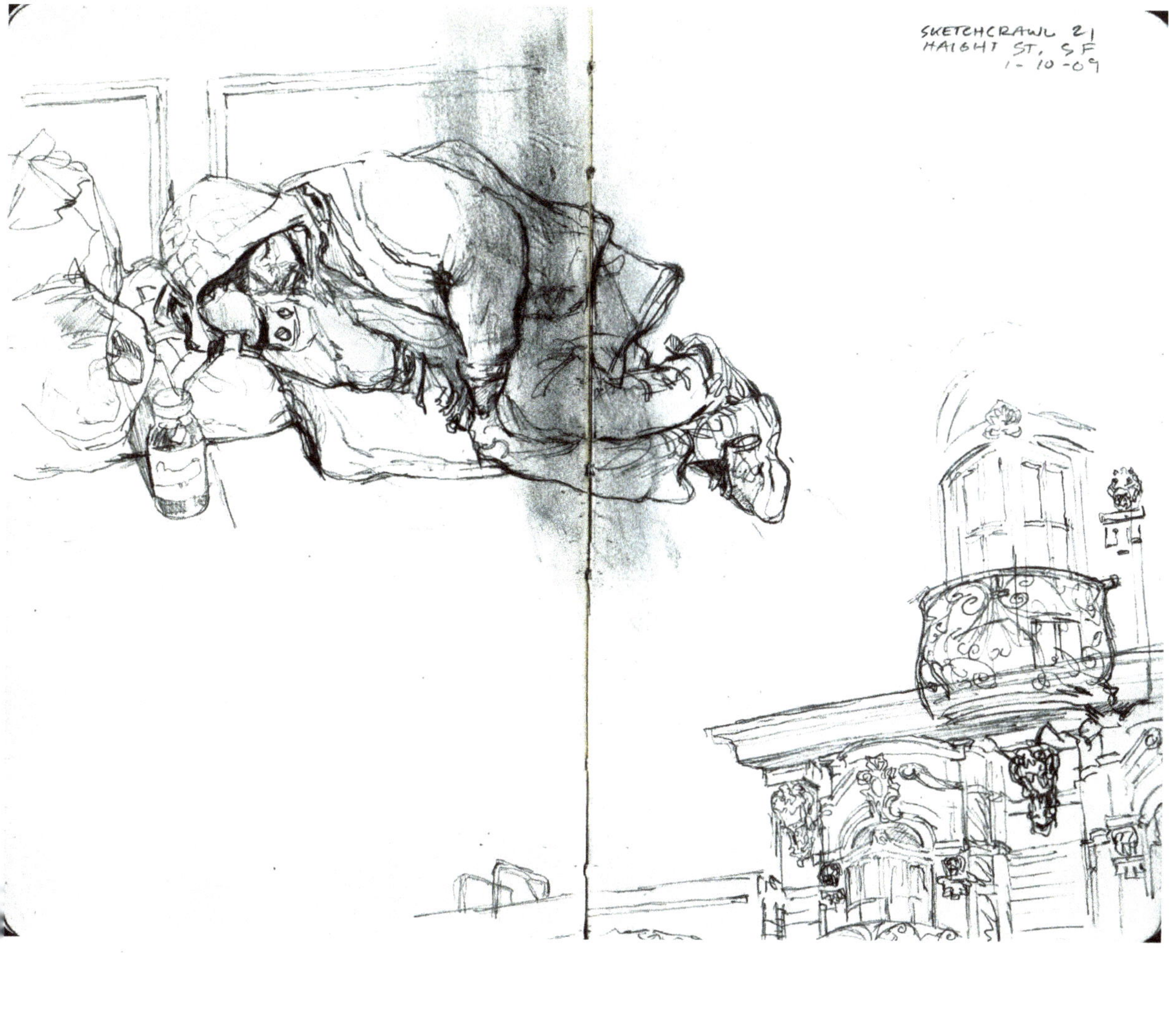
SKETCHCRAWL 21
HAIGHT ST, SF
1-10-09

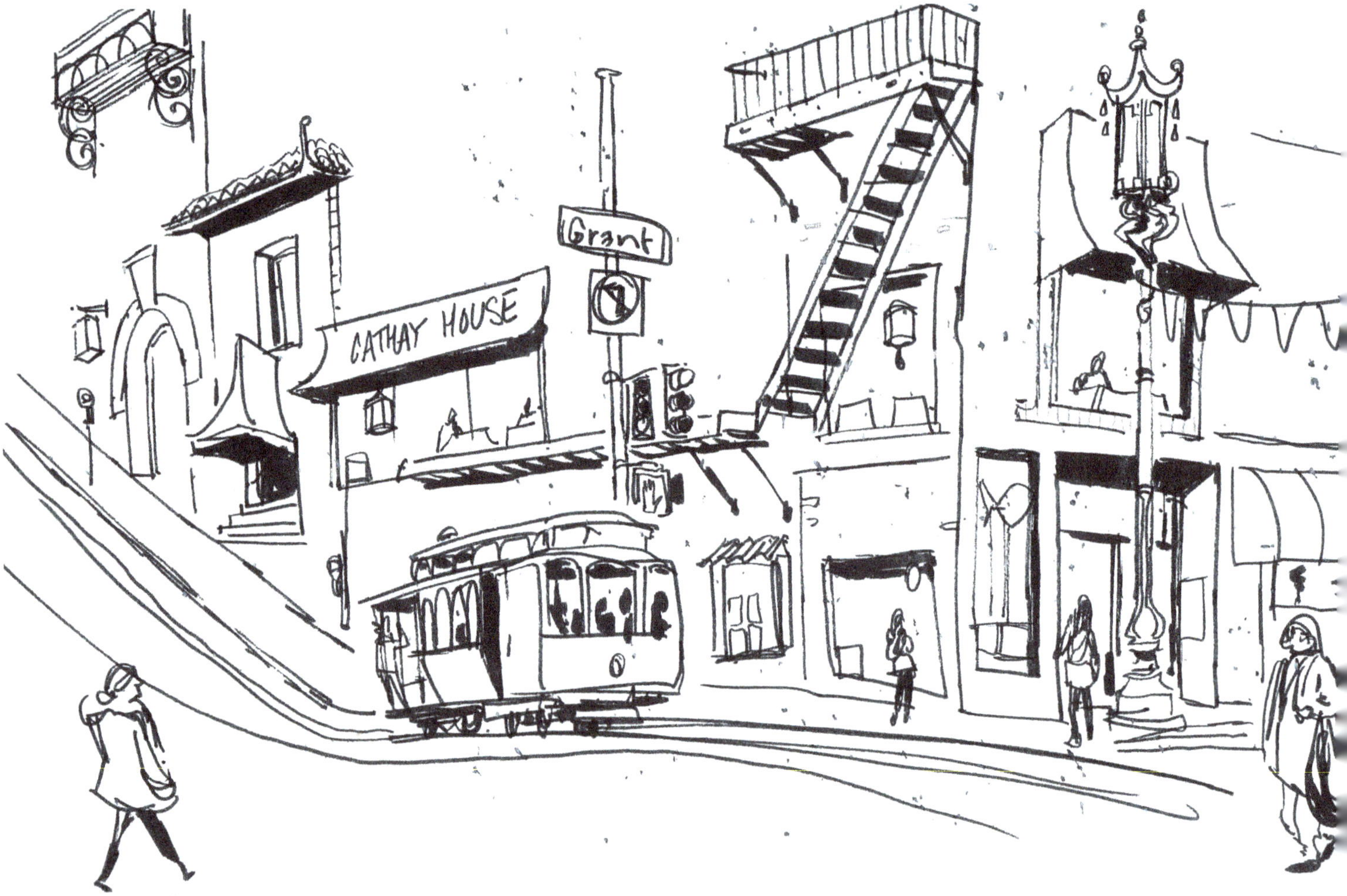

'Grant Ave.'

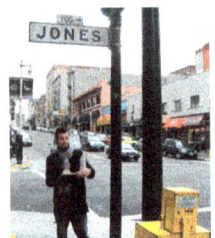

ARTIST PROFILE
Matt Jones

For me, urban sketching provides a visual diary of where and when I discovered a particular part of a city. I keep a sketchbook as a repository of visual ideas, notes, thoughts, and observations inspired by experience.

As a professional story artist for animated features, I find a sketchbook is invaluable as a resource of architecture, natural locations, and character studies. Places or people I've drawn often become the inspiration for ideas at work. San Francisco is unique, because the geography of the city offers wildly distinct vantage points. The steep hills, cable cars, and Victorian architecture make hugely interesting subjects to draw.

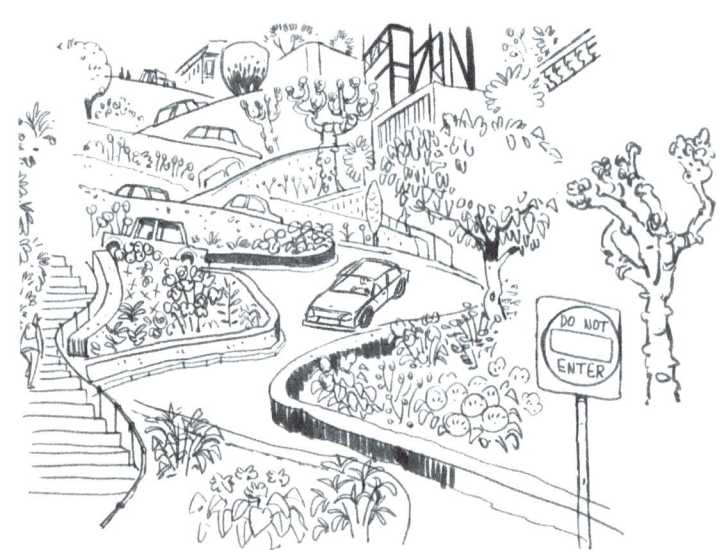

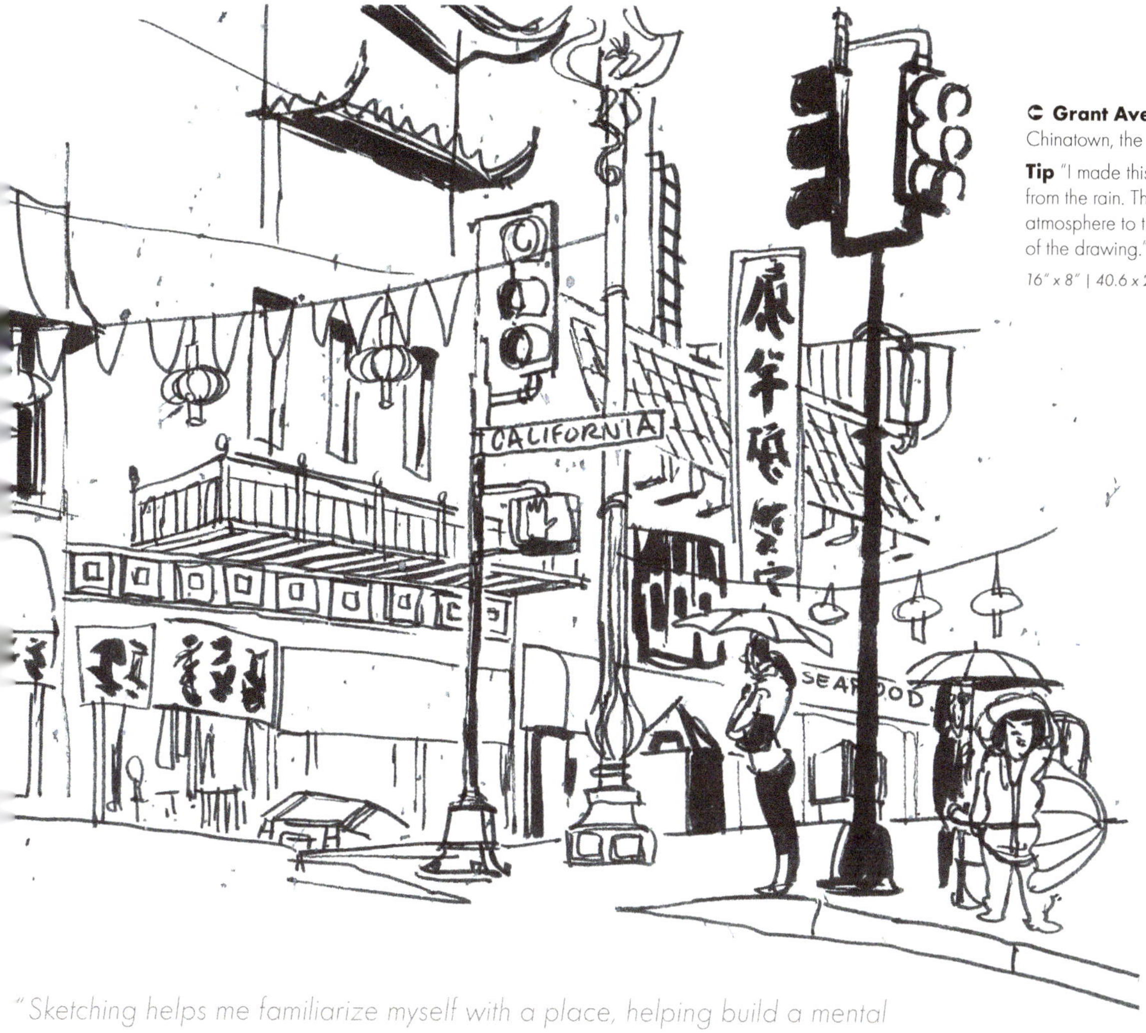

☾ Grant Avenue At a cable-car crossing in Chinatown, the umbrellas were out on this rainy day.

Tip "I made this drawing sitting in a bus stop to shelter from the rain. The damp conditions added some atmosphere to the sketch; rain drops literally became part of the drawing." — *Matt Jones*

16" x 8" | 40.6 x 20 cm; Tombow brush pen, rain, Moleskine; 1 hour

"Sketching helps me familiarize myself with a place, helping build a mental map and aiding me in learning street names and landmarks."

☾ Lombard Street The crookedest street in the world.

Tip "It was a complicated scene that needed careful simplifying of perspective and detail." — *Matt Jones*

11" x 8" | 28 x 20 cm; Tombow brush pen, Moleskine; less than an hour

☽ Oakland Bridge View across the East Bay from Emeryville. The Oakland span of the Bay Bridge links to Treasure Island and then to the city. Sutro Tower is just visible in the background.

Tip "The city is often shrouded in fog, but on a clear morning, I quickly made this sketch to capture the impressive sweep of the Oakland span of the Bay Bridge. I tried to focus on overall shapes and not get too caught up in details." — *Matt Jones*

11" x 4"| 28 x 10 cm; Tombow brush pen, Moleskine; less than an hour

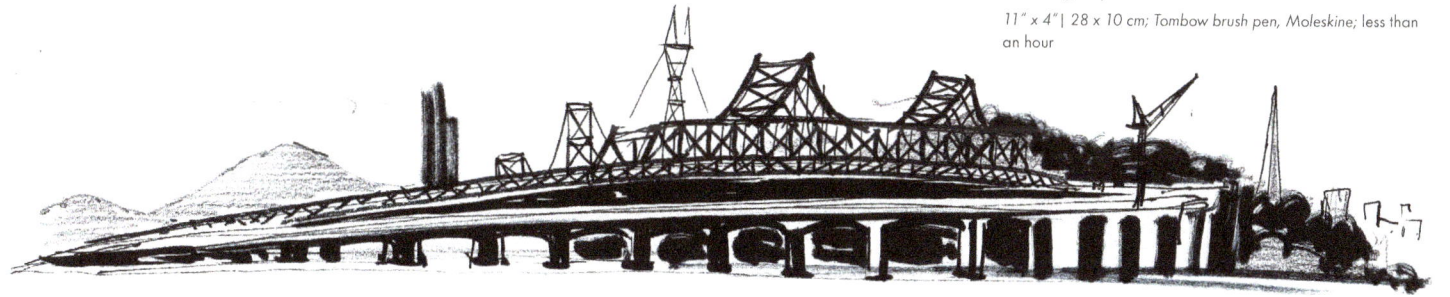

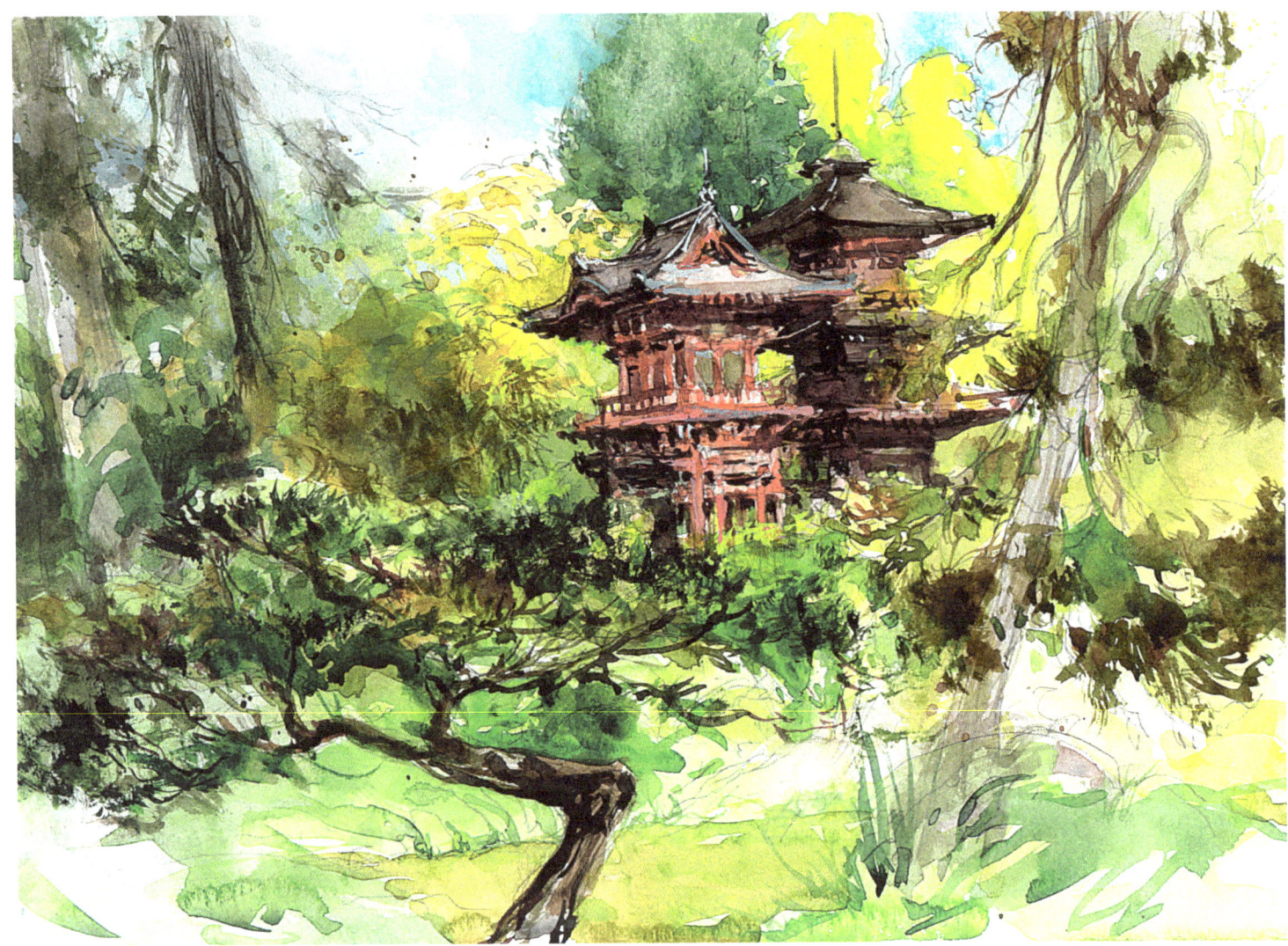

⌒ Japanese Garden, Golden Gate Park The Japanese Tea Garden at Golden Gate Park is a small, tranquil, park within a park just west of the De Young Museum.

Tip "The key to drawing trees is simplification. Create simple masses and reduce the trees to silhouettes, indicating some of the foliage at the edges."
— *Marc Taro Holmes*

11" x 14" | 28 x 35.6 cm; Winsor & Newton watercolor on Canson cold-press block, mechanical pencil in 0.7mm HB lead, sable brushes, faux squirrel brushes for larger washes, blotting and smudging with paper towels; about 3 hours

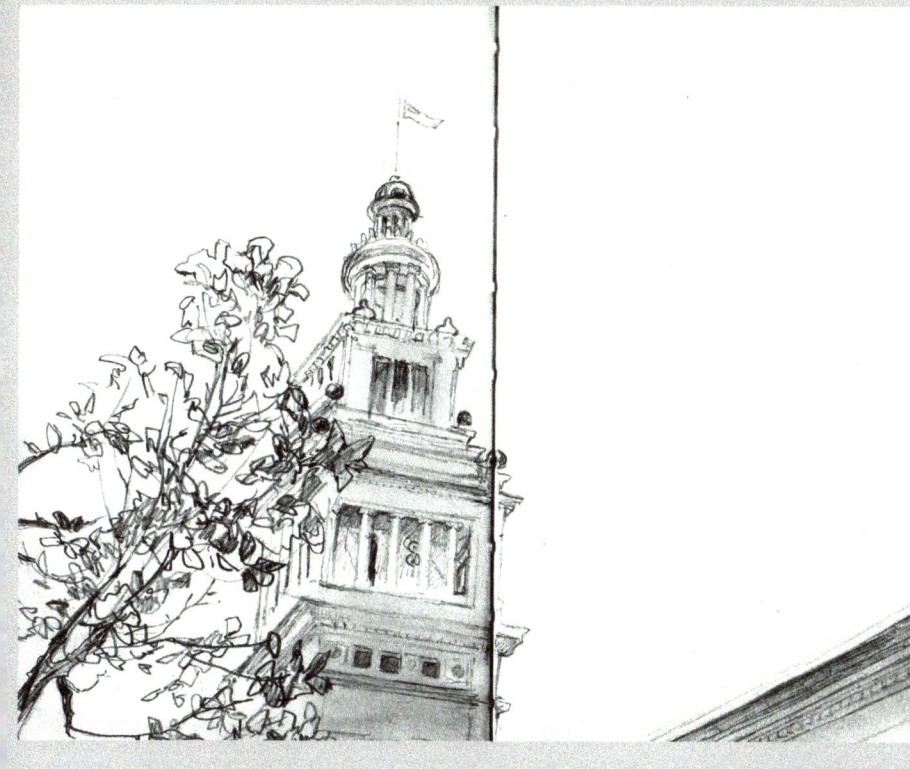

Ferry Building

"So what if it's a landmark that every tourist takes a photo of?" says Gary Amaro. "No one else will draw it like you."

↻ **From the Street** "These upward "shots" feel cinematic to me and can suggest a moving point of view. Along with the bulk of the building, any contemporary elements are also cropped off, giving this a timeless feel. The subtle tilt suggests that we are not centered on the building but are instead scanning past. This is a kind of photographic framing; I chose the angle looking through the tree for both composition and depth."
— Gary Amaro

5.25" x 8.25" | 13 x 21 cm; pencils, Moleskine large sketchbook; about 30 minutes

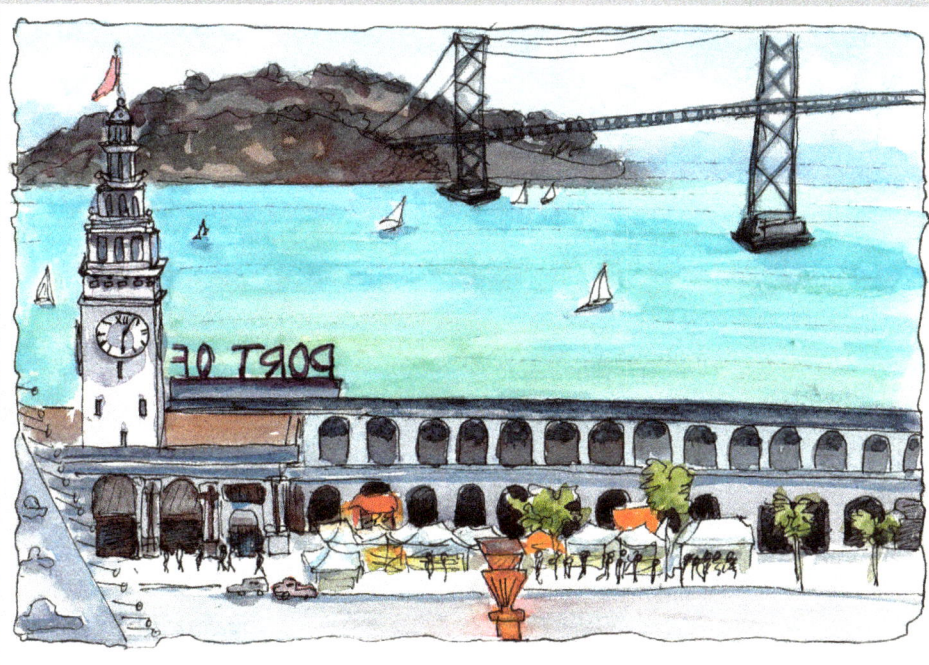

↻ **From the Hyatt Regency Hotel** "Some sketcher friends and I were allowed to go up to the private lounge on the top floor. First, I penciled in a rectangular window about half an inch smaller than the page. Then, I decided what was most important to include and made a few marks with pencil, to indicate where things started and ended, such as the top of the flag pole and bottom of the building. Finally, I drew directly with pen, going slowly."
— Jana Bouc

5.5" x 7.5" | 14 x 19 cm; Lamy Safari fine-point fountain pen filled with Carbon Platinum ink, Winsor & Newton and Daniel Smith watercolors, Niji waterbrush on a case-bound, sewn-signature journal that I made myself using 140-lb., cold-press Legion Multimedia paper; 30–40 minutes

DAVIS

The central California town of Davis is known for its university campus, ubiquitous bike paths, and highly educated population. British transplant Pete Scully is drawn to Davis's bright, small-town atmosphere, the American flavor of its residential neighborhoods, and the colorful accents provided by fire hydrants.

○ Old City Hall Scully sat in the shade on a mild January day to sketch the Old City Hall building. Built in 1938, it has also served as a fire station and a police station.

Tip "With golden light and blue skies, this is a very "Davis" scene. I think it's important to get a feel for your city's color palette and to represent it in your sketches." — *Pete Scully*

8″ x 4.5″ | 20 x 11.5 cm; Micron 01 pen, Winsor & Newton Cotman half-pan watercolors, Moleskine watercolor book; 90 minutes

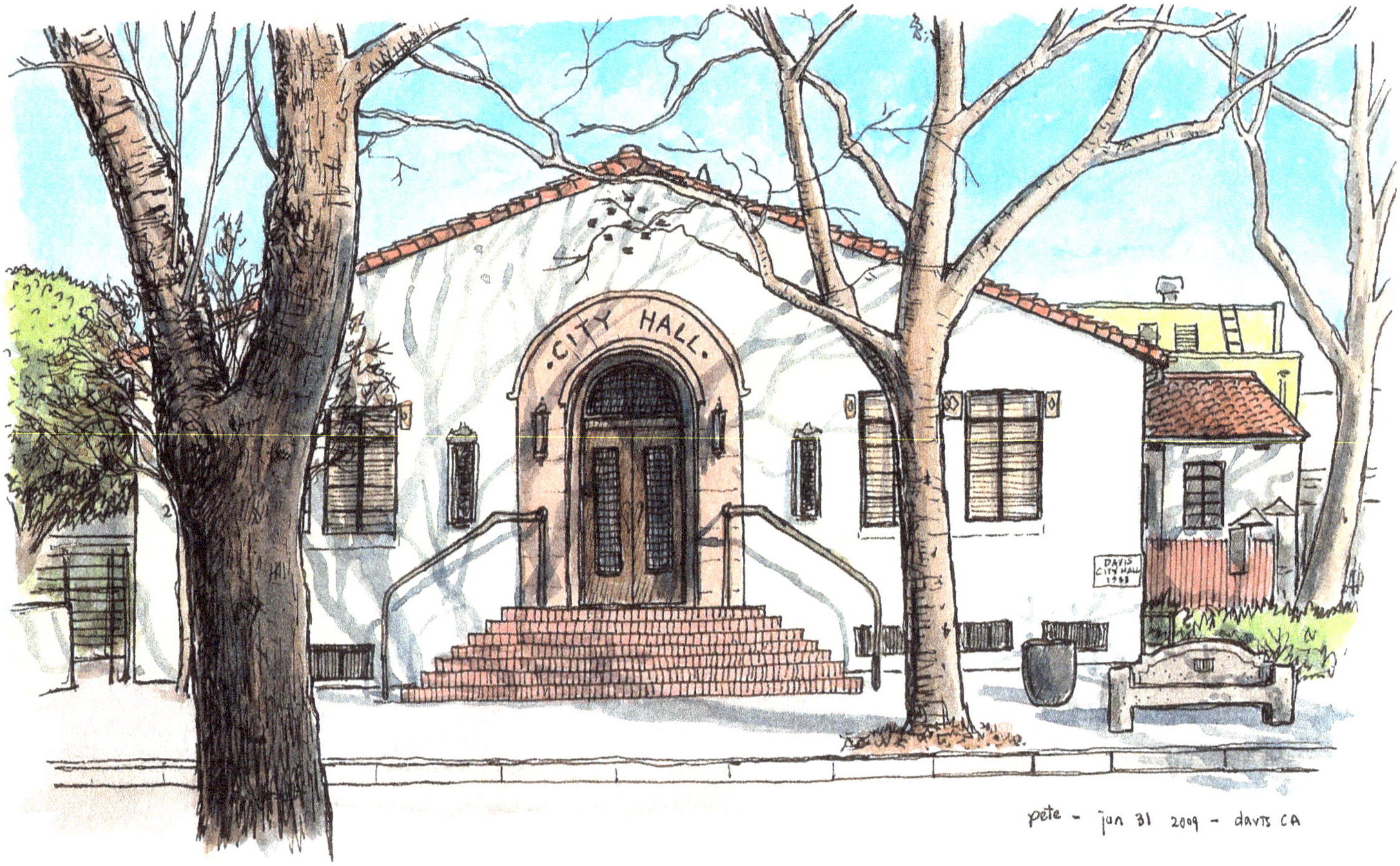

pete - jun 31 2009 - davis CA

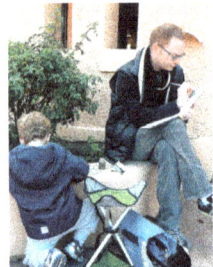

ARTIST PROFILE

Pete Scully

I am from urban north London but now live in urbane Davis, California. I sketch to remember where I am in the world; one day, I might forget. Urban sketching, for me, is the act of recording a place forever, so that in years to come, I'll have a visual record of where (and possibly who) I was. There is always something to draw; everything is interesting if you take an interest in it. I use the valuable lunch-hour break from my job at the university to catch some urban sketches. I often draw a frame around my sketches to limit my composition but rather enjoy letting objects, like trees and telegraph poles, pop out of the frame.

"I love to sketch buildings and trees, but I particularly like sketching fire hydrants."

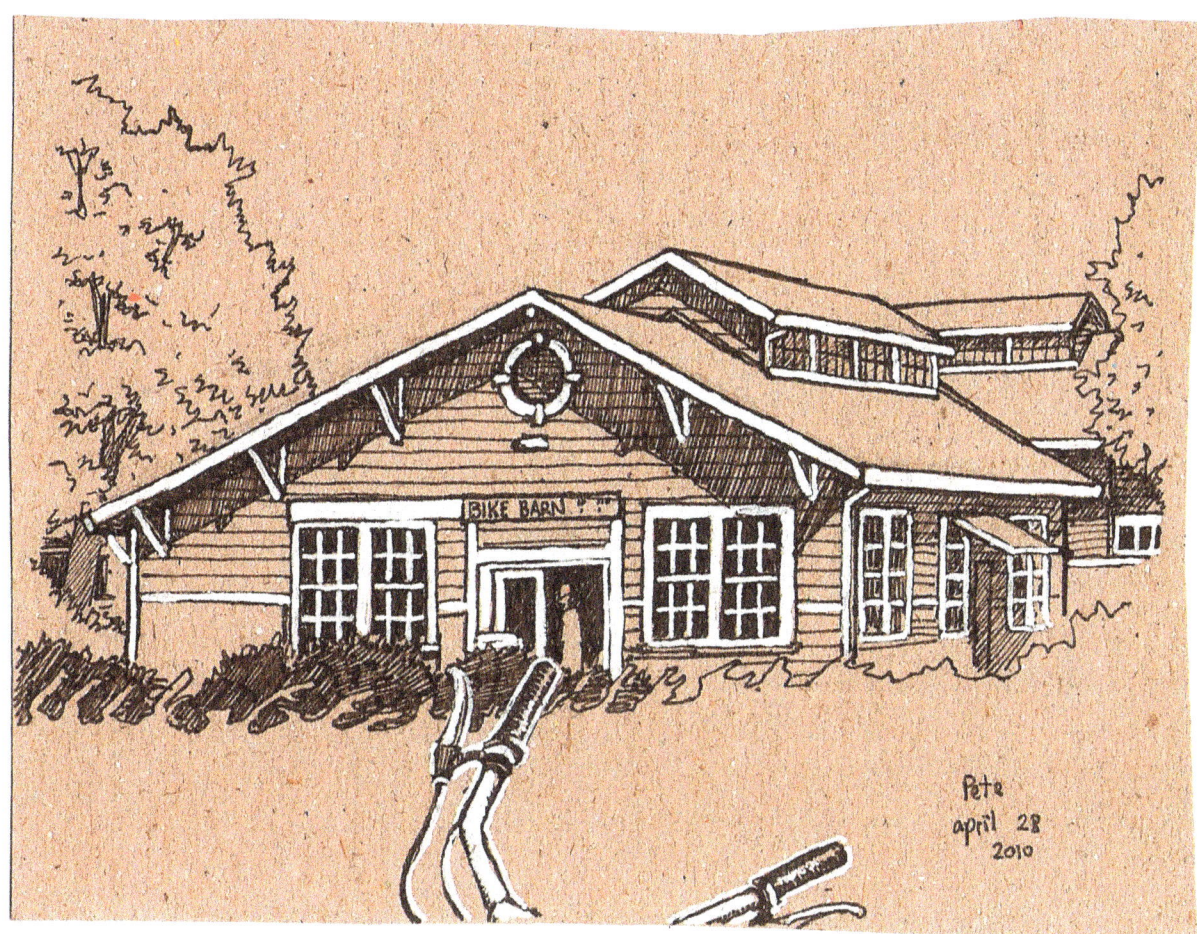

↻ The Bike Barn
Scully decided to start recycling the many envelopes that arrive at the university's graduate admissions office.

Tip "Sketching on brown paper, I'm less inclined to fill the whole space. Also, using a white gel pen can help emphasize some lines for contrast."
— *Pete Scully*

5" x 4" | 12.5 x 10 cm; Uni-ball Vision pen, Sakura white Gelly Roll pen, recycled brown envelope paper; about 15 minutes

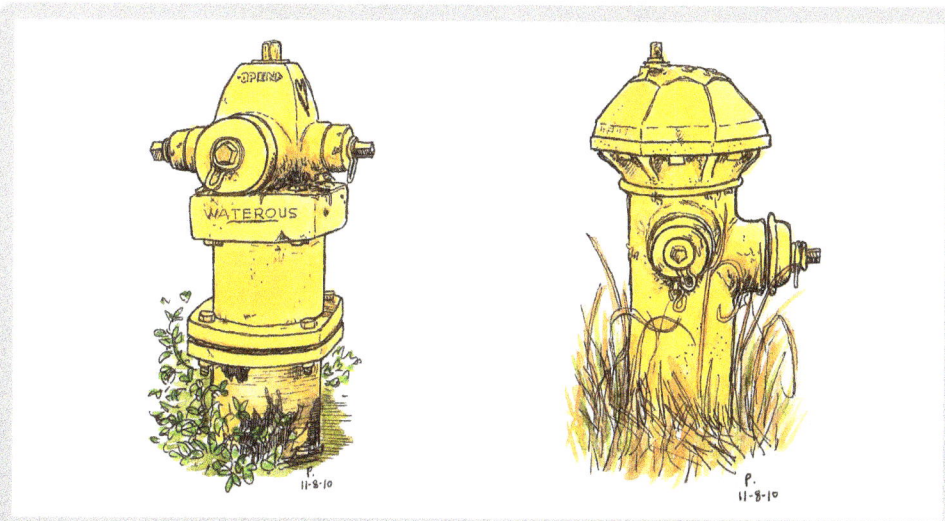

URBAN FURNITURE

Drawn to Fire Hydrants

by Pete Scully

I have a bit of an obsession with sketching fire hydrants. We don't get them in Britain—when people ask me how we put out fires, I tell them we just wait for it to rain. It's something else that, in my eyes, is very "America" and reminds me of those Richard Scarry storybooks I used to read as a kid. Fire hydrants are like little metal guardians but so common that nobody notices them and how varied they are.

LOS ANGELES

Sunny skylines, vintage cars, and movie-set action star in the sketchbooks of these Los Angeles–based artists. For French-born illustrator Stéphane Kardos, sketching on location in Los Angeles is much easier than in Europe. "The buildings are simple, streets are straight and wide, and there are more cars than people in the streets."

"The purpose of sketching is to record what I see in my own way, so I like having my own marks on paper, mistakes and all."

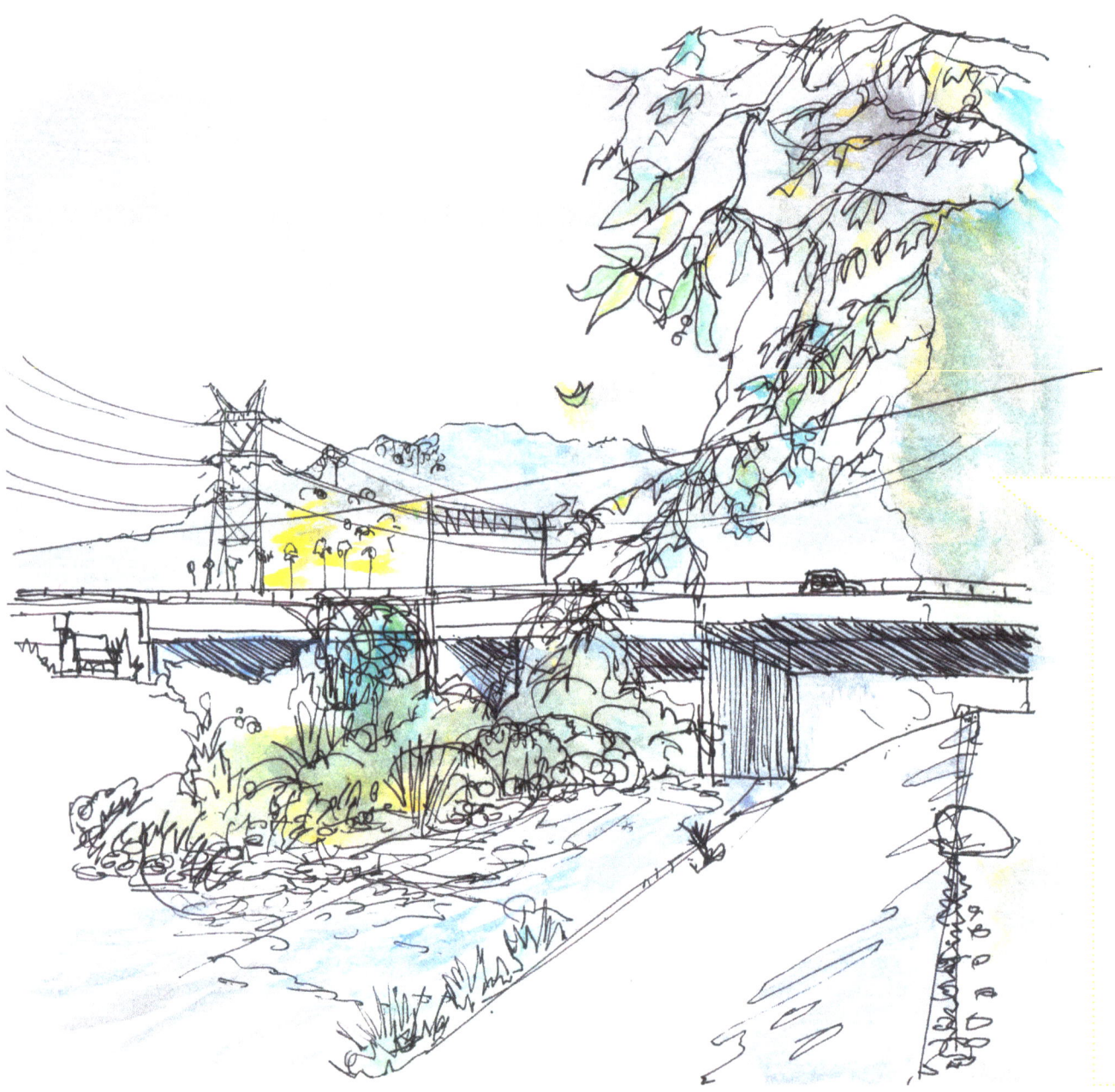

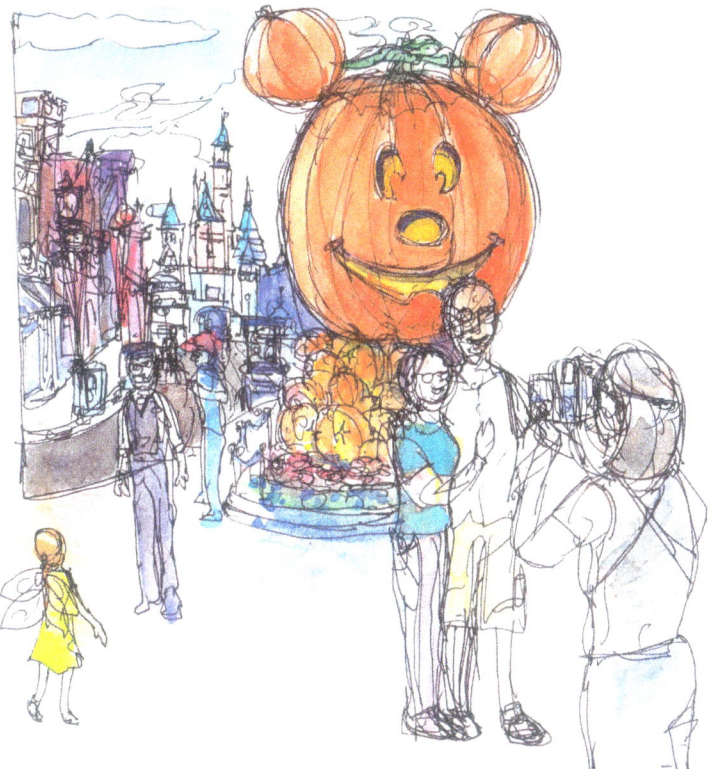

⟲ Birthday at Disneyland Nakaza celebrated her birthday at Disneyland, which she hadn't visited for more than ten years. Her sketch captured the spirit of the Magic Kingdom: tourists posing for photos, a little girl walking in costume, a large Mickey Mouse decoration for Halloween, and the park's cast members being attentive.

Tip "Instead of getting frustrated that people are 'blocking' your subject matter, I just treat them as part of the scenery—it makes the sketch more lively." — *Shiho Nakaza*

5" x 5" | 12.5 x 12.5 cm; Uni-ball Signo .38 mm pen, Sakura Koi waterbrush, watercolors on Holbein Multi-Drawing Book; about 30 minutes

U Food Truck at Night Lomo Arigato is one of many gourmet food trucks in Los Angeles. "Many are decorated to stand out from the crowd," says Nakaza, "and this truck had a 'knife' sticking out on the hood. You can see the flame that lights up when the chef is cooking up stir-fry."

Tip "I drew the two lines that form the top of the truck first, to establish perspective, and filled in the rest. I also like to draw shadows under cars to indicate how they are sitting on the ground." — *Shiho Nakaza*

4.75" x 3.5" | 12 x 9 cm; Uni-ball Signo .38 mm pen, Sakura Koi waterbrush, watercolors on Holbein Multi-Drawing Book; about 10 minutes and colored later from memory

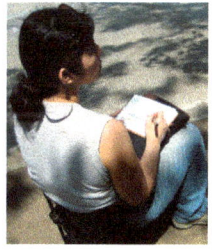

⋂ Shiho Nakaza found a shady spot to sketch this view of the paved Los Angeles River.

6" x 5.5" | 15 x 14 cm; Uni-ball Signo pen (sepia ink), watercolor; about 30 minutes

ARTIST PROFILE
Shiho Nakaza

My taste for sketching was piqued when I started studying animation and went on a drawing class to Italy. When I came back home to Los Angeles, I continued to sketch while pursuing a career in print design and illustration. In the process, I have learned to appreciate my city, with its quirks and beauty—people of multiple cultures, buildings with various architectural styles, nature that thrives, despite the city setting, and the near-perfect weather most of the year. One of my favorite places to sketch is the Santa Monica Pier, a beach in an urban setting with a great mix of tourists and locals, quaint wooden structures, and street performers.

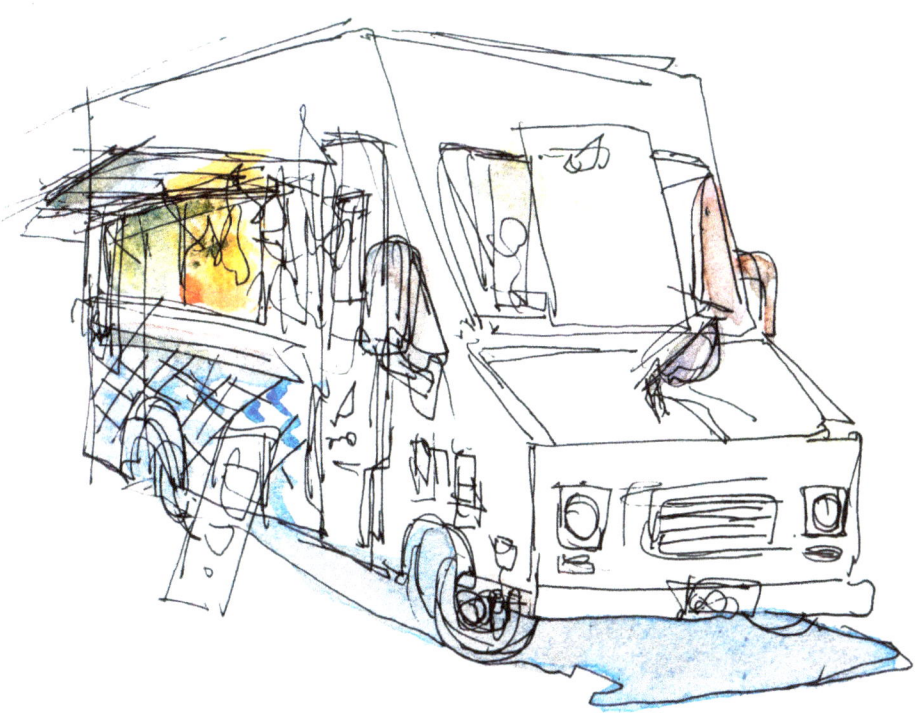

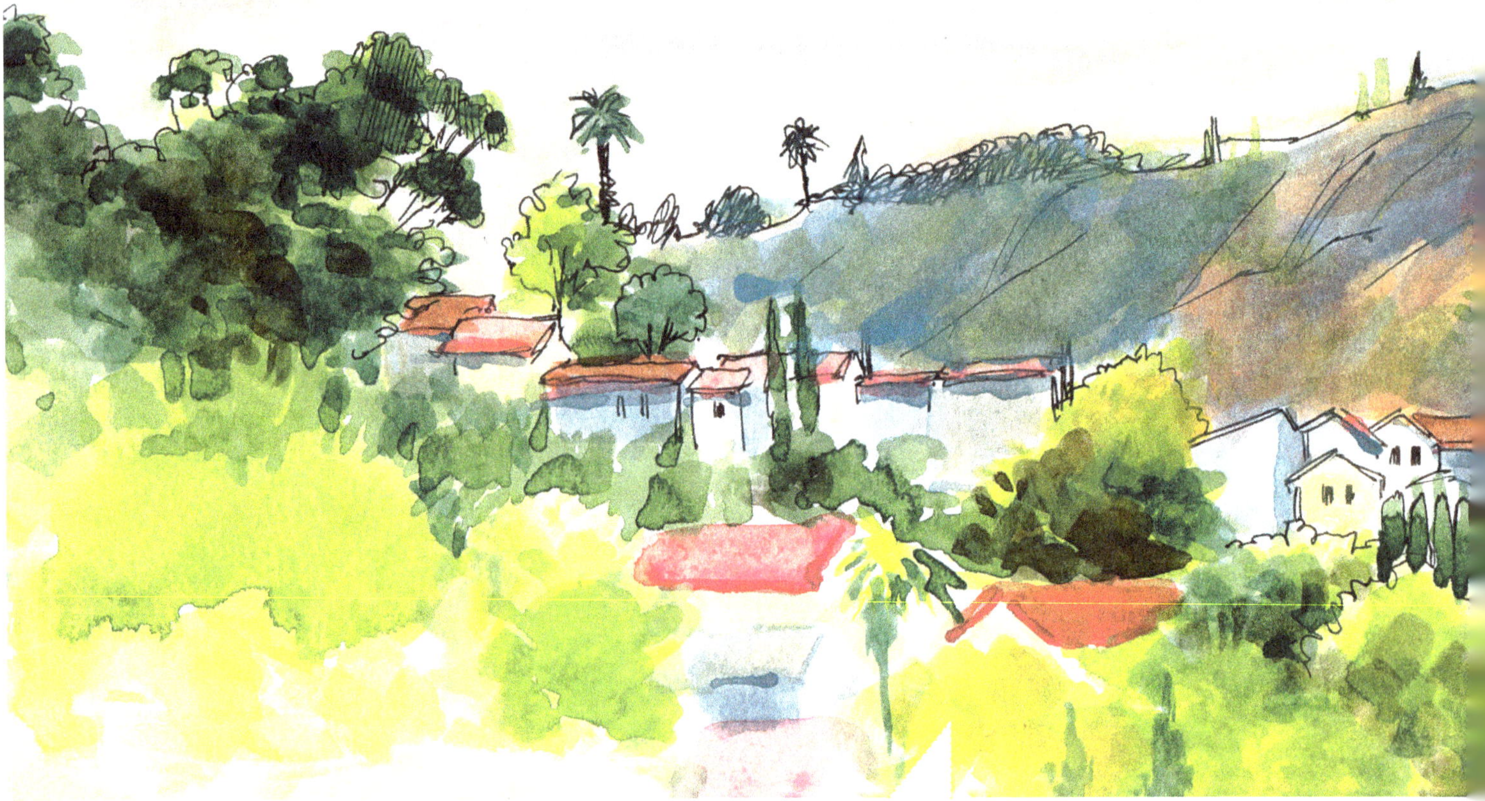

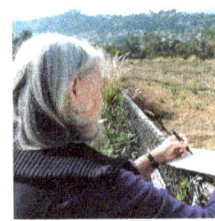

ARTIST PROFILE
Virginia Hein

I can't remember a time in my life when I wasn't drawing. I was trained in art school, but in truth, I've been learning to draw since I could pick up a crayon, and I still feel I'm learning every time I draw.

I was born in Los Angeles, and it continues to be a favorite subject. I never tire of the effects of atmosphere (what some unkindly call smog!), the verticals of the palm trees and horizontals of freeways, and the many brush-covered hills. As a toy designer, illustrator, and art teacher, I've always drawn and painted whenever possible; however, maintaining a constant sketchbook habit is something I'm doing now more than ever, especially since discovering the work of other urban sketchers online.

◑ Virginia Hein sketching in the hills at the northeast end of Los Angeles—Griffith Observatory is just barely visible, top center.

5" x 16" | 12.5 x 40.6 cm; ink and watercolor; about 2 hours

"Wherever I go, along comes the sketchbook. I fall in love with places through drawing them."

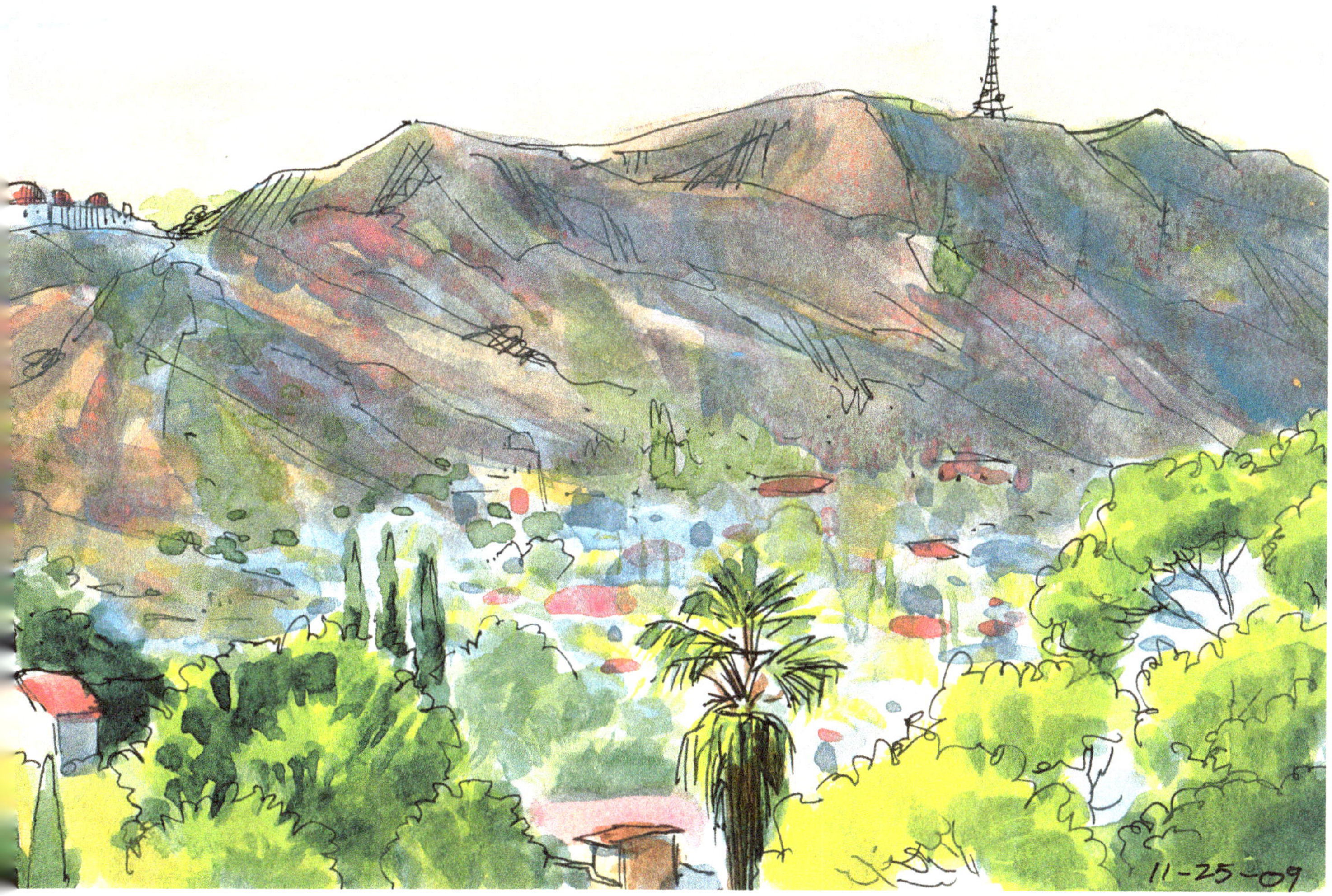

[Full-page watercolor sketch of mountains and city, signed 11-25-09]

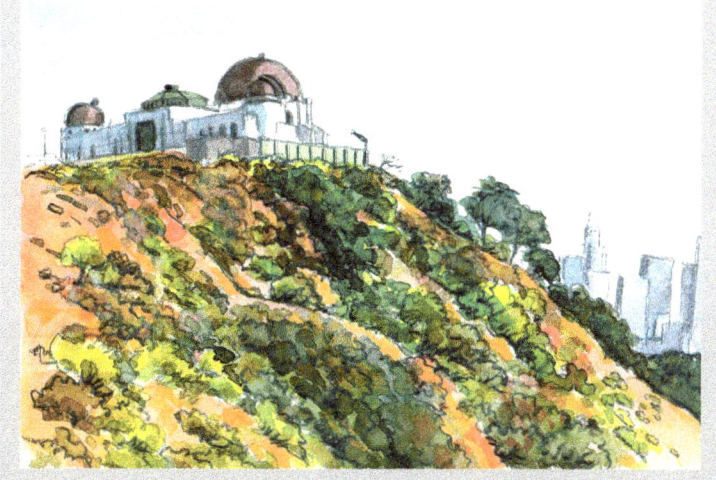

Sketching the Griffith Observatory

by Virginia Hein

On a beautiful day between rains, I went to sketch at my favorite building in Los Angeles, the Griffith Observatory. The observatory sits on top of Mt. Hollywood like a crown and looks out over the city. It first opened in 1935 and is visited by every Los Angeles schoolchild (including me). Many movies have been shot on location here, the most famous being *Rebel without a Cause* with James Dean. A monument featuring a bust of Dean now stands at the west side of the building to commemorate the use of the observatory in the film.

The observatory is the kind of place that's visited by many tourists, and so a sketcher might attract some attention. I've found that onlookers are generally politely curious, so I answer questions, but with practice have learned to stay focused on what I'm doing—most people respect that.

11.5" x 8" | 29 x 20 cm; HB, 2B, 4B, and 6B woodless pencils, Winsor & Newton watercolors, with some favorite Holbein colors (Lavender and Verditer Blue), on a Moleskine large watercolor book; about 1 hour each

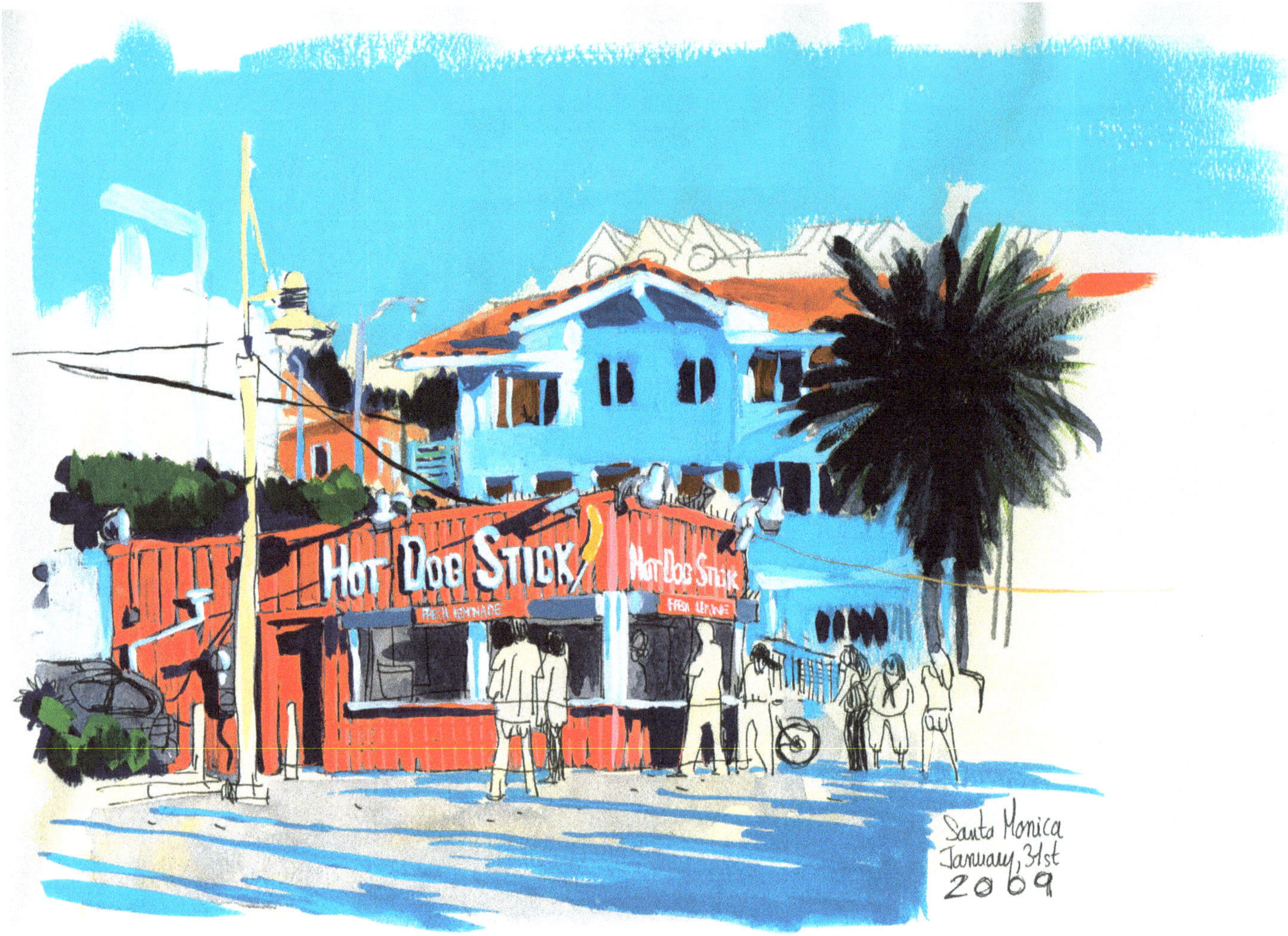

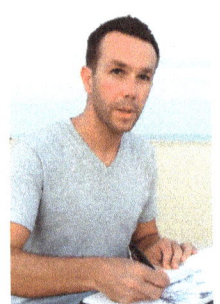

ARTIST PROFILE
Stéphane Kardos

I studied animation in France and, after living in Paris and London for years, I now live in Los Angeles, where I'm an art director for the Walt Disney Company. Los Angeles has great weather all year round (perfect for sketching on location), fantastic scenery, mountains, desert, and the ocean, as well as an interesting urban landscape and streets full of vintage American cars.

My line transformed over the years. I first wanted to record every detail of what I saw, but that wasn't spontaneous. I didn't feel the life in my drawings when I looked at them later. Now, my lines are looser; I just try to capture the essence of a subject. Sketching has a sense of urgency that I love. It's about spontaneity, enthusiasm, confidence. It's giving the feeling of a place, the illusion that every element is there.

"I always surprise myself, good or bad, by interpreting what I see as fast as I can."

🎧 **Santa Monica Hot Dog Stick** Kardos was drawn to the bright red of the hot dog stand against the blue sky as he walked with his wife and dog. "It struck me as very California, very L.A.," he says. "I wanted only to sketch it, but I had to add some color, too."

Tip "I used the long shadows on the ground to frame the composition and draw the eye to the red piece in the middle." — *Stéphane Kardos*

11" x 17" | 28 x 43 cm; Uni-ball Signo 207 ballpoint pen and Winsor & Newton Designers' gouache on Seawhite of Brighton sketchbook; 35 minutes

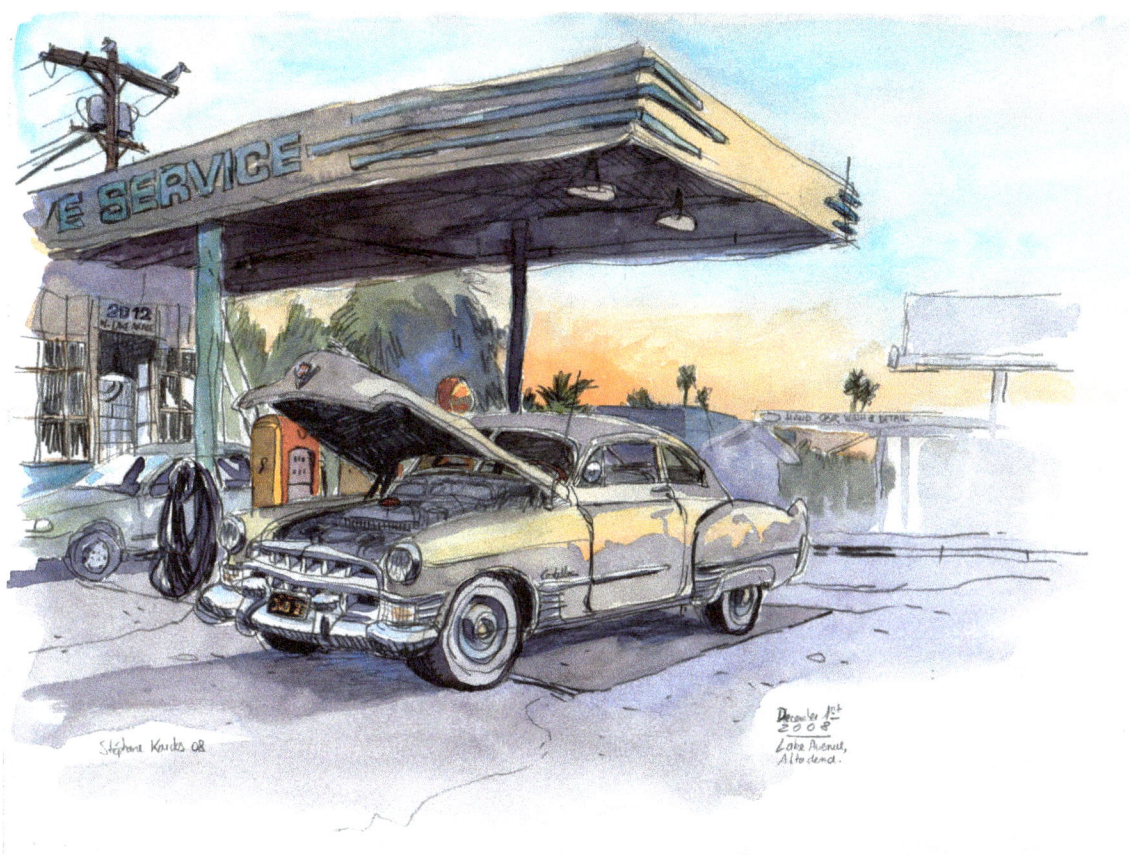

☾ At Ronnie's This old gas station on Kardos's street has been used in many movies, including the first Transformers film.

17" x 24" | 43 x 61 cm; pencil and Winsor & Newton watercolors on Daler-Rowney fine-grain, heavyweight paper; 45 minutes

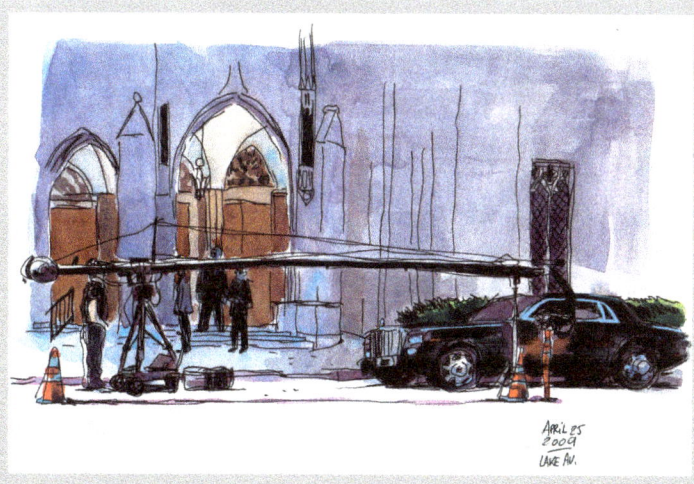

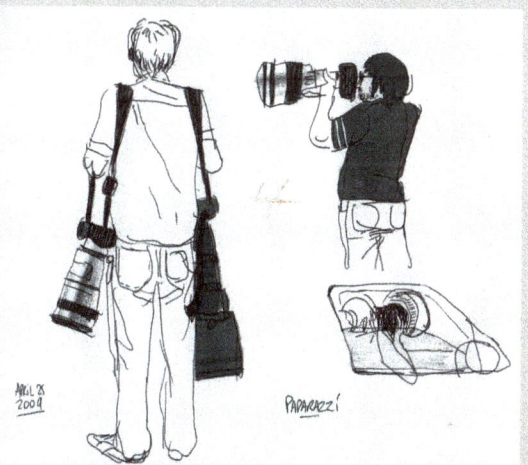

EYEWITNESS

Sketching the Paparazzi

by Stéphane Kardos

On my way to the post office one Saturday afternoon, I noticed more people than usual gathered around the corner from our house—in fact, quite a lot, with massive cameras. I'm kind of used to this, as it's common in L.A—you can't buy your bread without talking about the weather with Brad Pitt. But this time, I decided to stop and draw. I sketched mainly the paparazzi, because they are very interesting to watch.

They were not very happy that I was sketching them, which is funny for people who spend their time doing the same thing to other people: stealing their privacy.

8" x 11" | 20 x 28 cm; Seawhite of Brighton sketchbook

SAN DIEGO

San Diego's warm climate allows for year-round outdoor sketching. "We have beaches, mountains, and deserts that are all close enough for a day trip of sketching and painting," says local artist Lydia Velarde. Her favorite sketching locations are parks, including Balboa Park and the San Diego Zoo and Safari Park.

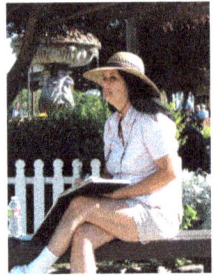

ARTIST PROFILE
Lydia Velarde

I started sketching in the early '70s, when an art teacher suggested we keep sketchbook entries on a daily basis. Initially, I kept sketching to improve my drawing skills. Later, my sketchbook became a constant companion, in which I documented my children's sports activities, places I went to dinner, and family events. I remember hiding my sketchbook under the table as I drew, later bringing it out as I got more courageous and realized no one really pays attention.

My sketch time is a time I can relax, because I seem to get lost in it and go to another place, forgetting anything that was on my mind. Sketching has also been a happy time for me to get together with other artists who enjoy sketching outdoors.

"If you are shy about drawing in public, you can position yourself against a tree or a wall and no one will bother you."

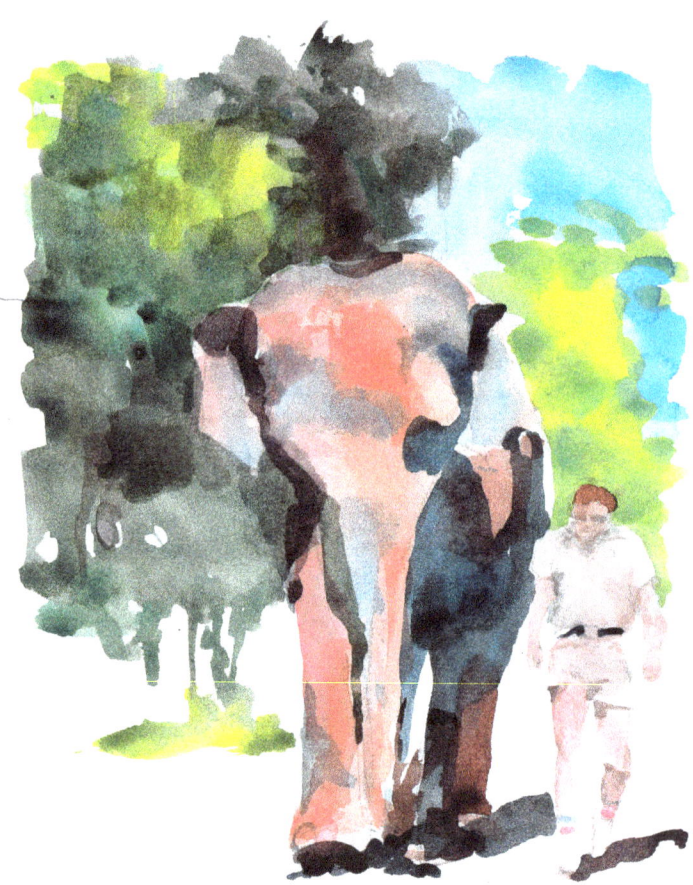

⌒ San Diego Zoo Lydia Velarde comes to the zoo with her season pass to draw people and animals. "People stand for long periods of time, and, even if an animal is moving, it repeats the movement, which makes it easy to draw" she says.

8" x 10" | 20 x 25 cm; watercolor in a classic black cover sketchbook, book bound

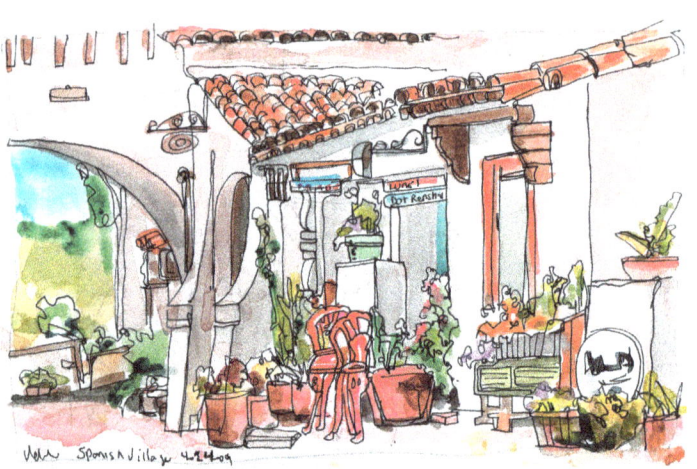

↻ Spanish Village at Balboa Park Sprawling Balboa Park features many gardens, museums, and Spanish Colonial-style buildings, such as the one Velarde captured here.

Tip "I like sketching the large shapes and creating a border on my page with a Sanford Design Ebony Jet Black pencil, which is extra smooth." — *Lydia Velarde*

5" x 8" | 12.5 x 20 cm; Koh-I-Noor Rapidosketch pen and Winsor & Newton Cotman compact watercolor set, Moleskine watercolor book

STYLE AND TECHNIQUE

Junipero Serra Museum in Pencil and Watercolor

by Lydia Velarde

For this kind of sketch, I first make a pencil outline or frame for the area I will draw. Then I start outlining the basic shapes from left to right and continue adding watercolor, working from light to dark. It's fun to paint white buildings and leave the white of the paper for the white of the building. It's a good lesson in negative shapes, because you draw the sky or shrubbery around the edges of the building, instead of the building itself.

7" x 7.5" | 18 x 19 cm; pencil and watercolor

⮎ **Hotel La Valencia in Pen** When I work with pen and ink, I just start at the top and work my way from left to right, as I would with handwriting, but first, I use a pencil as a guide for the main parts of the building. I used to do many detailed drawings like this, but it has gotten too tedious. I prefer loose work now.

9" x 12" | 23 x 30.5 cm; Koh-I-Noor Rapidosketch pen on Strathmore 400 series, spiral-bound sketchbook

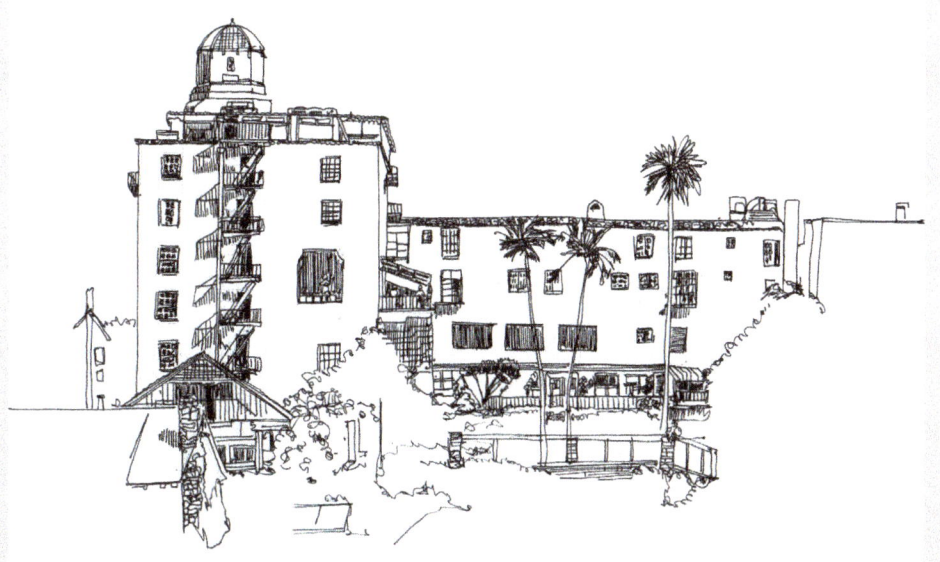

SAN ANTONIO

Corrugated tile roofs, centuries-old missions, and art deco architecture stand out in the urban landscape of San Antonio, Texas, a Southwestern American city, where Spanish explorers founded missions in the early 1700s. For local artist and teacher Paul Heaston, no amount of architectural detail is too daunting to draw, if you take it one step at a time.

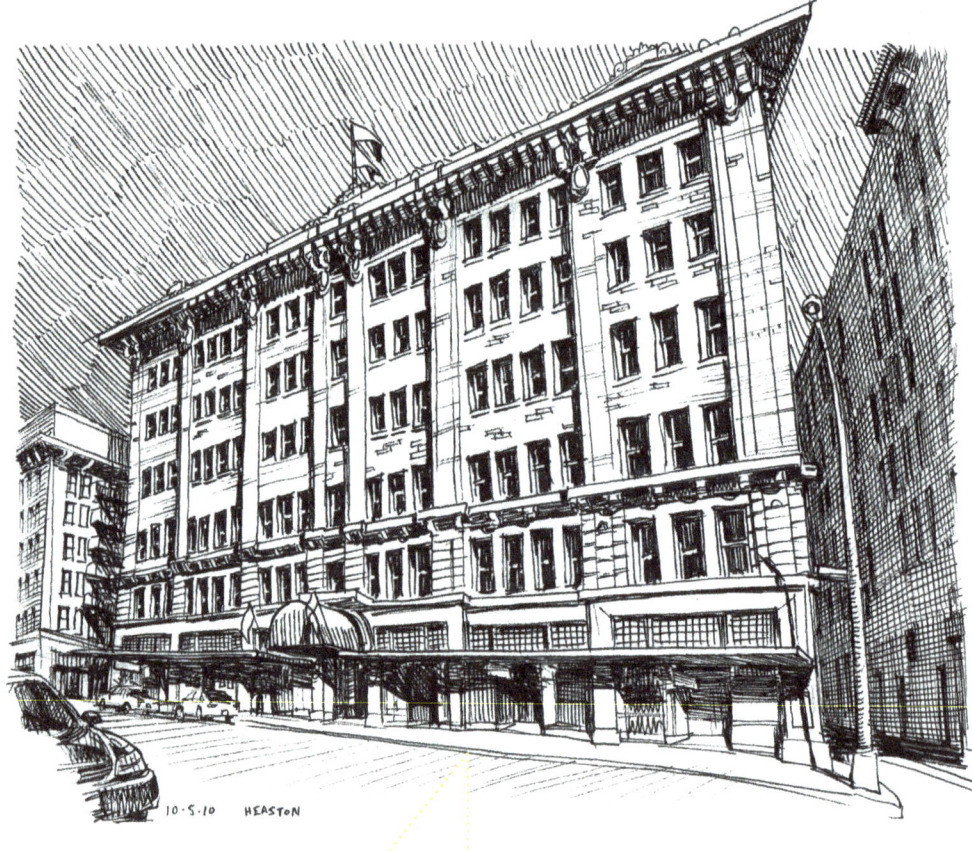

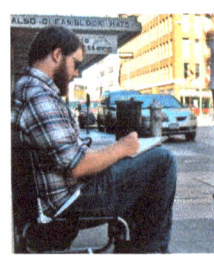

🎧 Paul Heaston sketches San Antonio's World Trade Center building on Broadway Street.

8" x 10" | 20 x 25 cm; Staedtler pigment liner pens; 2–3 hours

ARTIST PROFILE
Paul Heaston

I started sketching after years of having sketchbooks but never using them. I started out as an artist doing a lot of figurative painting, which can be a very deliberate and time-consuming process, so there's something about the spontaneous nature of location drawing that appeals to me.

At the same time, sketching allows you to really spend time seeing a place, unlike taking a photo. You get the feel of where you are—looking at a sketch can bring me back to all of the sensory experiences involved: the sounds, the smells, the sun in your face, or a brisk wind.

San Antonio's downtown is fortunate to have a pedestrian paradise in the beautifully landscaped Riverwalk, which is lined with shops and restaurants and towering cypress trees. I also find myself exploring the less well-known districts, trying to sketch areas that even locals aren't familiar with.

"I've never felt uncomfortable or unsafe sketching downtown, except of course when a thunderstorm blows in."

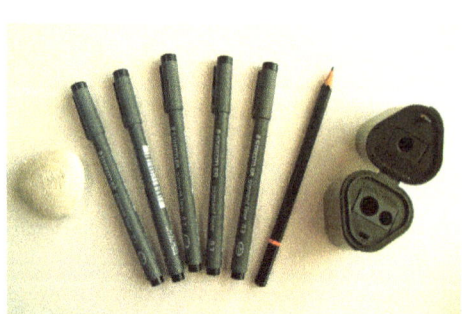

🎧 Heaston's pens

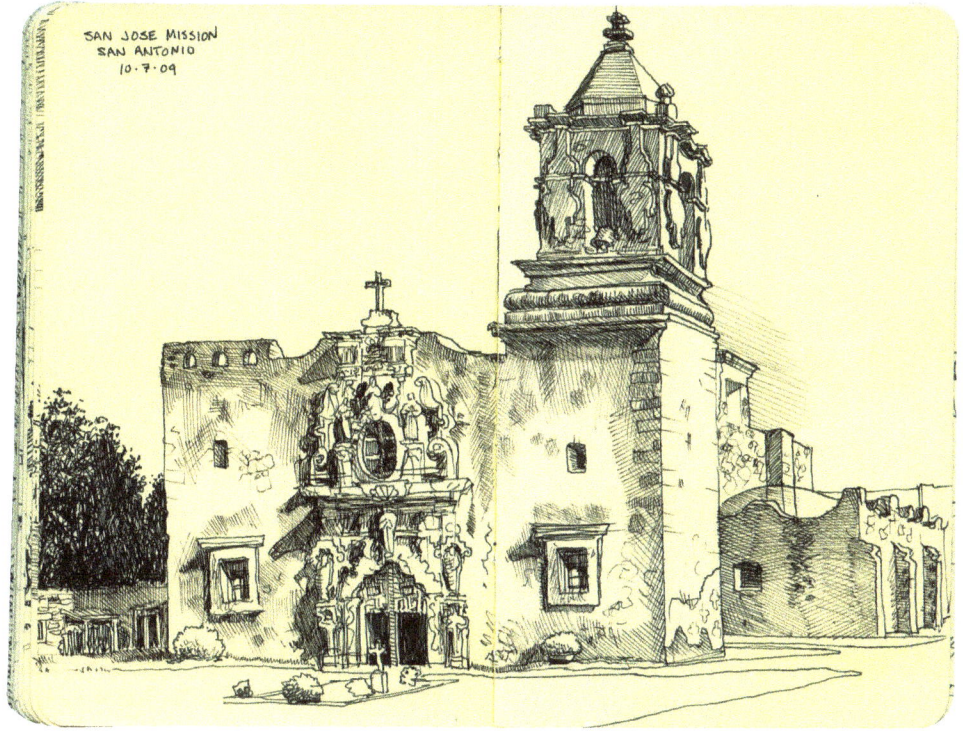

⊂ Mission San José While he sat and sketched on a hot October afternoon, Heaston tried to imagine this scene in the 1700s, "with no retirees wandering by listening to self-guided audio tours." The mission dates from 1720 and is still a functioning parish in the San Antonio archdiocese.

8" x 10" | 20 x 25 cm; Staedtler pigment liner pen on Moleskine sketchbook; 2 hours

⊃ Emily Morgan Hotel One of the many things Heaston likes about San Antonio is its fantastic stock of old buildings, many of which were constructed in the 1920s and '30s. "Though this sometimes makes me feel as though San Antonio is stuck in an older time (and in many ways, it is), I'm never at a loss for historic architecture to draw, so long as I can find some shade," Heaston says.

Tip "If I'm sketching ornate or elaborate architecture, especially on a small scale, I try to think less about the details and more about the big picture. What are the big shapes? How do I show the space? The detail usually emerges later." — *Paul Heaston*

8" x 10" | 20 x 25 cm; Staedtler pigment liner pen on Strathmore drawing pad; 3–4 hours

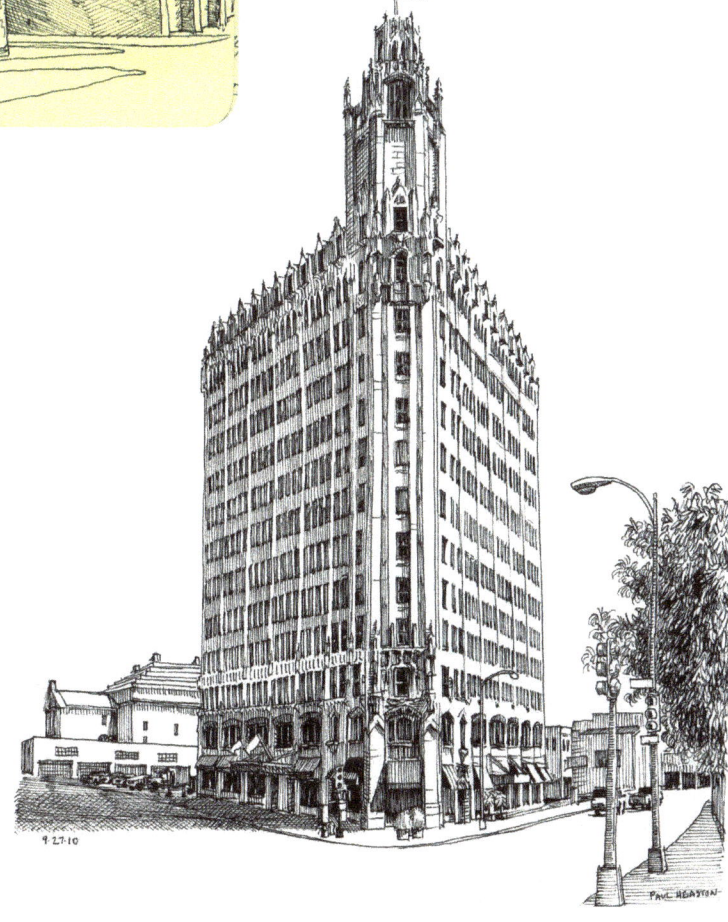

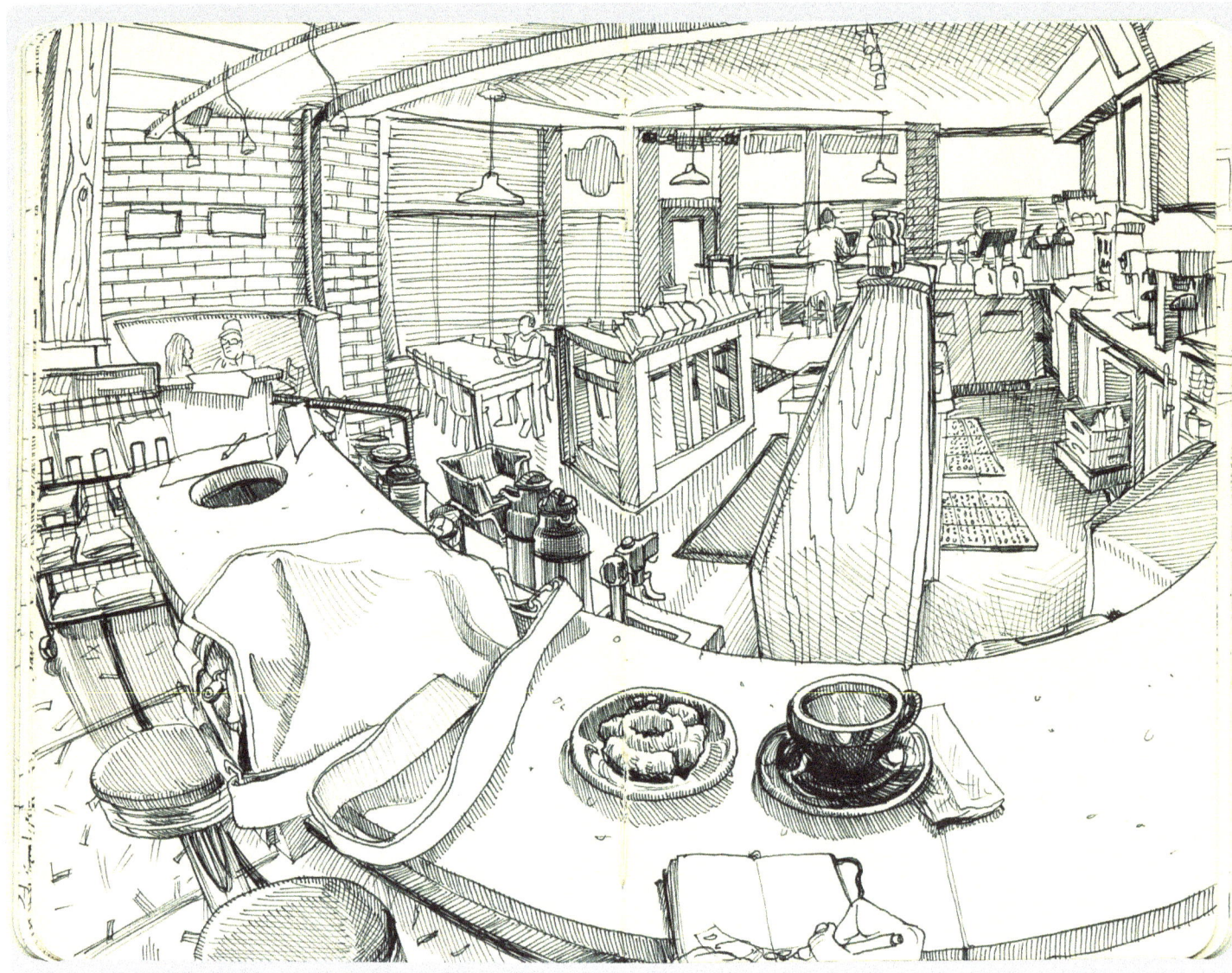

STYLE AND TECHNIQUE

How to Draw the Whole Picture

by Paul Heaston

I love the challenge of depicting as much space as possible and cataloguing everything within sight. These wide-angle views came out of an assignment I used to give to my drawing students, wherein they were to draw everything they could see—without turning their heads—until they had filled the frame. Because the eye is a wide-angle lens, one has to account for the way perspective changes as one gets further from the center of the composition, and I have found that curving the lines makes this a lot easier.

My approach has always been to start from the bottom, drawing my own sketchbook, and work my way up and out, and then hope for the best! Sometimes, the sketch works, and sometimes it doesn't, but it's a lot of fun to do.

5.5" x 7" | 14 x 18 cm; Staedtler pigment liner pens on regular and pocket-size Moleskine sketchbooks; 2–3 hours

↻ San Antonio from the Tower of the Americas Heaston first attempted this February sketch from the tower's outdoor observation deck sixty stories up but was quickly driven indoors by the cold winds. "I retreated indoors and drew with my Bristol pad leaning against the glass," he says.

8" x 10" | 20 x 25 cm; Staedtler pigment liner pen on Bristol pad; 3–4 hours

↻ The Tower of the Americas from Crockett Street This sketch was interrupted about halfway through, when Heaston realized he had to move his car from its two-hour parking spot.

Tip "I believe no amount of information or detail is too daunting if you take it one thing at a time. I just move from one thing to the next, foreground to background, and it usually comes together." *— Paul Heaston*

8" x 10" | 20 x 25 cm; Steadtler pigment liner pen on Strathmore drawing pad; 4–5 hours

KANSAS CITY

It is said that Kansas City has more fountains than any other city in the world but Rome. The Missouri city in the center of the United States is also the home of Hallmark Cards. Artists are almost part of the scenery, says Cathy Johnson, an artist and writer who's been sketching here since she was a kid.

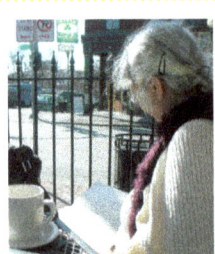

ARTIST PROFILE
Cathy Johnson

Once upon a time, I wanted to be an architect—until I discovered how much math was needed—not my long suit. But I never got over my love of buildings, of human habitations, whether cliff dwellings or crowded ocean-side cottages in

🎧 Johnson sketches Kelly's pub, one of the oldest buildings in town.
8" x 9" | 20 x 23 cm; watercolor; 45 minutes

southern California; the brownstones, cheek-by-jowl, in Washington D.C.; or the old hotels, public buildings, and museums in my native Kansas City, Missouri.

I've sketched ever since I was a kid—baby-book drawings from age two attest to that. And I've kept a journal for twenty-five years, or so, dragging it through airports, onto buses and into cars, along with whatever art supplies I absolutely had to have. No matter where I am, city or country, I sketch. And when I do, I take time to experience and respond to my environment in ways I couldn't begin to without pen in hand.

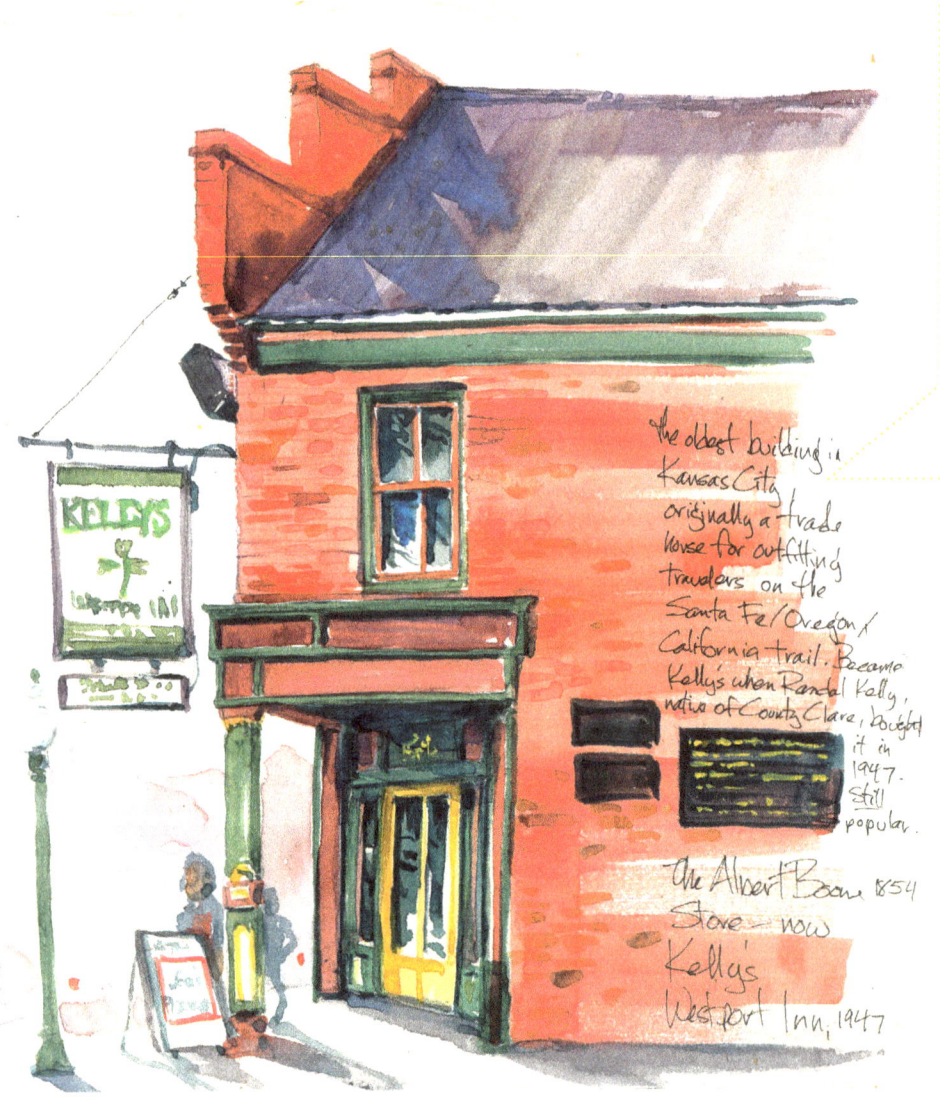

the oldest building in Kansas City, originally a trade house for outfitting travelers on the Santa Fe/Oregon/ California trail. Became Kelly's when Randal Kelly, native of County Clare, bought it in 1947. Still popular.

the Albert Boon 854 Store — now Kelly's Westport Inn, 1947

"I capture memories like a fly in amber."

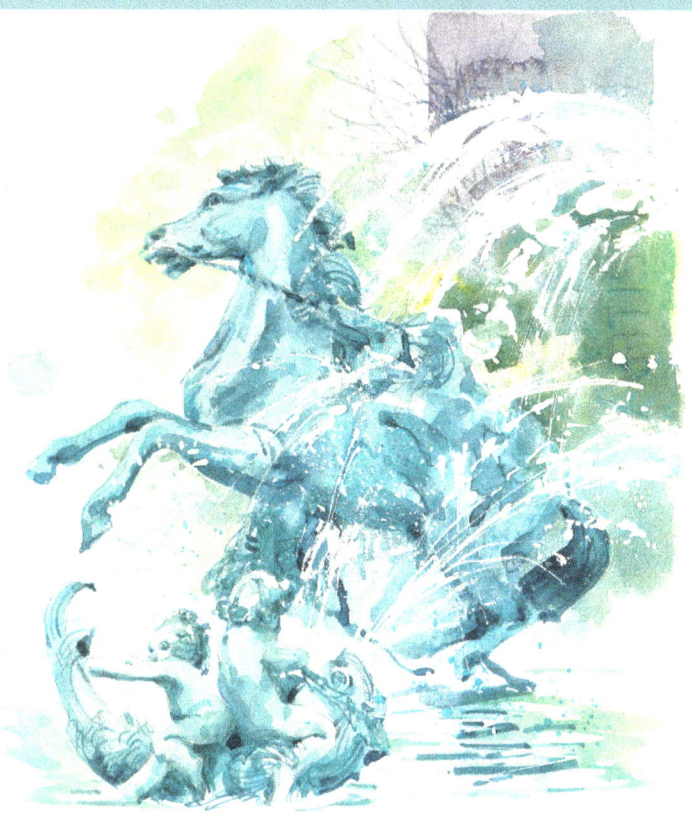

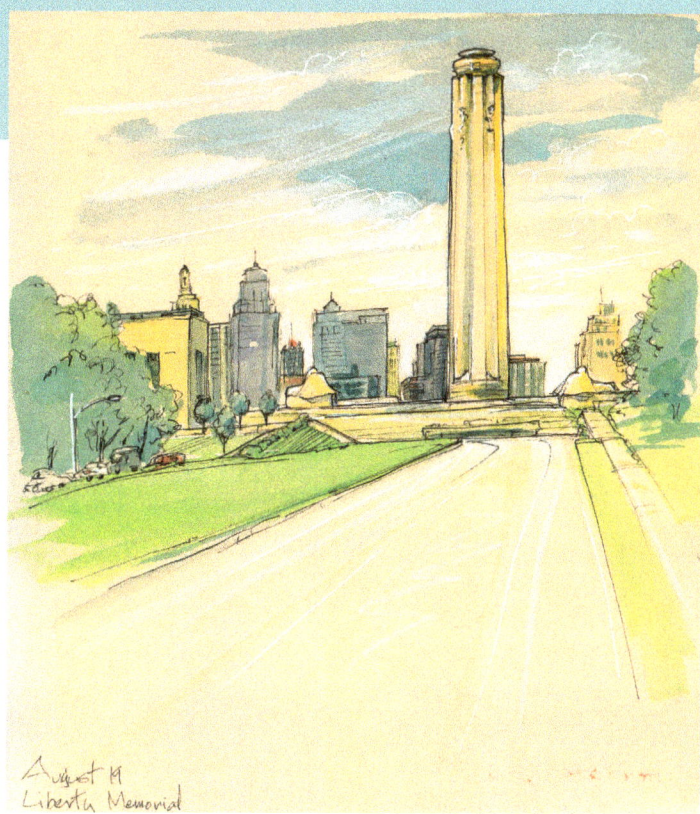

♠ City of Fountains One of Johnson's favorite fountains has been part of her life for decades, she says. "Candlelight vigils, demonstrations, and more, back in the early '70s . . . and now the fountain's waters are often tinted pink during October for Breast Cancer Awareness month."

Tip "Work as loose as you can, with big splashy arcs—think moving water! Spatter adds to the wet feeling." — *Cathy Johnson*

8" x 7" | 20 x 18 cm; watercolor, graphite guidelines, liquid mask on Fabriano hot-press paper; about 45 minutes

♠ Liberty Memorial—National WWI Museum The only American museum devoted solely to World War I sits on parklike grounds below the Liberty Memorial tower, which dominates the city's skyline. "When the flamelike light at the top glows against the night sky, it captures your attention from anywhere in the city," Johnson says.

Tip "I find sketching with ink first lets me work faster, which is good when the weather doesn't cooperate, when you don't have much time, or when you're with others who might not be sketchers. Then I splash in as much or as little color as I can and finish later." — *Cathy Johnson*

8" x 7" | 20 x 18 cm; .01 ZIG Millennium pen, Winsor & Newton watercolors and a few Daniel Smith colors, Zinc White gouache, white Gelly Roll gel pen, and Niji waterbrushes on fawn Stonehenge paper; 30–45 minutes

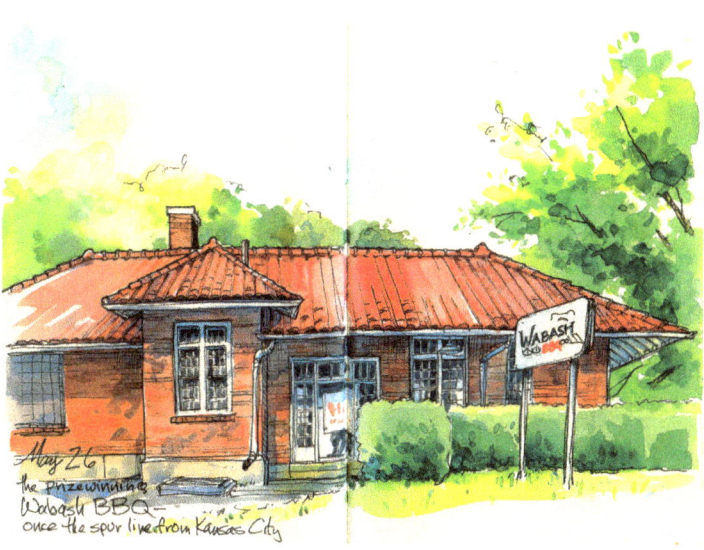

↻ Wabash BBQ Johnson likes to take visitors from out of town to this award-winning Kansas City restaurant. On this day, she drew while sitting on the grass under the shade of a huge sycamore tree. "It was very pleasant sketching here, with only the occasional passing car," she says.

10" x 8" | 25 x 20 cm; Pitt artist's pen and watercolor on hand-bound books with Arches hot-press paper; about 45 minutes

TORONTO

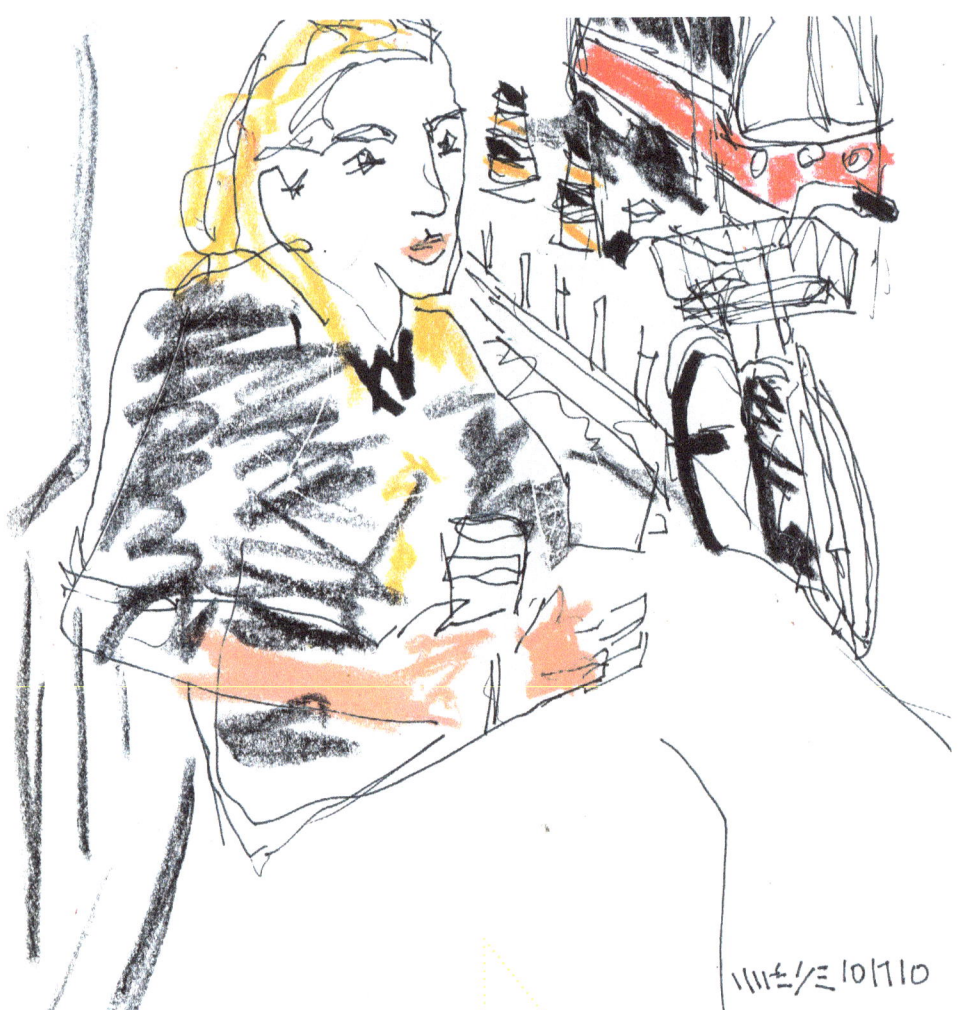

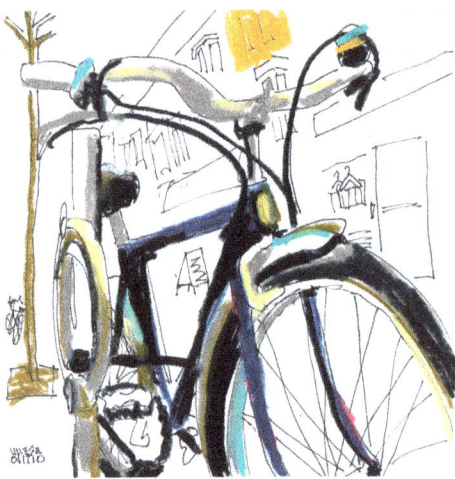

♠ **On College West** Waese calls this his favorite type of fender: classic, retro, and solid.

Tip "Special care is given to the foreground only, and just one rectangle touching the top edge and one line for the tree are colored in the surround." — *Jerry Waese*

7" x 7" | 18 x 18 cm; Pilot Hi-Tecpoint pen and Caran d'Ache Neocolor II water-soluble crayon on acid free paper in hardbound sketchbook; less than 1 hour

Canada's most populous city, Toronto sits on the northern shore of Lake Ontario, where architect Eugene Zhilinsky likes to sketch while strolling with his family. Farther away, in the Dundas Street neighborhood, artist Jerry Waese enjoys drawing the city's iconic red streetcars from the window of his studio.

"Every jacket I wear has at least some form of sketchbook in it and a pen or pencil and sharpener."

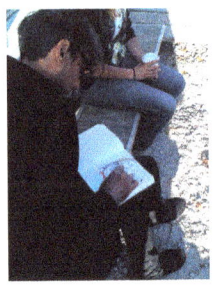

♠ Waese recalls his subject saying that being sketched was the most exciting thing that happened to her all day.

ARTIST PROFILE
Jerry Waese

Urban sketching is about making this place where I live home. I sketch the views that I see over and over, and though it is never the same twice, the recognizable people and places are a rich collage of my personal world. Most of what I draw is within a ten-block radius.

Because I sketch, I do see things differently; I find motif and beautiful rhythm in the mundane, and I look for composition clues in the flux of passing traffic. I draw daily, sometimes for hours—often before breakfast—but it could go on at any time that I am not busy with real work, such as programming, tax consulting, construction, marketing, websites, my wife's store, or local politics.

7" x 7" | 18 x 18 cm; pen and crayon; 10 minutes

STYLE AND TECHNIQUE

Sketching Fast-moving Streetcars

by Jerry Waese

When I do live drawing, my first concerns are the edges of the paper and the feeling of movement and tension in the scene. I let the pen go wherever, following the figures or streetscape approximately. I allow for areas of movement and, in so doing, I even draw some wriggling shapes. Then, I bring out the crayons, not necessarily retracing the same gesture at all, but attempting to show the feeling of the whole scene and binding the shapes to the whole picture area. You can't use pen after crayoning starts, or the pen tip gets wrecked. With the crayons, I mess it up as beautifully as I can, and I apply it very thickly and heavily, often erasing lines as I go.

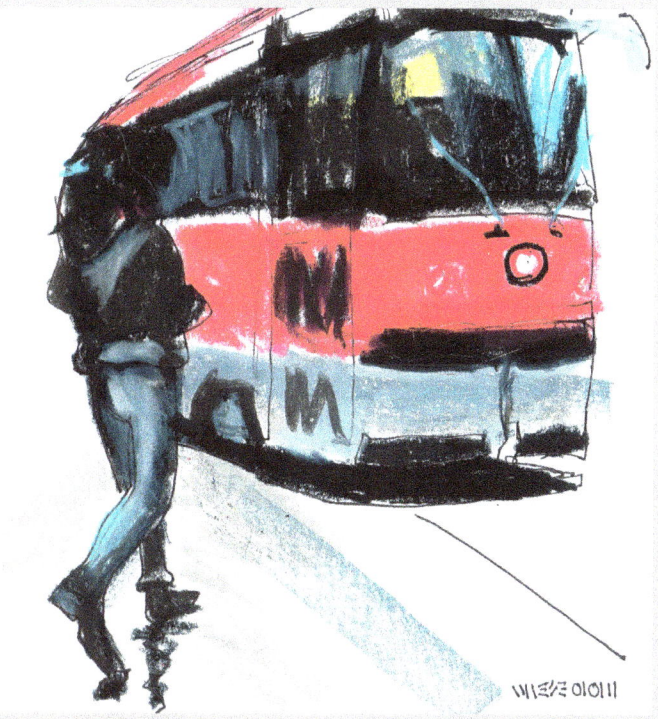

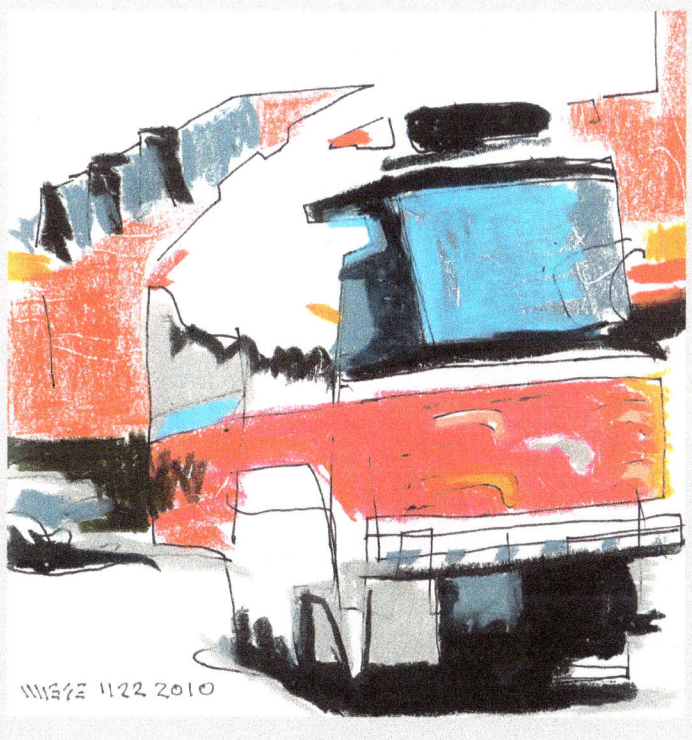

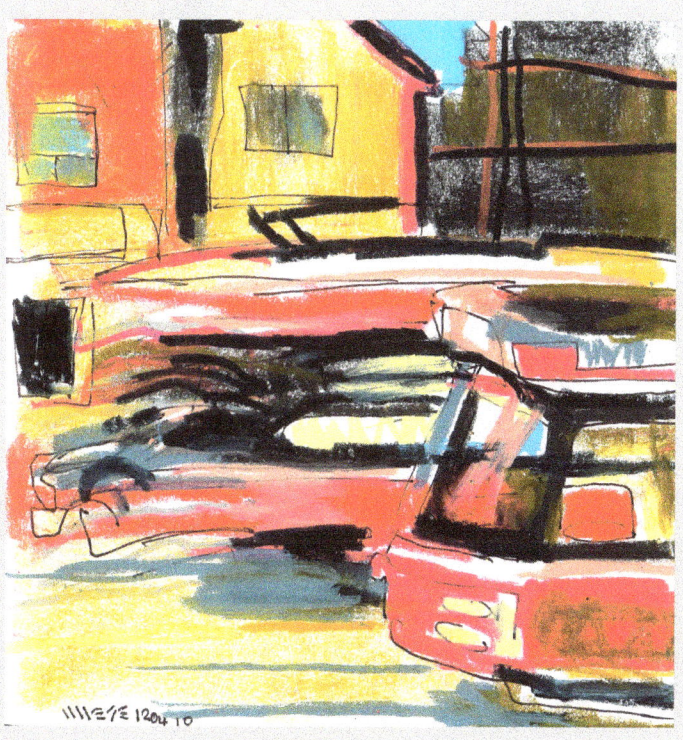

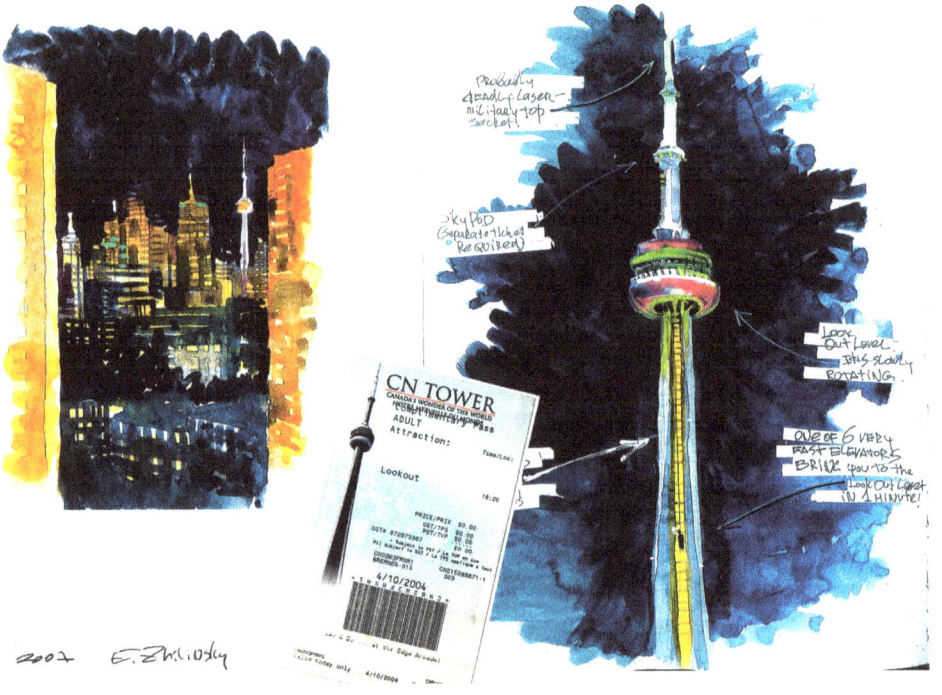

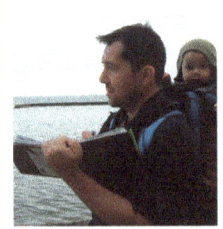

⟲ Eugene Zhilinsky sketches a view from West Beaches toward the Humber River Arch Bridge and the Long Branch area.

18" x 5.5" | 45.5 x 14 cm; pencil, Yarka watercolor set, white gouache; 10 minutes

ARTIST PROFILE

Eugene Zhilinsky

I am a Toronto-based, Russian-born graduate architect, artist, and architectural illustrator. Sketching comes naturally to me. I've painted, sketched, and drawn urban views all of my life. About five years ago, I became very interested in *carnets de voyage*, or the travel sketchbook genre. My sketches are accompanied by written comments, which become a part of the art. Those written observations help me share interesting facts I have learned while painting and sketching. It's also a fast genre, which is important, especially when you have a little child at home and only five minutes for your creativity.

⟲ **CN Tower** The Canadian National Tower (CN Tower) is part television antenna, part posh restaurant, and all Toronto landmark. Zhilinsky sketched it from the window of a friend's apartment. "It has superspeed elevators flying up and down between concrete structural columns. At night, it is always a light show," he says.

11" x 17" | 28 x 43 cm; pencil, pen, Yarka watercolor set. Ticket: 8.5" X 11" | 21.6 x 28 cm; Woodbridge black hardcover sketchbook; 25 minutes each

"Sketching makes life as exciting as an exotic voyage to a faraway place."

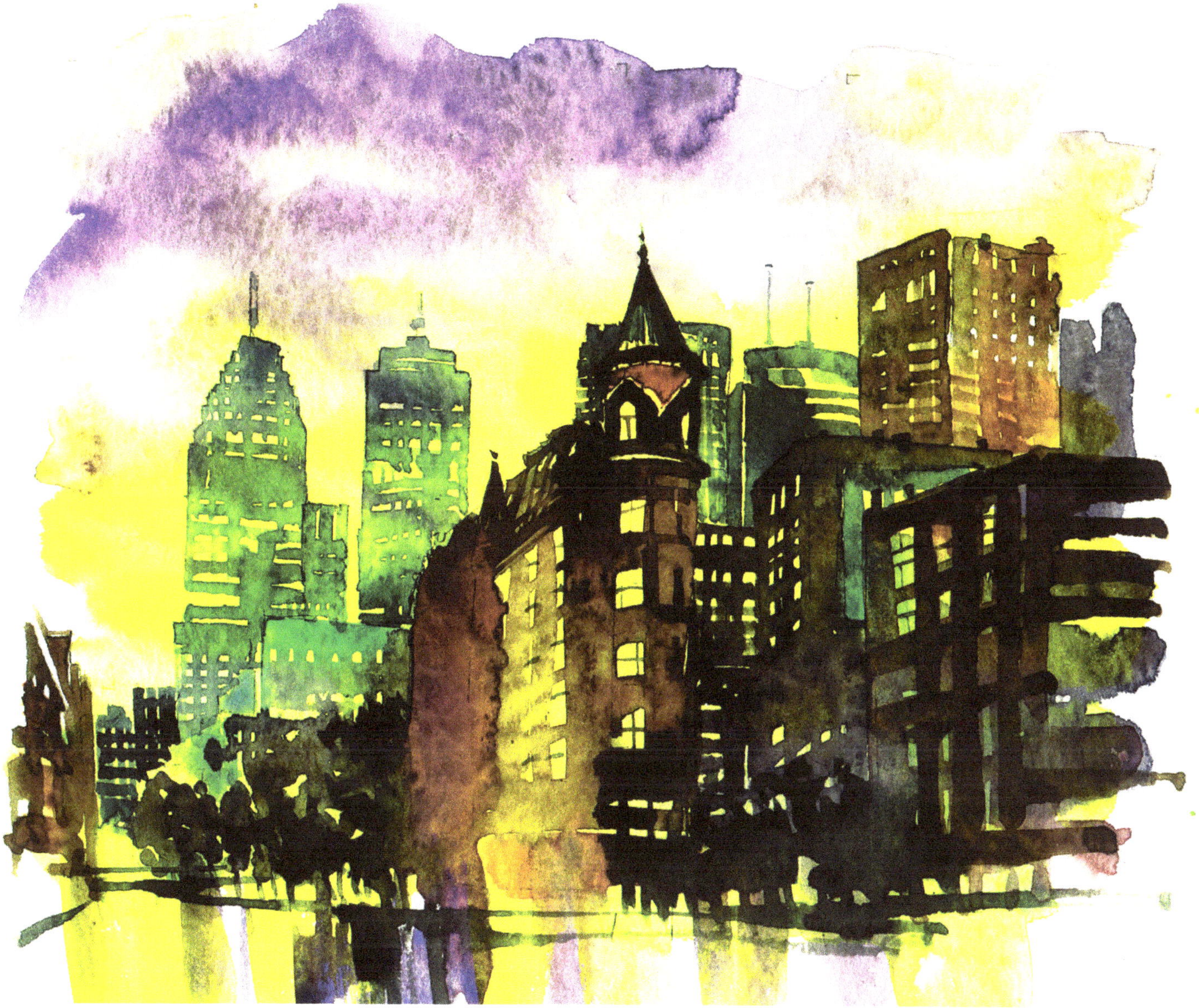

↑ Front Street at Dawn The building with the spiked roof is called the Flatiron, another Toronto landmark. "Everybody loves this view! The past and the present are side by side here," Zhilinsky says.

8.5" X 5.5" | 21.6 x 14 cm; pencil, Yarka St. Petersburg watercolor set on Canson watercolor paper block; 20 minutes

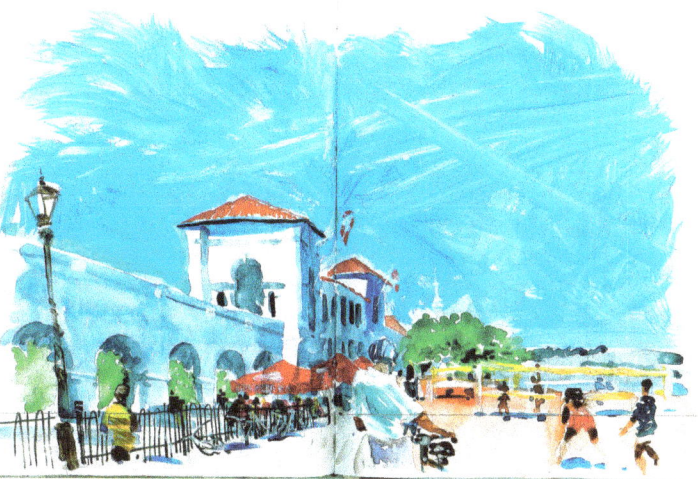

↩ Summer Stroll Zhilinsky favors West Beaches, a popular spot for locals, where you can draw under the shade of café terraces.

8.5" x 11" | 21.6 x 28 cm; pencil, watercolor set, blue acrylic color from a kids' color set on Woodbridge black hardcover sketchbook; about 15 minutes

MONTREAL

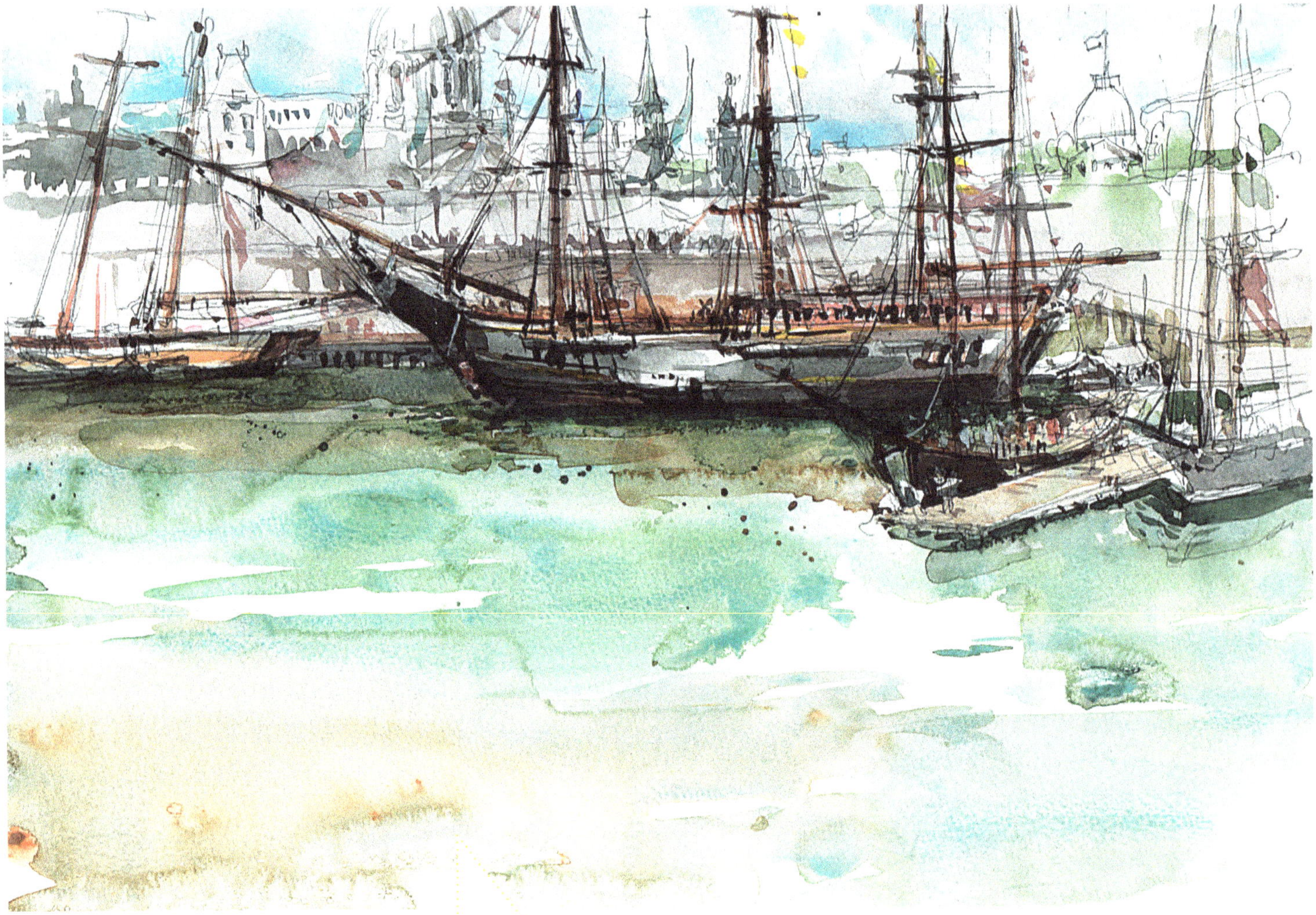

Montreal's small, walkable city center makes the second-largest city in Canada ideal for urban sketching. Local artist Marc Taro Holmes is drawn to the ornate architecture of French and English historic buildings around the Old Port, as well as the many intricate lines of cathedrals and churches, including a cathedral inspired by Rome's St. Peter's Basilica.

"I am drawn to the historic and the baroque."

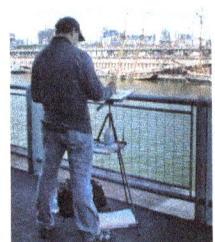

⌒ Holmes sketches the tall ships that come to the city's Old Port once a year.

9" x 12" | 23 x 30.5 cm; pencil and watercolor on a cold-press block; 40 minutes

ARTIST PROFILE

Marc Taro Holmes

I'm kind of a late-starter as an artist; finally becoming a full-time artist at age 40. Part of my method of self-retraining has been obsessive daily sketching—either from the model, from imagination, or by placing myself in exotic locales. After a few years of inveterate sketching, I think it's become a lifestyle.

I have a short attention span, so sketching and designing has always been my ideal form of expression. For me, the artist's gestural line carries a lot of feeling that can be lost in protracted work. I started keeping sketchbooks while traveling, as a way of recording my experiences in foreign cities, while simultaneously calming my fidgety attention. I can get mesmerized capturing all the little antique details on an old Gothic building, Victorian houses, sprawling mansions, and old stone bridges.

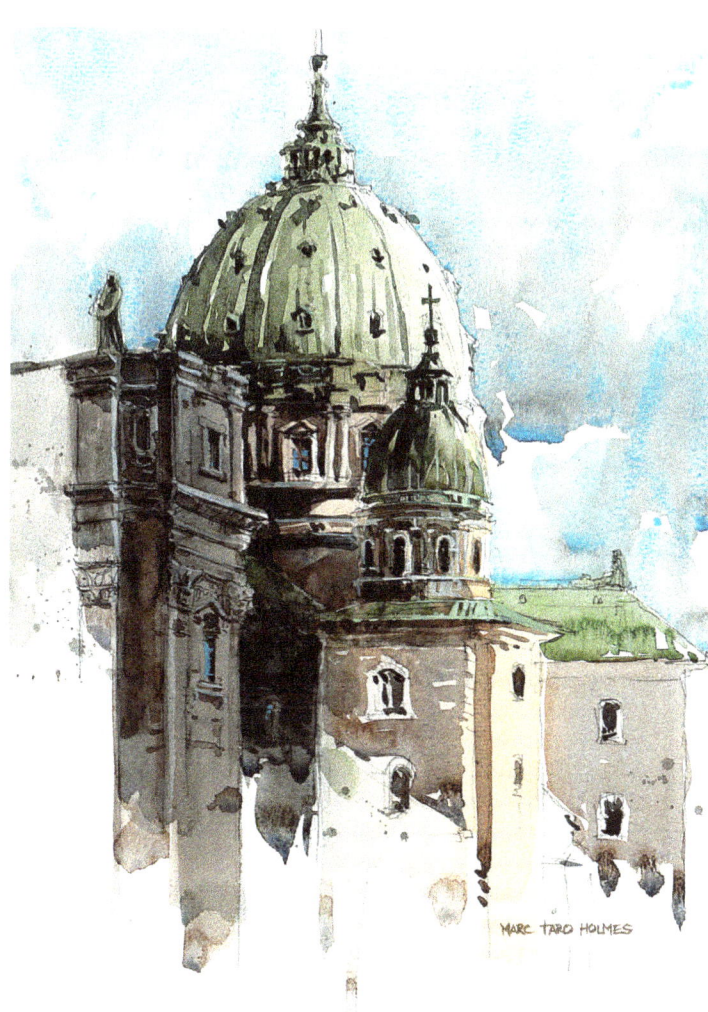

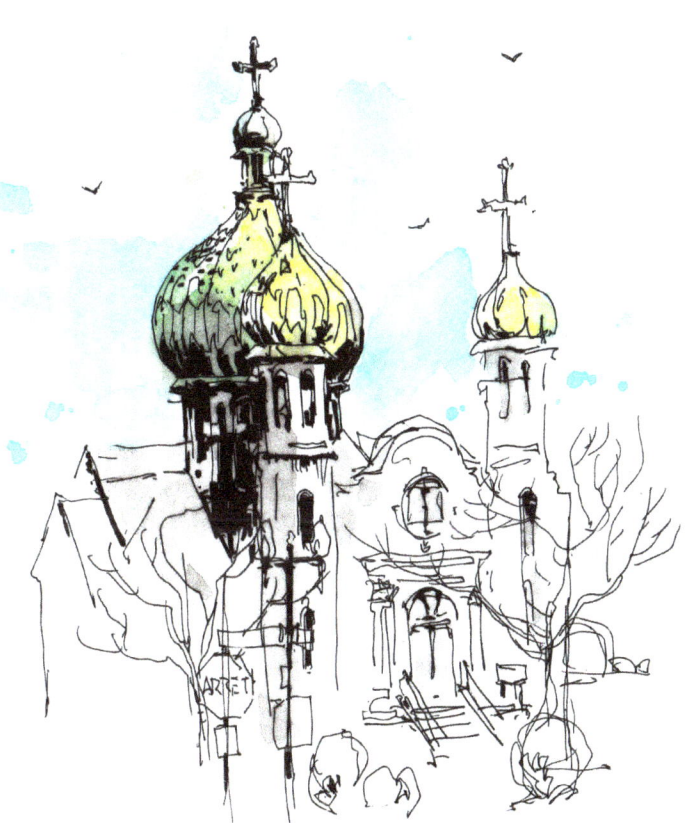

⋒ Mary Queen of the World Cathedral
This cathedral, whose design was inspired by St. Peter's Basilica in Rome, sits downtown, in the heart of Montreal's business center. Holmes says that even from a park across the street, it's hard to get an angle far enough back to sketch something this big.

Tip "Frequently, I don't even try to get the entire structure in the drawing. It's always the domes and cupolas that I enjoy anyway." — *Marc Holmes*

[AS] 11" x 14" | 28 x 35.6 cm; Winsor & Newton watercolors, with touches of white gouache on Canson Montval cold-press blocks; 2 hours

⋒ Onion-shaped Domes Holmes sketched this tiny Ukrainian church at Grand Trunk and Shearer while working temporarily in this part of the city.

Tip "If you're just doing a quick sketch, try splashing just a little color at the point of interest. It's not necessary to get it all—just hit the focus and draw the eye to what attracted you to that particular location." — *Marc Holmes*

11" x 14" | 28 x 35.6 cm; Pentel GFKP brush pen, Uni-ball Signo, and Cotman watercolor travel pans on 100-lb. Bristol cover stock; 15 minutes

NEW YORK CITY

It's hard to stop drawing in the city that never sleeps. Skyscrapers, architectural treasures, trains, buses, parks, performing arts, parades, crowds of people, and eccentric characters provide full excitement for these local sketchers, whose fast-moving lines match the energy of the world's capital. "As someone who loves drawing movement and excitement, I find it the best place in the world to be," says Veronica Lawlor.

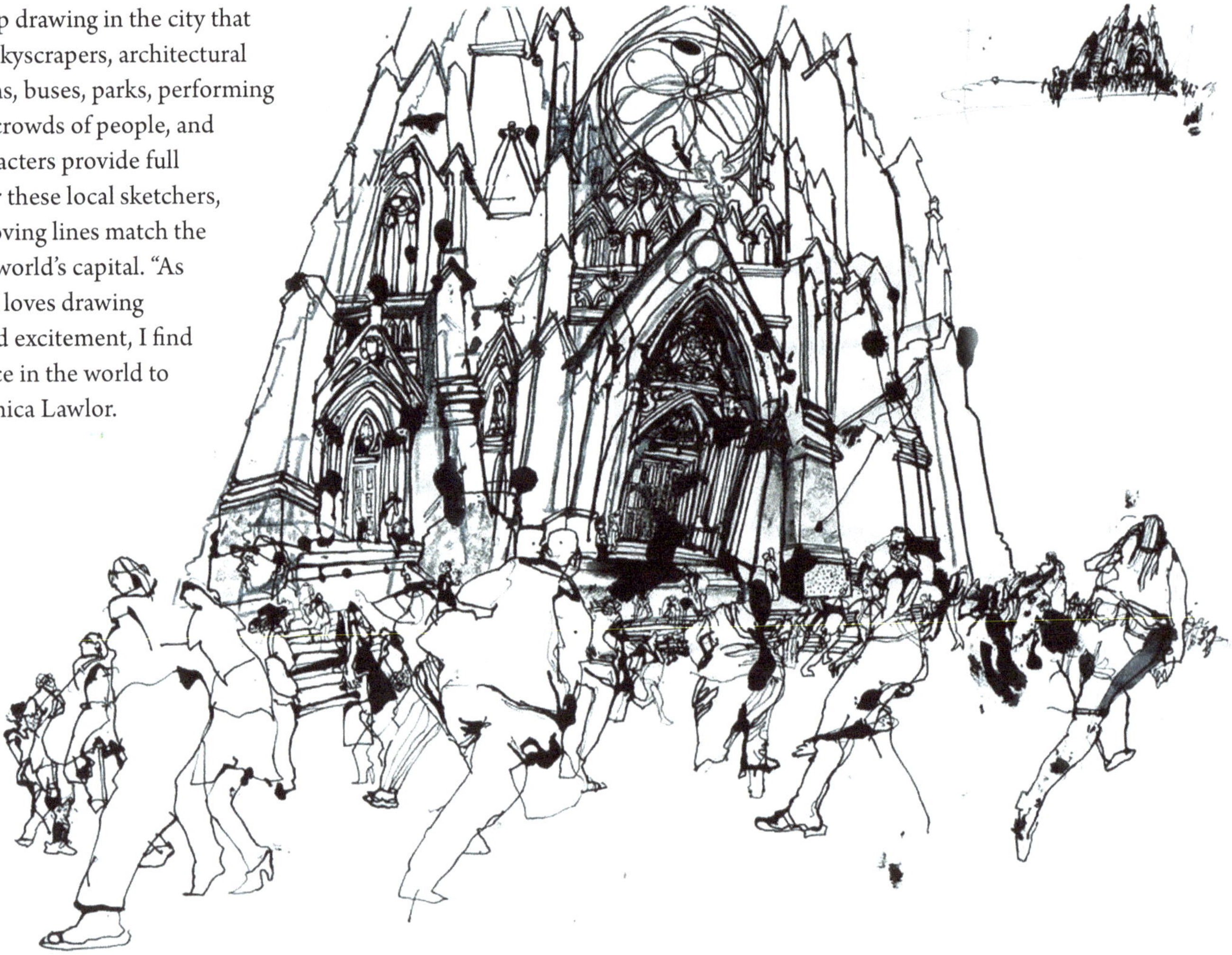

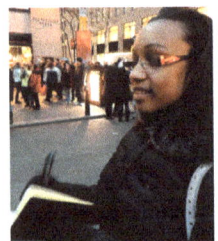

🎧 Danielle McManus sketching in the Rocke-feller Center area.
11" x 14" | 28 x 35.6 cm; Higgins pen and ink; about 3 hours

ARTIST PROFILE
Danielle McManus

When I was about seven or eight, I would sit on the front steps of my grandmother's house in Long Island with my colored pencils, crayons, and paper and draw the houses, trees, and cars across the street. I sketch because I simply just love to draw. It allows me to see the world differently and allows me to discover more about myself and the places that I am drawing. What urban sketching means to me is the joy of the artist going out and discovering a new place to draw.

My favorite sketching subjects are people. I love to capture their personalities and their body language. It's a thrill to expand on their personalities with the simple stroke of a line.

"Each time I go out and draw, it is as if I've got a new set of eyes."

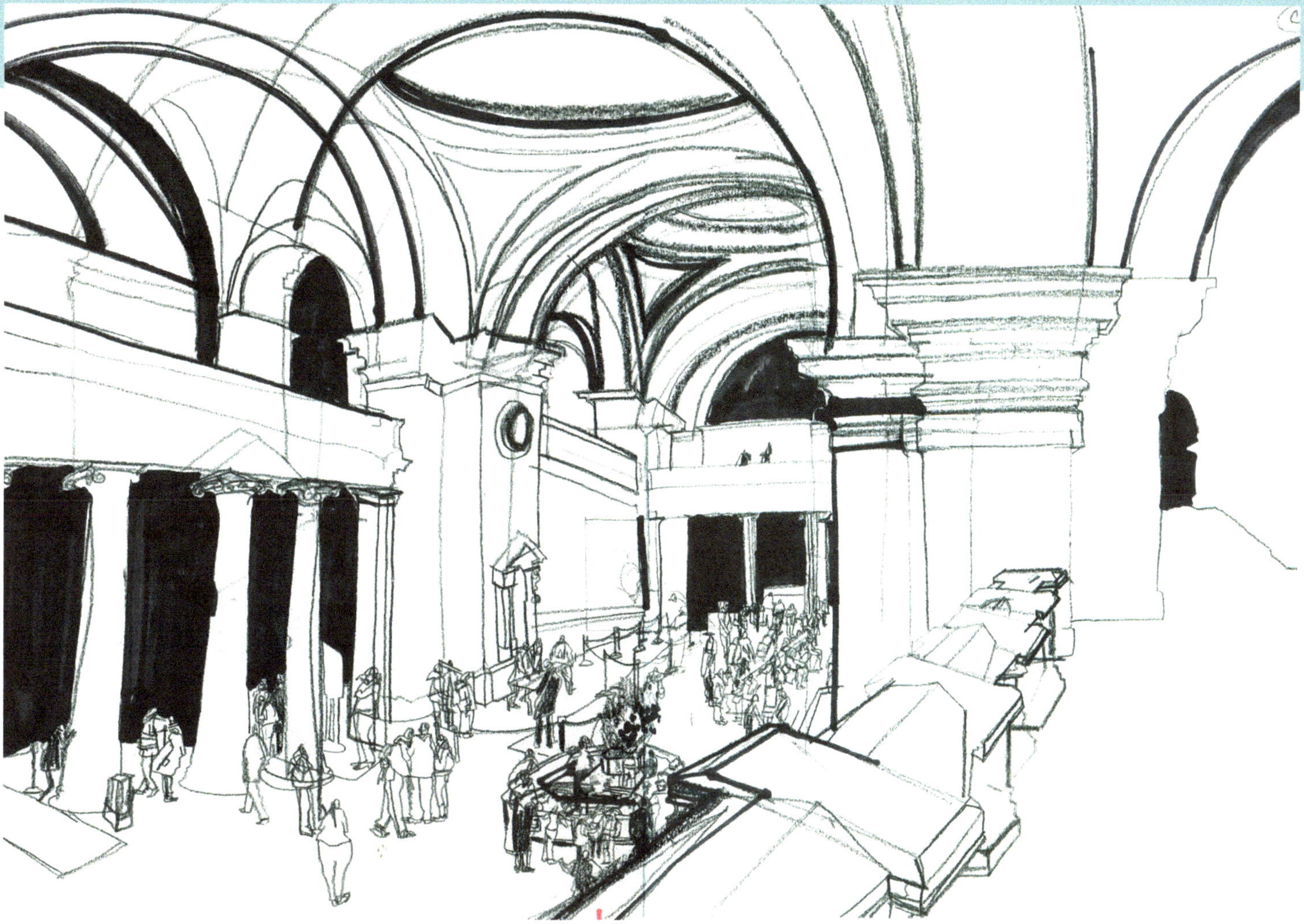

∩ The Metropolitan Museum of Art

McManus went to the second floor of the Metropolitan Museum of Art to get a different viewpoint of the lobby.

11" x 14" | 28 x 35.6 cm; Sharpie marker and Sanford china marker on 80-lb. Strathmore 400 Series white drawing paper; about 3 hours

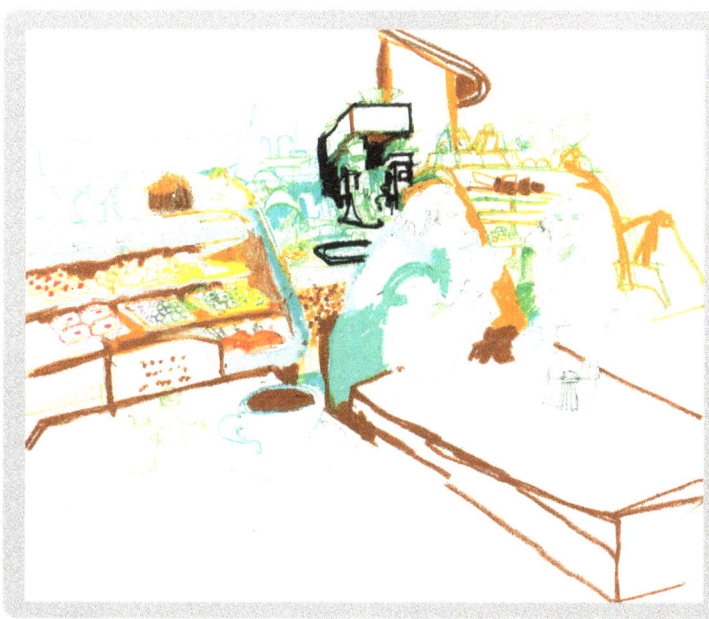

FIRST PERSON

Sketching in Harlem

by Danielle McManus

I spent three months in Harlem, thumbnailing and drawing various restaurants and people. In the beginning, I was a little nervous and didn't know what to expect, but the experience was great. I met many friendly people and became comfortable in a part of the city I never went to before.

This sketch shows Settepani Bakery and Café on 116th Street. I really wanted to go after all the textures, all the colors of the food, and the motion of the people enjoying their coffee, as I had my own cup.

11" x 14" | 28 x 35.6 cm; pencil, Prismacolor colored pencils, Neopastel on 80-lb. Strathmore 400 Series white drawing paper; about 2 hours

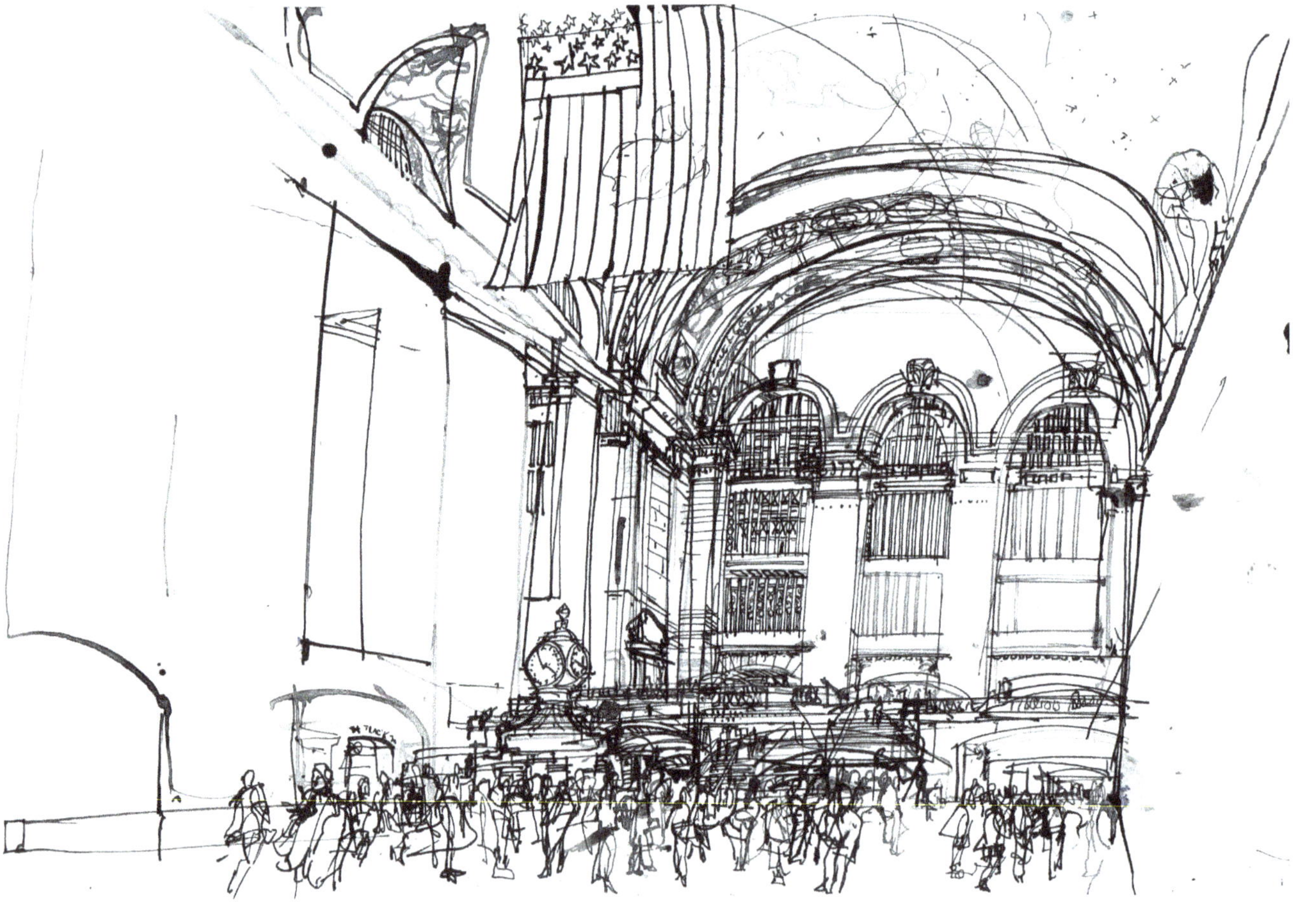

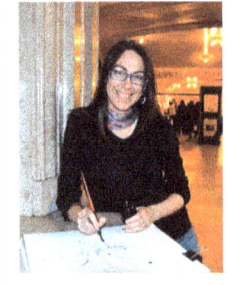

🎧 Vanderbilt Hall in Grand Central Terminal is a great place to go if you want to practice drawing people, Lawlor says. The terminal has zodiac constellations painted on the ceiling, gold chandeliers, and plenty of beaux-arts detail.

17" x 11" | 43 x 28 cm; dip pen and ink, 90 minutes–2 hours

ARTIST PROFILE
Veronica Lawlor

Reportage drawing—drawing on location—has been the lifeline of my artistic life. It's the way I was trained as a student, the way I work now as an illustrator, and the way I teach my students to approach their art. When I go on location to draw and paint, I experience the place and can feel a part of it in a way that is possible only through art. I have been plotzed on by pigeons in Venice, chased by an irate jazz musician in New Orleans, surrounded by curious tourists in the Forbidden City (who were scattered by the Chinese army, no less), spritzed by holy water at a Japanese temple, jostled by excited fans at a Spanish bullfight, and interrogated by a New Jersey highway patrolman. And I loved every minute of it—and the many, many personal stories related to memory and place that have been entrusted to me by people over the years, as I've wandered around the world, sketchbook in hand.

"I like to work quickly and keep it in the moment. I rarely add more to my drawings after I leave the location."

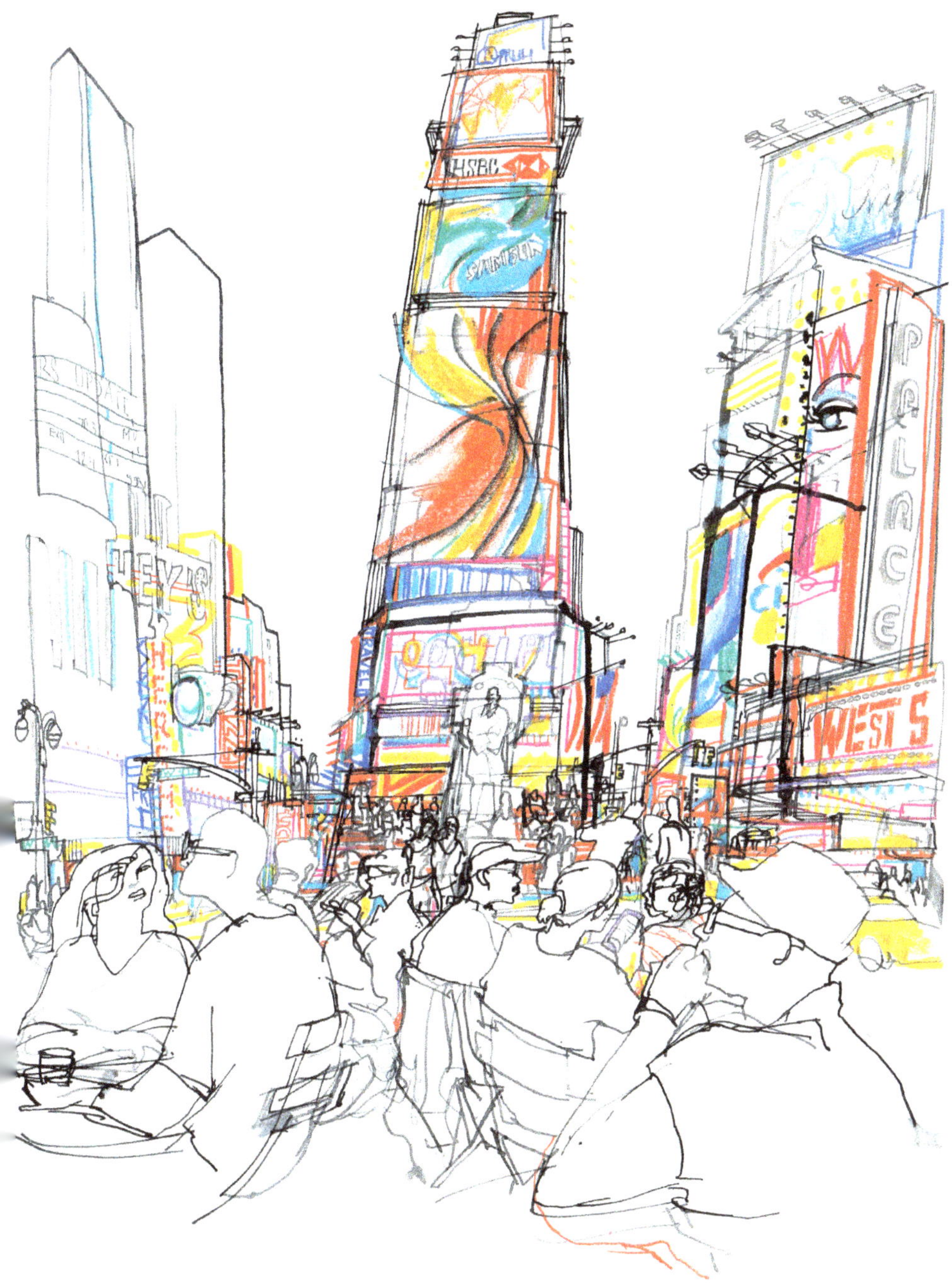

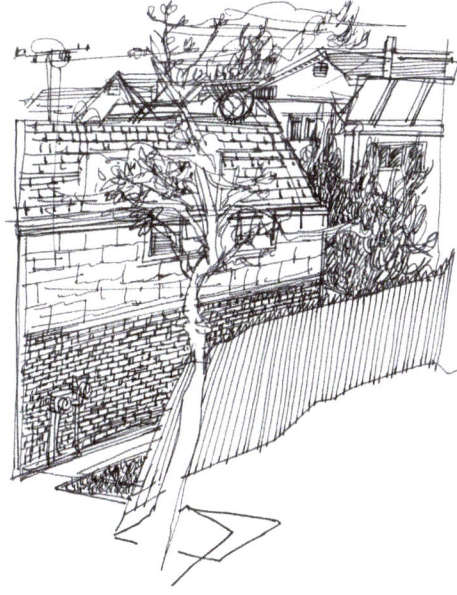

⋔ Times Square The city has closed off part of Times Square to traffic. Now, there are tables and chairs set up all over for the tourists to hang out, where there used to be traffic jams and honking horns.

Tip "Walk around first and make a few little thumbnails to decide which is the best point of view. If the crowd starts to watch and comment on what you're doing, relax and enjoy being part of the entertainment." — *Veronica Lawlor*

9" x 12" | 23 x 30.5 cm; pen and Higgins black ink with Prismacolor colored pencil and Nupastel pastel sticks on Canson pure white drawing paper; 1 hour

⋔ A Backyard in Queens The backyards in Queens, a borough of New York City, can be a little tight. Lawlor says she enjoyed the challenge of capturing all the different textures crammed into such a small space.

Tip "The true character of a city can be revealed in the most seemingly mundane scenes." — *Veronica Lawlor*

5" x 6" | 12.5 x 15 cm; Waterman fountain pen with ink, Moleskine journal; 15–20 minutes

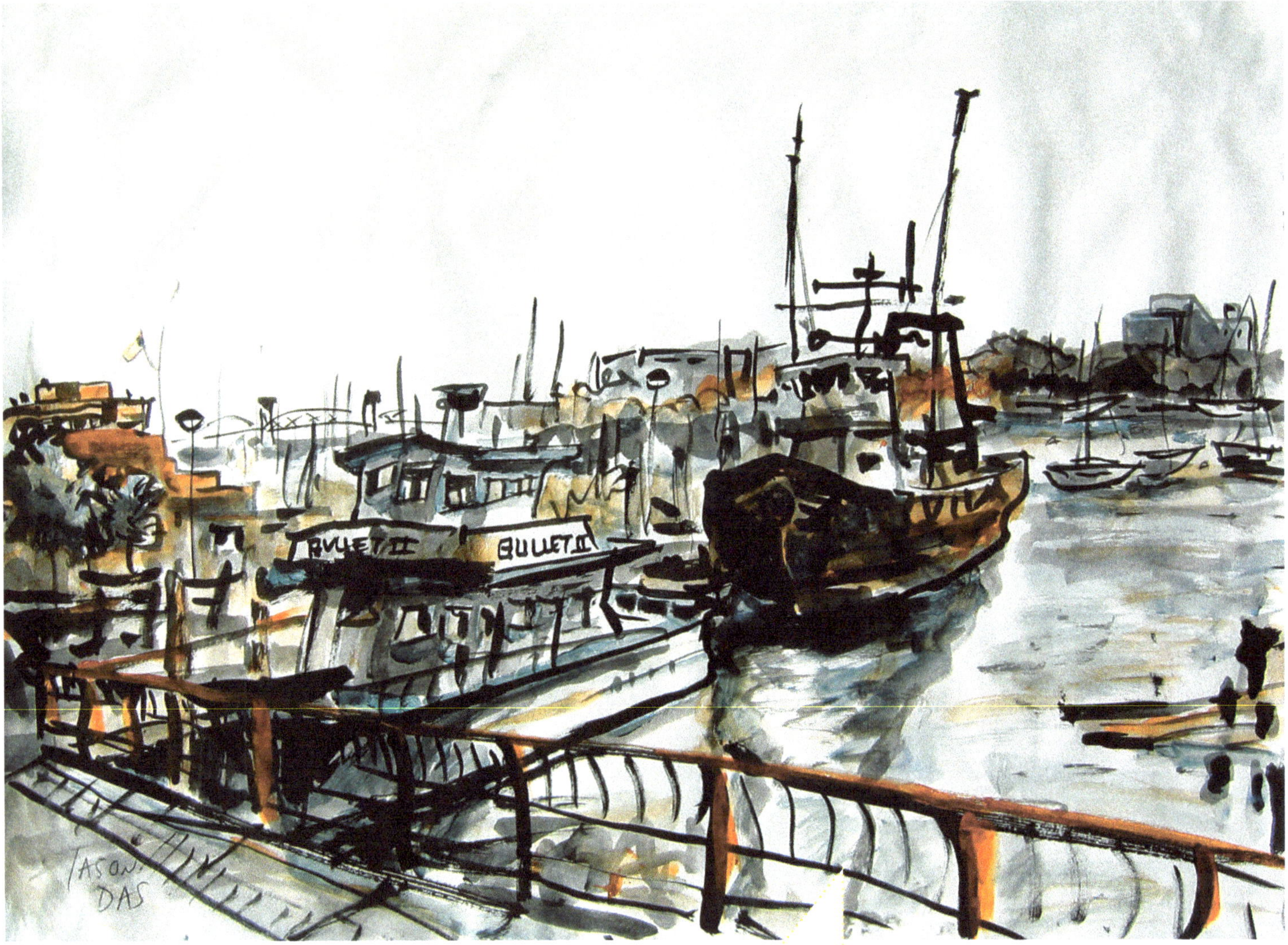

18" x 24" | 45.7 x 61 cm; Yasutomo Sumi ink (black), da Vinci watercolors on Canson Classic Cream drawing paper

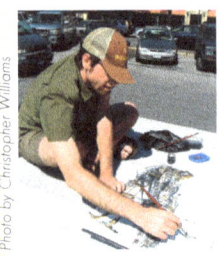

Photo by Christopher Williams

🎧 Jason Das sketching at Sheepshead Bay in Brooklyn.

ARTIST PROFILE

Jason Das

I'd always assumed I knew how to draw, but realized I didn't do much of it. Rather than attempting anything creative, I started carrying a sketchbook and drawing from life. It was wonderful to practice drawing so much more, but I was also pleased to discover how drawing from life could realign my engagement with my surroundings. It's a great way to learn more about my environment—architecture, botany, fashion—simply because I'm forced to pay attention to what I'm drawing. Then, at the end of it all, I get a drawing to show off! It's a pretty good deal.

Sometimes, I go out planning to draw, but generally I just try to keep a sketchpad with me whenever I can. I draw in offhand moments, in leftover time—while waiting for a train, eating a lonely lunch, or hanging out at a bar or coffee shop.

"A lot of my best sketches tend to happen when I should be doing something else."

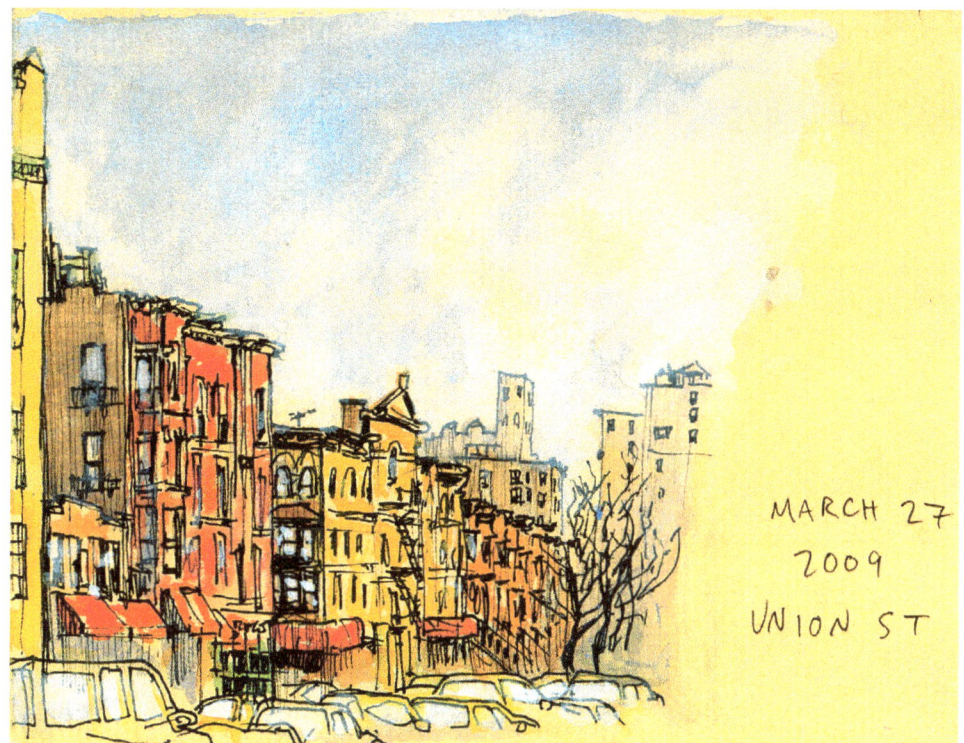

↻ **Union Street, Uphill** Jason Das's work shift at the Park Slope Food Coop sometimes leaves him standing outside long enough for a sketch. "I've done sketches looking every which way from this same spot," he says.

Tip "The nonwhite paper allows the translucent white paint to create highlights, including the windows and sky, but the white is also used to fade the background—a very easy way to depict atmospheric perspective."
— *Jason Das*

5" x 7" | 12.5 x 18 cm; black Pitt or Micron pen, watercolor on a handmade sketchbook bought at a craft fair

↺ **James J. Byrne Park** This is a view from Nice in Park Slope, one of Das' favorite places to get a sandwich or use the WiFi. "They've got great, big west-facing picture windows," Das says.

Tip "My goal was to capture the late-winter afternoon light. The yellow sky provides sharp contrast for the trees and distant buildings. Some branches are outlined; others are just done in watercolor. That's the binding string down the middle of the sketch!" — *Jason Das*

9.5" x 6.5" | 24 x 16.5 cm; Sakura Micron and Pigma Graphic black pens; watercolor on handmade book with Rives cream-colored cotton paper

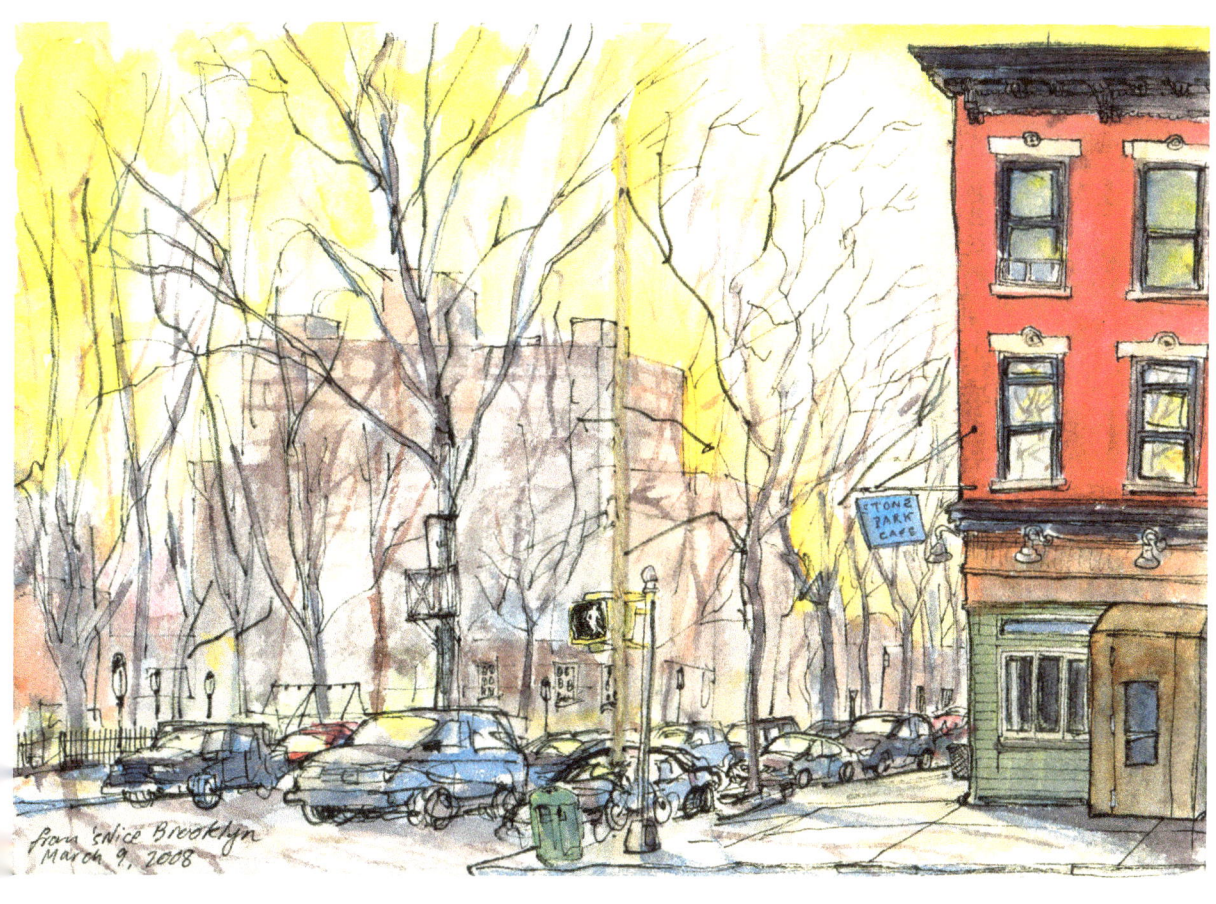

From one day to the next there are changes: just slow co-reality.

October 18. Saturday.

October 19. Sunday. 2008.

3.5" x 7" | 9 x 18 cm; Pilot ballpoint pen, Staedtler mechanical pencil, Lamy Safari fountain pen, various watercolor pencils (primarily Derwents), various water pens, Dove blender pens, Cotman watercolor field box on Moleskine plain notebook; about 20–30 minutes, plus some finishing at home

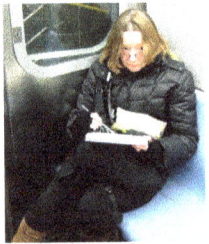

○ Sharon Frost has been sketching in the subway for more than forty years.

ARTIST PROFILE
Sharon Frost

I've been an artist all my life and have lived in New York City since I was in my twenties, when I did my grad work at Hunter College. I've been in the studio full-time since I retired, but I've become more and more dependent on my daily sketchbook activity, even as I continue to work on canvas. The sketchbook has become the heart of my studio practice. I'm becoming very attached to holding my work in my hand and thinking about how it fits in my brain.

I've been drawing in-transit for more than forty years now, most often in New York City subways and buses. I'm not that interested in portrait vignettes—more in the sense of isolation in a shared space and disparate attention. I try very hard not to let myself get caught. It almost never happens, and when it does, I stop.

"I'm an oil painter, and my drawings grow a lot like my paintings do. They grow from the page."

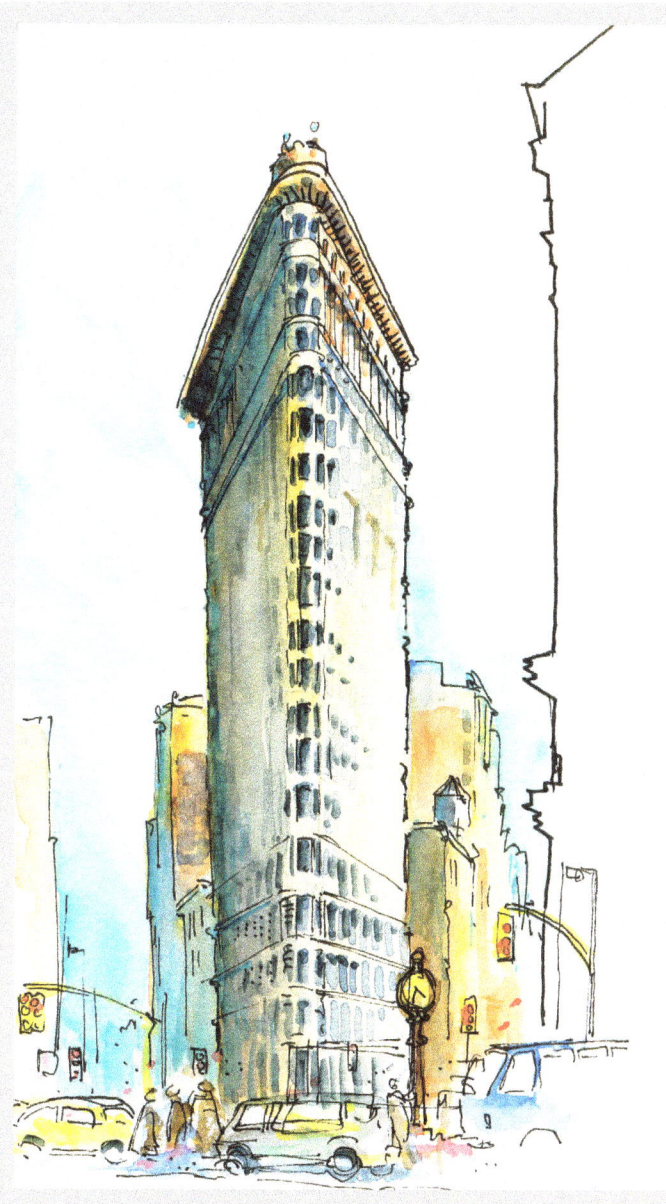

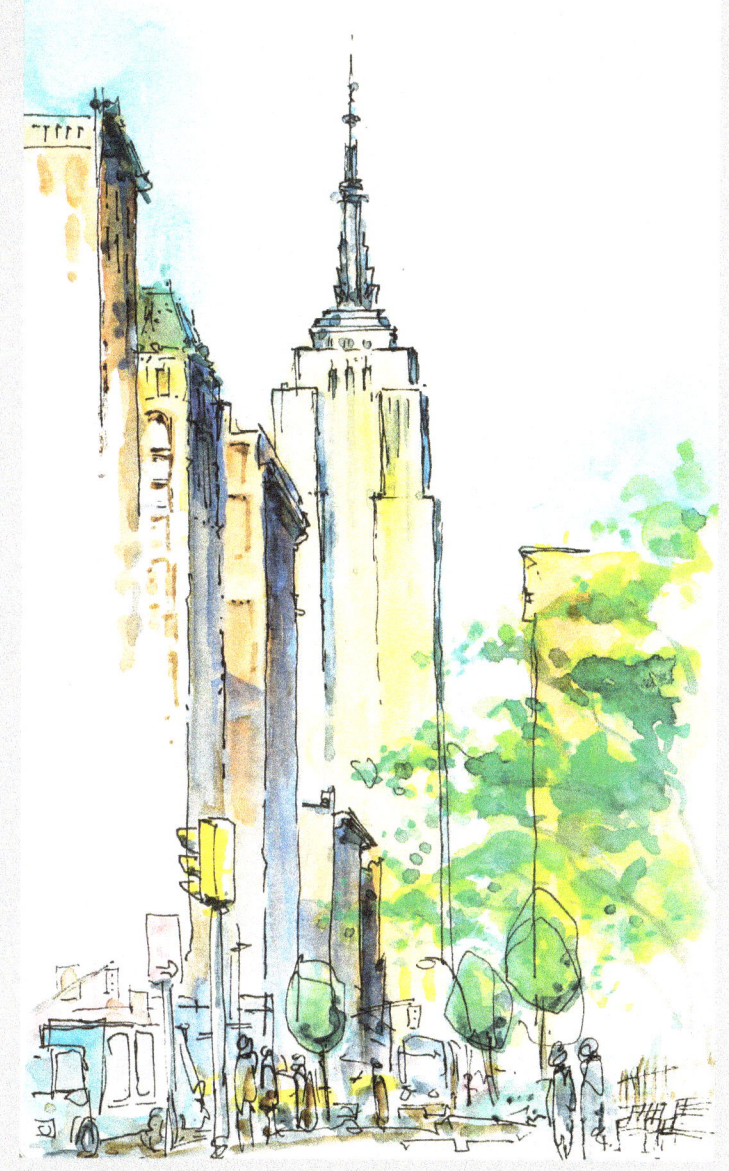

TRAVEL JOURNAL

Two Views from Madison Square

by René Fijten

It was our first time in New York, but at arrival, my wife suffered from severe jet lag and wanted to take a short nap. So I walked around the corner from the hotel and found this view. For me, the Flatiron is a mythical building; it represents the daring way New York transforms its urban tissue into buildings that reach for the sky. I found a chair and table in Madison Square, so I could sit quietly and draw this in the evening sun. Facing the opposite direction, I drew the Empire State Building while standing up and leaning against a lamppost on a traffic island with cars zooming by. After I returned to my wife, we walked to the Empire State Building, rose to the top floor, and enjoyed the most stunning view I had ever seen in my life.

5" x 8.25" | 12.5 x 21 cm; Edding 0.3 mm technical pen (waterproof), Van Gogh 12-color, portable watercolor set, Sakura Koi waterbrush on Moleskine watercolor book; 40 minutes

> *"The practice of translating what I see into something that communicates has taught me a great deal about myself and my reasons for creating art."*

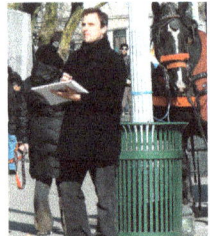

Greg Betza sketches in uptown Manhattan near the American Museum of Natural History (above).

14" x 17" | 35.6 x 43 cm; pen and ink on Canson drawing paper; 1 hour

ARTIST PROFILE

Greg Betza

I am an illustrator living in New Jersey, right outside of New York City. During my years studying in New York (at Parsons and the David J. Passalacqua School), I was introduced to the art of drawing on location, also known as reportage. What I love most about it is the opportunity to meet someone new, to discover a place I've never been, or to learn something new, just because I'm out there putting pen to paper.

New York is a city of movement, energy, and change. This has helped me grow as an artist, because I try to keep my art evolving to complement its constantly changing landscape. Whether I'm drawing the ships at the South Street Seaport or the crowds and skyscrapers of Times Square, or painting a landscape in Central Park, I am always challenged and inspired by this city.

VIEW POINTS

Flatiron District

by Greg Betza

I like to experiment with different graphics, to communicate the different feelings and energies of my subjects. Rather than treating the Flatiron Building like an architectural study, my aim was to convey its feeling amid the landscape of New York City. The contrasts between the dense lines and detail of the building, the loose lines of the people on the street, and the ornate shapes of the street lights are what make this an interesting and successful drawing, not how technically perfect I can copy the scene. When I turned to face uptown, the scene had completely changed and so did my graphics. There was energy, movement, and color, so my lines, strokes, and marks reflect that.

Right: 12" x 18" | 30.5 x 20 cm; Aurora fountain pen, Staedtler Marsgraphic 3000 duo marker, and Caran d'Ache Neocolor II water-soluble crayons on Borden & Riley #15 Tuppence Sketch Bond multiuse drawing paper; 30 minutes

Below: 12" x 18" | 30.5 x 20 cm; Caran d'Ache Neocolor II water-soluble crayons, Winsor & Newton Cotman portable watercolors, pencil, Borden & Riley #15 Tuppence Sketch Bond multiuse drawing paper; 30 minutes

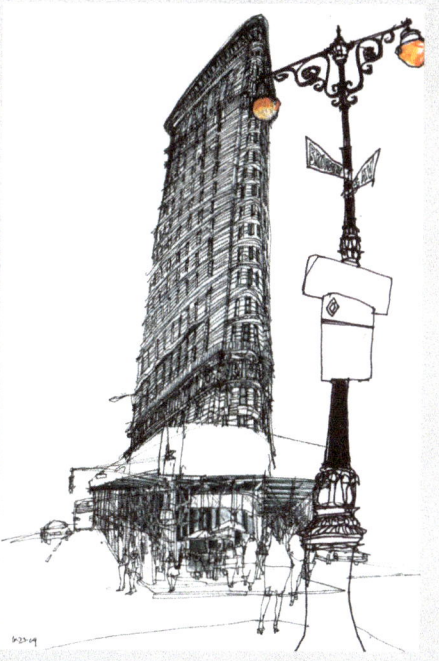

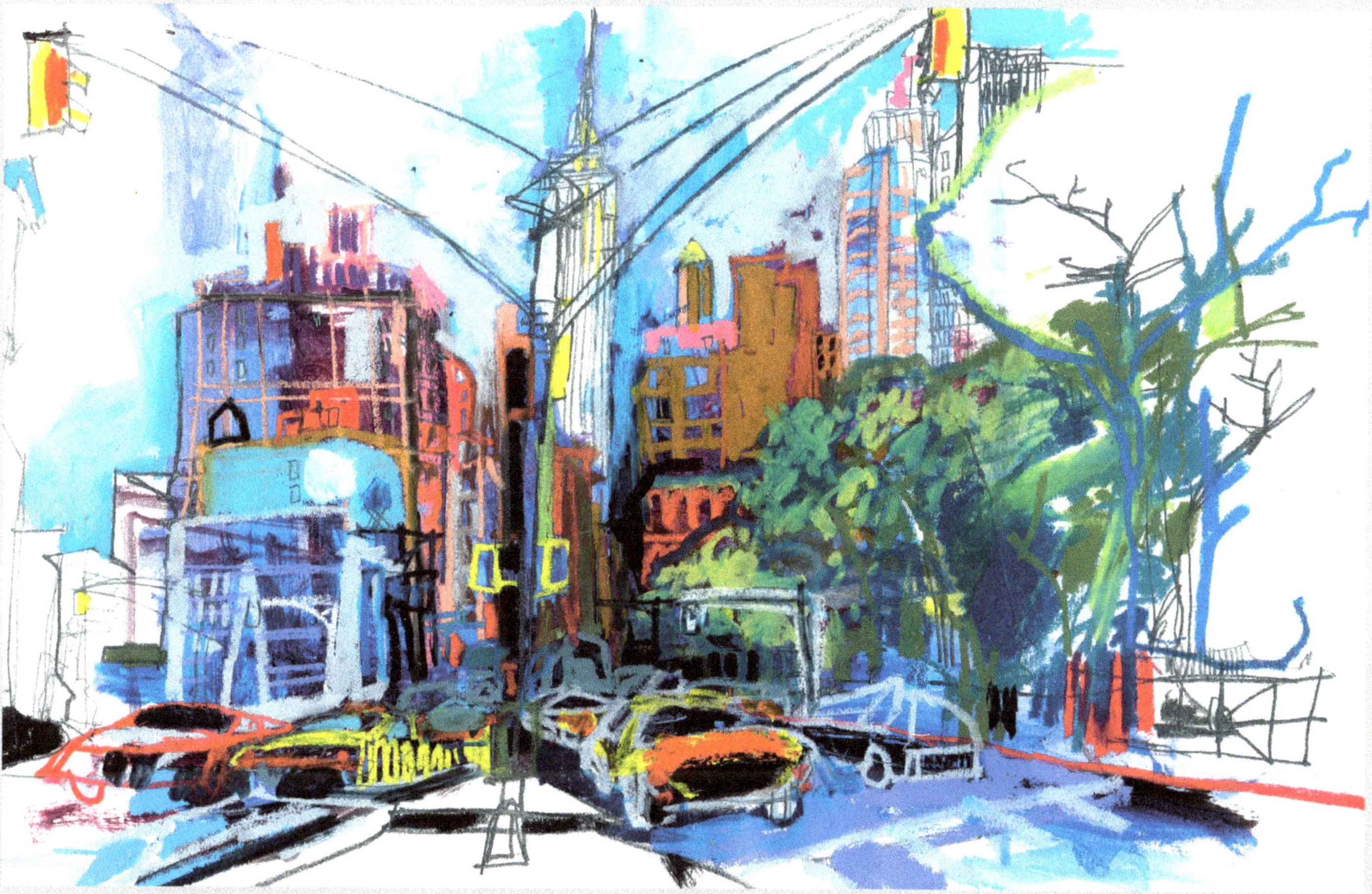

WASHINGTON D.C.

Museums, monuments, memorials, and government buildings on the National Mall are ideal for urban sketching. Local art teacher Christian Tribastone also mixes up drawing and eating, capturing the colorful and cosmopolitan variety of food trucks around the U.S. capital.

◑ Sâuçálito Dozens of high-end food trucks ply the streets of D.C., offering almost every kind of food, from Indian to barbecue, crepes to bhan mi. By the time Tribastone finished sketching the Sâuçálito truck, they'd sold out for the day and the staff was eating on the curb.

Tip "Learn to eat and draw! I love sketching food trucks, but I know they won't always be there long, so I tend to draw first and eat later." — *Christian Tribastone*

8.5" x 11" | 21.6 x 28 cm; pencil, Faber-Castell pens and white Gelly Roll pen on paper bag; about 1 hour

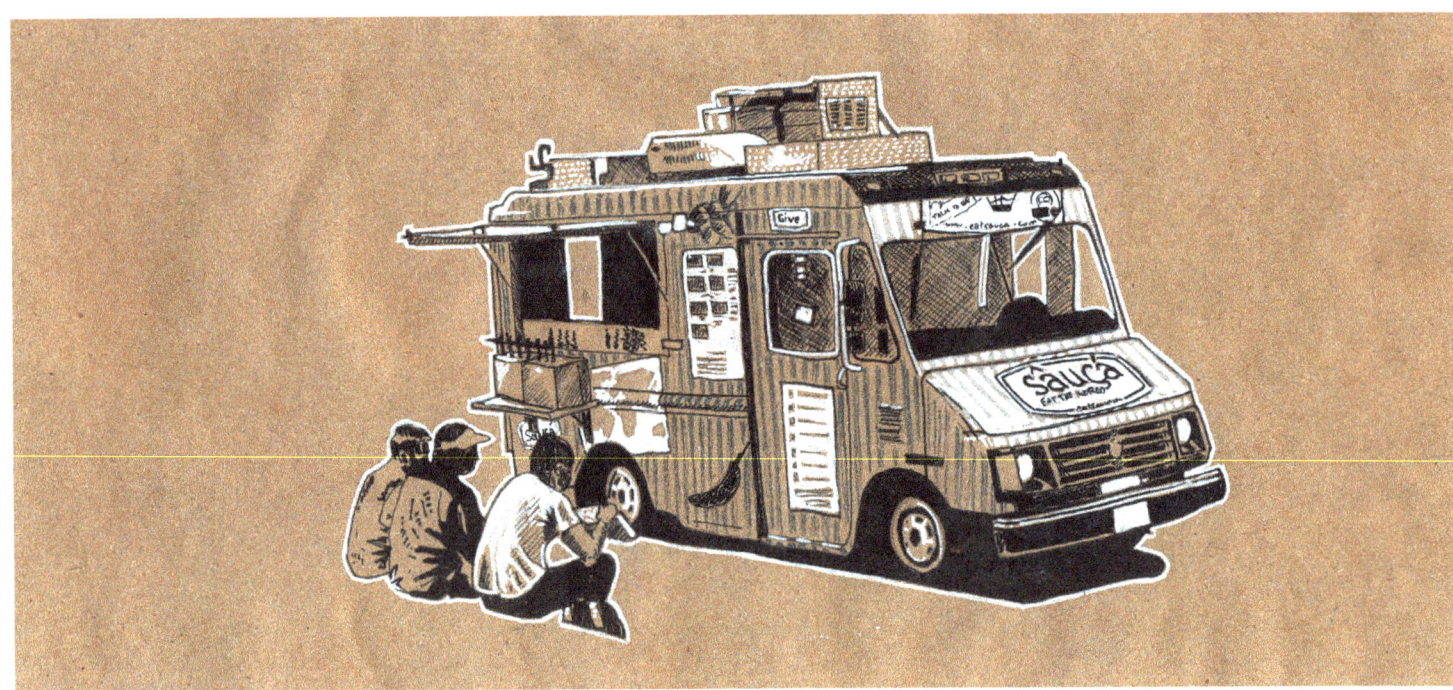

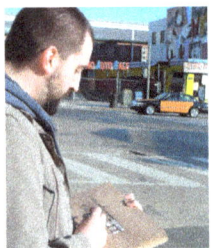

ARTIST PROFILE
Christian Tribastone

Making urban sketches has become both an act of meditation and exploration for me. It helps me seek out and discover new parts of this city I call home, as well as focus on spaces and places I might have never paid attention to otherwise. I am biased toward buildings of all sorts and any interesting sculptural or architectural elements that catch the eye.

I have loved making art since I was a child, and it became more and more of a focus in my life as I grew up, pursuing a degree in art and a career in art education. Urban sketching is a great way to connect with my environment, the city, and the community around me.

" I enjoy subjects that stay still for me as I draw them."

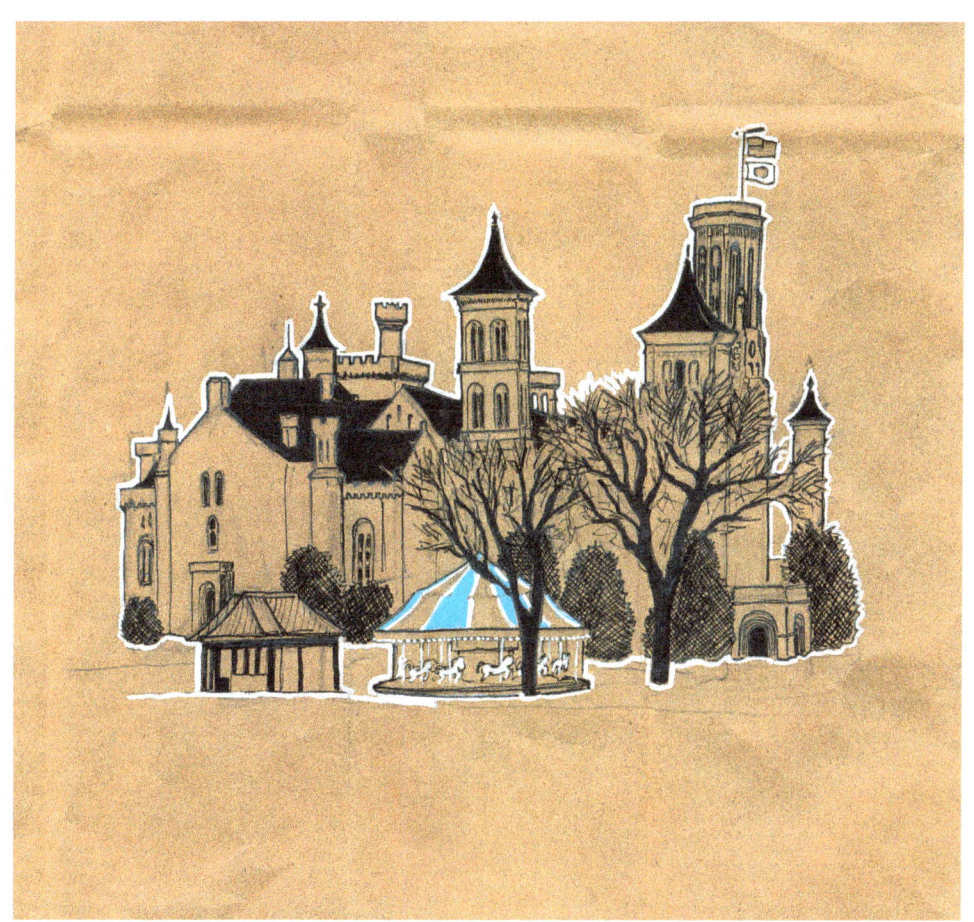

⌣ Castle and Carousel on the National Mall
Walking around the National Mall in December probably isn't the wisest choice, but even then, you will find crowds of people exploring the many museums and even riding the carousel.

Tip "When sketching in the cold, have a nice pair of fingerless gloves." — *Christian Tribastone*

14" x 11" | 35.6 x 28 cm; pencil, Faber-Castell pens, white Gelly Roll pen, and gouache on used paper bag; about 45 minutes

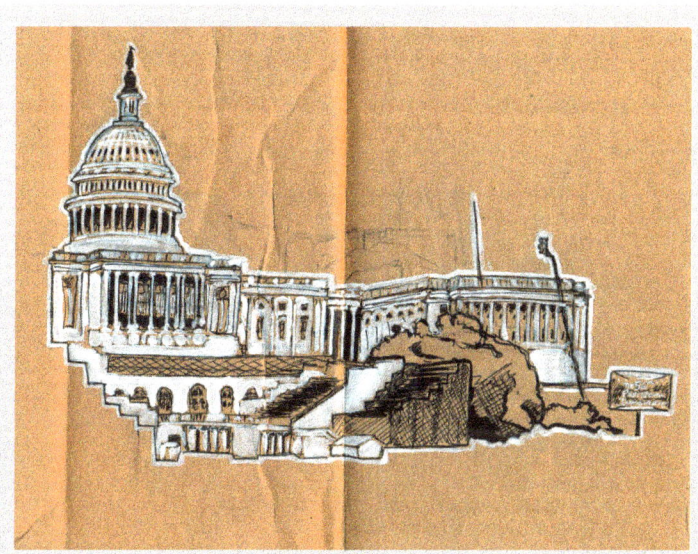

EYEWITNESS

Presidential Inauguration

by Christian Tribastone

I spent a couple of days prior to President Barack Obama's inauguration walking around the National Mall, taking in the area before millions of people came to the city. I was particularly happy to have walked by the main stage at the Capitol Building, because the workers testing the microphones were putting on a pretty good rendition of Abbott & Costello's "Who's on First" routine. With such a big event, I knew I'd want to spend extra time sketching before things got crazy. I was happy that I scouted the area and got to see and hear a lot of things I might have missed.

8" x 10" | 20 x 25 cm; pencil, Faber-Castell pens and white Gelly Roll and gesso on used cardboard; about 1 hour

NORFOLK

Just a few hours south of Washington, D.C., the naval-base city of Norfolk, Virginia, sits at the mouth of Chesapeake Bay. Local sketcher Walt Taylor describes it as a small town with no majestic vistas or baroque architecture. But once you scale your vision down to an appropriate level, he says, you can start discovering its charms: the working harbor, the reinvigorated downtown, and the waterways that insinuate themselves into the neighborhoods.

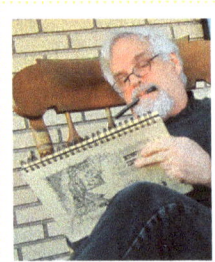

ARTIST PROFILE
Walt Taylor

When I was a kid, drawing was a way to get noticed by the popular kids and to avoid getting beaten up by bullies. Nothing much has changed since then. I'm fascinated by the way luxury and squalor, beauty and ugliness, hedge fund managers and junkies exist side by side in established cities, whose various constituncies have learned to accommodate each other over the generations. Newer communities try to exert too much control and are, therefore, much less interesting to observe and draw.

"I love the challenge of subjects no one else would think of sketching: a row of dumpsters, a chain-link fence, the side of a warehouse, a patch of weeds. It's a great exercise in seeing, in paying attention."

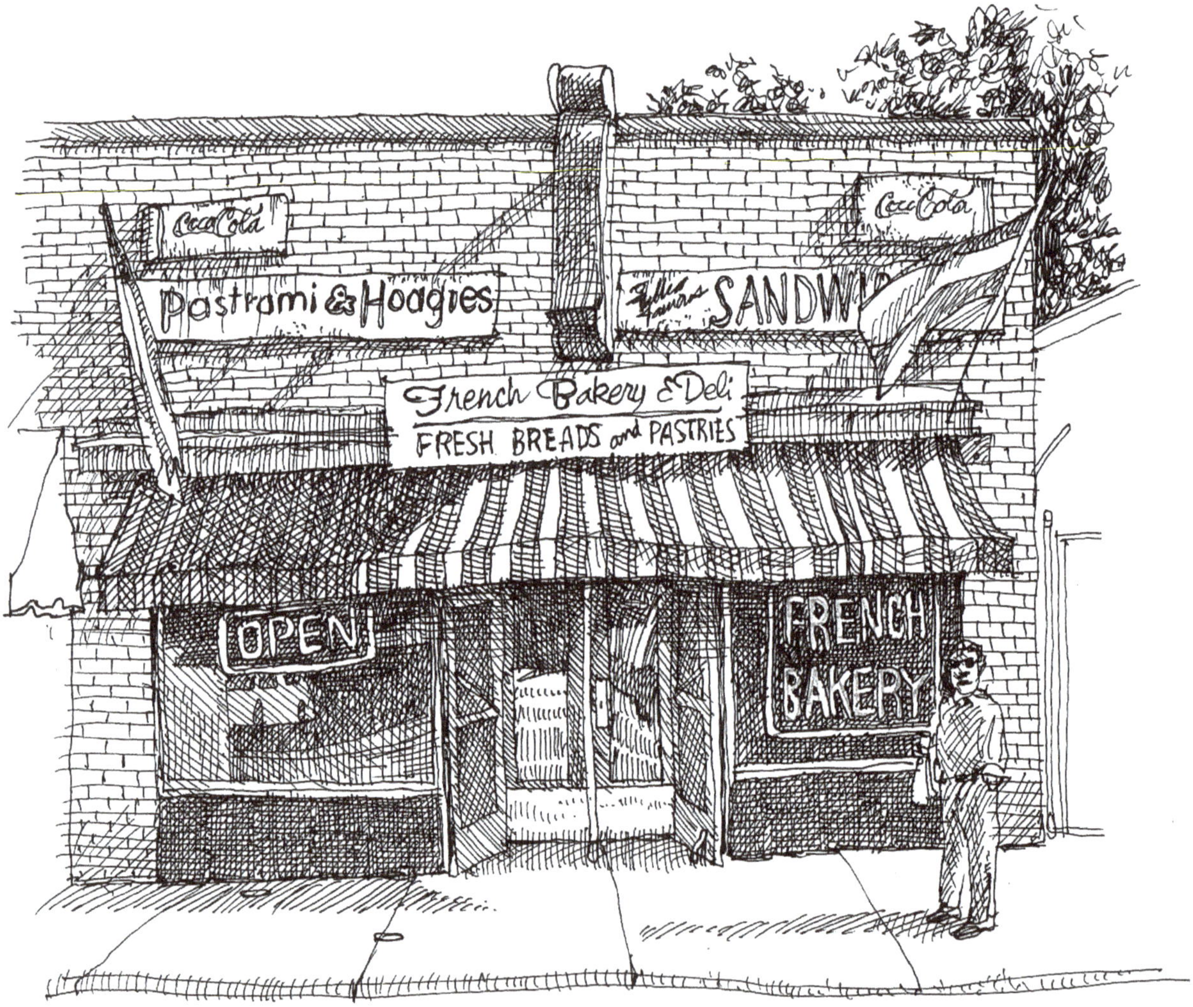

⊃ **French Bakery**
Taylor says he loves to draw buildings that have become unassuming neighborhood icons, that have, over the years, accumulated a wealth of utilitarian decorations, as if they'd grown organically on the spot.

Tip "When drawing a building façade head on, I always look for the little shadows and protrusions that give the scene a third dimension. Sidewalks are really good for this, too, as are trees in the background. What makes it interesting to me, though, is that splendid beat-up awning."
— *Walt Taylor*

8.25" x 7" | 21 x 18 cm; Copic Multiliner SP 0.2 on Cachet Classic ecru sketchbook; 1 hour

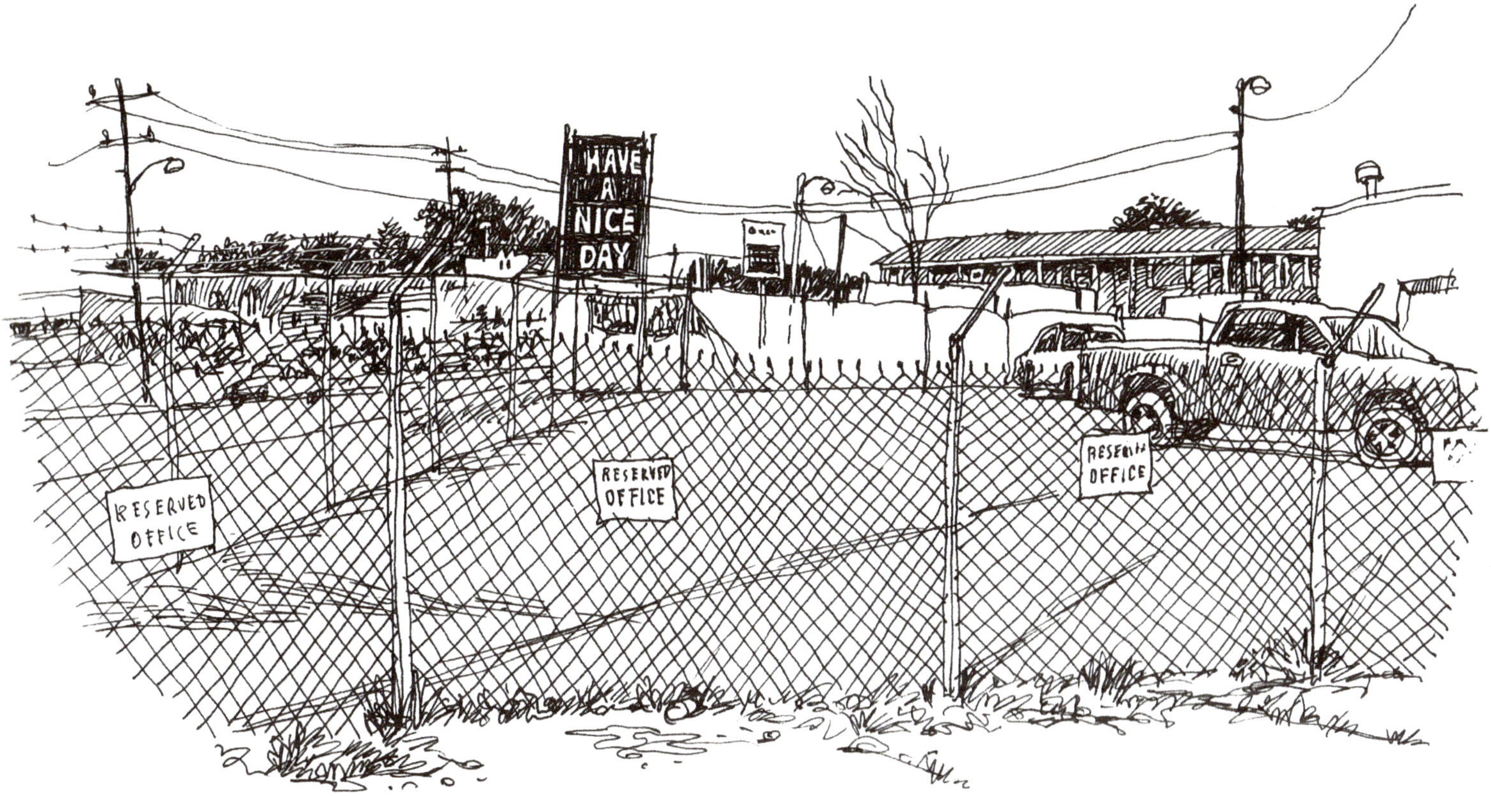

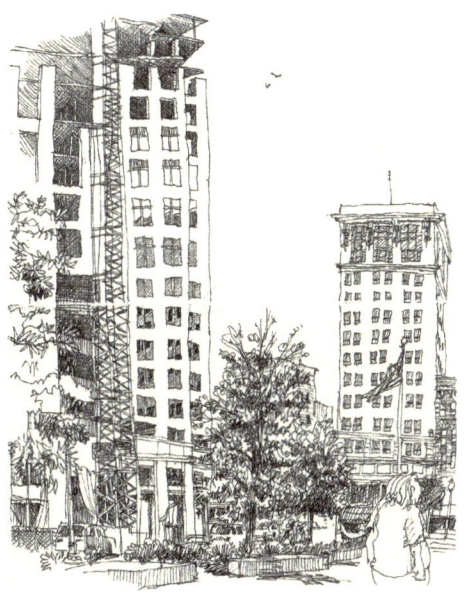

◖ Tall Buildings Walt Taylor says these buildings are tall by Norfolk standards. "Several hundred lines, and not a right angle in the bunch—one reason I've never been hired to do an architectural rendering. I like buildings to pulsate and wobble and breathe—as long as I'm not in one of them at the time," he says.

8″ x 10″ | 20 x 25 cm; Micron 02 pen on Moleskine large sketchbook; 1 hour

◖ Have a Nice Day Every city has miles and miles of vistas like this. "What sets it apart is this screwy sign rising from the clutter," Taylor says. "But I dutifully bent to its will and had a nice day."

Tip "For me, one of the highest functions of urban sketching is to find a locale that, at first glance, is completely devoid of interest, and looking and sketching until you see and feel the beauty of it." – *Walt Taylor*

10″ x 5.75″ | 25 x 14.6 cm; Copic Multiliner 0.2 on Cachet Classic wirebound sketchbook, ecru paper; 1 hour

ORLANDO

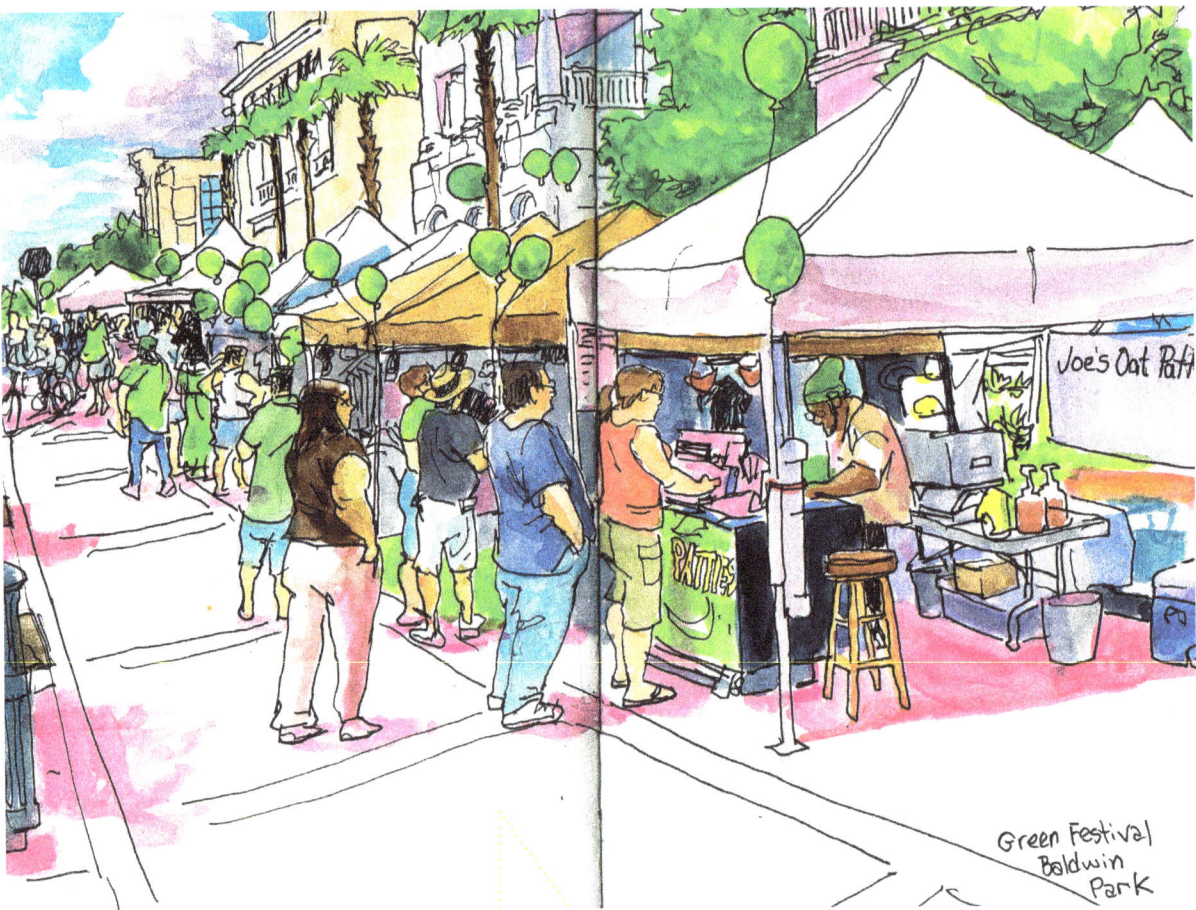

"I used to wear sunglasses, but now that I'm sketching every day, I no longer want to dim my senses."

Green Festival
Baldwin
Park

Orlando's sunny skies and world-famous theme parks aren't missing from the sketchbooks of journalist and illustrator Thomas Thorspecken. But the former Disney animator prefers to draw places, events, and art performances that are not covered in the news. "I am helping people see the true Orlando, the one that is hard at work every day, making this city an exciting place to live."

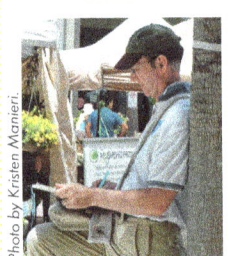

Photo by Kristen Manieri.

🎧 Thomas Thorspecken found a shady spot to sketch the activity at Baldwin Park during a green festival.

16.5" x 5.25" | 42 x 13.3 cm; Micron pens and watercolor; 1.5 hours

ARTIST PROFILE
Thomas Thorspecken

My feeling, when I first moved to Orlando, was that the whole town must be like the theme parks, a series of false façades, like on a movie set. I missed the culture and variety of New York City, from where I moved in the late '90s.

I have been using my sketches to discover the real Orlando. Sketching is offering me a way to finally put down roots, to become part of a vibrant community that I am uncovering one sketch at a time. People, for whatever reason, always seem to want to tell me their life's story when I am sketching, so my work puts me in contact with a wide variety of people around town. Sketching daily has also awakened a desire to further explore local news from an artist's perspective. I wake up every day wondering where my pen, watercolors, and sketchpad will lead me next. Every day is a safari, an adventure.

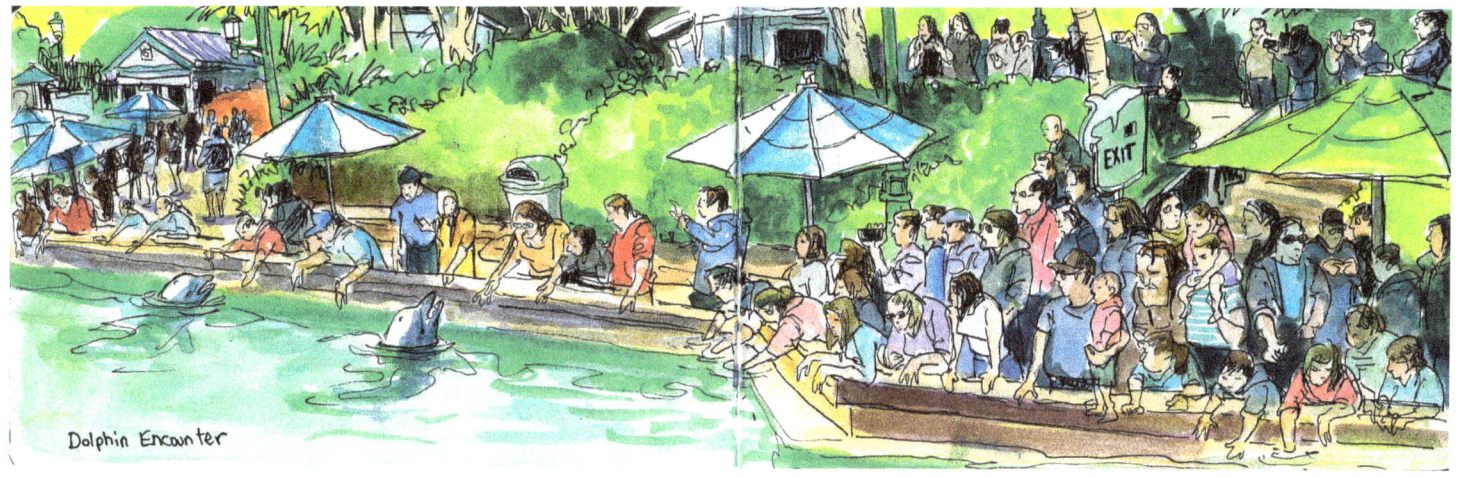

Dolphin Encounter

◯ The Dolphin Encounter at Sea World People buy fish to feed the dolphins at this popular attraction, then are guided by workers on how to attract the dolphins' attention. "I was standing next to a parks person whose job it was to watch the tourists and make sure they didn't have any personal items hanging over the water's edge," Thorspecken says.

Tip "Start with overall composition, then fill in the crowd, looking for individuals." — *Thomas Thorspecken*

17" x 5.25" | 43.2 x 13.3 cm; Micron pens, Winsor & Newton watercolors, Pentel waterbrushes, Hand-Book Travelogue Journal; about 2 hours

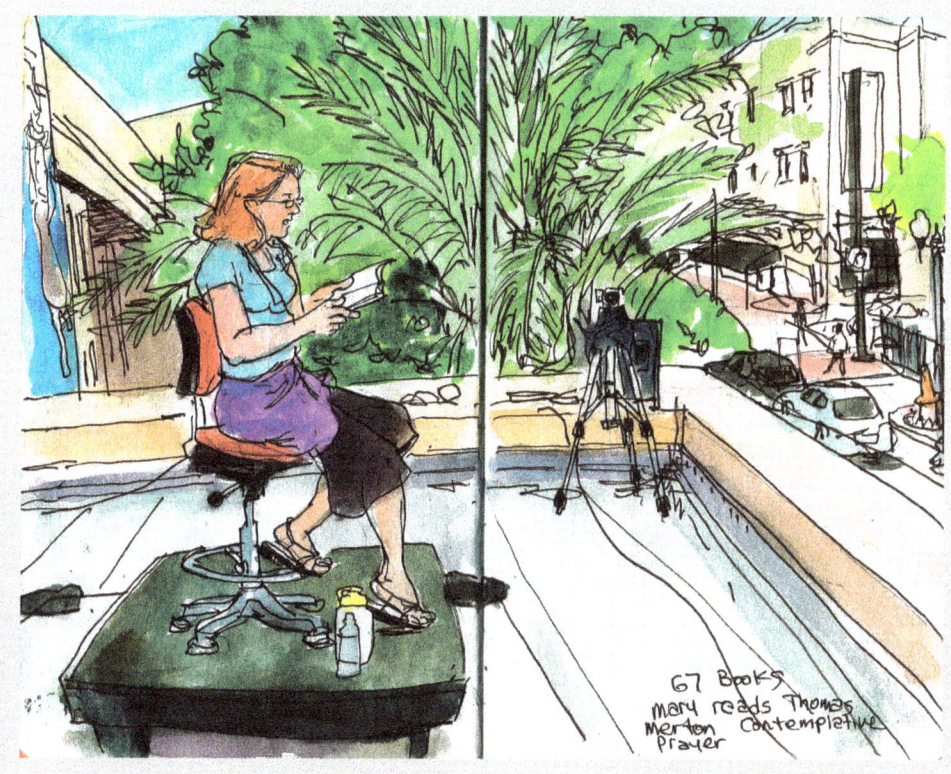

67 Books
Mary reads Thomas
Merton Contemplative
Prayer

SUBJECT MATTERS

Sketching Performers

Thorspecken likes to sketch art performances and other artists at work. "I visit painters in their studios, dancers and actors rehearsing, and authors writing," he says. "I have found sketching rehearsals and performances to be great sketching experiences." During National Library Week, people could read from their favorite book for one hour from the roof over the entry to the Orlando Public Library. "Sixty-seven readers participated, myself included," says Thorspecken. "The sun was pounding down that afternoon, and I sketched from the only patch of shade on the roof."

8.25" x 10.25" | 21 x 26 cm; Micron pens, Winsor & Newton watercolors. Hand-Book Travelogue Journal; 1.5 hours

SANTO DOMINGO

Sketchers in the Dominican Republic capital of Santo Domingo are blessed with year-round summer temperatures and plenty of beach scenes. Parque Colón in the Colonial Zone attracts colorful salespeople and performers, which makes for great urban sketching.

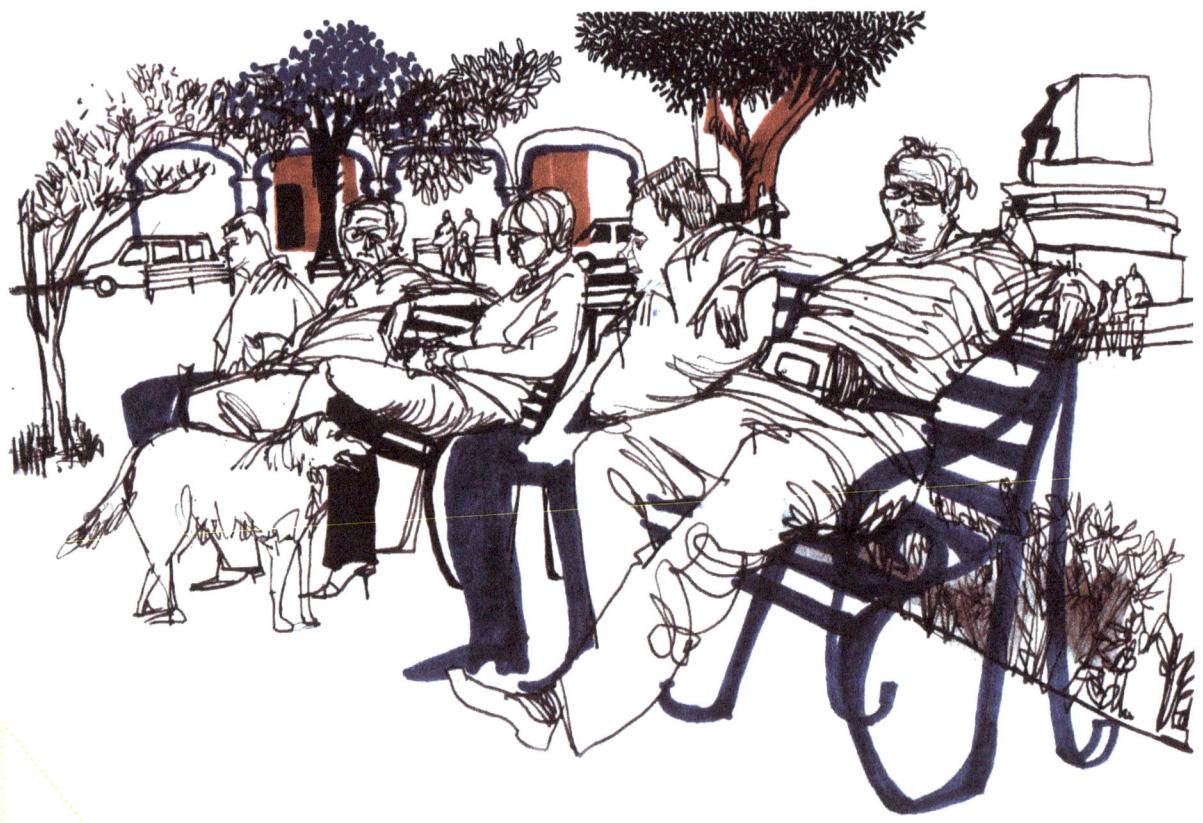

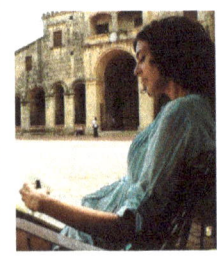

🎧 Nathalie Ramírez sketches at Parque Colón in the Colonial Zone.

8.25" x 5.5" | 21 x 14 cm;
Pelikan fountain pen with black
Chinese ink and Sharpies on
heavyweight bond paper;
about 45 minutes

ARTIST PROFILE
Nathalie Ramírez

I grew up surrounded by paintbrushes and music on this half-island called Dominican Republic. I carry this craving for art in my blood; my grandfather was a self-taught painter, my mother a painting teacher, my father an architect.

Sketching on location is important to me, because it's a way of relating to my surroundings. While sketching, I get to observe and learn more about the behavior of those around me and about the energy of a particular place. Drawing helps me interpret the world and communicate my visions and feelings about it. As a fine artist and illustrator, I find that urban sketching is closely related to everything I do; I dare say it is the very basis of my work. No matter what project I am working on, whether it be from my imagination or not, I always lean on the experience and training that reportage drawing has given me.

" I love sketching people as they interact, and I delight in their body language."

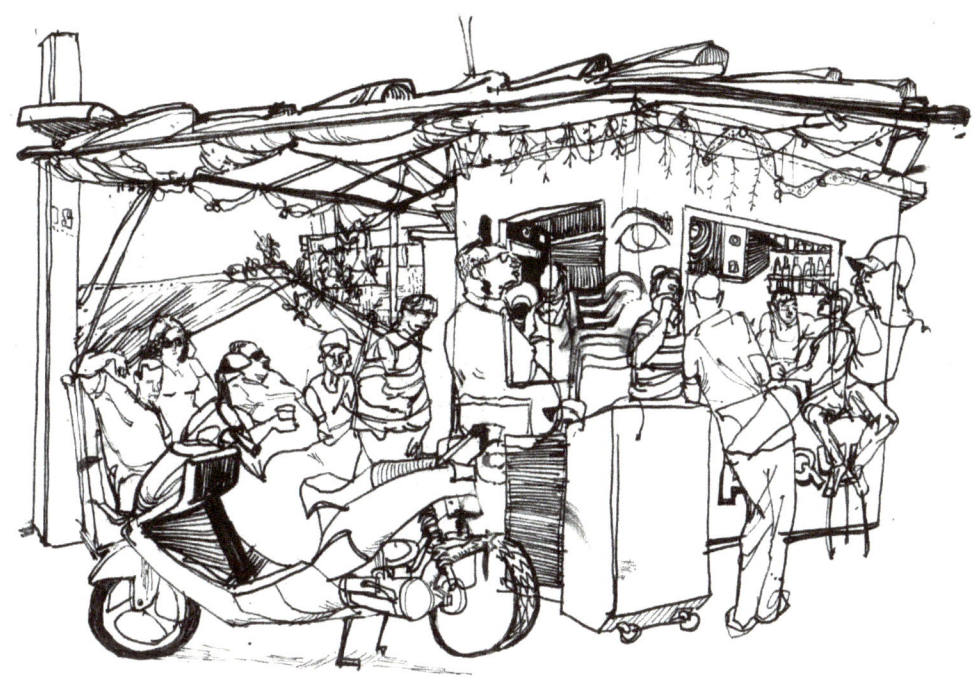

◅ **Colmado Ancla Aqui** *Colmados* are minimarkets, Nathalie Ramírez explains, in which everything from laundry detergent to salami can be bought. People tend to hang out there in the afternoons, especially on the weekends, to drink and socialize while listening to *bachata* at a deafening volume.

Tip "Don't be afraid to trust your gut instinct and put things down as they are happening. This gives the image that feeling of live energy that is common to drawings made on location." — *Nathalie Ramírez*

10.25" x 8.25" | 26 x 21 cm; Pelikan fountain pen, Chinese ink, Sharpie on Moleskine sketchbook; about 1 hour

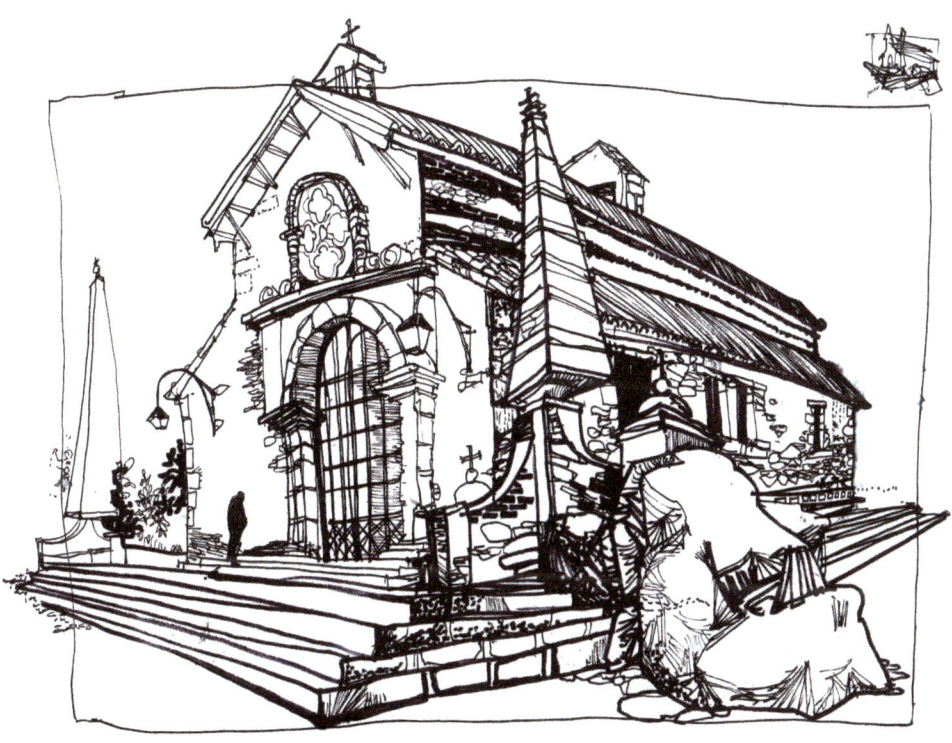

◅ **Church in Chavón** As Ramírez sat in front of this church at the place she once studied, she felt the familiar comfort you get from revisiting an old, dear friend. "The stones haven't changed visibly, the iron gates look just as quiet and heavy," she says. "It is only I that have changed, and that changes everything."

Tip "I think the best drawings come when you connect with the place, person, or activity you are drawing." — *Nathalie Ramírez*

11" x 14" | 28 x 35.6 cm; Pelikan fountain pen, black Chinese ink, black Sharpie on Strathmore Sketch premium recycled paper; about 1 hour

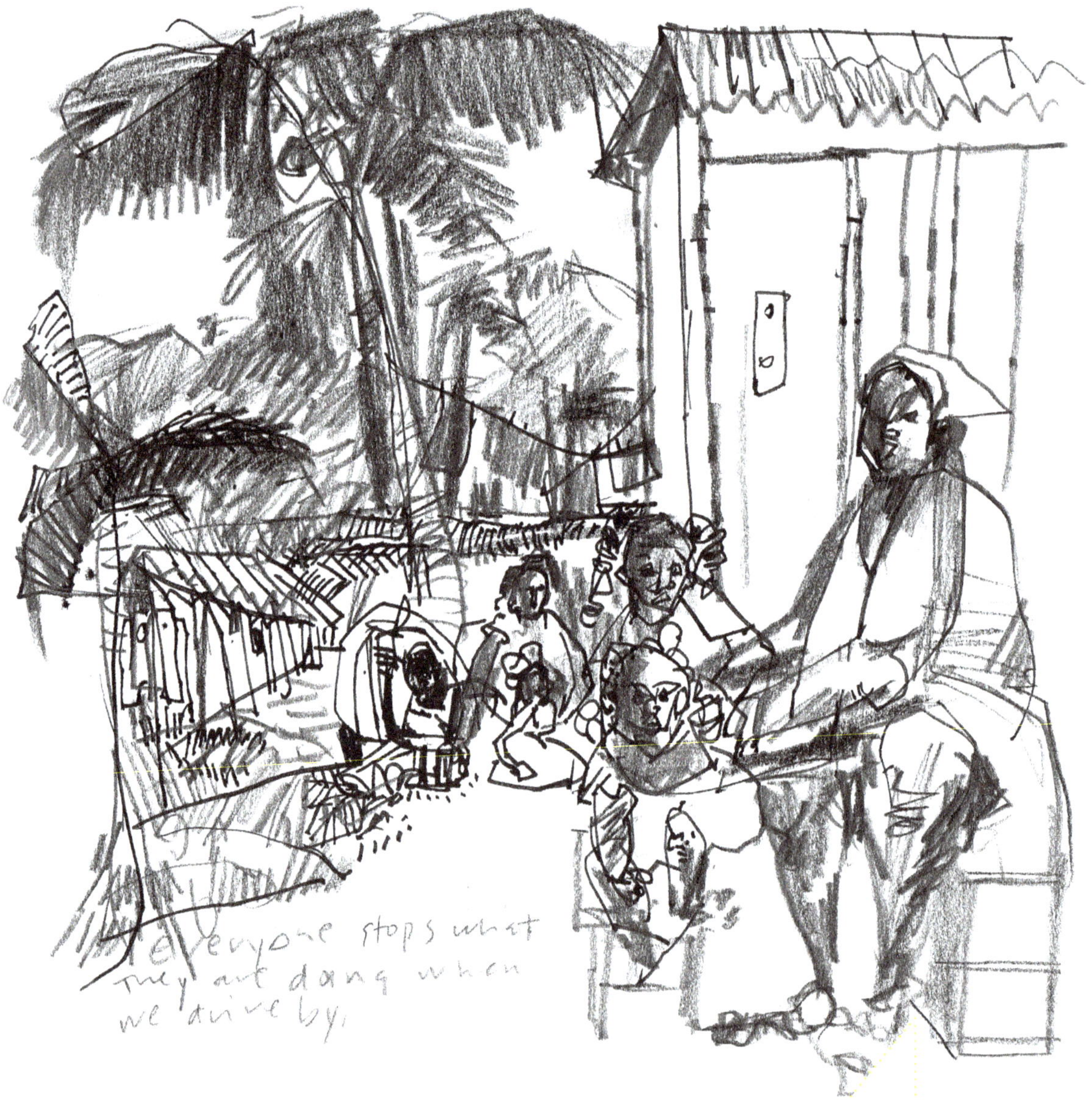

Everyone stops what they are doing when we drive by.

8" x 8" | 20 x 20 cm; Ebony
graphite pencil, Pelikan
cartridge pen on Canson
sketchbook; about 10 minutes

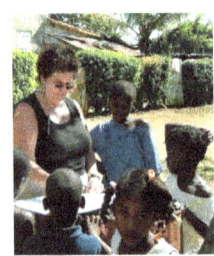

🎧 Melanie Reim sketch-
ing in the "batey," a
company town where
sugar workers live.

ARTIST PROFILE
Melanie Reim

Being able to travel and draw what I see is what makes me tick. My eyes
are bigger, my memories stronger, and my immersion in the environment
more connected for having spent the time to sit, absorb, and tell the story
of where I have been through my drawings. Although I am a born and bred
New Yorker, and there exists tons of subject matter just out my door, I am
more excited and inspired to draw out of my city, especially when in one of
my favorite places, La Romana, in the Dominican Republic. Perhaps it is
the wide-open, uninterrupted skies, or the rustling of the sugar cane or the
beauty of the people and the huge hug I get from this country every time I
visit. Being here never ceases to bring joy to my life and to my work.

"Simply put, I love to draw."

⤴ **Balloon Vendor**

Orling "Arty" Domínguez came across this street vendor making animal balloons at Parque Colón.

Tip *"I always take a few minutes to look at the person I will sketch, to observe the body language and the gestures and understand what are they actually doing."* — *Orling "Arty" Domínguez*

5.5" x 8.5" | 14 x 21.6 cm; Safari Lamy pen and Sakura Koi Watercolor Pocket Field Sketch Travel Kit on large Moleskine watercolor book; 20 minutes

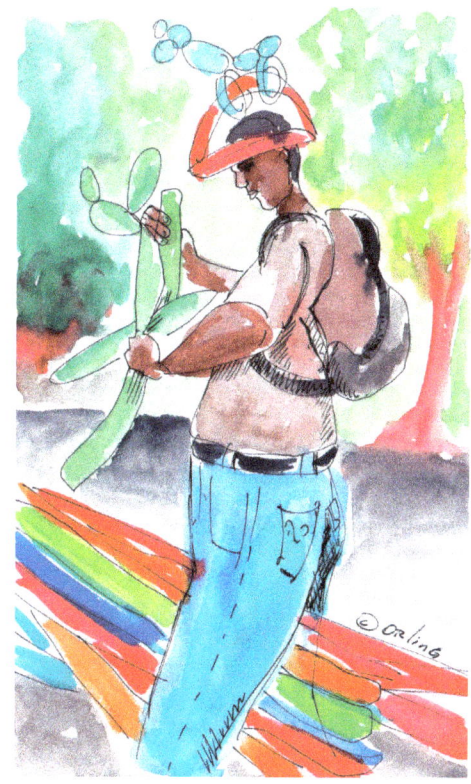

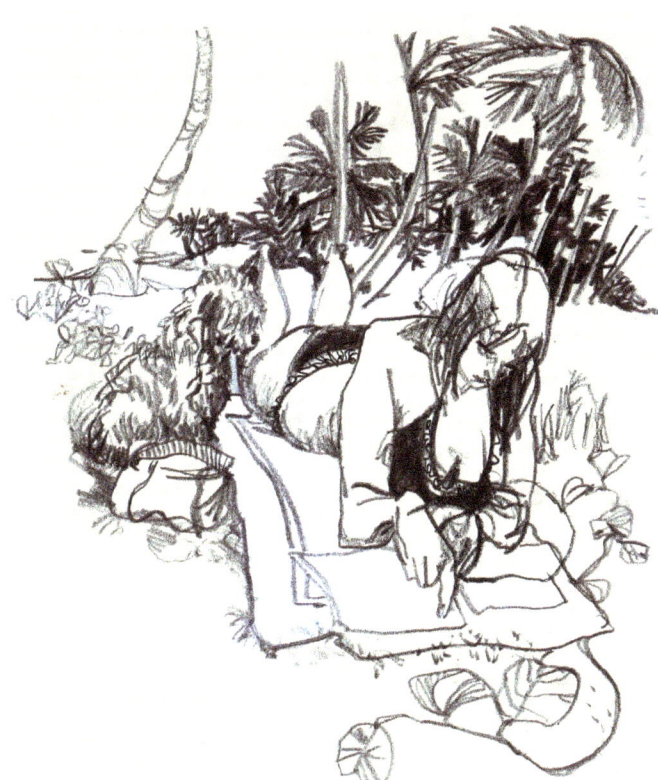

☊ Christmas in Nagua While northern countries were coping with icy roads and blizzards during Christmas, Ramírez sketched at the beach over a sun-kissed afternoon.

8" x 9.25" | 20 x 23.5 cm; black china marker, Pelikan fountain pen, black China ink, digital coloring, Daler-Rowney Cachet sketchbook; about 45 minutes

⤴ **Sporting Event**

Illustrator Jonathan Schmidt sketched a beautiful baseball night in La Romana, while getting beer knocked over him by fellow spectators.

5" x 8.5" | 12.5 x 21.6 cm; Caran d'Ache crayons and a few Faber-Castell colored pencils on no-brand, white loose paper on my homemade drawing board; about 20 minutes

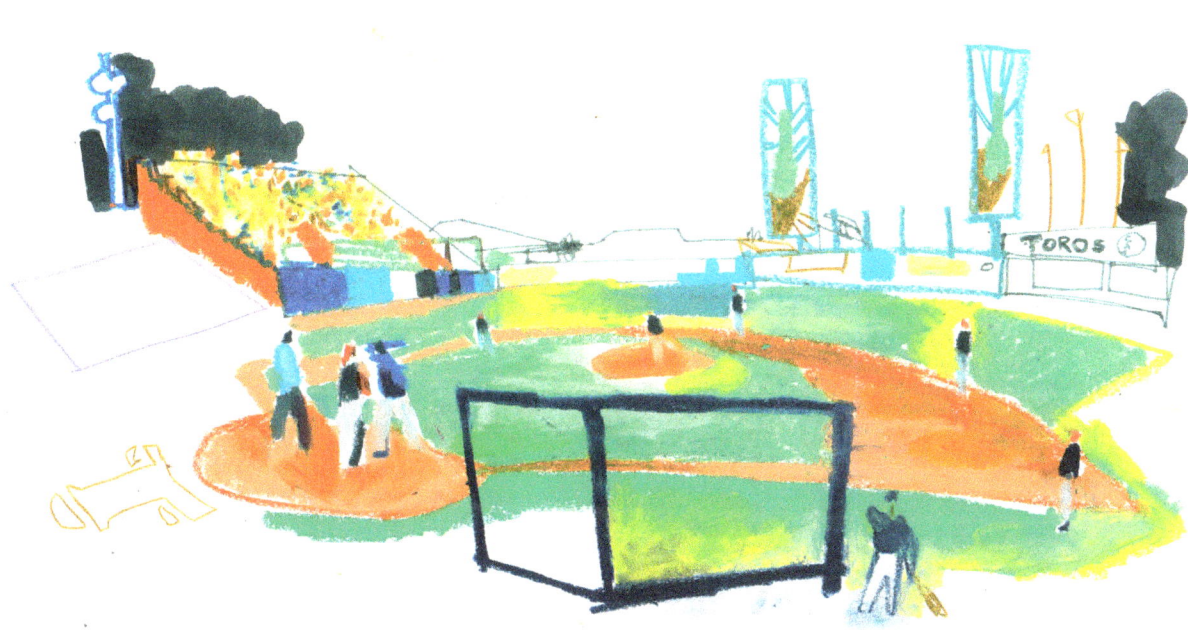

SÃO PAULO

Brazil's largest city is a hodgepodge of cutting-edge architecture, neo-Gothic cathedrals, skyscrapers from the 1920s, and densely populated bedroom communities. These artists cover the wide range of subject matter from their own points of view.

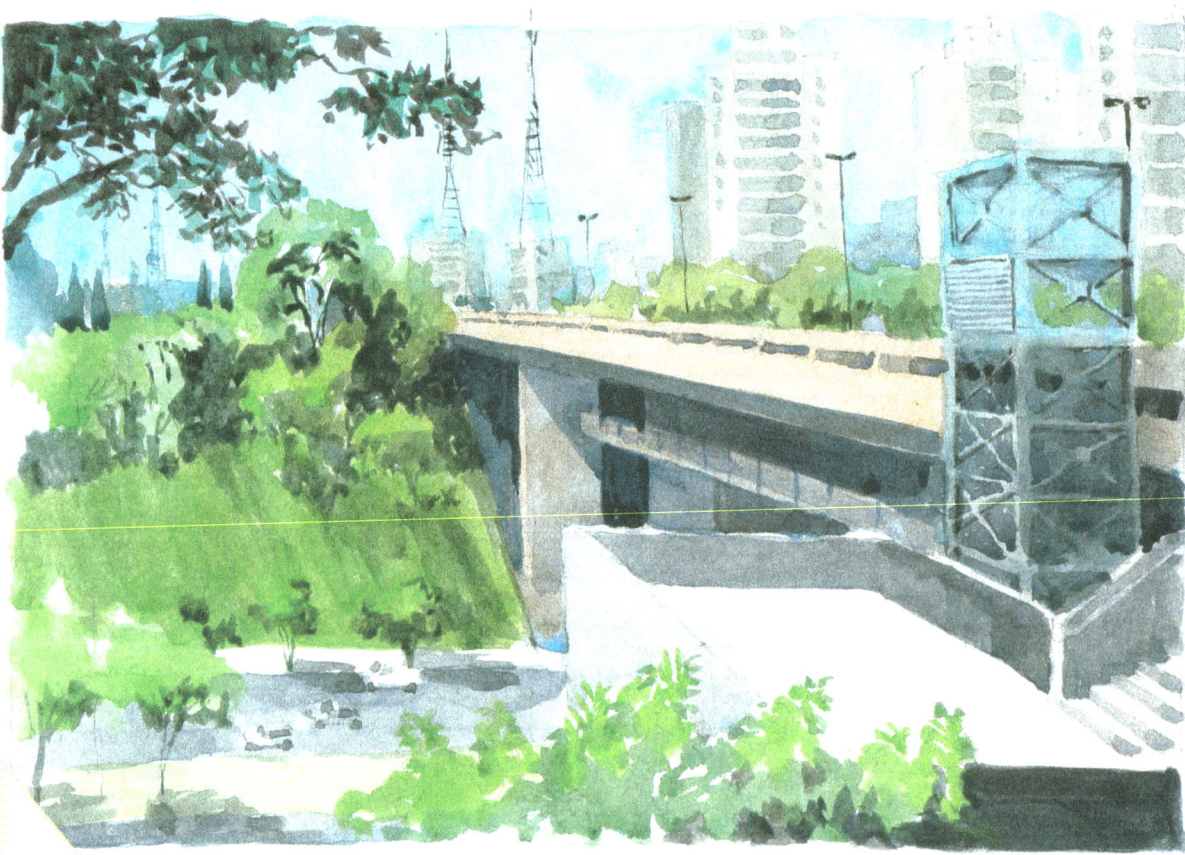

" The balance between loving and hating this big metropolis has changed since I started sketching in the streets."

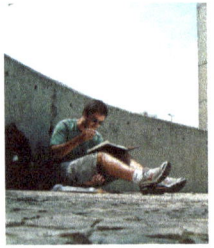

🎧 Eduardo Bajzek sketching the Viaduto Sumaré, an overpass and metro station in São Paulo.

8" x 11" | 20 x 28 cm; watercolor on Moleskine sketchbook; 1 hour

ARTIST PROFILE
Eduardo Bajzek

I was born in 1975 in São Paulo, Brazil, and I still live in this city. My passion for drawing led me to the architectural illustration field in my professional life. The work of Australian illustrator John Haycraft encouraged me to practice drawing on location. I started my first sketchbook during a trip to Italy and Switzerland a few years ago. Drawing in the streets in the middle of people, feeling and absorbing each particularity, was a fascinating discovery.

I have a personal rule of not adding to the sketches after I leave the spot, but I've broken this rule once or twice. When I'm traveling with my family, I don't have so much time to spend on each drawing. However, my wife has just started her own sketchbook, and she is very patient now.

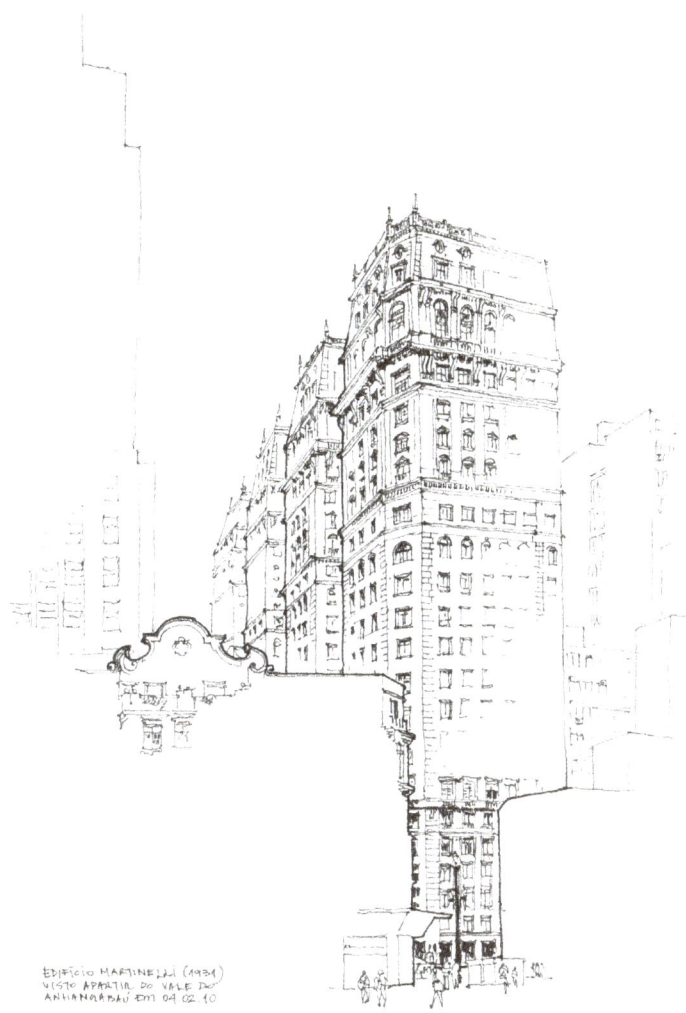

EDIFÍCIO MARTINELLI (1934)
VISTO APARTIR DO VALE DO
ANHANGABAÚ EM 04.02.10

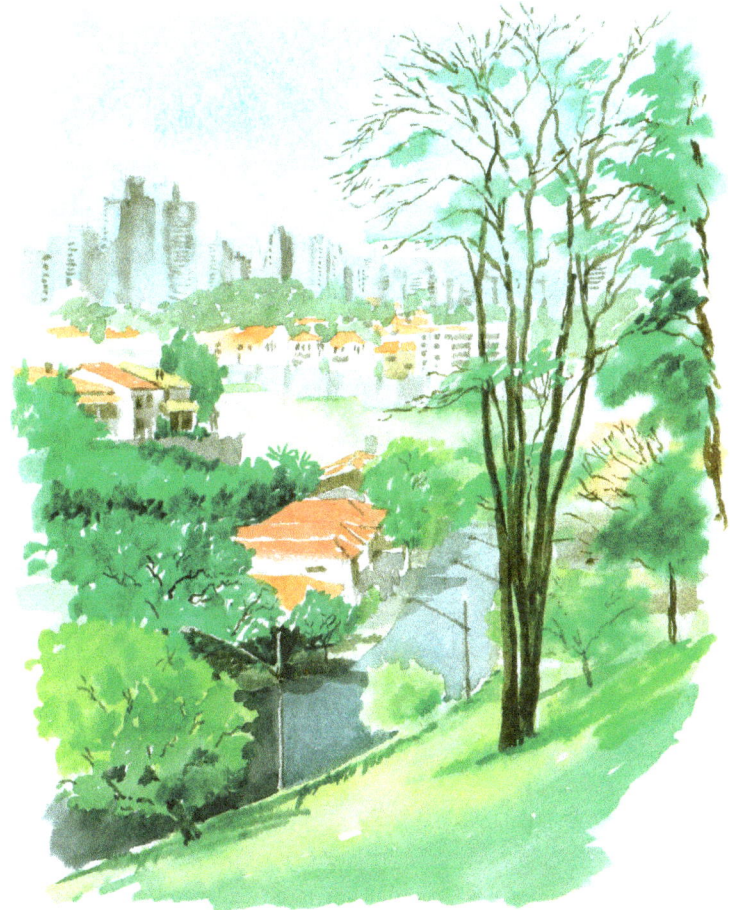

☊ **Martinelli Building** It was a huge effort sketching the Martinelli building, one of the first skyscrapers built in São Paulo, Bajzek says. It was "a challenge of perspective, attention and patience." While drawing, Bajzek says he realized that perception becomes more accurate after hours of drawing. "The lines become more intuitive, as the delay between seeing, thinking, and drawing lessens."

Tip "I used different thickness of lines to create the sense of depth because I decided not to make shadows or add colors." — *Eduardo Bajzek*

11.5" x 8" | 29 x 20 cm; 005, 01, and 05 Micron pens on Hahnemühle sketchbook, 140-gsm paper; 2 hours

☊ **Ladeira da Morte** Bajzek went skating here every week back in the '80s. The name translates roughly to "death slope," he says, adding that, though he couldn't get the whole street in the sketch, it does show the neighborhoods of Sumare, Perdizes, and Pacaembu.

Tip "I always try to avoid excessive detailing on the foliage of the trees when using watercolor. In this one, I like the vertical composition and the focus on the tree." — *Eduardo Bajzek*

9.5" x 7" | 24 x 18 cm; Winsor & Newton and Rembrandt watercolors, Princeton brushes on 270-gsm Fabriano Watercolor Studio Torchon block; 1.5 hours

CITY LANDMARKS

Drawn to Lina Bo Bardi's Architecture

by Eduardo Bajzek

Italian-born Lina Bo Bardi moved to São Paulo after World War II and created some of the city's most well-known architecture. The SESC Pompéia is an old factory converted into a sports and entertainment complex, with swimming pools, restaurants, and exhibit space. The huge blocks of concrete are connected by footbridges. Bo Bardi used this solution to solve a local problem: There is an underground stream just between the blocks. She could not build over it, but she was allowed to create the footbridges. There is a deck covering the stream, where I sat to make this sketch.

8.5" x 12" | 21.6 x 30.5 cm; ink and Prismacolor markers on Canson sketchbook; 1.5 hours

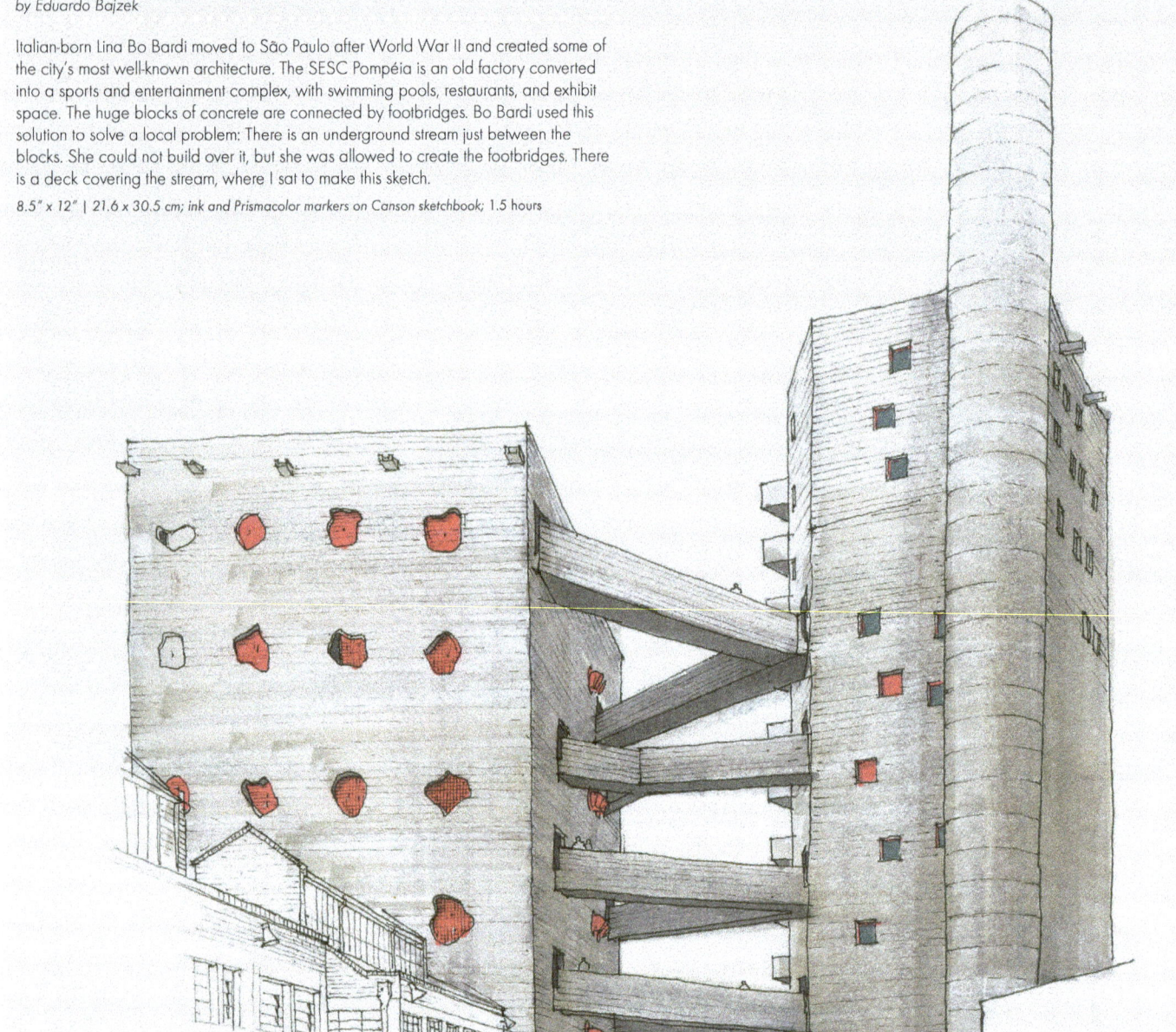

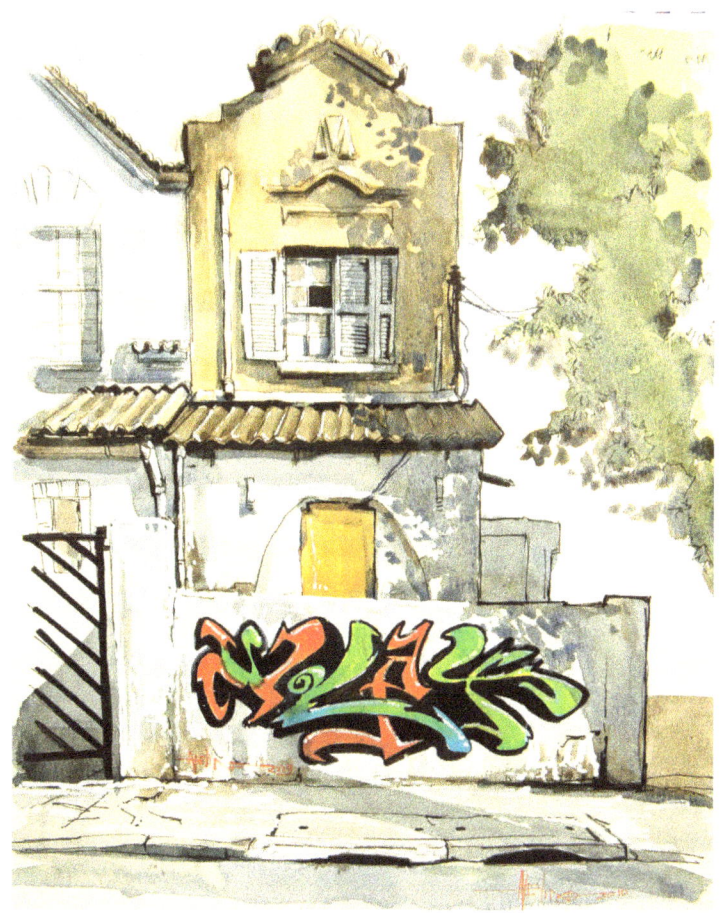

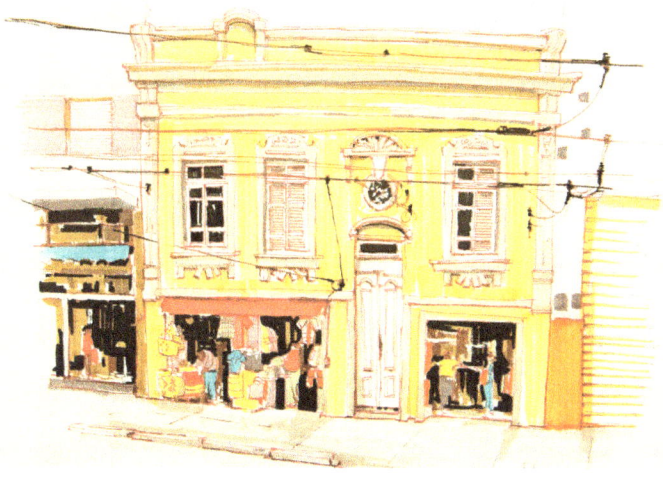

∩ Bráz Neighborhood This area is the main commercial center for clothing, and this is one of the few houses left, Carlos Avelino says.

Tip "I drew this during a weekday, without having a specific destination in mind. It's the best exercise to improve the way you see things, to develop your style through constant practice. Try to make drawing a habit." — *Carlos Avelino*

16.5" x 11.5" | 42 x 29 cm; Pantone and Prismacolor markers, pens (0.3, 0.5, 0.7), Winsor & Newton 60-lb. medium-grain paper

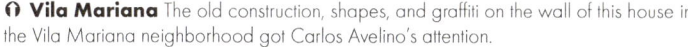

∩ Vila Mariana The old construction, shapes, and graffiti on the wall of this house in the Vila Mariana neighborhood got Carlos Avelino's attention.

13.25" x 11" | 34 x 28 cm; Pantone and Prismacolor markers, pens (0.5, 0.7), Winsor & Newton watercolors, Canson 140-lb. fine-grain, acid-free paper

∪ Guararapes Flood São Paulo artist Fabio Okamoto says the city is sprawling quickly, and tall apartment buildings are common in many areas. "Sometimes it is difficult to understand what is going on, and sketching is a way to try to understand it," he says.

Tip "Pay attention to the light conditions just before a tropical storm. The clouds become gloomy, and the light comes from below. During the rain, the scene becomes more mysterious." — *Fabio Okamoto*

16.5" x 5" | 42 x 12.5 cm; bamboo pen and ink on Moleskine notebook; 1 hour

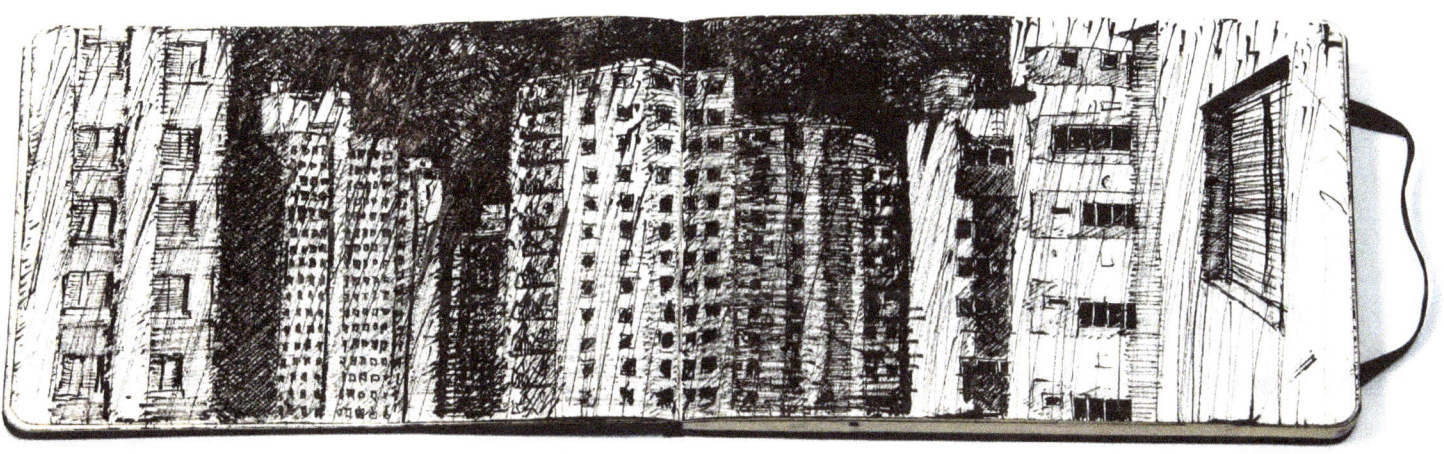

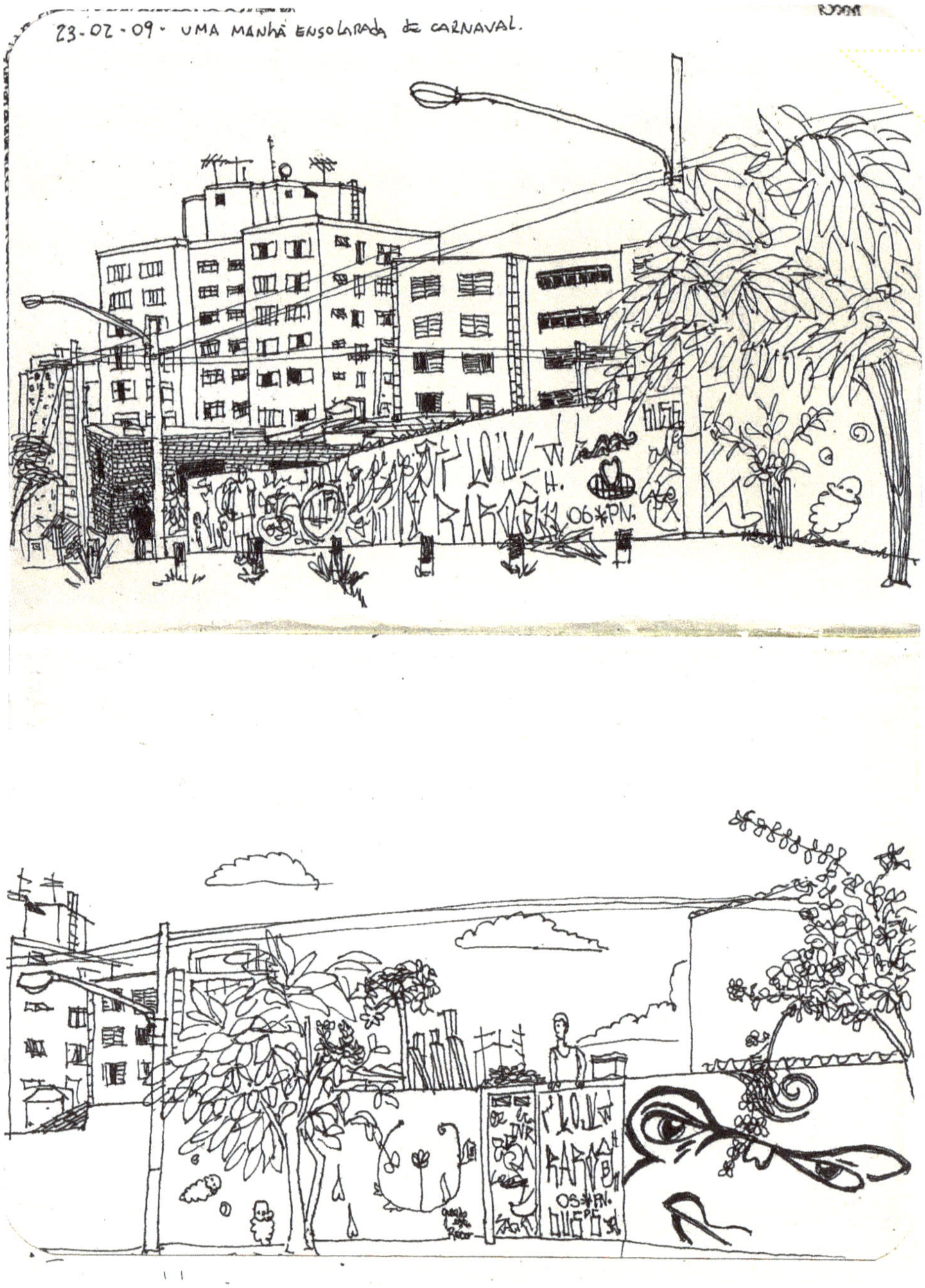

23·02·09· UMA MANHÃ ENSOLARADA de CARNAVAL.

ARTIST PROFILE
Juliana Russo

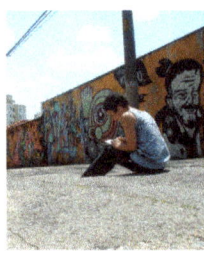

🎧 Russo sketches in her
São Paulo neighborhood,
Vila Madalena.

*5" x 7" | 12.5 x 18 cm;
Nankin Desegraph pen 0.3 on
Moleskine pocket sketchbook;
about 1 hour*

I walk the streets of São Paulo scrutinizing its disorganized architecture, its strange monuments of concrete, the graffiti, and the posters on the walls. It's the type of city that you love or hate. I started loving São Paulo when I started drawing it with my pen. My sketches are bringing me closer to it and helping me discover it.

I enjoy sketching the old buildings in the city center but also the disorganized architecture in the suburbs, the little houses and *favelas*. My own neighborhood, Vila Madalena, is one of the last remaining examples of old stores and homes from old dwellers.

I work as an artist and illustrator and have been observing and drawing my city ever since I started developing my own illustration style. In my work, there's always an underlying urban theme. The sketches are a way to look for the raw material for my installations and artworks.

"Sketching is something close to a spiritual experience, a state of meditation."

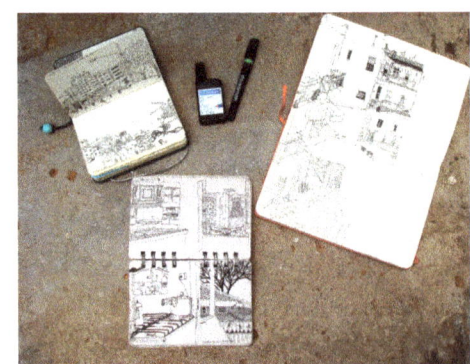

🎧 Russo's sketching tools and sketchbooks

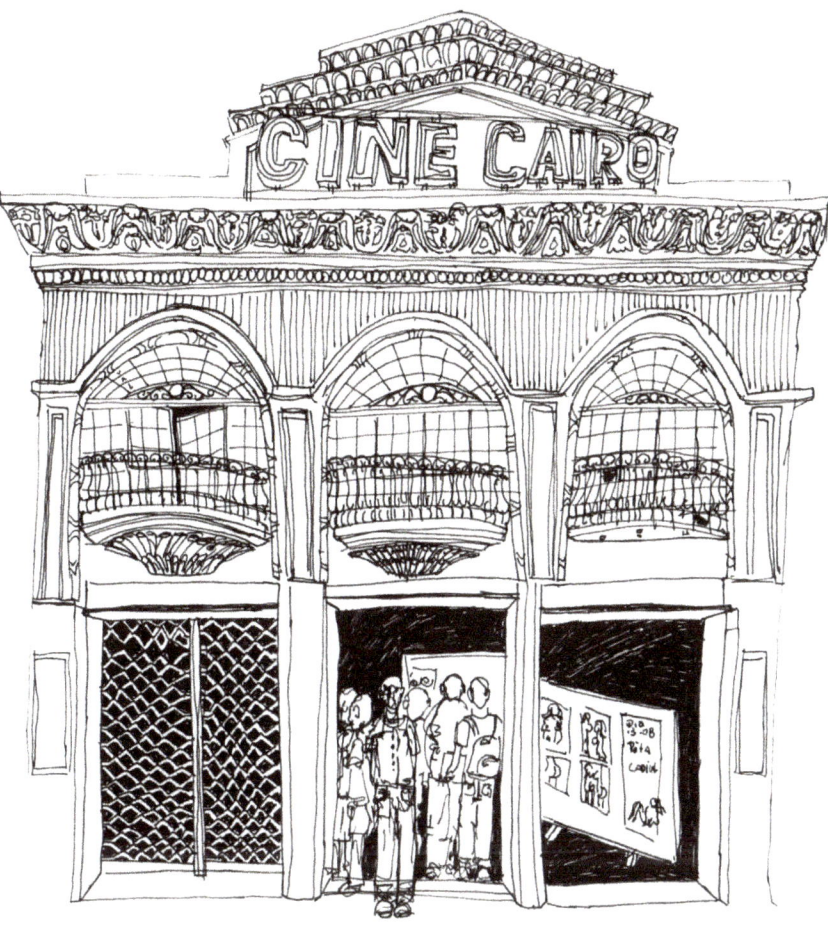

↻ **Cine Cairo** Only the façade remains of this fifty-year-old building, most recently a movie theater, in a square where a new cultural center is being built. "Little by little," Russo says, "many old buildings are demolished and replaced by modern, glass-covered buildings."

Tip "Draw old buildings as a way to keep a memory of them before they disappear." — *Juliana Russo*

5" x 5" | 12.5 x 12.5 cm; ; Desegraph 0.3 pen on 120-gsm sulfite paper; 1.5 hours

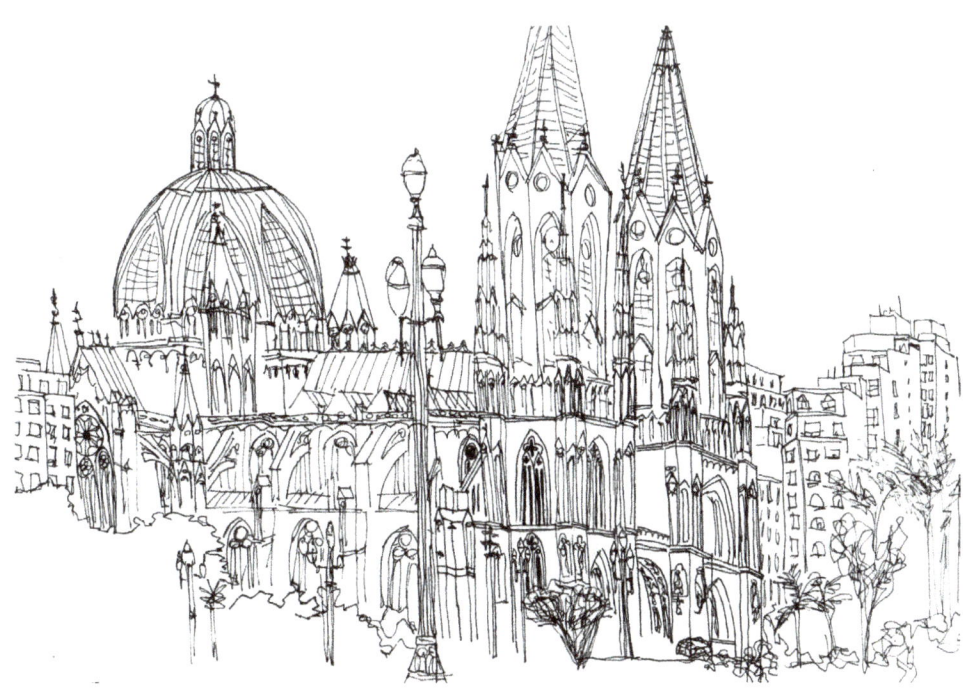

↻ **Catedral da Sé** São Paulo's cathedral dates from the sixteenth century and is one of the biggest neo-Gothic temples in the world.

Tip "I drew without much control and did not think about the structure of the page; therefore, I have no idea how the drawing will fill the page at the end. It's always a surprise. The calmer I am, the better it gets."
— *Juliana Russo*

8" x 5.5" | 20 x 14 cm; Desegraph 0.3 pen on 220-gsm Winsor & Newton smooth-surface cartridge pad (heavyweight); about 2 hours

"I draw everywhere: in the subway, on buses, at the bakery, and at home."

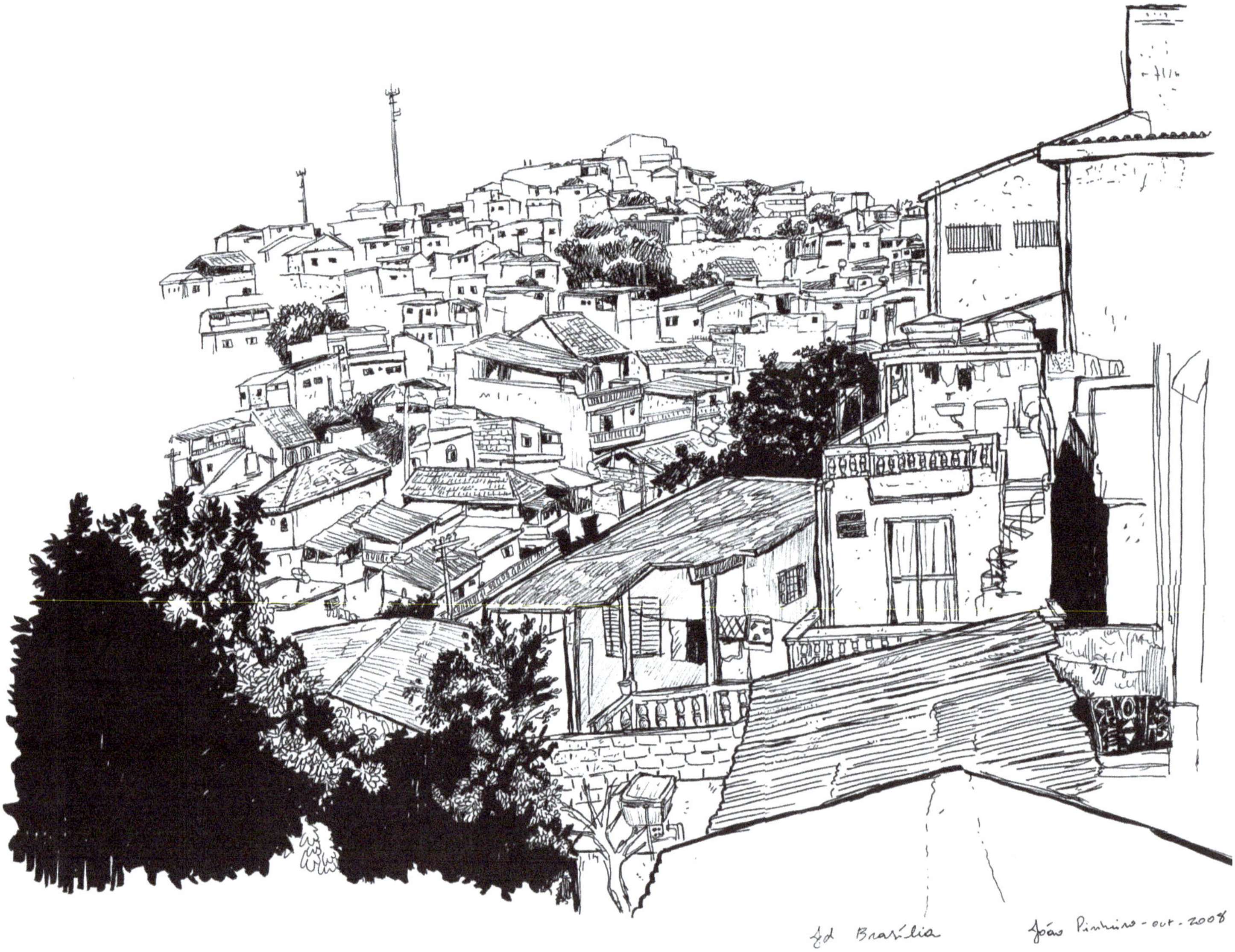

ARTIST PROFILE
João Pinheiro

I do not remember any time in my life when I did not practice drawing. Over the years, I only knew that the will to draw grew on me day after day. For more than ten years, I've recorded my impressions in notebooks of various sizes. I don't follow a single technique; I use graphite, ballpoint pen, China ink, gouache, or watercolor. In the sketch is explained my way of seeing the world. I believe that through the visual record we can see things that go unnoticed on other occasions.

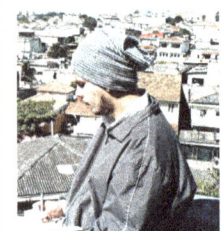

🎧 **Jardim Brasilia** During the week, the streets of João Pinheiro's neighborhood are empty. On weekends, however, the bedroom community springs to life, with kids playing soccer and people having a good time at the bars.

Tip "I set myself the challenge to do an elaborate drawing in a big format to explore new solutions for perspective and depth, light and shadow. It's important to take risks." — *João Pinheiro*

17.5" x 12.75" | 44.5 x 32 cm; Nankin Desegraph pen and brush pen on 200-gsm Debret paper; about 3 days

FIRST PERSON

Everyday Moments

by João Pinheiro

↻ At Home My father and uncle keep the tradition of authentic Brazilian music alive. This scene has repeated every weekend since I was a kid. My father grabs the guitar and starts singing with great emotion.

16.25" x 11.25" | 41.5 x 28.5 cm; Nankin Desegraph pen on handmade sulfite paper sketchbook; 1 hour

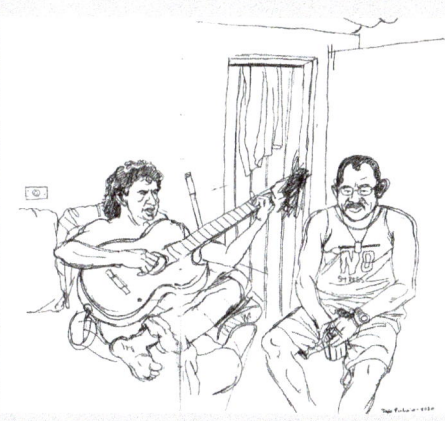

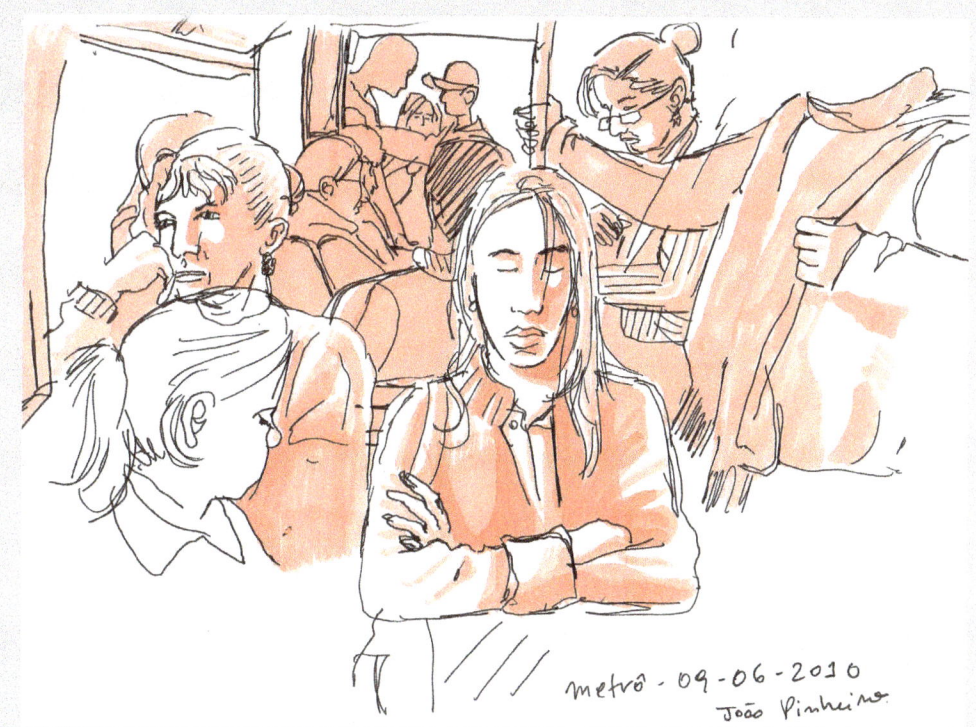

⌒ On the Subway I draw as much as I can between stations. Some people ask why I'm sketching or what I'm going to do with the drawings. Some ask for the drawing, and I don't mind giving it to them. I do these sketches as an exercise to learn different facial features.

7" x 10" | 18 x 25 cm; pen and marker, 20 minutes

⊃ At the Bar This beautiful girl is Stephanie. I was drawing the coffee machine and the bottles behind the bar, when the bartender became very interested in my drawing. He was so excited, he called out to the owner, who asked me if I would draw her daughter. "Come here, Stephanie, this fellow is going to draw you!" Then Stephanie came and posed timidly. "I'll try to be as fast as I can," I told her, and you can see her smile here.

16" x 8" | 40.6 x 20 cm; Nankin Desegraph pen on handmade sulfite paper sketchbook; 1 hour

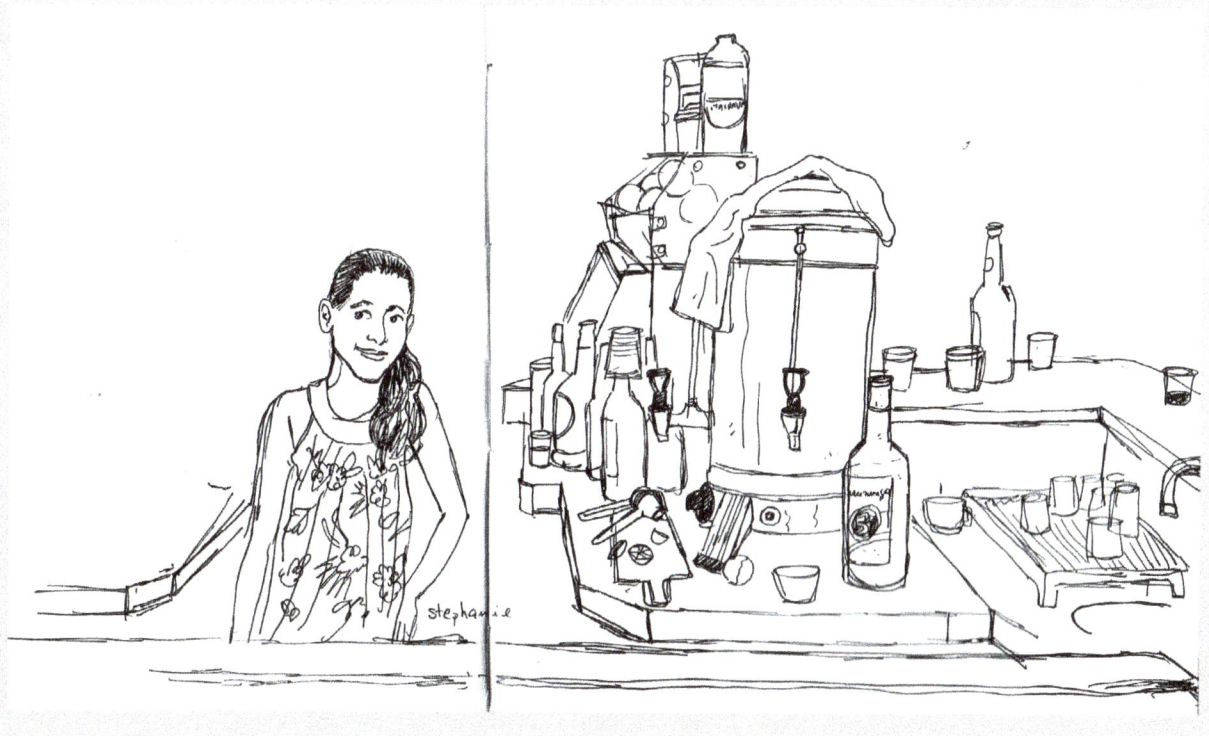

BUENOS AIRES

From the colorful painted houses of the La Boca neighborhood to Avenida Mayo, the boulevard that is the backbone of the city, Buenos Aires' many historic buildings and landmarks draw you in. "Europeanized culture, tango, barbecue, and football make this city a special place for everyday graphic records," says local architect Norberto Dorantes.

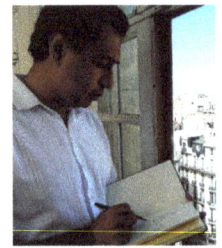

➲ Architect Norberto Dorantes sketches the Plaza del Congreso de la Nación from one of the domes of the buildings called La Inmobiliaria.

5" x 8" | 12.5 x 20 cm; ink, watercolors, and pencils on Moleskine sketchbook; 40 minutes

ARTIST PROFILE
Norberto Dorantes

I discovered as a child—in Mexico, where I was born—while copying all possible images from books, magazines, pictures, people, and even TV, that a few simple lines or spots might communicate many aspects of daily life and my own being. At the National University of Mexico, I was inspired to draw *en plein air*, and I currently teach architectural design and perspective.

As an architect, I am mainly interested in drawing buildings—their details, forms, and scale—as well as anything that helps me understand how a city has evolved over a period of time. But I'm also becoming interested in situations, the interaction of architecture, streets, cars, furniture, and people. Sketching is not just about copying a building but representing the life in the streets and their relationships to architecture.

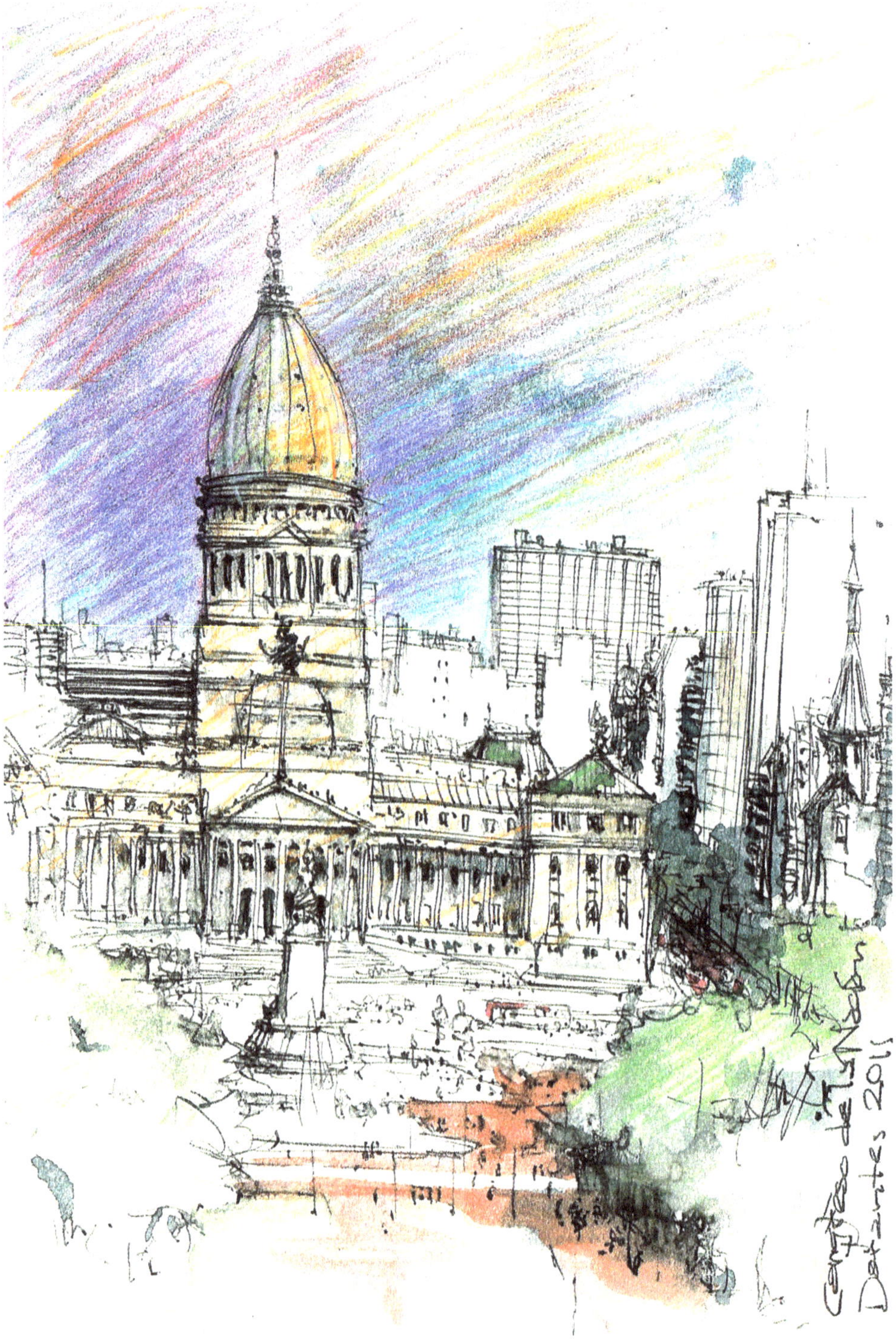

"I love the simple use of the pencil, the force and subtlety that can be transmitted in a few strokes."

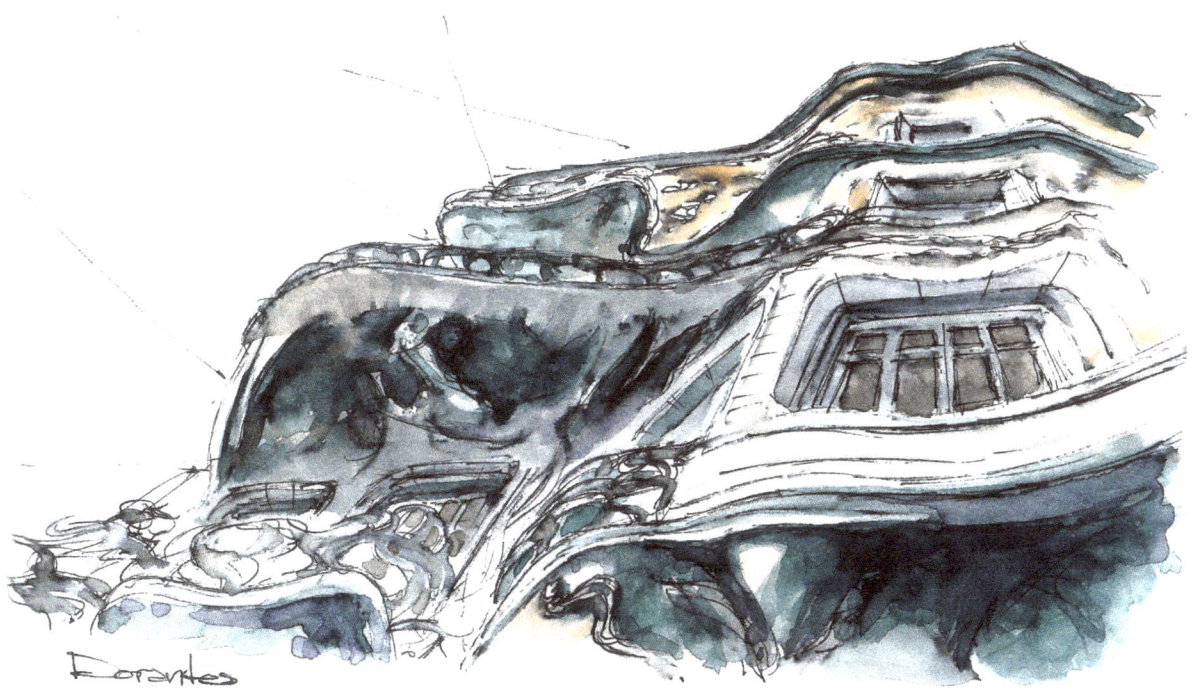

⊂ Casa de los Lirios

The art nouveau movement in Buenos Aires was prolific, Norberto Dorantes says. "These are the balconies of the Casa de los Lirios (House of the Lilies.) Their movement is very interesting and a good exercise in perspective."

8" x 5" | 20 x 12.5 cm; Rotring ArtPen F and Winsor & Newton watercolors, casanhair N10 brush on A4 90-gsm Canson sketchbook; 2 hours

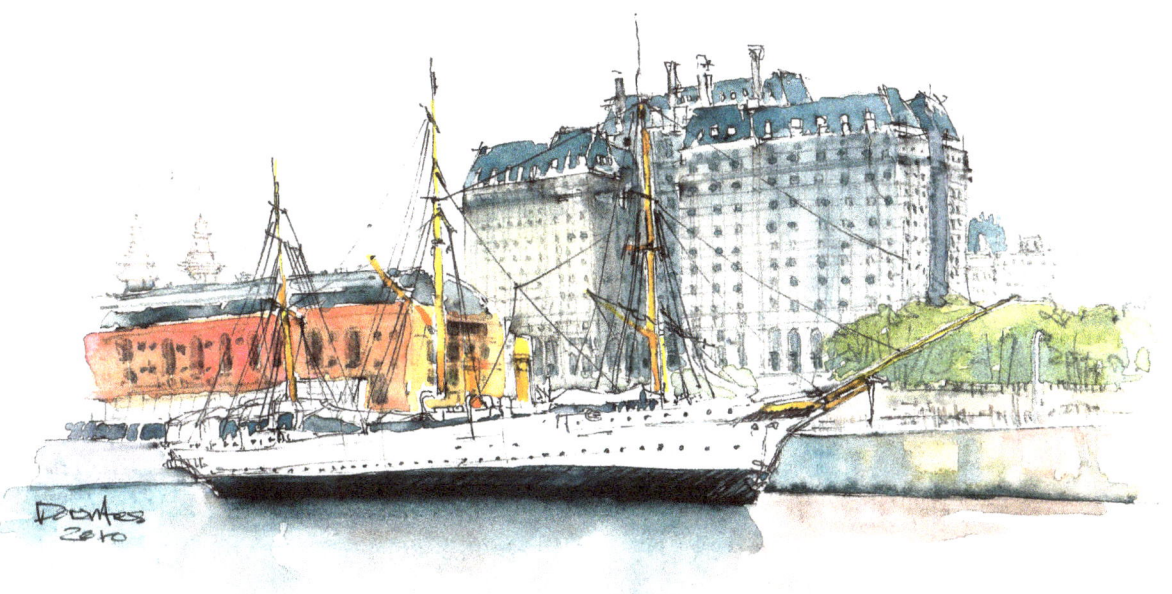

⊂ Puerto Madero

The famous frigate *Sarmiento*, the first modern ship in Argentina, is docked near red brick buildings and the remodeled building known as Libertador, is home of the Argentine army.

6" x 10" | 15 x 25 cm; Rotring ArtPen F and Winsor & Newton watercolors, casanhair brush on 90-gsm Canson sketchpad; 2.5 hours

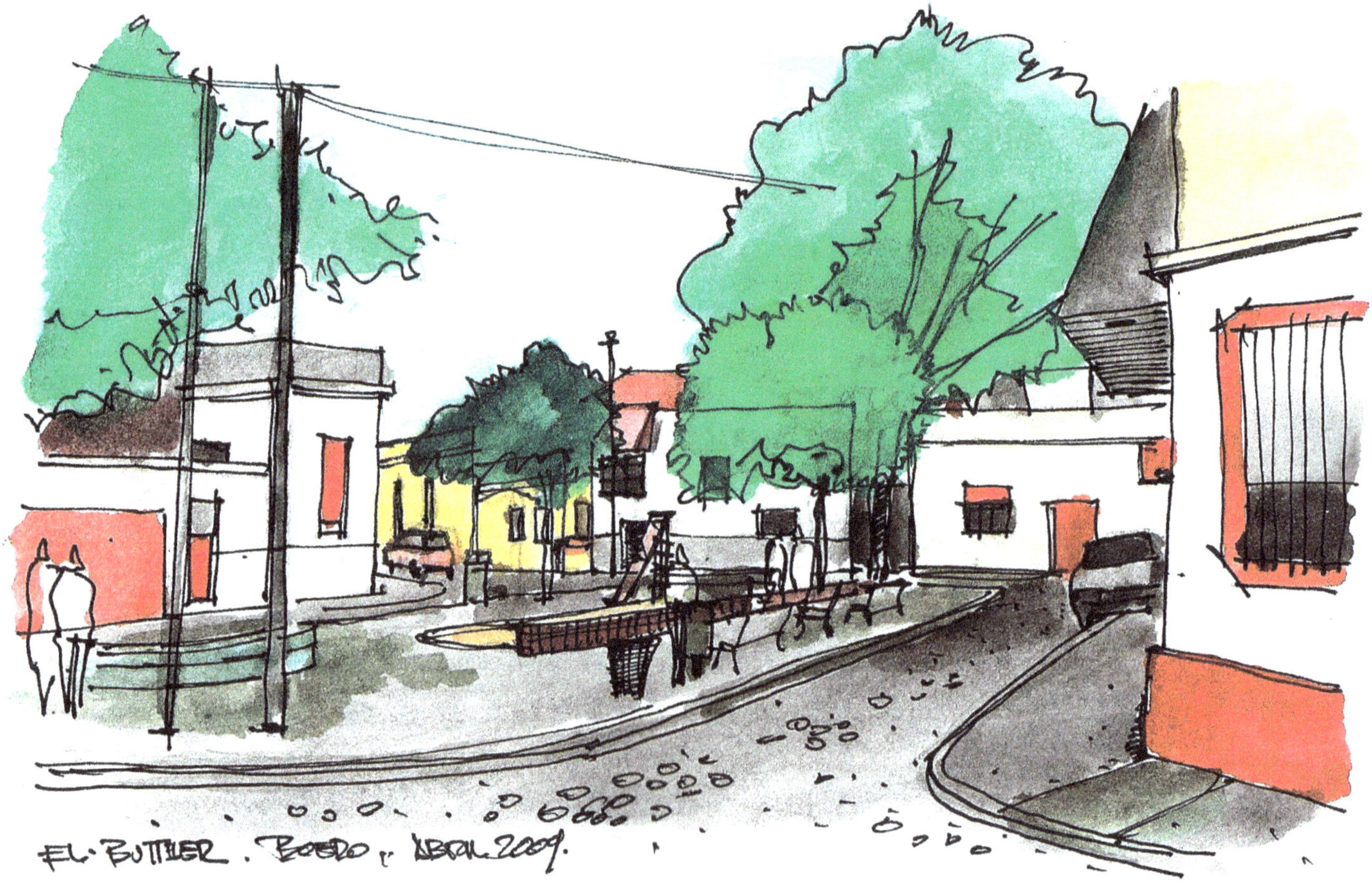

EL·BUTTLER · BOEDO · ABRIL 2009.

CITY LANDMARK

Callao Avenue, Buenos Aires

by Norberto Dorantes

Callao Avenue in the capital of Argentina is one of the most important and impressive. These streets I walk are a hybrid of modernity and tradition. I am very interested in the scale of the buildings and their impact on urban life. I chose these images that I drew from a café, leaving the subway, in a corner, waiting, walking.

It's very interesting to draw the same location at different times and using different media. Maybe the first time we get an incomplete impression of the site. Returning to observe and work with different media, we can discover new details. Each medium of drawing is a different form of expression and helps us create different atmospheres, too.

3" x 2" | 7.6 x 5 cm; ink with a Rotring ArtPen F and Winsor & Newton pro watercolors on 90-gsm Canson hardcover A4 sketchbook; 15 minutes

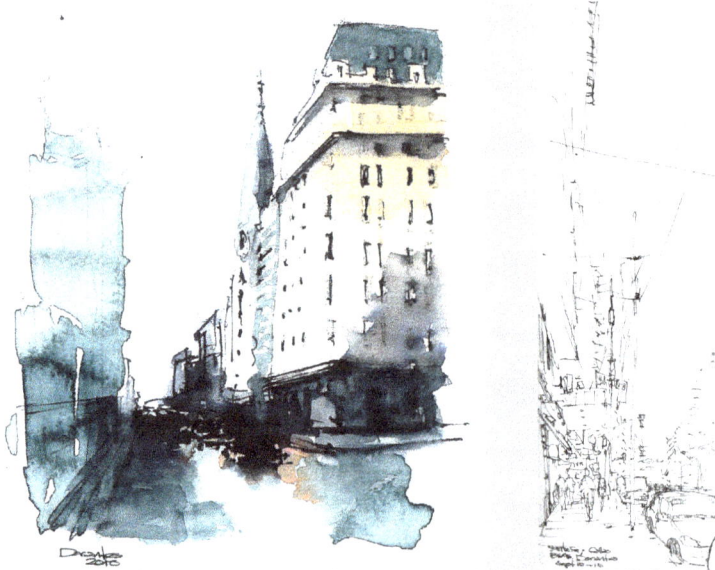

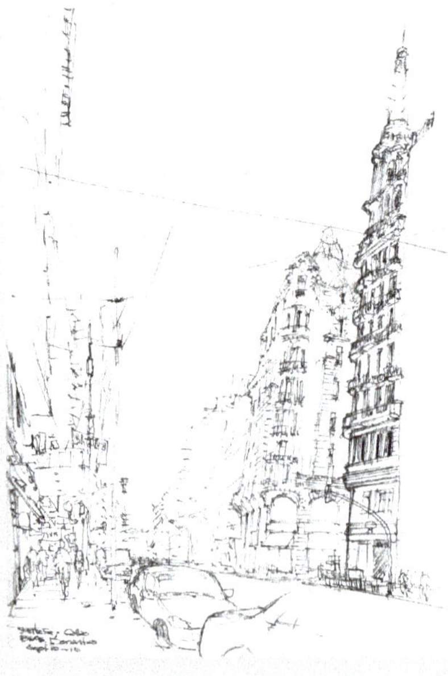

Caminito La Boca

Caminito is a popular street by the port. It's short—just 109 yards (100 m) long—its homes built from recycled materials, corrugated metal sheets, and wood painted with rich, vibrant colors. Here, visitors can enjoy tango dancers and singers, paintings, small sculptures, and live music. No doubt, this is an attractive promenade for sketching.

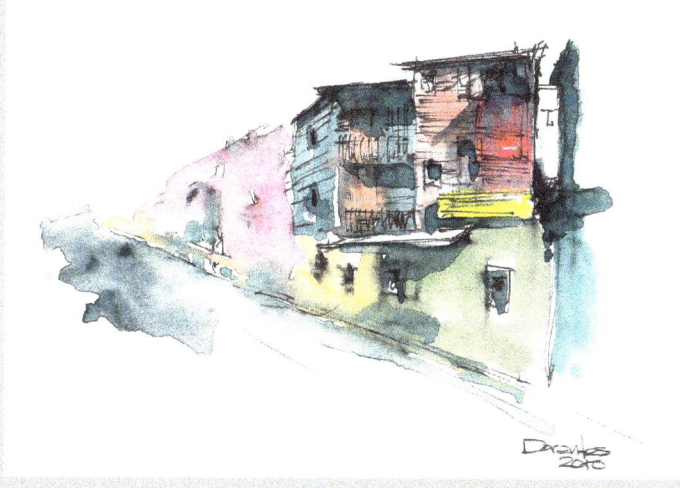

🎧 "I drew with quick strokes, trying to capture the color and texture of the street. I applied the ink while the watercolor was still wet, allowing it to merge with the water to create certain effects that blur the forms." — *Norberto Dorantes*

4" x 5" | 10 x 12.5 cm; Rotring ArtPen F and Winsor & Newton watercolors, #10 casan-hair brush on 90-gsm Canson sketch pad; 30 minutes

🔄 **"El Butteler" in the Boedo Neighborhood** Four narrow streets crisscross this small rectangular square dedicated to tango musician and composer Enrique Santos Discépolo. "It's an ideal place to draw, very peaceful," says local artist Diego Jappert. "While I sketched, a girl ran around the playground and neighbors were talking. I could hear tango music coming from a house."

Tip "Show the drawing to the curious neighbors for a more enriching experience." — *Diego Jappert*

5.5" x 8.25" | 14 x 21 cm; Rotring Tikky Graphic pen 0.3mm, Alba watercolors on Canson 160-gsm sketchbook; 30 minutes

Left, 11" x 8" | 28 x 20 cm; ink with a Rotring ArtPen F, Canson hardcover A4 sketchbook (90-gsm); 35 minutes

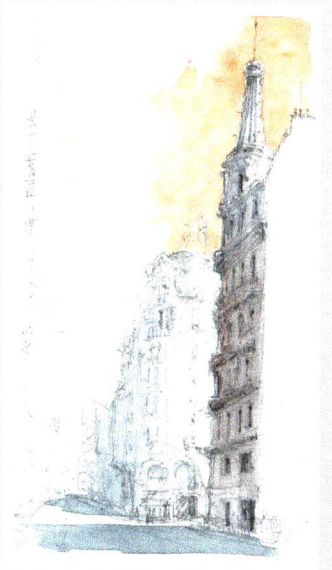

Right, 8" x 6" | 20 x 15 cm; 4B pencil and Winsor & Newton pro watercolors on 90-gsm Canson hardcover A4 sketchbook; 25 minutes

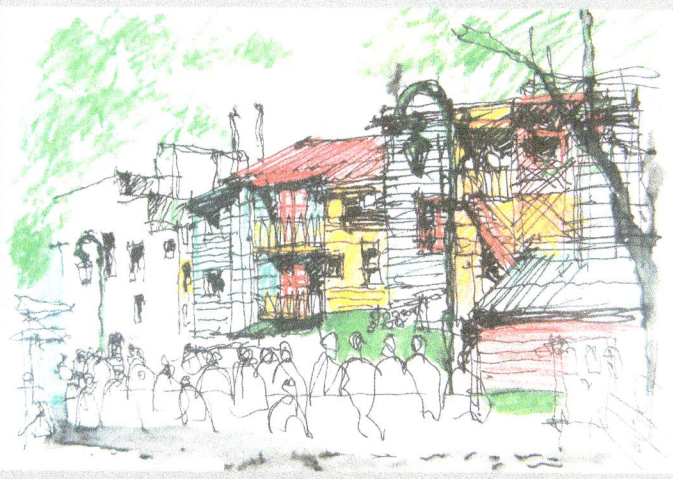

🎧 "I think the most important thing is to experience the site. Walk the place, feel the aromas and sounds, see the variations of light and shadow, watch the movement of people. The objective is to have a lengthy, immersed experience, then the sketch is a brief and concise graphic story, almost a flash." — *Carlos Marcelo Herrera*

5.5" x 8" | 14 x 20 cm; Rotring ArtPen (medium), Faber-Castell watercolor pencils, Winsor & Newton A5 sketchbook; 15–20 minutes

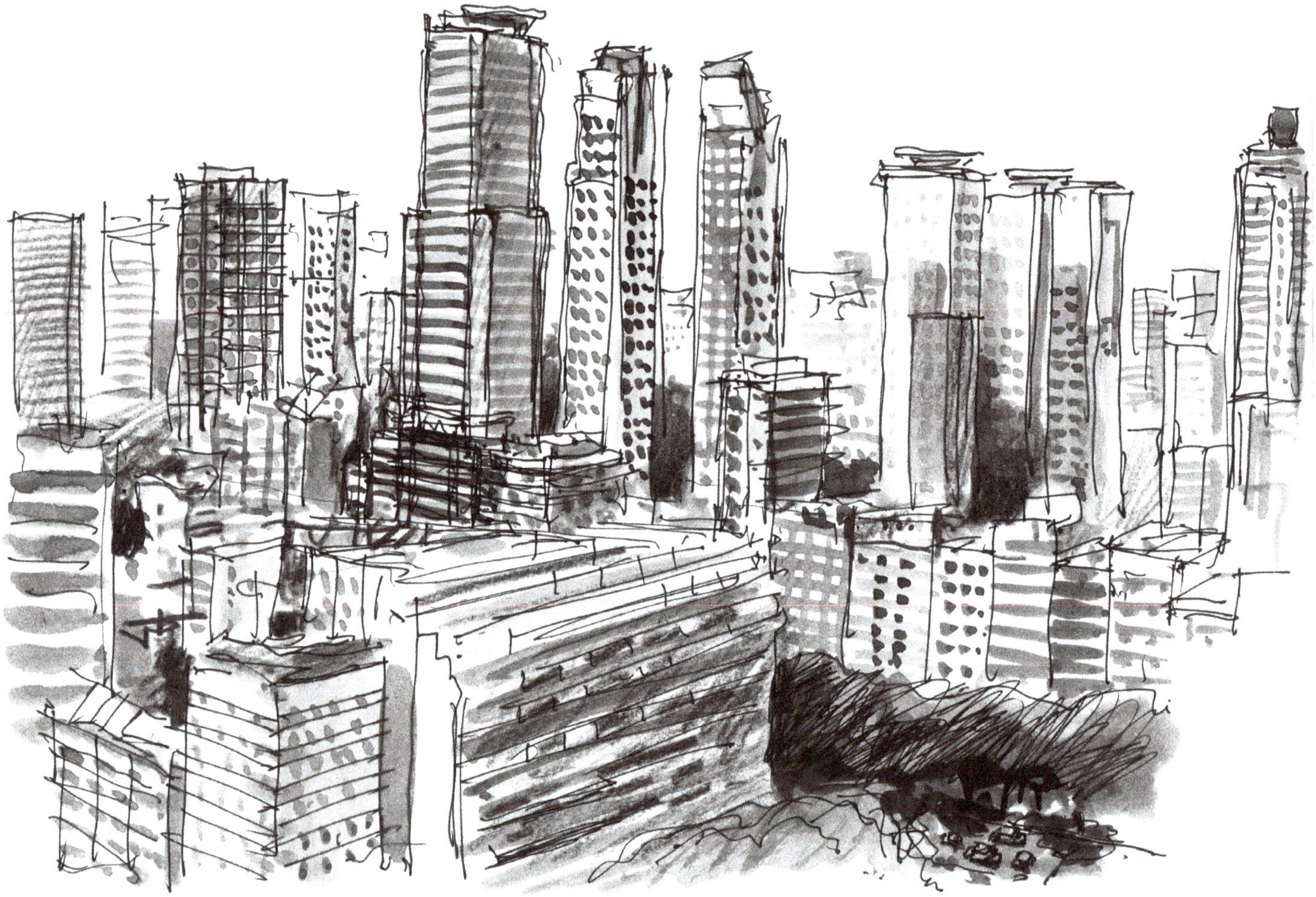

ARTIST PROFILE
Edgardo Minond

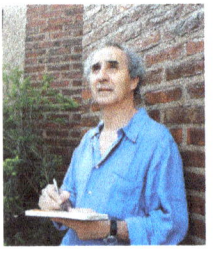

I've been interested in urban sketching since the beginning of my career as an architect. I was inspired by the book *The Concise Townscape* by Gordon Cullen. That's when I become really excited about drawing on location, which is a way to capture the spirit and atmosphere of a place. I love sketching from street corners, positioning myself so the main vantage point is not at the center of the scene but clearly to one side. I also enjoy looking up to find interesting perspectives.

Buenos Aires' diverse architecture and boulevards with trees make it a great city for urban sketching. Despite its flat topography, I always find exciting places to draw here.

☊ Libertador Avenue Edgardo Minond drew this skyline of Libertador Avenue from a twentieth-floor penthouse. "Sometimes, Buenos Aires can be seen as a massive shape of stiff, concrete buildings," he says, "but on a pedestrian level, we can enjoy many big trees alongside its sidewalks, as we can see at the bottom of the drawing."

11.75" x 8" | 30 x 20 cm; fountain pen with light Rotring black ink, brush strokes, and black Berol Prismacolor color pencil on cardboard mounted with 250-gsm Schoeller matte paper; 45 minutes

" A sketch can be more expressive than a written description or a photograph."

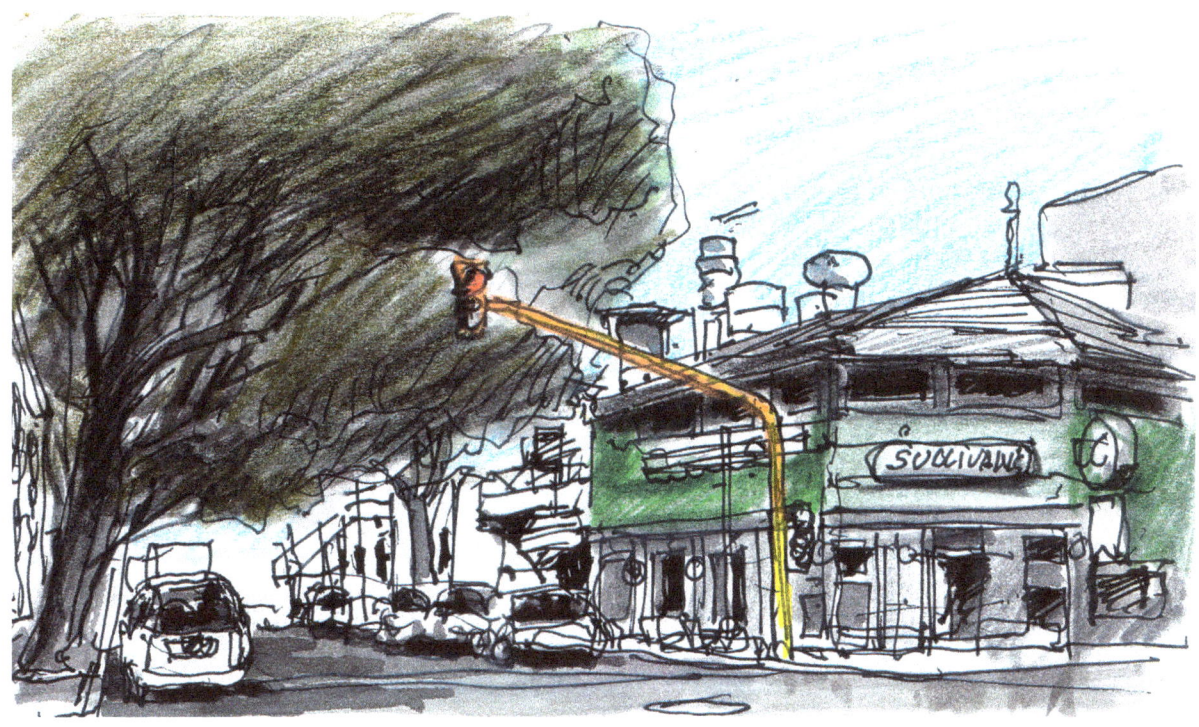

⟲ Palermo Viejo
Palermo Viejo is the most trendy neighborhood in Buenos Aires, Edgardo Minond says. "This corner, Borges and El Salvador Street, is a nice place to drink a *café con leche* on a mild spring afternoon. Both streets are lined with big *platanos* and *tipas* trees."

5.5" x 3.5" | 14 x 9 cm; Pentel 5-mm liquid gel pen, color pencils, and India ink on Moleskine sketchbook; 20 minutes

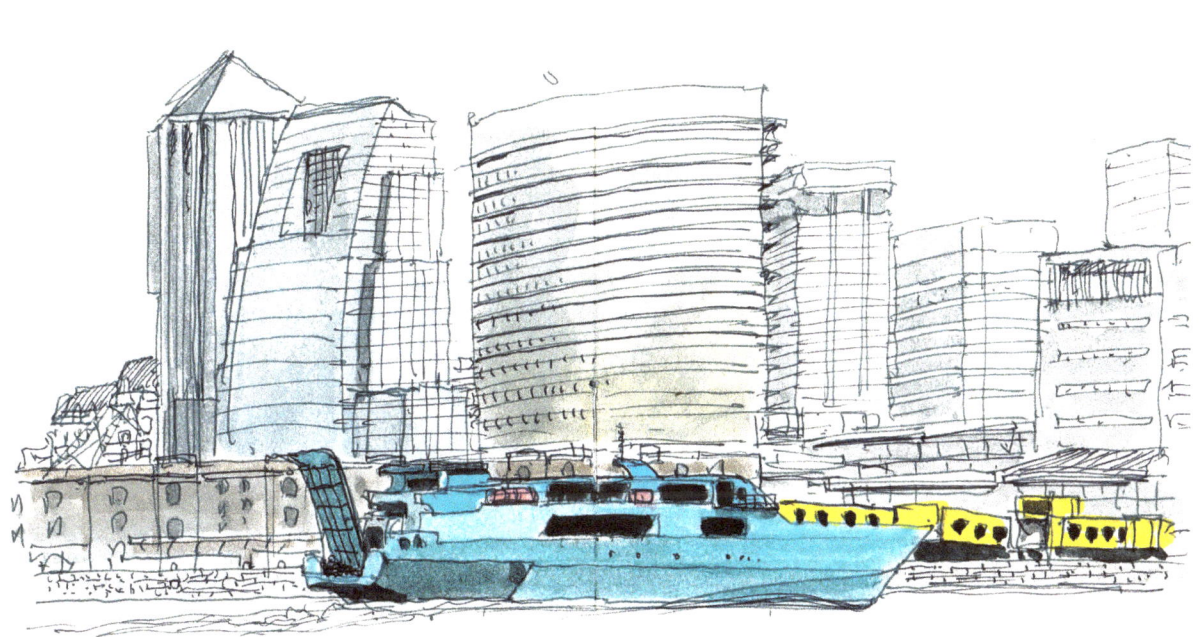

⟲ Skyline Edgardo Minond sketched the ferry that connects Montevideo with Buenos Aires as it drew near Buenos Aires' harbor. "I quickly drew its outline, which I later completed right at the port, seated in a small bar," he says.

Tip "Drawing with foreground objects helps realize where the vanishing points are."
— *Edgardo Minond*

5.5" x 3.5" | 14 x 9 cm; ballpoint, Winsor & Newton watercolors, on Moleskine pocket sketchbook; about 30 minutes

JOHANNESBURG

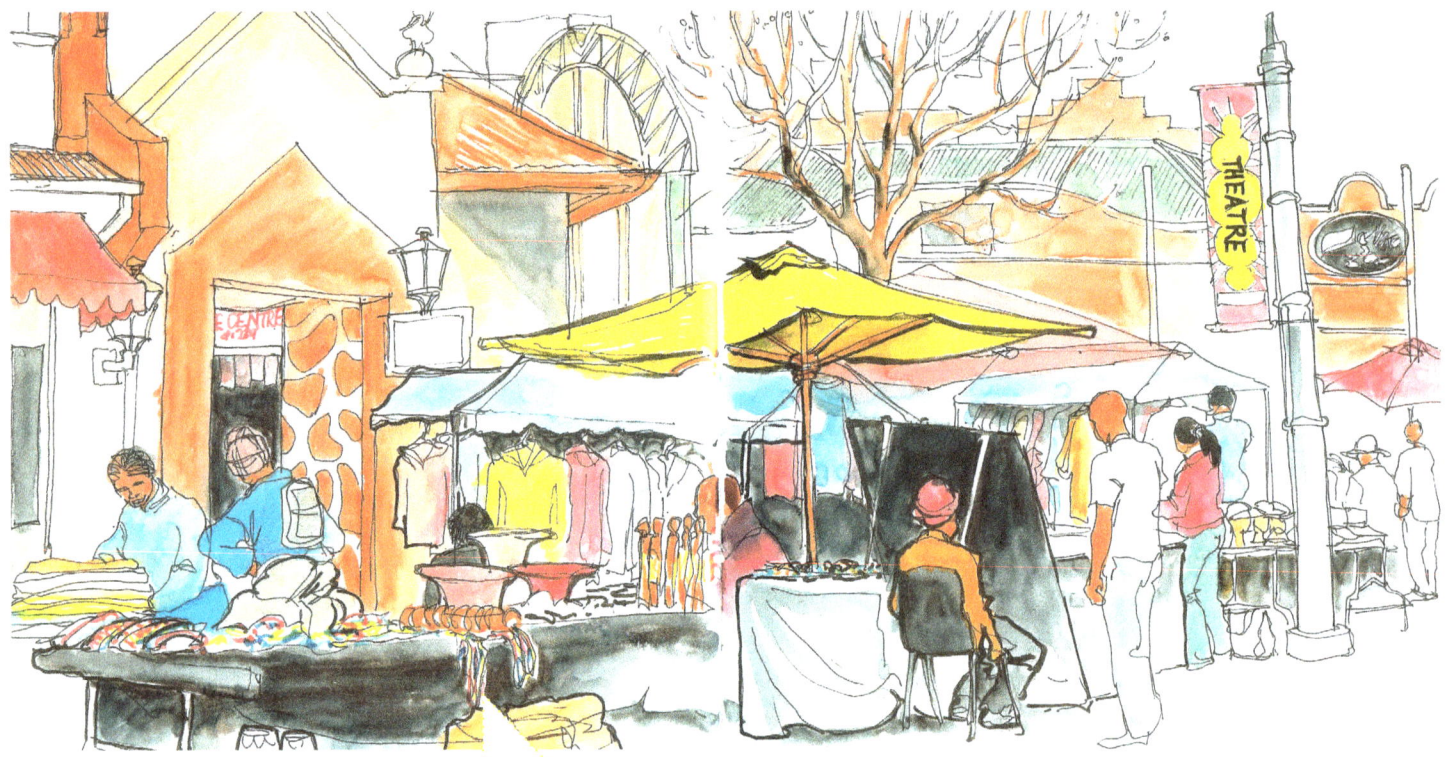

Illustrator Cathy Gatland took up drawing in the streets of "Joburg" in earnest after discovering the work of other urban sketchers on the Web. People are delighted to recognize themselves or the setting in her drawings, she says, and are amazed to find out she does it for fun and not to make money.

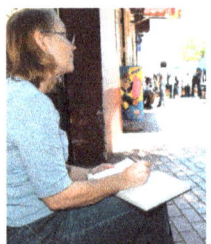

⋒ Cathy Gatland sketches the vendors and passersby at street markets.

ARTIST PROFILE
Cathy Gatland

When you examine faces, clothing, and surroundings closely enough to transfer your impressions onto the page, you can't help but see and love the humanity in your subject, the craftsmanship and care in a building, the life and humor in a street scene—and even feel sympathy for the circumstances that lead to decay and dereliction.

I enjoy sketching the small cameos of life around the streets—people going about their daily business, earning a living or just interacting with each other. The inhabitants of Joburg are diverse, from traffic-light beggars and basket weavers to platinum-dealing stockbrokers. The community spirit that is obvious among groups of people who spontaneously gather on pavements is almost a source of envy to those of us more privileged, confined behind our high walls and inside cars. I'm getting better and more adventurous at sketching buildings and architecture, but my focus always seems to go back to people and their activities.

"It's a challenge to me to try and capture movement and atmosphere, so I look out for lively scenes, which I sketch as unobtrusively as possible."

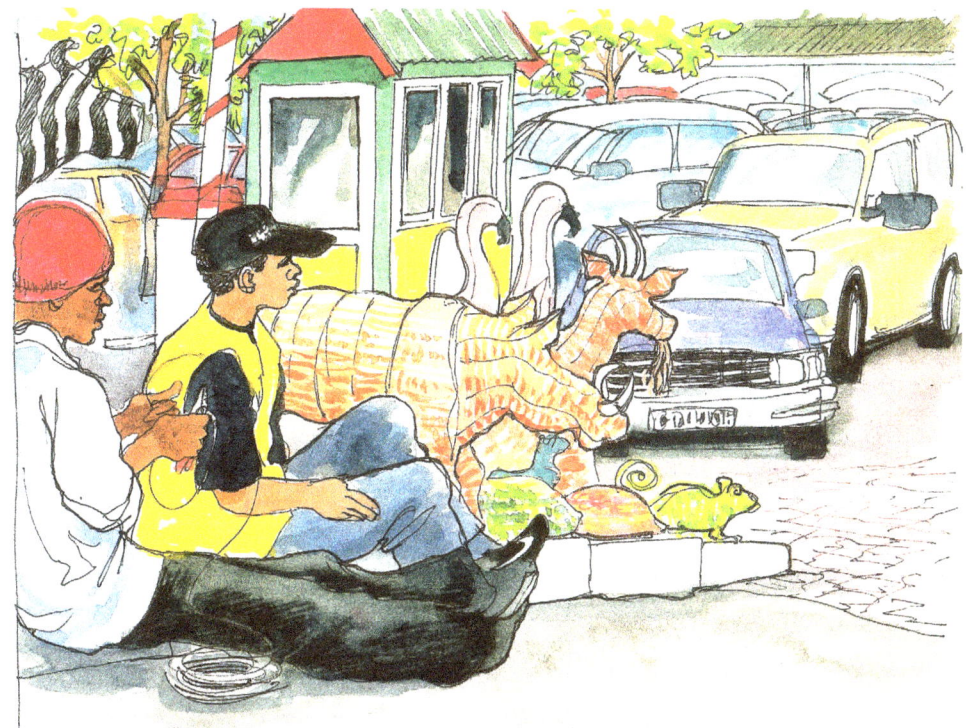

☾ **Bead Seller** "This guy with the red beanie sits outside a local shopping center's car park every day and makes and sells wire-and-bead animals, trees, flowers, and any special requests you might have," Gatland says. "There are lots of these craftsmen around the streets of Johannesburg, but I think this one is especially talented—There's always something different and unique on his patch."

Tip "On the street, people who are sitting relatively still and making repetitive movements provide good models if you're not ready to try and capture motion and bustle. His wares kept nice and still, and it didn't really matter if I started drawing one car and ended up with another." — *Cathy Gatland*

A5 (8.3" x 5.8" | 210 x 148 mm); Mitsubishi uni PIN fine line 0.2 pen, Cotman watercolors, Pentel Signpen blended with Pentel waterbrush on Canson spiral-bound A5 Visual Diary; 1.5 hours

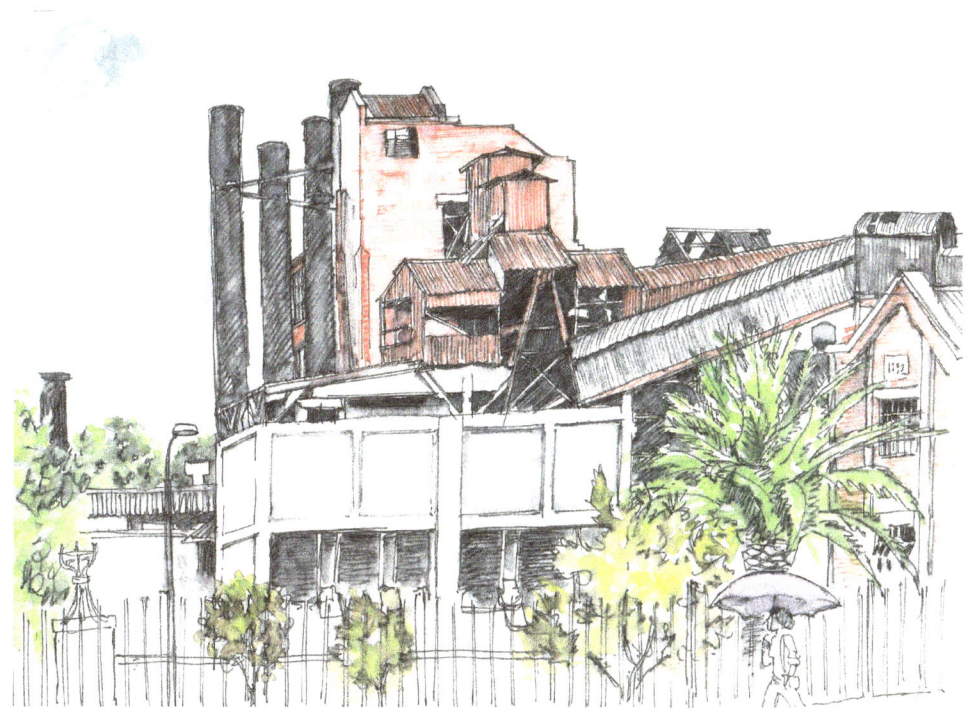

☾ **The Old Gasworks** Before 1964, gas to supply the city was manufactured from coal here, Gatland says. "Now abandoned, the Old Gasworks is a great drawing subject. Once I'd sketched out the shapes and angles of the chimneys and corrugated iron structures, I realized I was never going to fit the whole view onto my page, so it ended up being a sketch of just half of it."

Tip "Lightly plan out the whole drawing before getting caught up in the details." — *Cathy Gatland*

A4 (8.3" x 11.7" | 21 x 29.7 cm;); black and brown Pilot fineliners, blended with Pentel waterbrush, Mitsubishi uni PIN fine line 0.2 pen, Cotman watercolors on Ashrad cartridge sketchpad; about 2 hours

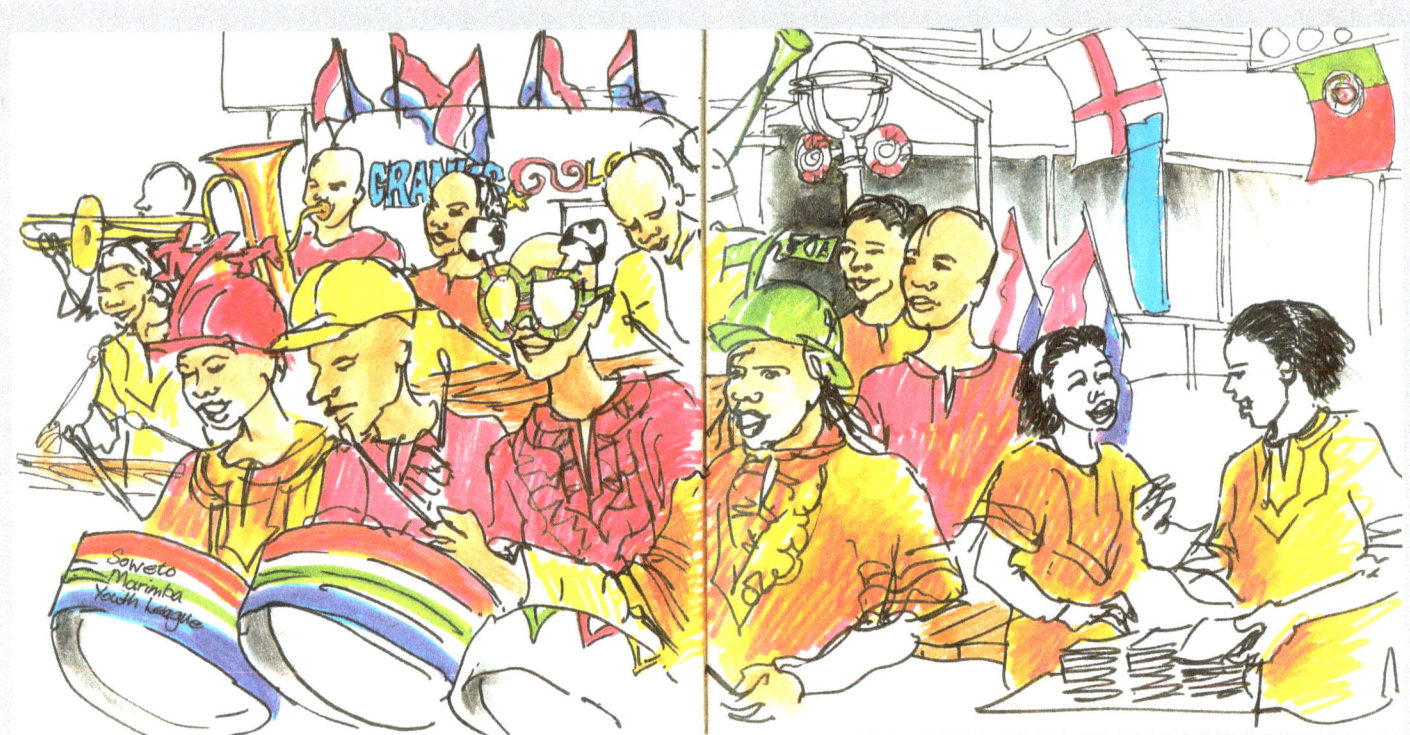

STYLE AND TECHNIQUE

Soweto Marimba Band

by Cathy Gatland

When sketching moving people, I watch for some expressive, demonstrative gesture or action and get the whole shape of it down as fast and simply as possible—the rounded curves of a back or a head thrown back. I draw important features that describe what they're doing next, such as hands and musical instruments, then connect them to the rest of the figure with arms or clothing. Similarly, if a wide, laughing mouth attracts my attention, I'll draw that first then build the rest of the figure around it. With a musical subject, wobbly or double lines just add to the impression of sound, vibration, and rhythm.

Top: 7.5" x 15.5" | 19 x 39.5 cm; Faber-Castell Pitt pens (Manga black set and basic color set) with smudged brown Pilot fineliner and Pentel Sign Pen, Seawhite of Brighton square clothbound sketchbook; approximately 40 minutes

Right: 7.5" x 7.5" | 19 x 19 cm; about 20 minutes

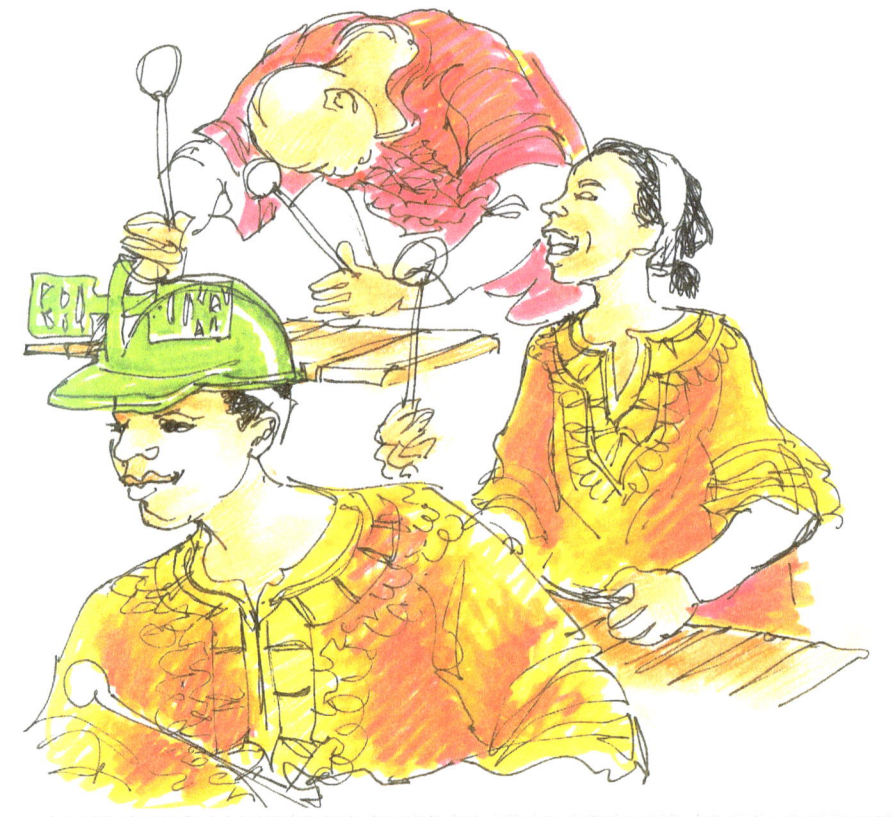

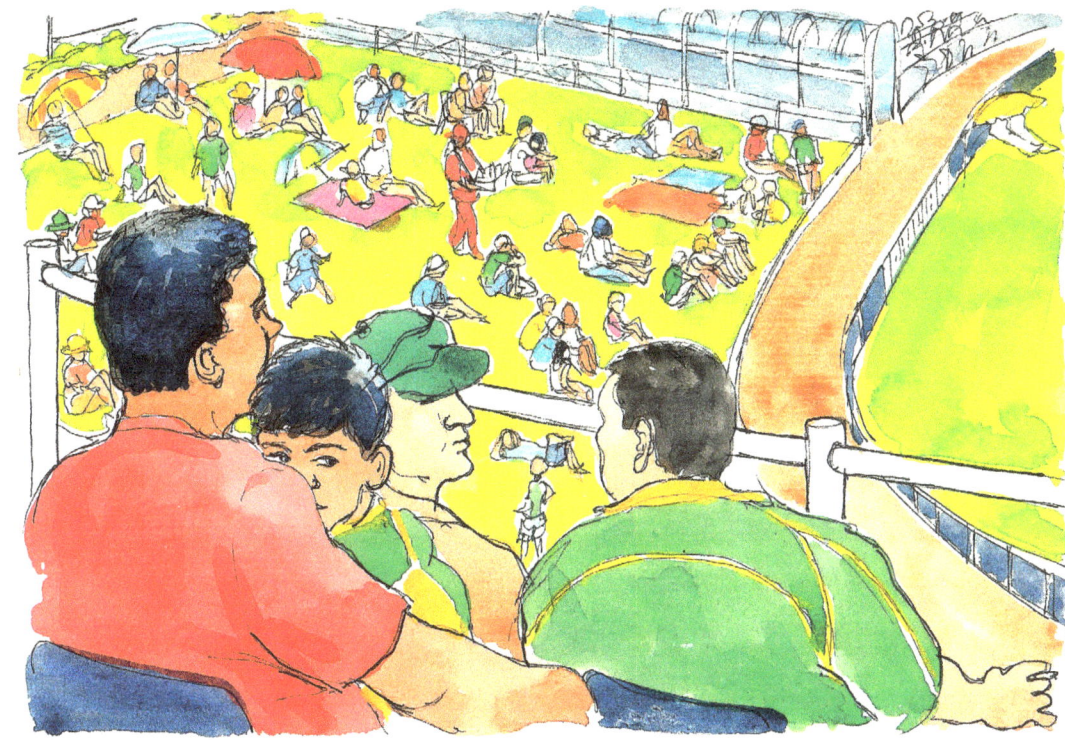

☾ Cricket at Wanderers "We went to watch the cricket—Australia versus South Africa at the Wanderers Stadium," Gatland says. "I started off trying to get the whole arena with buildings and stands, which was very ambitious, and I soon gave up and settled for the spectators around us. The little boy stared at me staring at him but didn't say anything to his dad or ask to see what I was doing, and eventually he nodded off and went to sleep."

Tip "You have to remind yourself to believe your eyes and that those figures in the distance do look only about as big as the front man's nose, and that, when you stop scribbling and sit back and take a look, it will all make sense!" — *Cathy Gatland*

A5 (8.3" x 5.8" | 21 x 14.8 cm); Mitsubishi uni PIN fine line 0.2 pen, Cotman watercolors and Van Gogh goat-hair brush on 110-gsm spiral-bound sketchbook; 30–40 minutes

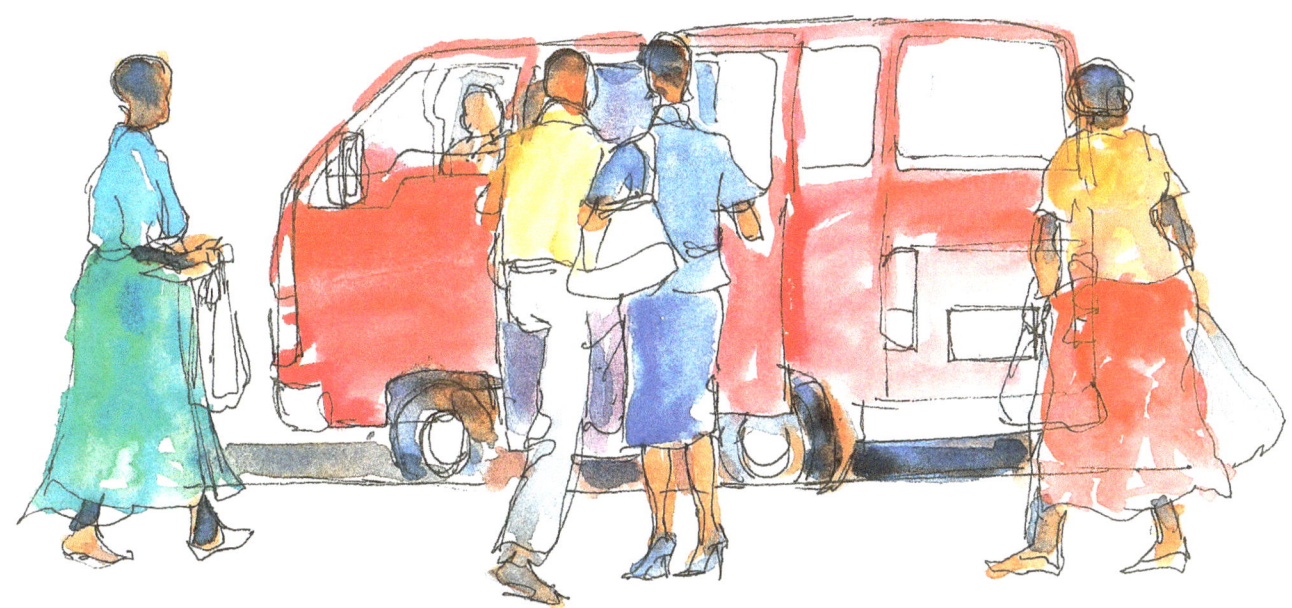

☎ Taxi Stop Unofficial minibus taxi stops like this are one of the most common sights in Joburg, Gatland says.

Tip "This is a sort of conglomerate sketch of a few different taxis that stopped for a couple of minutes each to offload and pick up passengers—the passengers weren't all in the same scene together at the same time but caught individually as I saw one cross a space that I wanted to fill." — *Cathy Gatland*

A5 (8.3" x 5.8" | 21 x 14.8 cm); Mitsubishi uni PIN 0.2 pen, Cotman watercolor travel set, Van Gogh goat-hair brush on Canson, 110-gsm, spiral-bound Visual Diary; 15–20 minutes

NOUAKCHOTT

Nouakchott was just a small oasis with some tents and mud brick buildings when it became the capital of Mauritania in 1960. The urban environment here lacks old buildings, and most streets are just plain earth and sand, explains local painter Isabel Fiadeiro. The color comes from the people, the markets, the street sellers, and the old cars driving around alongside the latest 4x4 models.

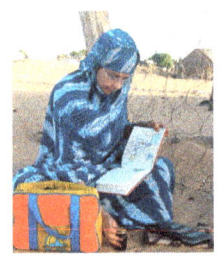

ARTIST PROFILE
Isabel Fiadeiro

When I arrived in Nouakchott for the first time, I became aware of how things can change so fast. I started recording things that might change or disappear in my sketchbooks. A year after I started sketching, a look at my first sketchbook made me realize how my drawing had improved. The sketches work also as a tool to develop my skills, but I still get days when sketching will just flow and others when it seems to be a struggle.

I'm interested in human beings and characters; it's not everyone I feel like sketching, but something about them. Little by little, I also started sketching the town, the markets, the crowds, and then the landscapes. It's like a new way of looking and revisiting places, plus it's a very good way of making contact with others.

◑ The Livestock Market Fiadeiro sat with two Mauritanian friends across the road to sketch the activity around the Marbat, a market on the outskirts of the city where you can buy live animals, such as goats or lambs.

11.5" x 6" | 29 x 15 cm; brush and metal tip using walnut stain on loose watercolor paper; 30 minutes

"People love to watch you draw, and most of them want to be drawn."

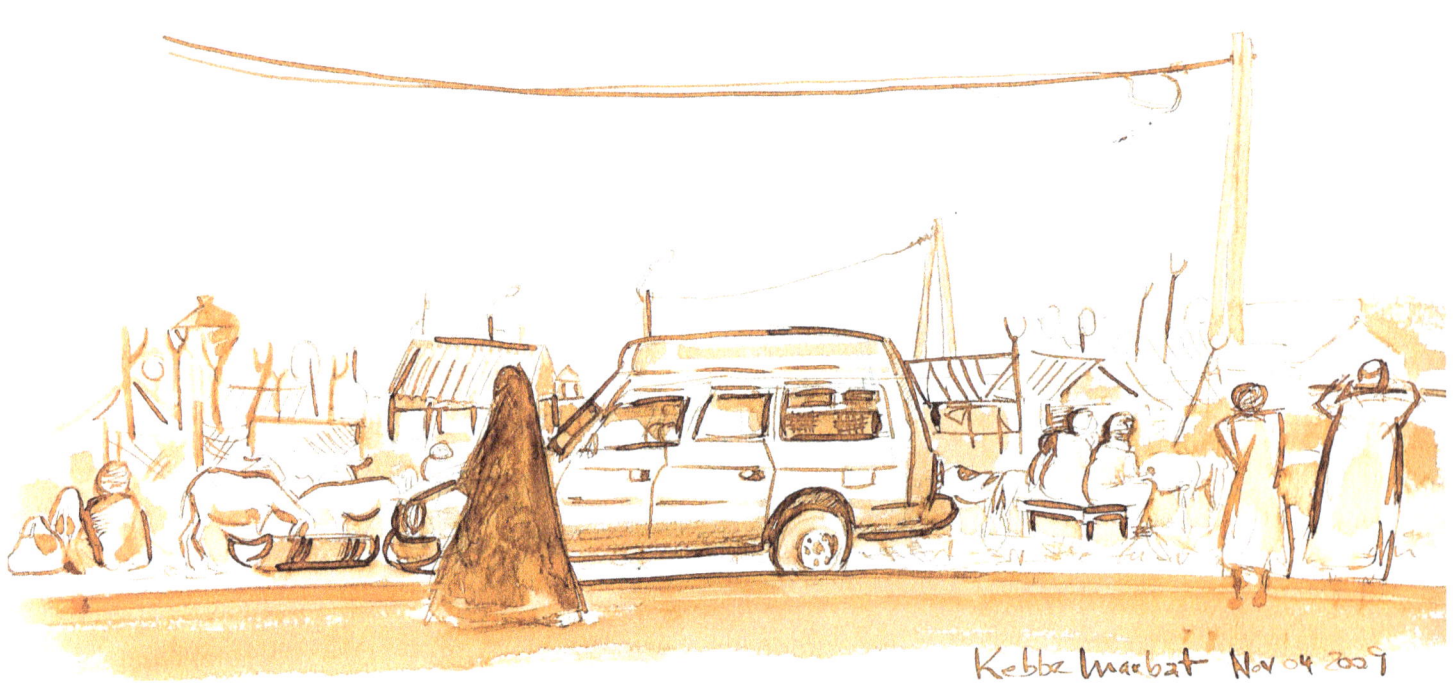

Kebbe Marbat Nov 04 2009

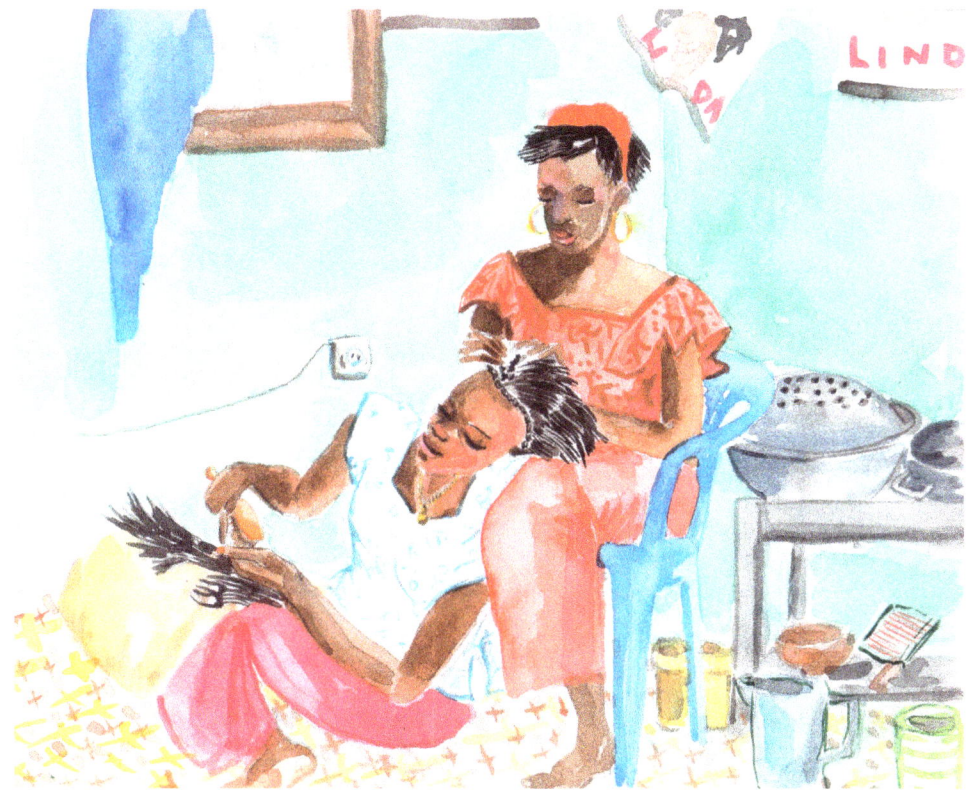

☾ **Hairdressers at "marché Cinquième"** Fiadeiro comes to the Salon of Mariam Si to have her hair plaited when the heat becomes unbearable. This market is also known as the "African," because most of the stalls are run by Mauritanians from different African ethnicities such as Wolofs, Peuls, and Soninkes; a few are run by the Moors.

6" x 8.25" | 15 x 21 cm; Clairefontaine smooth-grain, 180-gsm white paper, landscape format

☽ **Peugeot 404 and Fatima** This old car, a Peugeot 404, distributes gas to the small shops of Fiadeiro's neighborhood. Next to it is Fatima, a little friend who went to the shop to get a fizzy drink.

6" x 8.25" | 15 x 21 cm; Clairefontaine smooth-grain, 180-gsm, white paper, landscape format

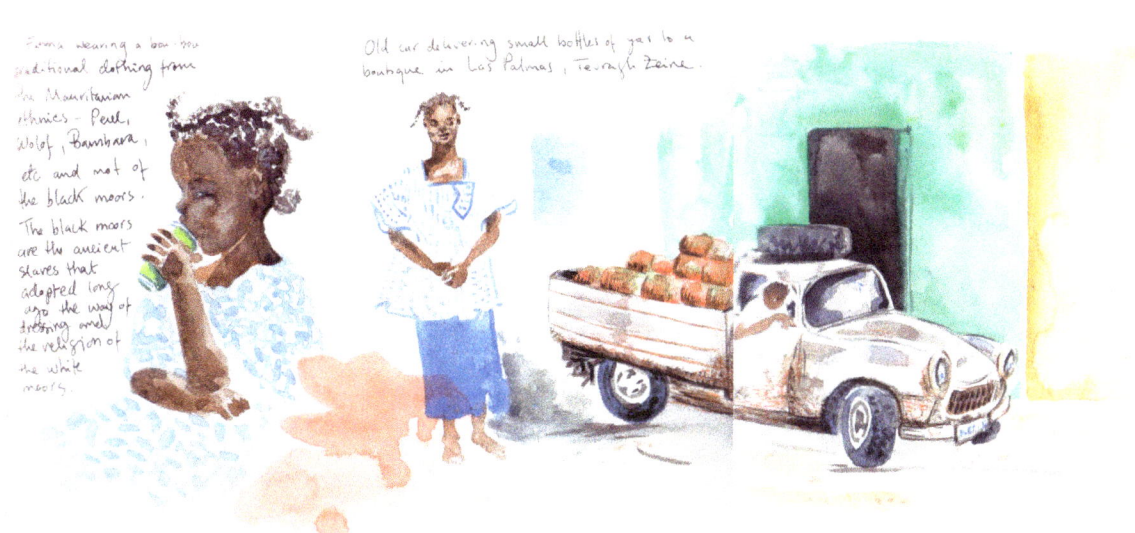

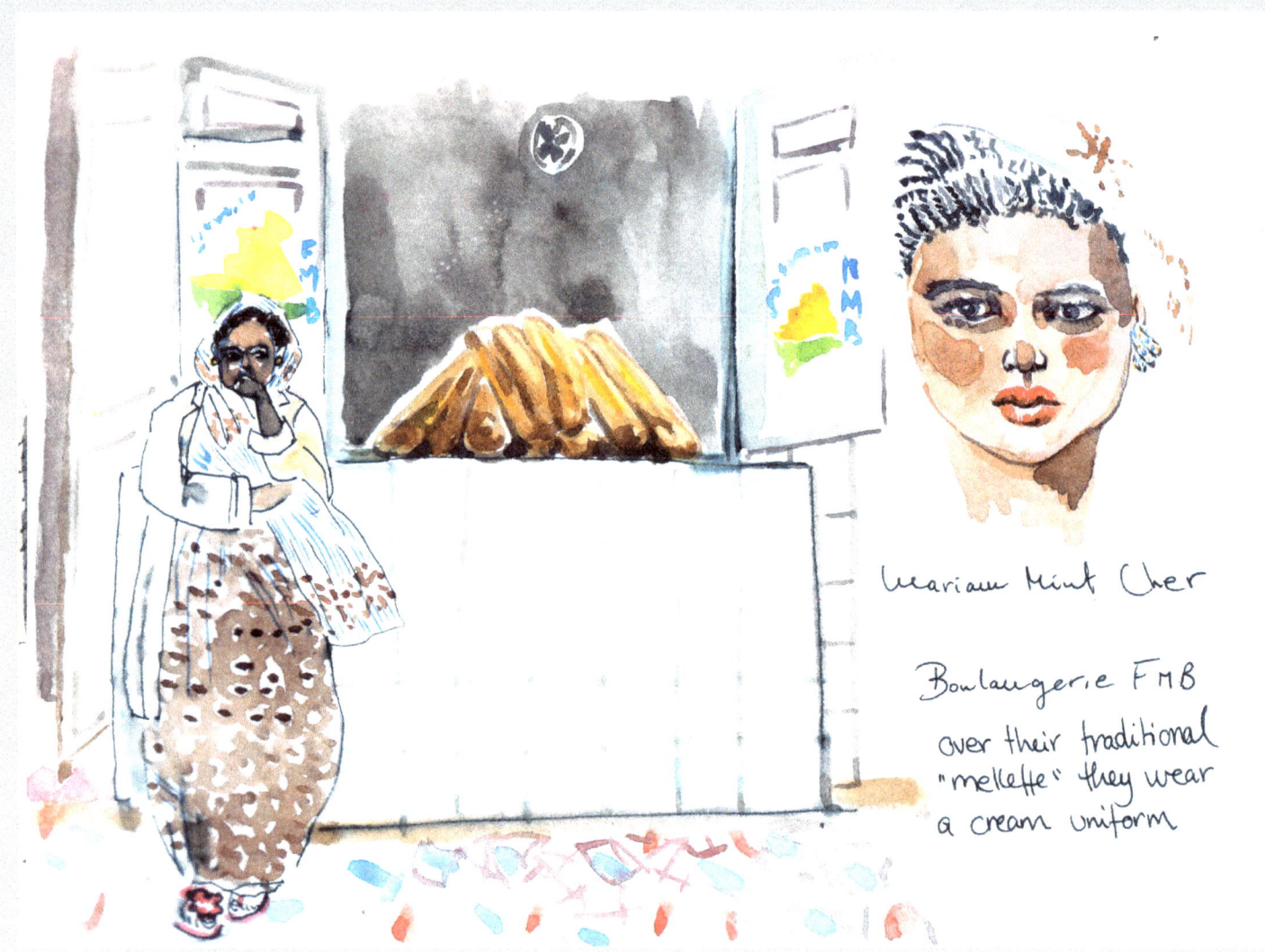

Mariam Mint Cher

Boulangerie FMB

over their traditional
"mellefte" they wear
a cream uniform

FIRST PERSON

Nouakchott's Markets

by Isabel Fiadeiro

For markets and busy places, I'll try to sketch at quieter moments. In Mauritania, between 2 p.m. and 4 p.m., it is so hot that people stay indoors. If I sketch at other times, I'll get too many onlookers, who block the alleyways, and then the sellers get nervous.

All over Nouakchott, you'll find bakeries where you can buy fresh bread in the style of the French baguette. Due to the particular climate–dry in the winter and humid during summer–these baguettes will go dry very fast in the open air or soggy when the humidity is high.

Fish is sold as well in the Cinquième, but this fish stall is in a big market close to the Moroccan mosque. Mauritanian waters are rich in fish; we have big fish, like tuna, all the way down to the "sardinella," from the sardine family.

6" x 8.25" | 15 x 21 cm; watercolor using different brushes (#00 and a bigger one for washes) on Clairefontaine smooth-grain, 180-gsm white paper, landscape format

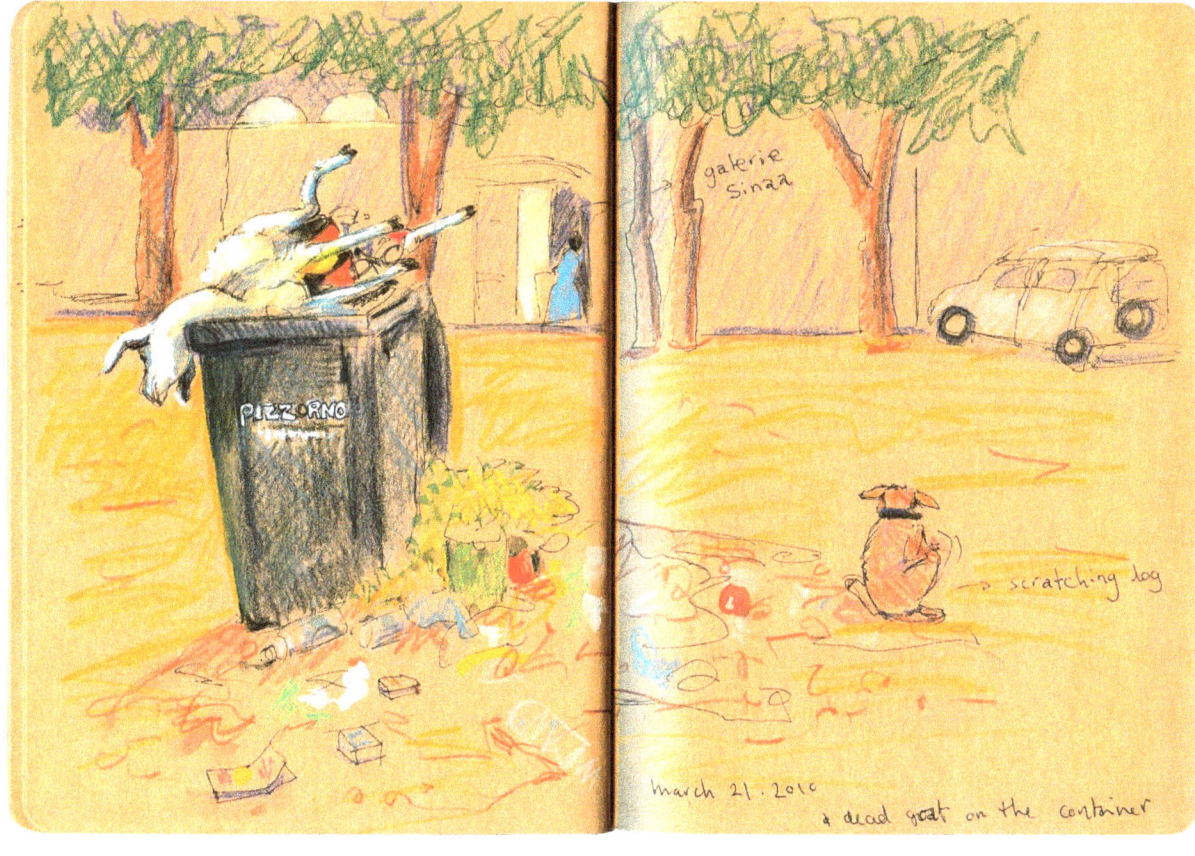

galerie Sinaa

march 21. 2010

a dead goat on the container

→ scratching dog

PIZZORNO

⊃ Dead Goat French waste company Pizzorno has been cleaning Nouakchott for the past few years, Fiadeiro says. They have distributed containers all around town, but they are not supposed to get rid of dead animals. Someone dumped the goat in this bin just across from Sinaa, and it kept swelling with the heat.

4.75" x 6.25" | 12 x 16 cm; Faber-Castell Polychromos colored pencil on Paperchase Kraft sketchbook

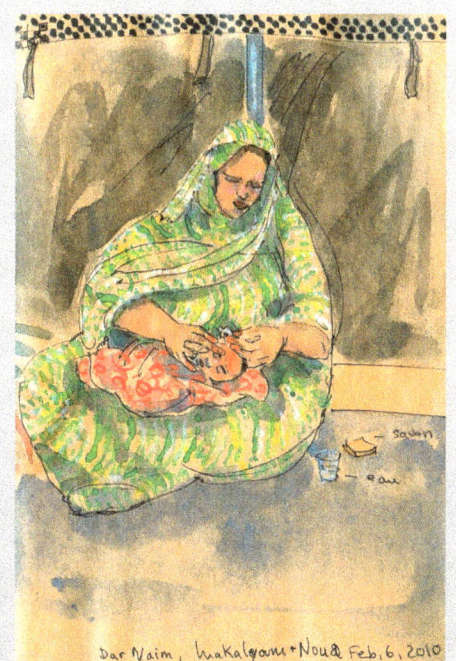

Dar Naim, Nakalyam+Noua Feb. 6, 2010

EYEWITNESS

Shaving the Baby's Head

by Isabel Fiadeiro

I went to the christening of a week-old baby named Nowa, which means "cloud." Her aunt had the task of shaving her head after smearing her face with a brownish red powder that was supposed to protect the child. She applied a bit of soap to the baby's hair and used a shaving razor blade. Her fingers had henna decoration on them, much the same color as the baby's face. The baby didn't suffer a single scratch!

Because it was a women's affair, we were mostly women at the party. We drank zrig—a mix of milk and water with sugar in it—and lots of small glasses of tea and ate a lot. In the afternoon, the young girls started singing and dancing, but I was too busy clapping my hands to draw.

4.75" x 6.25" | 12 x 16 cm; pen and watercolor on Paperchase Kraft sketchbook

MARRAKECH

The colorful Moroccan city of Marrakech is the first experience in Africa for many visitors. From different points of view, these artists captured the magical flavor of its streets and crowds. Their sketchbooks also sparked conversations in the street and made their travel experiences even more memorable.

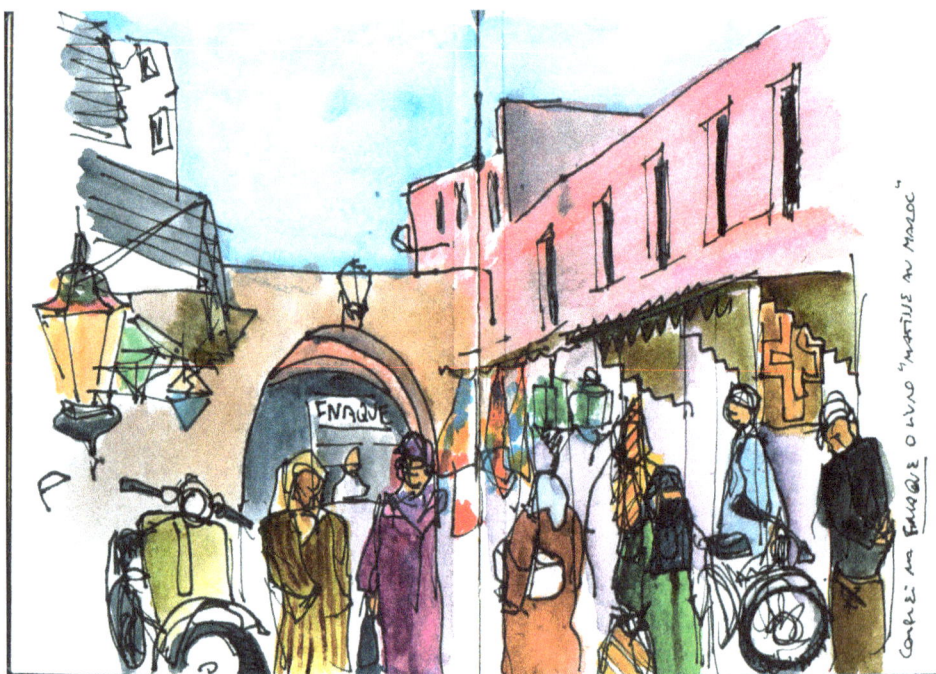

Busy Street Marrakech's streets are chaotic, from the point of view of a Westerner, says Lisbon's Eduardo Salavisa. "Motorcycles, donkeys with or without trailers, trucks and cars, and people going through the narrow streets all flash before my eyes," he says.

Tip "In these circumstances, where there is so much information and activity, I have to select and pay attention only to a few things. Here, I concentrated on the motorcyclists, the women wearing scarves, the archway, and the men in their djellabas." — *Eduardo Salavisa*

8.5" x 6" | 21.6 x 15 cm; 0.3 and 0.5 Rotring pens, Winsor & Newton watercolors on hardbound sketchbook; 20 minutes

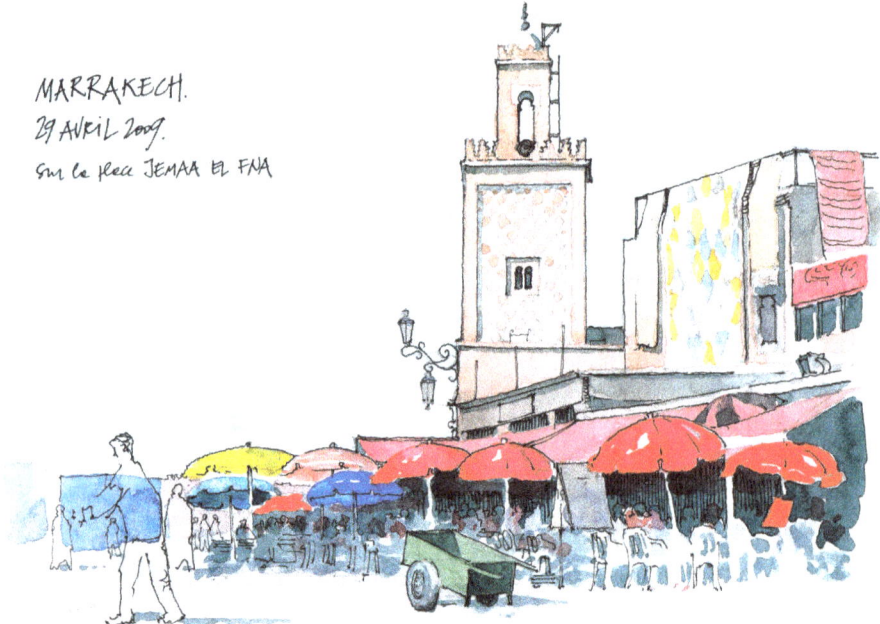

Sketch Location Revisited "My wife and friends had decided to visit Majorelle gardens," says Gérard Michel, "but I preferred to rest in the town to do some sketches. It was the second time we were in Marrakech; the first time, four years earlier, I had done a similar drawing without colors. This time, I was struck by the red Coca-Cola umbrellas and decided that they should be the focus of my drawing. I looked for a place to sit in the shadows, on the floor, against a wall."

8.5" x 11.75" | 21.6 x 30 cm; 2B pencil, Winsor & Newton watercolors, and Staedtler pigment liners on Seawhite sketchbook; about 1 hour

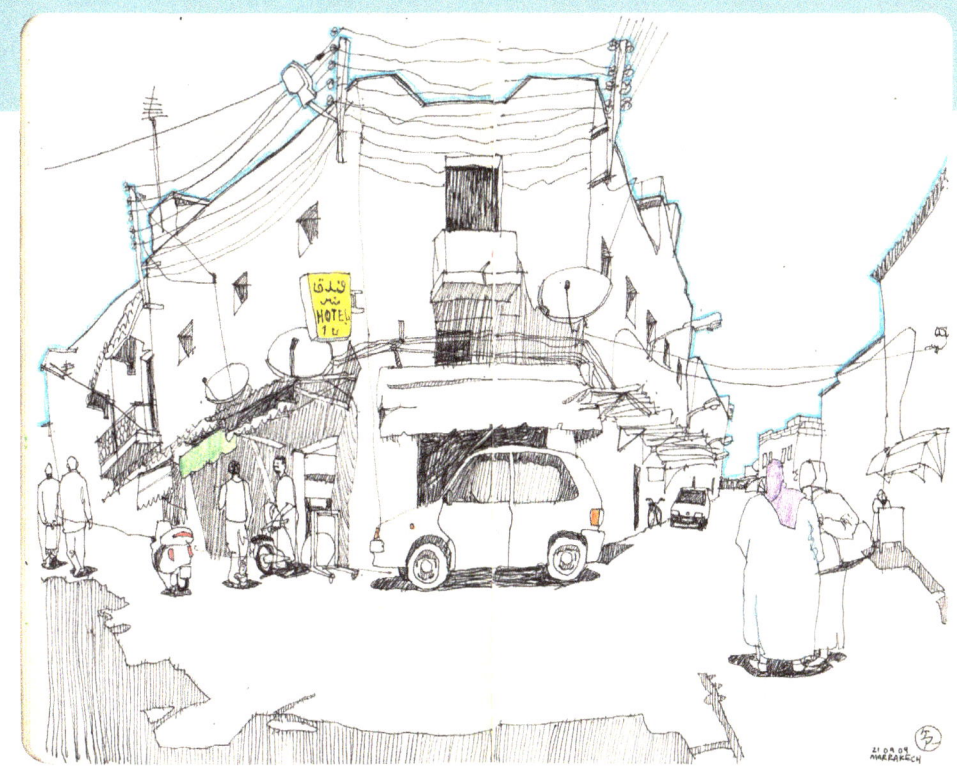

⟳ Streetscape Stuart Kerr says he felt a bit out of place in Marrakech, with his blonde hair, posh clothes, and sunburn, but the sketching soon had him squatting in the street, drawing with kids leaning up against him and having conversations in bad French with cigarette vendors.

Tip "In a new city, walk around a bit and search out a composition as you get lost (easy in Marrakech). Look for typical more than clichéd. I rough out the drawing in my head—but make sure I fit in the largest or most crucial section—in this case, the gable wall." — *Stuart Kerr*

10.5" x 8.25" | 26.5 x 21 cm; Pilot G-Tec-C4 pen, Holbein colored pencils on A5 Moleskine sketchbook; 35 minutes

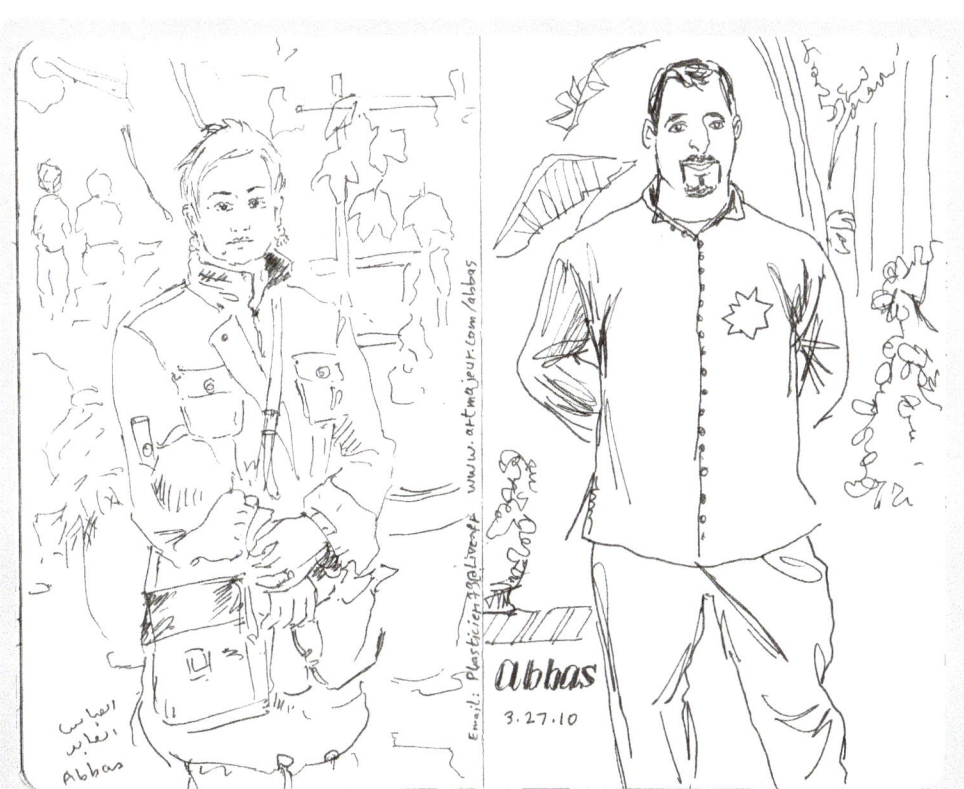

TRAVEL JOURNAL

Abbas, the Park Guide

Carrying her art supplies around opened up great conversations with the Moroccans Julie Johnson met, creating what she called a wonderful connection, even when there was no common language. She and Abbas, a park guide, took turns drawing each other, when he discovered Johnson was an artist.

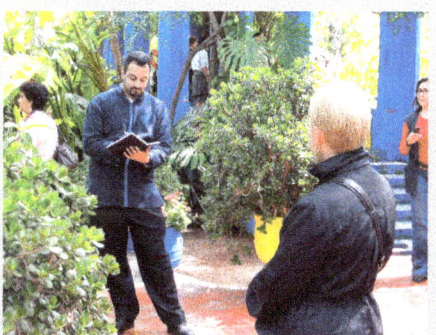

MÁLAGA

The city of Málaga in southern Spain is home to more than half a million residents and is a big tourist destination for its climate and beaches. Local sketchers, such as Luis Ruiz, are drawn to its busy harbor and panoramic views from the hill of Gibralfaro, where the Phoenicians first settled more than 2,500 years ago.

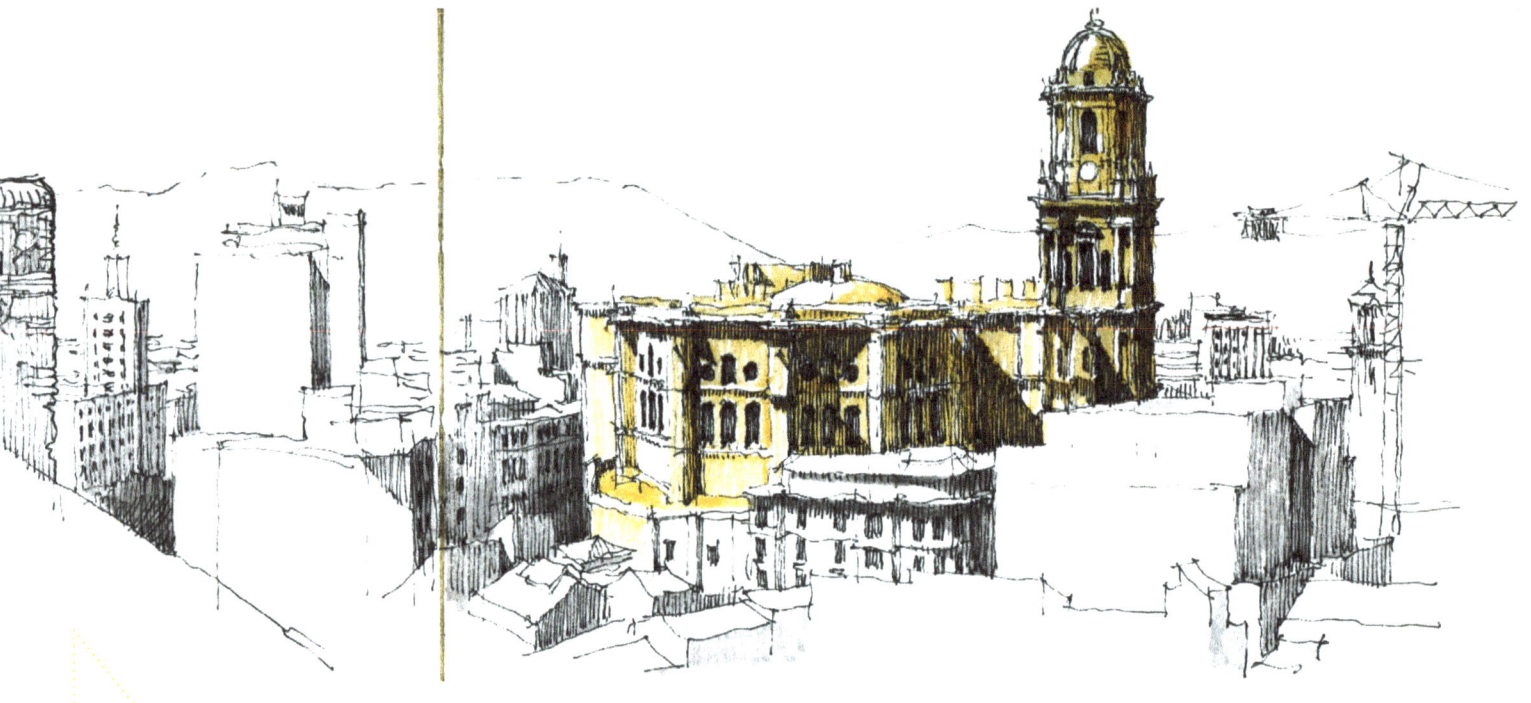

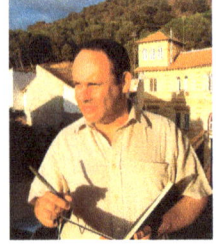

⌒ Ruiz sketches the cathedral of Málaga from the Alcazaba fortress.

12.75" x 5" | 32 x 12.5 cm; .05 Staedtler pigment liner and Tombow brush pens on Moleskine sketchbook; about 90 minutes

ARTIST PROFILE
Luis Ruiz

As an architect, I was trained to sketch on site in my first year of studies, and I have always considered sketching a wonderful tool in my job. But I have recently found the online urban sketchers community and discovered the immense joy of sketching outside with no particular task. I feel especially sensitive of keeping a record of time and place, and I'm changing from sketching just architecture to understanding the city as a big scenario for human activity. As an architect, I still cannot avoid putting a focus on buildings. Wherever I go, even in my own city, I am always looking upward, and I really enjoy discovering unnoticed details on façades or cornices.

"I see the city as a scenario of human life, and that's what I try to show in my sketches."

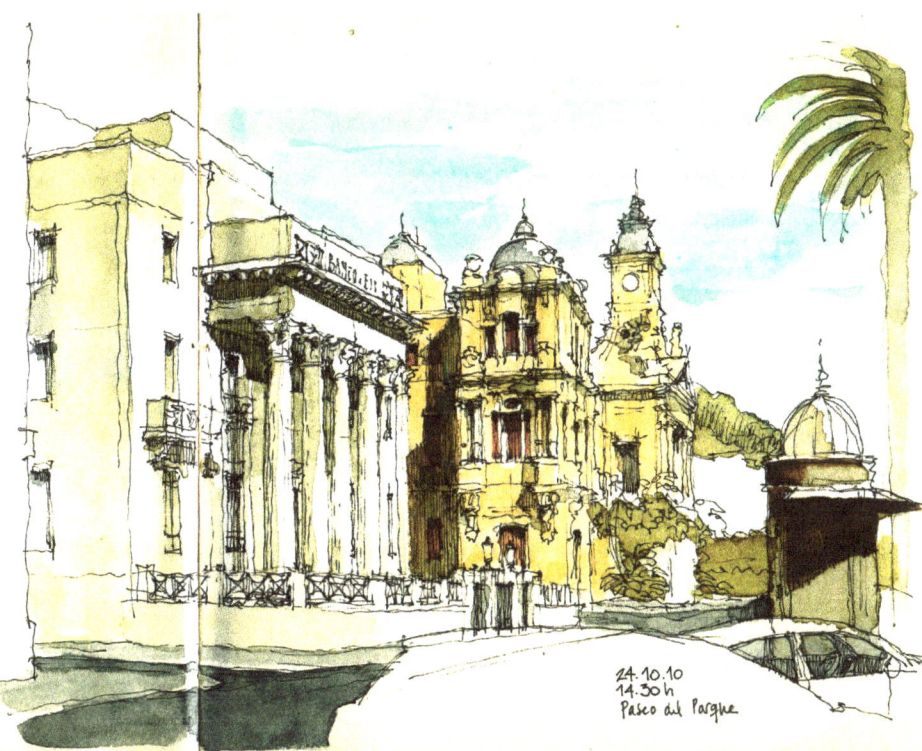

24.10.10
14.30 h
Paseo del Parque

☾ **The City in Autumn** Outdoor sketching is a pleasant experience in Málaga in autumn. The skies are incredibly clear, and the beautiful light draws attention to the architectural details of buildings such as the Banco de España and City Hall.

Tip "I choose a foreground element, perhaps a car or a group of people, first. I draw a few construction lines and then the shapes of the buildings, then add details after identifying the proportions." — *Luis Ruiz*

10.25" x 7.75" | 26 x 19.5 cm; 0.05 Staedtler pigment liner, Rembrandt watercolor set, Hahnemühle sketchbook; 90 minutes

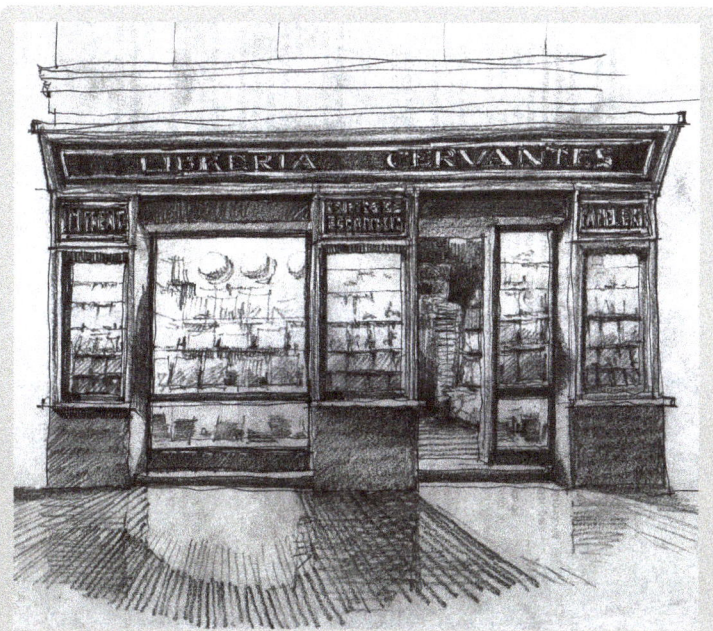

EYEWITNESS

The Old Bookshop Has Closed

by Luis Ruiz

Librería Cervantes was the oldest bookshop in Málaga. It was a magic place, delightfully old-fashioned in its style, with its row of globes on the upper shelf and its carefully displayed collections of the most beautiful fountain pens or luxury editions of poetry.

It was also one of the last family-owned shops in the main commercial area of the city, and when I drew this sketch, I feared it might disappear soon, in a changing streetscape where the price of the commercial real estate skyrockets, perhaps to be replaced by a plain store belonging to a big company or a franchise.

My fears came true. Librería Cervantes closed and that mysterious effect of the glowing glass is not there anymore.

9.5" x 6.75" | 24 x 17 cm; 2B pencil, office paper (A4 sheet); 30 minutes

VIEW POINTS

Drawing from the Gibralfaro Fortress

A climb up to the ancient fortress known as Gibralfaro offers one of the best sketching views in Málaga. Here's how different sketchers reflected the sights on paper.

⮑ Cristina Urdiales sketched the beautiful cathedral roofs in the middle of a sea of buildings. "On a sunny winter day like this, you can still draw in a T-shirt and sunglasses," she says.

5" x 7" | 12.5 x 18 cm; 0.1 Staedler pigment liner and Tombow brush marker (neutral gray), plain white paper

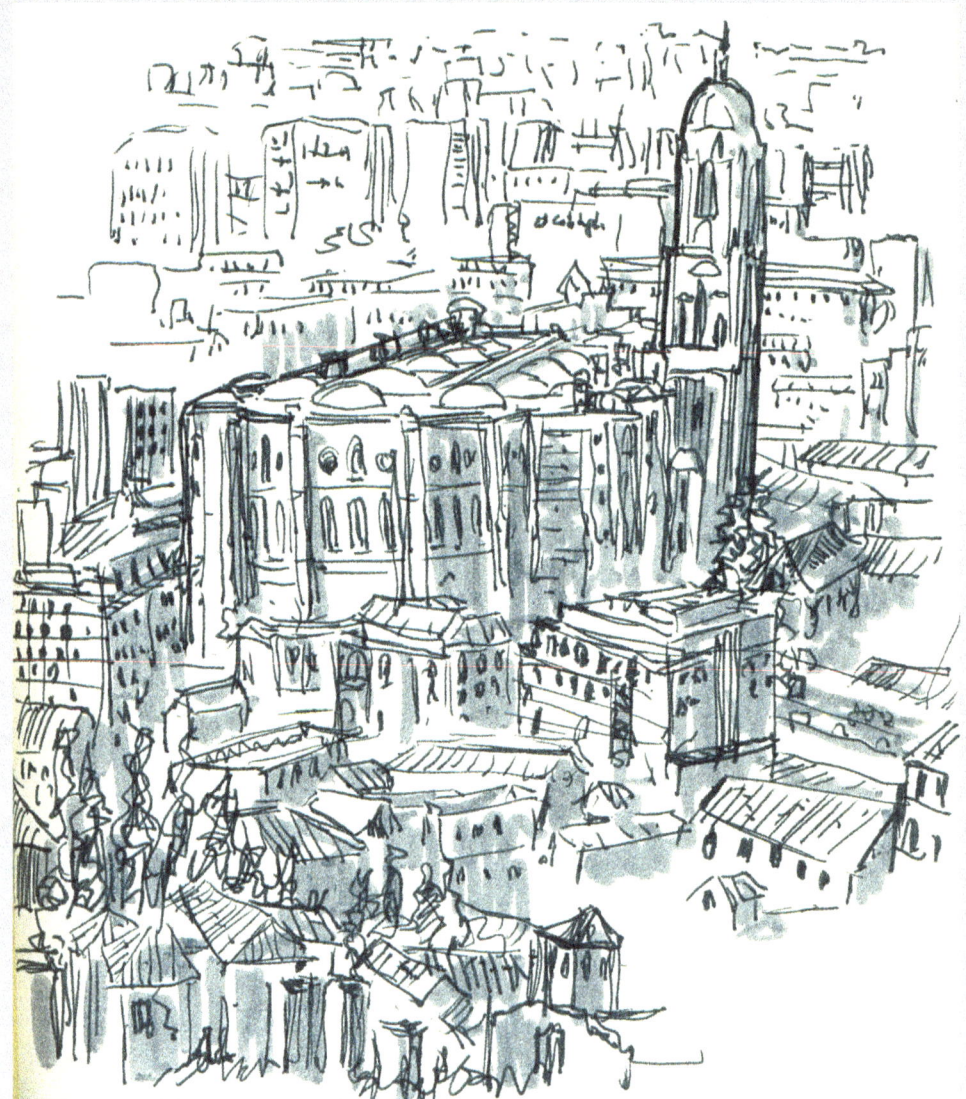

↻ Ignacio Dorao experienced a curious symbiosis of nature and city, feeling the birds, the fresh air, and the smell of pine trees, together with the distant sounds of the city, the harbor, and the view of aircraft taking off behind the mountains.

16.5" x 5.25" | 42 x 13 cm; 0.5 HB pencil, 0.1 and 0.2 Staedtler pigment liners, Winsor & Newton Cotman watercolor set on Moleskine watercolor book; 2 hours

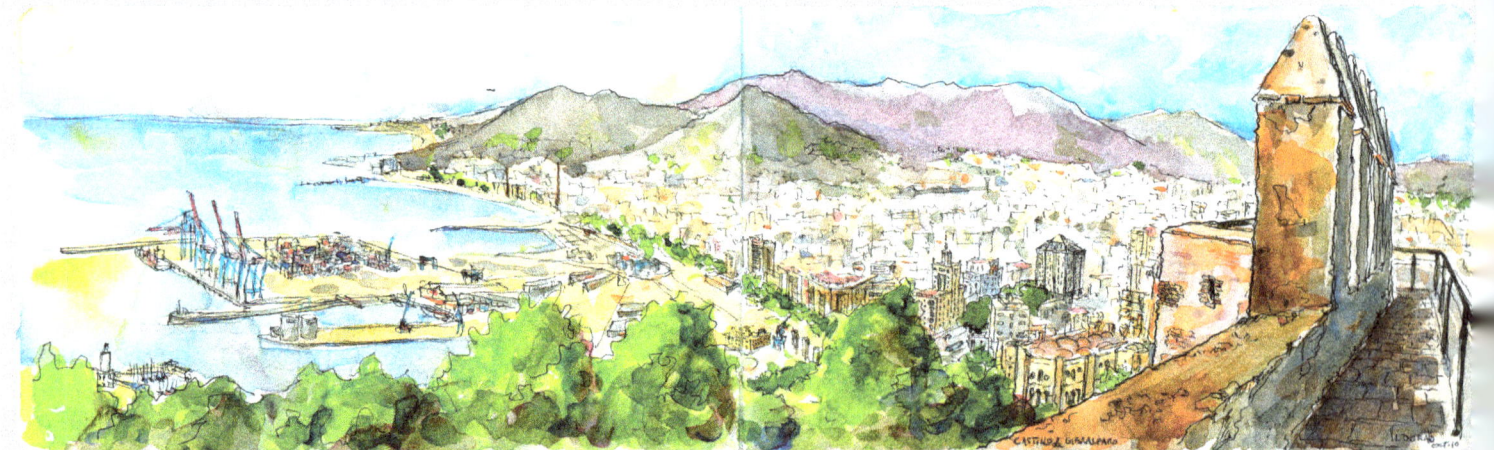

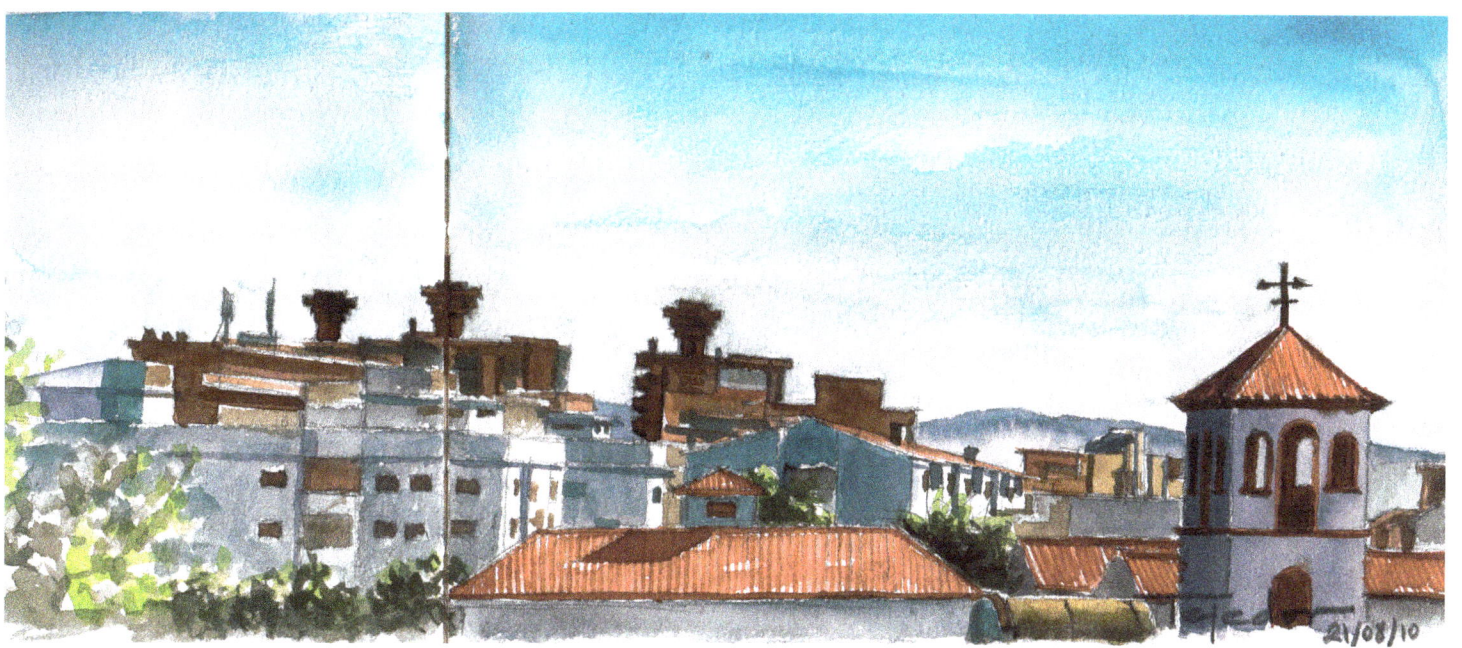

↺ **Skyline** "This view from the window struck me: an anonymous district in the outskirts of the city with a great contrast of ages, sizes, and shapes of architecture. I am fond of sketching roofscapes, so I could not resist the temptation of drawing it!" — *Paco Tejedor*

11.75" x 5" | 30 x 12.5 cm; HB pencil and Rembrandt watercolor set on Moleskine sketchbook; 45 minutes

↻ **Sunset in Málaga** "The colors of the beach were really difficult to draw because of the blending and changing colors of the sunset. But it was a magical moment. I was mostly looking at the sea, and I drew this watercolor in an instant with a very big brush and only two brushstrokes." — *Inma Serrano*

4.75" x 9.5" | 12 x 24 cm; Schmincke watercolors, #10 and #14 plain brushes, Talens white gouache, watercolor-paper handmade sketchbook; 15 minutes

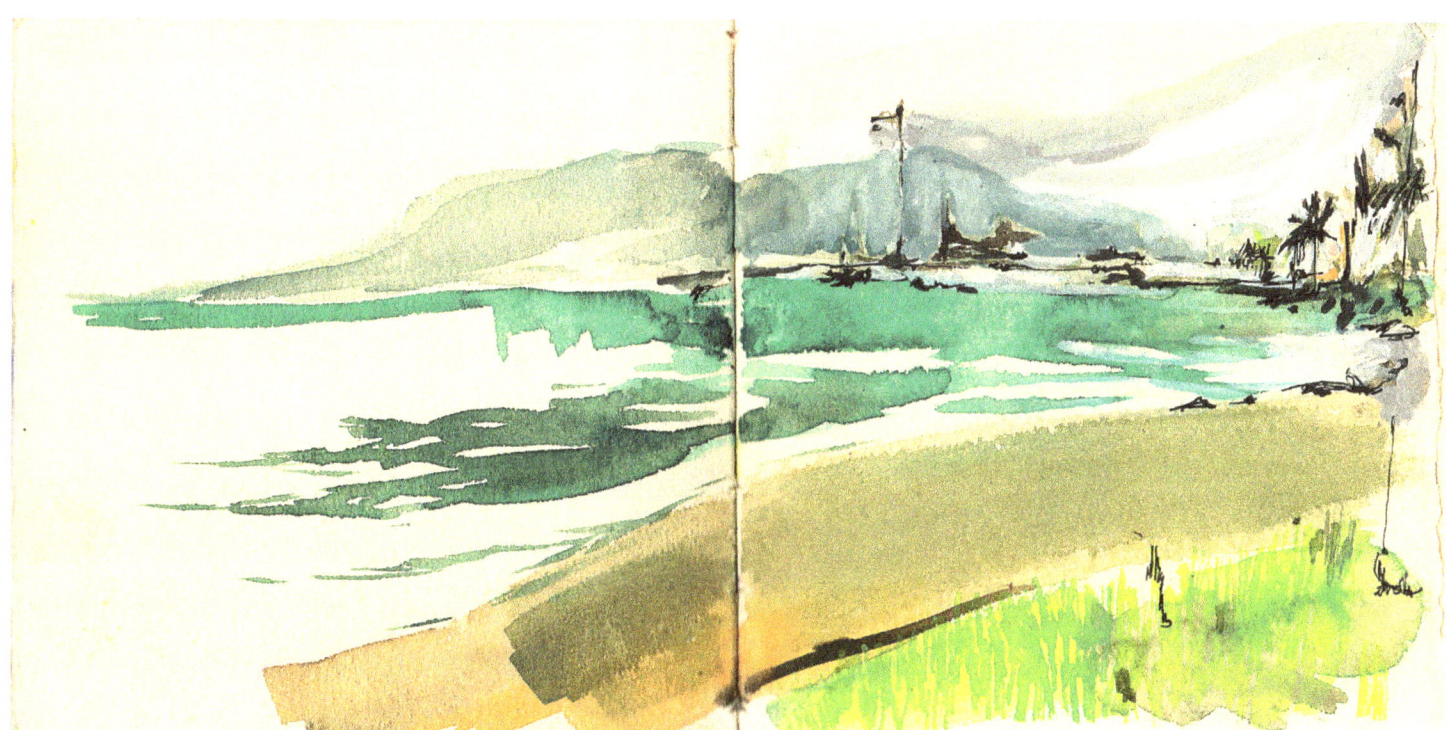

CÓRDOBA

Once a major capital under the Roman Empire and later under Islamic rule, the sunny Spanish city of Córdoba has preserved much of its unique architecture. Must-sketch sites include the Mosque-Cathedral complex and the impressive Roman bridge across the Guadalquivir River with its sixteen arches.

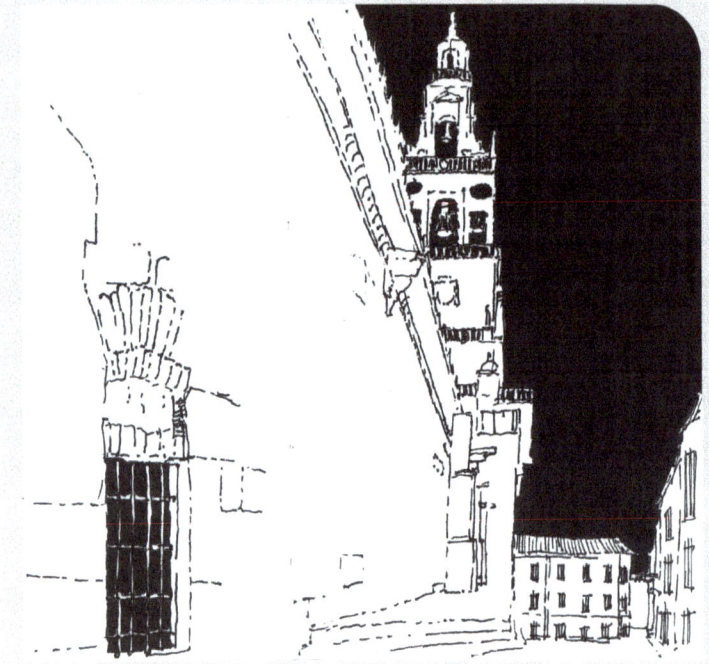

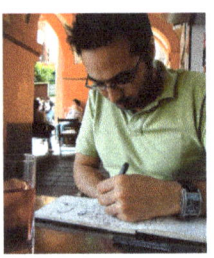

ARTIST PROFILE
Álvaro Carnicero

I went to study away from Córdoba, where I grew up, and for some years, I didn't want to return. Sometimes, it's enough to leave a place to realize the value of what you lose. That's what happened to me. I knew Córdoba was beautiful, that its old town was a World Heritage site, that the Mosque-Cathedral is one of the most fabulous, rich, and unique buildings in the history of architecture, and I knew most of its popular festivals and traditions. Yet, when I returned, I realized I still didn't really know my city.

Each walk out to draw is a journey into myself, and each time, I make a discovery—a street corner, an entrance to the porch of a house, a new terrace roof, a tower, or another old bar, in which I see the Córdoba from the last century.

⌒ Álvaro Carnicero enjoys sketching and a drink under the shade of the arches at the Corredera Square, which dates from the seventeenth century.

16.5" x 5" | 42 x 12.5 cm; Pilot G-Tec-C4 black pen, Winsor & Newton watercolors, Rotring ArtPen F, blue and black ink on Moleskine watercolor book; 30 minutes

" Drawing is a way to understand better a city, and it is perhaps the most sincere souvenir."

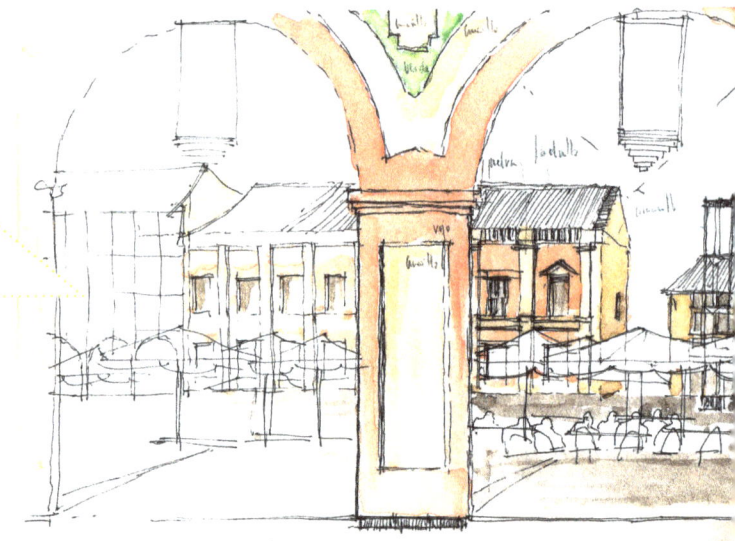

LA CORREDERA

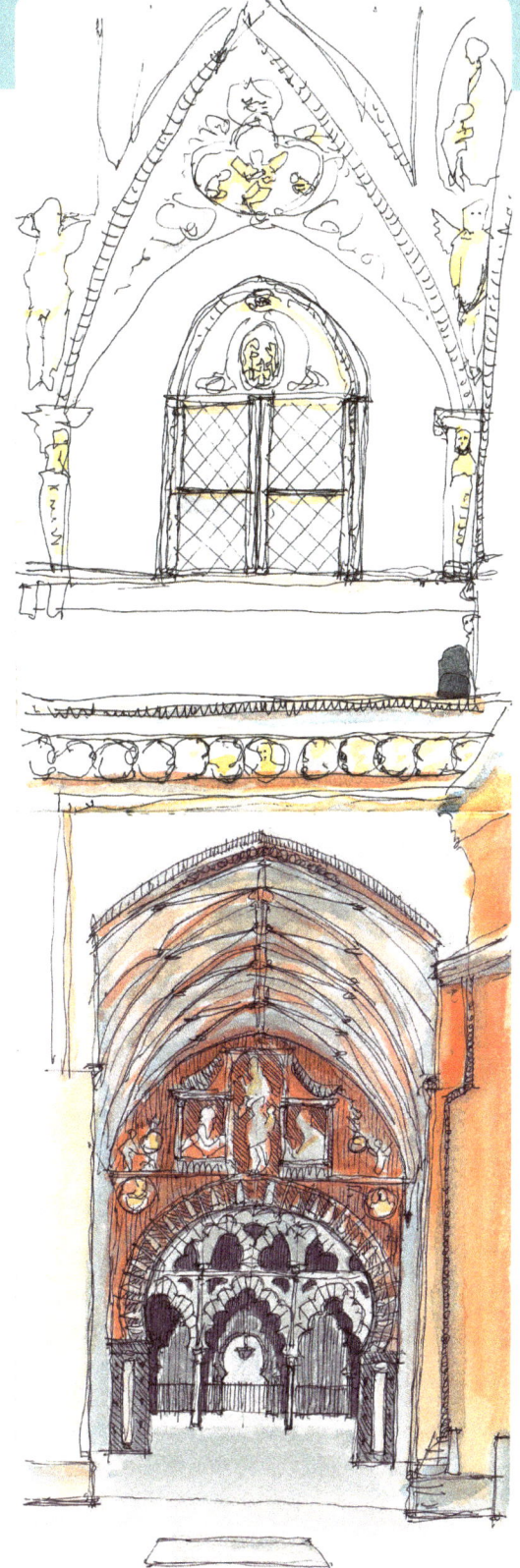

Sketch Interrupted

by Álvaro Carnicero

I had been sketching this view of the cathedral's tower for fifteen minutes, when my cousin showed up with some of his friends. The sketch was not finished yet, but I didn't want to be rude, so I stopped drawing. Later, I realized that this unexpected visit had favored me. Sometimes, we must leave the sketch before overdesign spoils it.

7" x 5.5" | 18 x 14 cm; 05 Pilot V-Ball Roller Ball, Pentel Pocket Brush (black) on white 200-gsm paper; 15 minutes

↪ From the Cathedral to the Mihrab

A cathedral was built inside the mosque in the sixteenth century, and Carnicero says the architect, Hernán Ruiz, understood perfectly the structural and aesthetic harmony that should exist between the two temples.

Tip "The vagueness of the details as the drawing is going deeper and the use of lines or increasingly austere color stains can be good resources to help show depth."
— *Álvaro Carnicero*

5" x 16.5" | 12.5 x 42 cm; Pilot G-Tec-C4 (black ink), Winsor & Newton watercolors on Moleskine watercolor book; 2.5 hours

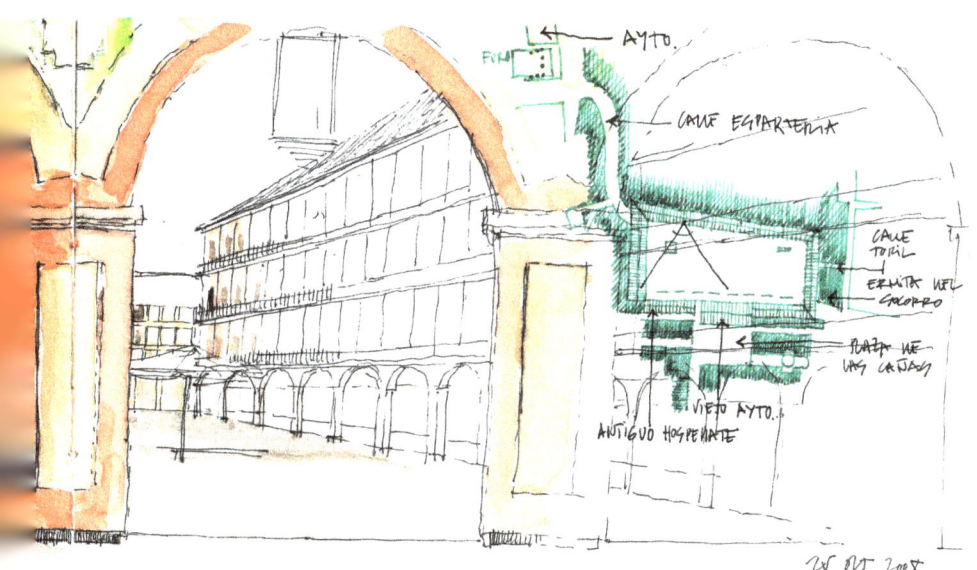

LISBON

From steep hills overlooking the mouth of the river Tagus, to narrow streets paved with cobblestones that lead to unexpected views: Lisbon provides its hometown sketchers with an abundance of views to draw. "With its terraces and gardens overlooking the river Tagus on one side, and hills with medieval castles on the other, Lisbon seems especially fitting to draw in a sketchbook," says local artist and teacher João Catarino.

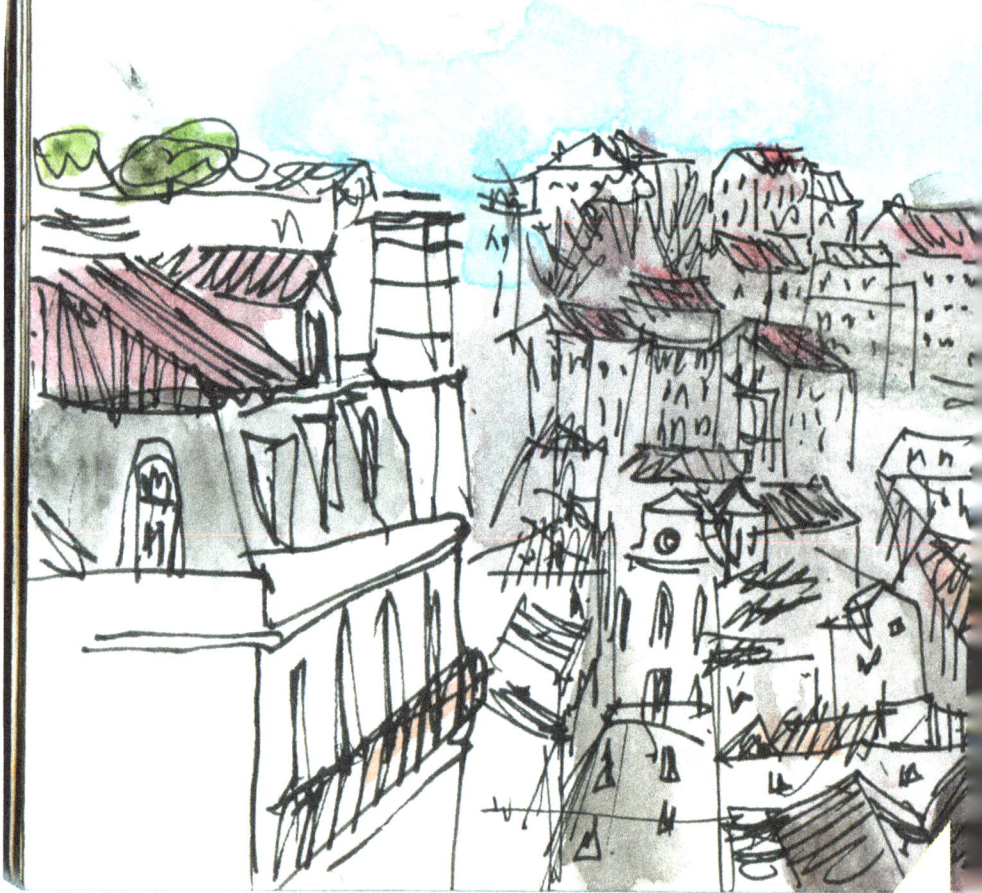

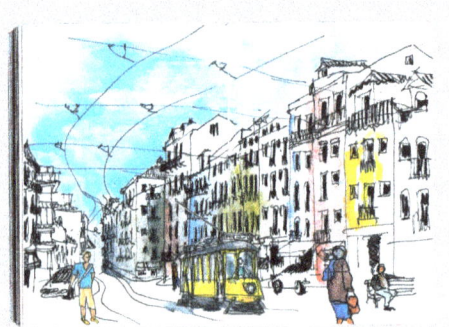

FIRST PERSON

Riding Lisbon's Historic Trams

by Eduardo Salavisa

Years ago, electric streetcars were the principal way of public transportation in Lisbon. But, as in many other cities, the choice of individual transportation, especially by car, won over the rails, and now only two lines remain in the city. One of them, Number 28, runs through several old quarters in the city center and attracts many tourists and people who live in those neighborhoods. A gratifying experience is to take that route and draw the interior of the tram, the commuters, and the tram operator, as well as a view from outside as the tram goes through streets full of activity. Just watch out for pickpockets.

4.25" x 6" | 11 x 15 cm; Rotring pen on Winsor & Newton hardbound sketchbook

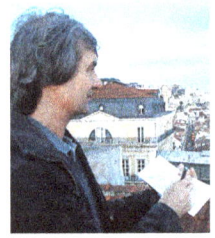

🎧 Eduardo Salavisa sketches a panoramic view of Lisbon and the Tagus River.

11.75" x 4" | 30 x 10 cm; Rotring pen on custom-made sketchbook by Laloran

ARTIST PROFILE

Eduardo Salavisa

I feel a close connection between traveling and drawing, a fact that has many advantages: I get lots of memories from my sketchbooks when I travel, and the fact that I feel I am traveling whenever I draw enables me to travel day after day, in my own town. What I like about my home town of Lisbon is the unexpected meeting of the alley, the old square, and the Tagus River, always peeking out at every corner of the street. Drawing every day in our own city is like traveling to a strange place, because the act of drawing forces us to be more attentive, and we notice situations that otherwise would not catch our attention.

"Carrying a sketchbook awakens the pleasure of drawing."

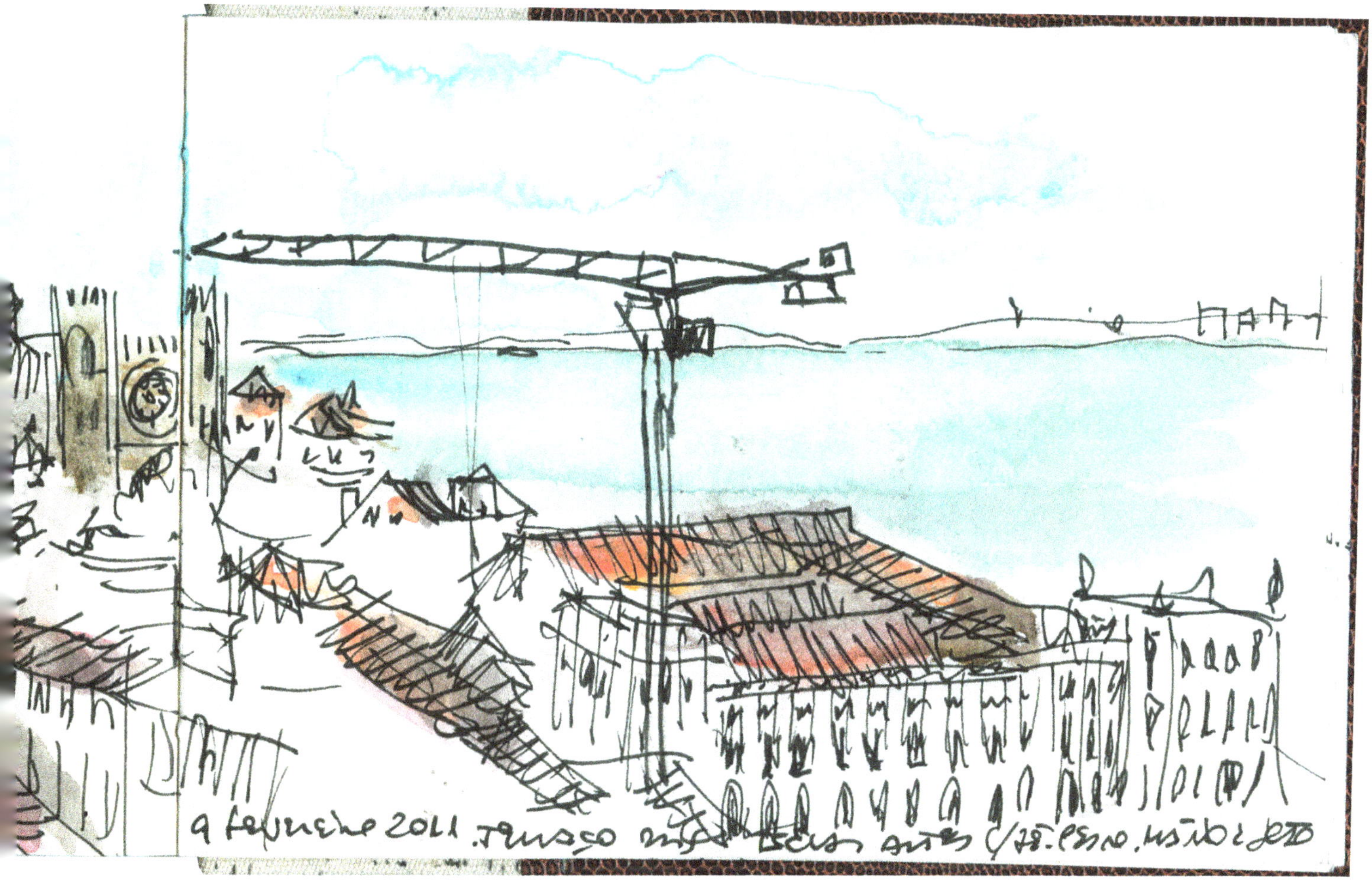

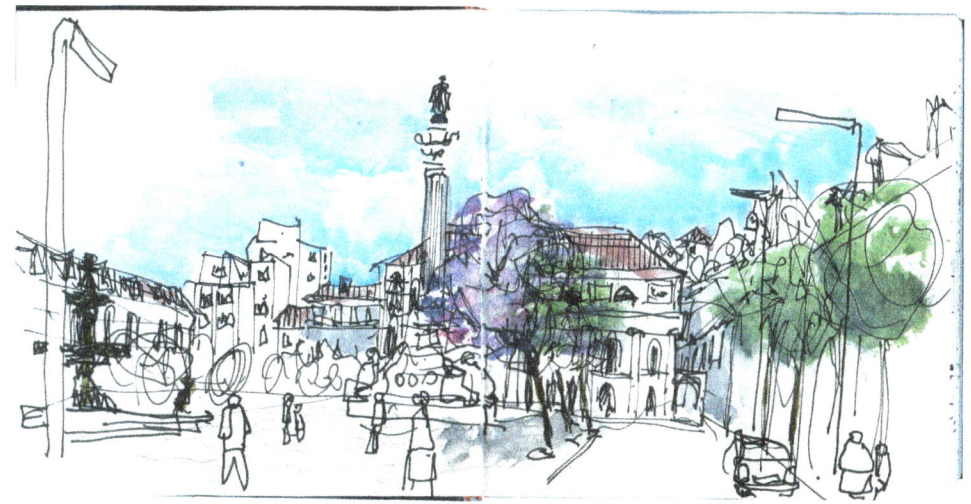

9 feureiro 2011. Jardim ...

↺ Rossio Square Baroque fountains, neo-Gothic architecture, and a monument to a Portuguese king are just a few features of Rossio Square, one of Lisbon's most lively spaces. Salavisa says he can't resist pulling out his sketchbook every time he passes by.

Tip "I did the drawing in a square sketchbook, which gives an excellent panoramic when you draw across the fold." — *Eduardo Salavisa*

10.75" x 5.5" | 27.5 x 14 cm; Rotring pen on hardbound sketchbook

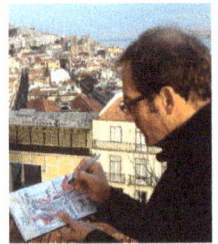

ARTIST PROFILE
João Catarino

Drawing everywhere is like traveling all the time. When you go out for a small walk, if you stop and give yourself some time to look around and make a drawing, you can have moments of total concentration and get a lot of pleasure from ordinary shapes and colors. You can also create your own view and interpretation of the world, so that it becomes accessible to others. Sketching is also a way to document and share our lives.

Lisbon is a city in which the traveler can get lost drawing and get lost for real. Wandering through the city, you can find a new experience awaiting at every corner. Some streets were planned with a rule; others are picturesque labyrinths dating from medieval times.

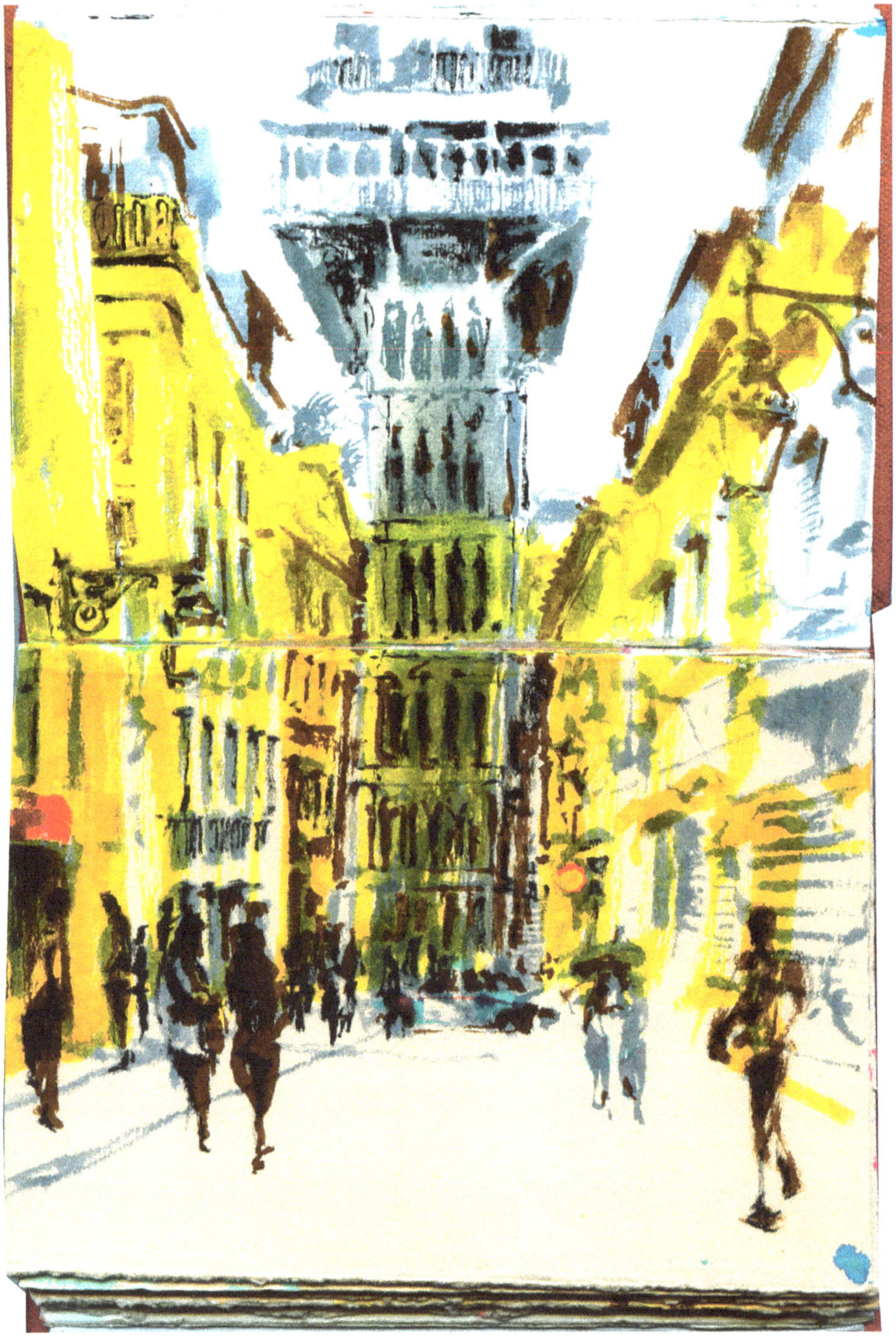

⊃ **Elevador de Santa Justa** This lift, built in 1902, connects the lower streets in Lisbon's downtown with the higher districts of Chiado and Bairro Alto.

Tip "This is on a handmade sketchbook with pages of different colors. I oriented the sketchbook with the light-colored page at the top of the drawing, for the area with most light, and the dark-colored page at the bottom for the area less illuminated." — *João Catarino*

8.25" x 6" | 21 x 15 cm; Ecoline liquid watercolor with waterbrush on handmade sketchbook with various watercolor papers; 25 minutes

"I look for details hidden in the contrast of light and darkness."

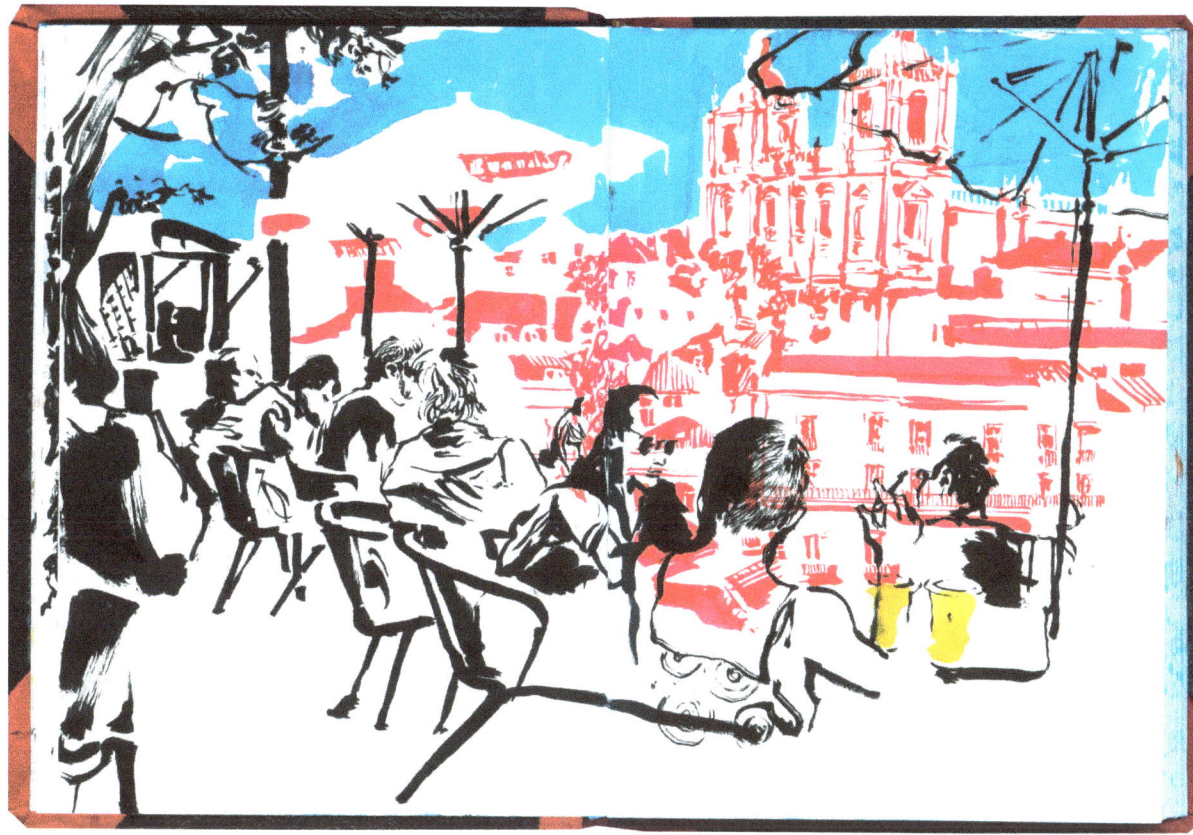

⊂ **Portas do Sol** "The Doors of the Sun" is the first hill that receives sunlight in the morning. "It's a fantastic place where every surface is full of color," says Catarino.

Tip "I started this drawing on the most improbable spot, the blue sky, then I did the red church, and I finished it drawing the foreground elements that were closer to me." — João Catarino

11.5" x 8.25" | 29 x 21 cm; Pentel brush pen on Clairfontaine sketchbook; 25 minutes

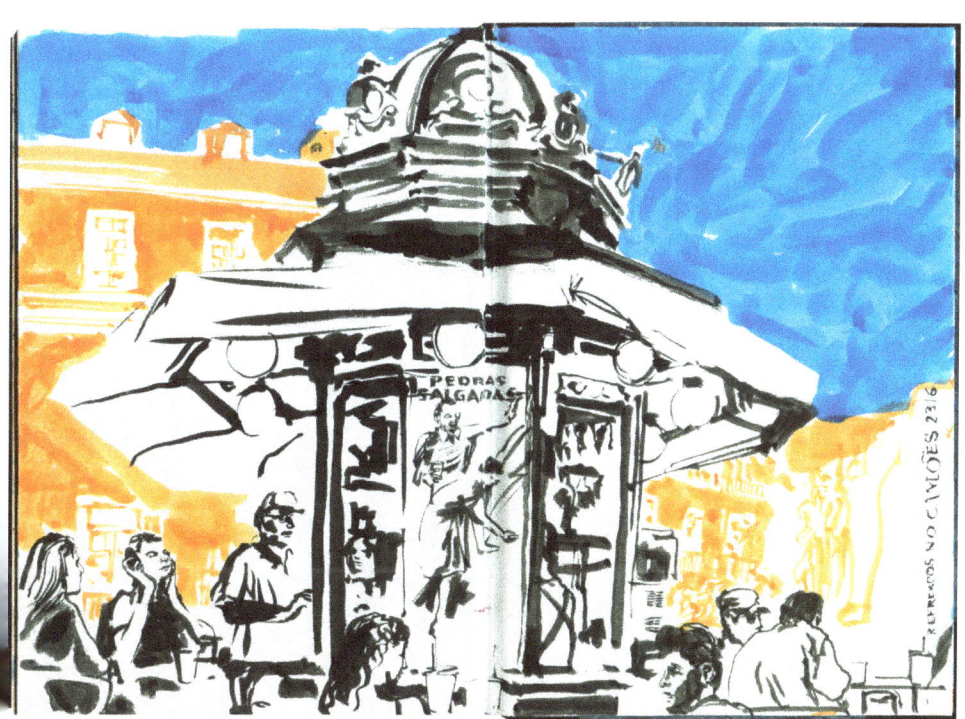

⊂ **Quiosque do Camões** Catarino did a series of drawings of *quiosques*, the traditional refreshment stands that sell "genuine, made-in-Portugal" beverages.

Tip "I started with the yellow of the building, then the blue of the sky, leaving enough white space to draw, in black, the spots with less light." — João Catarino

11.5" x 8.25" | 29 x 21 cm; Ecoline liquid watercolor with waterbrush, Pentel brush pen on "Papelaria Moderna" Lisboa sketchbook; 25 minutes

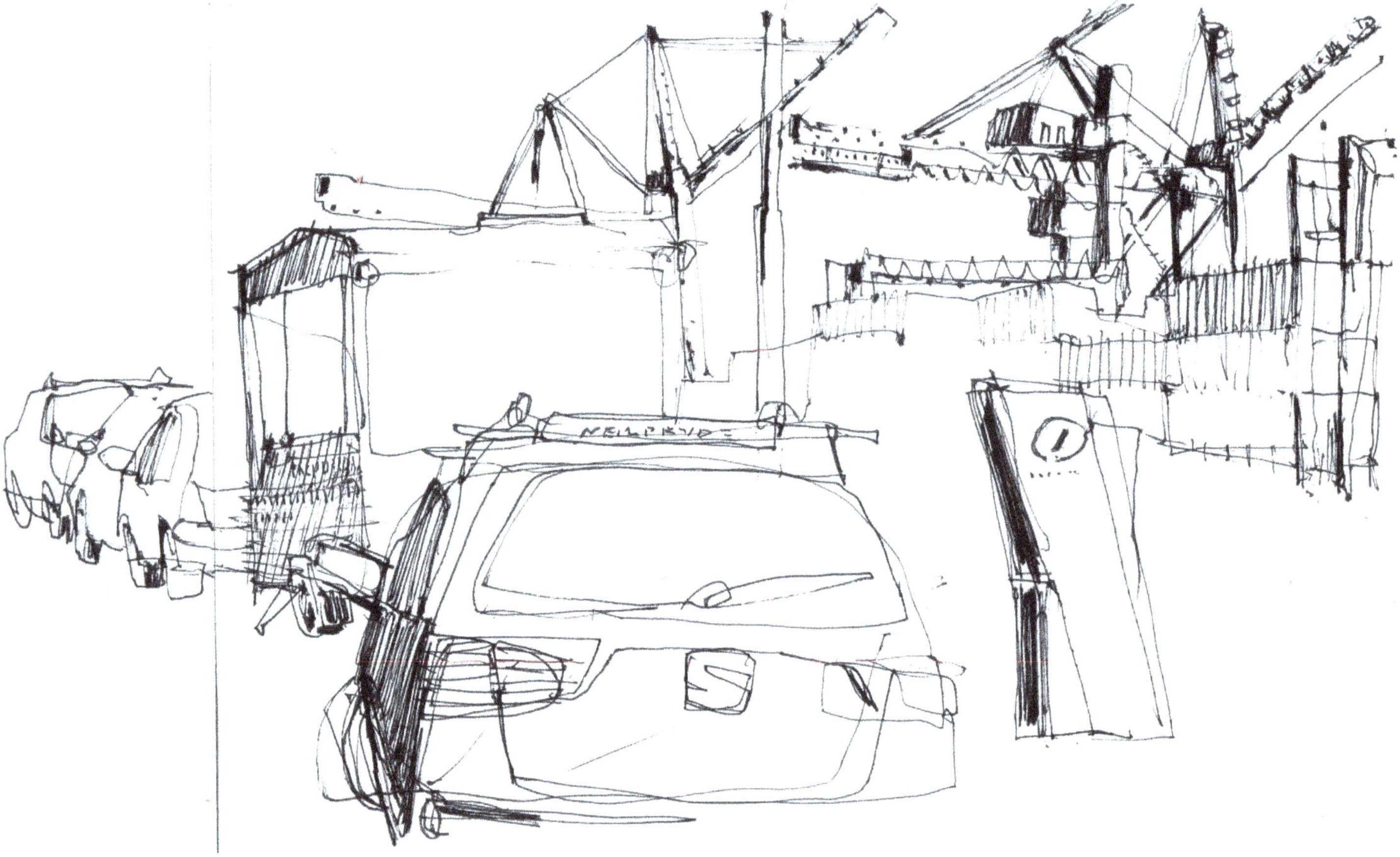

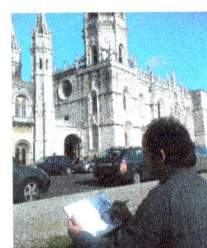

ARTIST PROFILE
José Louro

I draw, most of the time, for pleasure. That's why I rarely draw buildings. When it comes to buildings, drawing becomes more like a punishment. An urban city like Lisbon is about people's everyday life. I just sit and try to catch the moments that happen in front of me: my colleagues at the school, bars and bartenders, animals in the street, waiting for my daughter, people shopping, cars on the sidewalks, morning traffic from inside my car, people taking sunbaths on the beach. What interests me are the little things that, I think, no one really cares about. And, when my hand allows it, I put these little things on a pedestal.

⋒ **Lisboa Port** Louro enjoys drawing industrial equipment, such as cargo cranes, grain elevators, and ramps. This scene was sketched near the port from inside his car on a rainy day.

Tip "The white space highlights the figures that I want to be essential in the drawing. At the same time, I like that 'less is more' quality in a drawing." — *José Louro*

16.5" x 6" | 42 x 15 cm; Micron 0.8 pen on inexpensive school notebook; about 1 hour

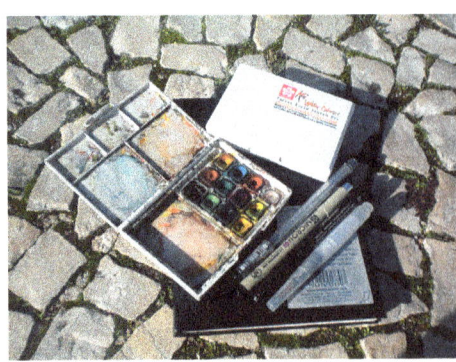

⋒ Louro's sketching tools

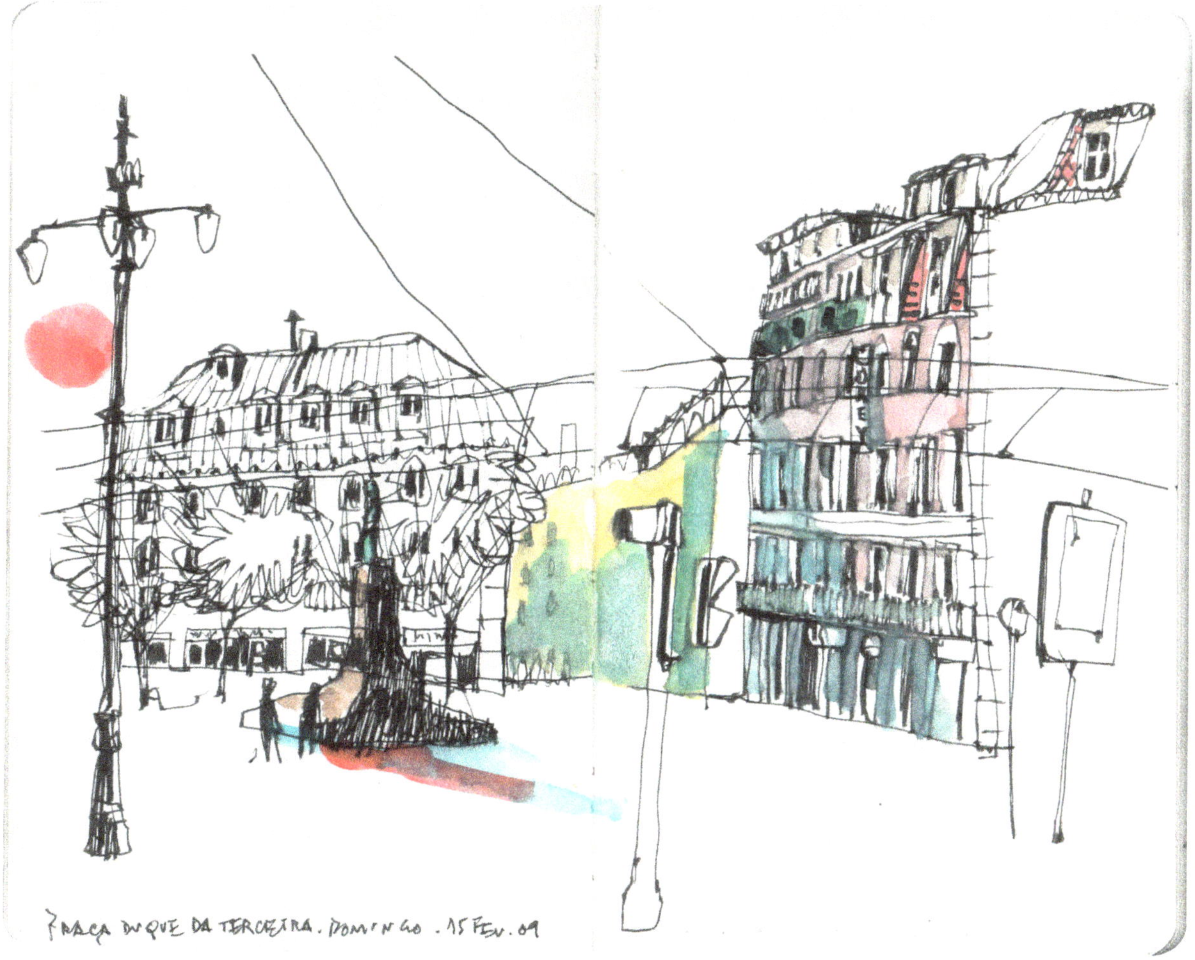

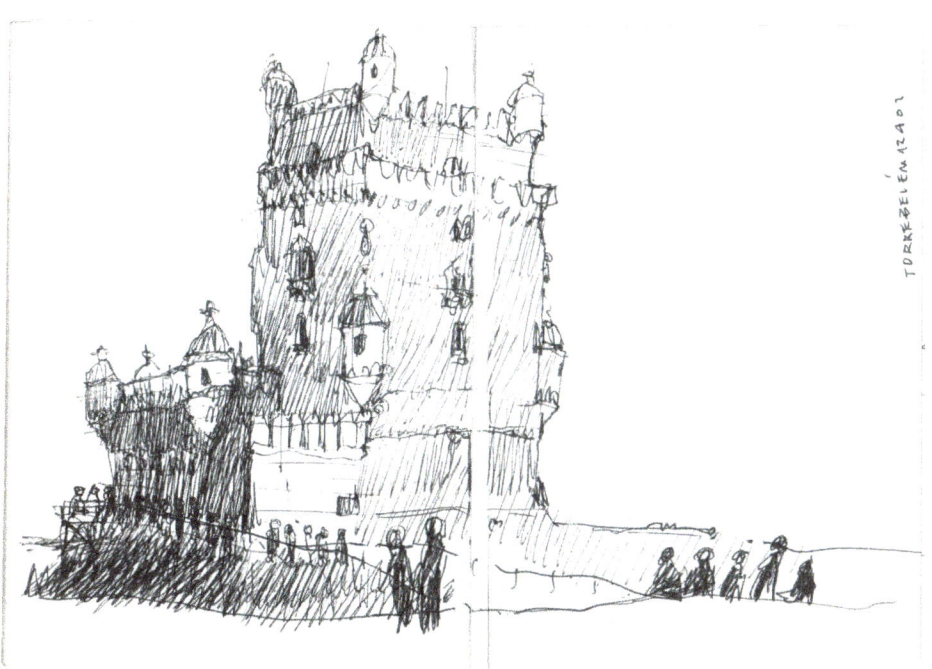

PRAÇA DUQUE DA TERCEIRA. DOMINGO. 15 FEV. 09

TORRE BELÉM AZADI

↻ **Cais do Sodré Square** This square is officially called Praça do Duque da Terceira, but since the sixteenth century, the people have called it Cais do Sodré. *Cais* means harbor and *Sodré* is the family name of an English family that had a business here. Many places in Lisbon have traditional names that are stronger than the official names, says Louro.

Tip "Like most of my street sketches, I just started by drawing an element on the left side of the page—in this case the street lamp—and then I drew the rest, taking measures and proportions from that first element."
— José Louro

10.25" x 8.25" | 26 x 21 cm; Sakura 12-color watercolor kit and gel ink pen on Moleskine sketchbook; about 30 minutes

↻ **Belém Tower** The Belém Tower is one the most famous monuments in Lisbon and a favorite sketching location for José Louro.

8.25" x 6" | 21 x 15 cm; Micron 0.8 pen on Winsor & Newton, 110-gsm A6 casebound sketchbook; about 30 minutes

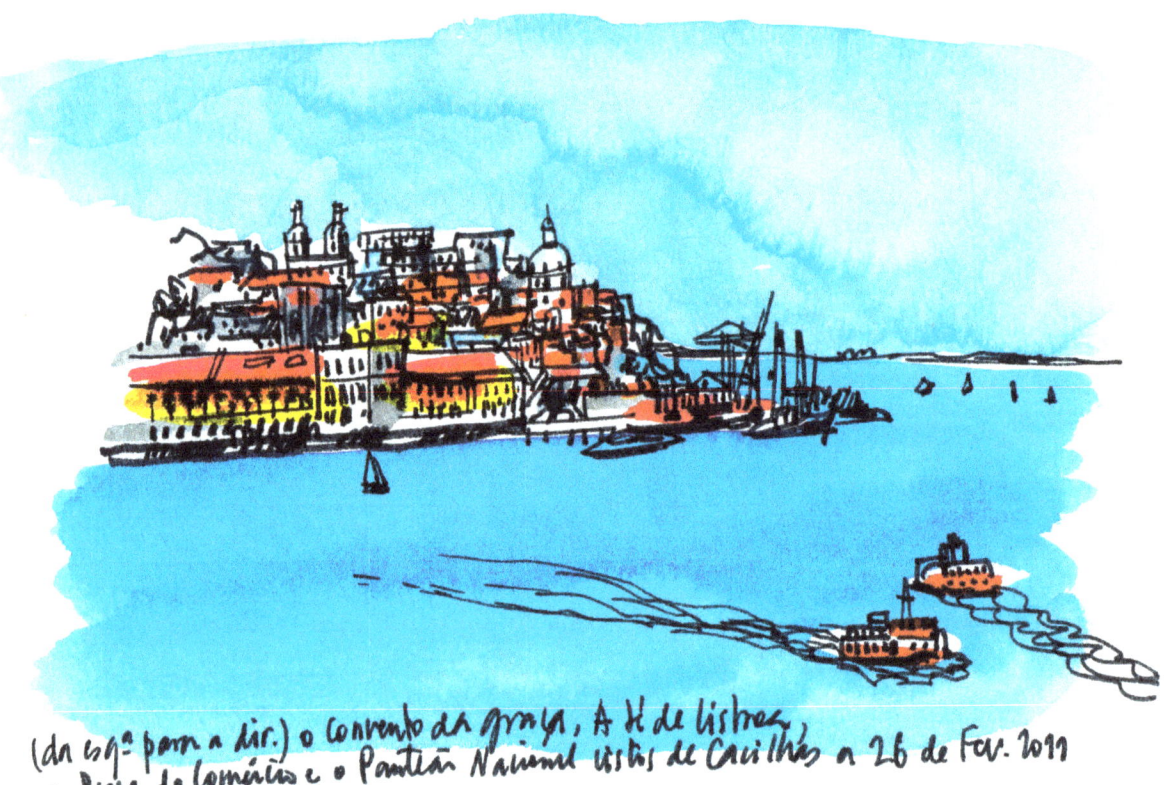

(da esq.ª para a dir.) o Convento da graça, A H de Listrea, a Praça do Comércio e o Pantião Nacional vistos de Cacilhas a 26 de Fev. 2011

⊂ Lisbon's River Gateway A different way to witness Lisbon's flirtation with its river is to cross over the Tejo River to Cacilhas. There, Câmara sat down at a restaurant's esplanade, ordered some seafood, and sketched the *cacilheiro*, the white and orange boats.

Tip "In some cases, choosing a narrow variety of colors works the best." — *Richard Câmara*

5.76" x 8.75" | 14.6 x 22 cm; Talens Ecoline watercolors with a MUJI black felt-tip pen on hardcover "TIGER" sketchbook with 150-gsm white pages; about 30 minutes

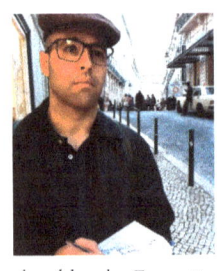

ARTIST PROFILE

Richard Câmara

Ever since I can remember, drawing has been part of my life. What seemed to be just a fun way to spend my time as a child, wound up being my profession. Today, I draw for a living, as a freelance illustrator on all sorts of exciting projects, among which are my personal sketchbooks. Every time I open one, I have the opportunity to work with different techniques, while observing and drawing little details that otherwise would most probably remain unnoticed. Drawing in these books allows me to witness what surrounds me and, in a certain sense, to take part in it.

"The sketchbooks are my mobile studio."

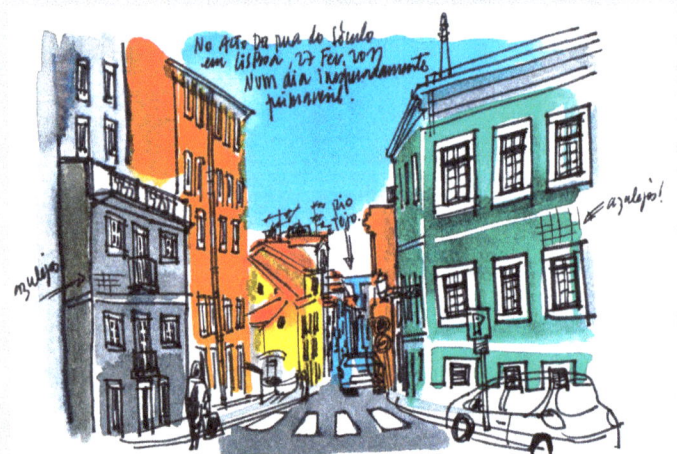

STYLE AND TECHNIQUE

Line over Color

by Richard Câmara

Identify the main colors and place them as filled shapes (leaving the windows and other details empty) before sketching any lines. Then, and only then, apply your linework on top of it. Don't worry if there isn't a precise match between the two. You'll soon discover other ways for them to meet and blend.

5.76" x 8.75" | 14.6 x 22 cm; Talens Ecoline watercolors with a MUJI black felt-tip pen on hardcover "Tiger" sketchbook with 150-gsm white pages; about 30 minutes

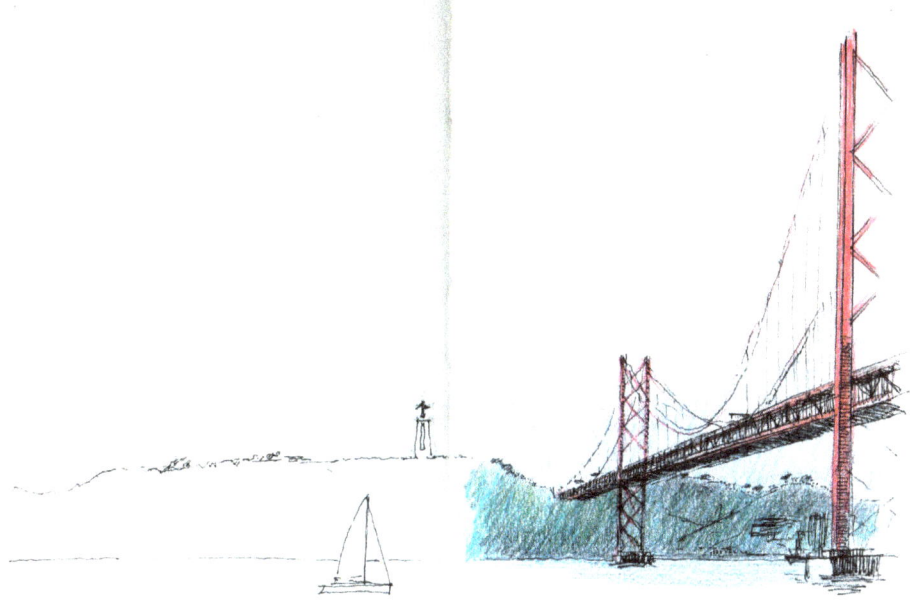

2019.01.10
Sketchcrawl

◔ **Bridge over Tagus River** "We gathered by the river on what was my first sketchrawl," Cabral says. "The view was obviously interesting, with the sailboats, the bridge, and the big statue on the other margin."

Tip "It was cold, but I was sitting against a wall facing south, so I could get some sun. First, I drew with pencil and pen, then colored onsite with pencils.

10.25" x 8.25" | 26 x 21 cm; pencil, colored pencils, Pilot DR 0.3 Pigment Ink Pen on Moleskine sketchbook; 20 minutes

" Mainly, I sketch because it gives me pleasure. The moment it turns boring, I will stop."

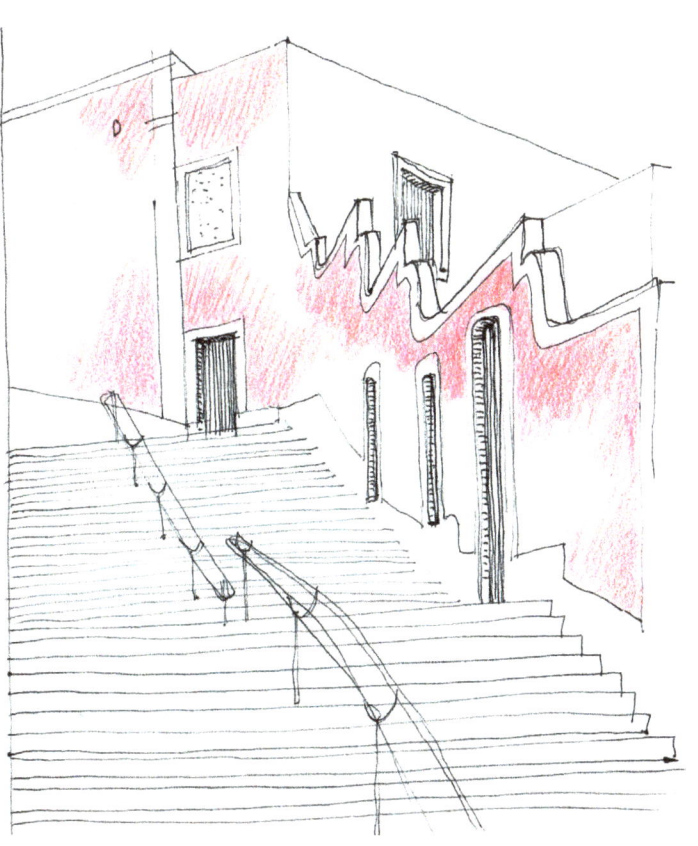

◔ **Escadinhas do Duque** This is why Lisbon will never be a bike-friendly town, says Cabral.

Tip "I was leaning against a wall on my left, and I decided not to draw any of it–just a line. I also forgot all the details, the people, the lettering, the textures, all the urban noise of the city. I was fascinated with the curved perspective of the pink wall and the stairs, which end where you cannot see."
– Pedro Cabral

6" x 8.25" | 15 x 21 cm; pencil, colored pencils, Parker Roller Ball pen, on 90-gsm Canson sketchbook; 15 minutes

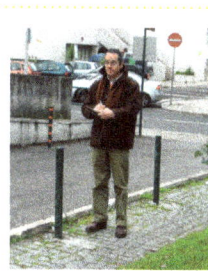

ARTIST PROFILE
Pedro Cabral
I do my best urban sketching when I visit a new place and get lost in the streets, exploring, discovering, just looking and drawing.

My urge to practice urban sketching grows out of the back and forth between "real" drawing and computer drawing, which I do as an architect. The more distant I am from old methods, the more I miss paper and pencils and all the related paraphernalia. I love sketching buildings, streets, and architectural details. Boats, nautical artifacts, and trees are also good themes. In Lisbon, I'm especially drawn to the relationship between old and new buildings, narrow streets that disappear from view before they end, and the mystery of narrow stairs that disappear after a corner.

BARCELONA

The colorful hues of the Mediterranean light blend with the magical forms of Gaudí's modernist architecture to captivate local and visiting artists who open their sketchbooks in Barcelona. From the narrow streets and Gothic cathedrals in the old town to modern architecture along the Diagonal Avenue, the second-largest city in Spain is as sketch-friendly as it gets.

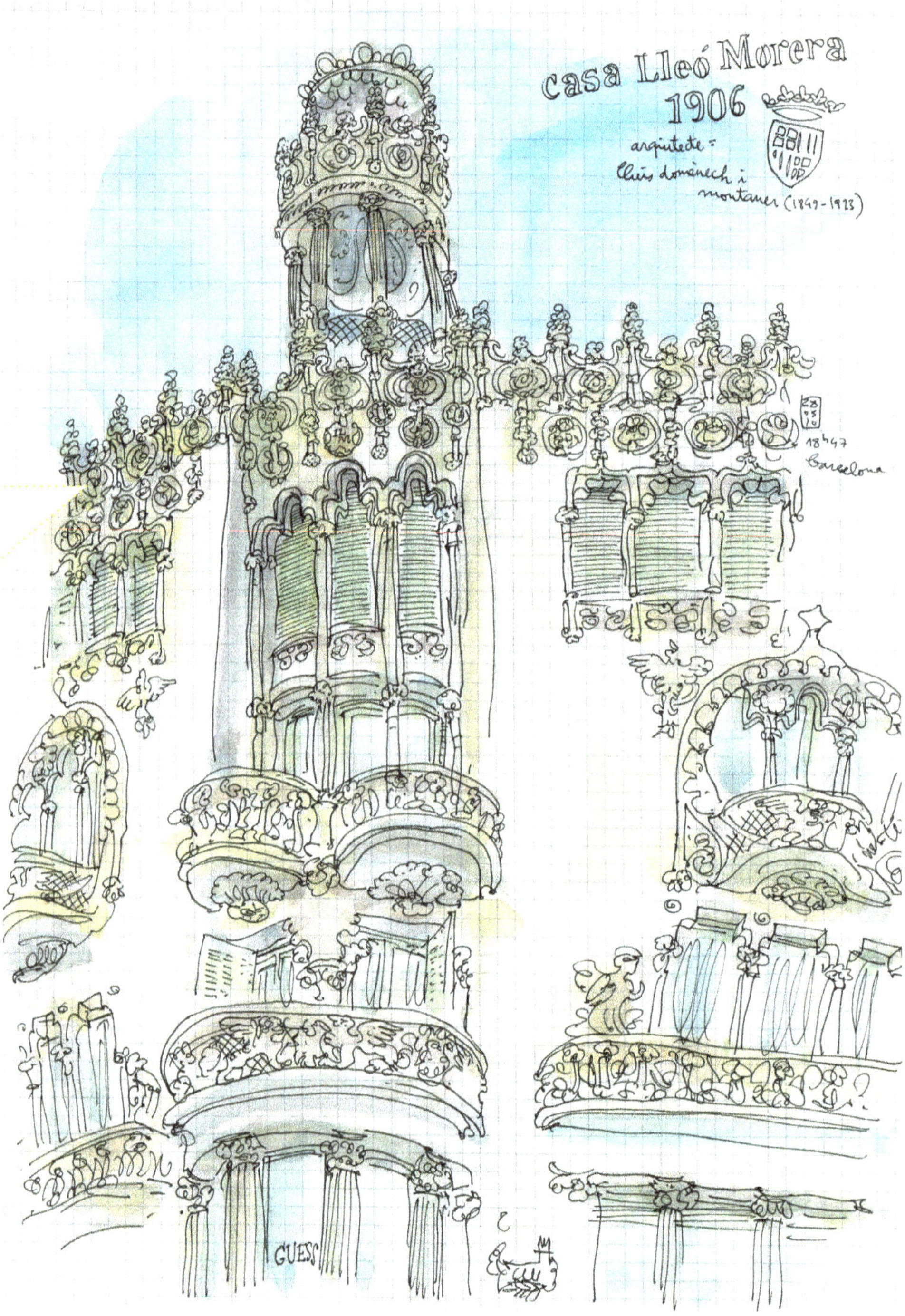

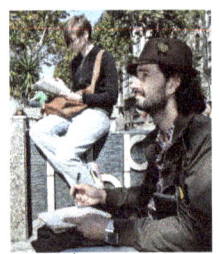

🎧 Barcelona-based French illustrator Lapin sketches Casa Lleó Morera, one of several modernist buildings along Barcelona's Passeig de Gràcia boulevard.

8.25" x 11.5" | 21 x 29 cm; 0.1-mm Mitsubishi uni PIN fine line pen, Daler-Rowney watercolors, Pentel waterbrush; 40 minutes

ARTIST PROFILE
Lapin

When I started working in a design agency, I felt bad that I did not draw anymore, spending days in front of a computer. I decided to start a notebook to sketch in the subway, to practice every day on my way to work. After nine years and more than 130 sketchbooks, I found my style. These fluid and vibrant lines are a transcription of my everyday life: an unpredictable collection of faces, an accumulation of objects, a projection of moments. I'm a diarist, drawing everyday things from life and creating a big library of images.

My favorite subjects in Barcelona are the modernist buildings, portraits, old vintage cars, people in the subway or in a restaurant, and a cup of tea.

casa Lleó Morera 1906
arquitecte = Lluis domènech i montaner (1849-1923)

"My memory is fixed in the pages of my sketchbooks."

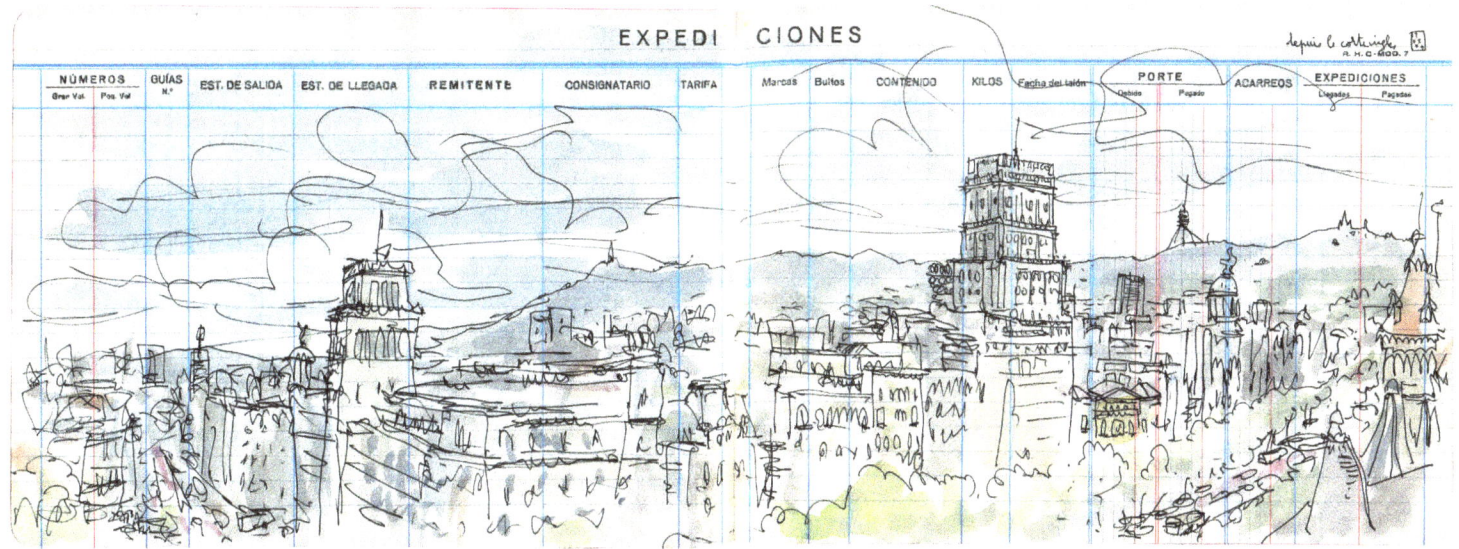

♫ Skyline from Plaça Catalunya Lapin likes to come to the cafeteria on the top floor of El Corte Inglés, a big department store on Plaza Catalunya for coffee, churros, and the panoramic view.

16.5" x 6" | 42 x 15 cm; 0.1-mm Mitsubishi uni PIN fine line pen, Daler-Rowney watercolors, Pentel waterbrush on vintage account book; 15 minutes

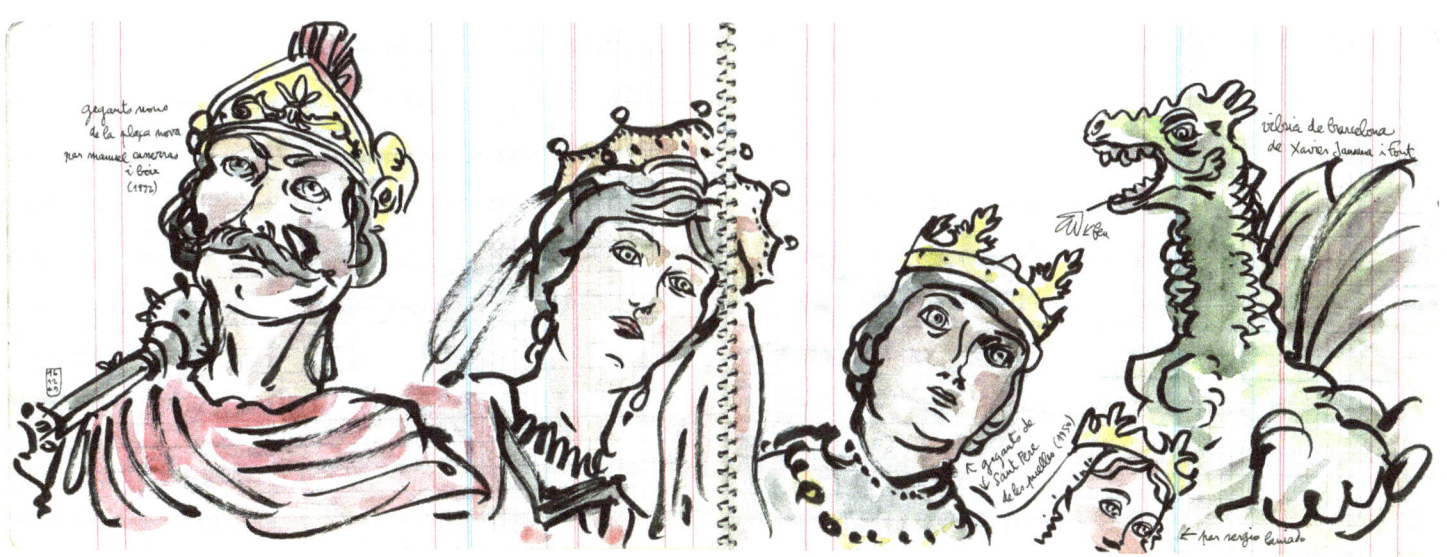

♫ The Giants of Barcelona The giants are a big institution in Spain; there seems to be no city festivity without giants walking and dancing in the streets, says Lapin. The tallest can be 13 to 16 feet (4–5 m) tall and are moved by one or several people hidden under the figures.

Tip "I'm still afraid to use different tools than my regular ones," Lapin says, "but I try to do it more often. It's a healthy way to reinvent your style and improve it. The brush pen is a lot faster than the ink pen; you have to be more synthetic and skip lots of details." — *Lapin*

16.5" x 6" | 42 x 15 cm; black MUJI brush pen, 0.1-mm Mitsubishi uni PIN fine line pen, Daler-Rowney watercolors, Pentel waterbrush on vintage account book; 10 minutes

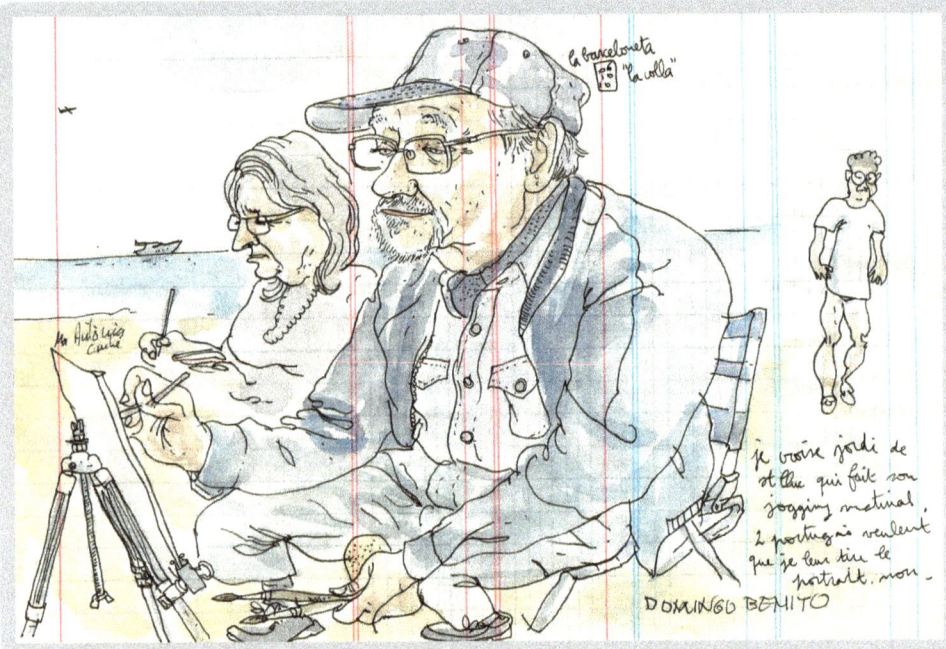

Arc de Triomf

This ornate arch is the centerpiece of an ample pedestrian boulevard in the heart of the city. It was built for the 1888 Universal Exhibition.

➲ "When I arrived in Barcelona, I remember it was the first place I visited as a tourist, because of the many comic book shops in the area. I have sketched this more than any other monument in the city. I consider myself a monochrome cartoonist, but I really enjoy playing with color—in this case, looking for the contrast of the red brick with the green environment."
— Sagar Fornies

3.5" x 11" | 9 x 28 cm; Schmincke watercolors and Pentel Aquash waterbrush on Moleskine pocket watercolor book; about 20 minutes

DRAWN TOGETHER

Sketching the Painters

by Lapin

La Colla Dels Dimecres (Wednesday's Gang) A group of watercolorists meets every Wednesday morning in a different part of Barcelona. When one of them invited me for the first time two years ago, I discovered a fantastic group of gifted painters sharing their passion for watercolor, for Barcelona, and for good food and beers after the work was done. Since that time, I try to visit them as often as possible. I have a lot to learn about conventional ways of painting with watercolor—and I am still amazed by how some of them catch the light in their paintings.

8.25" x 6" | 21 x 15 cm; 0.1-mm Mitsubishi uni PIN fine line pen, Daler-Rowney watercolors, Pentel waterbrush on vintage account book found in a Barcelona flea market; 20 minutes

➲ **Subway** Drawing on the city's clean and efficient Metro system is how Lapin started filling sketchbooks.

Tip "It's the best practice for me and all urban sketchers: very quick sketches done on the way to work every morning and on the way home every evening."
— *Lapin*

7" x 5.5" | 18 x 14 cm; 0.1-mm Mitsubishi uni PIN fine line pen on Moleskine A6 sketchbook; 3–5 minutes

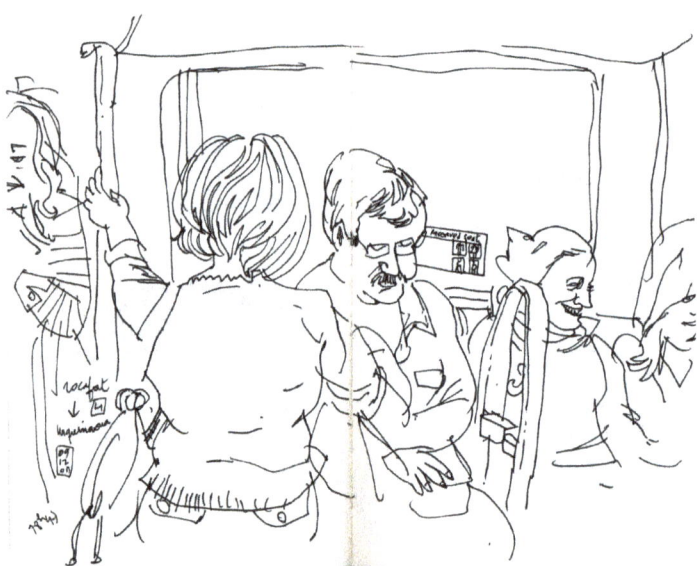

➲ "It's a challenge to sketch such an ornate building. I observed it many times before I dared to draw it. I started by drawing one little element with my ink pen, without any preparatory construction lines, and went from there." — *Lapin*

11.5" x 8.25" | 29 x 21 cm; 0.1-mm Mitsubishi uni PIN fine line pen, Daler-Rowney watercolors, Pentel waterbrush, acrylic paint for the sky, on vintage notebook; 1 hour

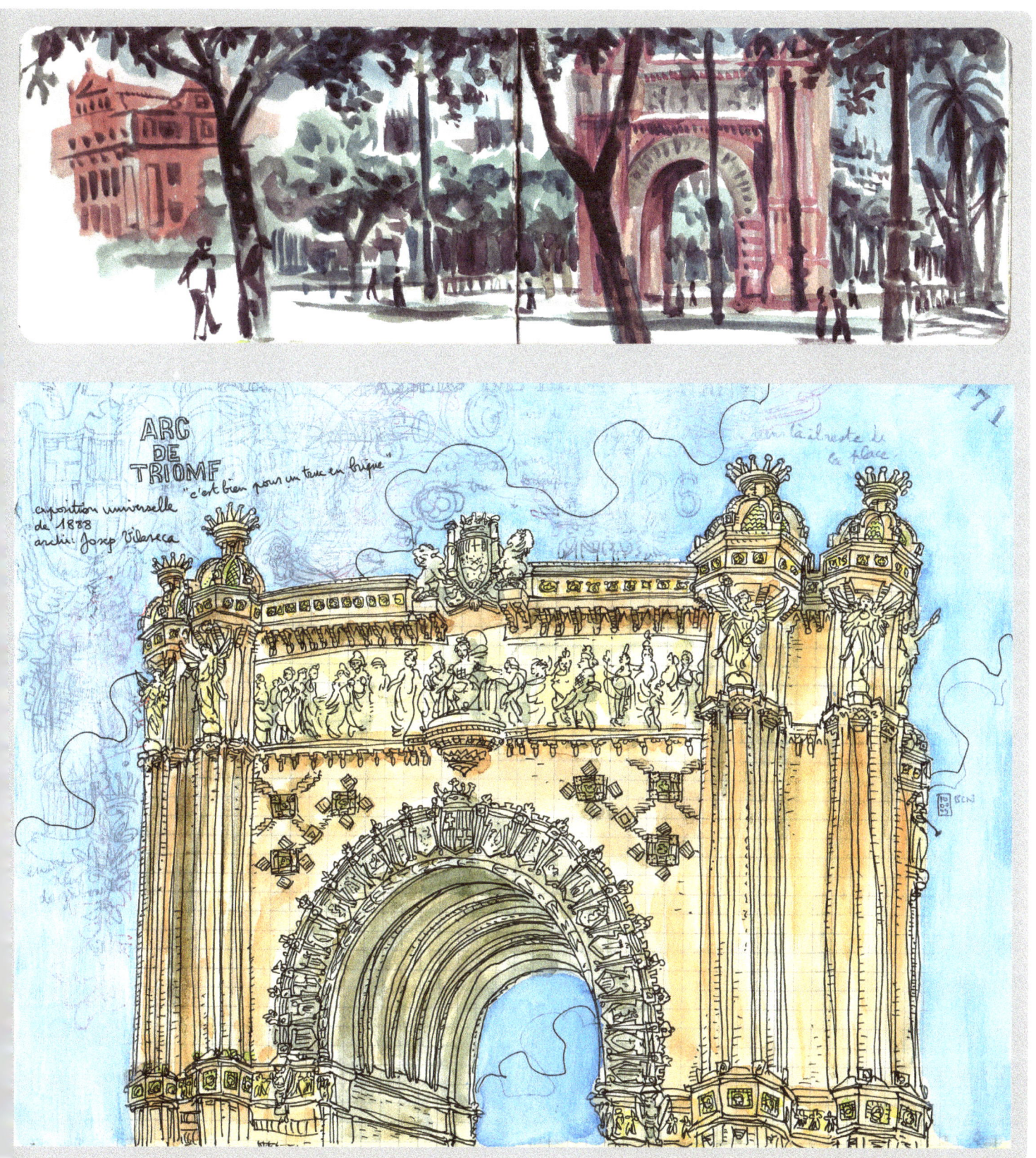

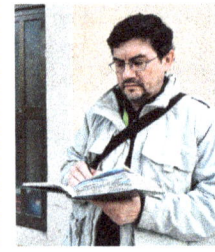

ARTIST PROFILE

Miguel Herranz

I always wanted to be an illustrator, but I detoured into graphic design. For more than twenty years, I killed the bug by sketching concepts for work, but it used to take me years to reach the last page of my sketchbook. Eventually, I became an illustrator but did not imagine that I would create everything directly on the computer with a tablet display. Drawing storyboards for commercials wasn't the same thing as drawing from life, so I started using my sketchbook more and more, especially after finding other people on the Internet with a similar interest.

Barcelona has the colorful Mediterranean liveliness, lots of history, and culture. Everything here has a drawing inside that I try to get out.

🎧 Barcelona-based illustrator Miguel Herranz sketches an ombú tree at Plaça de Prim.

Double A4 (8.3" x 11.7" | 210 x 297 mm); Pilot 78G fountain pen, Noodler's ink, liquid watercolor; 20 minutes

"The sketchbook is a door to escape to the world and from the world, to go back and look inside."

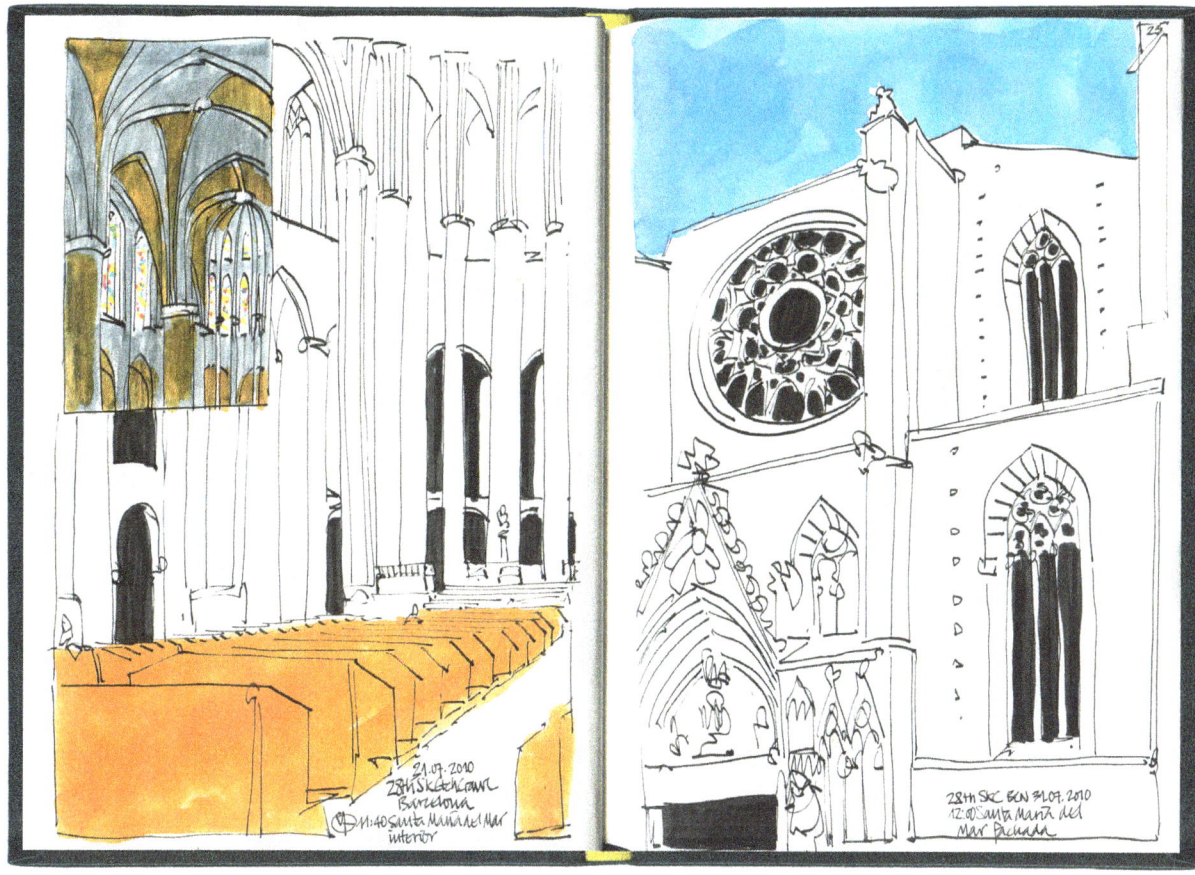

⊃ Santa María del Mar On the left side, Miguel Herranz tried to capture two of the main characteristics of this church: the solid lightness of the structure and the light entering from outside. "The right side tries to describe the façade, mainly the volumes rather than the details," he says.

A5 sketchbook (8.3" x 5.8" | 210 x 148 mm); Pilot 78G fountain pen with a calligraphic nib, Noodler's Bulletproof Black ink, Kuretake waterbrush loaded with liquid watercolor on Modir sketchbook by Ruggeri; 25 minutes each page

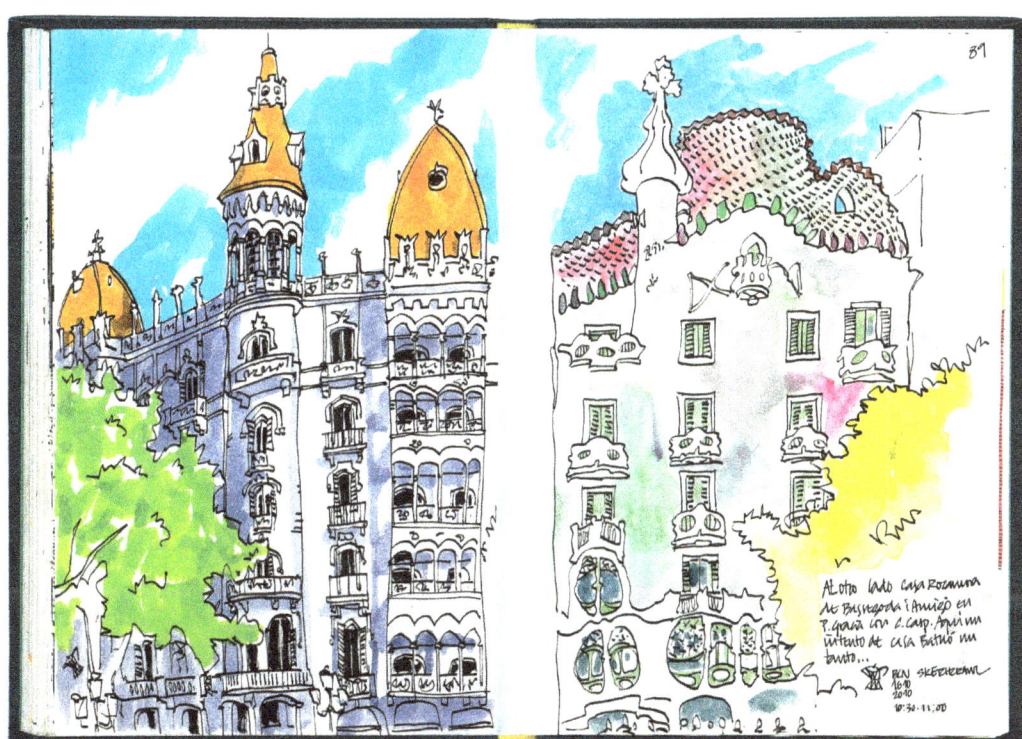

⊃ Two Houses in Passeig de Gràcia On the left page is the Rocamora House by Bassegoda i Amigò; on the right is the famous Batlló House by Antoni Gaudí. "I often see buildings as if they were sculptures," Herranz says.

Tip "I always do all the linework from life. The only postproduction I allow myself is coloring (when I can't do it from life) and writing." — *Miguel Herranz*

A5 sketchbook (8.3" x 5.8" | 21 x 14.8 cm); Pilot 78G fountain pen with a calligraphic nib, Noodler's Bulletproof Black ink, Kuretake waterbrush loaded with liquid watercolor on Modir sketchbook by Ruggeri; (left page) 45 minutes, (right page) 30 minutes

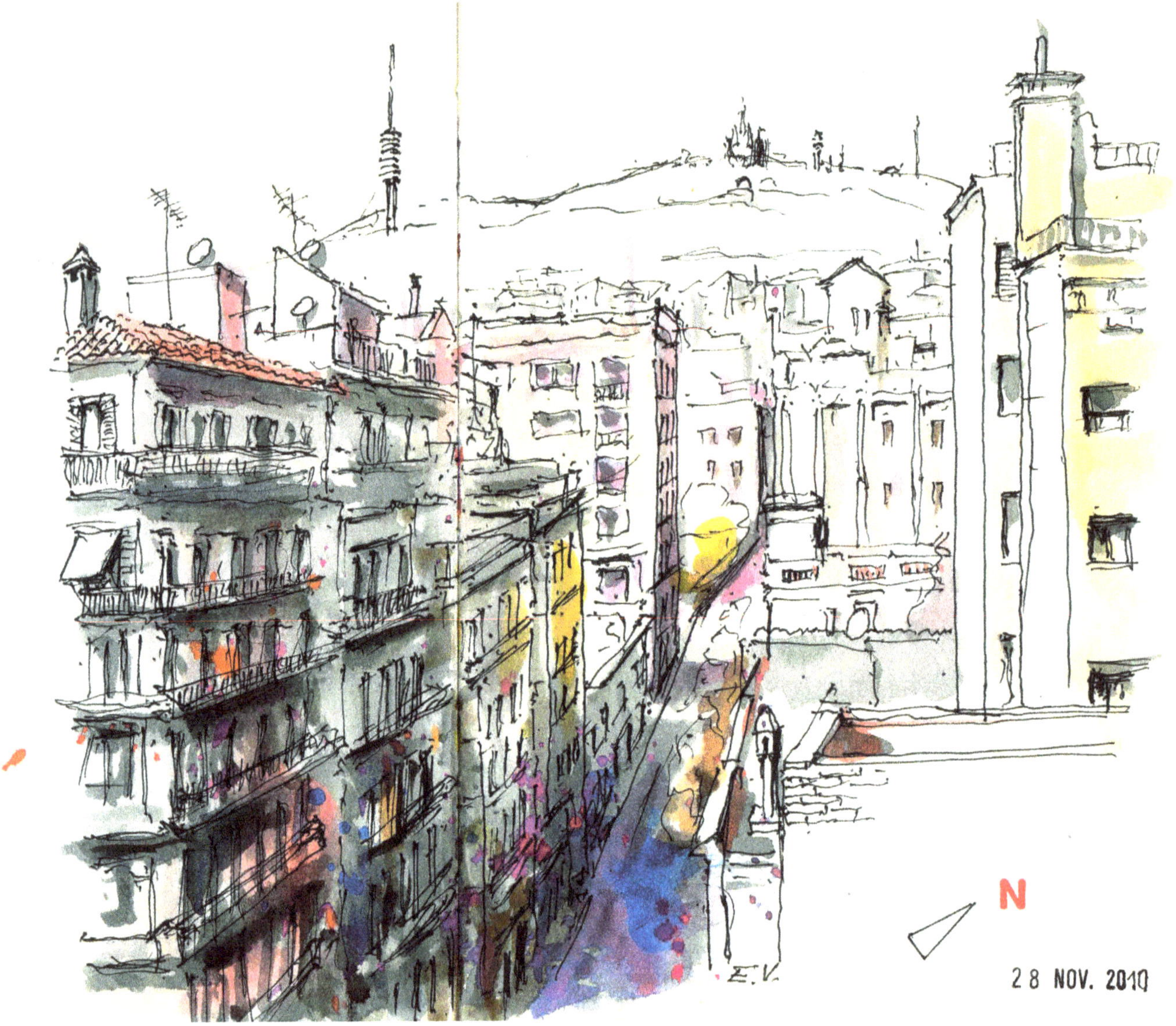

N

28 NOV. 2010

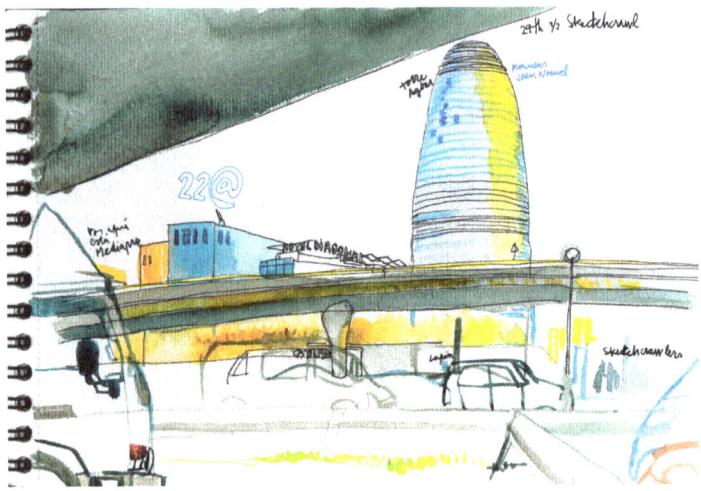

⌒ Tibidabo Mountain Eduardo Vicente sketched this view of the Sacred Heart of Jesus church and Norman Foster-designed telecommunication tower from his living room in the San Gervasio neighborhood.

6" x 8.25" | 15 x 21 cm; Uni PIN drawing pen (black, 0.2) and washes with colored India ink on Hahnemühle sketchbook; about 1 hour

⌒ 22@ District Swasky says that, although the main subject of this sketch is the Agbar Tower, designed by Jean Nouvel, he likes to keep his drawings organic and without framing. "Afterwards, I find treasures or little details I love, such as the watercolor truck on the left," he says.

Tip "Lately, I'm mixing ballpoint and watercolor lines; from my point of view, it's like working with layers. Depending on what I want to highlight, I'll draw using ballpoint (black line) or watercolor (more subtle)." — *Víctor Martínez Escámez (a.k.a. Swasky)*

11.75" x 8.25" | 30 x 21 cm; black and blue Uni-ball ballpoint pens and Winsor & Newton watercolor field box on Canson mixed-media paper; 20 minutes

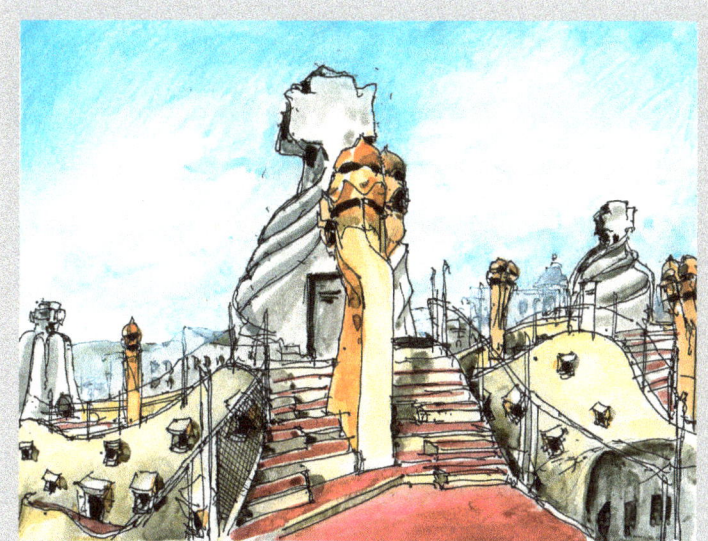

VIEW POINTS

Casa Milà's Roof

🎧 "I visited Antoni Gaudí's Casa Milà (also known as La Pedrera) in July. It was really hot up there, but it was impossible for me not to sketch such an amazing place as this top floor. Concrete waves were all around, chimneys hidden one behind another. I particularly love this point of view, with both patios in sight, surrounded by these twisted white volumes, crowned with a cross. I remember the light blue sky; the luminosity was so intense that the background seemed to be melting into the white horizon." — *Edgardo Minond*

9.5" x 8" | 24 x 20 cm; ballpoint black gel ink, Pébéo ink, and acrylic, on Schoeller 250-gsm watercolor paper; 40 minutes, plus 2 hours at studio

➲ "The roof of La Pedrera really blew me away. Apart from the substructure of brick arches, which creates a fascinating series of attic spaces, the culmination of the building (it hardly seems adequate to just call it a "roof") is a crazy, elevated, rollercoaster landscape with gaping holes, like volcanoes, dropping into the courtyards, twisting marshmallow stair towers covered in white tile fragments, and chimneys that rise like little groups of medieval warriors. I spent far more time up there than I had anticipated, because I simply didn't want to go anywhere else. The views of the Barcelona skyline were tremendous, the breezes were wonderful, and there was even a little music playing, as they were setting up for what must have been an incredible and elegant party." — *Matthew Brehm*

5" x 8" | 12.5 x 20 cm; Copic Multiliner Sepia, M. Graham watercolors, #6 round Connoisseur Kolinsky sable brush, Moleskine watercolor book; 30 minutes

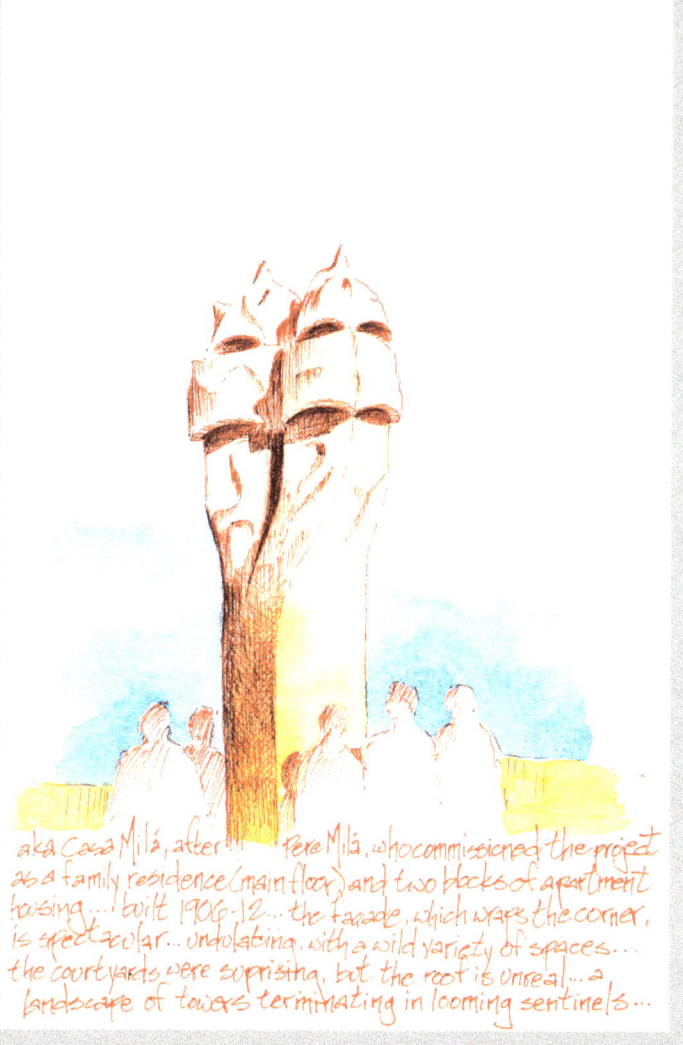

La Pedrera, Barcelona ———————— 7.2.09

aka Casa Milà, after Pere Milà, who commissioned the project as a family residence (main floor) and two blocks of apartment housing... built 1906-12... the facade, which wraps the corner, is spectacular... undulating, with a wild variety of spaces... the courtyards were surprising, but the roof is unreal... a landscape of towers terminating in looming sentinels...

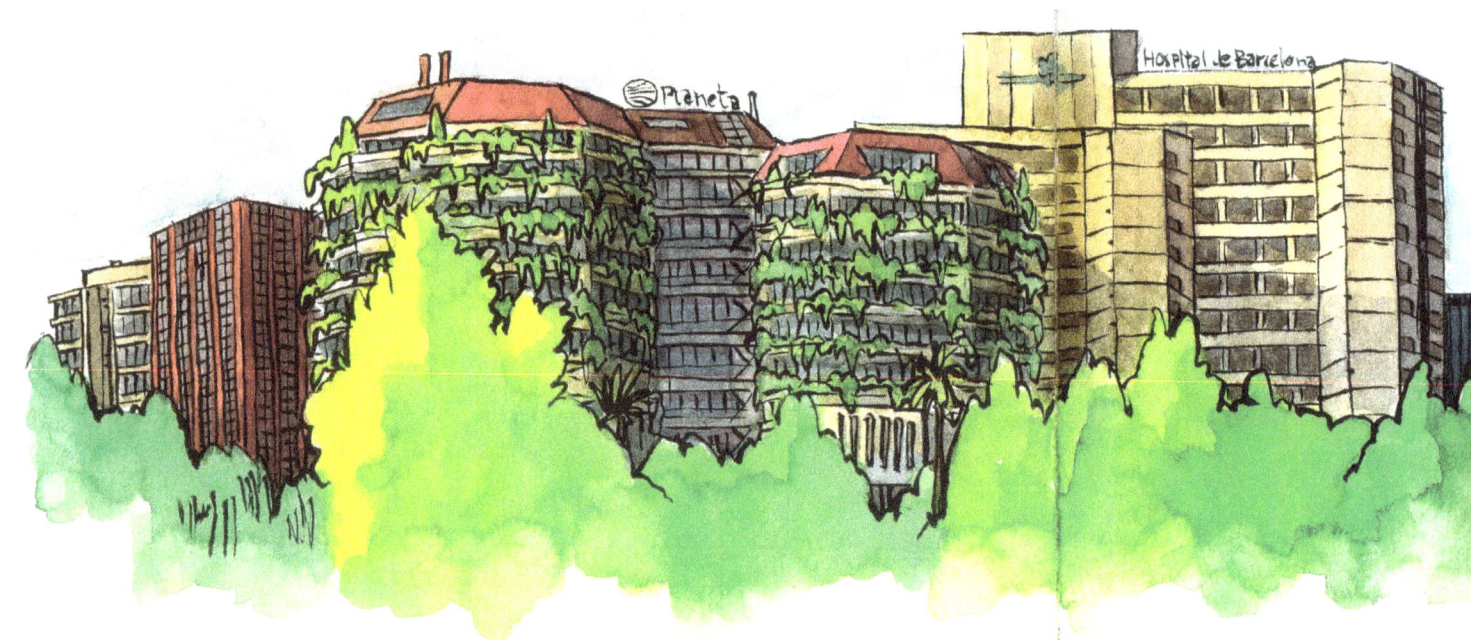

ᐱ Diagonal Avenue César Caballud sketched the buildings of Plaza Maria Cristina from afar. "That square has a hospital, a bank's central offices, and a building that has always called my attention for having loads of plants hanging from its balconies."

Tip "It was a bit of a challenge for me to draw a cityscape, because I usually draw people. But trying to draw subjects you wouldn't usually capture is a good way to learn new things and improve your skills." — *César Caballud*

8.25" x 10" | 21 x 25 cm; MUJI calligraphy brush pen and Schmincke watercolor metal box set of 12 half pans on Moleskine large watercolor book; about 2 hours

ᐱ Panoramic View The blue of the Mediterranean shows in the distance in this sketch from the hills along the northwestern edge of the city. Medieval castles inspired Gaudí to design La Casa Bellesguard, seen in the center of the image. The vertical shape and cross at the top have his signature style.

Tip "The secret is that when wet with water, the ink that washes away gives a shaded effect." — *Jose María Larrañaga*

16.25" x 5.25" | 41.5 x 13 cm; loaded fountain pen ink cartridge (ink is diluted by contact with water) on Moleskine sketchbook with paper that supports watercolor and washes; 30 minutes

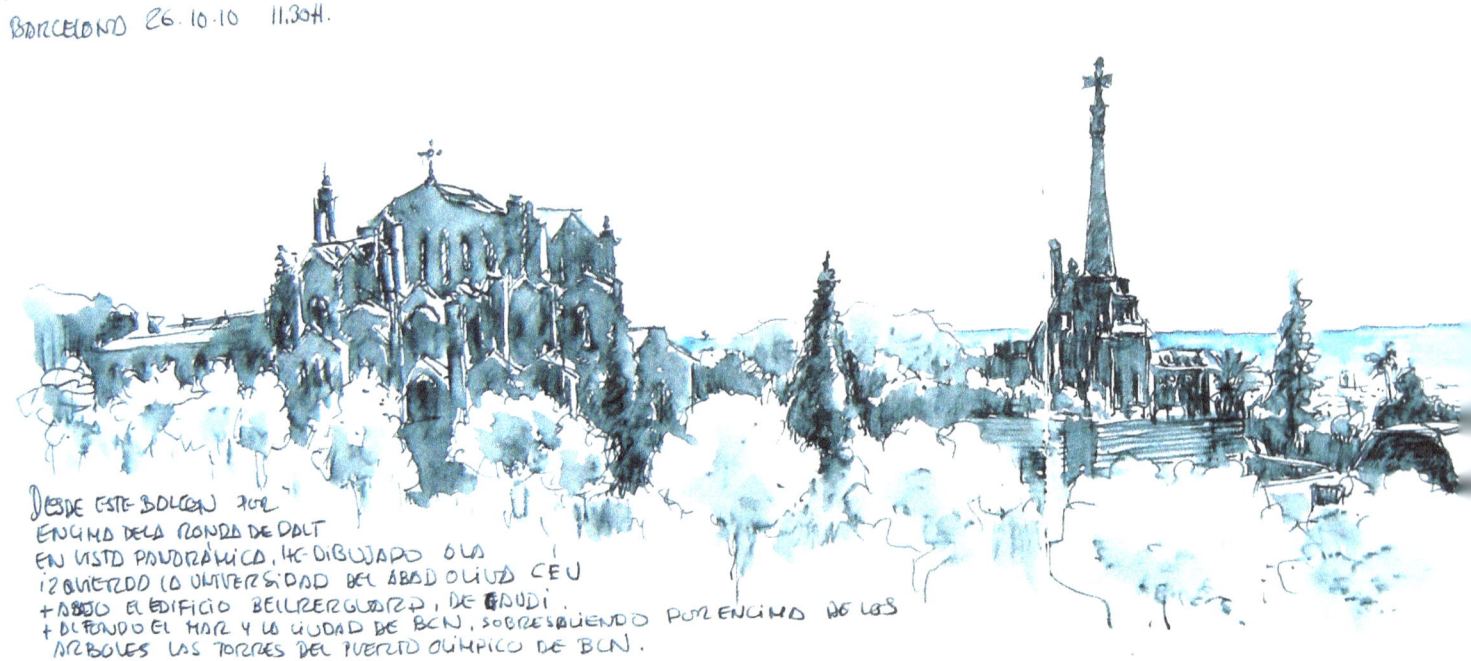

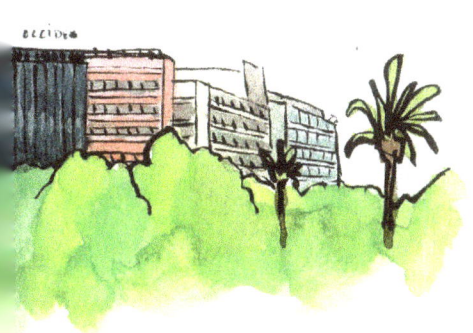

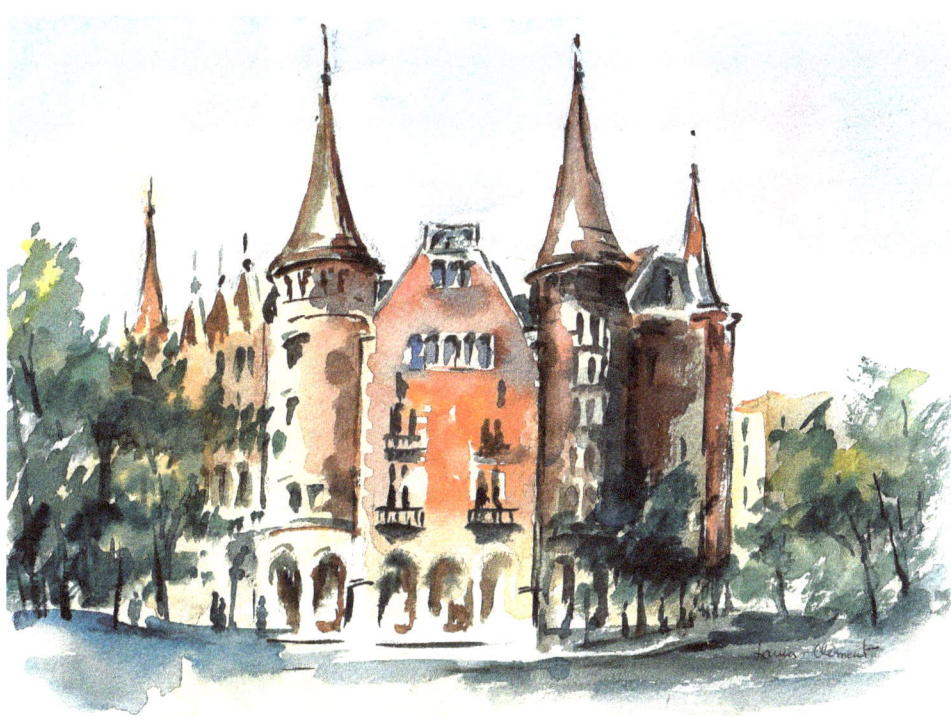

⋒ Casa de les Punxes This apartment-office building, one of the most emblematic of Barcelona, is located on the Diagonal Avenue. Translated from Catalan, its name means "House of Spikes."

Tip "Avoid overloading the picture with too much detail—it will lose naturalness." — *Laura Climent*

11.75" x 8.25" | 30 x 21 cm; Canson paper, Rembrandt brushes (#8 and #2) and watercolors; colors are cobalt blue, Naples yellow, yellow ocher, yellow-orange, burnt sienna, Hooker green, and Payne's Gray--all in a little box from Winsor & Newton that fits in any bag; about 1 hour

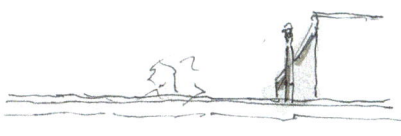

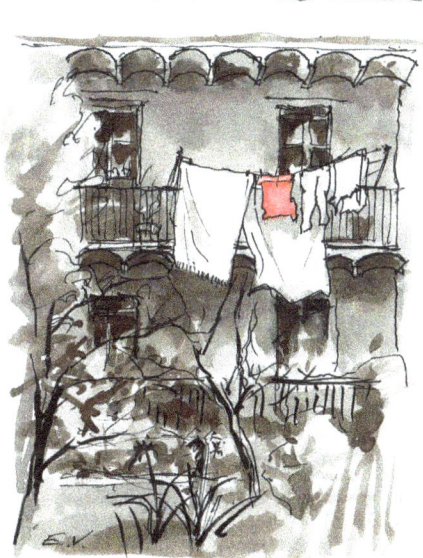

Jardins Portolá - Putxet

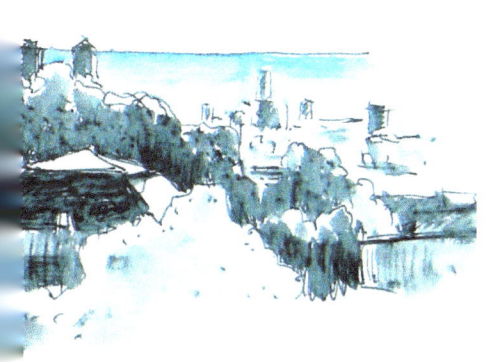

☾ Jardines de Portolá Struck by the red shirt between the white sheets, Eduardo Vicente sat on a low wall within the gardens of Portolá with the aim of capturing the simplicity of the scene.

6" x 9" | 15 x 23 cm; Sailor calligraphy pen and sepia wash with watercolor pencil, Montebello, Lefranc & Bourgeois sketchbook; about 45 minutes

BLOIS

Built on a hillside along the river Loire, the French town of Blois is a complex city of sinuous streets. According to local sketcher Guillaume Bonamy, the contrast in the size and height of its buildings and its green public parks make Blois a visual maze, in which the concept of distance and perspective is hard to grasp.

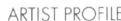

ARTIST PROFILE
Guillaume Bonamy

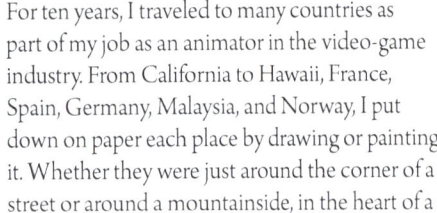

For ten years, I traveled to many countries as part of my job as an animator in the video-game industry. From California to Hawaii, France, Spain, Germany, Malaysia, and Norway, I put down on paper each place by drawing or painting it. Whether they were just around the corner of a street or around a mountainside, in the heart of a forest or in the bowels of a casino, I took note of those moments.

Now back in my country, sketching Blois has developed my passion and curiosity for its history. Each sketch brings new questions.

"Drawing has opened a door to a world where everyday life is synonymous with beauty and poetry."

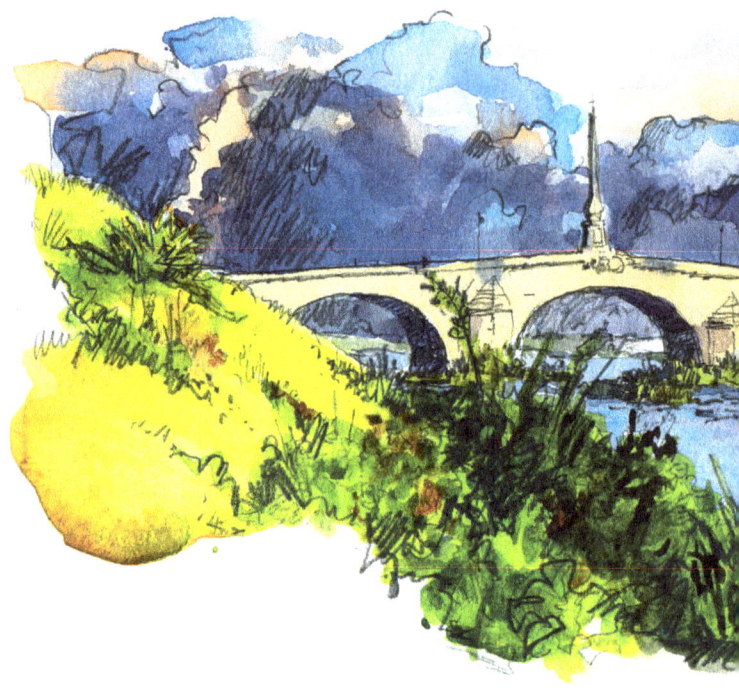

۝ Saint-Nicholas Church Bonamy enjoys sketching the Jacques Gabriel Bridge, which harmoniously unites the two riverbanks of the city. In this panoramic view, the changing light creates a silhouette of the city that's always different.

Tip "A few touches of color allowed me to highlight and clarify some of the buildings and their silhouettes." — *Guillaume Bonamy*

15.5" x 5.25" | 39.5 x 13 cm; watercolor over pencil drawing on Moleskine watercolor book; about 2 hours

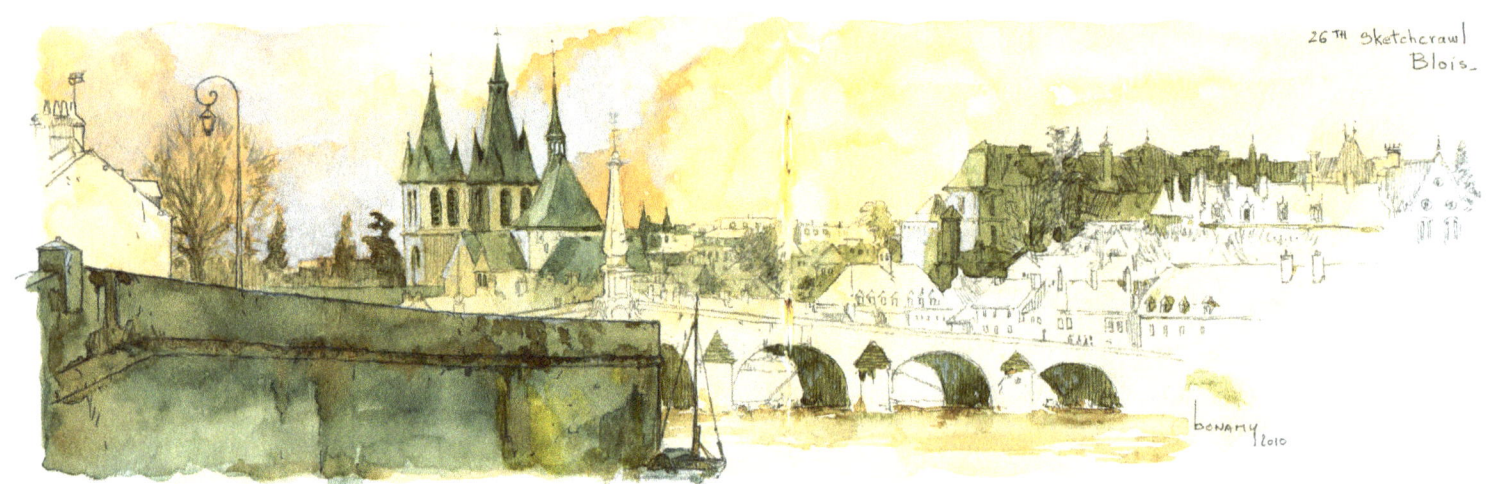

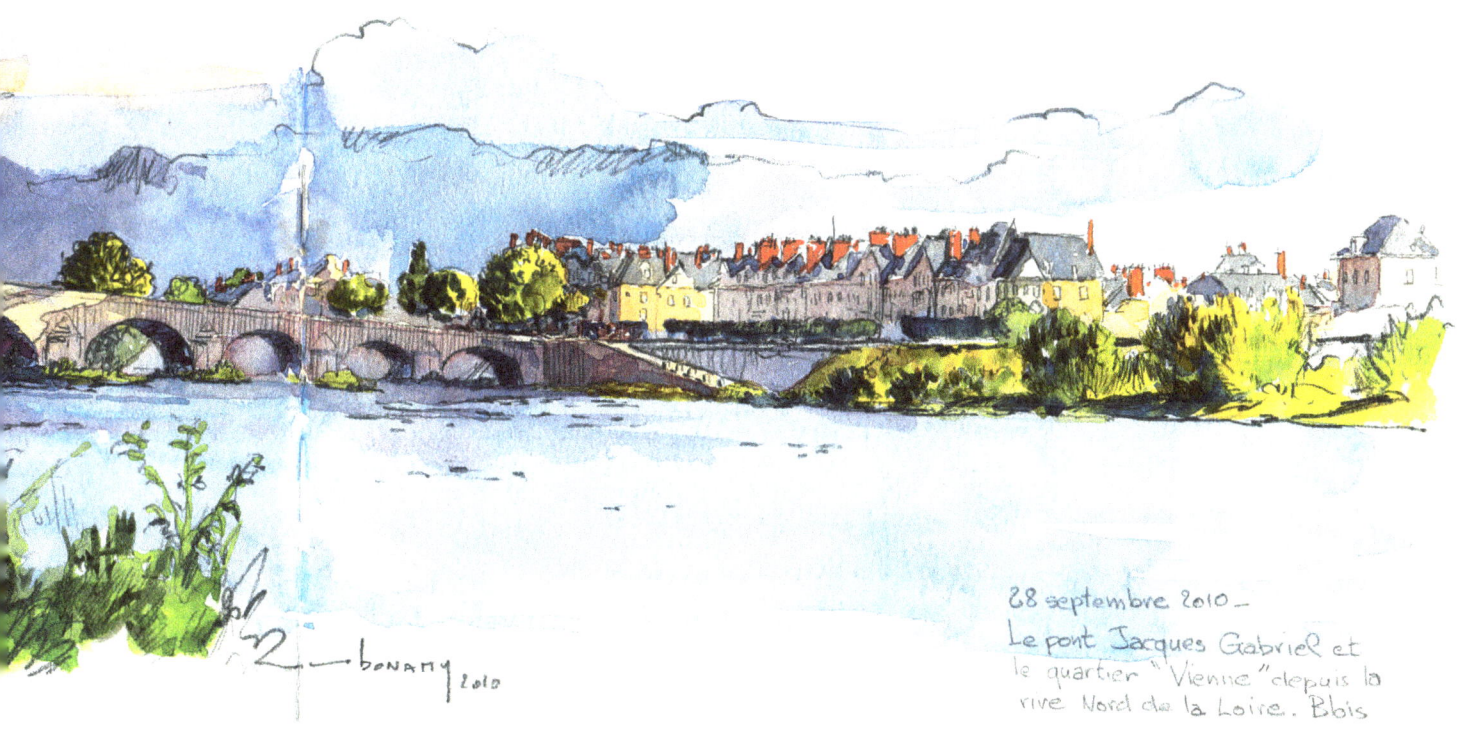

28 septembre 2010 –
Le pont Jacques Gabriel et
le quartier "Vienne" depuis la
rive Nord de la Loire. Blois

♉ Bar de l'agriculture Bonamy captured these two preoccupied characters—one a "regular" who always chose the same spot—while drinking an espresso.

Tip "Here, a few bottles are enough to re-create the atmosphere of the small café without developing a complex background." — *Guillaume Bonamy*

8.25" x 5.25" | 21 x 13 cm; pencil drawing on Moleskine Cahier notebook; 20 minutes

♎ From the Loire River Few people were around when Bonamy sketched this pastoral scene, apart from suspicious fishermen. "I guess I was occupying a good spot for fishing!" Bonamy says. "One of them came to speak to me for thirty minutes and told me the history of this bridge."

Tip "The view I chose allowed me to position the city as a final point of interest in the composition." — *Guillaume Bonamy*

16.25" x 5" | 41.5 x 12.5 cm; 2B pencil drawing and Winsor & Newton watercolors on Moleskine watercolor book; about 2 hours

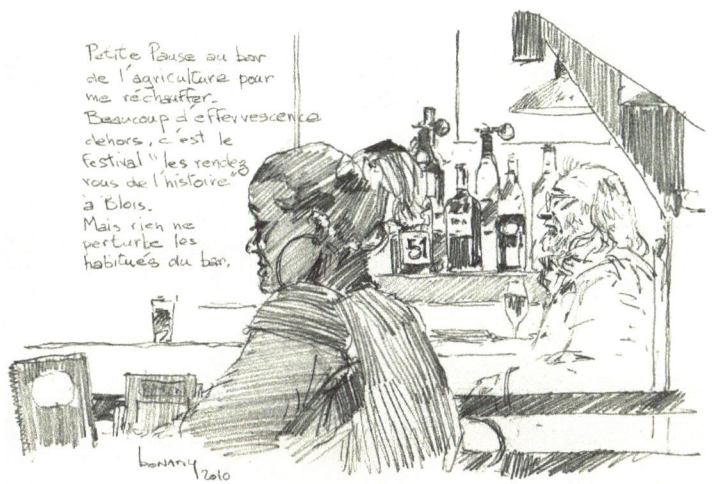

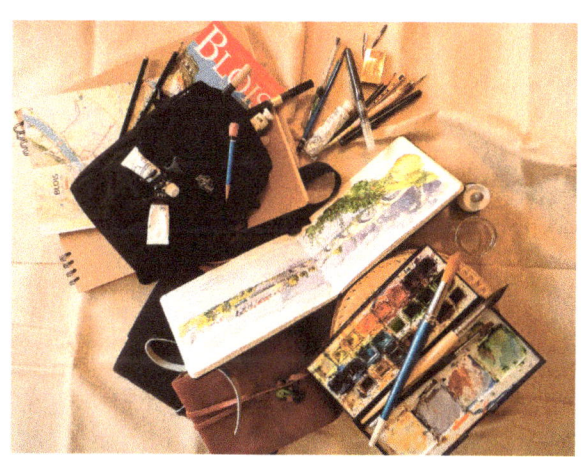

♎ Bonamy's sketching tools and sketchbooks

RENNES

The French city of Rennes is a university town, with picturesque places such as Place Sainte-Anne, with its cheerful cafés, boutiques, narrow cobbled streets, and brightly painted, ancient houses. Local artist Caroline Johnson enjoys drawing everything, from the medieval half-timbered buildings to the vast retail parks and housing projects.

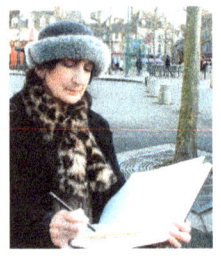

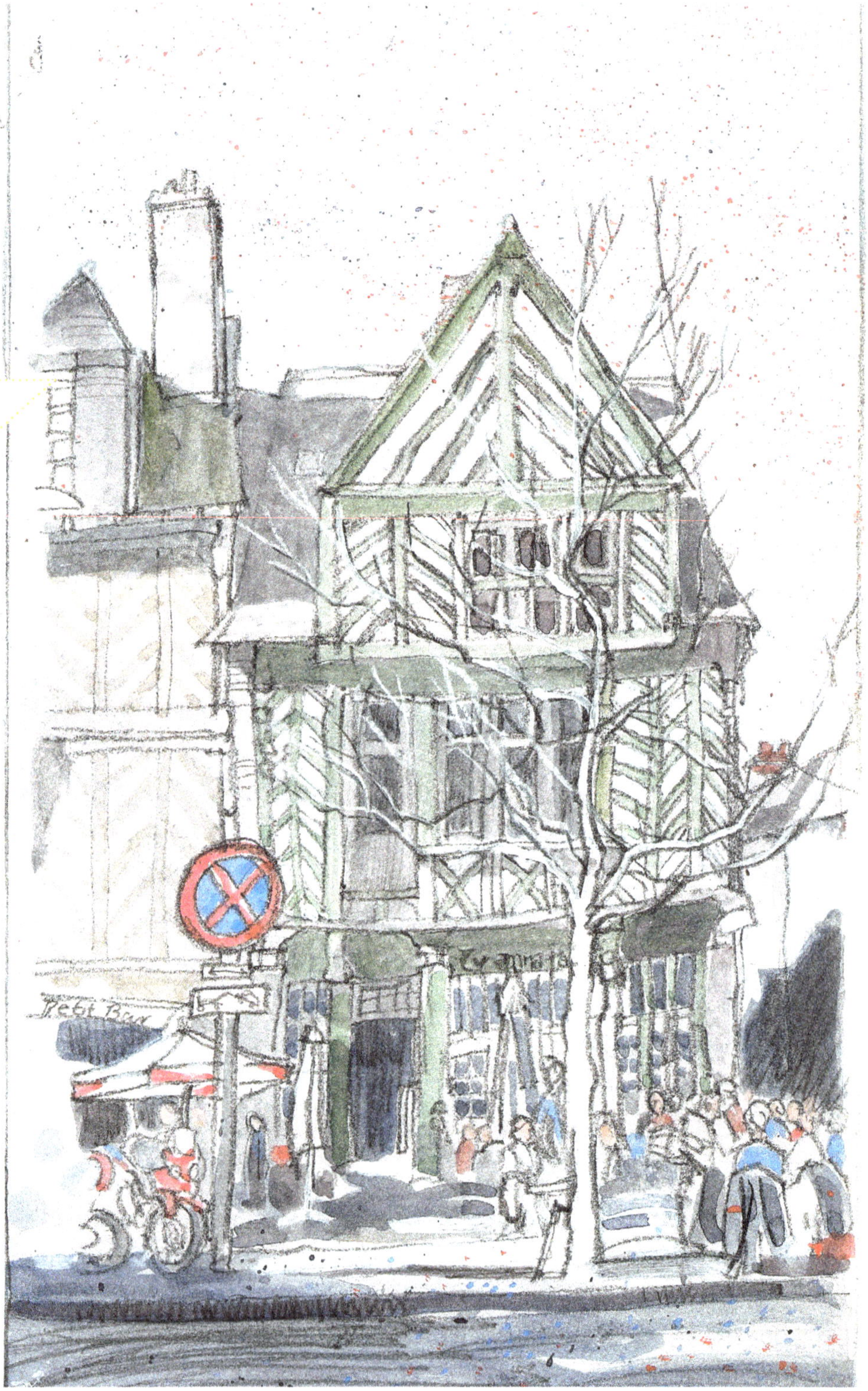

⌐ Johnsons sketches the Ty Anna Tavern in Place Sainte-Anne.

11.75" x 8.25" | 30 x 21 cm; Ivory Black Derwent drawing pencil, Winsor & Newton watercolors and linel gouache; 1.25 hours

ARTIST PROFILE
Caroline Johnson

I'm a tutor for painting and drawing workshops, in which I strongly encourage the use of sketchbooks. I'm drawn to the urban and the architectural and the people who inhabit these places, who are often quite unaware of their surroundings.

As an artist, I feel it's up to us to reveal the beauty of the mediocre and the overlooked. It's a challenge to show the charms of the urban, but there's a sense of urgency about drawing on location that's almost impossible to reproduce in the studio; one is less complacent and less in control, and that can only be good for the artist.

"Drawing on location produces lively work that is open to the accidental. Smudges, raindrops, coffee stains . . . all have to be welcomed."

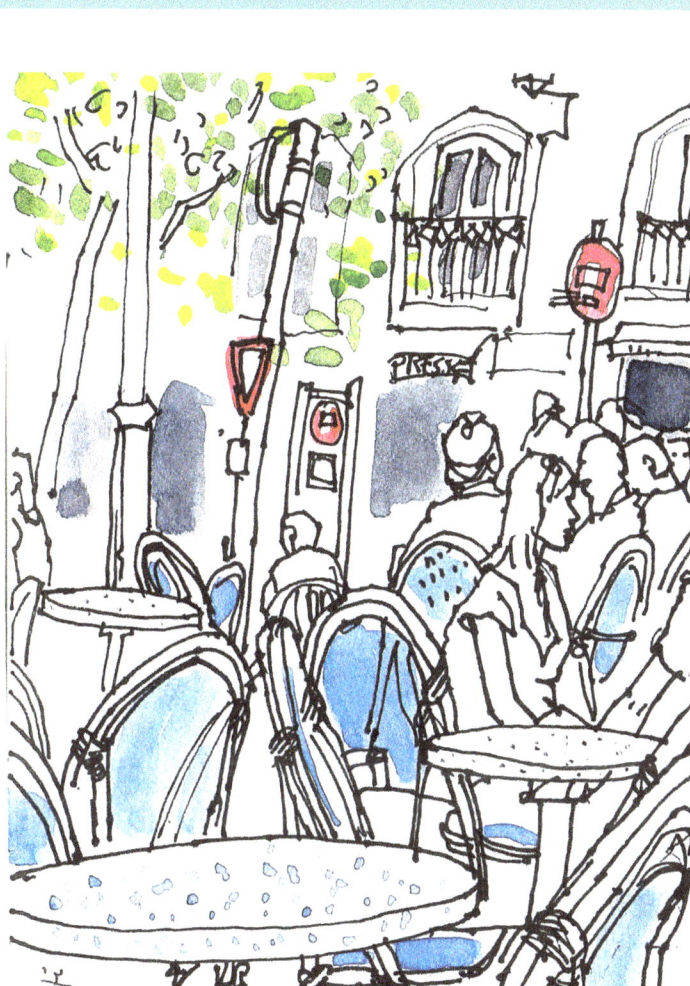

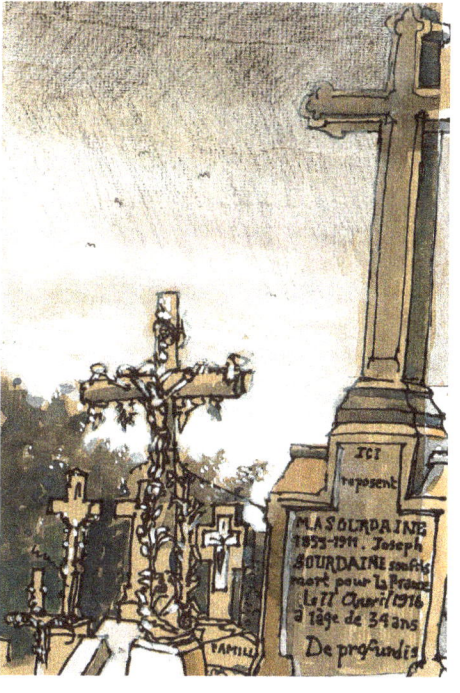

⊂ The Cemetery It started to rain just as Johnson settled under a huge, dark yew tree in the corner. "Here, I'm obliged to draw pretty much what's in front of me, so I go for what I think could be a dramatic composition," Johnson says.

Tip "Any unusual subject matter means new challenges for the artist and, from these, new abilities."
— *Caroline Johnson*

8" x 5.5" | 20 x 14 cm; Pilot drawing pen, Winsor & Newton black watercolor, Conté crayon and white gouache, various acrylic brushes, on Canson paper; 45 minutes

⊂ Outside the Ty Anna Tavern, Summer
Rennes is the capital of Brittany, and on Saturday afternoons, the cafés in the Place Sainte-Anne are buzzing with shoppers sipping drinks in the late-summer sunshine.

Tip "Sit in the shade and wear sunglasses or the white page is too bright!" — *Caroline Johnson*

6" x 4" | 15 x 10 cm; dip pen, Chinese ink, Winsor & Newton watercolors, Raphaël Petit Gris Pur brush, on WH Smith A6 sketchbook; 30 minutes

⊂ Butane Bottles at Ecomarché These colorful butane bottles are piled by the supermarket garage; there's no "town gas" in the area, and many folks rely on butane for cooking.

Tip "There are many subjects which, on first glimpse, are ugly and mundane, but inspiration can be found everywhere, if only we stop and look."
— *Caroline Johnson*

8" x 5.5" | 20 x 14 cm; Pilot drawing pen, Winsor & Newton watercolors, Raphaël Petit Gris Pur brush on Moulin du Coq sketchbook; 40 minutes

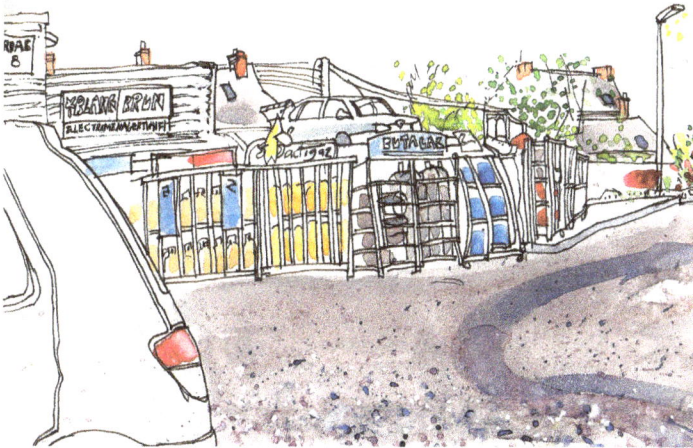

PARIS

Visitors come to sketch the Notre Dame cathedral by the river Seine, but for local architect Martin Etienne, sketching a view of the city skyline through his window can be just as fulfilling an experience. American artist Laura Frankstone's dream of sketching in Paris has come true several times. She's especially fond of drawing the play of water in the romantic city's majestic fountains.

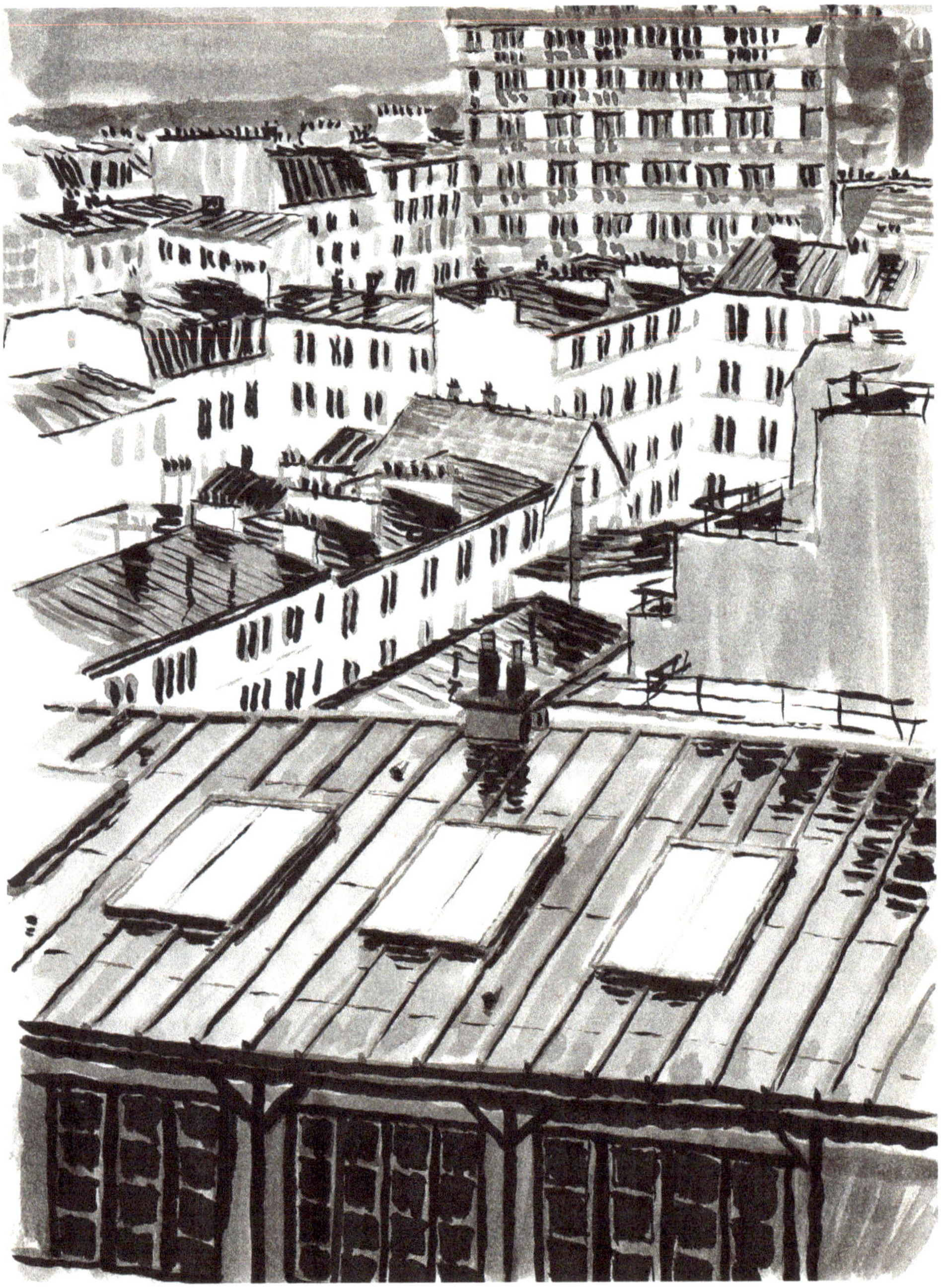

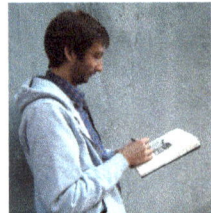

ARTIST PROFILE
Martin Etienne

I'm neither an explorer nor a traveler searching for something new all the time. I'm just a guy who loves to take advantage of his free time to draw. I like to draw everyday things, because I think if you look hard enough, you can find a source of daydreaming in the very simple things that are right in front of your eyes.

I don't know if I have a favorite subject to draw. But I can say that I have favorite moments to draw, so they determine the subjects. I like to sketch when I'm in quiet places and when I'm alone. Most of my sketchbooks represent people traveling on trains, people in restaurants or bars, and people reading in gardens; when I stay at home, I love to draw the view from my window.

" Sketching can transform moments of boredom or waiting times and make them pleasant."

↻ **On a Rainy Day** Martin Etienne says the weather on this day was too ugly to go outside. "So this is the view from my apartment on a rainy day: wet zinc roofs," he says.

Tip "It's easier to catch the light on an object or a face if you sketch in monochrome, because you don't have to think about the color of the subject and you can concentrate on the brightness or darkness of its different parts." — *Martin Etienne*

10" x 7.25" | 25 x 18.5 cm; black Pentel brush pen with ink cartridge and India ink diluted with water for the gray parts on Moleskine notebook; about 30 minutes

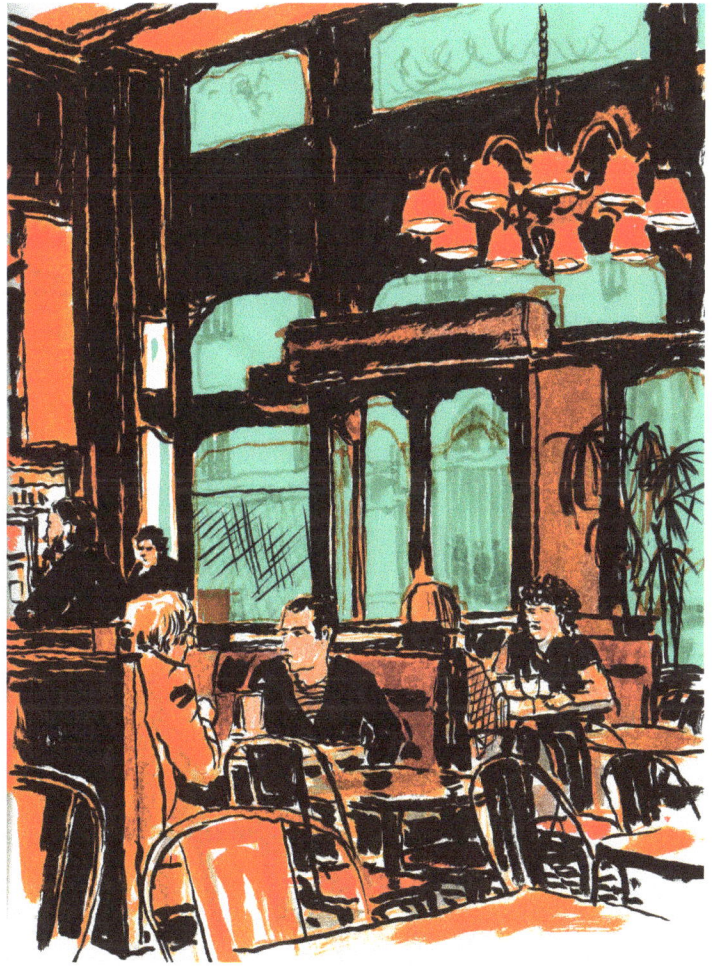

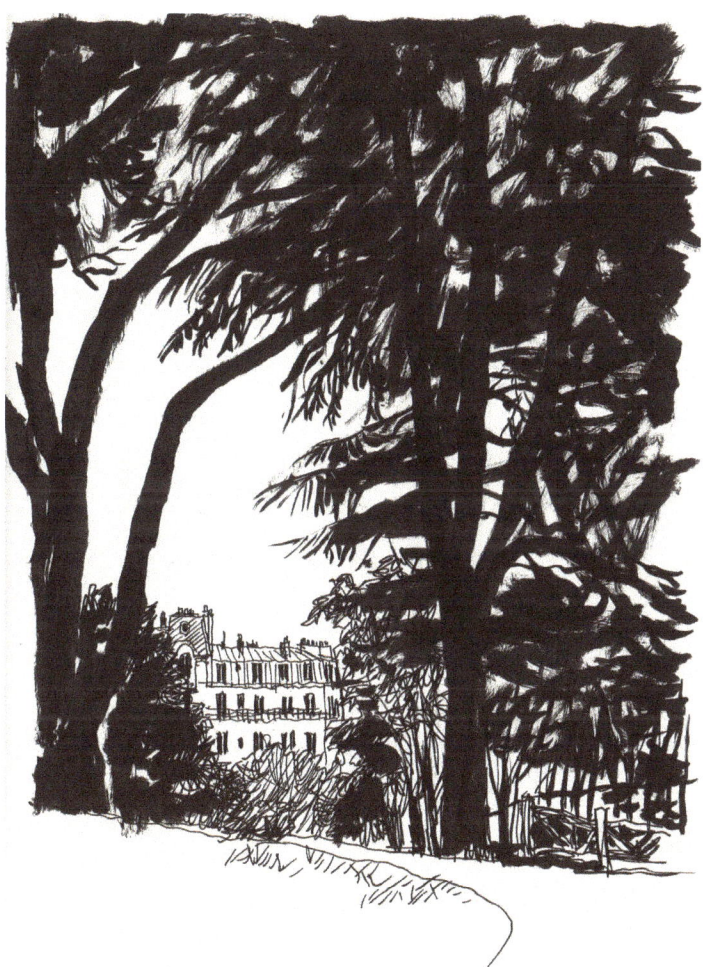

⋂ **Le Café Charbon** Etienne drinks a coffee every day at this café and restaurant near his home.

Tip "I started this drawing directly with the brush pens. I don't like to make construction lines with pencil beforehand, because after, I feel like I'm just coloring. So sometimes the drawing is not so good, and with the brushes, you can't erase, but it doesn't matter. You have to find solutions to minimize the drawing's mistakes. At the end, it's always a surprise." — *Martin Etienne*

10" x 7.25" | 25 x 18.5 cm; Pentel brush pen with ink cartridge on Moleskine Cahier notebook; about 30 minutes

⋂ **Le Parc des Buttes Chaumont** A typical Haussmann building seen from the Parc des Buttes Chaumont in the 19th arrondissement.

Tip "Using the brush pen is, for me, the best and easiest way to draw trees. The question when I want to represent a tree is always the same: I can't draw all the leaves of the tree, and I don't want to do just a contour line of the foliage. So I think the brush is a good way to represent the thickness and the lightness of the foliage at the same time." — *Martin Etienne*

10" x 7.25" | 25 x 18.5 cm; Pentel brush pen with ink cartridge on Moleskine Cahier notebook; about 15 minutes

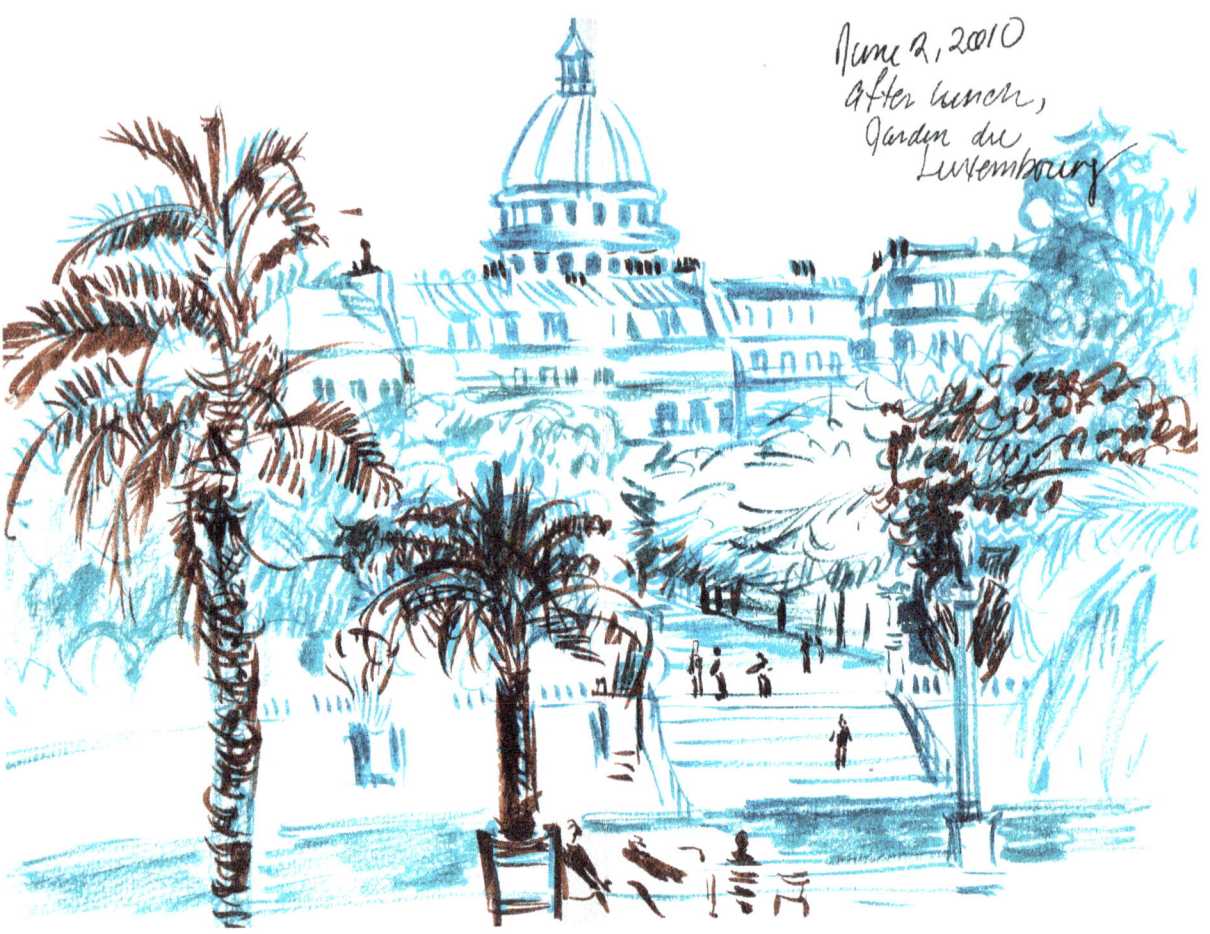

June 2, 2010 after lunch, Jardin du Luxembourg

◒ Jardin du Luxembourg The Pantheon seen from Luxembourg Gardens in late spring. It was early in June, Frankstone says, so the crowds were smaller, the foliage on the trees was not so dense, and there were longer vistas available to sketch.

Tip "Using one warm-toned ink and one cool tone allows you to create more depth than you can with one color. And there's enough color in this kind of sketch that you don't feel compelled to add watercolor washes, which are easily overworked."
— Laura Frankstone

4.5" x 6.5" | 11.5 x 16.5 cm; Niji waterbrush with acrylic ink, in this case, Payne's Gray and Sepia on a Maruman accordion sketchbook; about 20 minutes

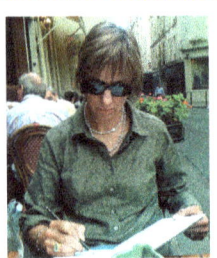

ARTIST PROFILE

Laura Frankstone

I left my birthplace, a tiny island in the middle of the Bering Sea, when I was a baby, and I've been traveling ever since. I've been drawing almost ever since, too. Paris was my first city, and it remains the one I know best. I was four when I first visited Paris, and I've been going as often as I can. I spent a month sketching there recently by myself, the fulfillment of a long-held dream.

Sketching in city settings, I use a close- to mid-range focus, emphasizing more intimate, less panoramic subject matter: wine glasses, plates, cutlery—the remnants of a bistro meal; people caught in ordinary, oblique moments; figural sculpture; and fountains that animate public spaces and remind us of the human presence behind the scenes.

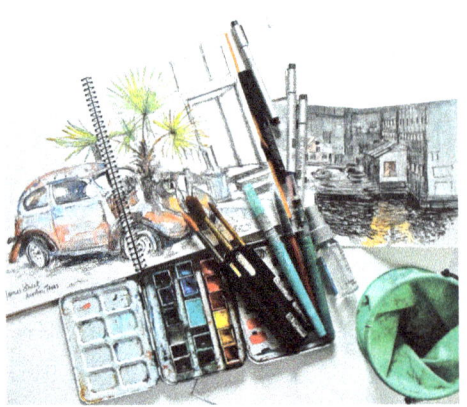

◑ Frankstone's sketching tools

"Sometimes, I get a big kick out of getting just the gesture of the scene. Other times, I love to lose myself in slow, contemplative drawing."

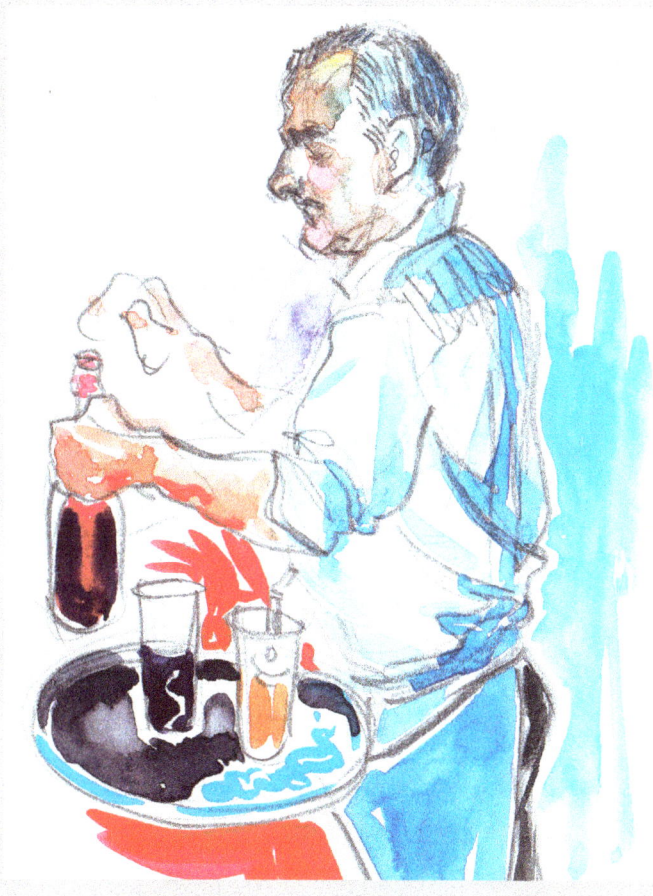

FIRST PERSON

Impressions of Paris

by Tatyana Sasha Yuditskaya

In France, being a waiter is a career—not just a student job, as in North America. Waiters are mostly men. They are real professionals; their work is very hard. Many of them are true philosophers, and they possess a great knowledge of human nature. Non-French tourists largely misinterpret the French waiter's professional poise and dignified appearance—thus, the stereotype of the "arrogant French waiter" was born. This stereotype is due to not knowing the language. If one speaks French, one has a totally different picture of what a French waiter really is. While living in France, I had a chance to become a friend of an old Parisian family of bistro keepers. Those people were like a family to me. And, after I left France, they still are. There is true camaraderie and real support among bistro patrons in France.

5" x 2" | 12.5 x 5 cm; greasy lead pencil, watercolor on Sennelier sketchbook

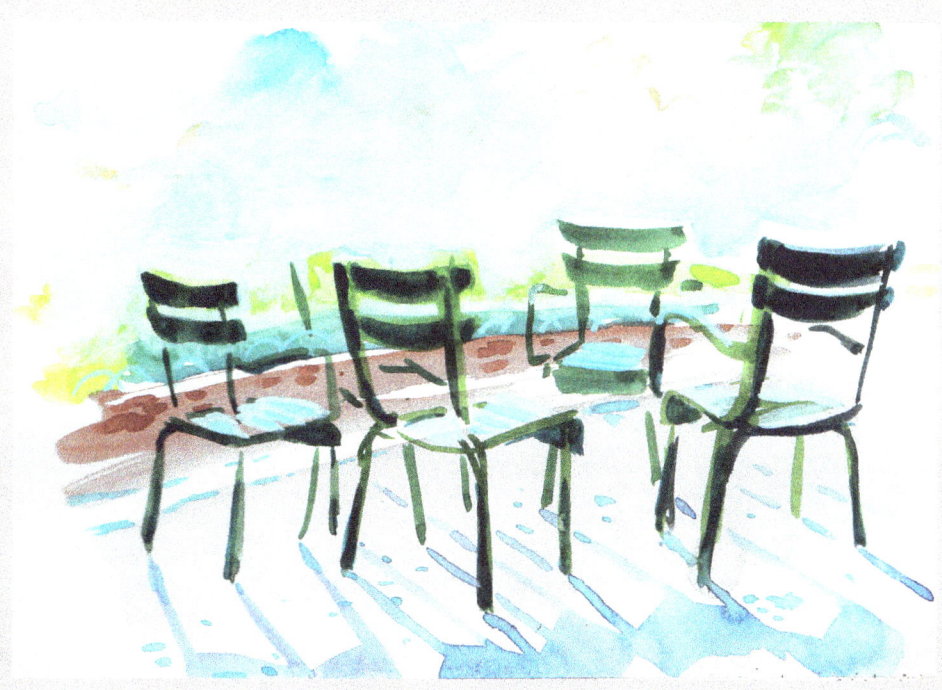

↺ Parisians come to Jardin du Luxembourg on a sunny day; they pull up the famous, green wrought iron chairs and form groups. They sit and talk like only the French can. The sun goes away, the Gendarmes sing-song *"On ferme! On ferme!"* (Closing time!), and people start leaving. The chairs are left empty in groups, and the conversations seem to linger in the twilight garden air.

6" x 8" | 15 x 20 cm; watercolor, brushes, white gouache on Sennelier sketchbook; 30 minutes

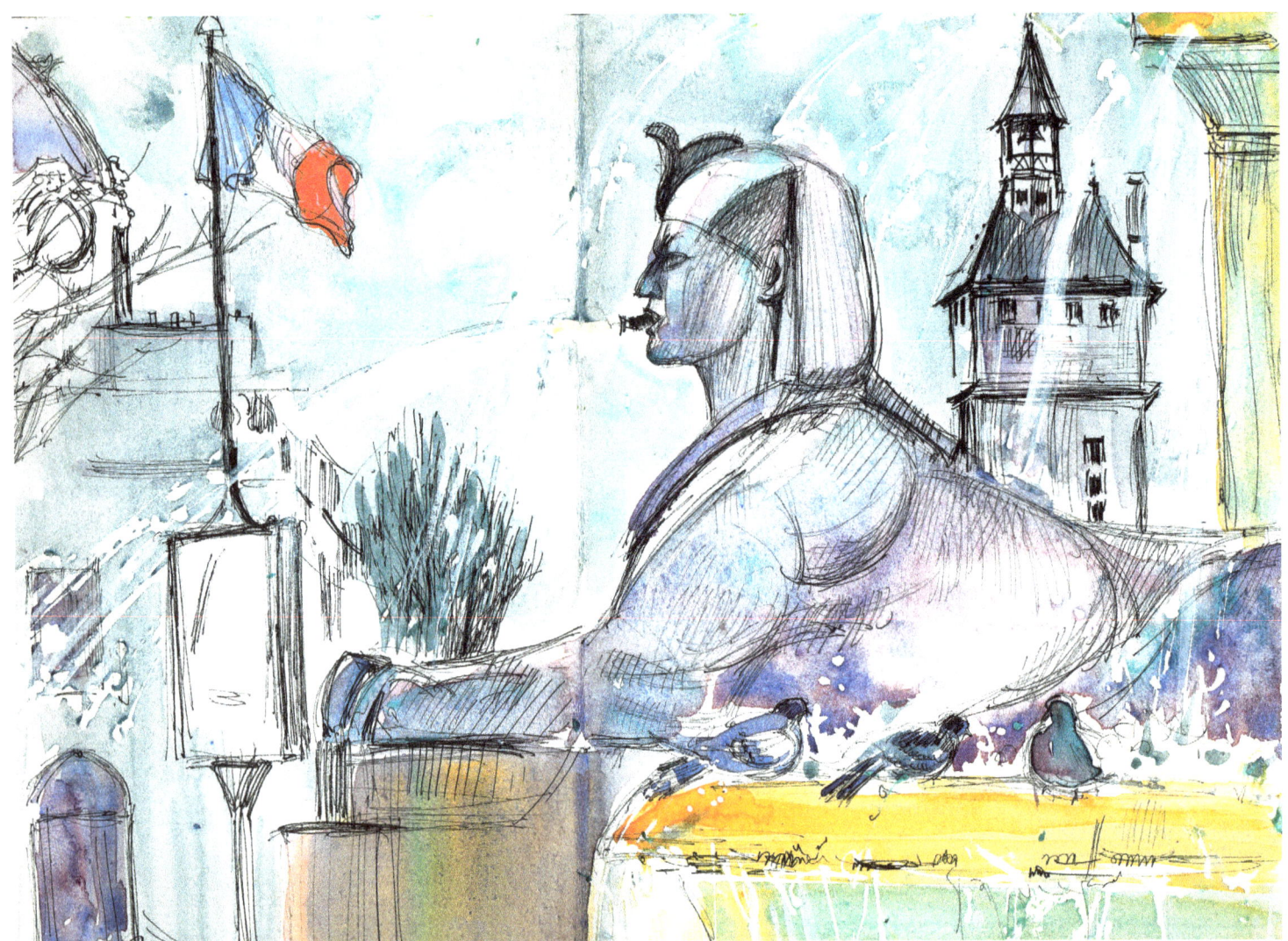

⌒ **Palmier Fountain at Place du Châtelet** "I love the play of water against sculpted, figural shapes, so I seek out fountains to sketch wherever I go," Frankstone says. "Paris is heaven for a fountain person, like me."

Tip "Try to find a time of day when such a public square is not crowded, so you have room to see and draw."
— *Laura Frankstone*

9" x 13" | 23 x 33 cm; Faber-Castell Ecco Pigment liner pen with Schmincke watercolor washes, accordion sketchbook custom-made with Fabriano cold-press paper; about 45 minutes

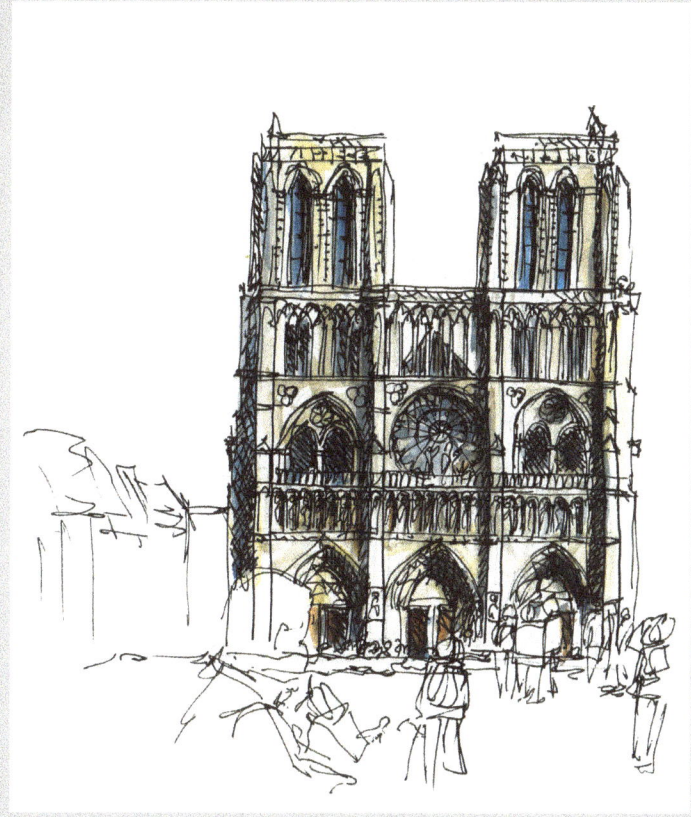

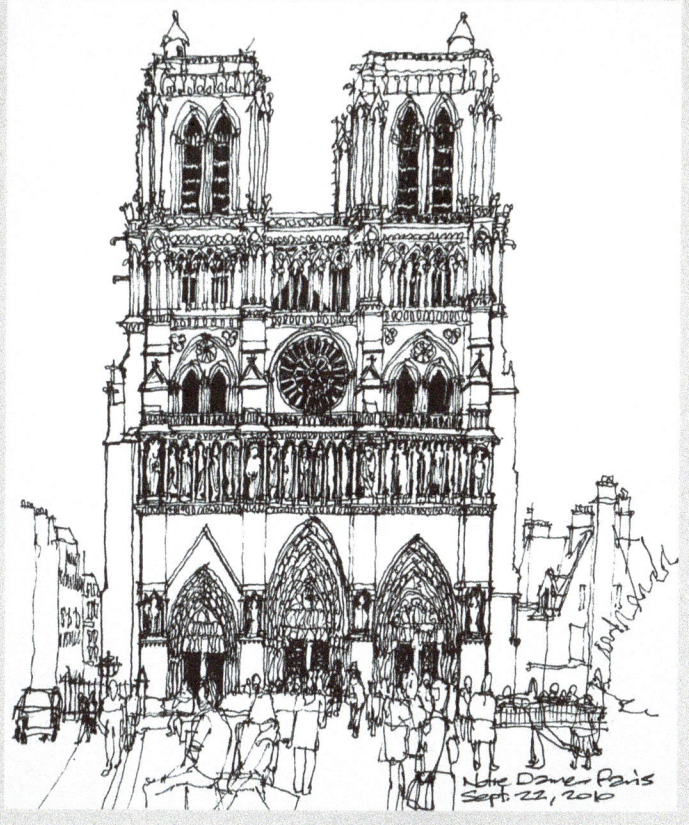

VIEW POINTS

Notre Dame

🎧 "As an architect, I really love sketching complicated buildings but also enjoy drawing the many tourists that often obscure, temporarily, part of the view. Tourists getting in the way would annoy me if I was taking photos, but, as a sketcher, including them is a great way of adding context. I always start by looking for a square to get the main proportions right and then break the building façade into bays and storys. Next, check that the windows fit into the bays and then just go for it!" — *Liz Steel*

8" x 8.5" | 20 x 21.6 cm; Lamy Safari pen with Noodler's ink, Winsor & Newton Artists' watercolor, Daler-Rowney Ebony sketchbook (150-gsm cartridge paper); 45 minutes

🎧 "Given that Paris is where Gothic architecture was born, I had to do a sketch of the great cathedral there. This sketch took so long that a constantly changing group of bystanders looked over my shoulder and sat beside me. At one point, a whole class of Russian schoolgirls sat around me and watched me work very closely. They were generally silent and very attentive. I checked the proportions by eyeing the building, with my pen used as a scaling device for the major structural bays. Luckily, the building is relatively simple in layout, and, with the double arched windows drawn roughly correctly on the spires, it was just a matter of following these down to the ground." — *Matthew Cencich*

6.5 "x 9.5" | 16.5 x 24 cm; Pentel black, fine-point, felt-tip pen, Holbein small multidrawing book; 2.5–3 very focused hours

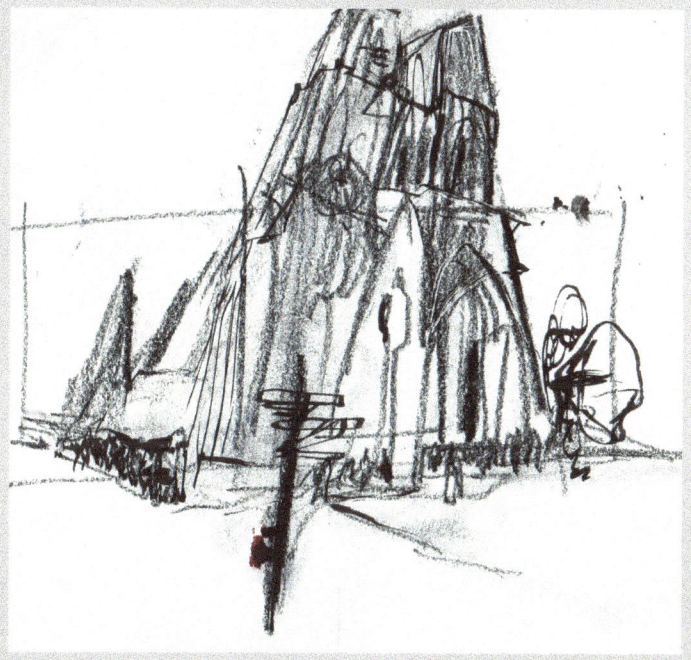

🎧 "I walked around the cathedral and made a few thumbnail drawings of the outside first. Thumbnails are great because they give you a chance to just play around with different points of view and ideas." — *Danielle C. McManus*

14" x 17" | 35.6 x 43 cm; Sanford Paper Wrapped Marker (china marker) in black, Canson premium 80-lb white, smooth-surface drawing pad; about 5 minutes

LIÈGE

Born in A.D. 558, in the valley of the river Meuse, the Belgian city of Liège has a lot of historical monuments, some 1,000 years old. Local architect Gérard Michel often takes his bike on sketching excursions, exploring steep hills and climbing stairs, in search of interesting views to draw.

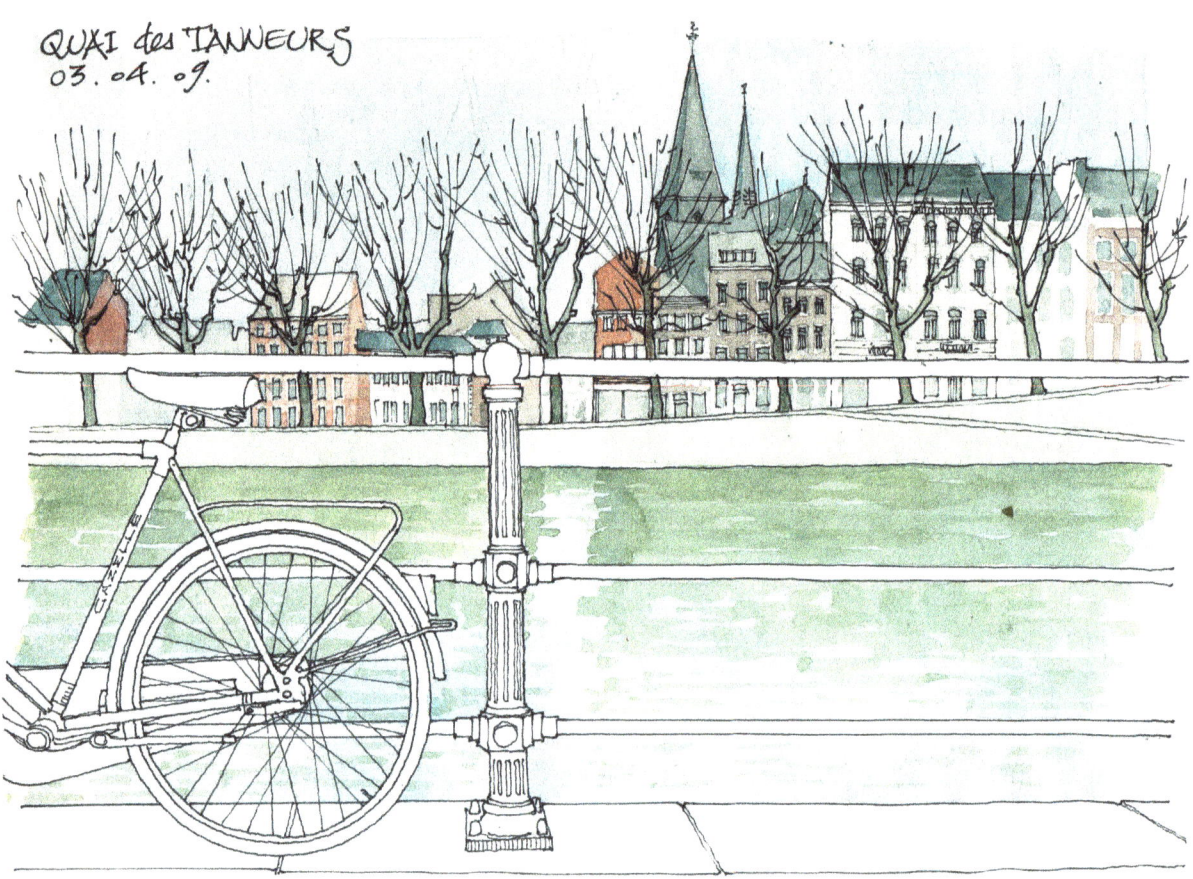

QUAI des TANNEURS
03.04.09.

↺ **River Meuse** The first tower is the steeple of the Saint-Pholien church. In the foreground is Michel's bike, on the bank of the Meuse.

Tip "I liked drawing the guardrail and the bike to give depth to my drawing."
— *Gérard Michel*

8.25" x 11.75" | 21 x 30 cm; pigment liner and watercolor on A4 sketchbook; 1–2 hours

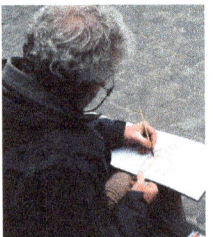

ARTIST PROFILE
Gérard Michel

I was fifteen when I did my first architectural sketches, clumsily, during bike rides. Today, I'm sixty-four, and I have taught drawing and sketching to architecture students for more than thirty years.

I'm impressed by man's actions on his environment to live in it. Landscapes and architecture are the most obvious result. To see, to understand, to record—what medium is better than drawing? Taking time, trying to see everything; my drawing is never quick. Time to draw—it's canned pleasure! My sketchbook is always with me.

At first, my drawing was linear, but today I often use color: pencil or liner for the lines, watercolor for the tones. With experience, I've gained easiness. Very few construction lines are necessary; my drawing is woven like a net, with a virtual weft.

"My eye goes from one point to another, measuring angles and distances without necessarily drawing a line."

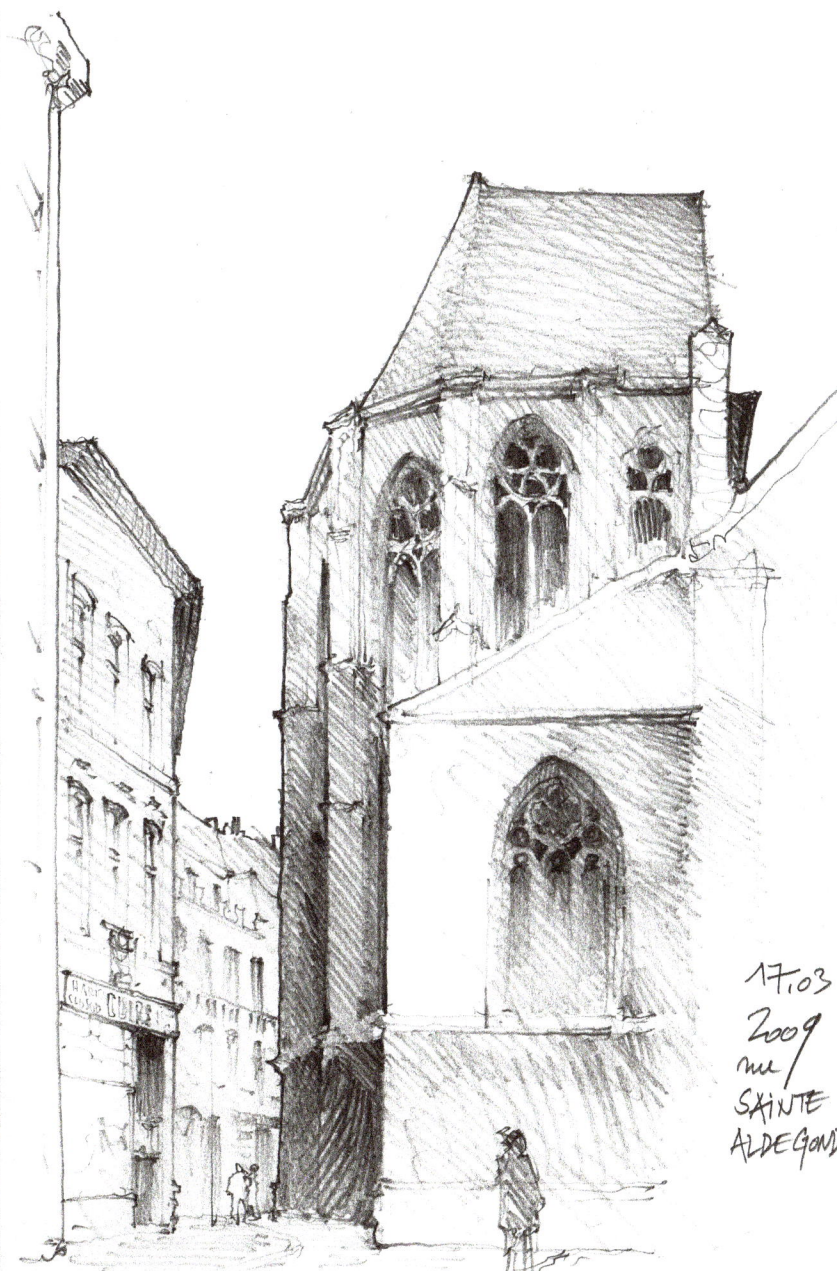

17.03
2009
rue
SAINTE
ALDEGONDE

↻ The Viaduct The weather is sulky, and the street is glum, Michel says. "Only the advertising sign is like a sun."

Tip "I liked how the bridge cuts the sky!"
— Gérard Michel

8.25" x 11.75" | 21 x 30 cm; pigment liners and watercolor on A4 sketchbook; about 2 hours

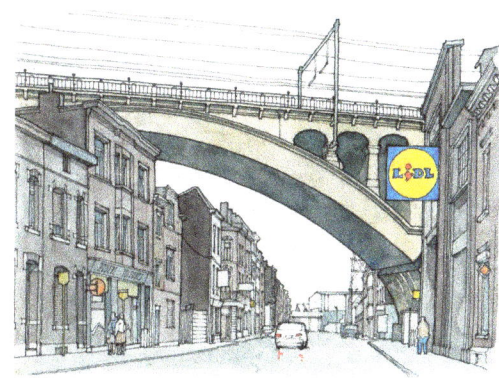

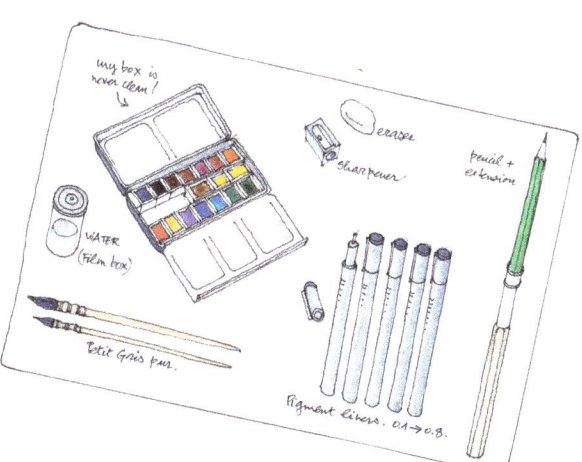

↻ Michel's sketching tools

↻ In Pencil Under what Michel called a timid sun, he took his students to draw outdoors in Liège one morning. He calls the silhouette of this church—with the big Romanesque tower and the high Gothic choir—typical.

Tip "When I draw with my students, I always draw with a pencil on ordinary paper, as it's quicker and easier."
— Gérard Michel

8.25" x 11.75" | 21 x 30 cm; 2B pencil, 90-gsm typing paper; 30 minutes

LONDON

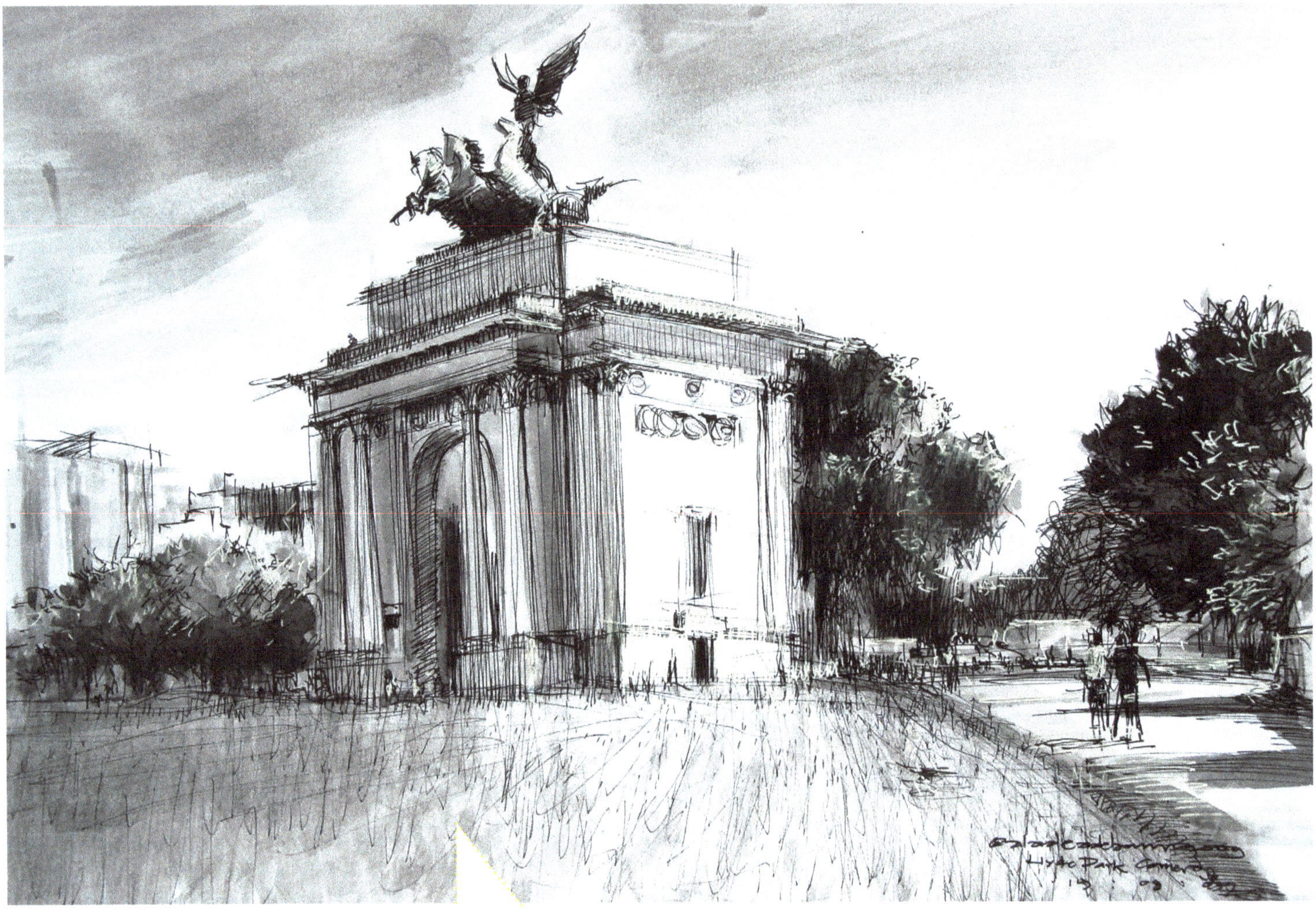

Big and bustling, London has world-famous sketchworthy sites, such as the Houses of Parliament, the Tower Bridge, the Tower of London, and St. Paul's Cathedral. The Tube, the oldest underground rail system in the world, also becomes a fast-moving studio for sketchers such as Adebanji Alade, who's fond of drawing commuters.

"Urban sketching means drawing anywhere in my immediate environment."

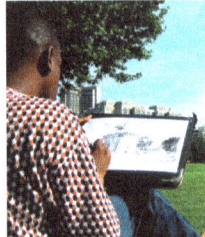

Adebanji Alade sketches the Wellington Arch in London's Hyde Park.

15" x 10.5" | 38 x 26.5 cm; pen and ink wash; about 1.5 hours

ARTIST PROFILE
Adebanji Alade

I love the look of an empty spread on my sketchbook. It gets me hungry to fill it with the people I see every day on the trains, Tube, and buses in London. I go through the London Transport System armed with my biro or pencil and an A6 sketchbook, looking at people's faces, and I get high! I love everything about the human face, and going through a multicultural city like London serves me with all I need to see, feel, and explore.

I love sketching on location, because it trains my hand-eye co-ordination, something useful for me as a figurative painter. But most of all, I just enjoy the experience of sketching, with the people all around me watching, peeping, making comments, getting cross, smiling, and, best of all, asking me to send the sketches to their mailboxes for their personal use.

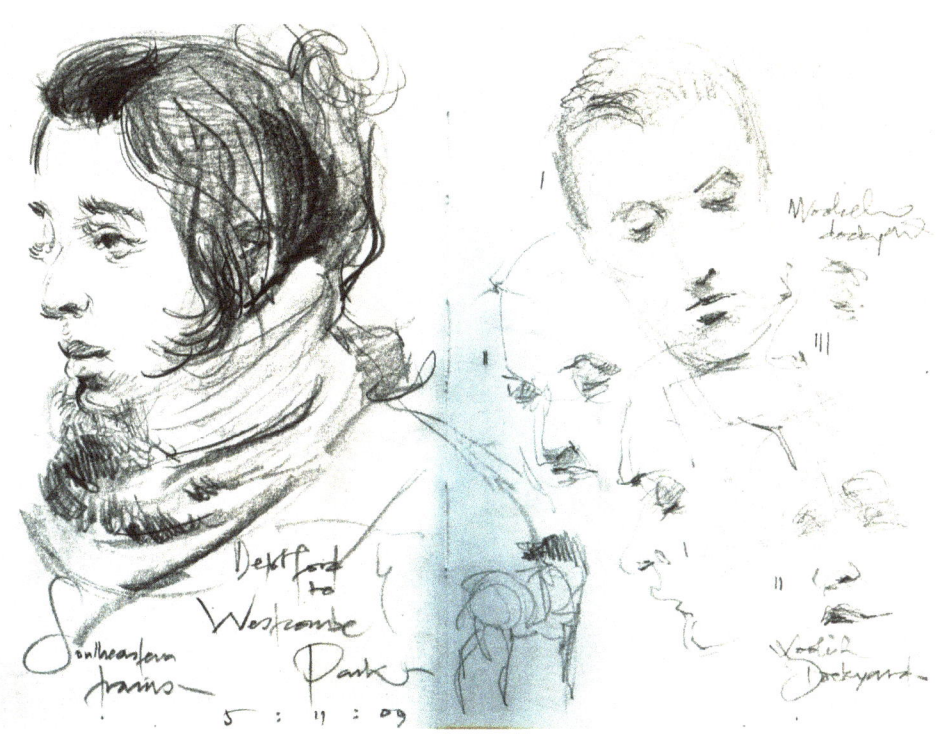

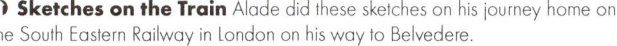

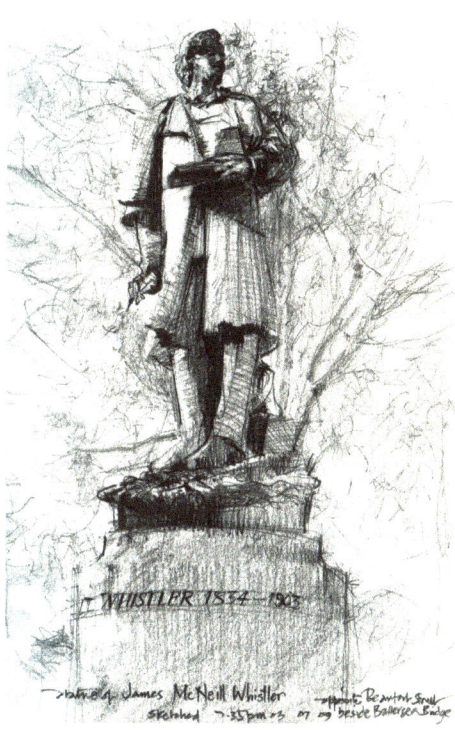

⋂ Sketches on the Train Alade did these sketches on his journey home on the South Eastern Railway in London on his way to Belvedere.

Tip "I love sketching on public transportation, because if ever I need to sketch a face, these are the places to be: a wide variety of people in different moods from different walks of life, from all over the world! It's a gold mine for me." — *Adebanji Alade*

8" x 6" | 20 x 15 cm; Faber-Castell TK400 mechanical pencil holder with TK 9071, 2-mm, 3B leads on a Daler-Rowney sketchbook with 150-gsm, acid-free cartridge paper; about 10–13 minutes

⋂ Statue of James McNeill Whistler This statue celebrates the time the American painter spent living in Chelsea. Alade, who lives nearby, was drawn to it because the artist appears to be holding a thick sketchbook in one hand and a pen in the other.

Tip "I pitched myself just below the statue and took measurements to get the proportions right. I started by sketching lightly, then, when I was sure of the drawing, I became far looser and freer with my shading, which helped add a three-dimensional feel to the subject." — *Adebanji Alade*

8" x 11" | 20 x 28 cm; Faber-Castell graphite 3B-TK 9400, TK 9071 (lead and leadholder); 1.5 hours

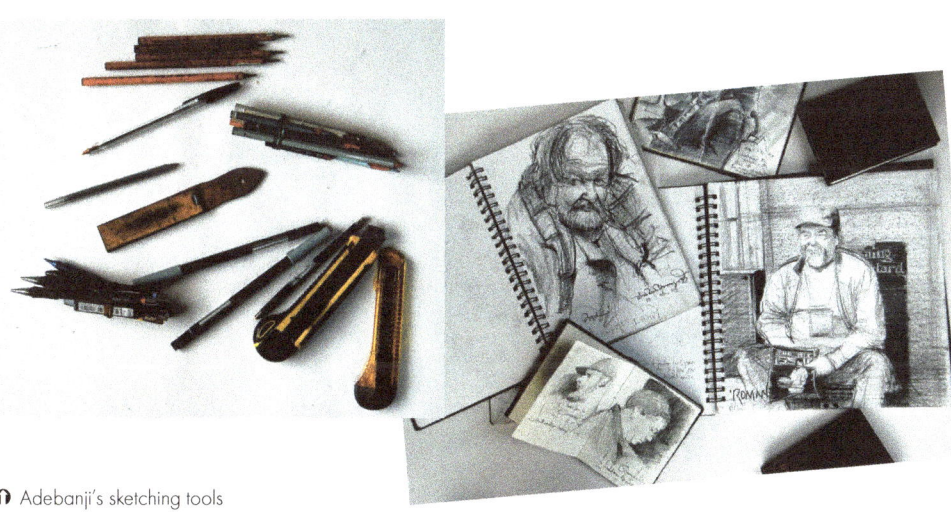

⋂ Adebanji's sketching tools

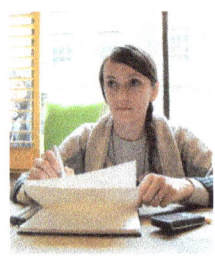

ARTIST PROFILE
Olha Pryymak

I am a painter working in oils on the subject of urban life. My choice of subject matter revolves around my own life in the city. My favorite places here are the nooks and crannies of the East End and its various street markets; my second favorite place is the National Gallery, offering a great place to study the masters.

I also like to sketch the city—the business district, a very dramatic place in the oldest part of town, which crosses with the East End, where the artsy types blend in with the office folk—and Shoreditch in Hackney, full of people with great ideas, art galleries, and old masters' paintings.

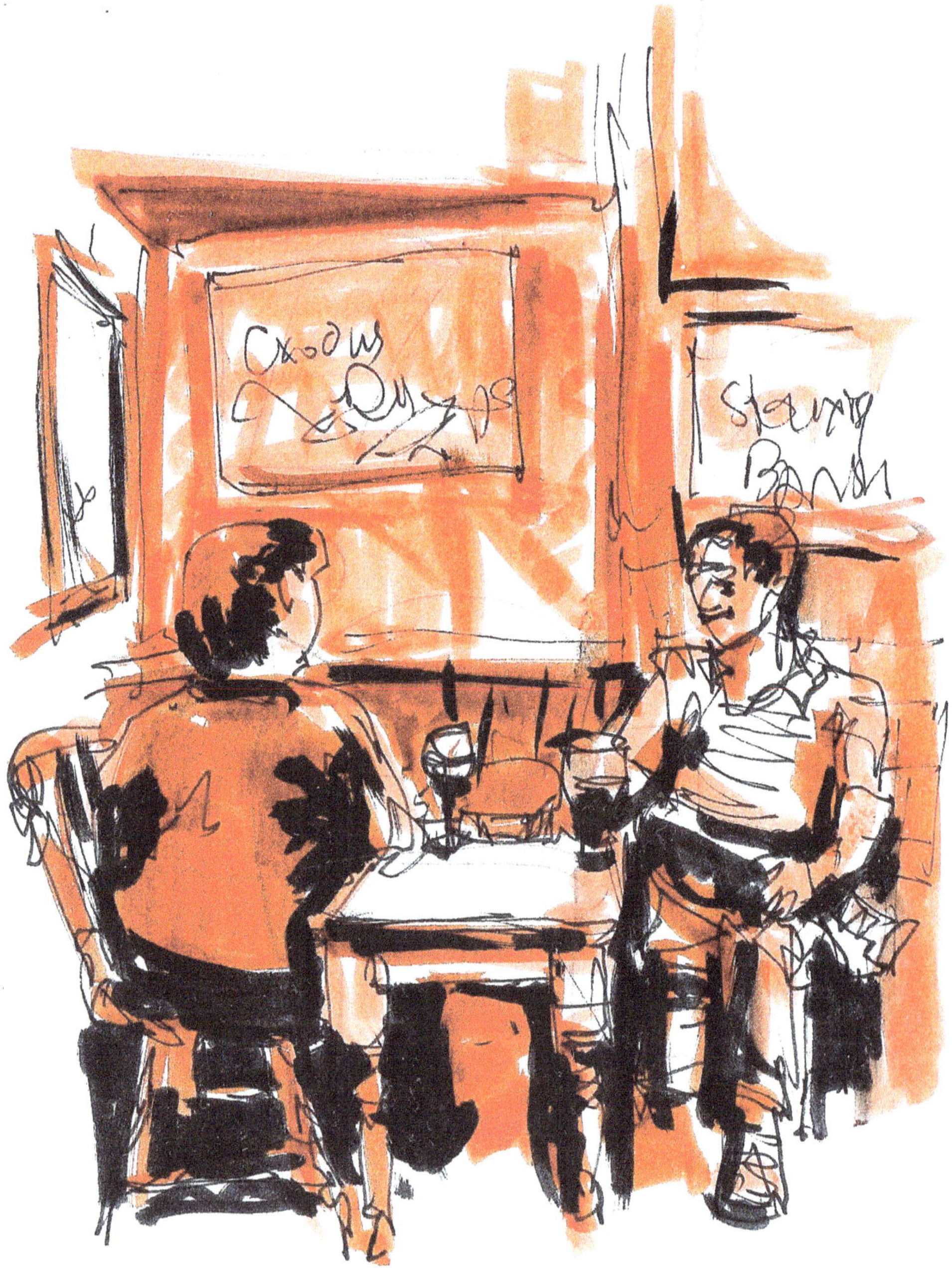

⤴ **At the Pub** London painter Olha Pryymak was stupefied by the name of the pub Filthy McNasty's, but it turned out to be a laid-back, hip, local kind of place, full of people not minding being sketched.

A5 (8.3" x 5.8" | 21 x 14.8 cm); Copic color marker, Pentel 0.2 ink pen, Daler-Rowney sketchbook; 15 minutes

"Sketching for me is about highlighting the noteworthy and the beautiful in everyday life with help of paper and pen."

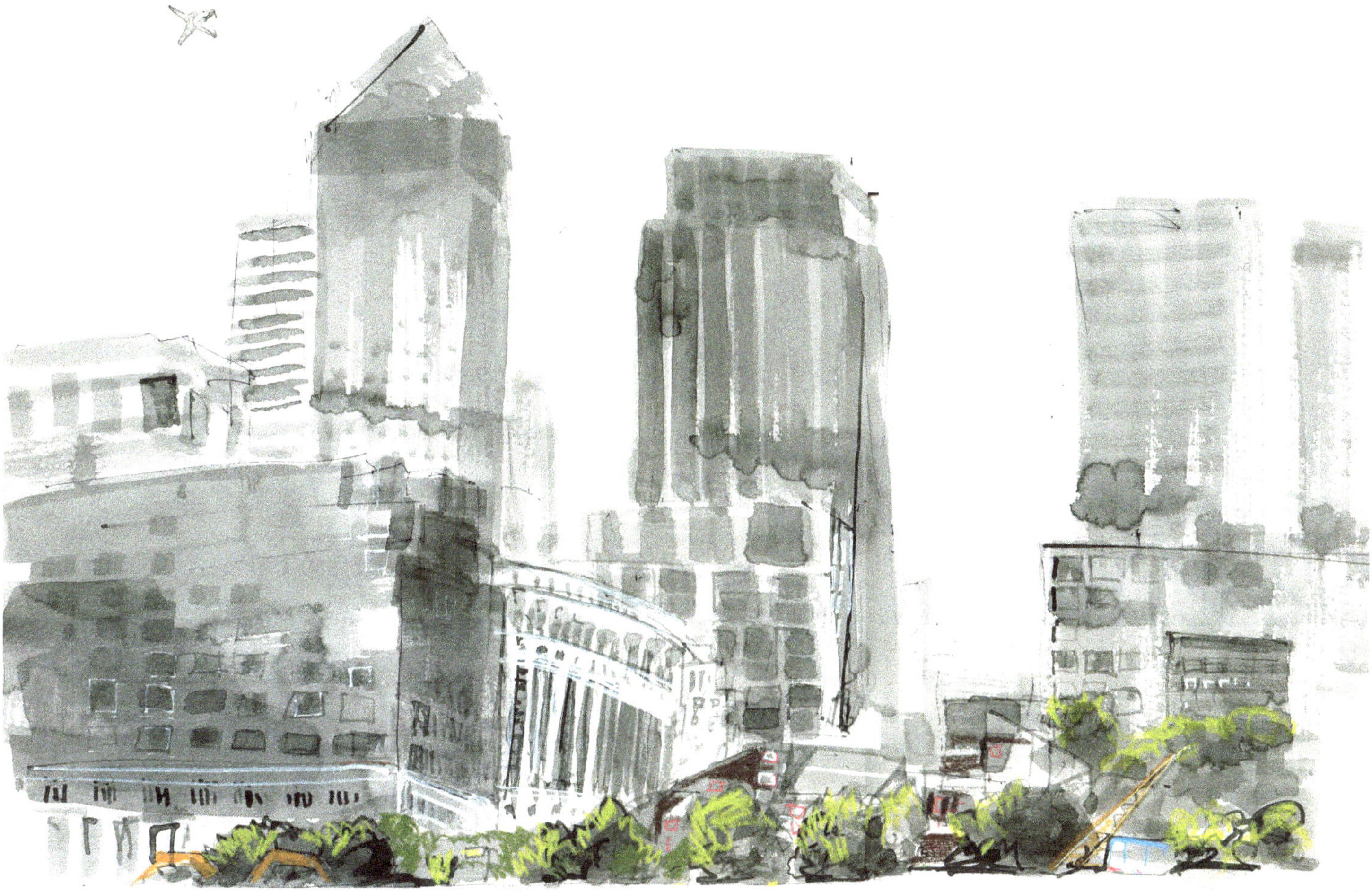

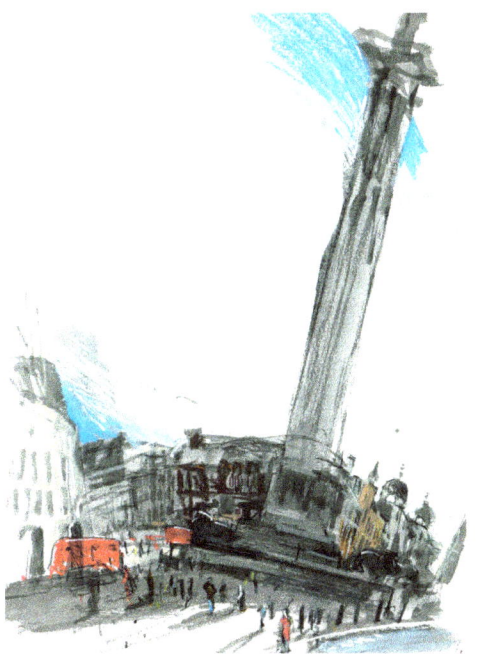

⌂ Isle of Dogs Jackson explored a bit of the Thames along the Surrey side, between Deptford and Rotherhithe. "There are some interesting relics of the old docks, among acres of unimaginative faux-Georgian housing developments and tower blocks," he says. Across the river is the Isle of Dogs—formerly docklands, now a habitat for venture capitalists, with planes frequently taking off from London City airport.

Tip "This is the kind of location where drawing in a sketchbook is quite limiting. There is something liberating about sitting down with big sheets of paper and using different media almost in a painterly way to make a drawing." — *Barry Jackson*

A2 (23.5" x 16.5" | 59.4 x 42 cm); diluted Indian ink; brush, reed pen, Neocolor wax crayon, Snopake correction pen on 200-gsm cartridge paper; about 1 hour

↻ Trafalgar Square This is looking down on Trafalgar Square from the terrace in front of the National Gallery. Barry Jackson wanted to somehow include Nelson's Column as a presence in the drawing.

Tip "I didn't want to 'fill in' the whole sky, just make a note that it was a stunning blue sky. I used a white correction pen to clean up some edges and add some highlights. I find that correction fluid is a really useful tool, but be careful not get it on your clothes—it doesn't wash out." — *Barry Jackson*

A3 (16.5" x 11.7" | 42 mm x 29.7 cm); Pentel brush pen filled with diluted Higgins Chinese ink, 6B pencil, Conté charcoal pencil; Neocolor II nonsoluble wax crayon; Snopake correction pen, single-sheet Fabriano 200-gsm drawing paper; about 30 minutes

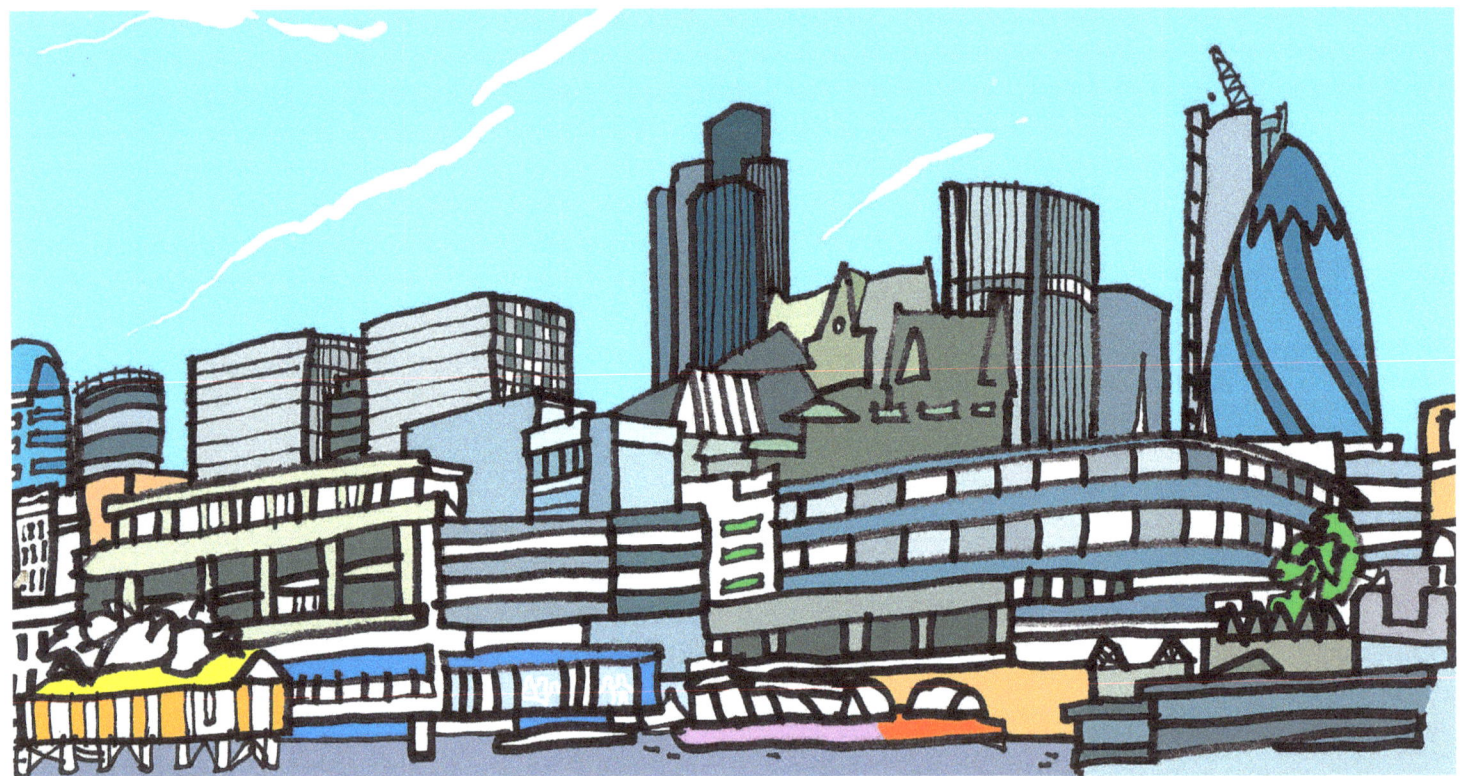

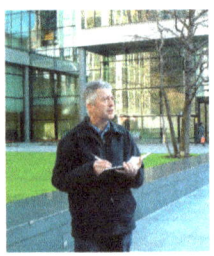

ARTIST PROFILE
James Hobbs

I've lived in London for more than twenty years, having spent most of my youth in relatively rural parts of the U.K., but the buzz of city life gets me like it always did. I often cycle past St. Paul's Cathedral, the London Eye, the Houses of Parliament, and the buildings along the Thames, and I can still marvel at what a great city I live in.

When it comes to drawing, though, I am as likely to be taken by the more mundane things going on. I like to stand before the great city sights, remove the workbook from the bag, uncap the marker, and then turn around before starting to draw. It's the street furniture, the every day, the easily overlooked ubiquitous stuff that makes a city what it really is. It's a kind of anticelebrity view of the world that I like. They creep in, of course; the Post Office Tower, Canary Wharf, and the Shard crane their necks to get a look in, but I try, at least, to keep them in their place.

"The idea of a drawing being 'finished' suggests to me a kind of polished death. I would rather have four quick drawings than one 'perfect' work."

City Skyline This view of London, Hobbs says, makes the city look as if it has been built in the last ten years (and much of it has), but this is actually one of the oldest parts of the city; the venerable old Tower of London is just out of view to the right.

Tip "The digital color decisions are made back in the studio. Getting the balance right is more important than capturing accurate colors." — *James Hobbs*

4.25" x 8" | 11 x 20 cm; Edding 400 and Edding 404 permanent markers, digital color on Seawhite sketchbook, 140-gsm cartridge paper; 20 minutes

Peter Jones Department Store James Hobbs found himself Christmas shopping in this large department store in west London and needed a restorative cup of tea.

Tip "Empty chairs in any work can be an inviting sight, as we imagine sinking into one of them to relax. I chose my seat because of this view. The baubles immediately appealed to me as a lively, decorative backdrop to a drawing." — *James Hobbs*

4" x 6" | 10 x 15 cm; Edding 400 and 404 permanent marker pens, Seawhite sketchbook; 20 minutes

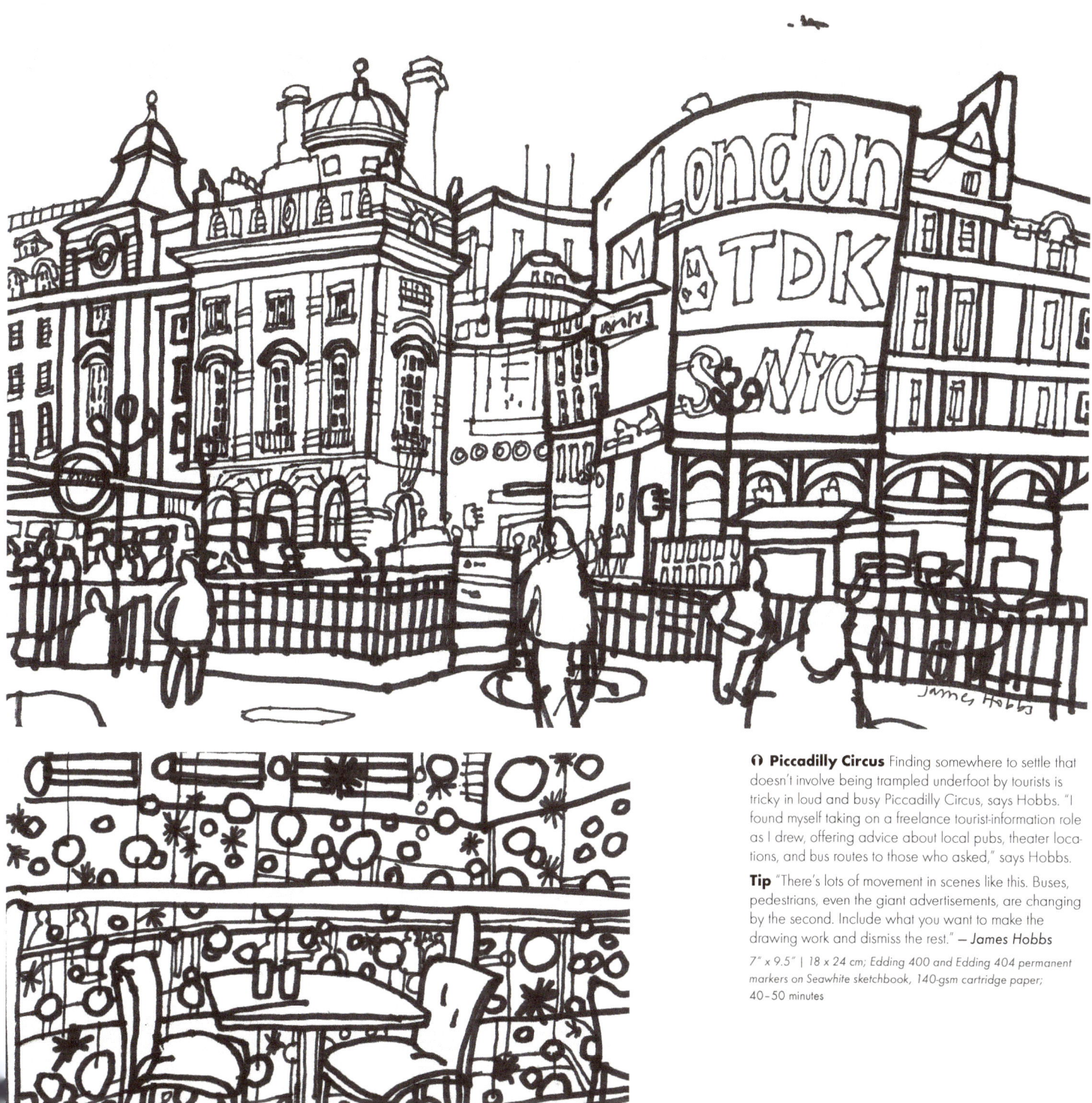

Ω Piccadilly Circus Finding somewhere to settle that doesn't involve being trampled underfoot by tourists is tricky in loud and busy Piccadilly Circus, says Hobbs. "I found myself taking on a freelance tourist-information role as I drew, offering advice about local pubs, theater locations, and bus routes to those who asked," says Hobbs.

Tip "There's lots of movement in scenes like this. Buses, pedestrians, even the giant advertisements, are changing by the second. Include what you want to make the drawing work and dismiss the rest." — *James Hobbs*

7" x 9.5" | 18 x 24 cm; Edding 400 and Edding 404 permanent markers on Seawhite sketchbook, 140-gsm cartridge paper; 40–50 minutes

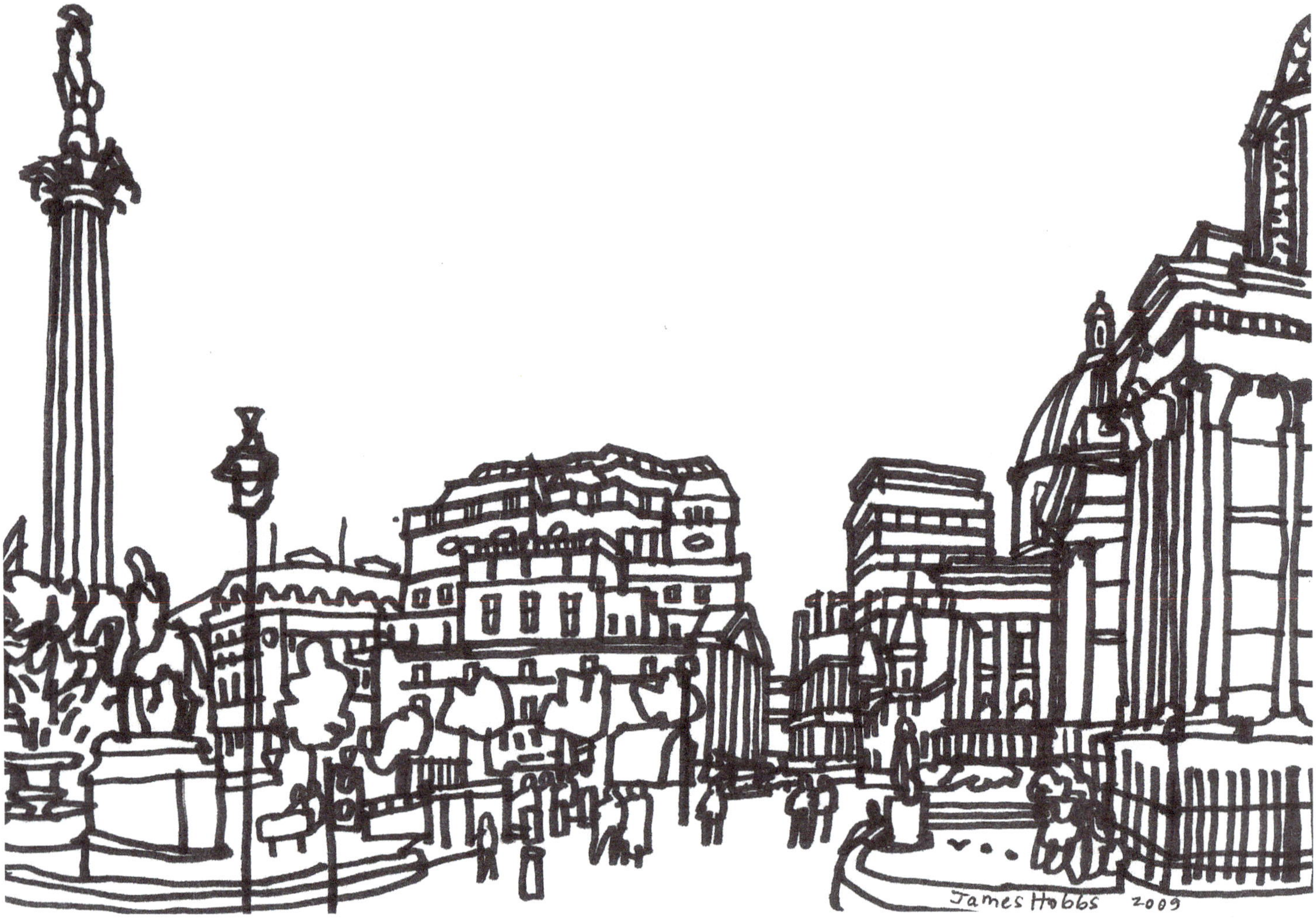

◠ **Trafalgar Square** Trafalgar Square was a glori-
fied roundabout until 2003, when the north side was
closed to traffic, thus allowing a relaxed stroll across the
square and up the steps into the National Gallery, on
the right-hand side of this drawing. Suddenly, instead of
it being a place to endure, it became a place to linger,
reflect, and watch the world go by, says Hobbs.

Tip "The problem with this drawing, and similar ones, is
that it is easy to get the scale wrong and thus crop off
something vital, in this case running the risk of leaving
Nelson's Column without Nelson. A degree of creative
editing has gone on to ensure the main subjects fit on
the page." — *James Hobbs*

*5.75" x 8" | 14.6 x 20 cm; Edding 400 and 404 permanent
marker pens, Seawhite sketchbook; 35 minutes*

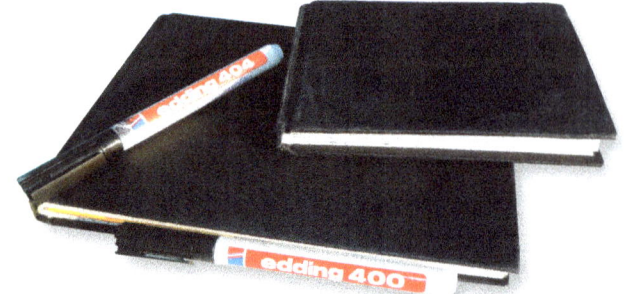

◠ Hobbs' markers and sketchbooks

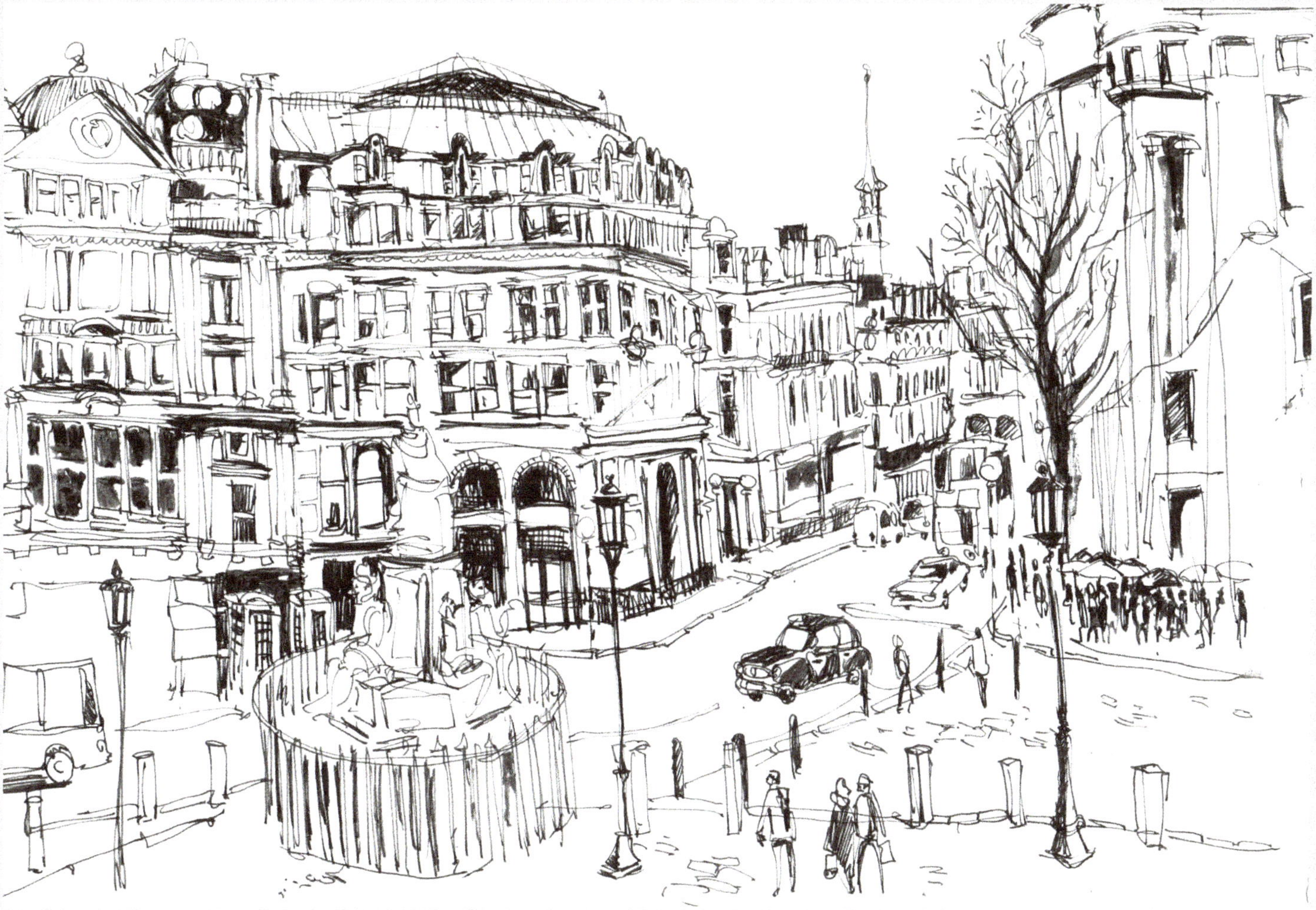

VIEW POINTS

St. Paul's Cathedral

🎧 Zhenia Vasiliev sketched the view one usually sees when coming out of the cathedral.

Tip "Sketching a street filled with plenty of decorated houses like these is hard, because you might be carried away by drawing small details and forget the drawing as a whole. I always try to limit myself, sketch only the necessary, and allow for blank areas where possible."
— *Zhenia Vasiliev*

A4 (8.3" x 11.7" | 21 x 29.7 cm); Lamy Safari fountain pen, Noodler's black ink, John Purcell sketchbook, 190-gsm, 100% cotton, mould-made watercolor paper; 40 minutes–1 hour

➲ Despite seventy-six consecutive nights of bombing raids during World War II, St. Paul's Cathedral miraculously survived, while thousands of buildings around it were reduced to rubble. It is surrounded now by not entirely unsuccessful modern developments. Their stark, angular lines in this view contrast with the curvier elaboration of the 300-year-old temple, says Hobbs.

Tip "Forget vanishing points and 'how to learn perspective' lessons. Look closely and draw lots."
— *James Hobbs*

5.75" x 8" | 14.6 x 20 cm; Edding 400 permanent marker, Seawhite 140-gsm, cartridge paper sketchbook; about 20–30 minutes

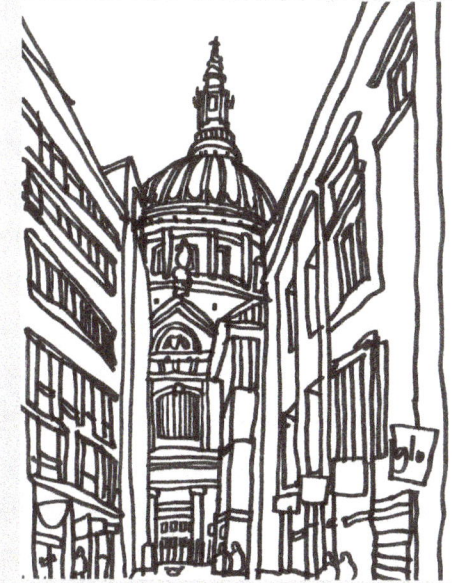

SHEFFIELD

The English city of Sheffield is known for its past as a center of steel production during the Industrial Revolution. These days, rather than making smoke, the old factory chimneys make interesting subjects to sketch. Victorian houses and steep hills also contrast with ultramodern architecture in the city center, where local sketchers meet to draw.

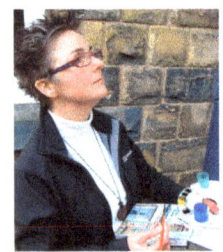

ARTIST PROFILE
Lynne Chapman

When I lived in London, my hometown, I worked as an editorial illustrator, but I moved to Sheffield many years ago, and, these days, I specialize in children's picture books.

My illustration is very different from my sketching: I illustrate mainly from my imagination, drawing in pastels, but I fill my sketchbooks with places and people I observe directly, usually standing on a street corner or sitting on a train—trying in vain to look as inconspicuous as possible. I keep these two very separate, so that my sketchbooks remain "fun," purely for me, and don't get sucked into "work." Until recently, the sketches remained hidden away on a shelf, so I'm thrilled that the Urban Sketchers online community gives me the opportunity to share them.

" I don't have a stool, so I often draw standing. I like the restriction of having to finish before my arms drop off."

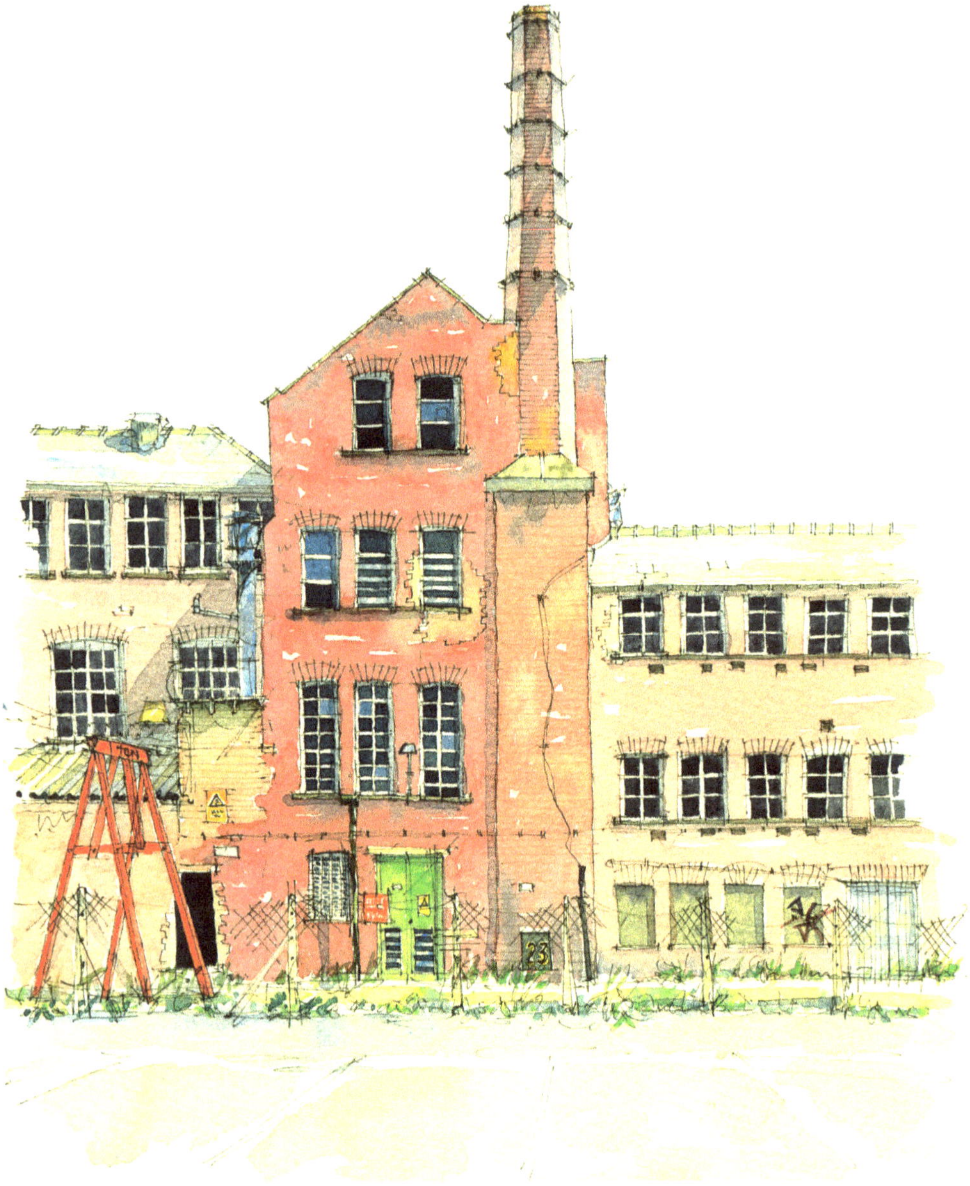

⟲ Egerton Lane Bryn Hughes's first memory when he first came to Sheffield was the red brick of terraced houses and small factories, weathered by decades of grime. Craftsmen known as "little mesters" manufactured stainless steel products, such as knives and scissors, in buildings like this one.

Tip "I drew directly with pen, filling in the dark windows first, before painting the red brickwork and dropping in yellow ochre and ultramarine blue to provide the texture."
— *Bryn Hughes*

8.25" x 11.75" | 21 x 30 cm; 0.1 Pilot DR pen, Rembrandt watercolors and sable brushes on Daler-Rowney "The Langton" watercolor paper

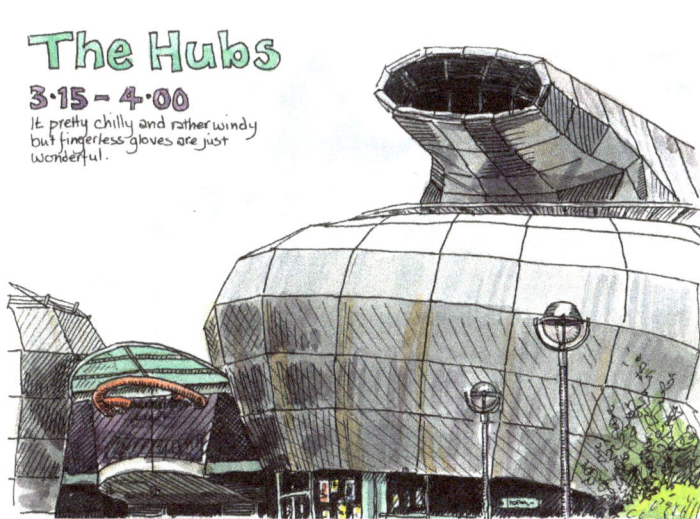

The Hubs

3·15 – 4·00
It pretty chilly and rather windy but fingerless gloves are just wonderful.

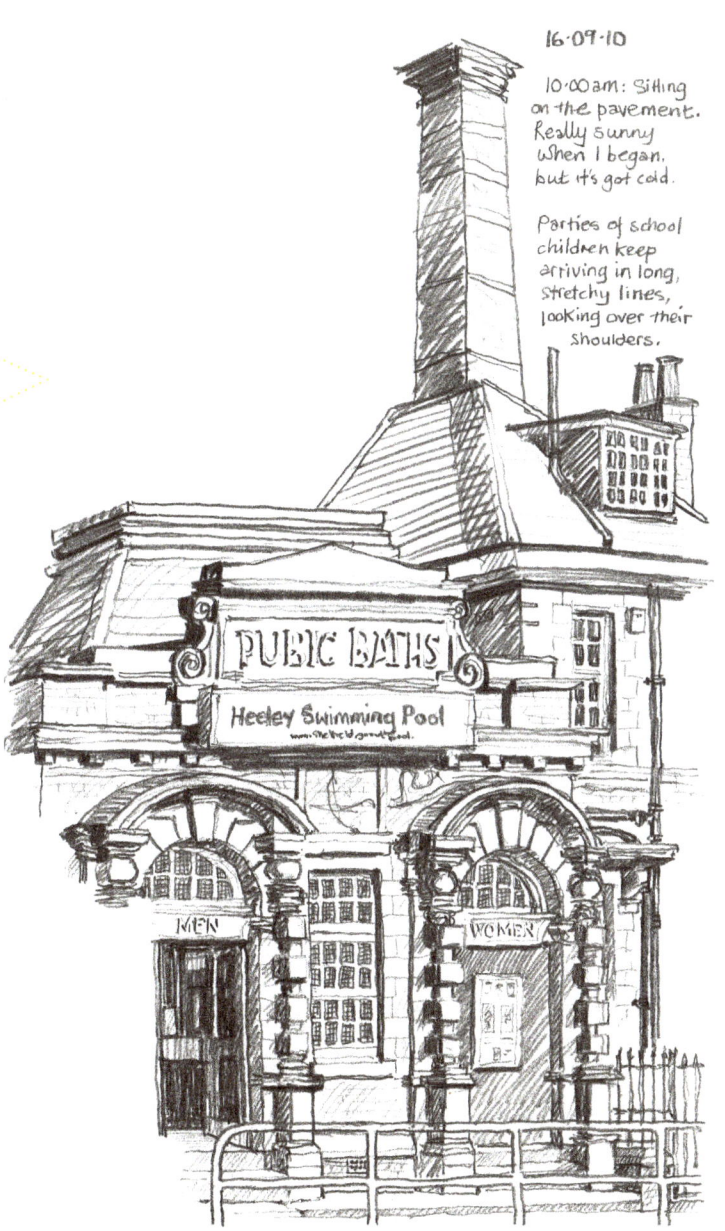

16·09·10

10·00am: Sitting on the pavement. Really sunny when I began. but it's got cold.

Parties of school children keep arriving in long, stretchy lines, looking over their shoulders.

PUBLIC BATHS

Heeley Swimming Pool

MEN   WOMEN

The Hubs This curiously four-headed, metallic building is known locally as the kettle-drums, Chapman says. It was designed as a museum but is now part of the university.

Tip "It was tricky to draw because of the tilted angles and slight twist, so I decided to just begin at one end and see if it all joined up. Mercifully I gauged things pretty well, because drawing the tiles in pen was totally unforgiving." — *Lynne Chapman*

6" x 8.25" | 15 x 21 cm; Staedtler pigment liner and watercolor on Daler-Rowney 150-gsm, acid-free cartridge paper; 45 minutes

Heeley Baths This 100-year-old building stands incongruously on a fairly ugly road at a busy junction, Chapman says. Once a slipper-bath house and laundry, for those with no bathroom at home, it is now a public swimming pool and gym. Chapman loves the beautiful brickwork, the name in carved stone, and the old, segregated entrances.

Tip "Composition can make the difference between a successful or disappointing drawing. I walked back and forth in front of the building a few times, before picking my viewpoint, because the section with the chimney was set slightly back, so a few inches this way or that made an enormous difference." — *Lynne Chapman*

10.25" x 6" | 26 x 15 cm; 3B pencil, line color slightly tinted later in Photoshop, Daler-Rowney 150-gsm, acid-free cartridge paper; 1 hour, 15 minutes

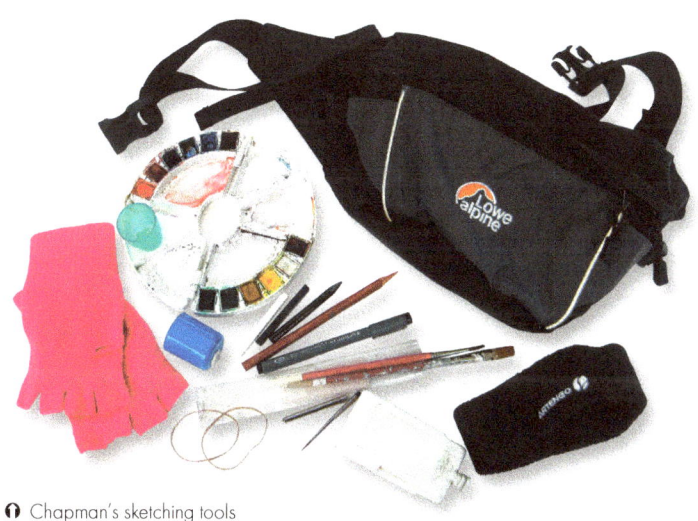

Chapman's sketching tools

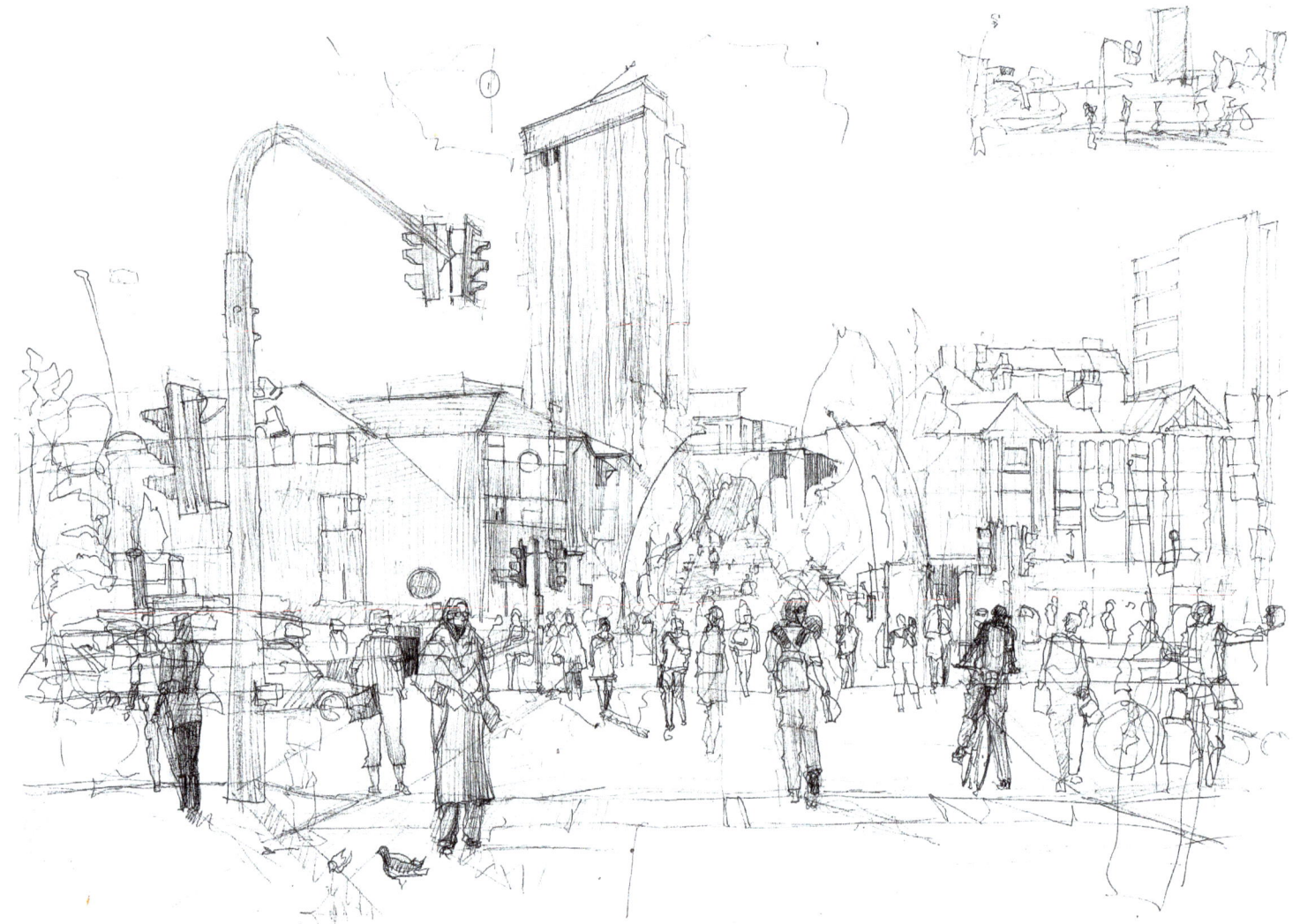

⋒ The Crossing Sheffield artist Tim Rose has sketched this pedestrian crossing many times. "I like the design of shapes and am interested in the light at different times of day and the effects on the people crossing," Rose says. "People stop to watch . . . it goes with the territory, but it is all good humored."

Tip "When drawing outside, always stand, rather than sit. Look serious and you won't get bothered too much." — *Tim Rose*

16" x 20" | 6.25 x 8 cm; 2H and HB pencil; Daler-Rowney 150-gsm, A2 sketch pad; 90 minutes

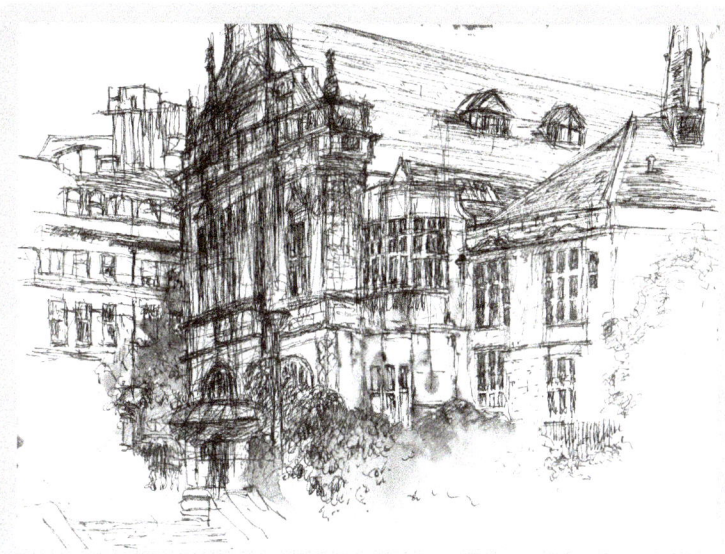

DRAWN TOGETHER

Sketching with Strangers at the City Center

More than twenty-five people who didn't previously know each other attended the first Sheffield sketchcrawl, organized by Lynne Chapman. They met in the city center to sketch landmarks, such as the Town Hall and the Giant Ball-bearing fountains at the Peace Gardens. "People started coming over to ask what we were doing. The security guards were dead impressed, and another man took a photo of me with his girlfriend! A photographer from the local press was so interested that he hung around to watch for 2 hours." Chapman says she finished her drawings "just in time for the scurry for the pub, to thaw out and compare the day's sketches."

↻ "I was in a very cold and windy spot and was trying to work as quickly and freely as possible, moving my whole arm vigorously in a vain attempt to keep warm."
— *Colleen Penny*

11" x 15" | 28 x 38 cm; 1.0 Uni-ball Gel Impact pen on black, 140-lb. RKB Bockingford Fat Pad; 60 minutes

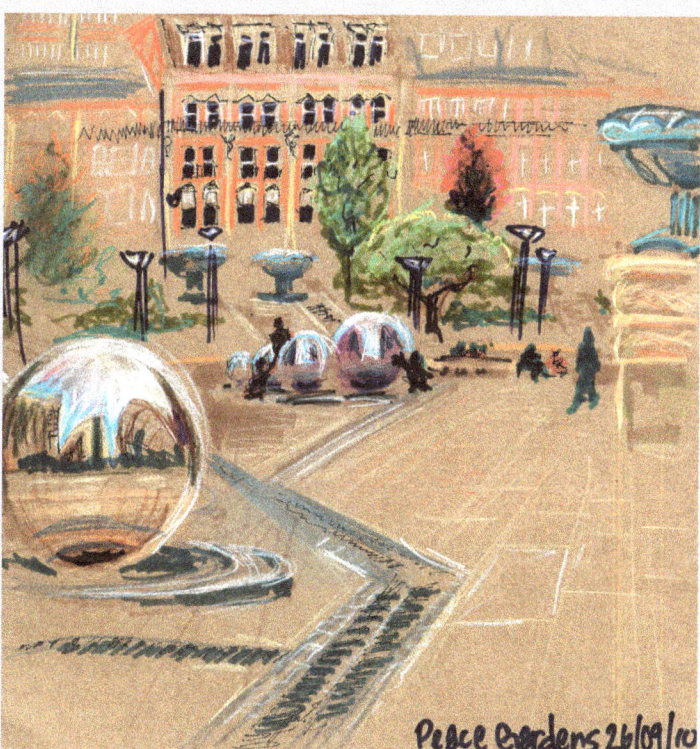

Peace Gardens 26/09/10

🎧 "I'm studying architecture and am supposed to keep a sketch journal. Events like this get me out and doing something, and I got to meet some lovely and talented people in the process." — *Nic Kirkman*

11.5" x 11.5" | 29 x 29 cm; Caran d'Ache Classicolor pencils, Zig Kurecolor Twin S felt-tip pens, and Rotring Rapidograph pens on square, Seawhite, spiral-bound Kraft book; 1 hour

↻ "I was pleased to capture the big wheel behind the town hall: old and new juxtaposed. Using the 'negative space' between the buildings helps you to create a more interesting composition than if you simply place one building in the middle of the page."
— *Lynne Chapman*

6" x 8.25" | 15 x 21 cm; Staedtler pigment liner and watercolor on Daler-Rowney 150-gsm, acid-free cartridge paper; 50 minutes

11·00am

Lots of people come to look and some take photos. The security men are lovely and very impressed!

1st venue of the day: the Peace Gardens but I have to stop for a photo call with the Star.

DUBLIN

Ireland's capital is a low-rise city of one million people, with few buildings extending beyond six floors. Local sketcher Roger O'Reilly is drawn to the buzzing streets and cosmopolitan atmosphere of the inner city, as well as quieter scenes of leafy squares in the suburbs and coastal districts.

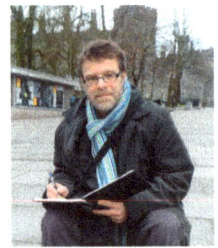

ARTIST PROFILE
Roger O'Reilly

Like many professionally employed in the creative industry, I draw every day as part of my work and found little inclination to sketch, until I went on a lengthy sojourn to India. Immersed in an amazing and unfamiliar environment, with plenty of time on my hands, I found myself filling in a sketchbook a week. I've never looked back.

Dublin's city centre, with its old Georgian squares, parks, and long-established shopping streets, is a constant flurry of activity and spectacle. It's a great place to just sit, watch, and draw.

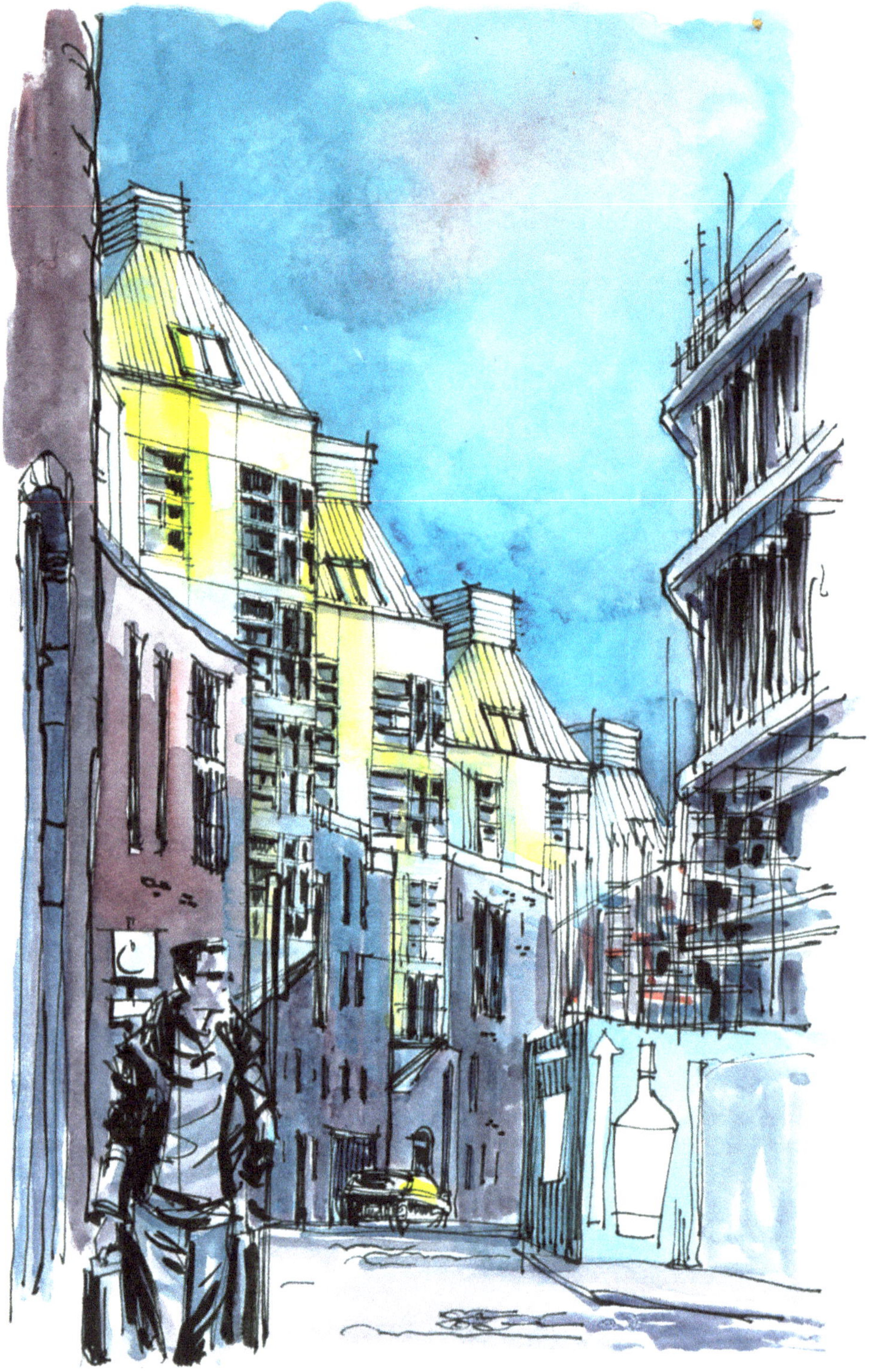

⮌ **Apartments, Smithfield** Just after a downpour, the sun came out and washed its watery light across these rooftops near the Irish Distillers building in Dublin's Smithfield.

Tip "I started by quickly laying in the line with an 03 liner pen, always aware that the main contrast in the picture was going to be the dark sky butting up against the illuminated rooftops, so I kept the detail up there simple."
— Roger O'Reilly

5.5" x 8" | 14 x 20 cm; liner pen, brush pen, and Canson A5 watercolor heavy-cartridge sketchpad; 40 minutes

⊙ O'Connell Street The city's main street, drawn from O'Connell Bridge.

Tip "I started with the lanterns and the monument, both to frame the picture and because I knew they would impose very little on any sketches of pedestrians, which are composites of scores of people wandering up and down the street." — *Roger O'Reilly*

6" x 6" | 15 x 15 cm; waterbrush filled with diluted black, liquid-acrylic ink, Canson A5 heavy cartridge sketchpad; 20 minutes

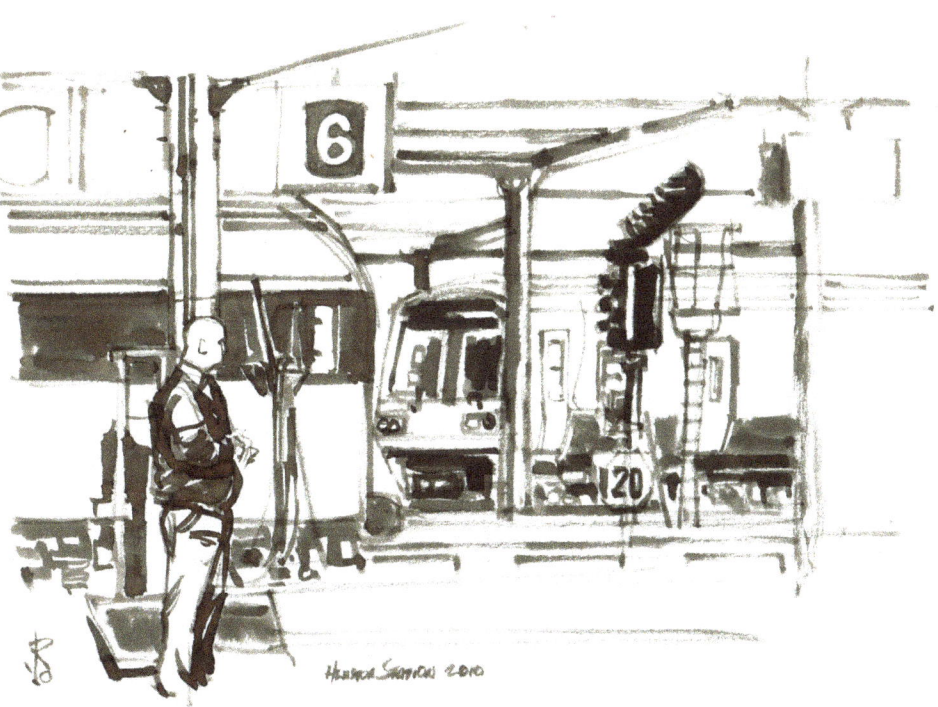

⊙ Heuston Station O'Reilly sketched while waiting for the train to Kilkenny. Heuston Station is the point of arrival or departure for rail routes west or south of Ireland's capital.

8" x 10" | 20 x 25 cm; waterbrush filled with diluted black, liquid-acrylic ink and calligraphic ink on Daler-Rowney heavy cartridge artists' block; 30 minutes

"I'm not a particular fan of the 'empty-street' genre of sketching. The ebb and flow of human traffic is what brings the landscape to life."

GLASGOW

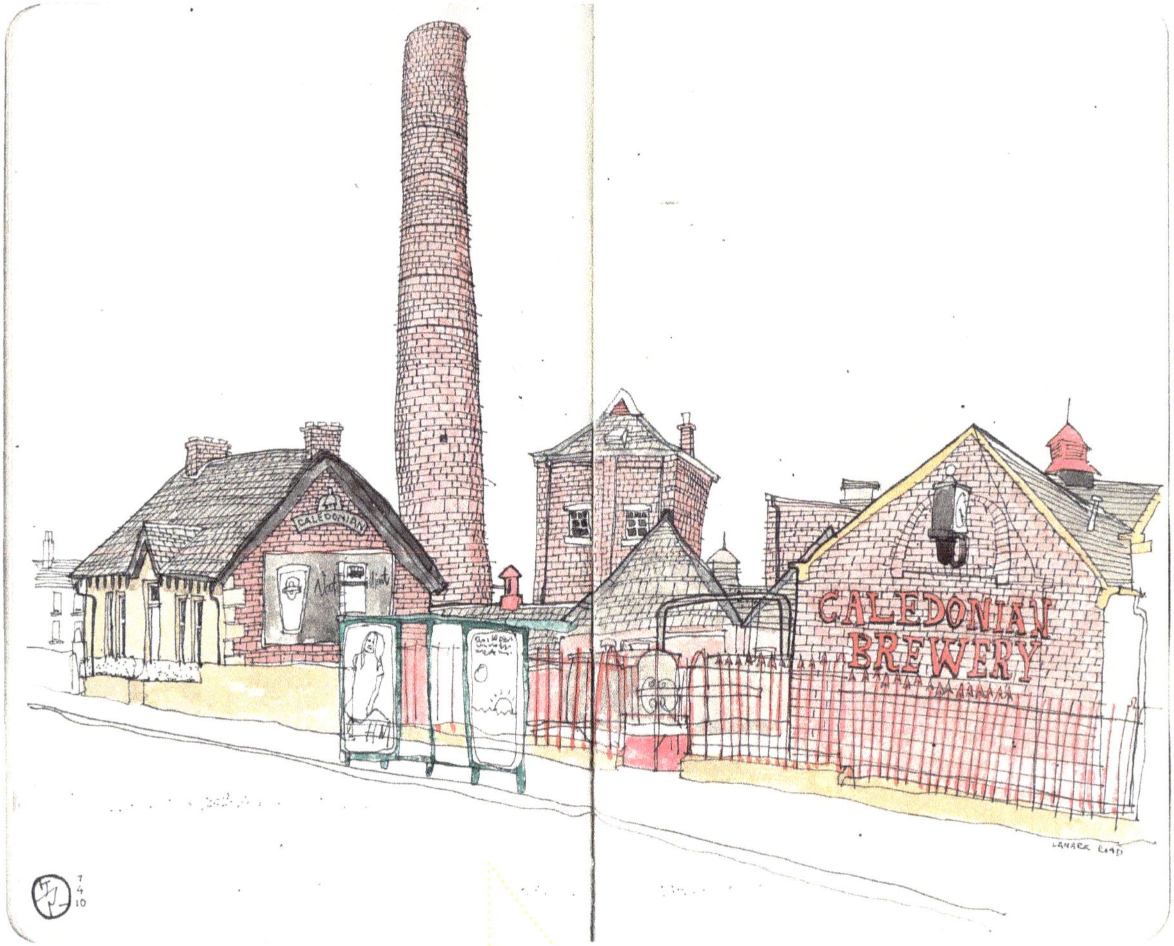

"Out-of-the-office sketching gives me a great sense of relaxation and contentment."

The largest city in Scotland is defined by red-and-blonde Victorian sandstones, says local designer Stuart Kerr. He enjoys drawing the detailed, refined masonry of building façades, even in the unpredictable weather. Illustrator Wil Freeborn usually takes cover sketching in museums and cafés, keeping an eye on the newspapers for different types of events to draw.

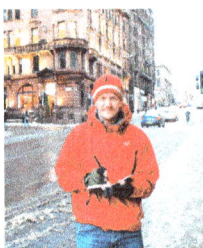

◑ Glasgow designer Stuart Kerr sketches the Caledonian Brewery.

10.25" x 8.25" | 26 x 21 cm; 0.4 Mitsubishi uni PIN pen, Holbein colored pencils, Moleskine sketchbook; 40 minutes, with color added later

ARTIST PROFILE
Stuart Kerr

I've been drawing obsessively in the last six years. I draw much more than I ever did at art school, where I studied product design. I am now an illustrator and exhibition designer and regularly use drawing to convey concepts. I enjoy drawing buildings, because I find the straight lines easier than drawing people. I'm quite easily distracted, so drawing allows me to focus. It also means that situations in which I'm waiting for appointments or transport become ideal opportunities for sketching.

Glasgow has had to reinvent itself since the heady days of shipbuilding, but the legacy lives on through the rich architecture of the city.

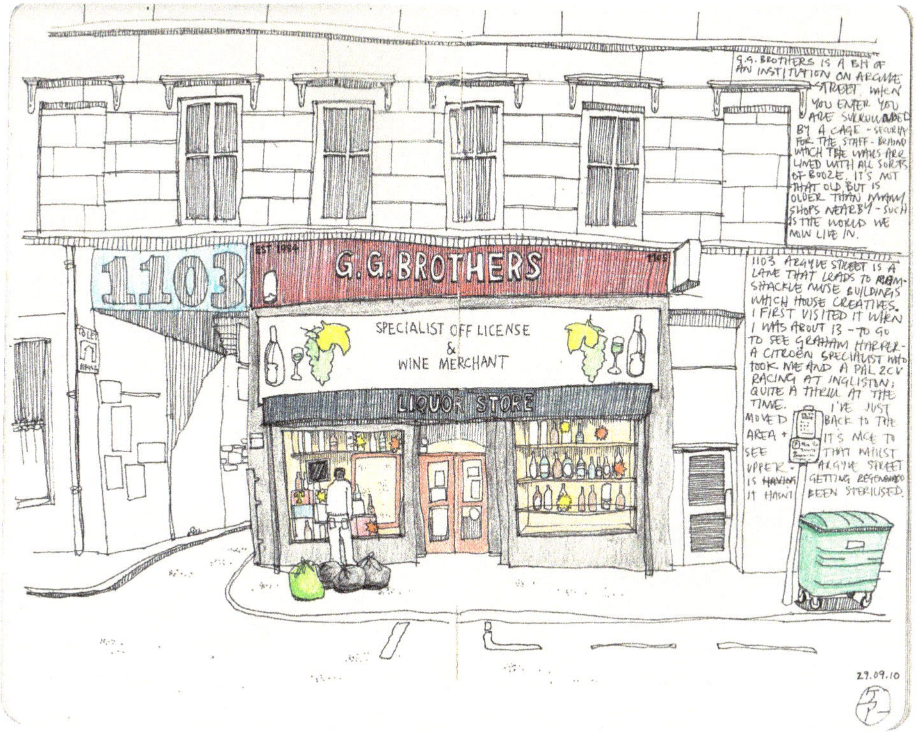
G.G. BROTHERS IS A BIT OF AN INSTITUTION ON ARGYLE STREET. WHEN YOU ENTER YOU ARE SURROUNDED BY A CAGE - SECURITY FOR THE STAFF - BEHIND WHICH THE WALLS ARE LINED WITH ALL SORTS OF BOOZE. IT'S NOT THAT OLD BUT IS OLDER THAN MANY SHOPS NEARBY - SUCH IS THE WORLD WE NOW LIVE IN.
1103
EST 1964
G.G. BROTHERS
SPECIALIST OFF LICENSE
&
WINE MERCHANT
LIQUOR STORE
1103 ARGYLE STREET IS A LANE THAT LEADS TO RAMSHACKLE MUSE BUILDINGS WHICH HOUSE CREATIVES. I FIRST VISITED IT WHEN I WAS ABOUT 13 - TO GO TO SEE GRAHAM HARPER - A CITROËN SPECIALIST WHO TOOK ME AND A PAL 2CV RACING AT INGLISTON; QUITE A THRILL AT THE TIME. I'VE JUST MOVED BACK TO THE AREA + IT'S NICE TO SEE THAT WHILST UPPER ARGYLE STREET IS GETTING REGENERATED IT HASN'T BEEN STERILISED.
29.09.10

⊂ GG Brothers Kerr finds the signs and full-window display with fluorescent stickers at this well-known, local off-license pleasing. "When you step through the door, you enter a cage and are surrounded by product. It's very functional," he says.

Tip "As subject matter, the bland can often be just as interesting as the grand." *– Stuart Kerr*

10.25" x 8.25" | 26 x 21 cm; 0.4 Mitsubishi uni PIN pen, Holbein colored pencils, Moleskine sketchbook; 40 minutes, with color added later

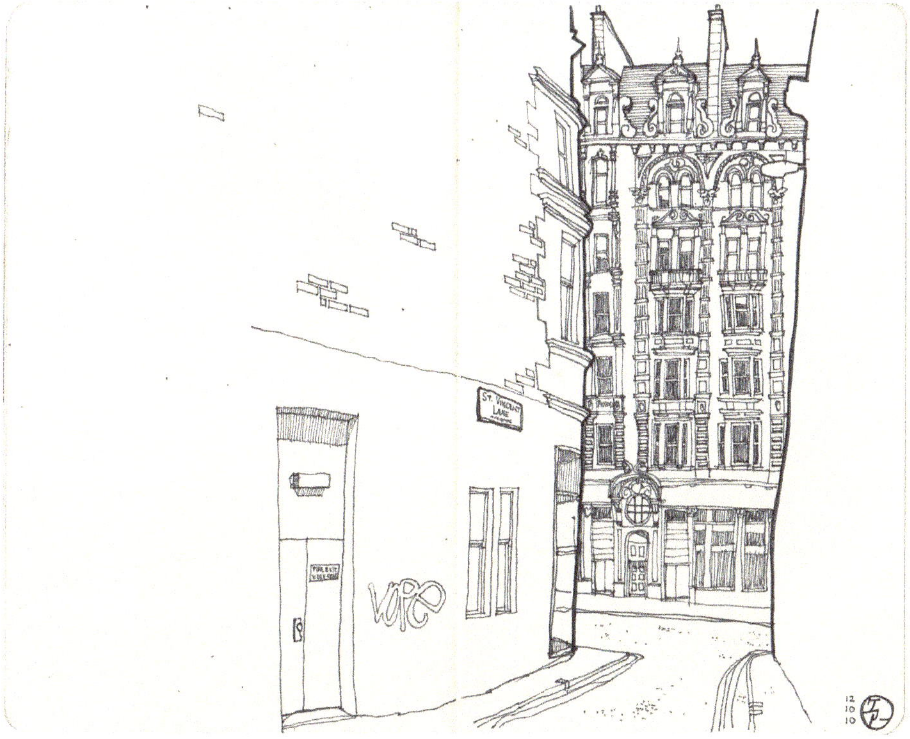
ST. VINCENT LANE
12
10
10

⊂ St. Vincent Lane There's not much of medieval Glasgow remaining, Kerr says, but the impressive Victorian mark is still firm here. This Liverpool and London and Globe Insurance Building has been renovated with a modern interior and mason work on the exterior that Kerr finds truly incredible.

Tip "I used a composition that had proved successful once before: letting the foreground leak into the second page." *– Stuart Kerr*

10.25" x 8.25" | 26 x 21 cm; 0.4 Mitsubishi uni PIN pen on Moleskine sketchbook; 1.5 hours

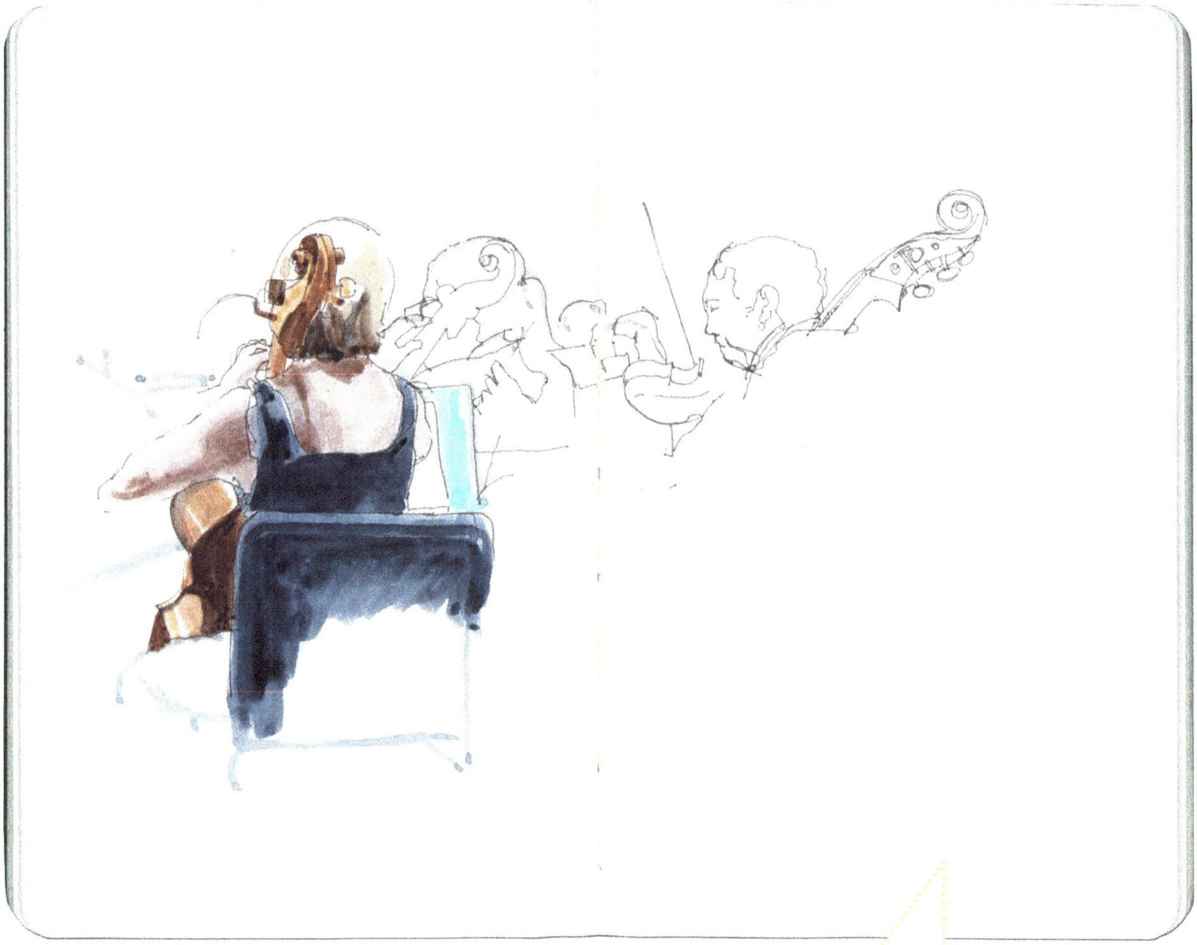

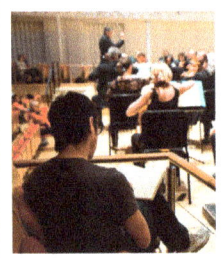

ARTIST PROFILE

Wil Freeborn

I started drawing again with my daily commute, and it really snowballed from there. Once I got the feel of drawing again, I looked farther afield for new places and events to record and experience. In many ways, it has broadened my outlook on life, as well as offering me an opportunity to meet new people and other urban sketchers. It's been a great way to explore and find out more about where I live. I've never really been one to draw buildings; I prefer small scenes, where people are doing something—small snapshots of day-to-day life.

I have found that people of all backgrounds are interested in drawing. It's something we can all relate to and recognize.

🎧 Will Freeborn sketches the BBC Scottish Symphony Orchestra at the City Hall in Glasgow. "It felt like a privilege, because I got great access to draw very close to the orchestra."

10.25″ x 8.25″ | 26 x 21 cm; Faber-Castell Pitt Artist pen (brown, fine) and watercolor; 30–40 minutes, longer with watercolor

" I prefer to draw during events and choose places that are a bit sheltered, like cafés and museums."

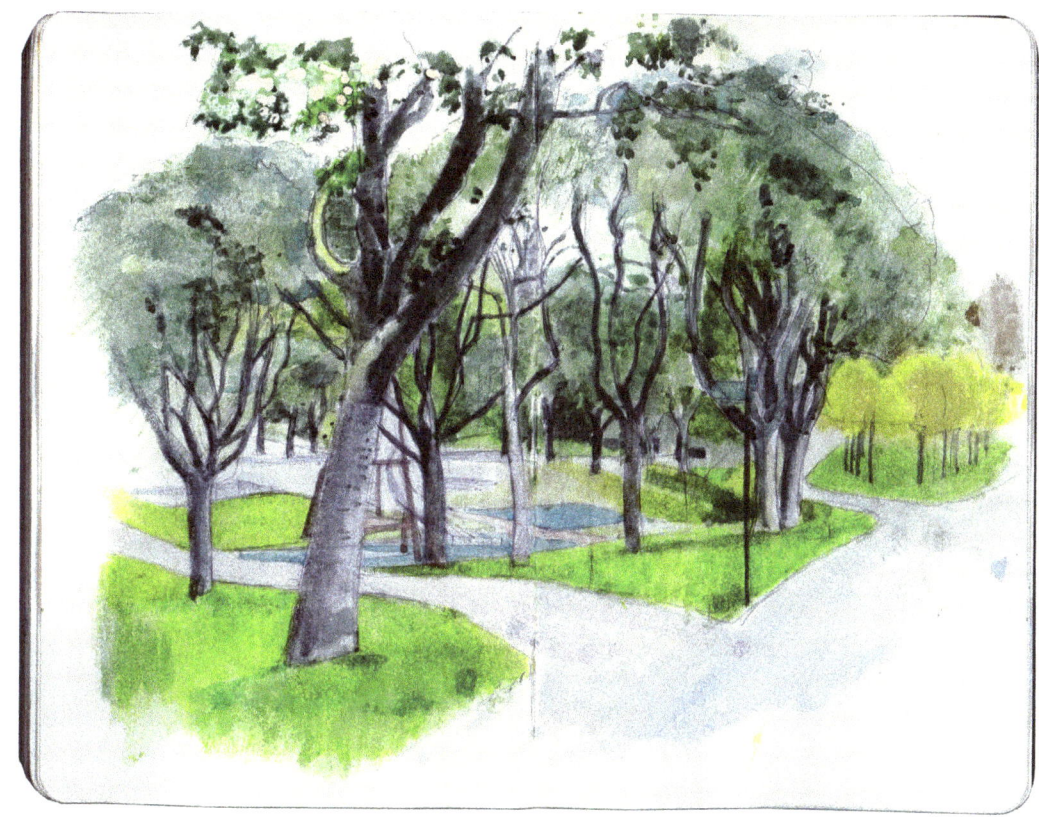

☾ Kelvingrove Park "Sometimes, living in a city is as much about the parks and open spaces as it is about the buildings," says Freeborn.

10.25" x 8.25" | 26 x 21 cm; pencil and watercolor, Moleskine large sketchbook; 30–40 minutes, longer to add watercolor

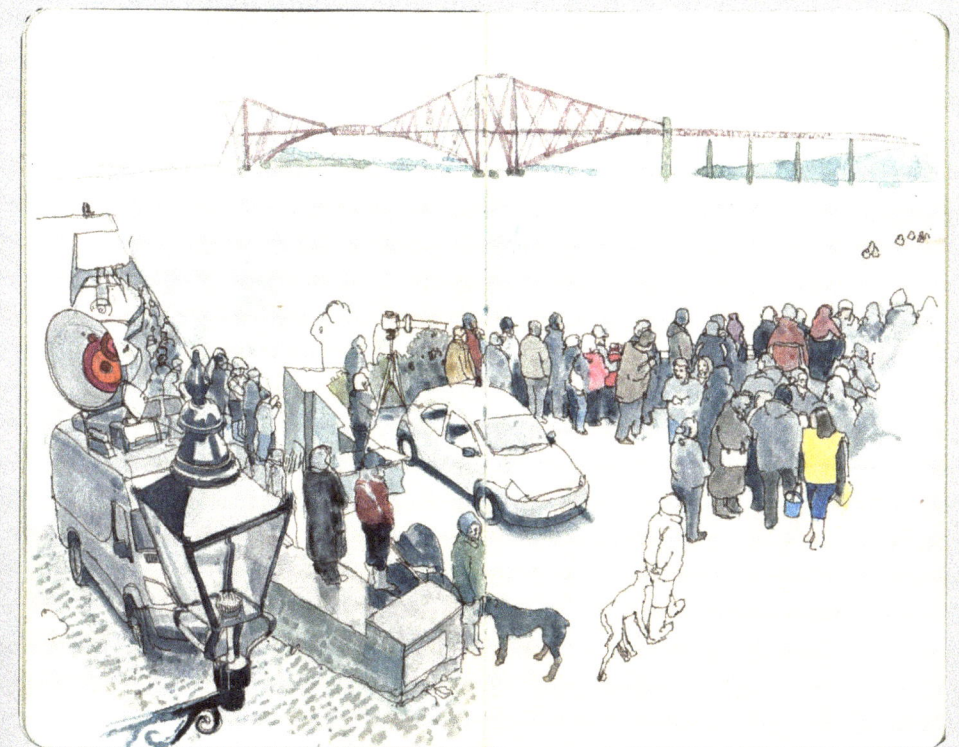

EYEWITNESS

Loony Dook

by Wil Freeborn

I went to "Loony Dook" at Queensferry, where brave souls jump into the Firth of Forth to wash out the old for New Year's Day. It was a great day for it, with the coast covered in snow. They say about 3,000 folks came down to see it, with 800 jumping into the freezing water.

It was a very cold day and very crowded, with thousands coming to this tiny port from all over Scotland. It was difficult to get a view, so I climbed up some stairs to see the crowd, the TV crew, and the scenic Forth Road Bridge. It meant I missed drawing the people, but, as with so many events, being part of a crowd allows you to capture the atmosphere.

10.25" x 8.25" | 26 x 21 cm; Faber-Castell Pitt Artist pen (brown, fine) and watercolor, Moleskine sketchbook; 30–40 minutes, longer to add watercolor

AARHUS

Denmark's second-largest city, Aarhus sits at the base of a bay facing the inner straits between the Danish islands. Its wet and mild climate includes long, dark, and rather chilly winters that make outdoor sketching a seasonal activity, says local sketcher Ea Ejersbo, who nonetheless seldom goes anywhere without a sketchbook.

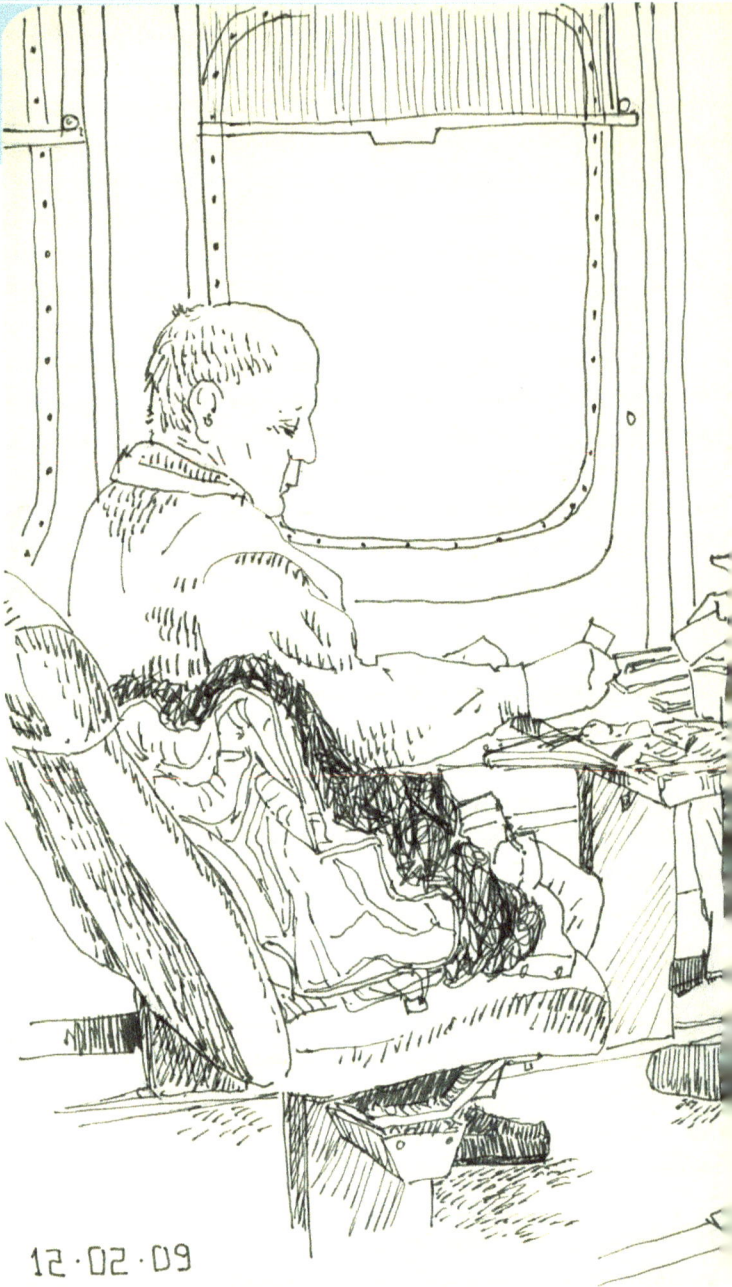

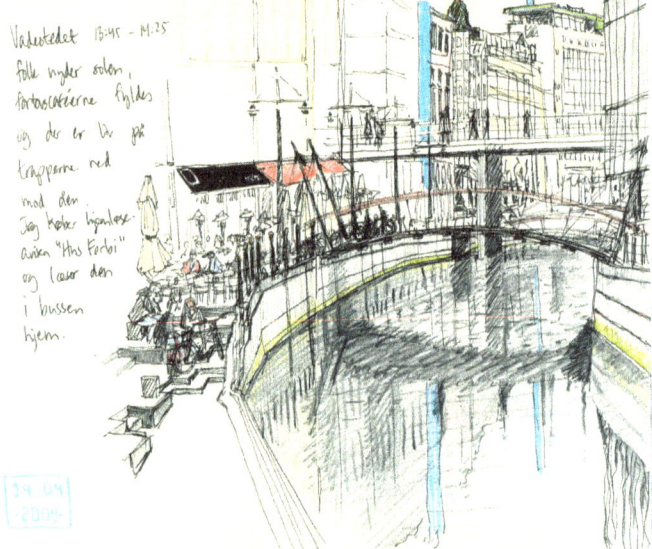

⋂ Vadestedet In the pedestrian area of central Aarhus, Vadestedet ("the ford"), is one of Ejersbo's favorite places to sketch. "The place is always full of life—people hanging out on the stairs, sitting outside cafés, hurrying across the bridges, or strolling along the banks of the canal," Ejersbo says.

Tip "Focus on the larger elements and lines present—the expanse of the canal, the bridges, and the buildings that frame them—and let details, such as people, poles, and café fixtures, add a bit of texture and life." — *Ea Ejersbo*

6.25" x 8.25" | 26 x 21 cm; mechanical pencil with HB lead, Shachihata Artline pen, Faber-Castell Pitt pen, and color pencils, on Moleskine large sketchbook; about 20 minutes

⊃ Mols-Linien Ferry The Mols-Linien ferry sails between Aarhus on the east coast of Jutland and Kalundborg on the west coast of Sealand, carrying passengers and cars. "This is the old, slow ferry I've been traveling on since childhood, as opposed to the newer catamarans that also service the route," Ejersbo says.

Tip "The composition is very simple, composed of just sea, sky, and the bulk of the ferry jutting in from one side. Once the elements are placed, use your time to advantage by focusing on the details—in this case, the ferry." — *Ea Ejersbo*

7" x 5.5" | 18 x 14 cm; Faber-Castell Pitt pens, colored pencil, and mechanical HB pencil on Moleskine pocket sketchbook; 10 minutes, some color added later

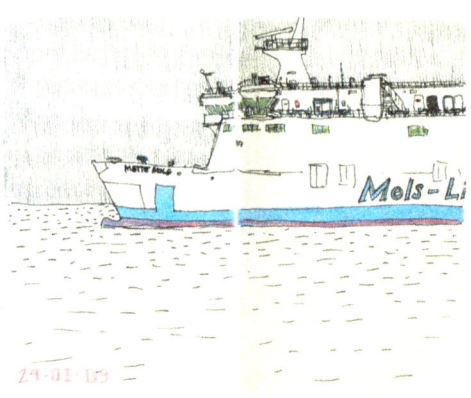

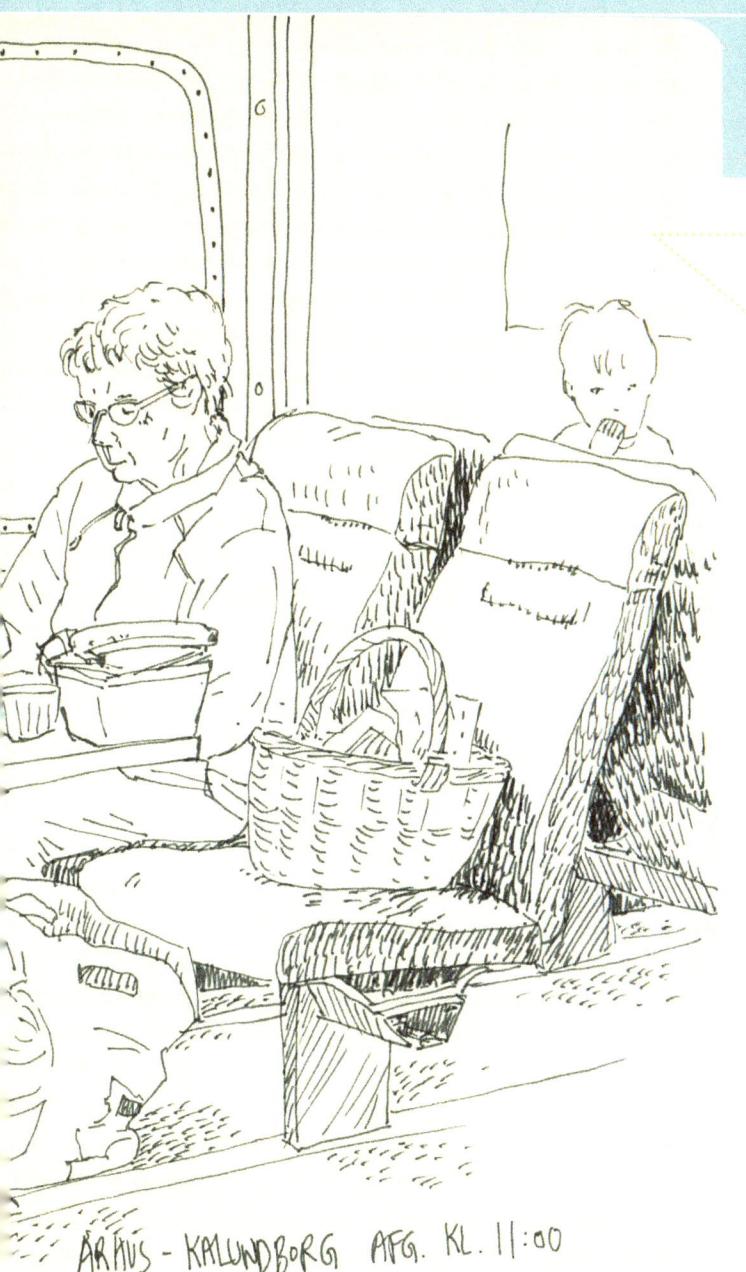

ÁRHUS - KALUNDBORG AFG. KL. 11:00

"I like sketching directly in pen; it forces me to be bold and direct and to observe with presence and precision."

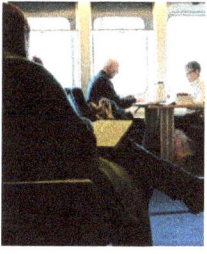

🎧 Ejersbo sketches a couple on the Mols-Linien Ferry between Aarhus and Kalundborg playing cards over coffee.

10.25" x 8.25" | 26 x 21 cm; Shachihata Artline pen on Moleskine large sketchbook; about 30 minutes

ARTIST PROFILE
Ea Ejersbo

I like to observe and register the things that surround me and that I'm a part of, and sketching is a way to experience and share my appreciation of life. One of the things I like about sketching in town is the many layers present everywhere, the history and different functions inherent in the buildings and spaces, the many lives being lived each moment, intersecting with each other or passing unnoticed right under other people's noses—sketching makes me slow down and see these things in a way I otherwise wouldn't.

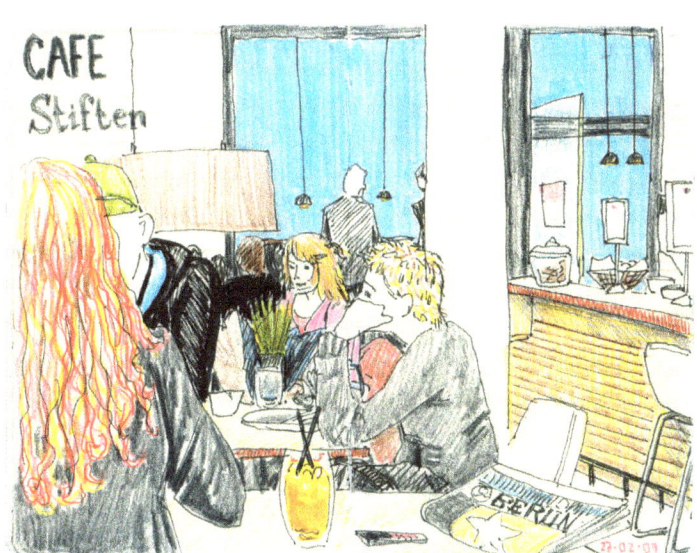

🎧 **Café Stiften** The café gets top points from Ejersbo for its deliciously thick and creamy hot chocolate.

Tip "When sketching with colored pencils, focus more on contrasts and mood than on matching the actual colors of the scene." — *Ea Ejersbo*

7" x 5.5" | 18 x 14 cm; Faber-Castell Pitt pens, graphite pencil HB, and colored pencils on Moleskine pocket sketchbook; about 20 minutes, some color added later

STOCKHOLM

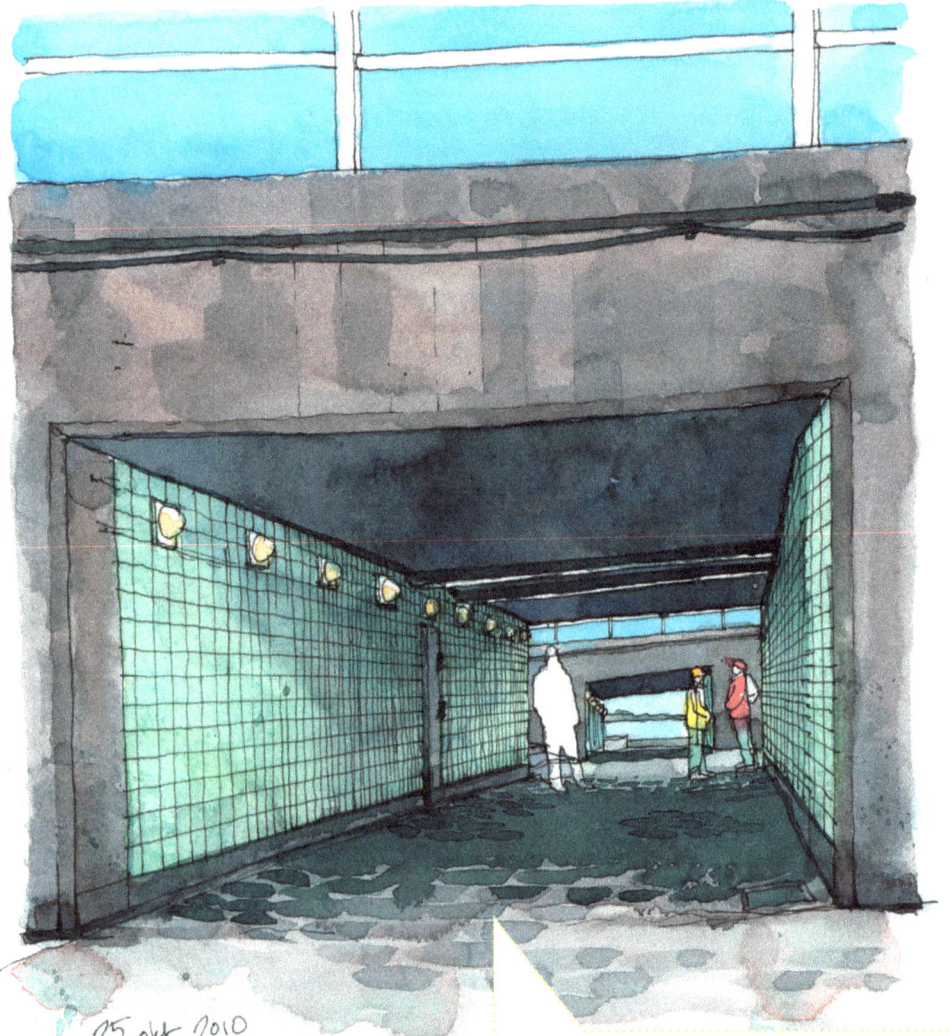

25 okt 2010
Slussen nere vid
nytorstatyn.

6.75" x 8.75" | 17 x 22 cm; Lamy Safari pen with Noodler's
Lexington Grey ink, Winsor & Newton watercolors on 300-gsm
Arches Satine watercolor paper; about 1 hour

To arts teacher Nina Johansson,
Stockholm is an inspiring city in which
to draw. "It's a beautiful place, with lots
of water and layers of architecture from
different periods," she says. "I like that
there are still places where things are not
quite perfect; it's a bit worn down and
unfinished here and there. And cold, very
cold, in the winter."

*"Drawing a city isn't just capturing it on
paper; it's really about getting to know
it, to feel it, to make it your own."*

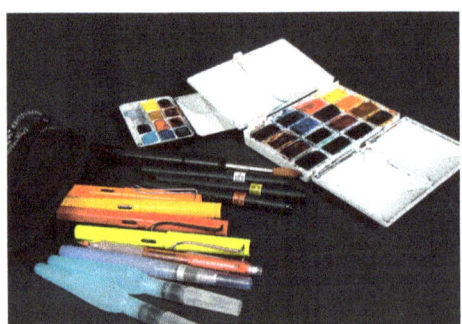

♪ Johansson's sketching tools

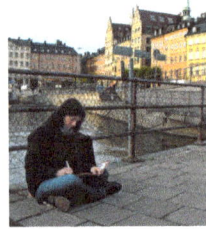

♪ Nina Johansson
sketches one of many
walking tunnels in the
Slussen area of
Stockholm.

ARTIST PROFILE
Nina Johansson

I've been drawing for as long as I can remember, but when I started using
sketchbooks some years back, I suddenly started drawing much more. It's as
if the idea of filling that darned book creates a drive to draw. A filled
sketchbook gives a great feeling of accomplishment, and since I keep all
my books, I can literally see my own work grow and develop.

I like to draw directly in ink, because that makes me look harder and
concentrate more on placing my lines on the paper. I don't mind mistakes;
I just draw over them and try to incorporate them into the drawing. Then, I
either color my drawings with watercolors or use crosshatching to get some
shading and texture.

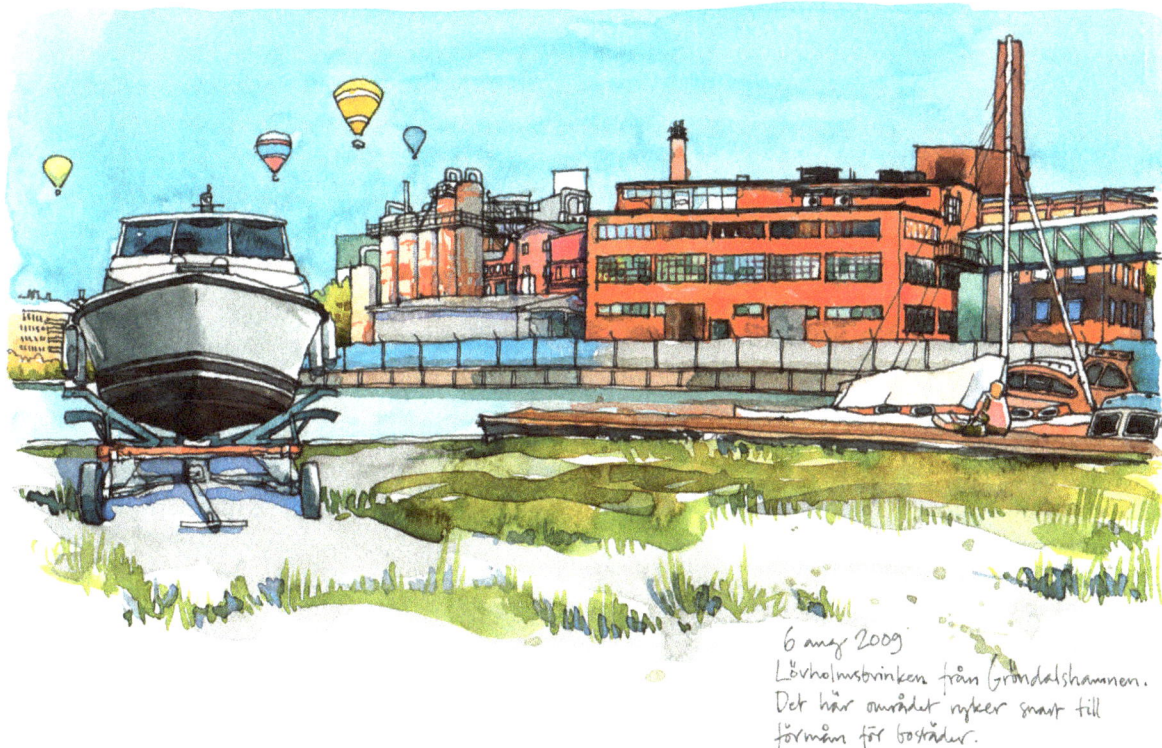

6 aug 2009
Lövholmsbrinken från Gröndalshamnen.
Det här området ryker snart till
förmån för bostäder.

↻ Farewell Lövhol-msbrinken These old industrial buildings at Lövholmsbrinken in Stockholm are soon to be torn down to make room for apartment buildings.

Tip "Watercolors always dry much lighter than they look when they are wet, so I lay them down quite strong. I like spattering paint here and there, using a fan brush, or even a toothbrush, for oil paint, to add some texture and randomness to parts of the image."
— *Nina Johansson*

10.75" x 7" | 27.5 x 18 cm; Lamy Safari fountain pen with EF nib, Noodler's Lexington Grey ink, and mainly Winsor & Newton watercolors, Moleskine Folio A4 watercolor album; about 1.5 hours

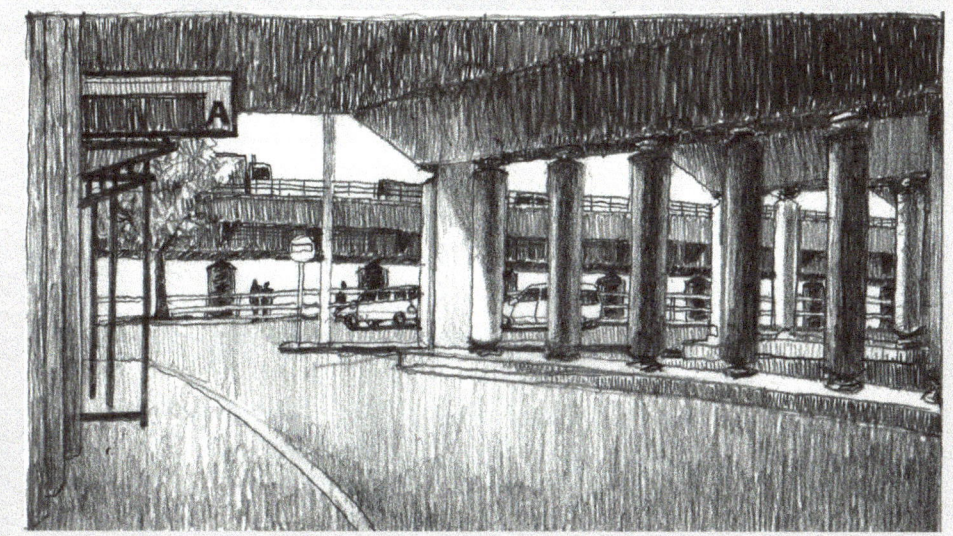

STYLE AND TECHNIQUE

Capturing Values with Pencil

by Nina Johansson

Concrete might not be all that beautiful at first glance, but I love the values in this bus terminal in Slussen. The play of light here is what caught my eye, and all the rows of pillars make an exciting perspective. A camera would hardly capture this successfully, because of the strong contrasts, but with a pencil, it's a really fun drawing challenge. Pencil is not my usual choice of drawing tool, but I love it for its wide grayscale possibilities.

6.75" x 3.75" | 17 x 9.5 cm; 2B mechanical pencil on Arches Satine 300-gsm watercolor paper in hand-bound sketchbook; 40 minutes

Aspudden Public Bath Demolition

by Nina Johansson

The old public bath in Aspudden, Stockholm, was torn down to make room for a new kindergarten. Many people, including me, were incredibly upset about this. Built in 1919, the bath was a pearl, a unique piece of history, offering bathing experiences that you don't find anywhere else. How about a swim and a movie, or ladies' night, with lit candles around the edge of the water? Because the pool was rather small and not so deep, this place was a favorite for families with young kids.

After fifty-nine days of occupation by neighbors, who tried to stop the demolition, the police put a high fence around it, pointed a floodlight at it, and posted two guards in a car outside. The cars parked in the middle of the street to prevent the excavators from reaching the bath were moved. At midnight, a large number of people from Aspudden marched past the police guards to lay down roses in front of the bath.

It was a very sad moment, and many of us had tears in our eyes. A few days later, the last walls of the building were torn down, and now the site is just a pile of dust and snow.

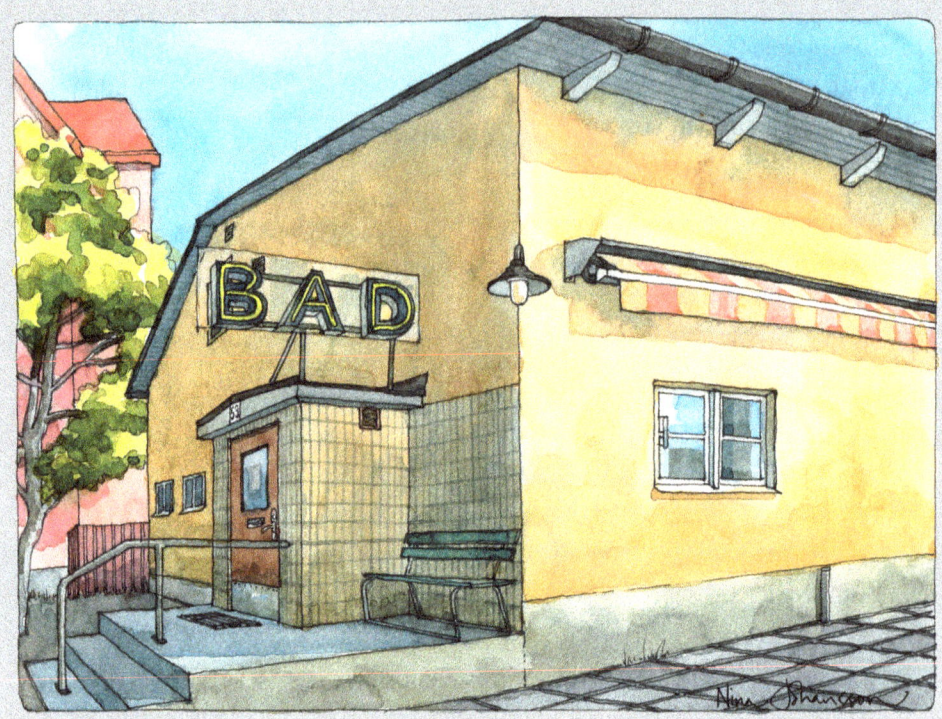

10.5" x 7.75" | 26.5 x 19.5 cm; Lamy Safari pen with Noodler's Lexington Grey ink, Winsor & Newton watercolors on Moleskine Folio watercolor page; about 1 hour

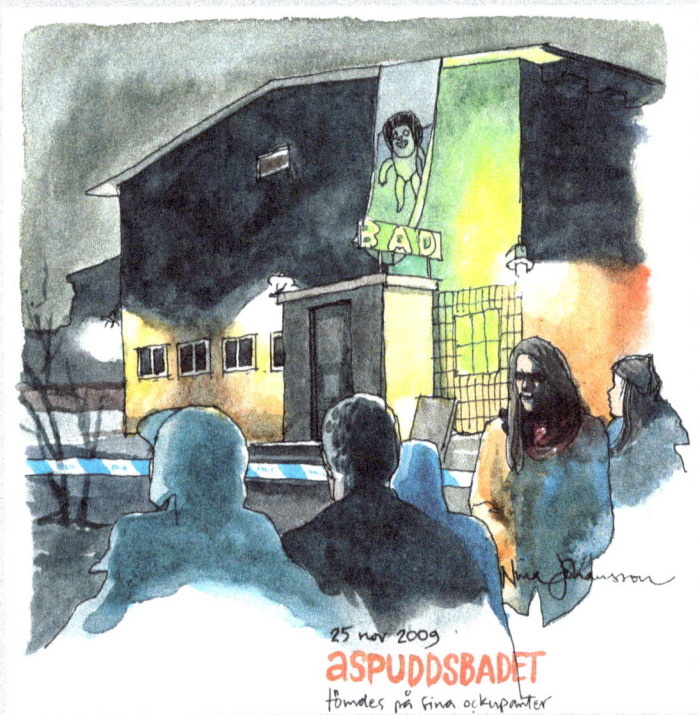

25 nov 2009
aspuddsbadet
försvaras på fina ockupanter

6.25" x 7" | 16 x 18 cm; Uni-ball eye pen, Winsor & Newton watercolors, Fabriano Rosaspina printing paper in hand-bound sketchbook; 45 minutes

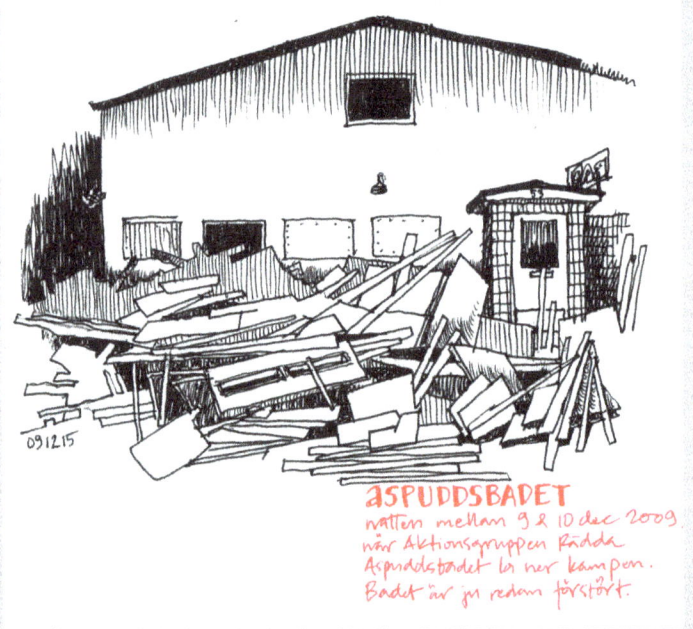

091215

aspuddsbadet
natten mellan 9 & 10 dec 2009
när Aktionsgruppen Rädda
Aspuddsbadet la ner kampen.
Badet är ju redan förstört.

6" x 5.25" | 15 x 13 cm; Uni-ball eye pen and Copic marker on Fabriano Rosaspina printing paper in hand-bound sketchbook; 30 minutes

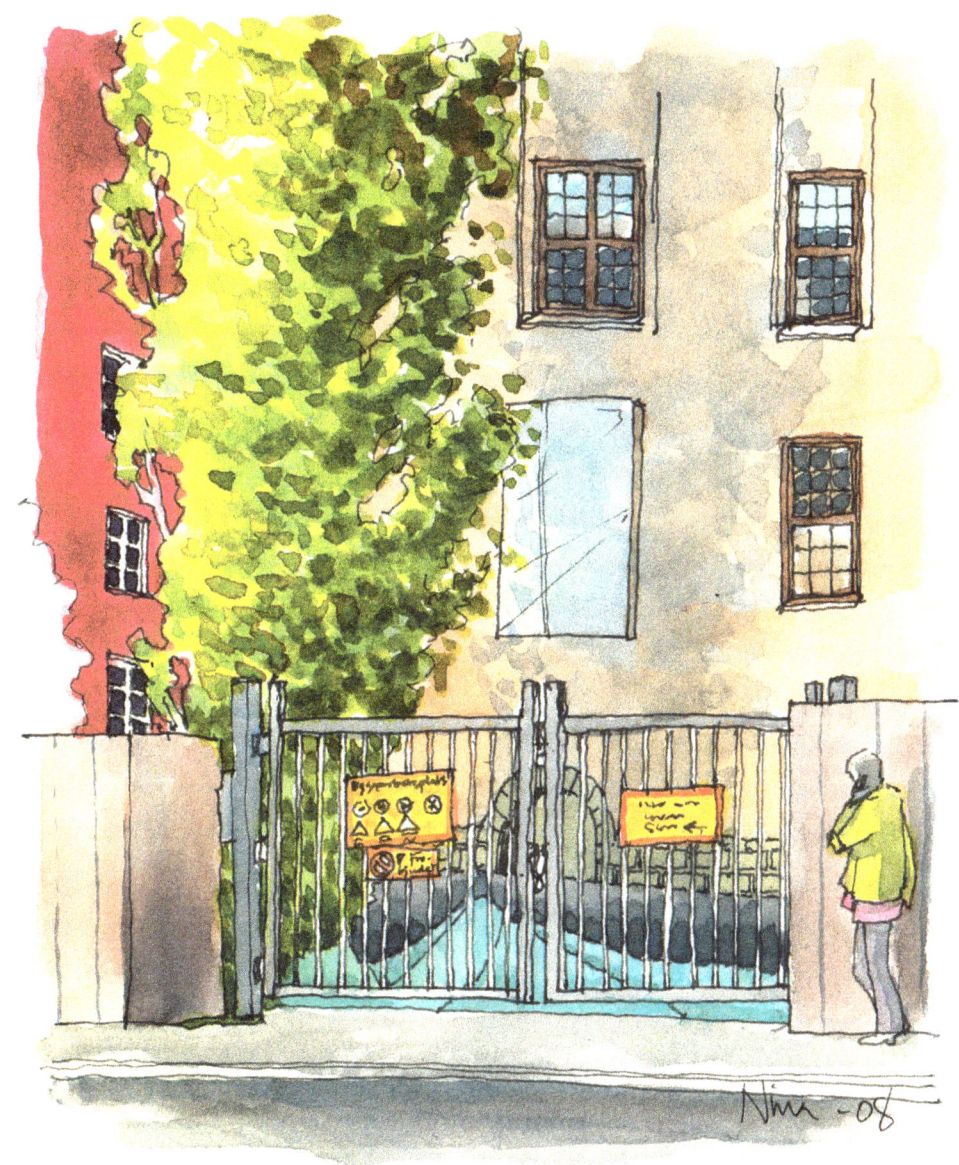

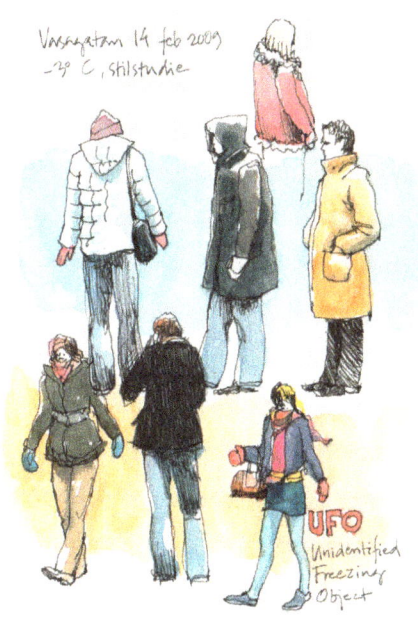

∩ UFOs Stockholm's residents are usually decked out for winter in padded jackets, thick knitted caps, and huge scarves, Johannson says, but she often spots "half-wits, dressed as if it were the middle of summer."

Tip "When I draw people from life, I don't care about page layout; I just draw them as fast as I can before they move out of sight." — *Nina Johannson*

5" x 6.75" | 12.5 x 17 cm; Lamy Safari pen with Noodler's Lexington Grey ink and Winsor & Newton watercolors on cheap, no-name paper, in hand-bound sketchbook; 20 minutes

∩ On a Backstreet Johansson visited one of her favorite cafés and discovered that the renovation of a courthouse had left a huge hole across the street. "I'm sure this is very disturbing for the neighbors, but this is part of what I like about living in a city—things change," Johansson says. "Sometimes, it's sad when things you like disappear, but, on the whole, this is what makes a city."

Tip "Don't just draw pretty scenes—draw anything and everything." — *Nina Johansson*

5" x 6" | 12.5 x 15 cm; Lamy Safari with EF nib, Noodler's Lexington Grey ink, Winsor & Newton watercolors, Fabriano Artistico 200-gsm, hot-press paper, in hand-bound sketchbook; about 45 minutes

MOSCOW

Russia's capital city might be filled with repetitive blocks of flats, says illustrator Zhenia Vasiliev, but the spirit and mood of each place can be quite different; the sketcher should aim to find that uniqueness. But beware of the cold weather, Vasiliev says, when ink can freeze inside the pen. Illustrator Olga Prudnikova visits her hometown often and records how much the city has changed in her sketchbooks.

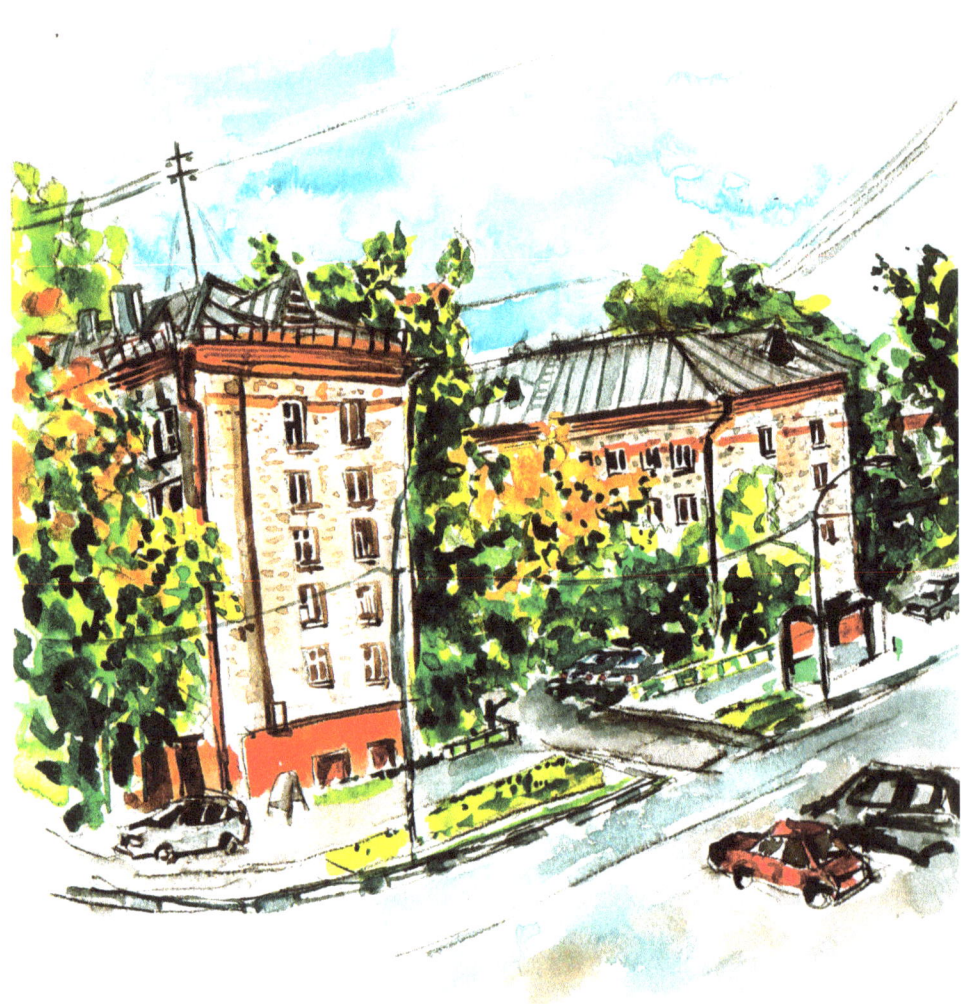

" Sketching in a big city is the chance to take a closer look at its small parts, which otherwise would go unnoticed."

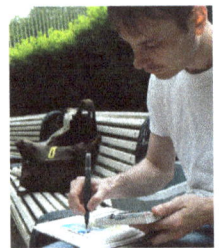

ARTIST PROFILE

Zhenia Vasiliev

When you sketch, you force yourself to be attentive to the details and start noticing how little you actually know of familiar places: the street you walk down every day, the bus you're riding, or the café where you have a quick coffee.

One of my favorite places to sketch in Moscow is the yards around the Novokuznetskaya metro station. I like also sketching the green space around the VVTs (All-Russian Exhibition Center), which is directly connected to the Botanical Garden and its Soviet-era monuments and pavilions.

⋒ **Moments of Golden Autumn** At the time of this sketch, Vasiliev lived near a railway line and captured the street below from the platform. "I was feeling a bit sad when sketching, because I knew I was going to leave Moscow (for London) and wouldn't see this quiet street for some time," he says.

11.75" x 8.25" | 30 x 21 cm; Winsor & Newton Cotman Sketchers' Pocket Box Set and Pentel Aquash waterbrush on 300-gsm, cold-press watercolor paper; about 40–60 minutes

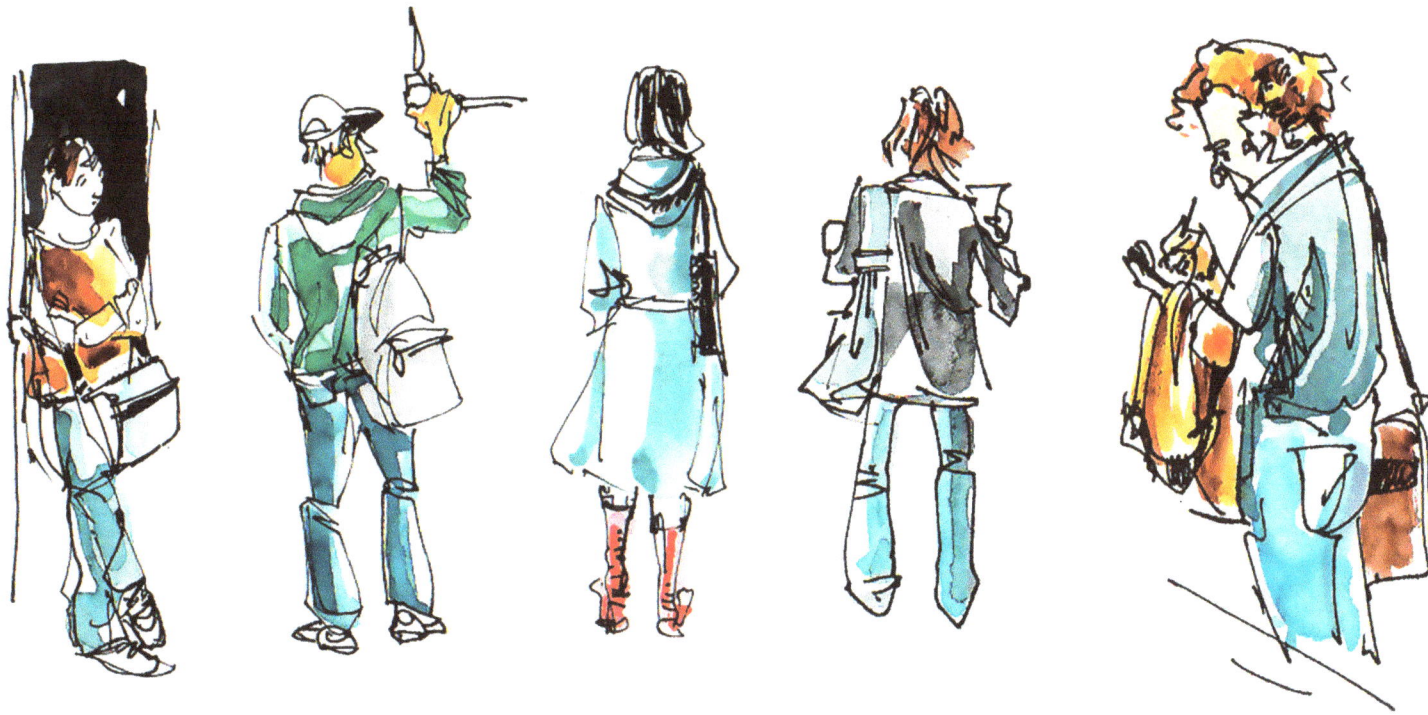

🎧 **People Sketches on the Go** Zhenia Vasiliev says he's been turning boring moments of waiting into hundreds of quick sketches on the go.

Tip "I cut plenty of A6 sheets of cheap paper and take a pack with me when I go out. I attach the pack of paper to a piece of cardboard with a stationery clip. It's cheaper than a soft-cover sketchbook and more convenient, because the cardboard provides a firm base for drawing." — *Zhenia Vasiliev*

A6 (5.8" x 4.1" | 14.8 x 10.5 cm) Lamy Safari fountain pen, Noodler's black ink, Winsor & Newton Cotman Sketchers' Pocket Box Set and a Pentel Aquash waterbrush on Whatman drawing paper; 1 minute for each figure

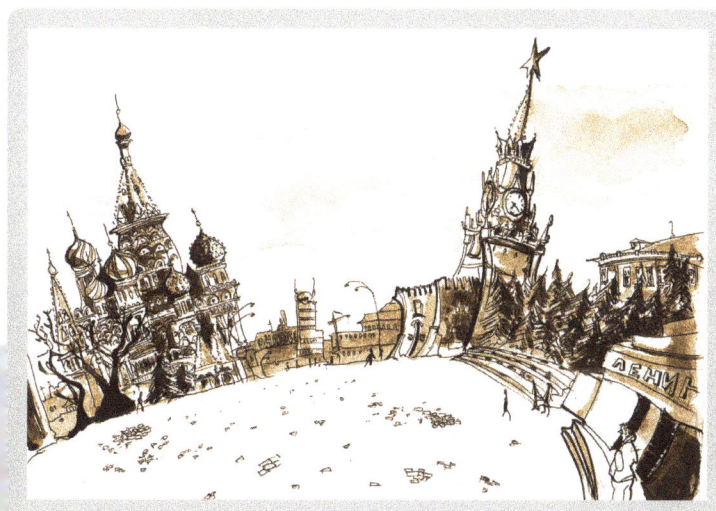

CITY LANDMARK

Red Square in Sepia Tone

by Zhenia Vasiliev

I was standing while drawing, and it was quite chilly, as the beginning of October in Moscow often is. Surprisingly enough, this was actually the first time I had an opportunity to look at the familiar buildings without being in a hurry. Landmarks are rarely things you stop to look at when you pass them every day. Red Square is even more unlucky in this case, because you normally don't go through it to get somewhere. With the fisheye angle, I could include Christ the Saviour, a major Kremlin tower, and the Mausoleum in one picture.

4.25" x 5.75" | 11 x 14.6 cm; ballpoint pen, Winsor & Newton nut brown ink on Whatman 200-gsm watercolor paper; 30 minutes

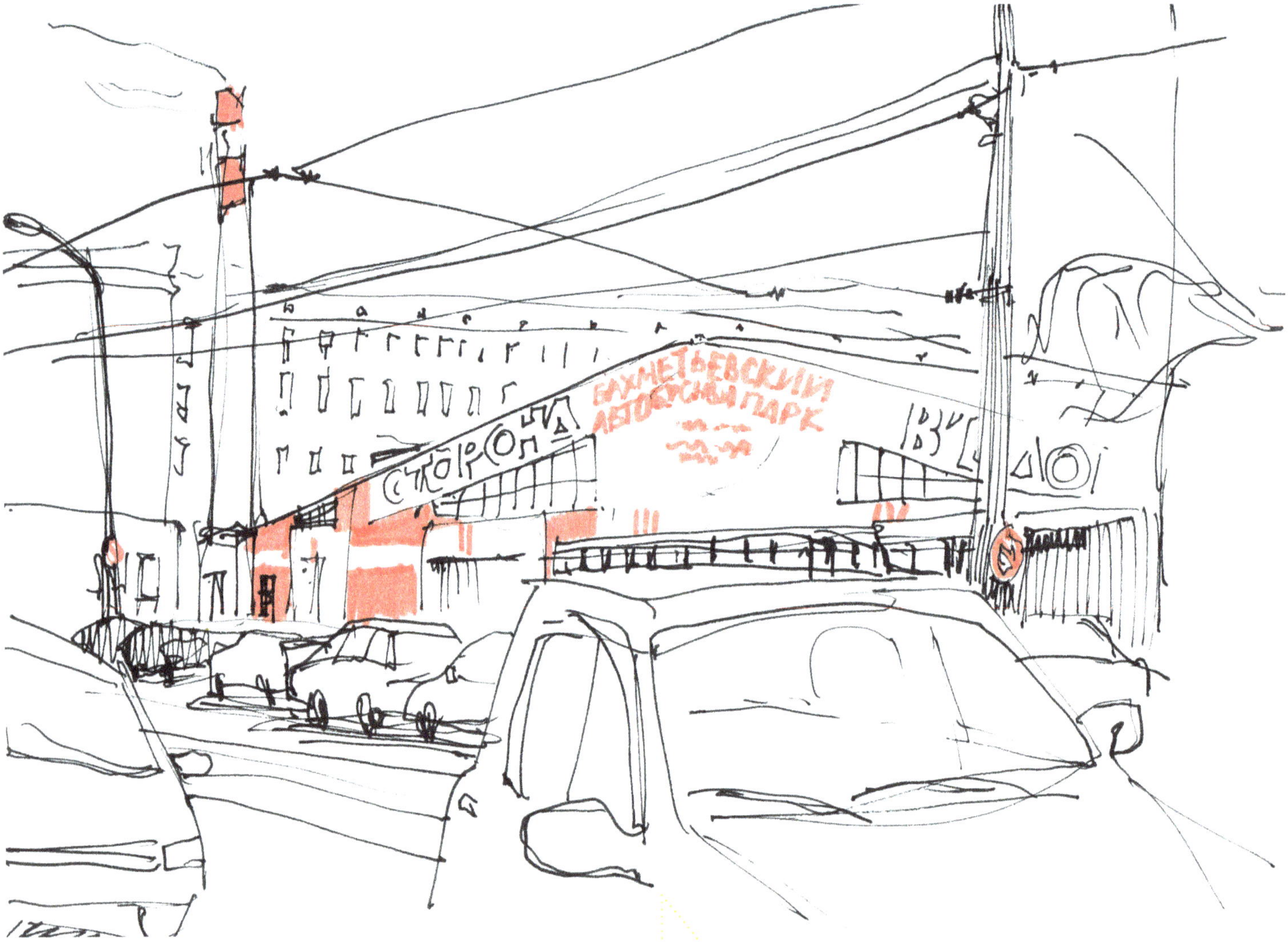

5.25" x 7" | 13 x 18 cm; opic 0.5 liner and Faber-Castell brush marker; about 10–12 minutes

"By looking with the eyes of a traveler, it becomes easier to portray the face of the city."

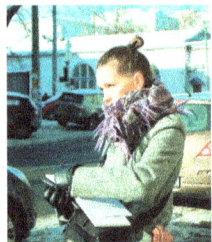

🎧 Prudnikova sketches the former Bakhmetevsky Bus Garage in Moscow, which now includes a gallery of contemporary art, a café, and a nice bookstore.

ARTIST PROFILE
Olga Prudnikova

I started to sketch while traveling, and, since then, I've brought the same attitude of a traveler to my everyday life. I found that I can even look at my hometown, Moscow, with different eyes. It's a city with urban objects, faces of people, and simple moments that fill my sketchbooks and help me notice more around me.

As a freelance illustrator and artist, I use some of my sketches when I prepare material for my work, and I think sketching is definitely the best way to develop strength in your hand and lines.

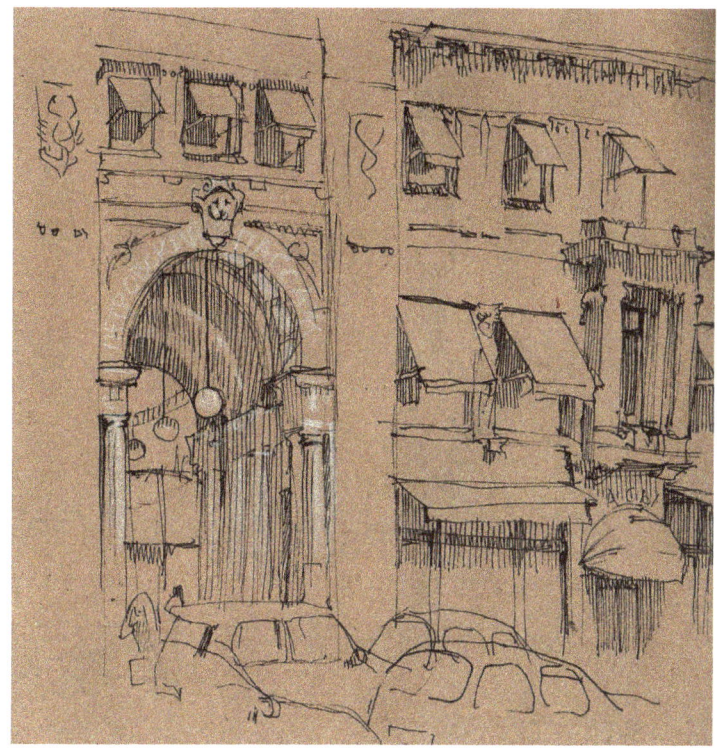

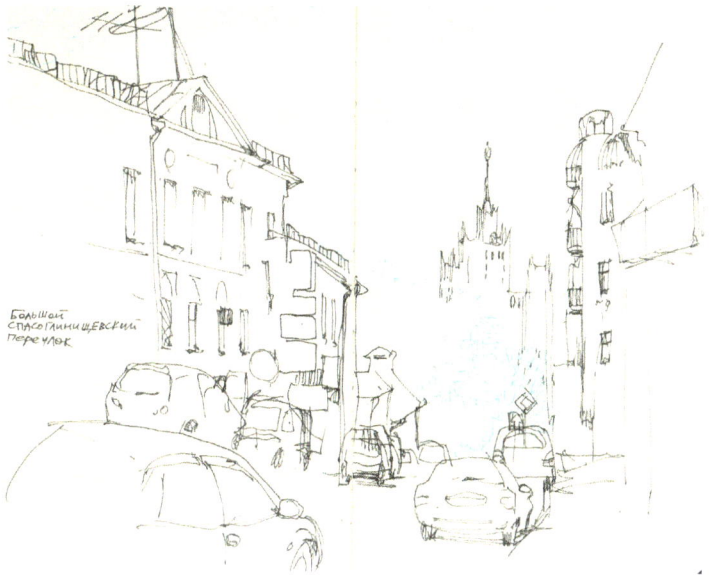

∩ Petrovsky Passage The shopping arcade Petrovsky Passage was opened at the beginning of the twentieth century. It's still one of the most expensive trade areas in Moscow, Prudnikova says.

7.25" x 7.25" | 18.5 x 18.5 cm; Faber-Castell 0.3 black liner, white color pencil on Kraft paper pad (Russia); 15 minutes

∩ Bolshoi Spasoglinitshevsky Pereulok The sidewalk on which Olga Prudnikova stopped to draw a view of an old "skyscraper" and the trees behind a hill was so narrow, she had to sketch standing in a phone booth.

10.25" x 8.25" | 26 x 21 cm; Copic 0.3 liner, MUJI .38 pen on Moleskine large sketchbook; 15 minutes

∪ Business Lunch at the Vnukovo Airport Olga Prudnikova took advantage of the wait for her flight from Moscow to sketch people in a café, though she says the man in the uniform noticed her drawing them, and she had to stop.

Tip "If I draw a group of people, I like to see their relations and capture the feeling of the dialogue." *— Olga Prudnikova*

11.75" x 8.25" | 30 x 21 cm; 5B pencil on 96-gsm Lana sketchpad; 10 minutes

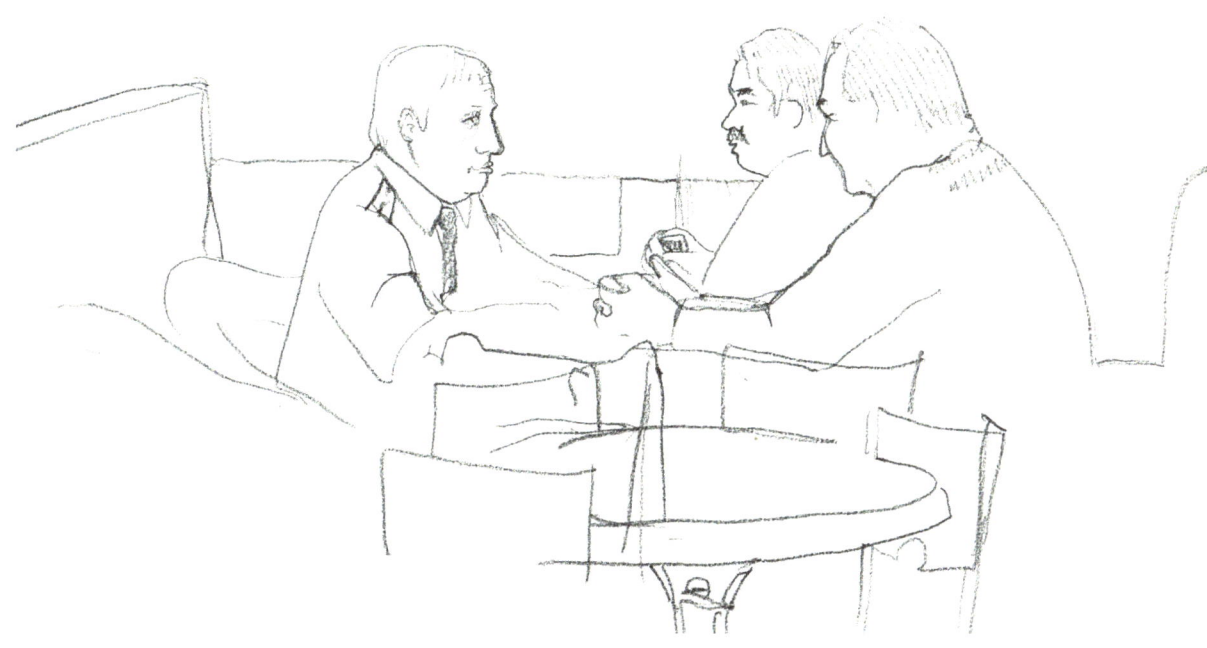

BERLIN

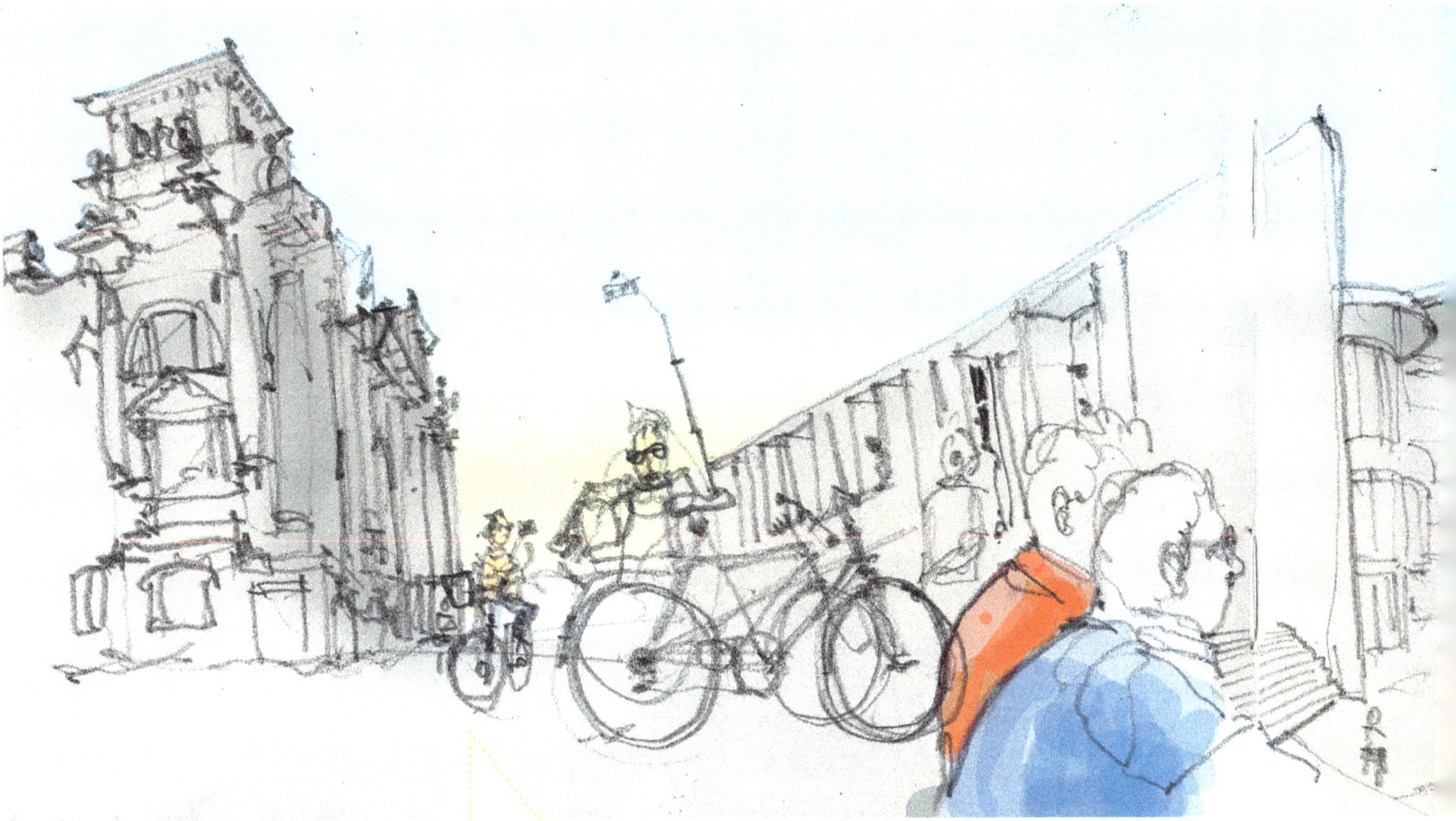

On first view, Berlin is not a beautiful city, says architect and illustrator Rolf Schroeter. "It has lots of breaks, empty spaces, and few 'scenic' places. But that's what makes it a good place to sketch." The breaks and gaps in the city are often spatially and historically interesting, he says. By sketching, "one can discover things one did not know before and maybe uncover some specific beauty."

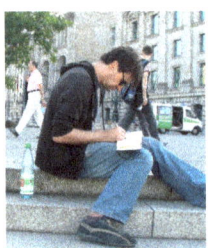

🎧 Rolf Schroeter sketches a view of the Reichstag in Berlin on German election day. Schroeter used the computer to add color to the pencil sketch.

ARTIST PROFILE
Rolf Schroeter

I rarely go out for the exclusive purpose to draw, but I always carry a sketchbook and pen with me and use them on every occasion. Most of my sketches are done in short breaks during my typical, everyday movements. I choose topics and views spontaneously and try to let a place flow with as little resistance as possible on the sheet, trying to get "disturbing me" out of the way. I like this state of concentrated self-unawareness. I hope that occasionally something of common interest emerges from that practice.

I am a stone mason and architect but am working as an illustrator now. My professional work deals mainly with computer graphics, mostly executed using 3-D techniques. Location sketching is a useful practice to develop a feeling for composition and to explain the narrative quality of images. But, above all, I enjoy making images that are totally self-driven, without aim, guide, or deadlines.

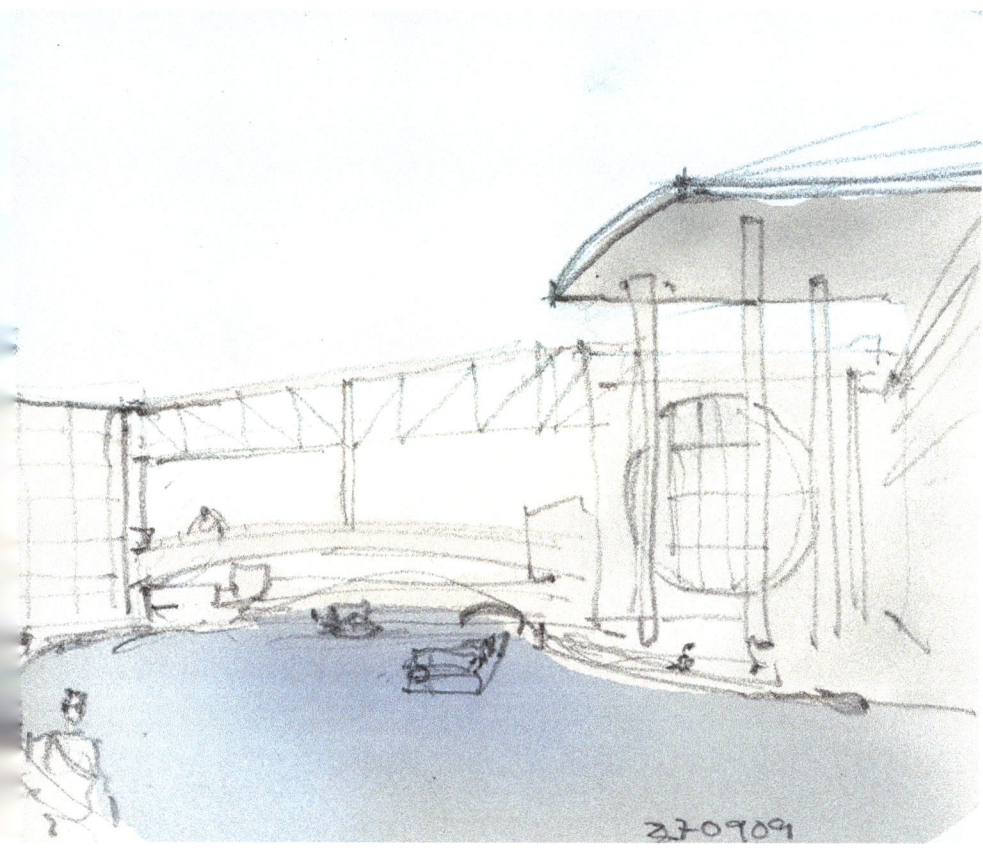

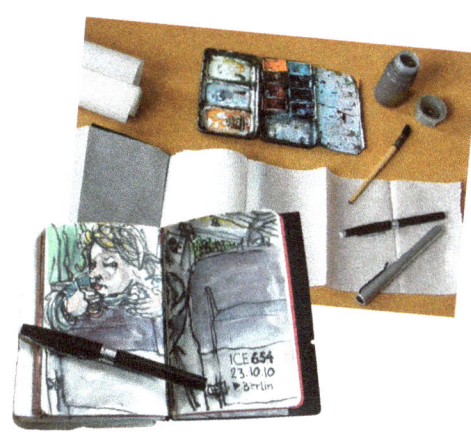

⋂ *Schroeter's sketching tools*

⋃ **Bode-Museum, Berlin** On his way to the museum, Rolf Schroeter's plans changed when he spotted a beautiful evening light. He stopped to do this sketch, instead.

Tip "I always like to work from special viewpoints that I find accidentally or by strolling around a place. They are much more interesting than the obvious, multi-photographed views, especially at scenic places." — *Rolf Schroeter*

5" x 8.75" | 12.5 x 22 cm; 4B graphite pencil in KOH-I-NOOR leadholder, Winsor & Newton watercolors on Hahnemühle 140-gsm Travel Journal

"Since I reactivated my sketching, my relation to Berlin intensified, and I got somehow involved in the city."

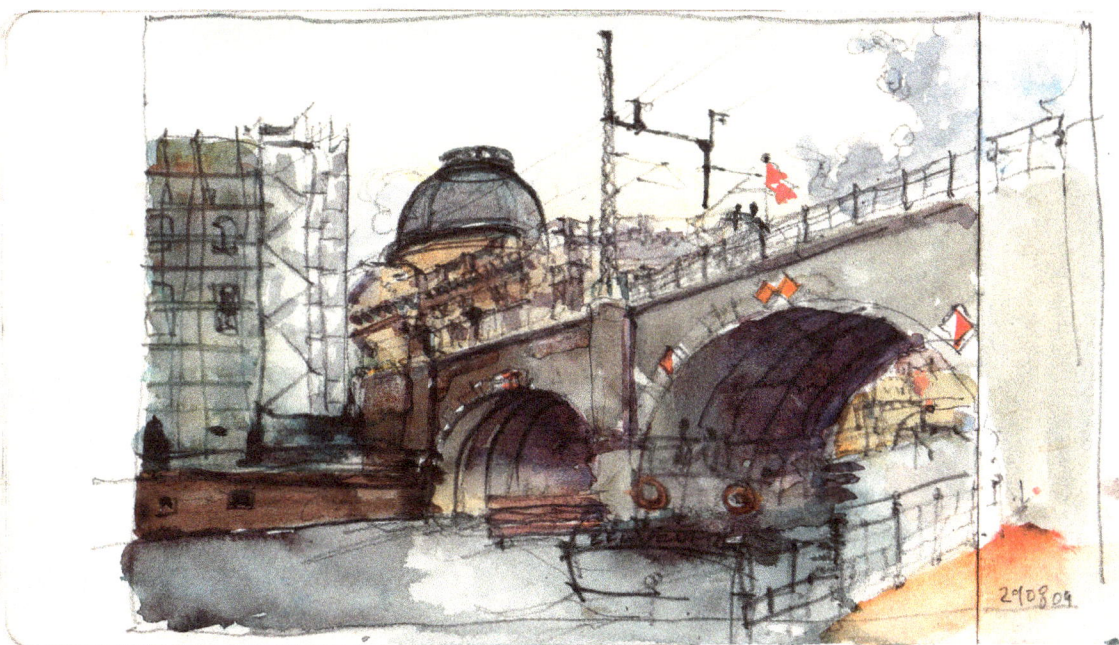

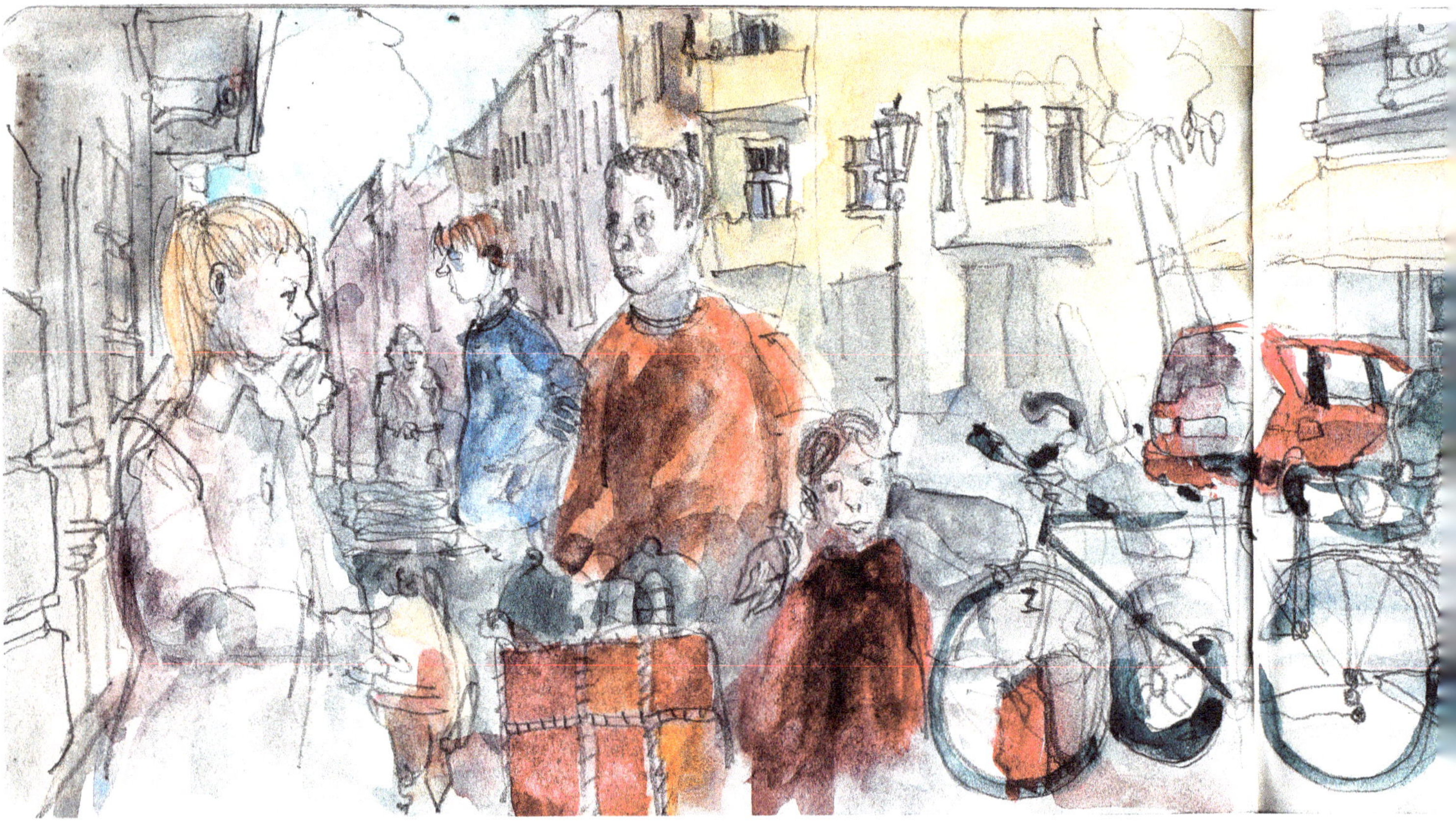

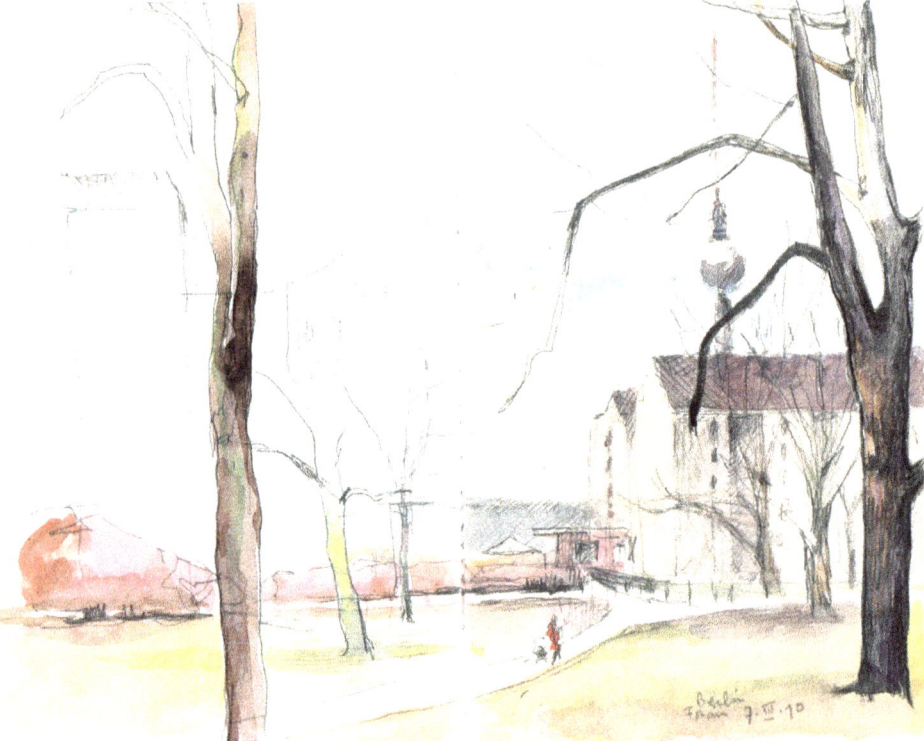

☾ Berliner Fernsehturm Catalina Somolinos was attracted to the emptiness of the park, the naked trees, the simple gray houses, and the view of the Berliner Fernsehturm over the roofs, in the faraway distance, pinching the pasty, dense sky.

Tip "Try to catch the subtle winter tones, as fast as the frozen air allows you to keep your hand drawing."
— *Catalina Somolinos*

10.5" x 8.25" | 26.5 x 21 cm; Winsor & Newton watercolors, white tempera, and pencil on 140-gsm Hahnemühle Travel Booklet, portrait size; 15 minutes

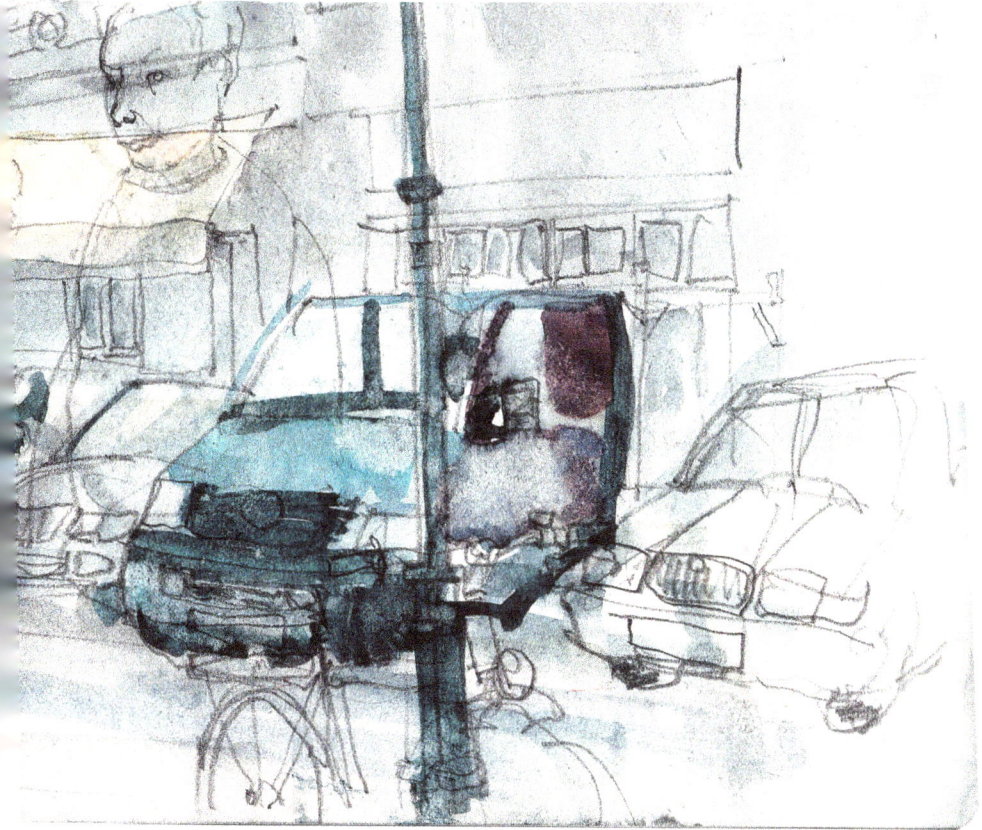

☾ **Flea Market, Klausenerplatz-Kietz** Rolf Schroeter's children were trying to sell some of their old toys at the neighborhood flea market; he took some time to sketch while caring for their stand. "It was a very comfortable sketching situation, with a seat and a table in front, but I could not move around to search for a better viewpoint, so I just took what I got."

Tip "In streets with houses, I always try to get the "negative" shape of the sky right. Even if I have a vanishing point in mind, I think it's much easier to get the angles right when concentrating on the abstract shape of the sky." — *Rolf Schroeter*

16.25" x 5.25" | 41.5 x 13 cm; 4B graphite pencil in KOH-I-NOOR Hardtmuth leadholder, Winsor & Newton watercolors, traditional French watercolor brush (no waterbrush) on Moleskine Reporter notebook (plain); 45 minutes

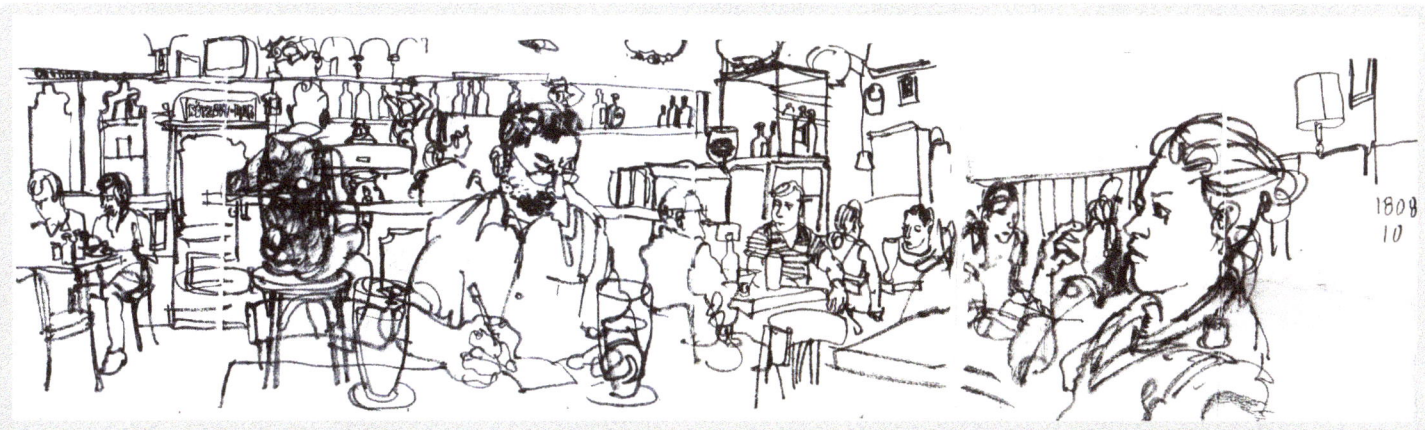

DRAWN TOGETHER

Meeting Fellow Urban Sketchers at a Pub in Linienstrasse, Mitte

by Rolf Schroeter

Urban sketcher Gabriele Orlando visited Berlin, so I got to know him that evening. We met with Berlin sketcher Olga Prudnikova, sketched together in the Tacheles, and then dropped into this pub. It was very enjoyable to meet other sketchers, exchange ideas, and sketch together. I started this without an idea about composition, just with the image of Gabriele, but then continued, partly on an additional sheet, and wound up with a roughly 170-degree panorama. Sometimes, it is nice to doodle without concept and continue just for the joy of "writing down a place."

6" x 21.25" | 15 x 54 cm; Pentel brush pen with Pentel ink cartridges, ink thinned with water, sandwich wrapping paper; 30 minutes

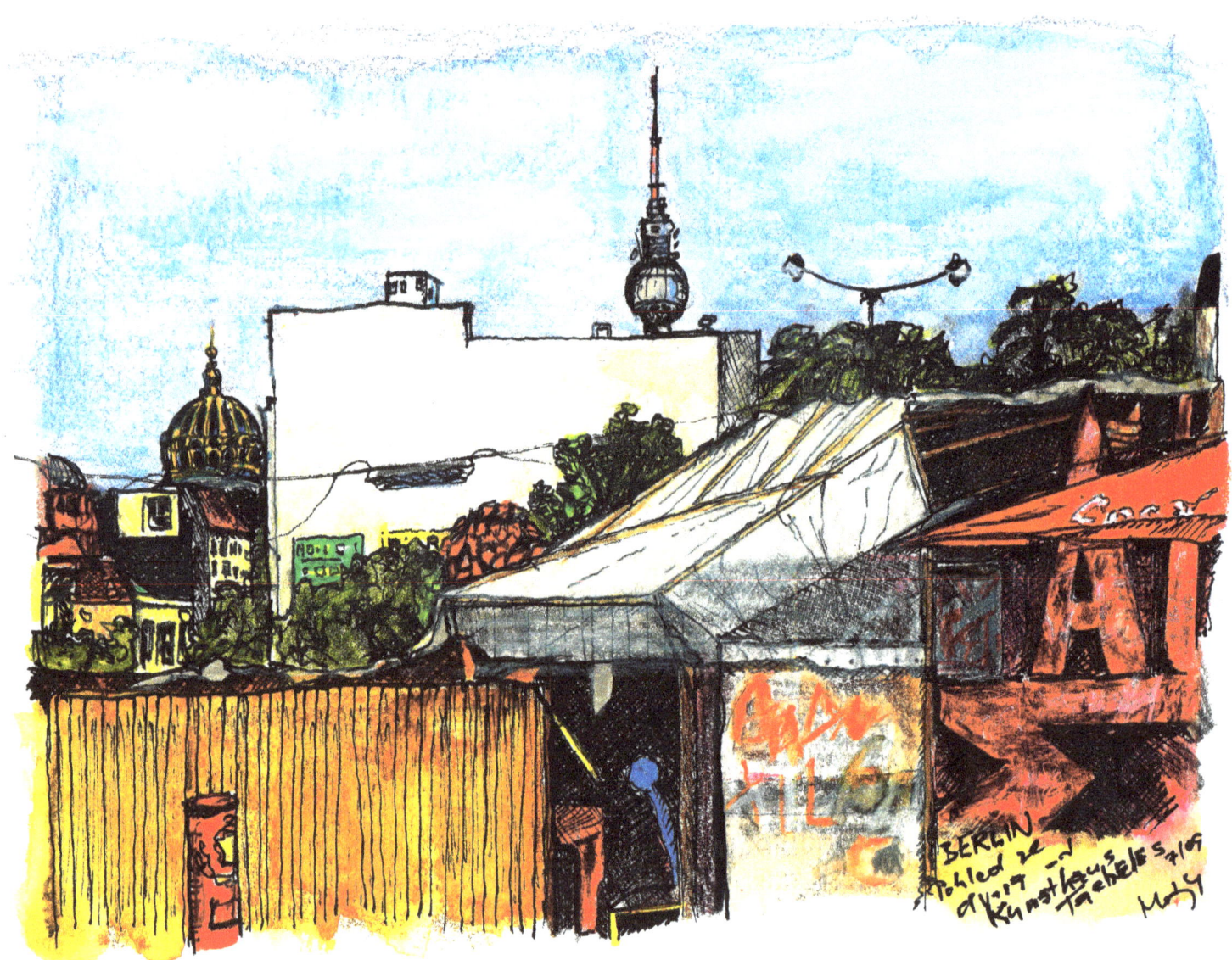

⋒ View from the Courtyard of Tacheles Kunsthaus The Tacheles art center is situated in a ruin in Berlin Mitte in East Berlin. The area was a Jewish quarter in the past and has now become a meeting point for people interested in arts and culture, says Czech artist Aleš Motýl.

Tip "For me, it is important to search out quiet places and artistically interesting perspectives that differ from conventional views of the city." — *Aleš Motýl*

7" x 10" | 18 x 25 cm; Copic 0.3 Multiliner, Faber-Castell Albrecht Dürer watercolor pencils, Hahnemühle Britannia watercolor block (natural white, matte, 300-gsm); 1 hour

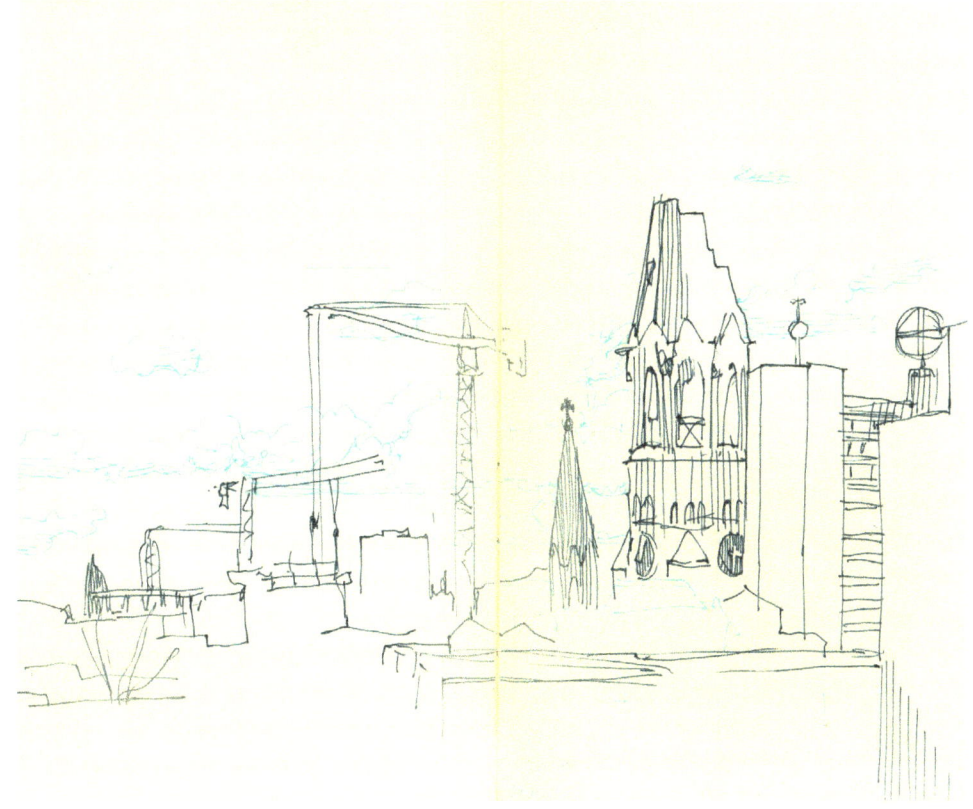

↺ The Kurfürstendamm Known locally as the Ku'damm, The Kurfürstendamm was the center of nightlife during the 1920s and has now become a huge shopping street in Berlin. You can see the ruins of the Kaiser Wilhelm Memorial Church, which was damaged during a bombing raid in World War II.

Tip "The best location for sketching a busy urban street is often not on the street itself but rather looking out from a higher floor in one of the buildings. A great sketching spot on this usually very crowded street offers itself in a chocolaterie on the top floor of the KaDeWe shop center." — *Olga Prudnikova*

10.25" x 8.25" | 26 x 21 cm; MUJI pen on Moleskine sketchbook; 15 minutes

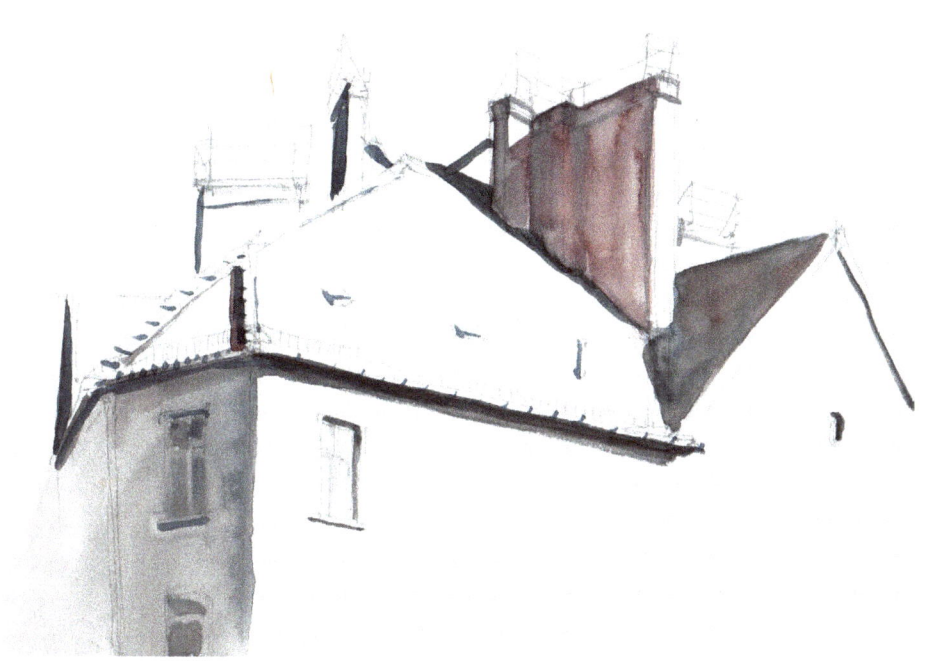

↺ Corner of Seumestrasse and Simplonstrasse Oona Leganovic recommends drawing the forms of the object first and then coloring in only the parts in shadow.

Tip "Try to wet each shadow part completely. That way, you can push around the paint and let it flow, which makes the shadows come alive a bit. You don't have to draw in every detail of the house; you can just focus on the parts you find interesting." — *Oona Leganovic*

7.5" x 5.5" | 19 x 14 cm; Schmincke tube watercolor and 0.7 Pentel GraphGear 1000 mechanical pencil on landscape-format Boesner watercolor book with 250-gsm Canson C paper, on the smooth side; 20–30 minutes

STUTTGART

Stuttgart is the cradle of Porsche and Mercedes, so it's no surprise to find artists here who enjoy drawing cars. But the industrial city has more to offer. Architectural drawer Florian Afflerbach enjoys sketching around the densely populated area of Stuttgart-West. "There are ancient façades from the period of promoterism next to blocks of flats from the 1950s, when living space was needed after the Second World War," he says.

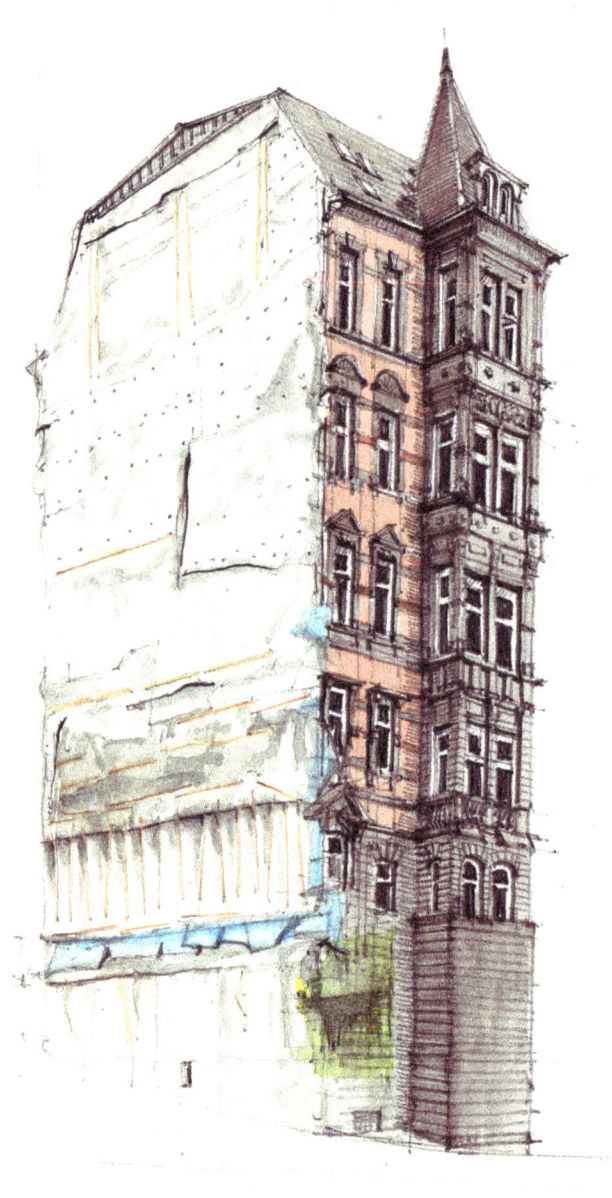

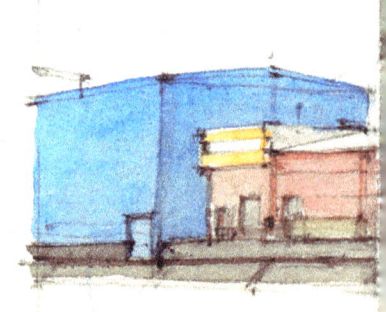

☾ Gaisburgstrasse Afflerbach saw a terrific opportunity to sketch a view of this building from the promoterism era (after the Franco-German war of 1870–1871). "A new housing area was built on the hillside next to this house, so this scene can't be seen or drawn anymore." he says.

Tip "Drawing construction sites is always fantastic and an outstanding situation, because it is very temporary. The construction site changes every day, and you can come back to see what has happened, so far. So, you have to decide quickly if you want to do a sketch."
— Florian Afflerbach

10" x 13.75" | 25 x 35 cm; 4B Faber-Castell pencil, Schmincke watercolors, #4 and # 6 da Vinci brushes on 170-gsm Boesner sketchbook; about 2 hours

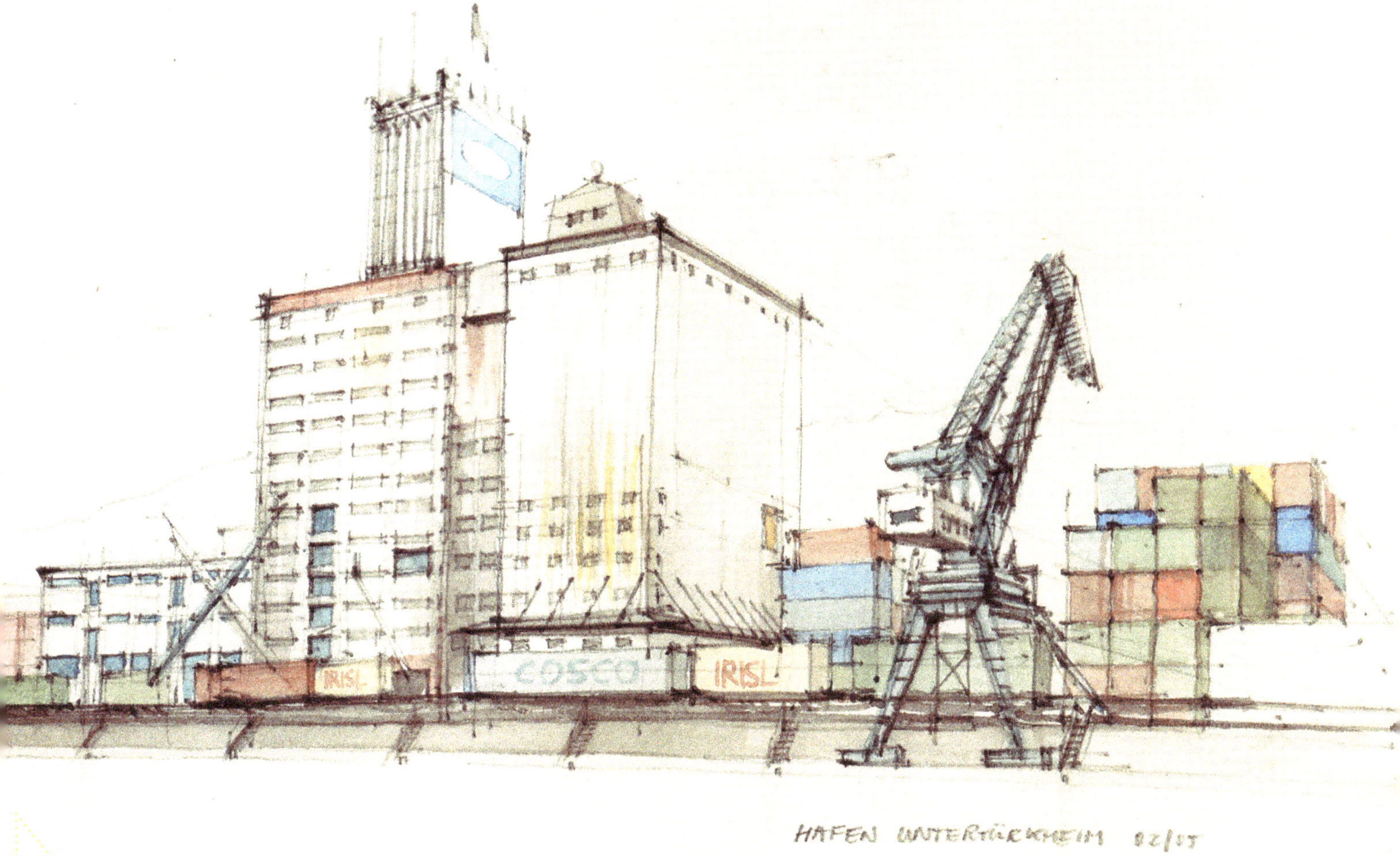

HAFEN UNTERTÜRKHEIM 02/15

11.75" x 6" | 30 x 15 cm;
4B Faber-Castell pencil,
Schmincke watercolors, #4
and #6 da Vinci brushes,
170-gsm Boesner sketchbook;
1 hour

ARTIST PROFILE
Florian Afflerbach

I've drawn ever since I can remember, but through my studies in architecture, I learned to construct and engineer a drawing. A stay in Paris during my studies was an influential time in my development as an artist, because I had the time to do whatever I wanted. I found two friends, and we explored the city together. I learned something very important: always look at what other people do. Drawing has become something fundamental to me—it brings satisfaction and happiness to me in my daily routine.

I often spend the weekend exploring Stuttgart by bike or on foot with my sketchbooks. The inner city is surrounded by steep hills, where the upper-class neighborhoods are located. That makes it even more interesting, socially, spatially, and architecturally. I think I got to know Stuttgart like the back of my hand.

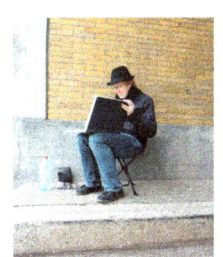

Florian Afflerbach enjoys drawing industrial settings, such as the Port of Stuttgart.

"Drawing brings satisfaction and happiness to me in my daily routine."

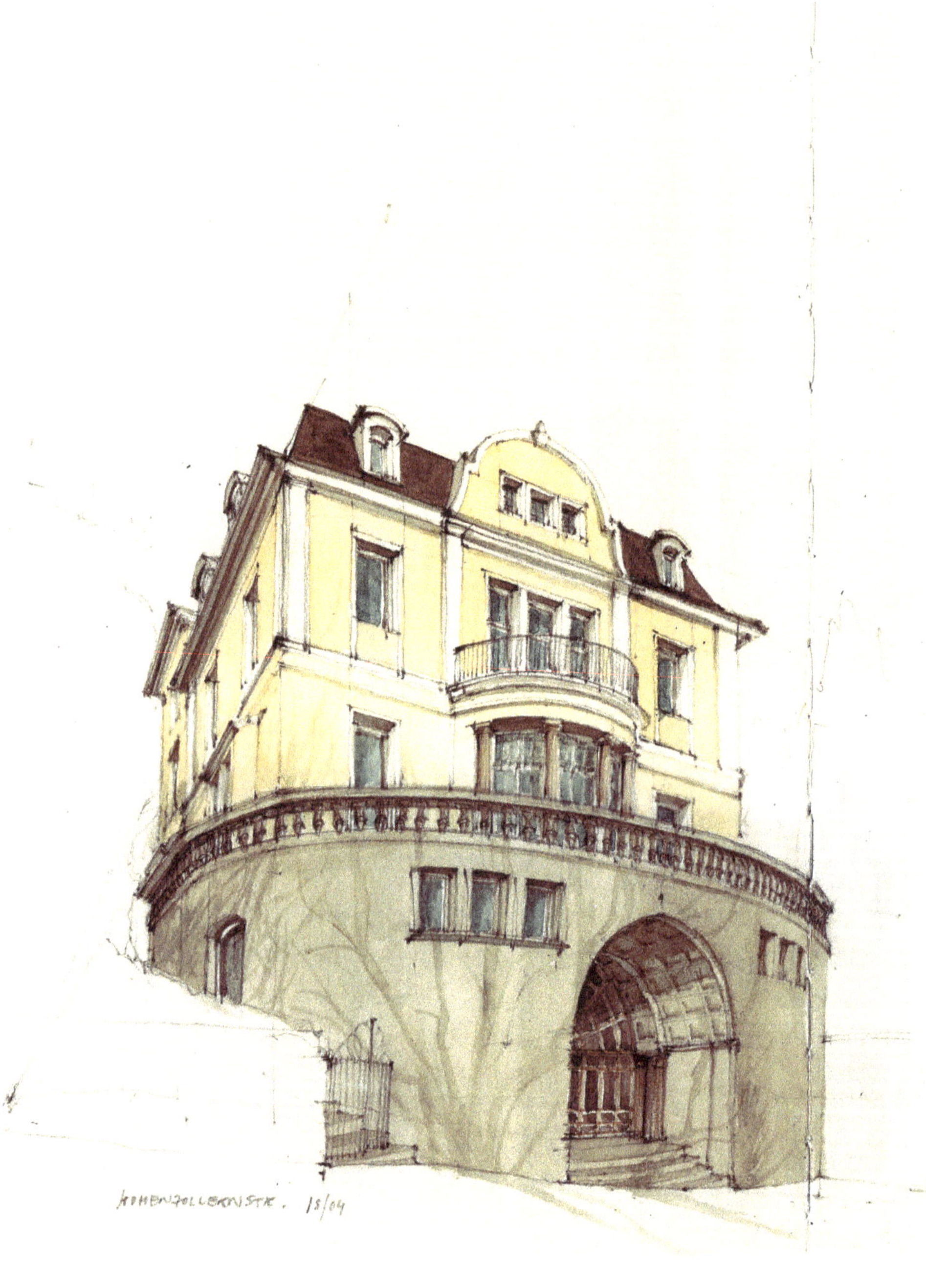

↻ **Hohenzollernstrasse** Afflerbach calls this a truly masterful building, representative of its 1900s era. "The huge entrance arch seems to correspond to the so-called Schwabtunnel, a tunnel that connects two Stuttgart quarters, he says. "The trees on the other side of the road created beautiful shadows on the façade."

Tip "In many cases, the arches, ellipses, and decorated risalits [projections] of a house from this period will be symmetrical, which can help you better reconstruct its form." — *Florian Afflerbach*

8" x 6" | 20 x 15 cm; 4B Faber-Castell pencil, Schmincke watercolors, #4 and # 6 da Vinci brushes on 170-gsm Boesner sketchbook; 1 hour

↪ **At the Mercedes-Benz Museum** Afflerbach recommends a visit to the car company's museum, which opened in 2006. "When I was a child, I wished to be a car designer and made little models of my own designs— they were called Flaf," says Afflerbach.

Tip "Don't hesitate to carry a sketchbook into a museum. Drawing is usually more tolerated than taking pictures with a camera. I always get a better understanding of the exhibited objects when I draw them." — *Florian Afflerbach.*

21.5" x 13.75" | 55 x 35 cm; 4B Faber-Castell pencil, Schmincke watercolors, #4 and # 6 da Vinci brushes on 170-gsm Boesner sketchbook; 15 minutes per sketch

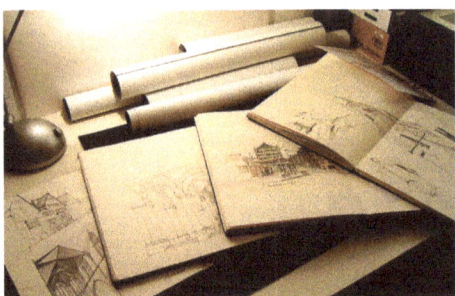

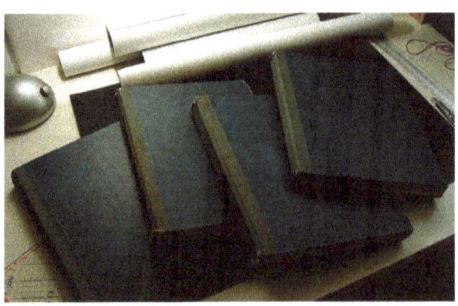

↻ Afflerbach's sketchbooks

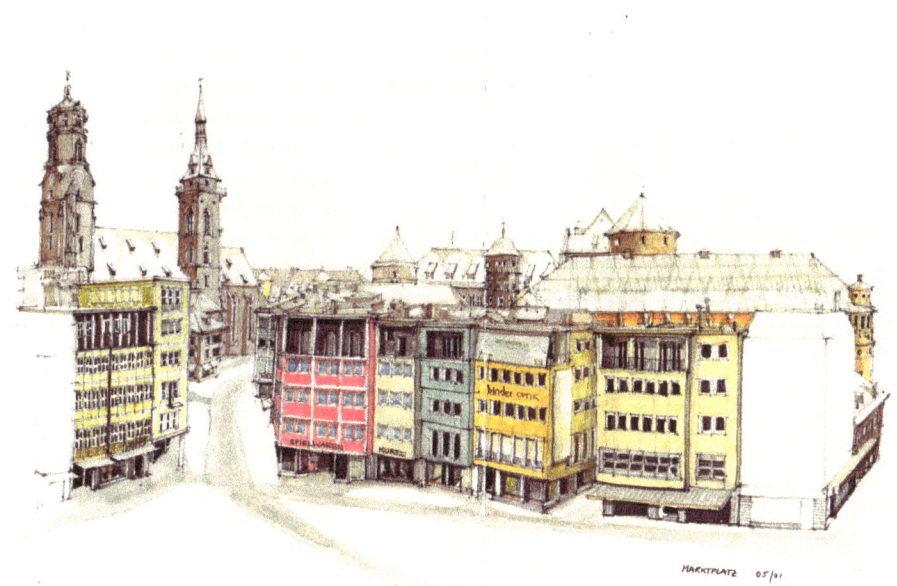

ᴄ Marktplatz In early 2009, the season's first snow fell on Stuttgart, and Afflerbach took the chance to visit Stuttgart City Hall, one of few buildings in Germany with a paternoster—a continuously moving passenger elevator with a series of open compartments. Afflerbach rode it up to the council chamber on the top floor. "From there, I had a wonderful view over the market square, with its beautiful and important buildings from different periods," Afflerbach says. "The whole market square of Stuttgart was destroyed in the Second World War. As you can see here, the neighborhood buildings and the city hall on the market square were built in 1950s style."

19.5" x 11.75" | 50 x 30 cm; 4B Faber-Castell pencil, Schmincke watercolors, #4 and # 6 da Vinci brushes on 170-gsm Boesner sketchbook; 3 hours

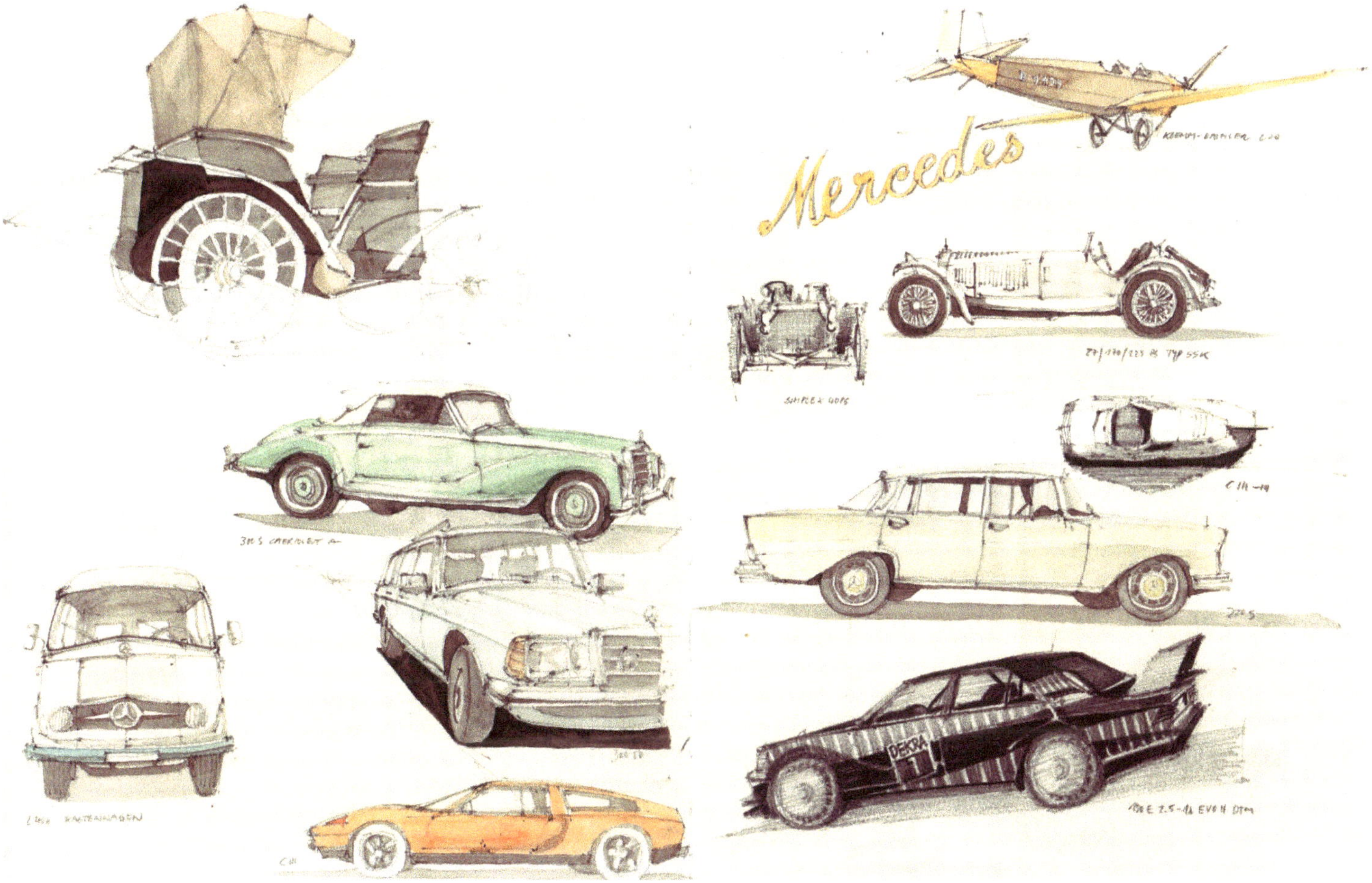

KANDERN

Kandern, a small town at the southern edge of Germany's Black Forest, is surrounded by wooded hills, vineyards, orchards, and farms. Elementary school teacher Rob Carey enjoys drawing its picturesque half-timbered houses and shops—some dating from the 1500s—and indulging in detailed renderings of their tiled roofs and arched windows.

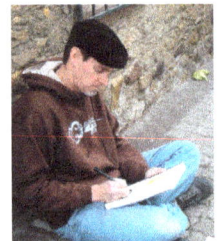

ARTIST PROFILE
Rob Carey

Urban sketching forces me to sit still and really look at details I wouldn't normally notice. I become detached, yet very connected with my environment at the same time. Although it's relaxing, I also find it incredibly challenging. When you're sketching, you're staring at a complex scene of intersecting lines and unusual shapes and figuring out how to record them on paper. The goal is communicating your experience at that time with whoever sees the sketch later. It's the same as telling a story.

I enjoy sketching scenes with interesting details. I look for old shutters, drain pipes, telephone poles, balconies, and shadows. I am constantly looking around me for subjects to draw. In fact, at times, I have to force myself to stop seeing everything as a possible sketch.

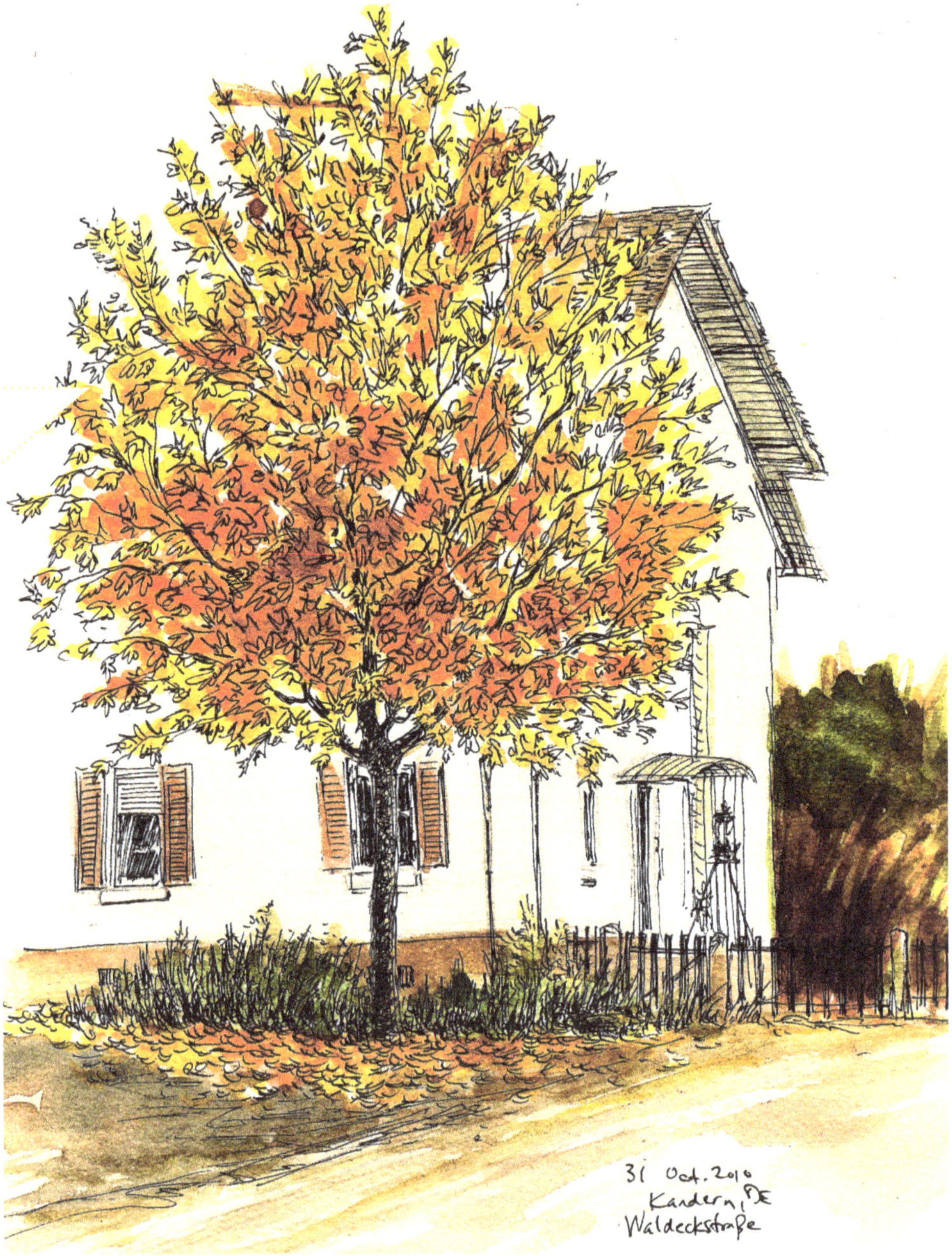

🎧 Carey captures the fall colors of Kandern.
8" x 10" | 20 x 25 cm; Faber-Castell SX Pitt artist pen, watercolor; 2 hours

"Communicating a geographic experience through art is a way to make connections with people around the world and develop one's understanding of others."

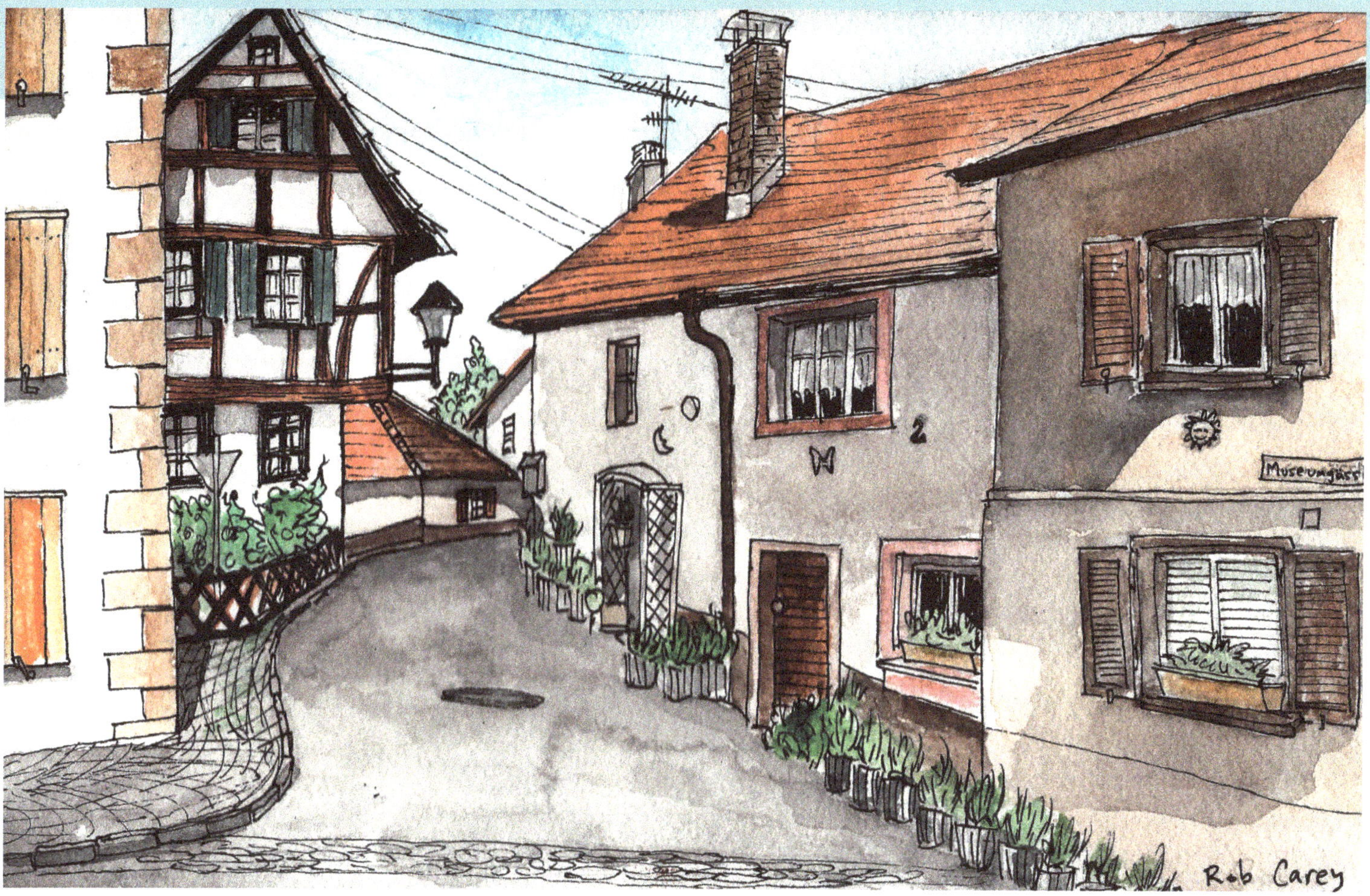

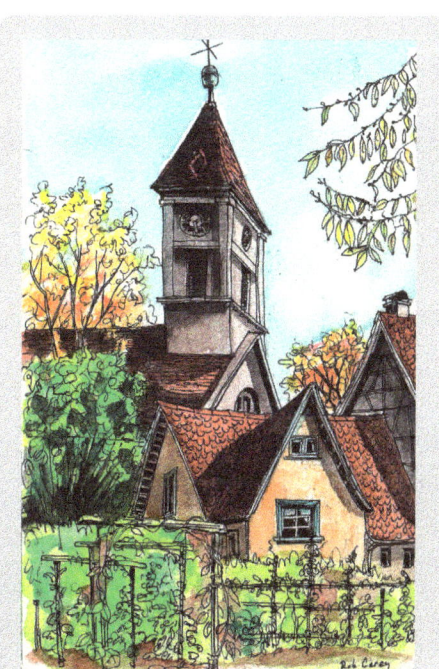

Welcome to My Backyard

by Rob Carey

I was standing on the street, trying to sketch this church tower during my lunch break. It was a terrible vantage point, really, but I just wanted to draw. A local man came out to see what I was doing then asked me to follow him to the back of his house, where there was a beautiful garden. As we walked into his garden, he told me to turn around and look at the tower from there. This was the view. He says, "Anytime you want to come in my backyard and draw, just go ahead." A few days later, the sun was out again, I had a lunch break, and there I was, sitting at his garden table, paints and pens all over the place, with my Moleskine in hand.

6" x 8" | 15 x 20 cm; Winsor & Newton watercolors, Micron pen on Moleskine large watercolor book; 1.5 hours

☊ Kandern Alley German expressionist August Macke painted many scenes in Kandern, including this street near Carey's first home. "Macke's paintings are displayed along a walking route, so you can see where he got his inspiration," says Carey, who was inspired to draw the street from the opposite angle.

Tip "Before sketching, I rough out the composition in pencil, to see if everything I want to include actually fits onto the page." — *Rob Carey*

6" x 8" | 15 x 20 cm; Winsor & Newton watercolors, Micron pen on Moleskine watercolor book; 1.5 hours

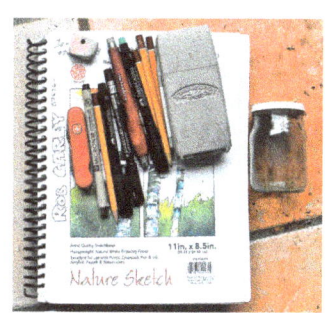

☊ Carey's sketching tools

VENICE

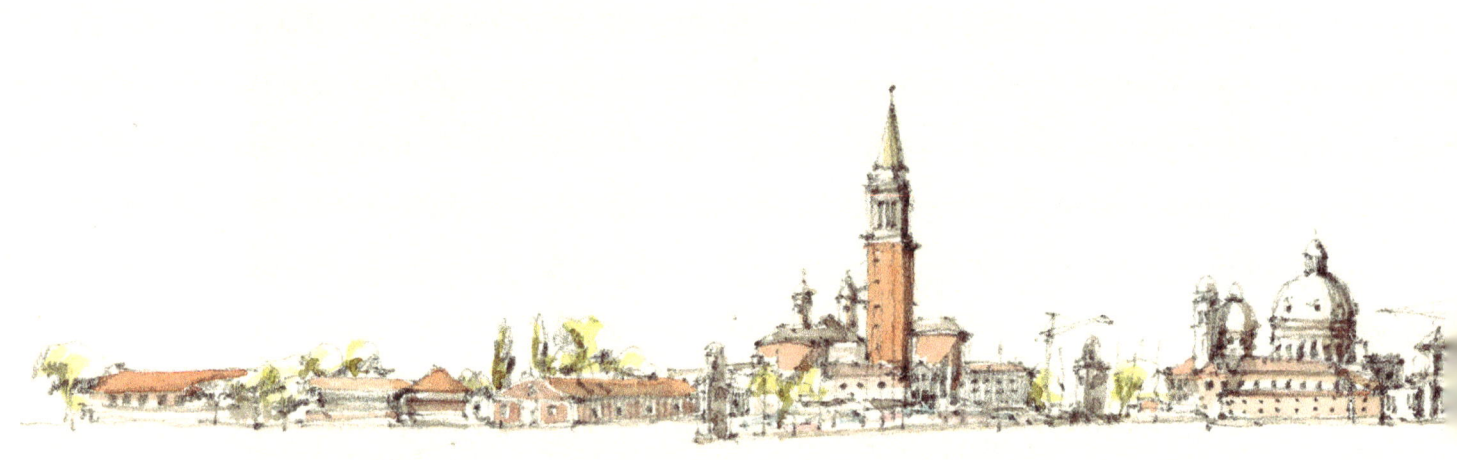

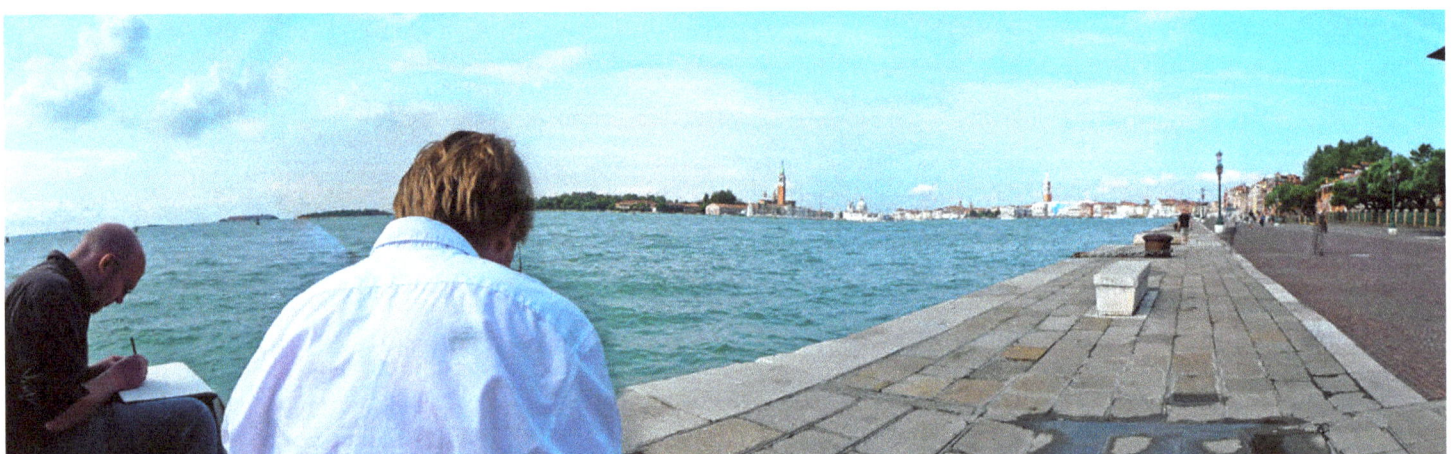

Venice is a mecca for sketch travelers. The City of Canals offers a walkable environment that is as picturesque as it gets. The gondolas and boats, weathered architecture, and pedestrian streets make it idyllic for urban sketching. The images these artists produced left them wanting to book their next vacation right away.

Panorama Sketching from the waterside at Riva Dei Sette Martiri, German architect Florian Afflerbach remembers the day being windy, with the sun coming from the left. "Interesting for right-handers and the construction of shadows," he says.

Tip "When drawing a city's silhouette, take care with the proportions of the important landmarks, and don't count all the windows. The execution of water is a separate mastership, so why not leave it empty? Adding some boats or waves could solve the problem." — Florian Afflerbach

19.5" x 4" | 50 x 10 cm; 4B Faber-Castell pencil, Schmincke watercolors, #4 and #6 da Vinci brushes on Boesner sketchbook; 1 hour

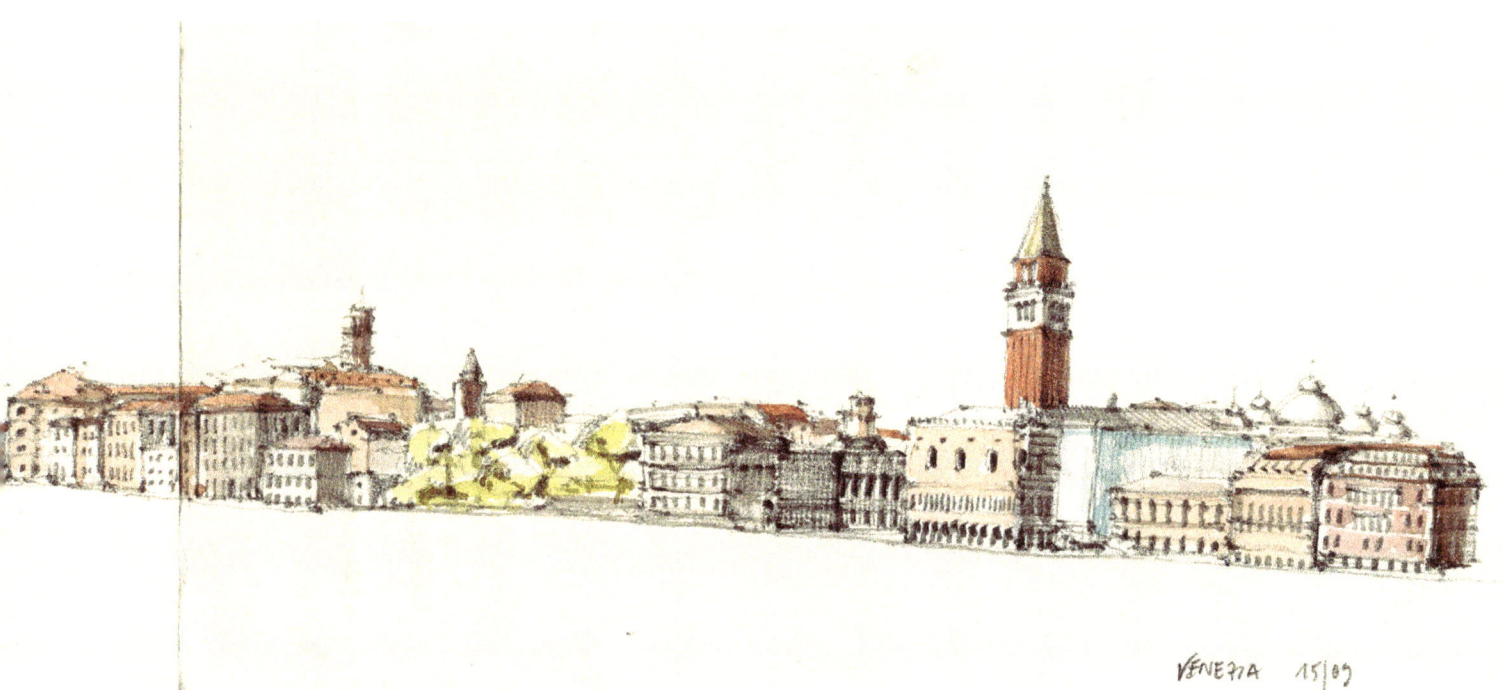

VENEZIA 15/09

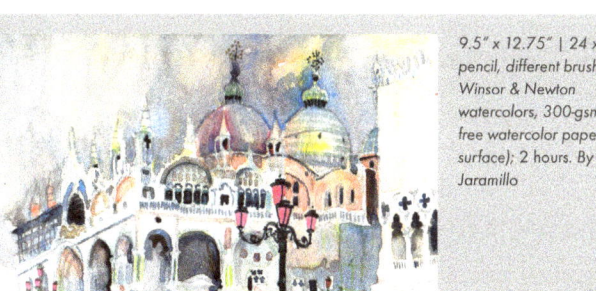

9.5" x 12.75" | 24 x 32 cm; pencil, different brushes, Winsor & Newton watercolors, 300-gsm, acid-free watercolor paper (matte surface); 2 hours. By Omar Jaramillo

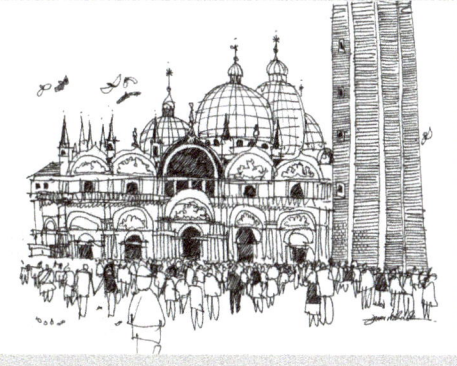

Size: 8" x 10" | 20 x 25 cm; Uni-ball Vision Micro ballpoint pen on Strathmore hardbound sketchbook; 25 minutes. By James Richards

STYLE AND TECHNIQUE

People Bring Streets to Life

These sketches capture the relation between St. Mark's Cathedral and the crowds of people in the square. "The people were drawn very quickly as a texture across the bottom, to try to convey the energy of the crowd," says James Richards.

The heads of the people are at the same height in this type of perspective, explains Omar Jaramillo. "When drawing people, usually the heads are at the same height in a perspective, varying just the size, to indicate depth. For painting a crowd, I usually spread different spots of color, let them slightly mix; when dry, I will paint, with a dark color, hair, bags, and clothes. Don't forget their shadows on the ground."

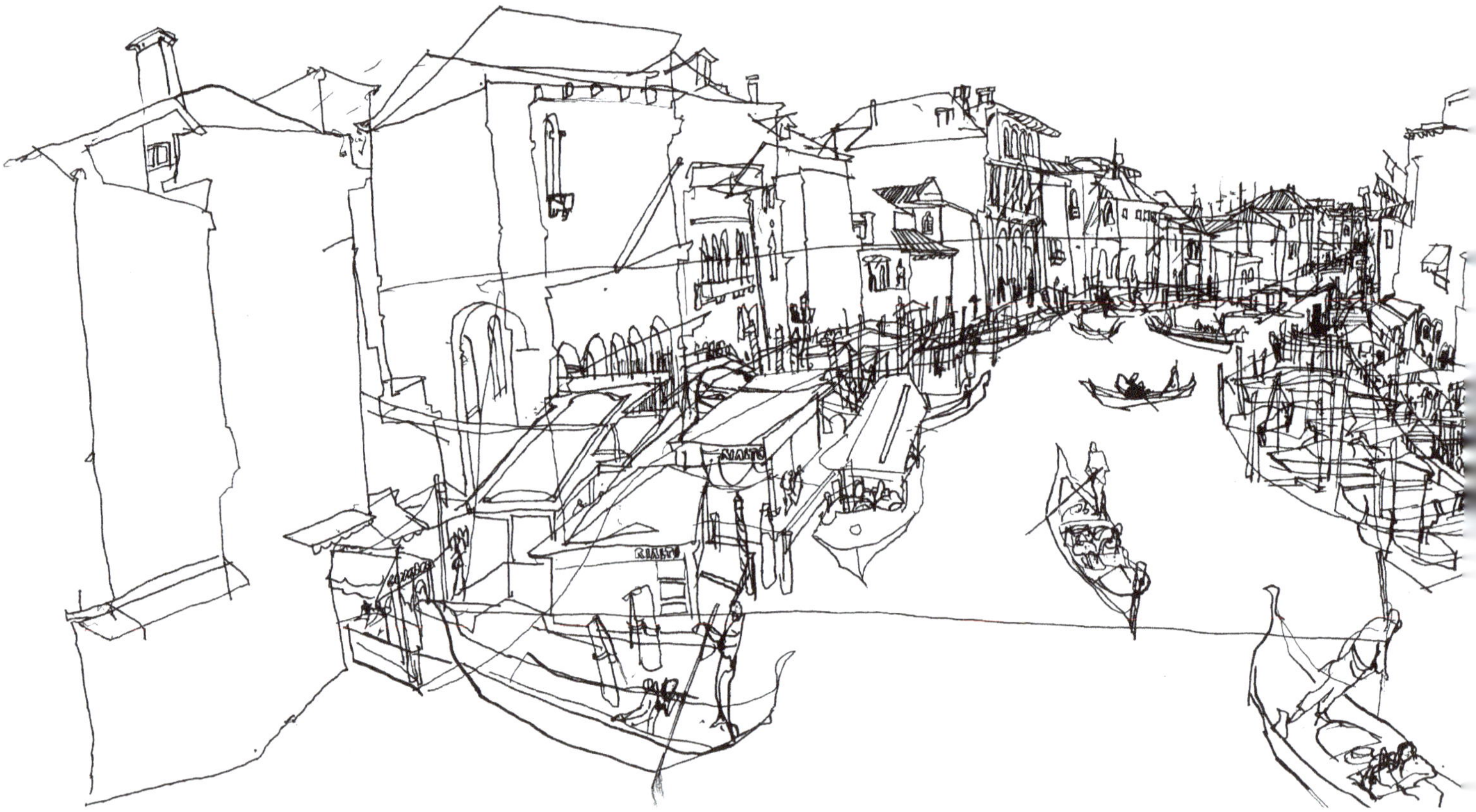

ᴖ Grand Canal New York illustrator Veronica Lawlor made this drawing of the Grand Canal from the Rialto Bridge. "I stood in the middle of the bridge, leaned my board on the side, and got busy," she recalls. "I remember a small old woman, about 4 feet (1.2 m) tall, dressed all in black, shoving me and hurling some sort of Italian curse at me for standing still on the bridge and drawing. I was right in her way–ha! Boy, was she angry with me. She was a piece of work, all right, but most Italians were eager to give me the thumbs up or to signal some form of appreciation for drawing there."

Tip "I didn't add any color because I wanted the boats and activity to stand out against the architecture. The black-and-white feeling really expresses the character of Venice. It's dilapidated but beautiful, and the agitation of the drawing of the canal in contrast to the grand design of the buildings in a way represents the life of today against the historical backdrop of the city." — *Veronica Lawlor*

17" x 11" | 43 x 28 cm; ink and dip pen on plain white paper clipped to a board; about 1.5 hours

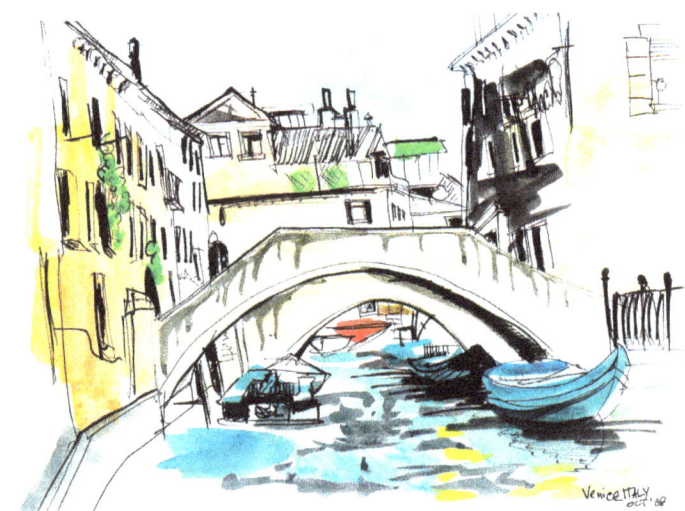

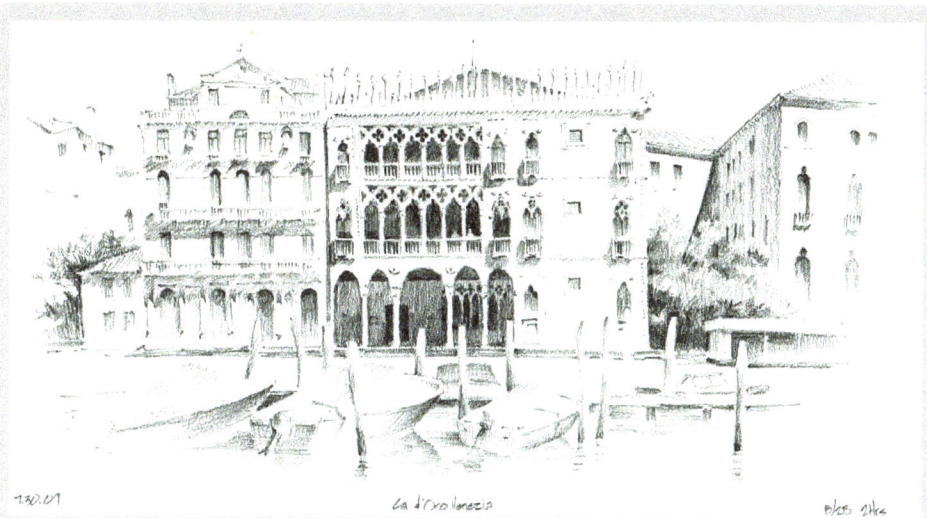

8.25" x 11.75" | 21 x 30 cm; Staedtler Mars Lumograph, B and 2B, on loose-leaf sketching paper; 2 hours

FIRST PERSON

Sketching Ca d'Oro 23 Years Apart

by Matthew Brehm

I drew the Ca d'Oro, also known as Palazzo Santa Sofia, as a student in November 1986 (below), when I was just learning how to sketch. I remember the drawing being very enjoyable, despite the fact that it was cold that day, and my hands were numb by the time I finished. The memory stayed with me until I had a chance to visit Venice twenty-three years later, in July 2009. I was eager to get back to this very spot and draw again. When I returned home a few weeks later and compared the two sketches side by side, I was happy with the progress I had made over the years. But more important, I was feeling fortunate to get two chances to draw such a wonderful subject.

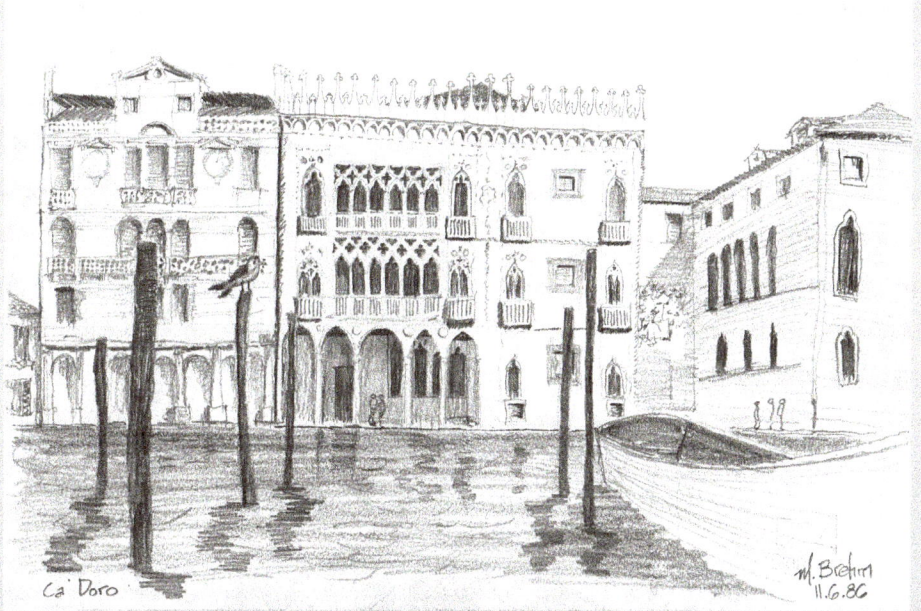

9.5" x 13" | 24 x 33 cm; pencil on Fabriano Ruvido paper, 1-2 hours

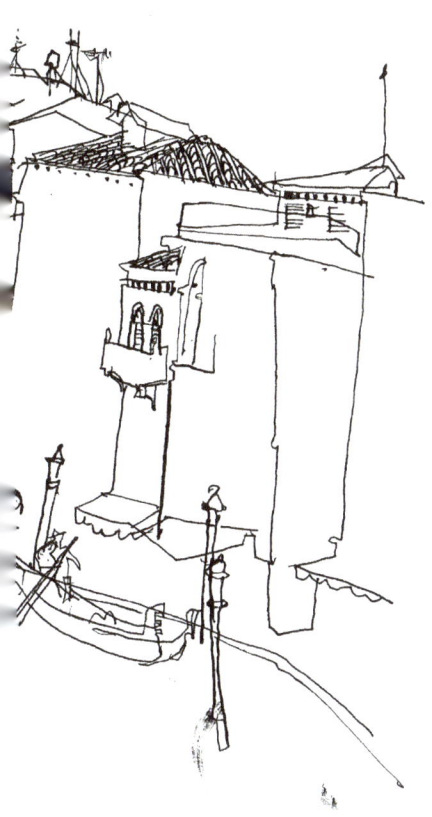

◔ **Venice Canal** Russian illustrator Zhenia Vasiliev appreciated Venice's lack of cars—and car noise. "With only boats and pedestrians—and warm weather—Venice is a real paradise for an urban sketcher," he says.

Tip "Watercolor works best for me when drawing water, because it very nicely reproduces water's transparency and depth. In the boats sketch, I even put some yellows in the channel to show reflections of the buildings."
— Zhenia Vasiliev

6" x 8.25" | 15 x 21 cm; ink and watercolor on A5 drafting paper

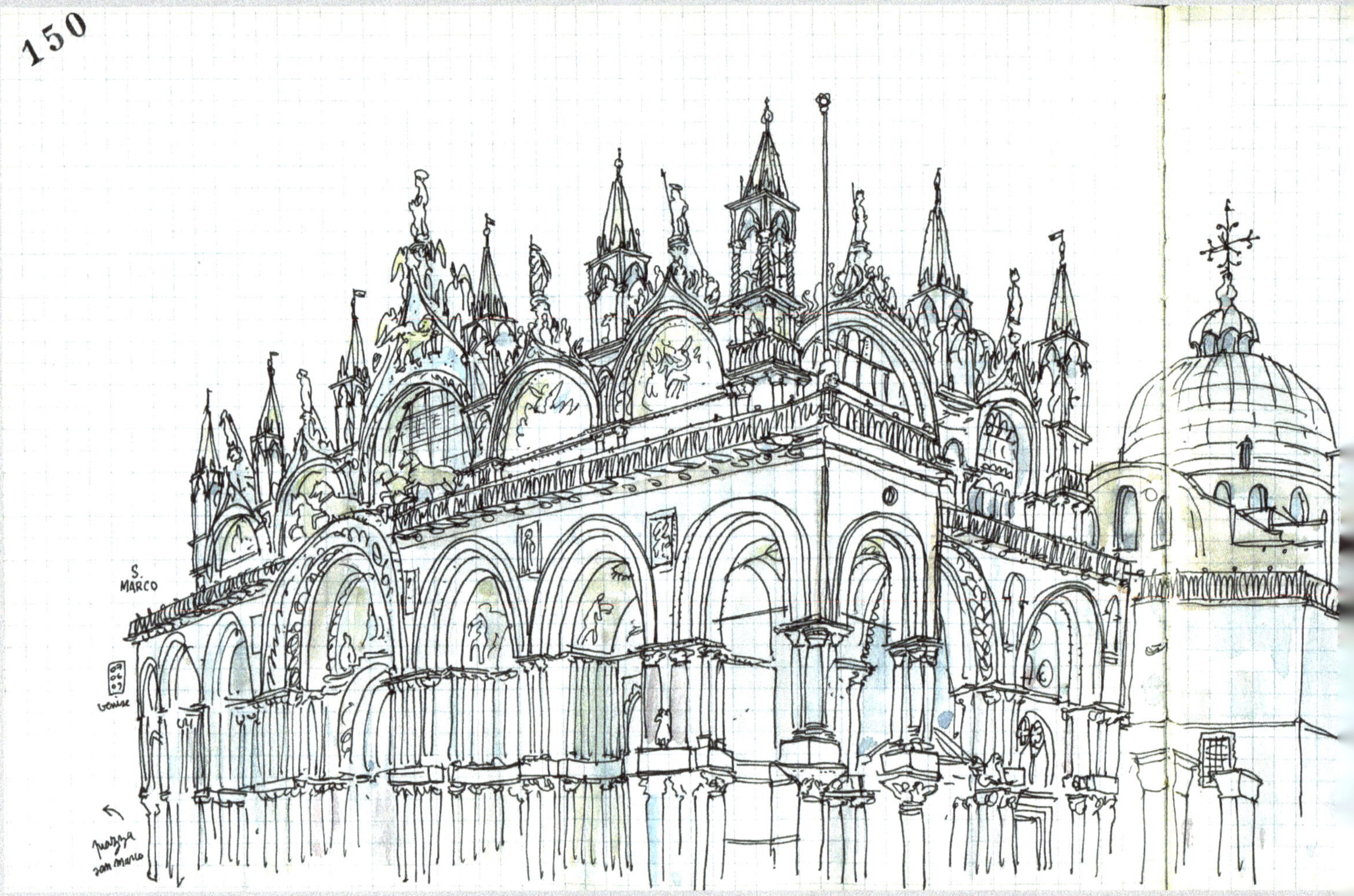

150

S.
MARCO

VIEW POINTS

Piazza San Marco

I woke up at 5 a.m. to sketch at St. Mark's square. A friend told me that it's the best way to meet Venice, face to face. He was right. To be alone here is something precious. I totally fell in love with the cathedral, so colorful. Walking in the street, I contemplated the city sleeping, but after 10 a.m., all was so different: it was too warm and loud, with thousands of tourists escaping from giant boats to invade the island. The day was neverending, and I enjoyed that I could see so much."
— *Lapin*

21.5" x 8.25" | 54.5 x 21 cm; Mitsubishi uni PIN fine line 0.1 ink pen, Daler-Rowney watercolors, and Pentel waterbrush on vintage notebook; 1 hour, 15 minutes

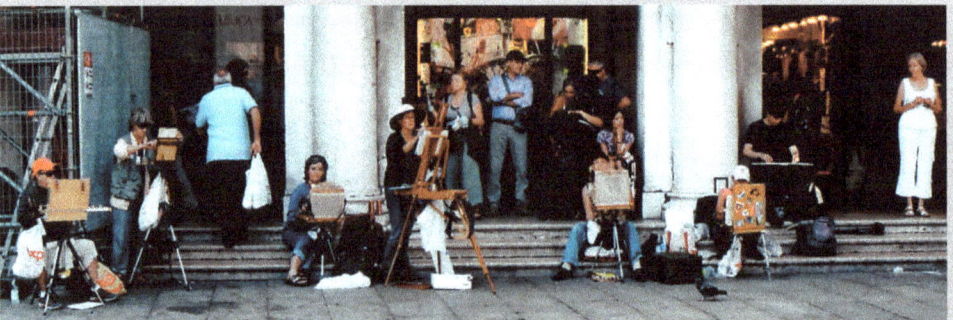

There were more than ten other sketchers and painters next to us, expressing the same location on their paper and canvas, but always in a different way. Another thirty people were looking on. What a great feeling! The only thing I didn't like were the pigeons sitting right above us! As we were drawing, the flood came, and people's feet were in water." — *Florian Afflerbach*

11.75" x 6" | 30 x 15 cm; 4B Faber-Castell pencil, Schmincke watercolors, #4 and #6 da Vinci brushes on Boesner sketchbook; 2.5 hours

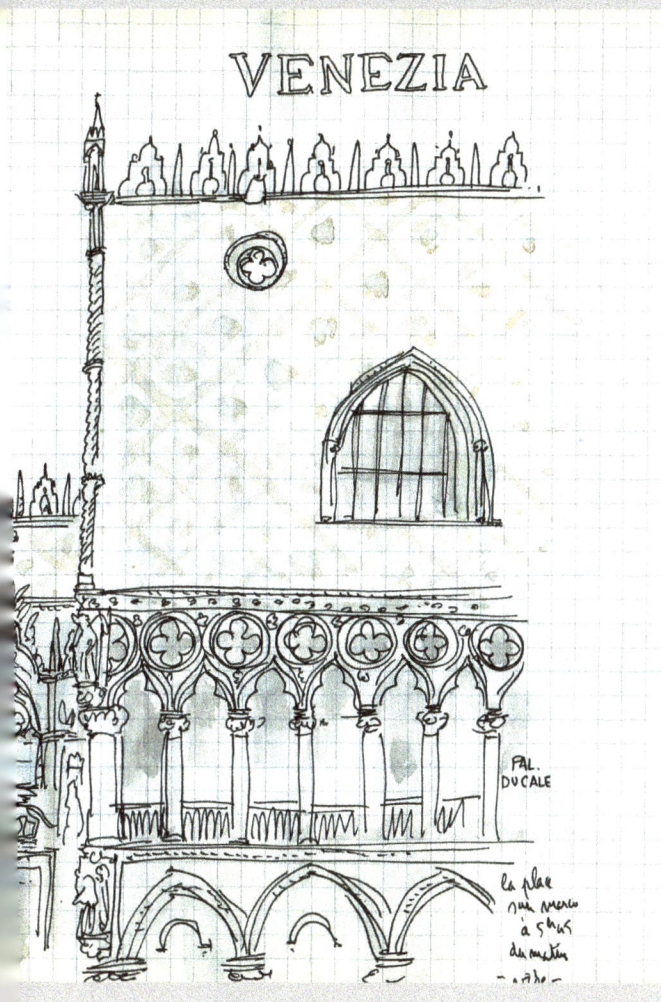

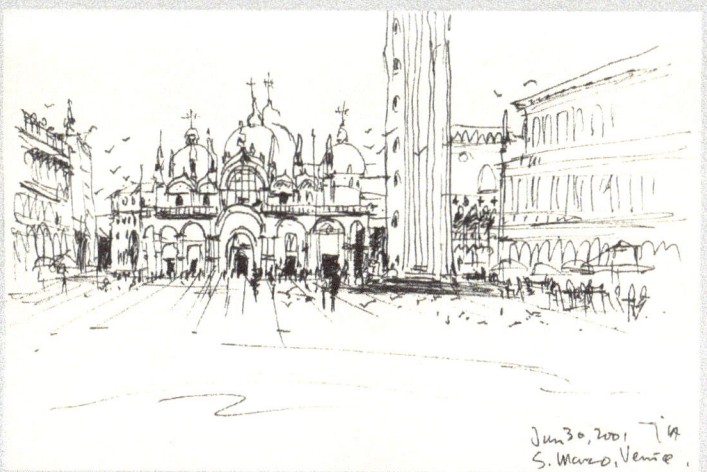

🎧 "This was done in the summer, with four or five American friends. We only had a short window of time to rest at the famous St. Mark's Square. I sat and sketched very quickly, while the rest waited for me to finish. I let the pen glide across the surface of the paper and added dark tones where suitable. The domes were the first elements to be put on the paper before I added the vertical and horizontal lines. Adding the birds with a few short lines and many dots was done last in one quick movement, and that was really fun."
— *Tia Boon Sim*

8" x 5.5" | 20 x 14 cm; Pilot drawing pen on sketchbook made by Lo Scrittoio, Italy, for Cavallini & Co.; 15 minutes

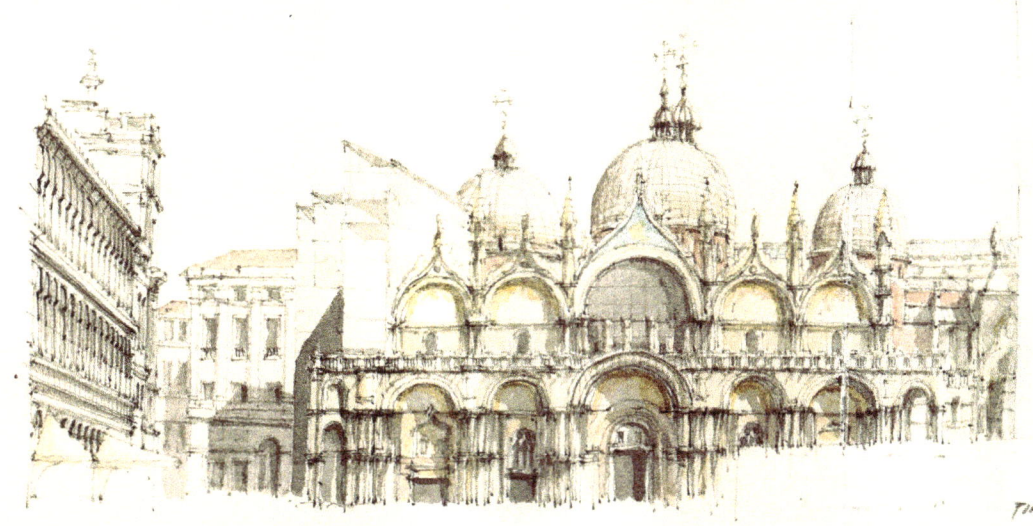

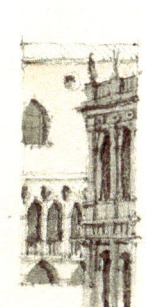

ROME

⤵ al Velabro

According to myth, says Benedetta Dossi, Romulus and Remus—the founders of Rome—were brought here by the overflowing Tiber River and raised by a she-wolf, who, in reality, was likely a courtesan.

Tip I distort buildings because I think it's more fun to interpret the reality instead of reproduce it. Before I start to draw, I have a general image of what I want to realize, and then I start directly with a permanent pen."
— *Benedetta Dossi*

10.25" x 8" | 26 x 20 cm; Bic pen, Maimeri acrylics, Winsor & Newton brushes, on Moleskine sketchbook (thin paper); 30–40 minutes

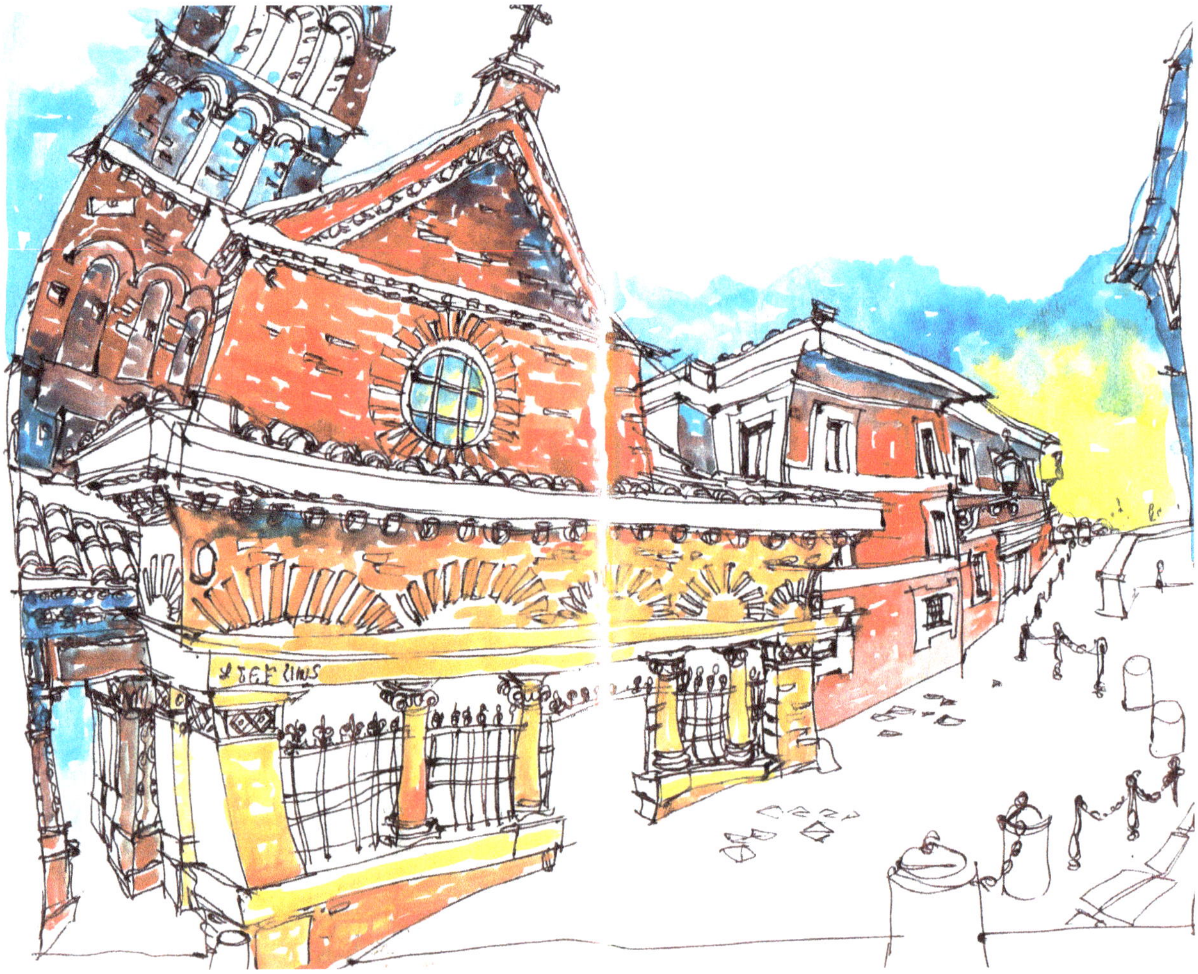

Rome's mix of ancient ruins and architecture styles that span centuries has made the Italian capital a magnet for artists past and present. American teachers Matthew Brehm and Fred Lynch find the city an ideal location to teach drawing to their students every summer. No matter where you choose to sketch, says local artist Benedetta Dossi, it's important to feel the environment before you put pen to paper.

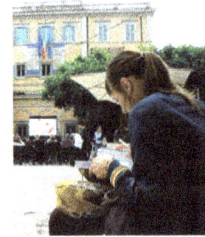

ARTIST PROFILE
Benedetta Dossi

I love to draw. I express myself with strong lines and quick color. I try to sketch buildings, people, furniture, and cars, as if they were always on the go. I take my notepad with me on the bus every day and draw looking through the window: people running, reading, standing, taking the dog for a walk, laughing, talking. On the weekend, I walk around Rome, reading books about its popular legends and drawing its bridges, squares, monuments, and walls.

My dream is to travel and embrace other cultures and capture their vitality in my sketchbooks. I would explore the world slowly, open my arms, breathe in deeply, and listen.

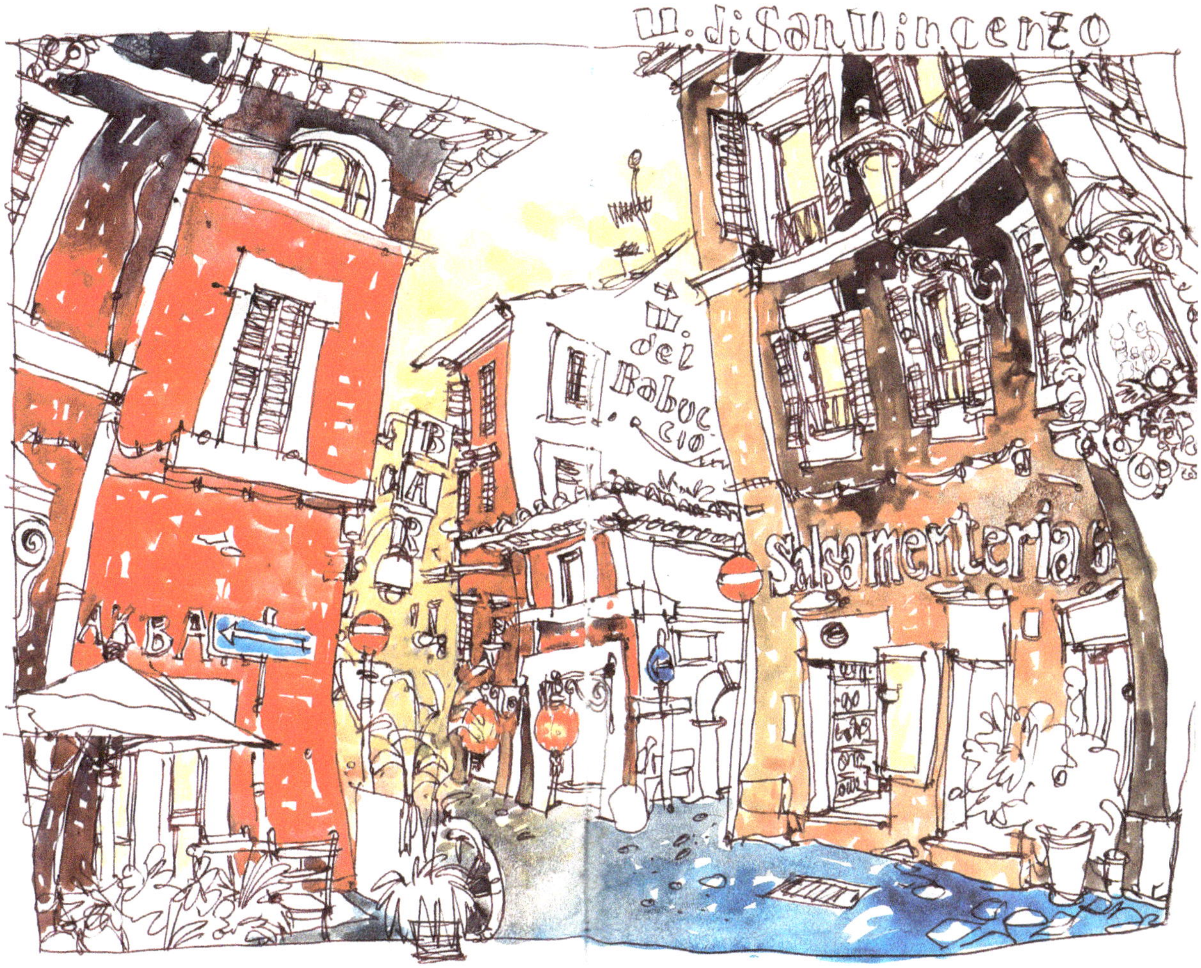

San Vincenzo

On a cold morning in the area of Trevi, Benedetta Dossi spent some time looking around to catch the atmosphere and the spirit of the scene.

Tip "To stay there and listen to the street's conversations, looking for the details, like a ruined sign, allows you to connect with the surroundings."
— Benedetta Dossi

8.5" x 6.75" | 21.6 x 17 cm; BIC pen, Maimeri acrylics, on Moleskine thin paper; 30–40 minutes

Tiberina Island Surrounded by three bongo players, two Chinese artists, some hopeless fishermen, and a lot of happy tourists, Dossi sketched peacefully under the sun on Tiberina Island in the river.

8.75" x 6.75" | 22 x 17 cm; Bic pen, Winsor & Newton watercolors, on Moleskine thin paper; 30–40 minutes

"I suggest taking time to hear the sound and the spirit of your surroundings. Drawing for me is simply listening."

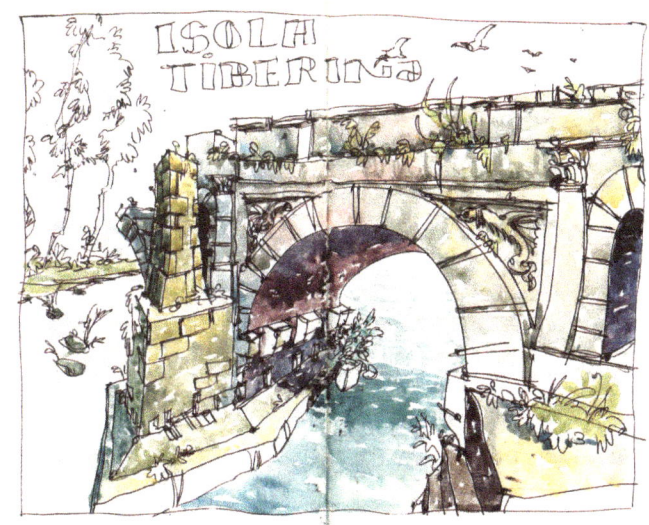

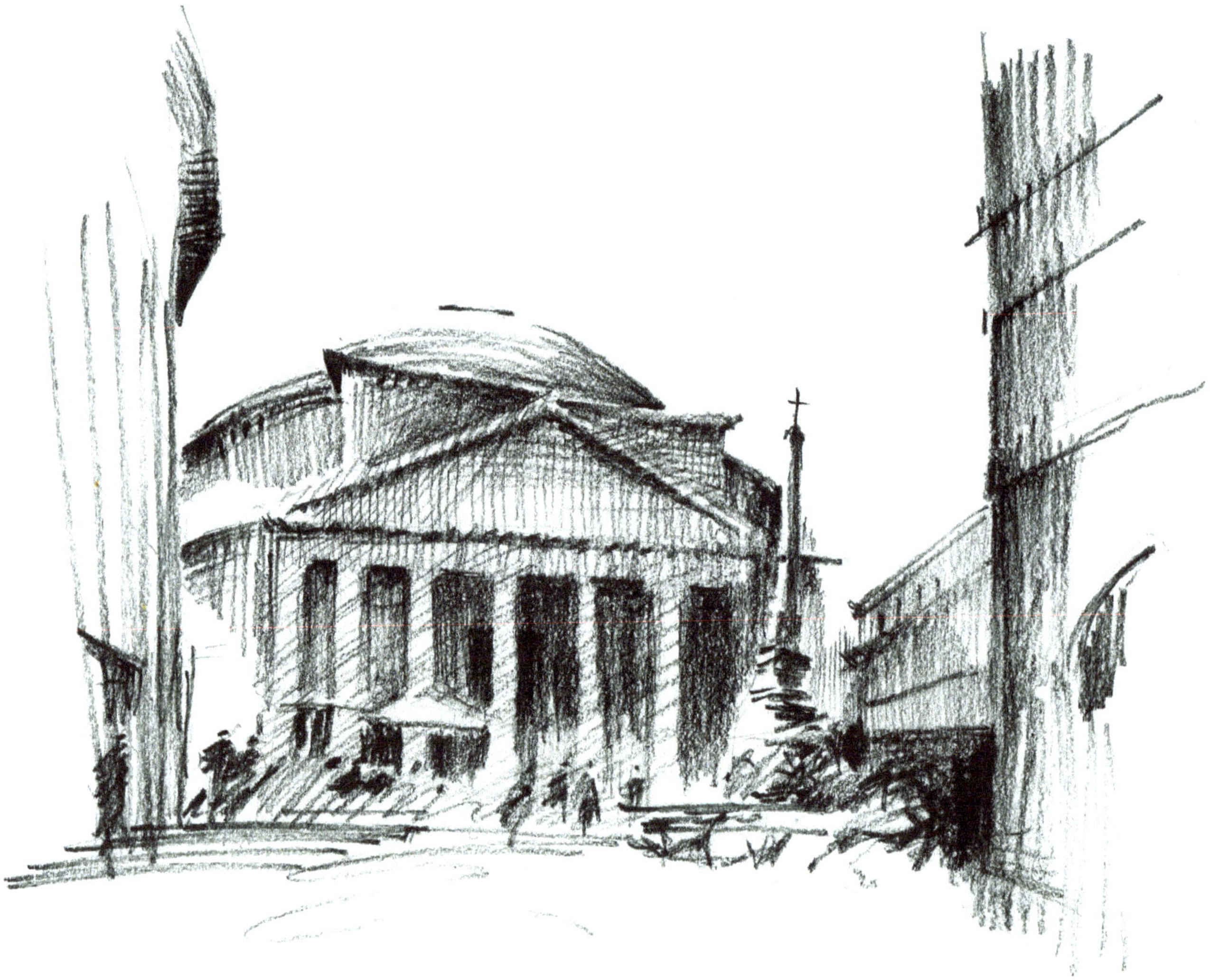

Matthew Brehm

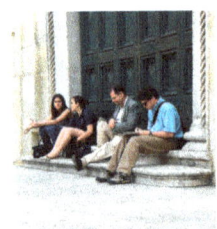

I did little observational sketching while working in architecture firms, but once I began teaching, I rekindled my interest in the practice. Now, it's an important aspect of what I do for a living. Architecture students rely heavily on computers, these days, but there is still strong interest in sketching by hand, for the unique value it brings to the design process.

I spend two months teaching in Rome every summer. My students and I spend a few mornings each week exploring and sketching the streets and *piazze* throughout the city. Sketching in Rome puts us in touch with the city, its history, its art and architecture. Rome has been studied in this way for centuries, by countless artists and architects, because it possesses a unique blend of ancient, medieval, renaissance, baroque, and modern urbanity."

"It's important to put yourself in the best position possible for a sketch, instead of finding a comfortable place to sit."

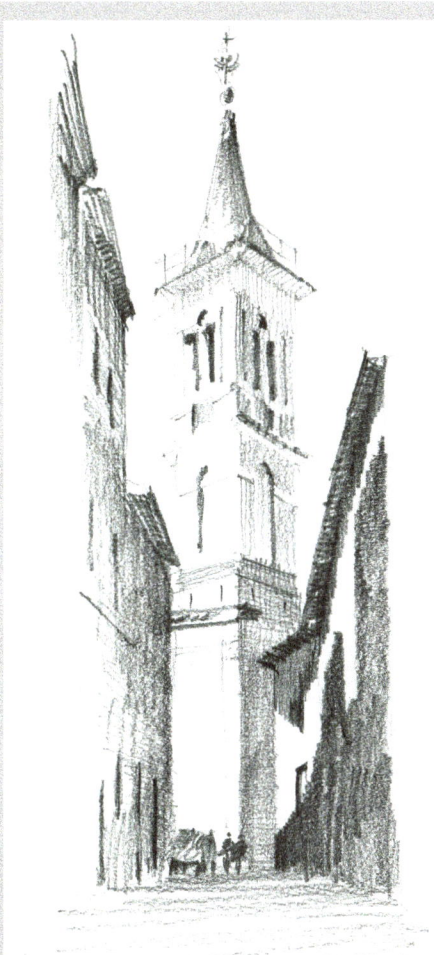

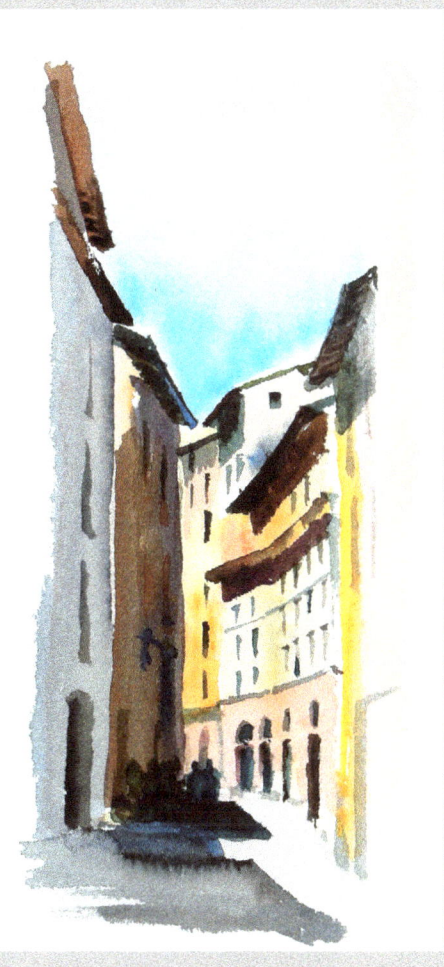

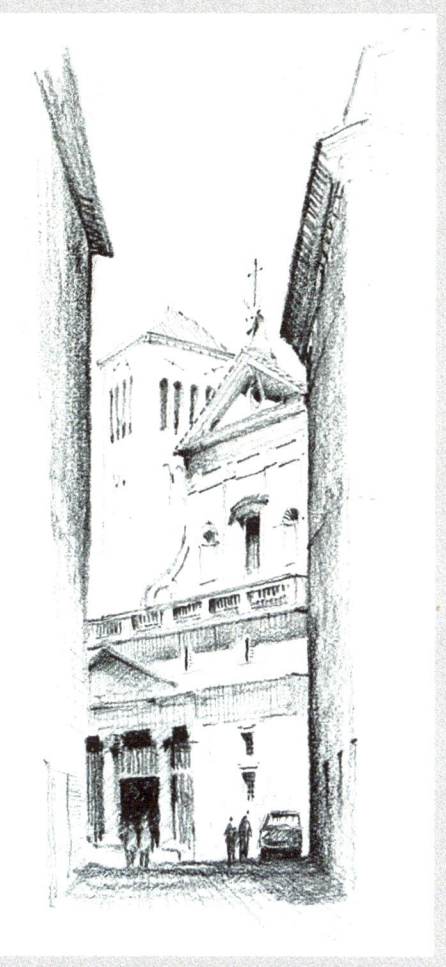

1. Vicolo della Volpe *Staedtler Mars Lumograph HB pencil, Aquabee heavyweight sketchbook; 20 minutes*

2. Via delle Vacche *M. Graham watercolors, #6 round Connoisseur Kolinsky brush, Arches cold-press watercolor pad; 45 minutes*

3. Sant'Eustachio *Pitt oil-based, extra-soft pencil, Canson Classic Cream drawing pad; 30 minutes*

VIEW POINTS

Narrow Streets

by Matthew Brehm

The narrow streets of Rome (or any city with some medieval character) offer delightful surprises—they are like slot canyons, often with glimpses of bell towers or church façades.

Perspective is a real challenge in these situations, because we often have the tendency to raise the eye level and draw too much of the ground plane, or we run out of space on the page for such dramatically vertical compositions. So it is always important to take time in setting up the sketch—to visualize it on the page and to begin with light guidelines that establish the limits of the entire drawing. Once this is achieved, it can be great fun to go very dark with the shading, to give a strong sense of clear sunlight and spatial depth.

↻ **Pantheon** Matthew Brehm had just a short time after helping his students with their sketches of the Pantheon to try this drawing amid a crowd of tourists and students.

Tip "I remember doing the quick hatch pattern across the columns at the very end because I thought they were a little too stark and as a way of emphasizing the importance of speed and looseness in making a sketch."
— *Matthew Brehm*

9" x 12" | 23 x 30.5 cm; General's medium charcoal pencil, Fabriano 4 Ruvida pad; 20 minutes

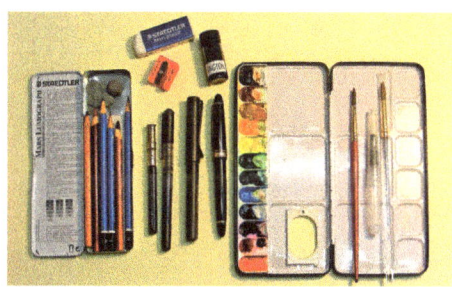

♁ Brehm's tools

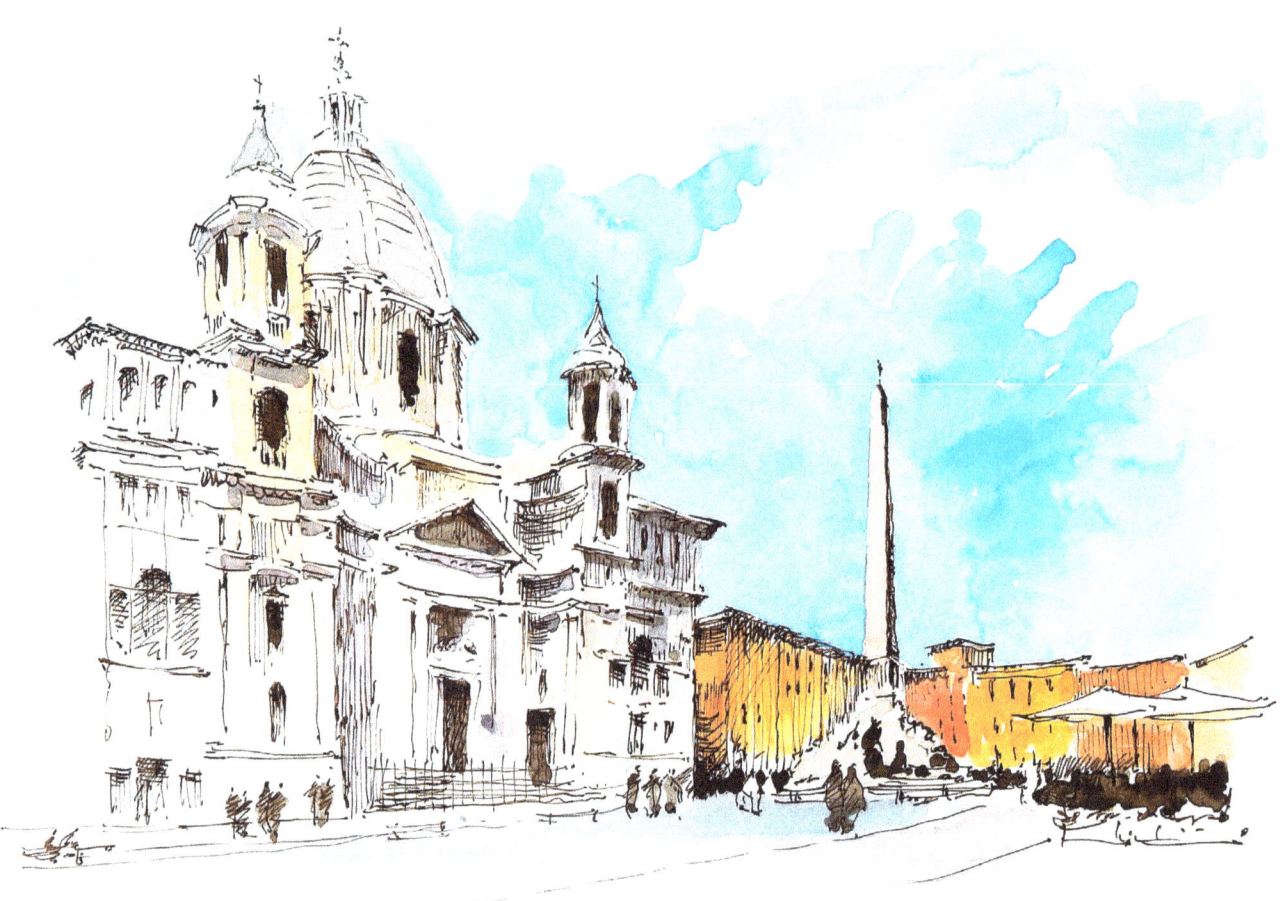

⋒ **Piazza Navona** Brehm calls Piazza Navona, in the heart of Rome, one of the most fascinating large urban spaces he's ever encountered. "Just as I was finishing, a pigeon very nearly hit me from an eave above where I stood—just one of the hazards of urban sketching," he says.

Tip "I started with very light pencil lines, then added sepia ink with a dip pen, and finally added the splashes of watercolor. I like the dark brown tone of this sepia-colored acrylic ink, but using a dip pen can be tedious. I'd prefer to use a fountain pen but haven't yet found this color in a waterproof ink." — *Matthew Brehm*

9" x 12" | 23 x 30.5 cm; HB pencil, Speedball pen with a Hunt extra-fine nib and FW sepia ink, M. Graham watercolors, basic #6 round brush on Aquabee Plate Bristol pad; 45 minutes

⊃ **Portico d'Ottavia** The Portico d'Ottavia is a fascinating ruin from the time of Augustus, built around 27 BC. The surrounding street level is about 15 feet (4.5 m) higher than the ancient ground level, but because the portico has been excavated, it is now possible to get down and view the ruin from more or less the "intended" viewpoint.

Tip "One shouldn't be afraid to get up close to imposing subjects like this. If you stand back too far, the perspective has a tendency to 'calm down' and become less dramatic." — *Matthew Brehm*

9" x 12" | 23 x 30.5 cm; Staedtler Mars Lumograph 2B pencil, Canson Classic Cream drawing pad; 30 minutes

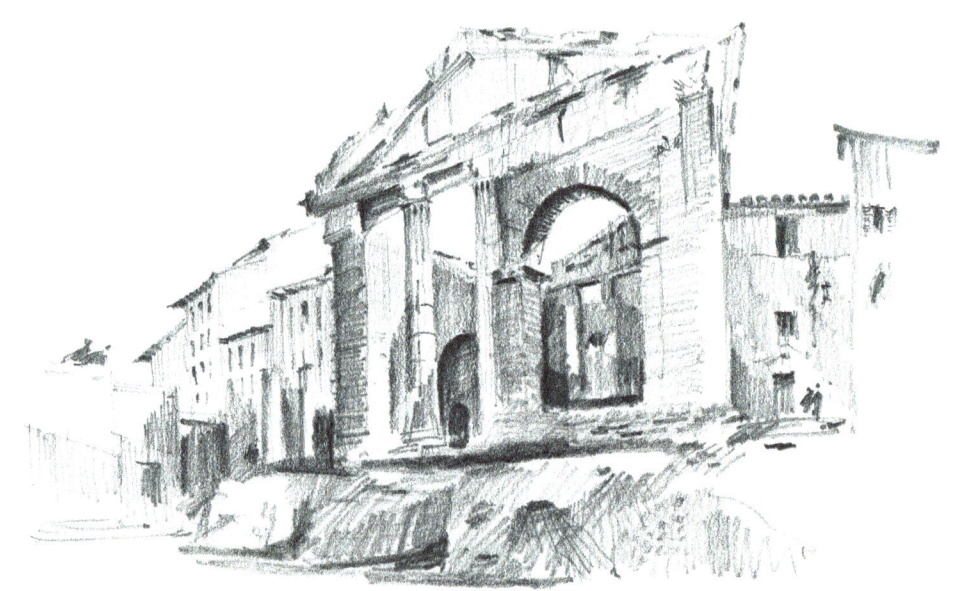

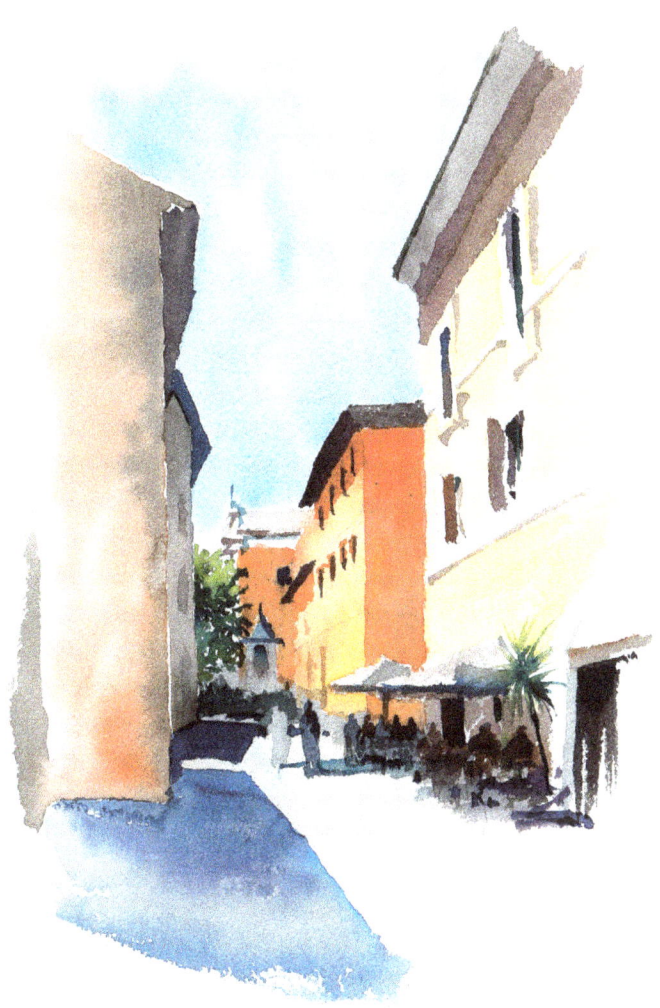

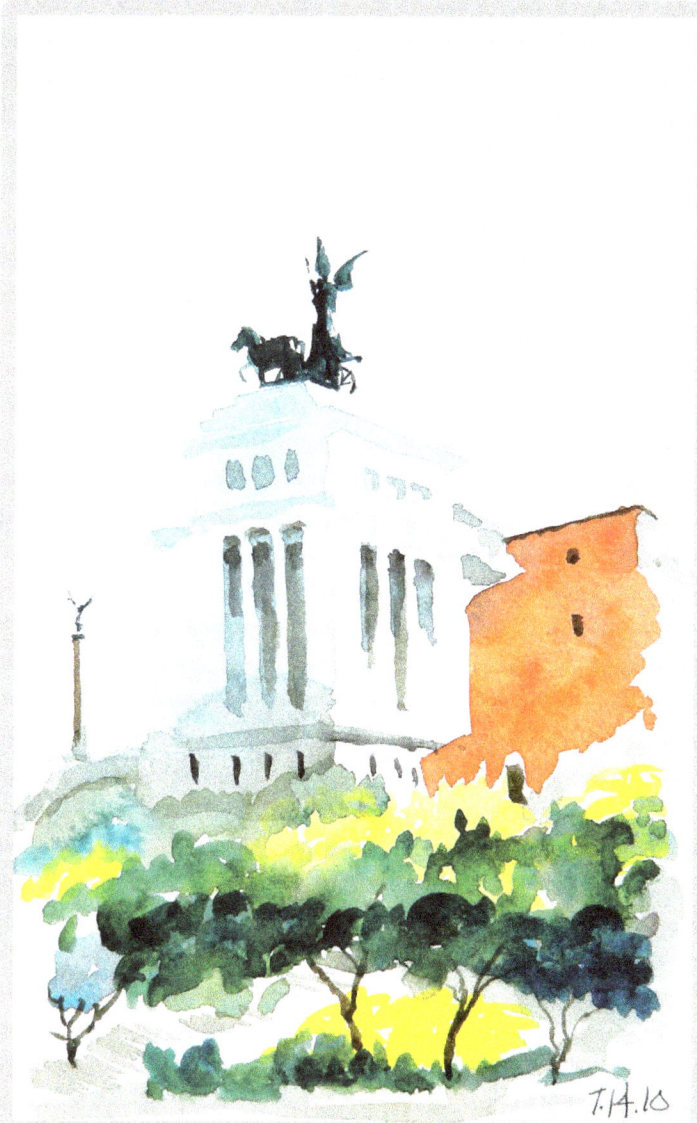

∩ **Via della Scala** Brehm and his wife spent most of one summer people-watching in and around this busy bar and crossroads, lingering in the shade of the umbrellas to stay out of the brutal sun.

Tip "I had been experimenting with a 'wet-into-wet' technique, and I used it here to create the sky and the wall on the left. It has the power to create some atmosphere in a watercolor. Generally, I recommend starting with light washes and working up to the darker tones. If the lights are kept very light (the sky, the walls on the right, and the street) and the darks are made very dark (the shadows on the left and under the umbrellas, and the eaves against the sky), a strong impression of sunlight can be created."
— *Matthew Brehm*

9" x 12" | 23 x 30.5 cm; M. Graham watercolors, #6 round Connoisseur Kolinsky brush, Arches cold-press watercolor pad; 60 minutes

STYLE AND TECHNIQUE

Quick Watercolor Sketch of Vittorio Emanuele Monument

by Matthew Brehm

This was an attempt to show my students how to sketch directly in watercolor, without any guidelines in pencil. Several of my students were struggling with it, going over the same washes too many times, using two or three different brushes, and trying to show detail throughout their sketches. They were spending too much time on their sketches and were generally unhappy with the results. So this was an exercise in quickness, focused detail, and the great versatility of a single brush.

5" x 8" | 12.5 x 20 cm; M. Graham watercolors, #6 round Connoisseur Kolinsky brush, Moleskine large watercolor book; 15 minutes

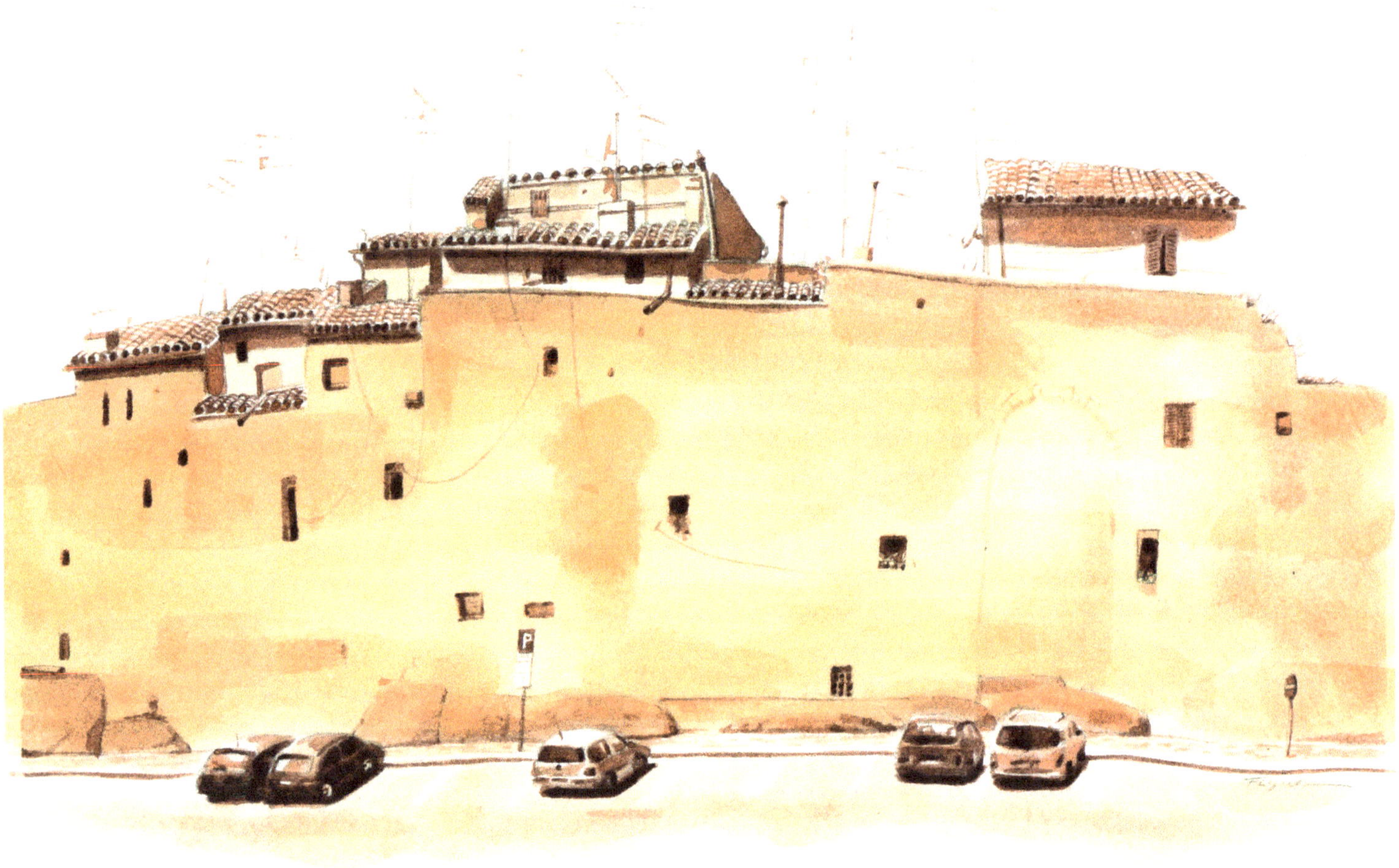

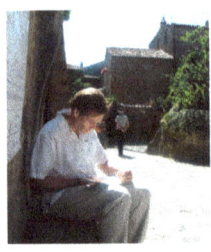

ARTIST PROFILE

Fred Lynch

For as long as I can remember, I've been creating pictures. Sketching onsite, however, is relatively new to me. As an illustrator, I've spent the better part of my professional life creating imagery to communicate, entertain, and inform, the primary focus being on imagination and message.

My foray into the sketching world happened later in life. Sketching more directly addresses my surroundings, and I've found there is nothing quite like the challenge of capturing a witnessed scene and an experience, with limited time and materials. Each July, I sketch with my students in Viterbo, a small city in central Italy; the rest of the year, I can be found in and around Boston, often on the sidelines of a soccer field, hunched over a Moleskine as my children play."

∩ **Wall by Porta Romana, Viterbo** Ironically, this ancient wall was painted from the back lawn of a McDonald's restaurant in Viterbo. "What struck me was the amusing composition formed by the arrangement of four items: cars, windows, houses, and antennas," Lynch says.

Tip "Whenever I'm sketching, I address first the thing that I fear could leave the scene. In this case, it was the cars." — *Fred Lynch*

12" x 9" | 30.5 x 23 cm; Winsor & Newton nut brown ink, Winsor & Newton Artists' watercolors, sable and Cotman brushes, Arches Aquarelle hot-press watercolor block; 2 hours

"In a foreign place, one's senses are heightened and almost everything is interesting to draw."

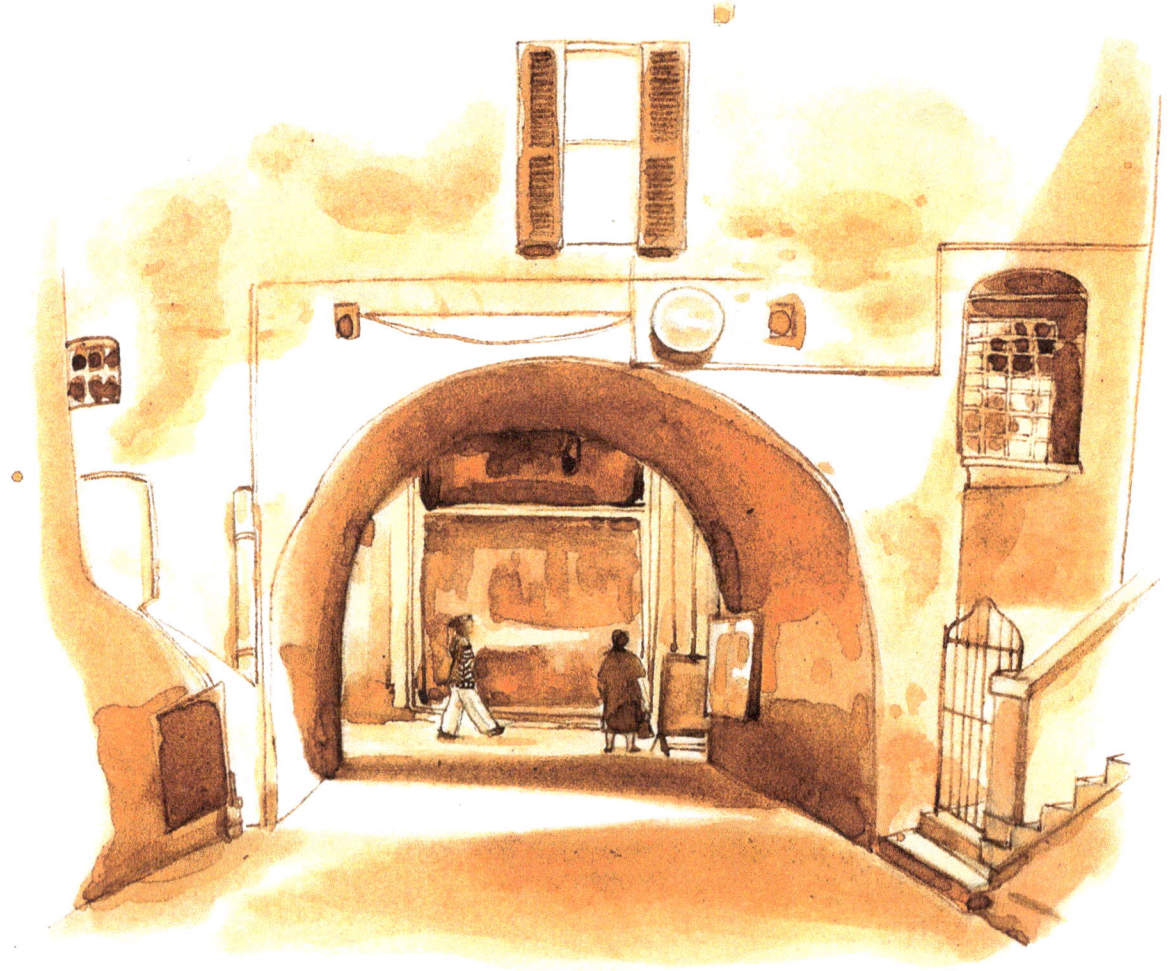

↺ Approaching the Corso Fred Lynch says he's a big fan of arches and loves to capture the transitions and contrasts of light below them.

Tip "This sketch, one of my favorites, is lucky to exist at all. After unfolding my stool and setting up my materials, a dump truck backed up slowly through the tunnel until it stopped in my lap. For days, I walked by and the truck was still there, seemingly permanently. Not until a week and a half later did I return and discover the truck was gone. Finally, I could finish my drawing!"
— *Fred Lynch*

10" x 7" | 25 x 18 cm; Winsor & Newton nut brown ink, Winsor & Newton Artists' watercolors, sable and Cotman brushes, Arches Aquarelle hot-press watercolor block; 2 hours

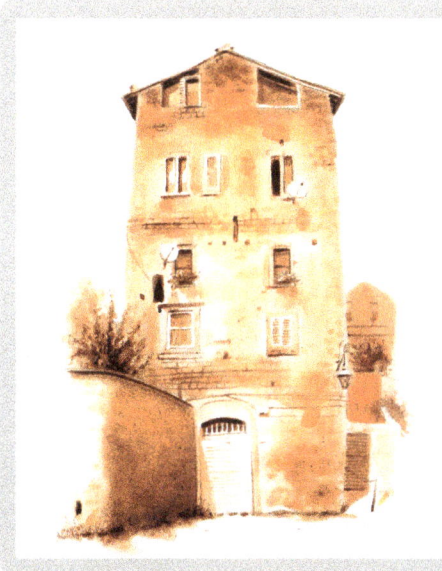

FIRST PERSON
Via delle Mole, Viterbo

by Fred Lynch

I'll always remember this drawing because of the friend I made that day. While sitting in the shade, looking up and sketching for well over an hour at this odd house on the edge of town, I heard singing—opera singing—not particularly good opera singing. Where was it coming from? Finally, a middle-aged man, wrapped only in a bath towel, came to the open window, having finished his aria. I looked up; he looked down, sensing he was being watched, and we both smiled. I held my drawing for him to see, and he nodded.

For the next two weeks, we passed each other on the streets of Viterbo, exchanging more smiles and nods but nothing more. We had a bond. We had exchanged our art and perhaps shared that vulnerable feeling of having done so.

7" x 10" | 18 x 25 cm; Winsor & Newton nut brown ink, Winsor & Newton Artists' watercolors, sable and Cotman brushes, Arches Aquarelle hot-press watercolor block; 2 hours

NAPLES

Naples's geography is ideal for sketchers who love cityscapes. "I can walk along the sea front, following several bays where the city faces the Mediterranean Sea, or walk on Corso Vittorio Emanuele, a street halfway up the hills that surround the whole city," says local architect and teacher Simonetta Capecchi.

"I draw to remember and to share with others, but, most of all, I draw what I'm curious about."

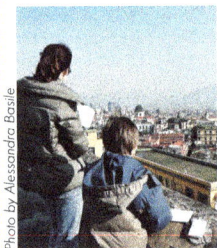

Photo by Alessandro Basile

🎧 Simonetta Capecchi sketches with her son from the roof of a church on a cold January day. "My son made a watercolor panorama as well, much faster than me!" says Capecchi.

ARTIST PROFILE
Simonetta Capecchi

To keep an illustrated journal is just a pleasure. I like that moment when I'm perfectly concentrated on what I see in front of me. Drawing means staying longer in places, and this always makes a difference in the way we perceive things or situations; we understand them better.

Sketching in the street is unusual, so people stop and talk to me. Sometimes, they get annoyed, like the fishmonger, who said, "She is drawing, drawing—but she doesn't buy anything!" It also scared someone who thought I was a municipal officer reporting an improper use of public space. Once I was approached by someone who recognized my sketches: "I know you from your blog; thanks to you, I started drawing again after years!"

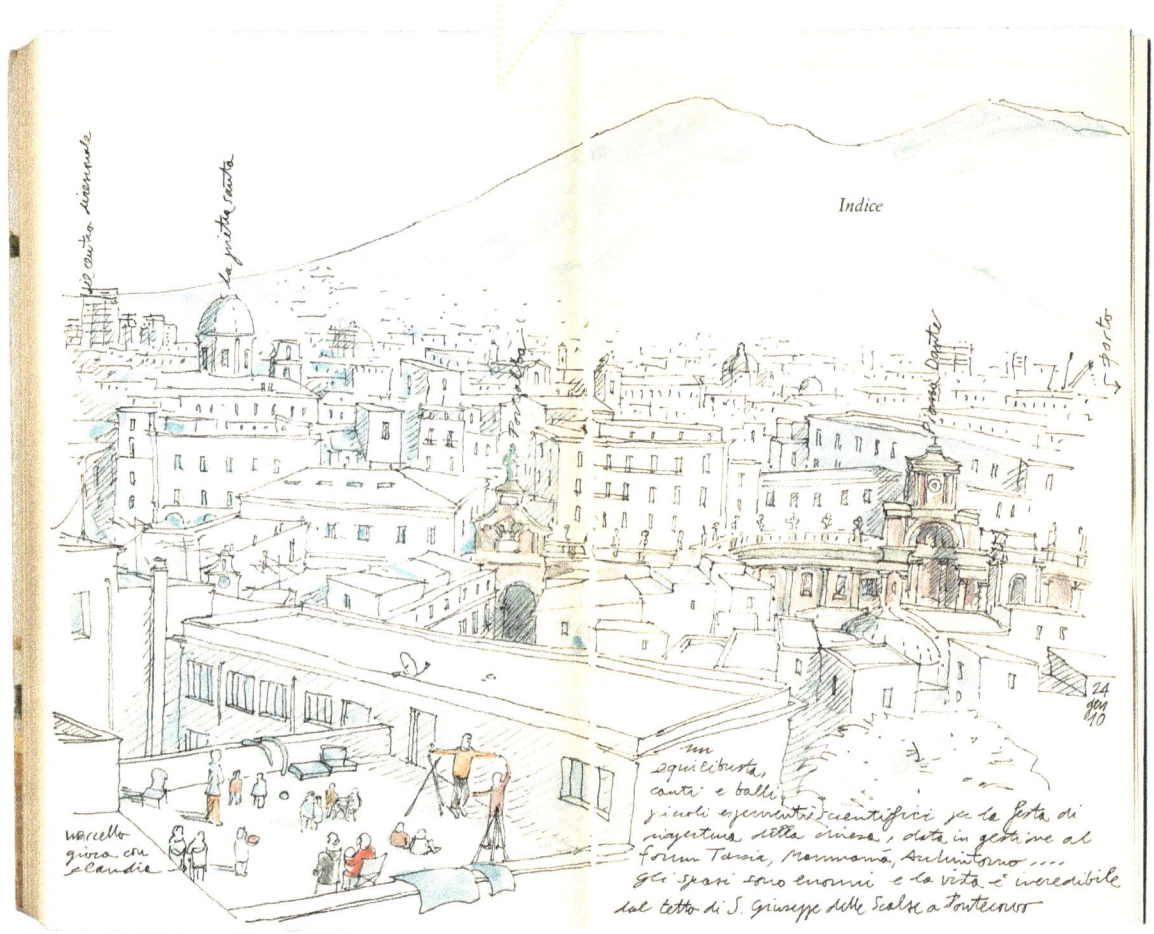

10" x 8" | 25 x 20 cm; Uni-ball ultra-fine waterproof pen and watercolor on a printed book by Fabrizia Ramondino titled *In viaggio*; about 30 minutes

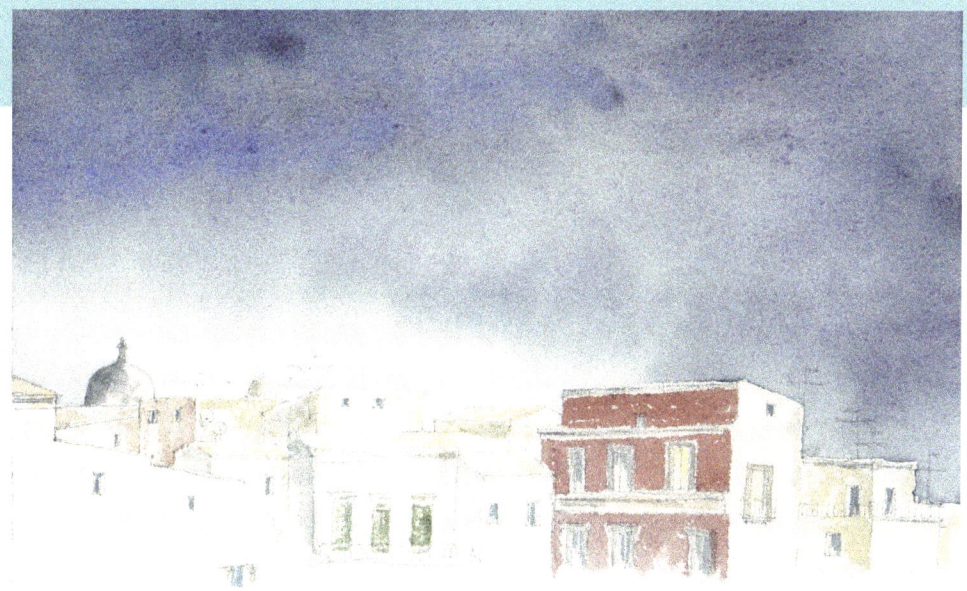

↻ Above, Roofs and Clouds Because of the sea winds, the sky changes fast here, Capecchi says, and clouds can be a great subject. "I had been inspired by a book on Constable's clouds—I read he used to paint studies for his oils on the beach in a winter storm."

Tip "I remember that day with a great pleasure. I was concentrated on painting only, taking my time to wait for the right light, trying papers and brushes, instead of drawing quickly, standing in the middle of a street. I should do it more often." — *Simonetta Capecchi*

10" x 6.25" | 20 x 16; Winsor & Newton watercolor set, #18 round Vang Jax-hair brush, Pentel waterbrush, 4B pencil, Arches 140-lb. cold-press watercolor paper; 1 hour or more

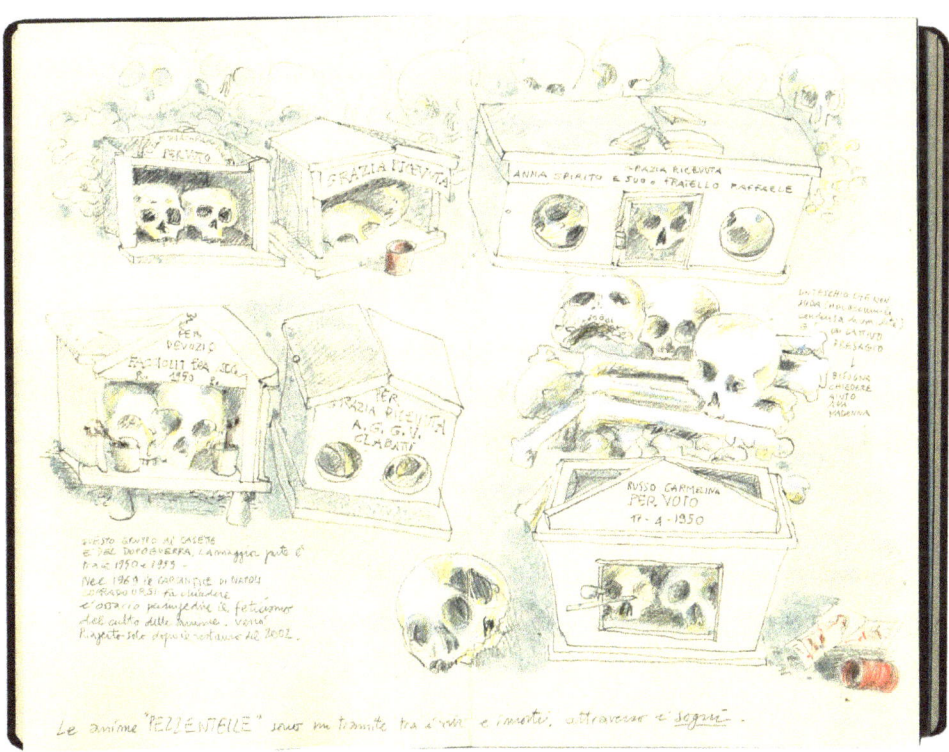

↻ Underground, Skulls and Devotion The Fontanelle Cemetery is an ancient cave in the Sanità district, used as a graveyard centuries ago.

Tip "To draw skulls in this dark and damp space was strange and not very comfortable. I tried to be as quick as possible, which is not necessarily a bad condition for drawing. Luckily, I brought a portable chair and a heavy jacket. I also took some pictures, but they came out blurry, so once again, drawing was the best way to record such an interesting experience." — *Simonetta Capecchi*

10" x 8.25" | 25 x 21 cm; 4B and 6B pencils, Winsor & Newton watercolors, Pentel waterbrush on Moleskine large Japanese album; for seven spreads, color added later

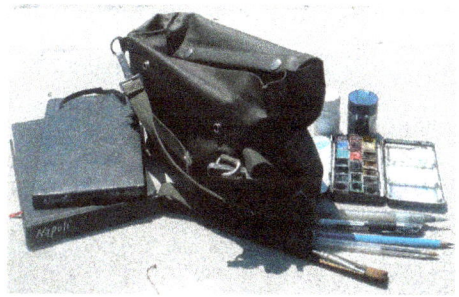

⋂ Capecchi's sketching tools and sketchbooks

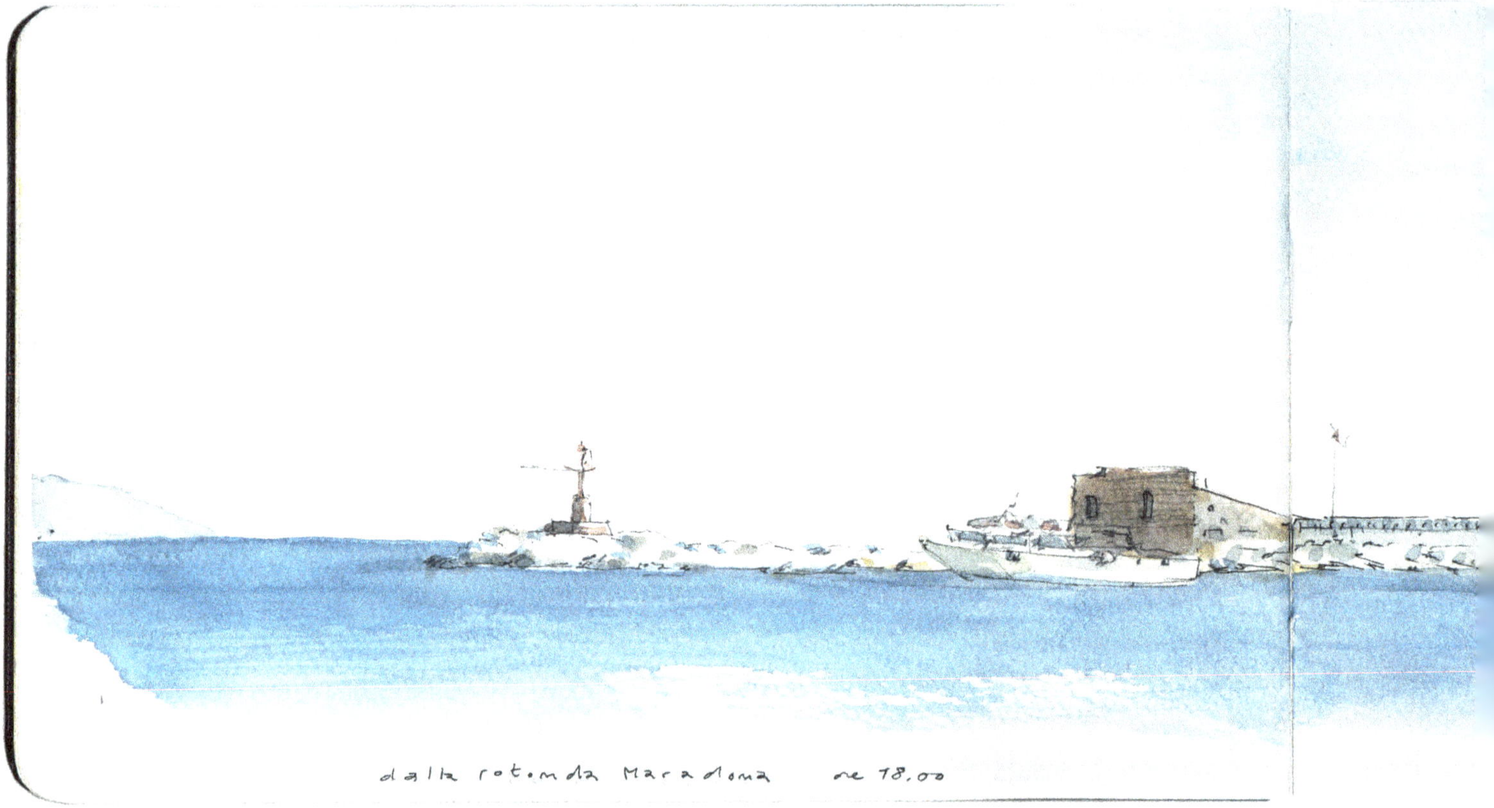

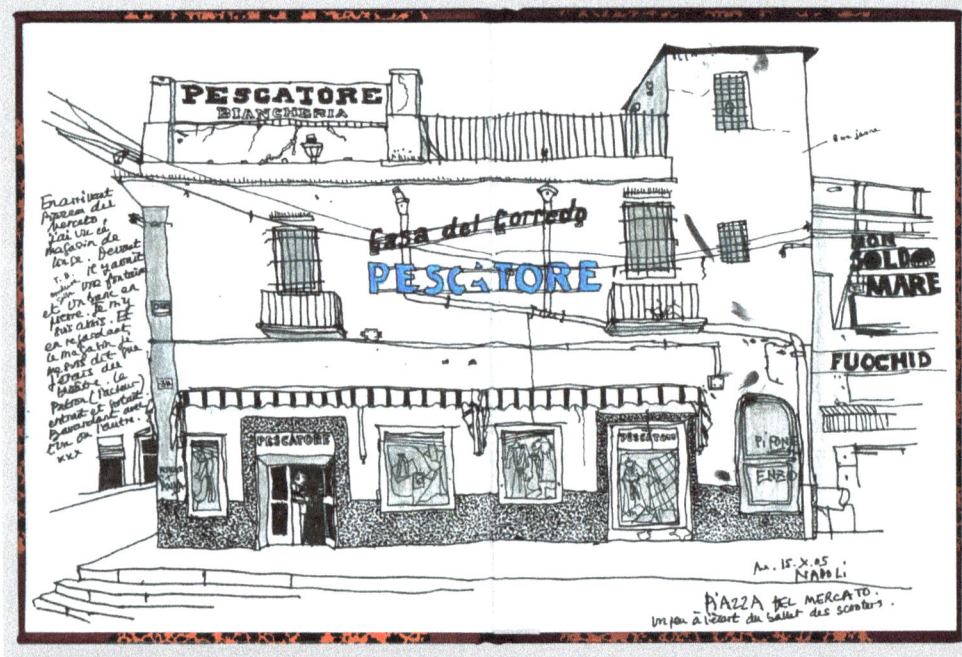

TRAVEL JOURNAL

Michel Longuet's Sketchbook of Naples

During a visit to Naples, French illustrator Michel Longuet shared one drawing a day on Simonetta Capecchi's blog, In viaggio col taccuino. "I like Michel's drawn reportages of Paris, so I was curious to see my own city through his eyes," says Capecchi. "Michel's work has a great narrative quality. He draws slowly but daily, and each drawing or small group of drawings has a story to tell; his words are chosen with humor and attention."

⟳ "In piazza Mercato, I saw this clothes and brides' dresses shop. A fountain with a stone base is in front of it. I sat there and watched the building. I thought it was like a theatre stage. The owner (the actor) came in and out, chatting with people passing by." — *Michel Longuet*

⟳ "There are several public elevators like this one in Naples. In this popular neighborhood, there is not an inch of space to spare. Pedestrians, scooters, and cars are moving like in a silent film—very fast. Very alive." — *Michel Longuet*

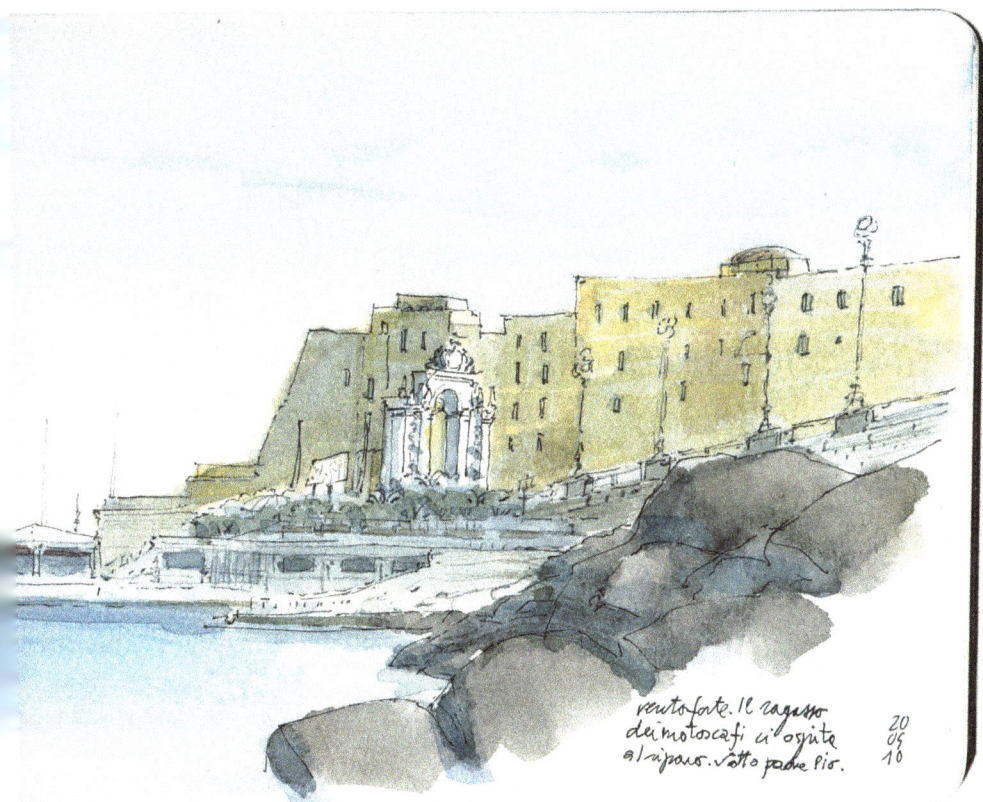

↻ **Horizon, Boats, and Castle** The Castel dell'Ovo is an ancient fortress partly carved on tufaceous rock and surrounded by the sea. Its irregular shape, visible from almost everywhere in town, is one of my favorite subjects, says Capecchi.

Tip "This sketch was made as an example of how to give a sense of depth in a seascape. You need a detail in the foreground so that you can measure distances."
— *Simonetta Capecchi*

8.25" x 5" | 21 x 12.5 cm; Mitsubishi Uni-ball ultra-fine, waterproof ink pen, Winsor & Newton watercolors, Pentel waterbrush on Moleskine watercolor book; about 30 minutes

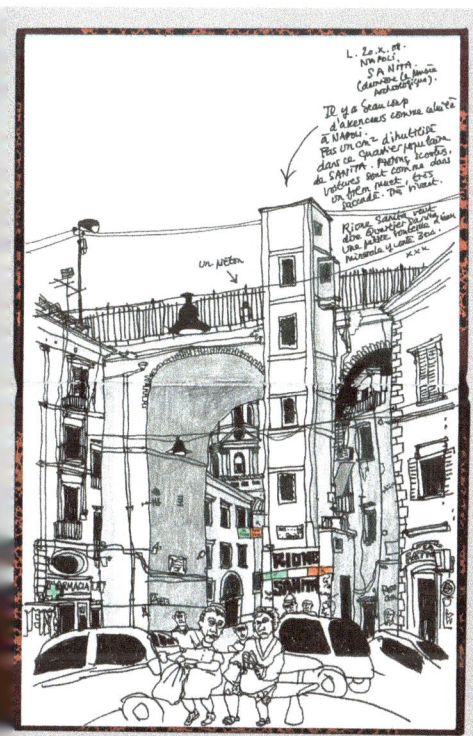

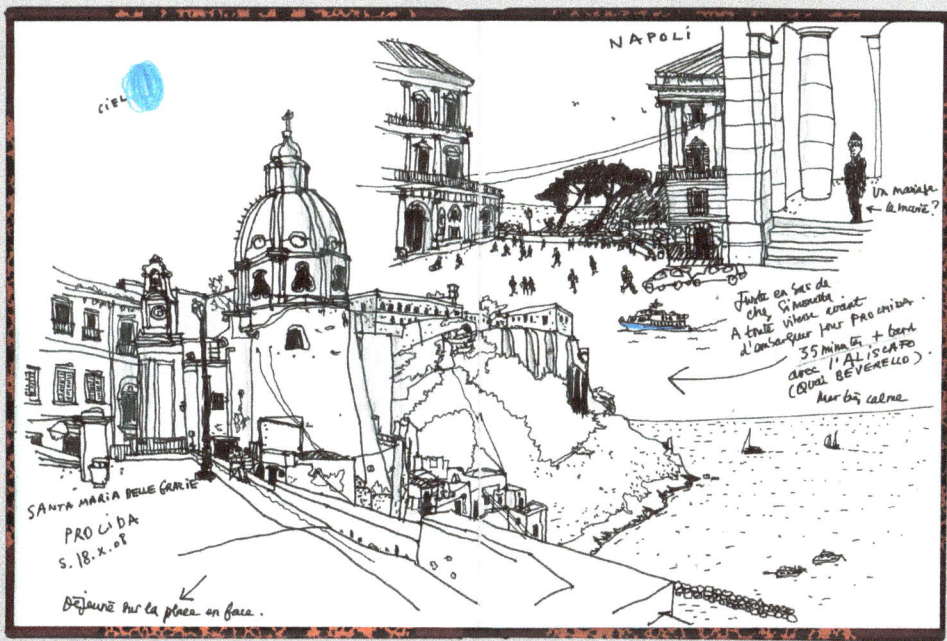

🎧 "On the right is a view of Plebiscito Square before taking the ferry to Procida Island. The sea was calm. In Procida, I had lunch in a square near Santa Maria delle Grazie." — *Michel Longuet*

ISTANBUL

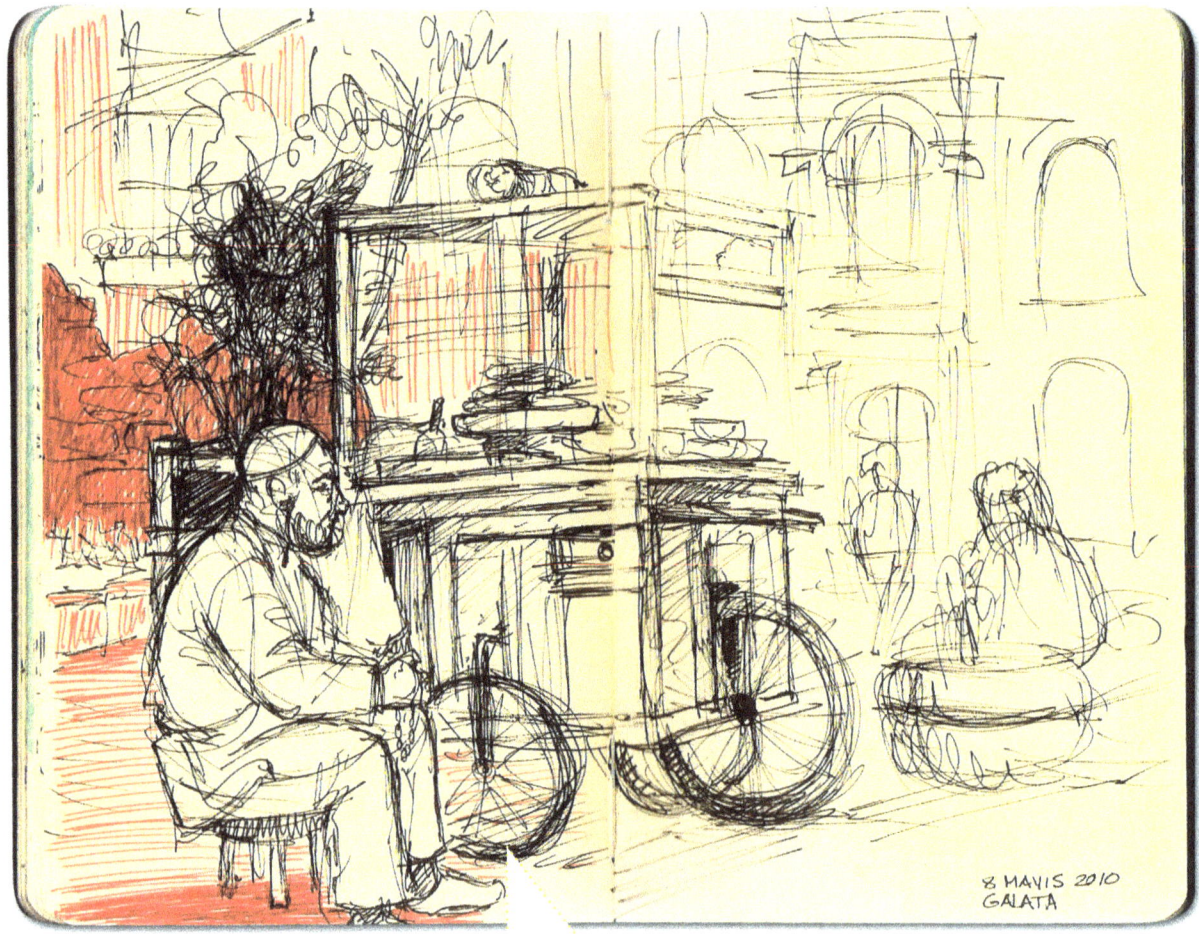

"I'm a compulsive sketcher; I have to sketch or I feel like there's something missing in my day."

At the crossroads of Europe and Asia, Istanbul's multiple layers of history are guaranteed to overwhelm the senses of any sketcher visiting the former capital of the Ottoman Empire. From the silhouette of Eminönü Mosque to lively scenes at markets and cafés, the sights, smells, colors, and sounds of Istanbul create vivid memories for the artists who sketch here.

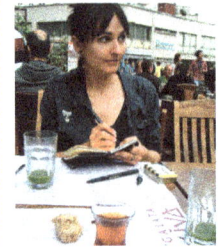

⌒ Istanbul illustrator Samantha Zaza enjoys a vegetable juice while sketching a familiar street vendor from an outdoor café.

Pigma Micron pens on Moleskine sketchbook; about 15 minutes

ARTIST PROFILE
Samantha Zaza

Urban sketching is more than drawing the buildings in a city; it's capturing its soul and rhythm. I strive to convey a sense of the feeling of Istanbul, not just to record the shapes of structures and anonymous people. I particularly love drawing people in those forgettable moments: the unremarkable daily coffee at the usual café, the metro ride home, the walk to work. Those private situations seem so intimate. You really catch a glimpse of someone's self, forgetting their surroundings, their façades, and being fully immersed in their thoughts.

Istanbul is never short on inspiration. There's always something to discover. A walk to the supermarket is never just a walk to the supermarket—there will be singing fishmongers, pushy old ladies in tiny shoes, suspicious cats, and lots and lots of emptied tea glasses.

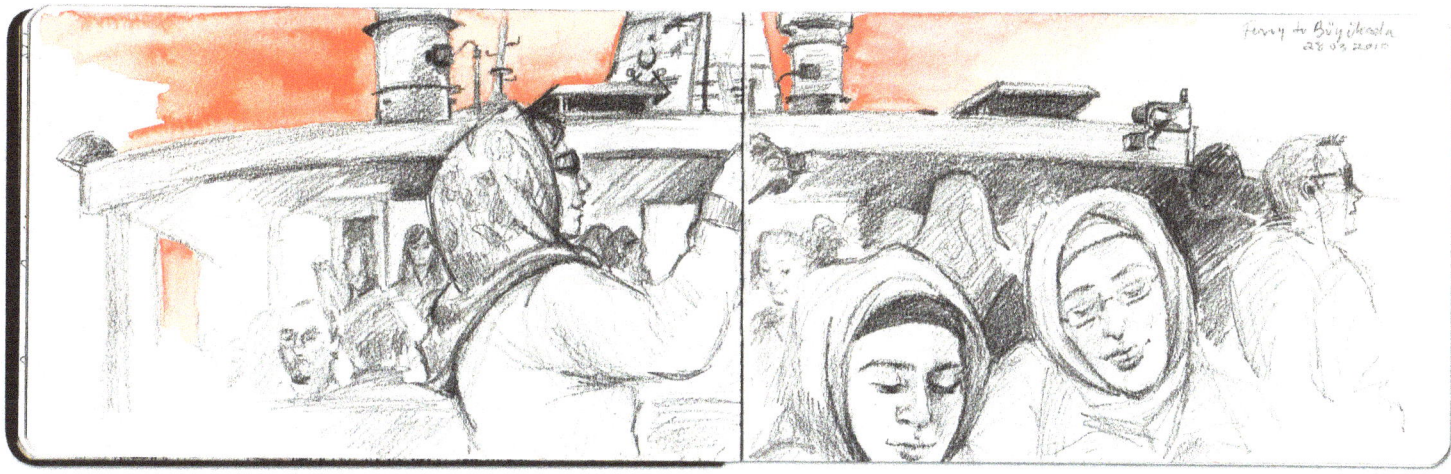

The Bosphorus Zaza remembers this as a foggy, hazy day with a little chill in the air. She spent a couple of hours in the afternoon lazily sketching on the balcony with a cup of hot tea. On the left is Asia, and, on the right, curving around to where Zaza sat, is Europe. "I love watching the men on the fishing boats casting and pulling up their nets and the big tankers carefully winding their way up and down the Bosphorus," Zaza says.

Tip "To create a sense of distance, I add more details in the foreground and less in the background. I also play with value, lightening things as they move farther away from me." — *Samantha Zaza*

10.5" x 8.25" | 26.5 x 21 cm; Sanford Design Ebony pencil; Moleskine sketchbook; about 2 hours

The Ferry to Büyükada Riding on the packed ferry to the Prince's Islands, these two girls in the foreground were so sweet, Zaza remembers. "After watching me sketch, they bought me a tea," she says.

Tip "Fingerless gloves make sketching on breezy ferries a lot easier." — *Samantha Zaza*

16.5" x 5" | 42 x 12.5 cm; Sanford Design Ebony pencil and Winsor & Newton gouache on Moleskine large watercolor book; about 20-25 minutes

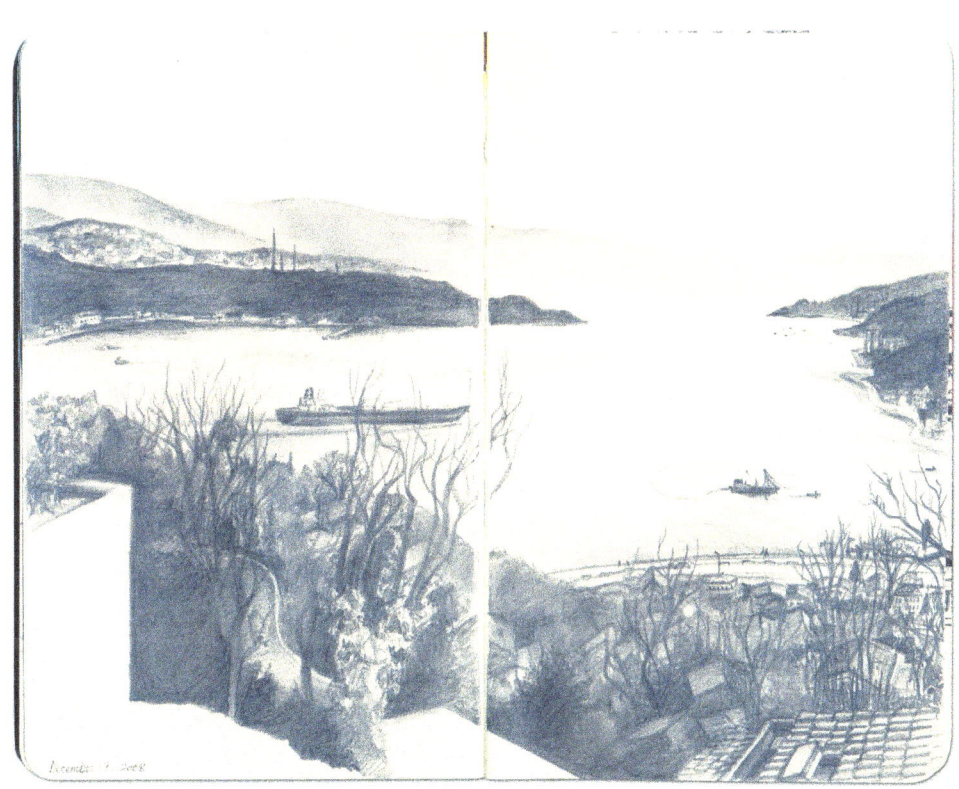

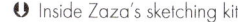 Inside Zaza's sketching kit

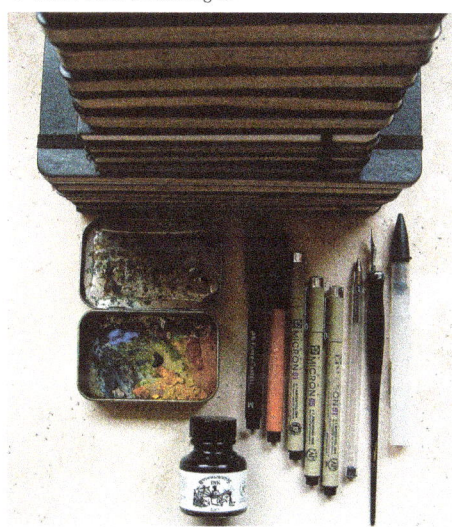

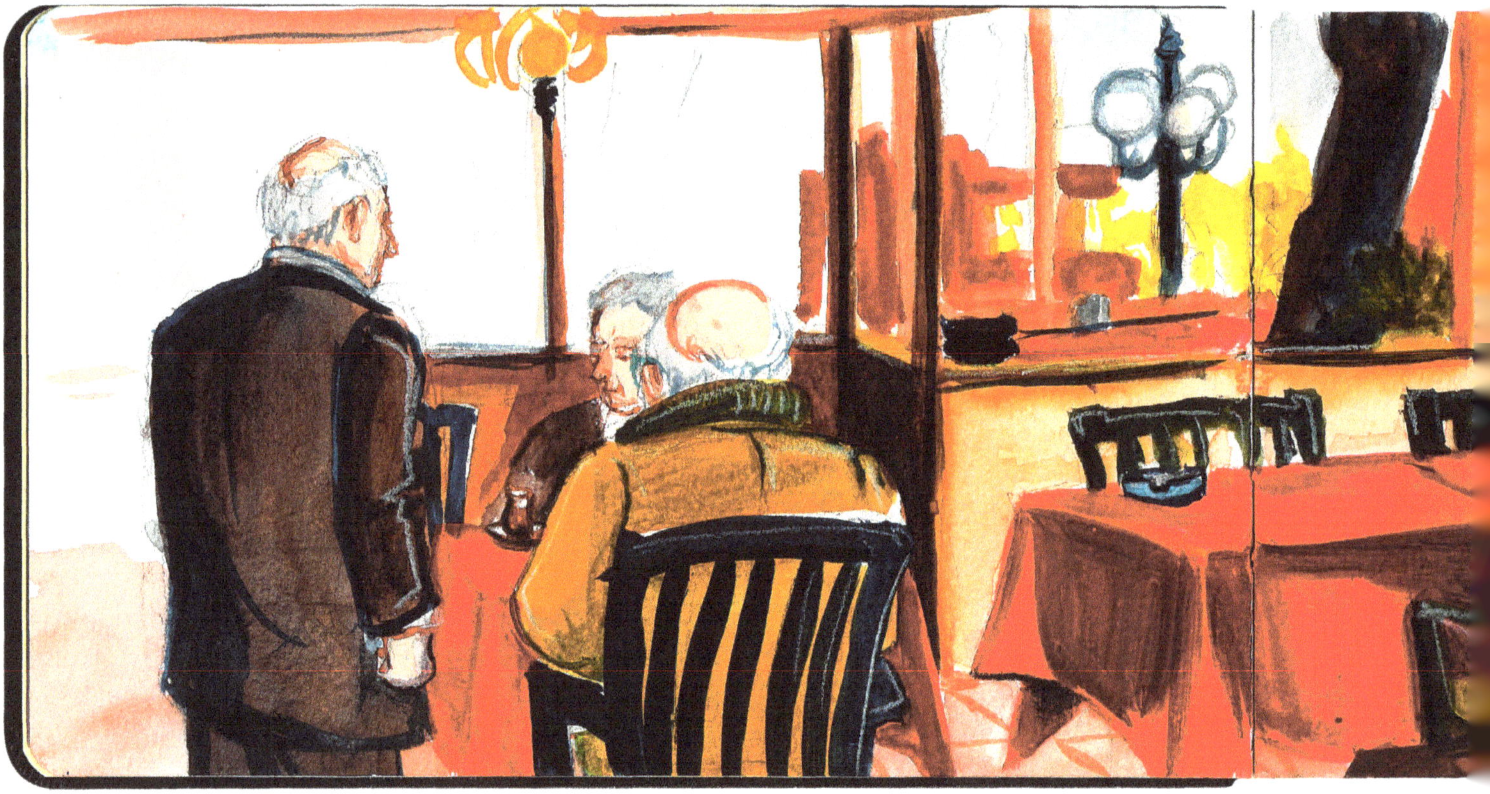

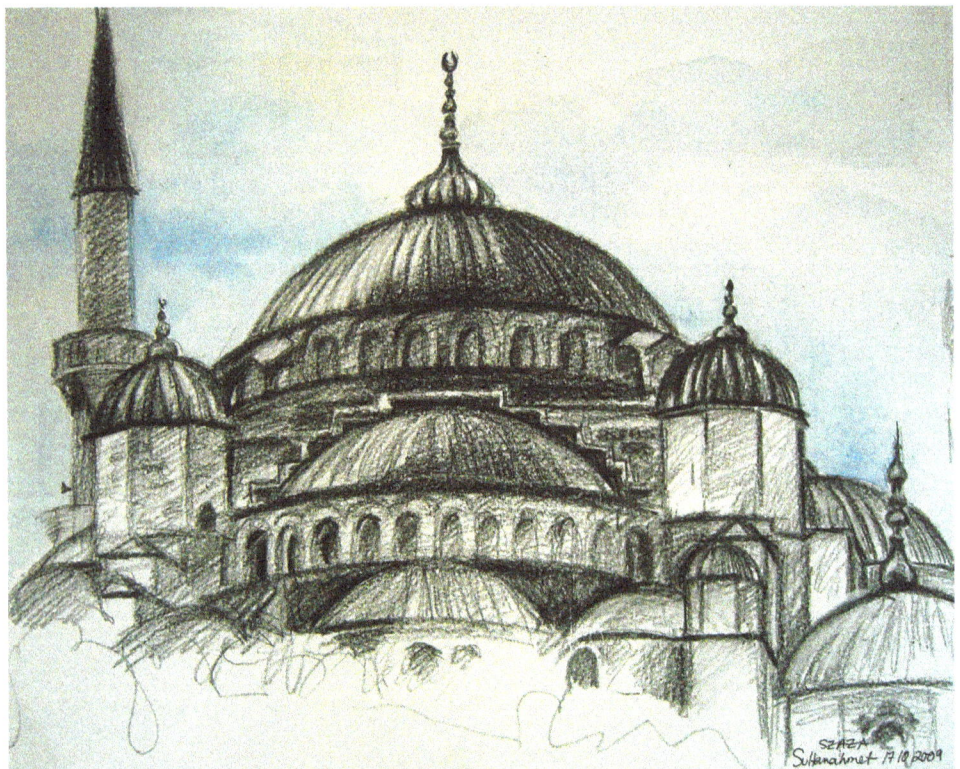

↻ **Sultanahmet Camii** "The benches in front of Sultanahmet Camii, also known as the Blue Mosque, are a great place to sketch people," says Samantha Zaza. "With a tiny paper cup of tea from the çay guy, you're set to draw the afternoon away!"

Tip "Observing which direction the light is coming from and where the shadows fall will helps give shape to objects, buildings, and people." — *Samantha Zaza*

9" x 12" | 23 x 30.5 cm; Sanford Design Ebony pencil and Winsor & Newton gouache on Boesner Aquarelle 300 paper; about 30 minutes

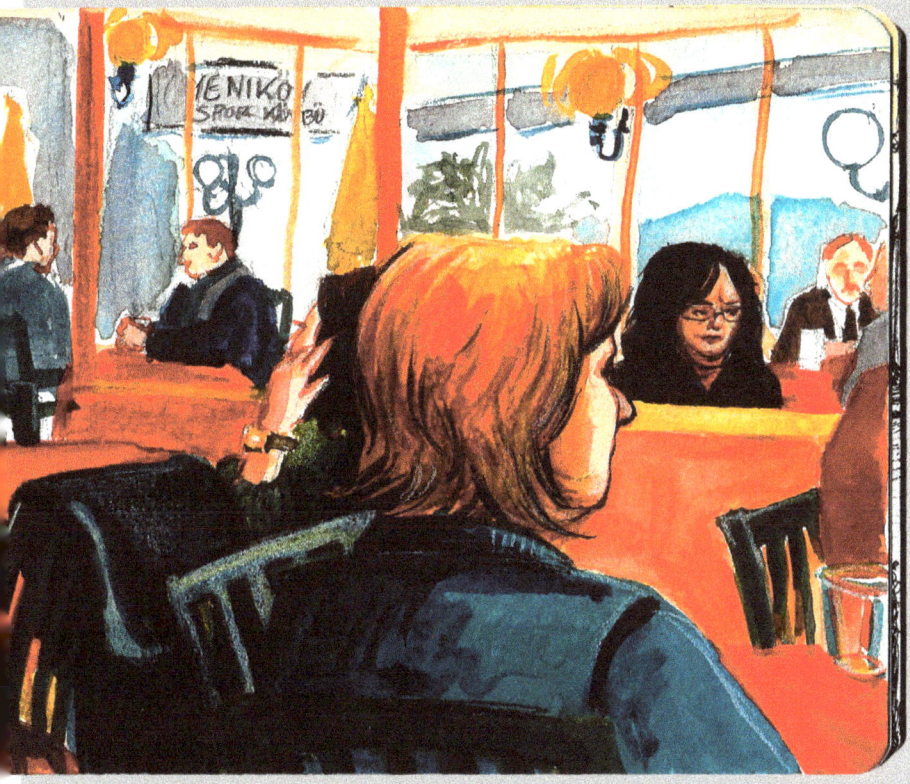

FIRST PERSON

Sketching Stories from Café Yeniköy Spor Kulübü

by Samantha Zaza

↻ Yeniköy Spor Kulübü café is right on the Bosphorus—in the summertime you can sit out on the terrace and watch the boats go by. People often get together here to play mah-jongg, Okey (a Turkish tile-based game), and cards with their lunch. It is imperative that any sketcher have within reach a delicious Turkish coffee, or *kahve*.

16.5" x 5" | 42 x 12.5 cm; Winsor & Newton gouache, a random chalk pencil I found; Moleskine watercolor book; about 25 minutes

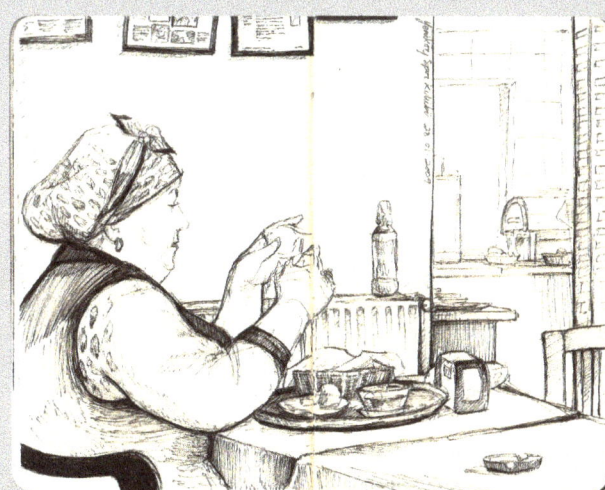

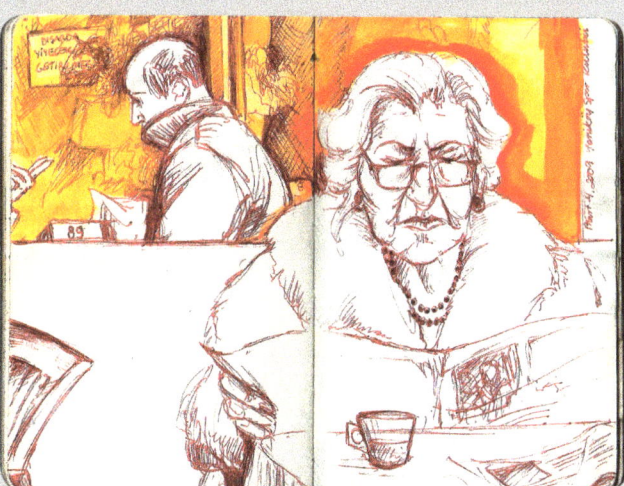

∩ I was told that this lady takes care of the bathrooms in the café. She has so much character, and is usually moving about, but on this day, she sat down and had a breakfast of bread, butter, cheese, and tea. Her hands were so quick, they were difficult to draw. Once again, a waiter whisked away my Moleskine, and, when he showed it to her, she started smiling and said all sorts of things to me that I didn't understand. I was told one of them was "health to your hands."

10.5" x 8.25" | 26.5 x 21; Sakura Pigma Micron pen on Moleskine sketchbook; 15 minutes

∩ This elegant lady was in her usual spot at the café, frowning over the news in her fur coat and coral necklace. A kind, elderly gentleman, who I believe is the owner, presented me with a sheet of paper from the copier and motioned for me to draw her for him. After I finished, he picked up the paper and excitedly ran off to give the drawing to the lady. A smile grew over her face, and she thanked me for the drawing, declaring it was *"çok güzel"*—"very nice." It made my day.

5.5" x 7" | 14 x 18 cm; Sakura Pigma Micron pen, Winsor & Newton gouache on Moleskine Istanbul City notebook; 10 minutes

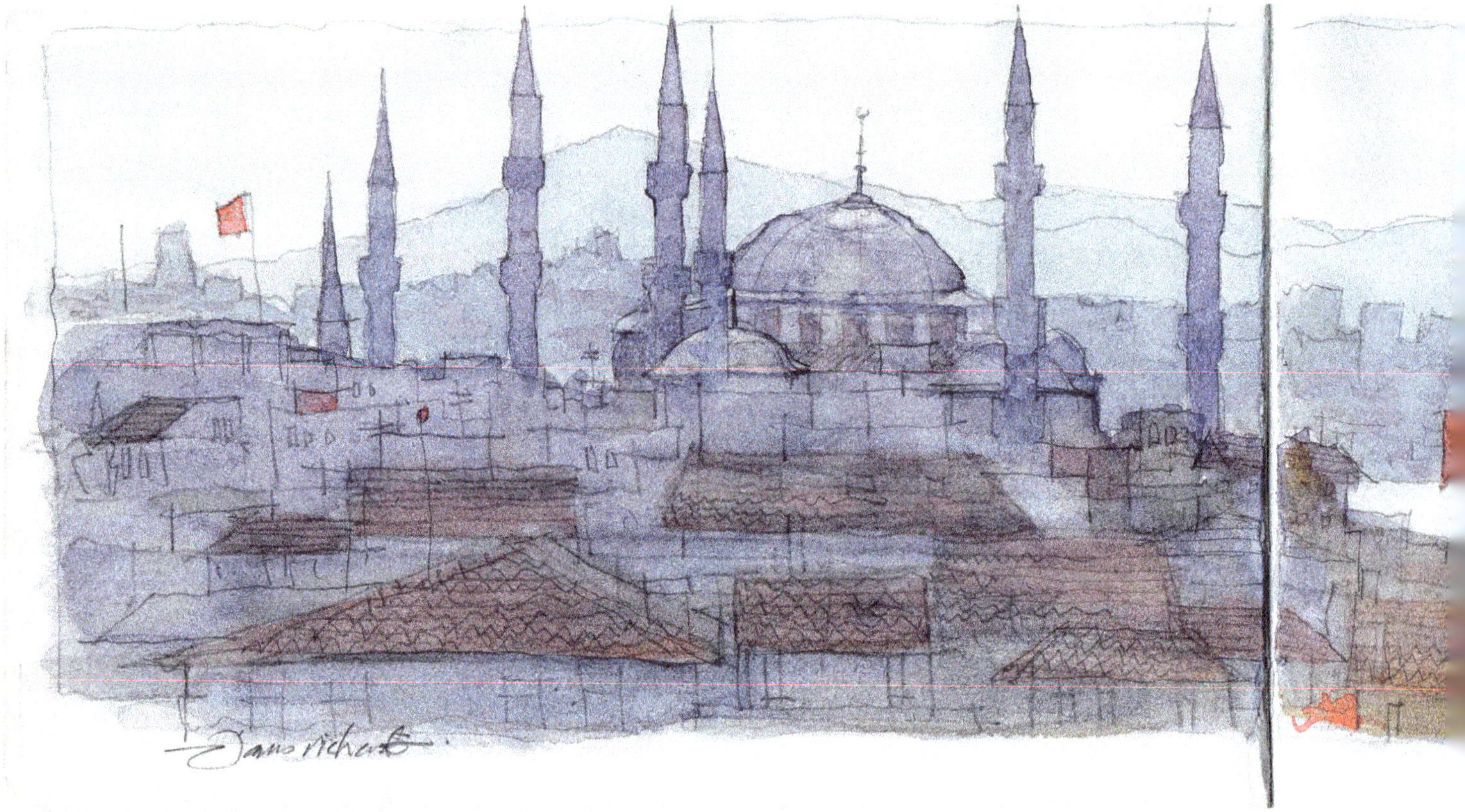

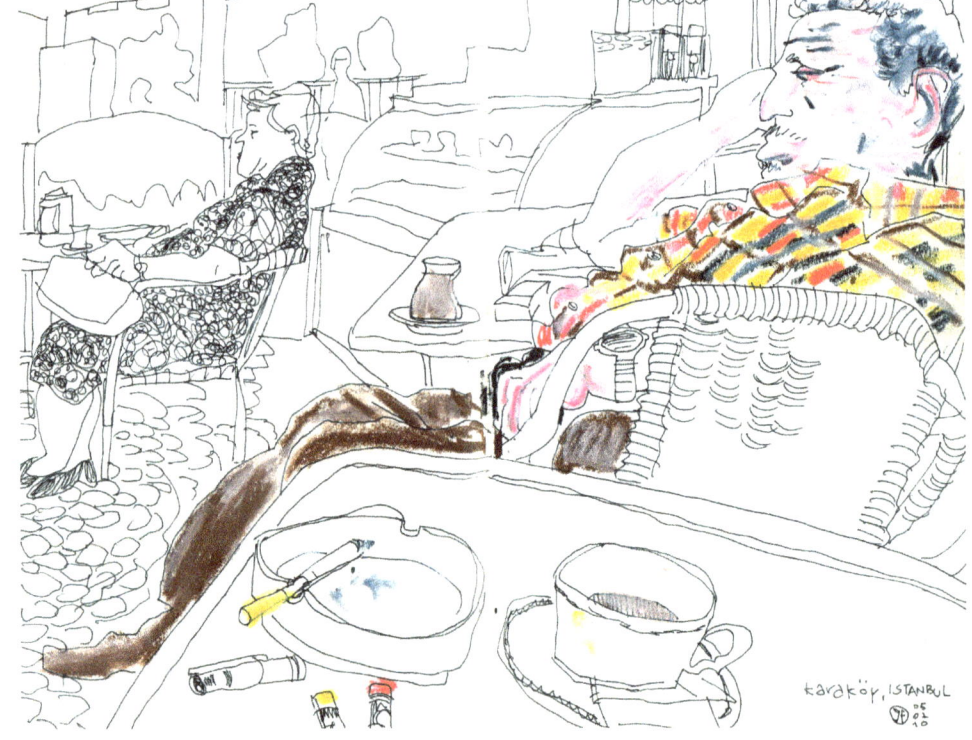

⋒ Early Morning "I hiked, crossed bridges, and climbed towers across Istanbul's historic peninsula, looking for a scene that captured Istanbul's riveting silhouette," says James Richards. "I finally found it from my hotel roof."

Tip "I added the watercolor as a series of washes, light to dark, background to foreground, allowing each wash to dry before applying the next." — *James Richards*

5.5" x 16.5" | 14 x 42 cm; .07 BIC Velocity HB pencil, Winsor & Newton travel watercolor kit on large, landscape-format Hand-Book Travelogue Journal; 15-minute pencil sketch, 25-minute watercolor

⊃ Sleeping Man in a Café Giorgio Fratini says he usually sketches with just a black pen, but this man had a beautifully colored shirt, so he used a wax pastel for the first time. "It was my first drawing of a series that I did during a recent trip to Turkey," Fratini says. "It's a good way to start a trip: with a nice drawing."

Tip "Sketching sleeping people is simple. They don't look at you, and they usually stay still." — *Giorgio Fratini*

6.75" x 8.75" | 17 x 22 cm; black Pilot G-Tec-C4 and Caran d'Ache Neocolor II water-soluble wax pastels; handmade sketchbook bought on a street in Istanbul; about 15–20 minutes

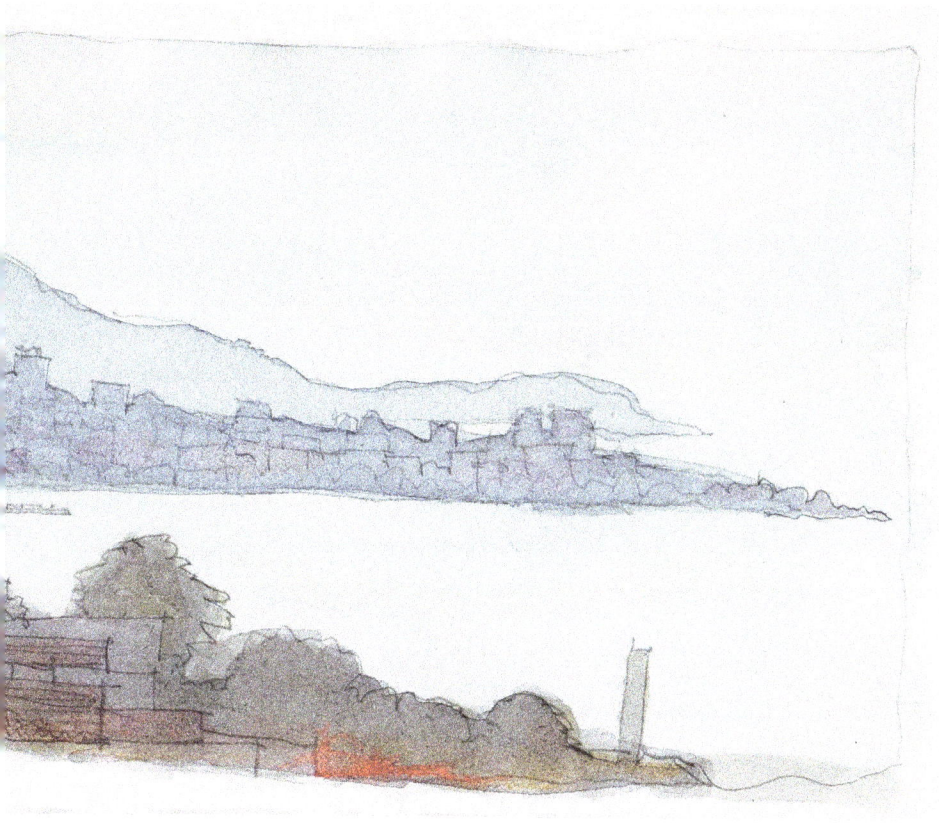

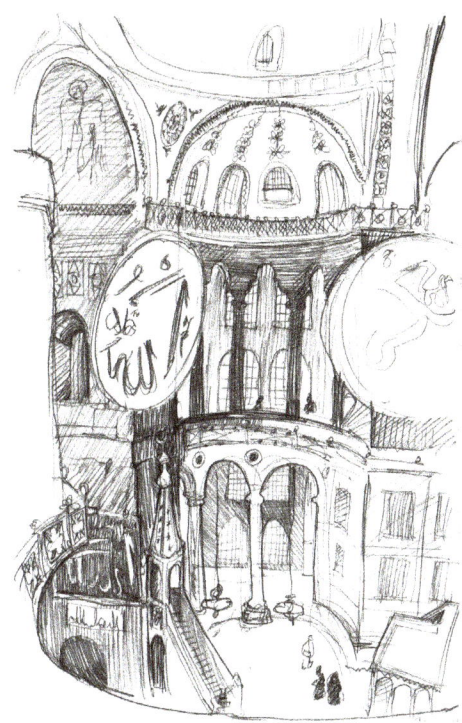

∩ Inside the Ayasofya Murray Dewhurst was captivated by the sheer size of Hagia Sophia. "The enormous dome, combined with layers of Christian and Islamic elements, is hugely evocative of the many centuries that have passed since its completion in AD 537 but also a big challenge to get down on paper," Dewhurst says. "I chose a quiet spot upstairs and singled out a manageable section of the interior to capture."

5.75" x 8.25" | 14.6 x 21 cm; Staedtler .05 technical pencil on A5 basic spiral-bound sketchbook; 30 minutes

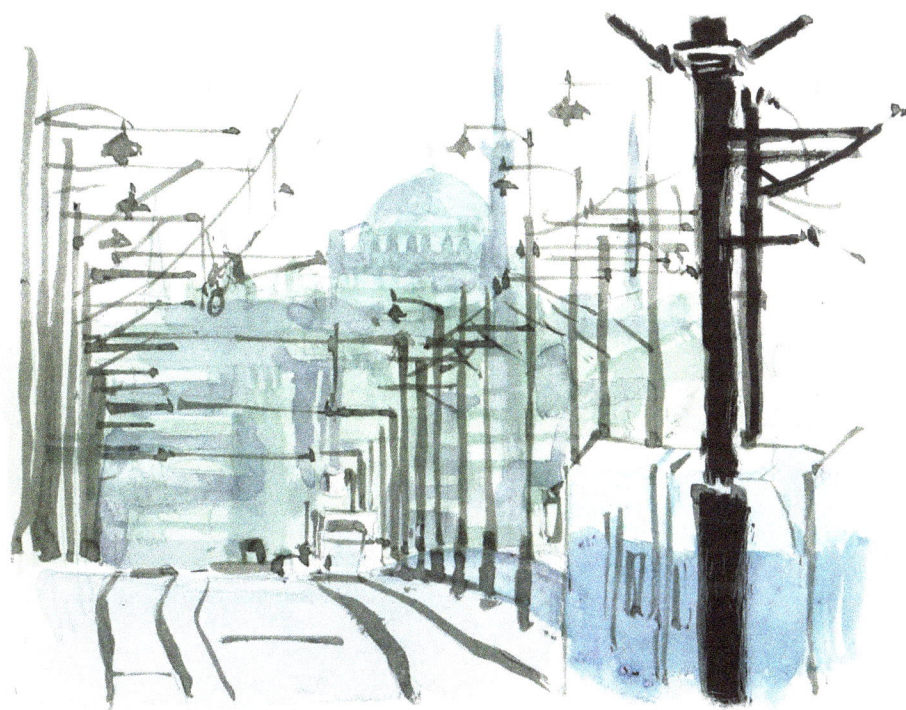

⊂ Tram Across the Bosphorus Roger O'Reilly sketched this standing on a traffic island with cars and trams whizzing by and curious onlookers momentarily distracted from casting their rods from the bridge's upper deck.

Tip "The most important part of the sketch was to create a sense of depth with the power lines. These were drawn in first. The background was washed in next, and while I was doing this, the tram to right pulled into view, so I quickly penciled it in. The final touch was to strengthen the sense of hazy light by rendering the nearest two poles in black." — *Roger O'Reilly*

5.75" x 8.25" | 14.6 x 21 cm; Pentel brush pen, pencil, and watercolor on 150-gsm A5 cartridge paper sketchbook; 15 minutes

TEL AVIV

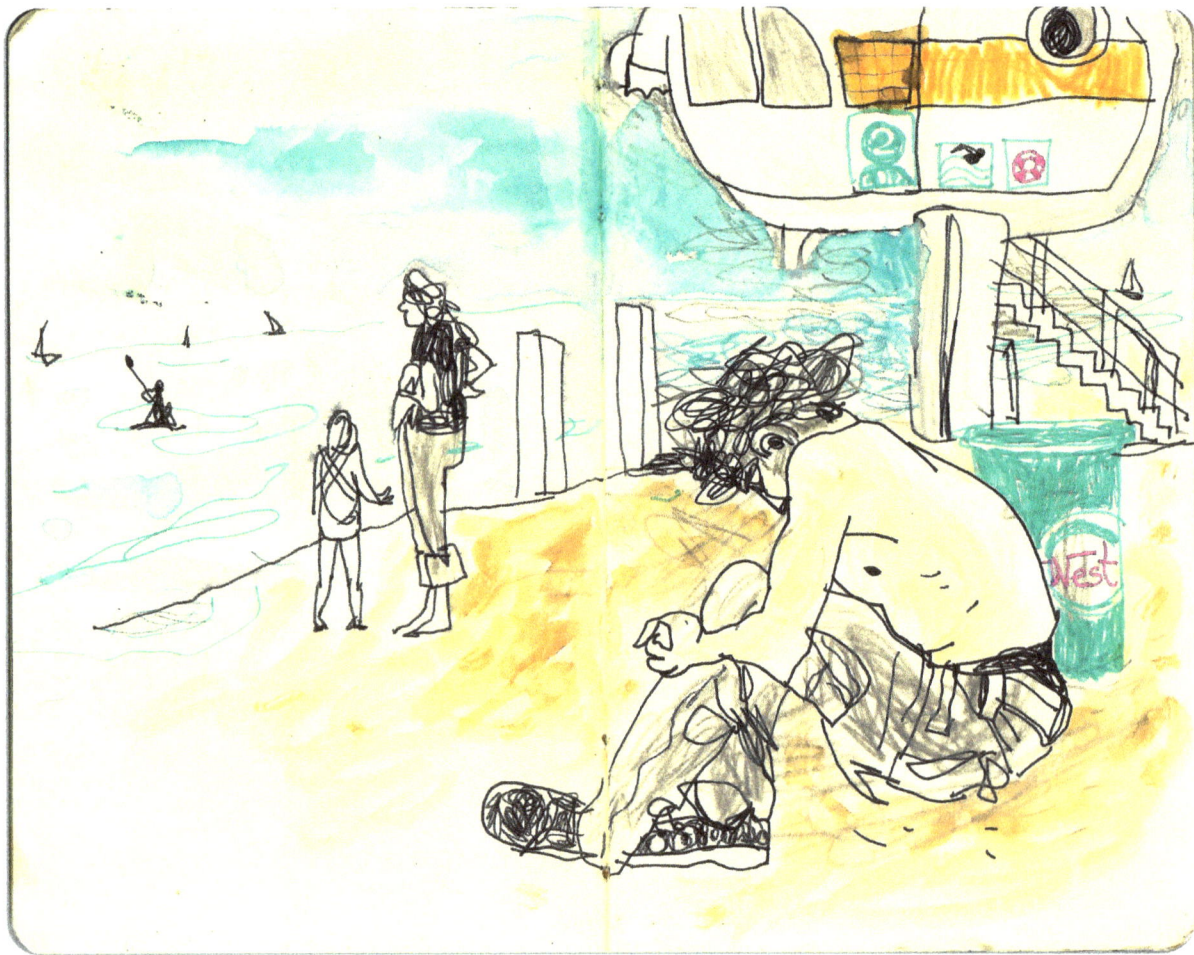

☾ Kite at the Beach
Grechanik dashed off a sketch of a not-so-successful attempt to fly a kite at Sharon Beach on a windless Israeli winter day.

Tip "I did a quick sketch with black pen only, trying to catch the human figures first, because they could move every moment. Afterward, I added more details and watercolor."
— *Marina Grechanik*

5.5" x 7" | 14 x 18 cm; Faber-Castell fiber-tip pen, Van Gogh 12-pan watercolor pocket box by Royal Talens, synthetic brushes, Derwent Inktense colored pencils on Moleskine pocket sketchbook; 15 minutes

Israel's capital of Tel Aviv has a beautiful coastline, with beaches and promenades that are crowded and hot in summer and quiet and calm in winter. Local illustrator Marina Grechanik is drawn to the contrast between the bright blue sea, the soft white sand, and all the activity around the waterfront.

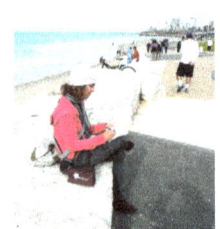

ARTIST PROFILE
Marina Grechanik

My sketches serve as a big bank of ideas for my work as a graphic designer and illustrator. They also help me balance my need for creative hand work, as opposed to the mostly computer-produced graphics in my job. Sketching keeps my hands flexible and my eyes fresh. I don't feel comfortable when I leave home without a sketchbook and some pens in my bag.

I love to sit in a corner of some Tel Aviv coffee shop and explore the relationship between people, the environment, and myself. This unique local mix of cultures, languages, and styles is always a great source for inspiration. Sometimes, I find some usual items, like sugar bags or napkins. I use them in my drawings to show the atmosphere. Sometimes, I draw directly on placemats.

"My way to observe things and to save them in my memory is to draw them."

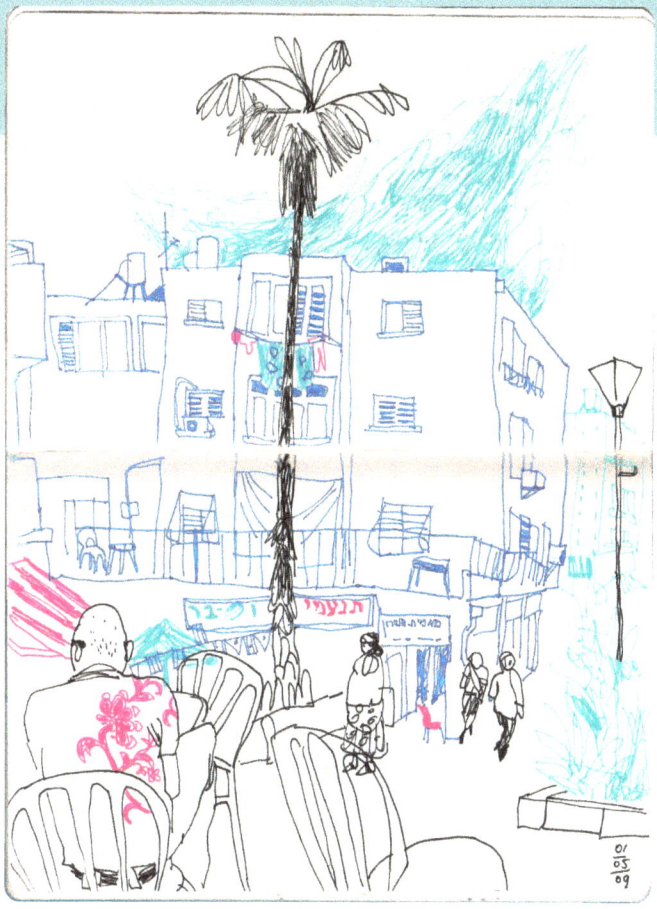

⌒ Ahuza Street in Ra'anana This small suburb of Tel Aviv is Grechanik's hometown. Although she says there's nothing special in Ra'anana's straight, clean streets, for her, sitting at the coffee shop, sketching and observing people, is always a special experience.

Tip "I had in my bag only four colors. So I chose to make a line sketch using my colors alternately. I didn't get a realistic color sketch, but I did transfer the atmosphere and the feeling I had." — *Marina Grechanik*

10.5" x 8.25" | 25.6 x 21 cm; Stabilo 0.4 color pens on Moleskine Cahier notebook; 20 minutes

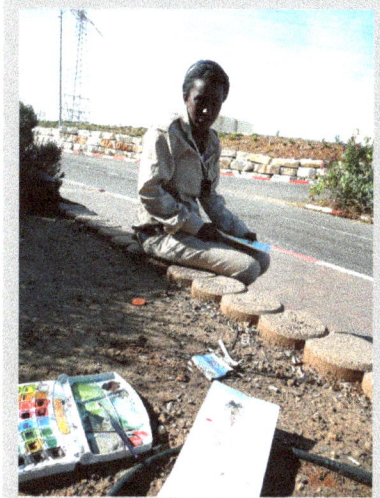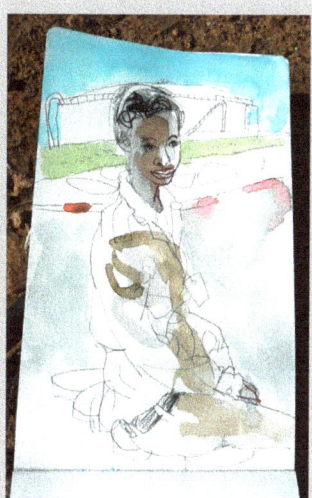

FIRST PERSON

Drawing Openly in Public

by Marina Grechanik

When I draw in public places, I usually try to avoid people seeing me in action, but once I dared to draw in the middle of the street. It was a fantastic experience! I went together with my friend, Harriet, so it gave me some courage. People were passing by, stopping from time to time and giving us some comments. It was quite nice. Suddenly, a young soldier girl, who stopped to watch us drawing, asked, "Would you be interested in drawing me?" Obviously, we agreed. We drew quick sketches and gave them to the girl. She was so pleased! And so were we! Then I felt like I was a real urban sketcher!

[AS] 8.25" x 5.25" | 21 x 13 cm; Van Gogh 12-pan watercolor pocket box by Royal Talens, synthetic brushes, pencil on Moleskine watercolor book; 10 minutes

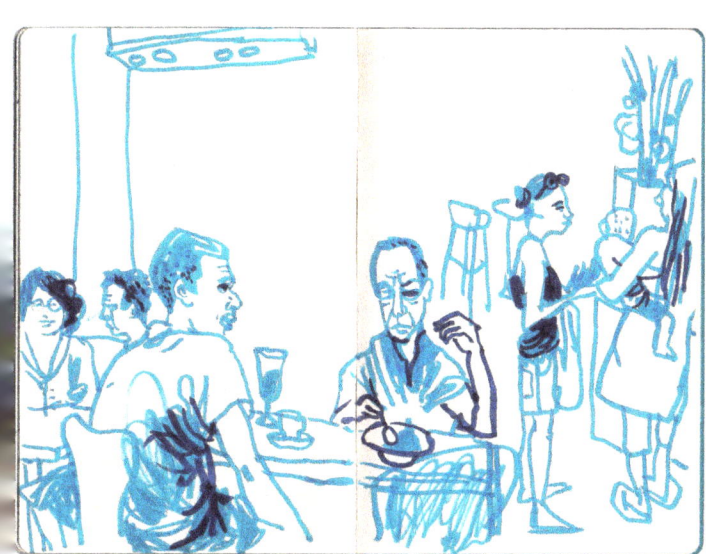

⌒ People at Arcaffe Coffee shops are Grechanik's favorite kind of location. "People are busy making orders, chatting, getting their drinks," she says. "I liked [the men's] expressions and started my sketch by putting them at the middle of the scene."

Tip "It's important to think about a composition, to choose the 'heroes' of your sketch." — Marina Grechanik

10.5" x 8.25" | 25.6 x21 cm; Sakura brush pens on Moleskine Cahier notebook; 15 minutes

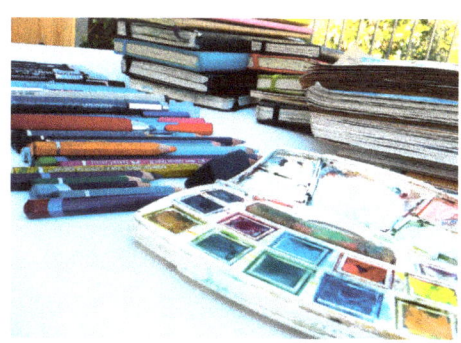

⌒ Grechanik's sketching tools

AL AIN

Palm trees, sand dunes, and old fortifications made of mud don't usually come to mind when you think of "urban" sketching, but such is the landscape in Al Ain, a city in the United Arab Emirates, where finding a shady spot to sketch is a must if you don't want to get a sunburn.

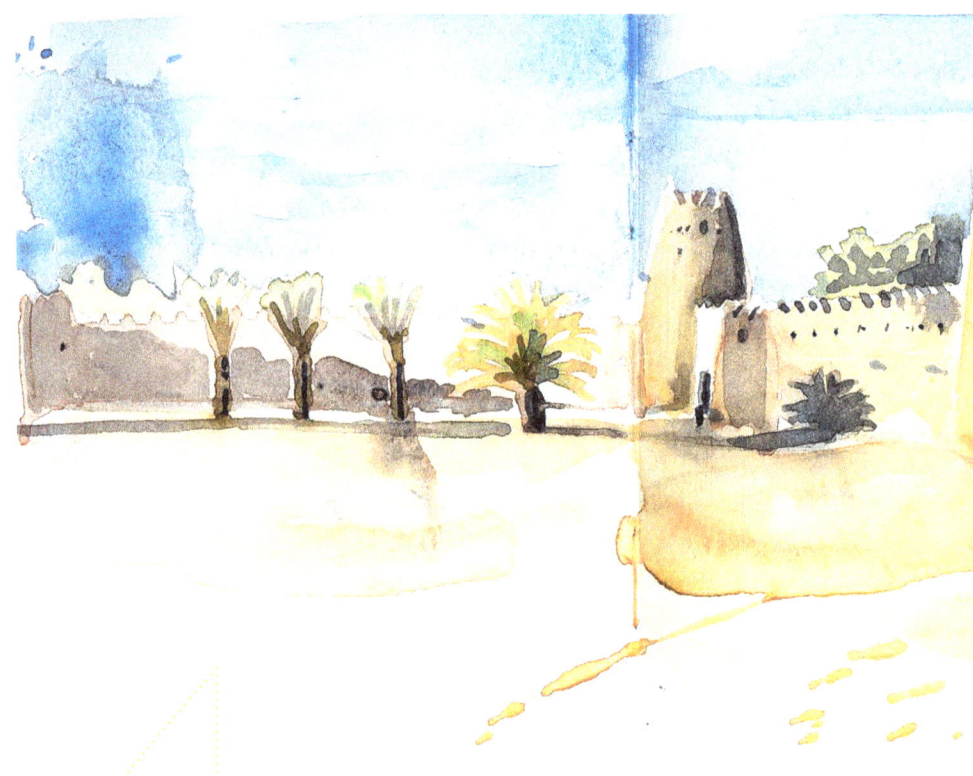

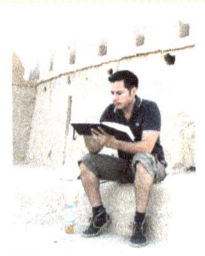

🎧 Omar Jaramillo sketches some of the buildings inside the Al Jahili Fort, a United Arab Emirates landmark.

16.5" x 5.25" | 42 x 13 cm; watercolor; 20 minutes

ARTIST PROFILE
Omar Jaramillo

In the last decade, I have been on a long journey. I was born in Guayaquil, Ecuador, where I studied architecture. I moved to Kassel, Germany, to accomplish a master's degree. Later, I moved to Catania, Italy, and, since recently, I have lived in the United Arab Emirates.

For me, drawing is a way to learn why a place is the way it is and what makes it different from others. It's a way to love a place, to become part of it. I like to draw architecture, but I am more attracted to urban scenery, portraying how people live in the city. Since I'm a foreigner in this country, everything that locals find normal and take for granted, for me, is exotic.

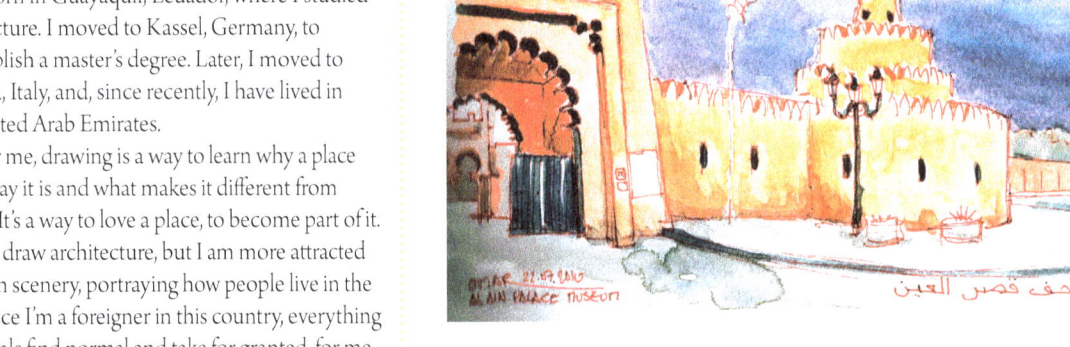

🎧 **The Museum Palace** It was late and the museum was closing as Jaramillo sketched the former residence of Sheik Zayed, the first president of the UAE. "When I finished, the sun was gone and the moon was shining," Jaramillo says.

Tip "Be sure you are working with a waterproof ink. You don't want ugly surprises." — *Omar Jaramillo*

8.25" x 5" | 21 x 12.5 cm; Faber-Castell Pitt pen (sanguine), Winsor & Newton pocket watercolor set, waterbrush on Moleskine large watercolor book; 20 minutes

"I always thought that drawing was a solitary experience, until I found the online urban sketchers community."

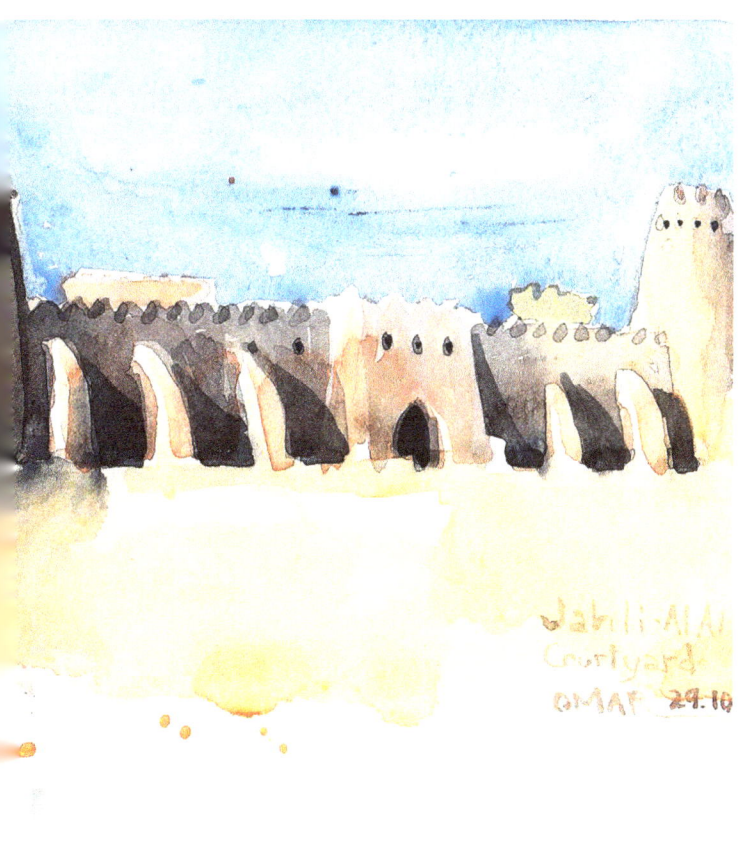

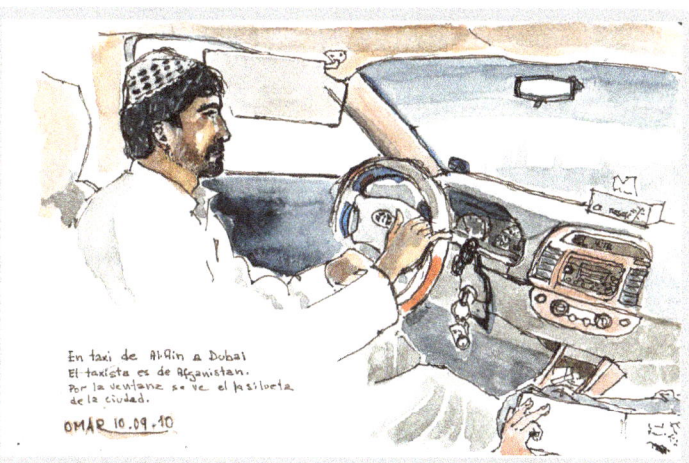

FIRST PERSON

Taxi Ride to Dubai

by Omar Jaramillo

I discovered at the bus station that there aren't any buses from Al Ain to Dubai, just some small minibuses, with no space for luggage. I took a taxi, instead. It cost a little more, but it took me directly to the airport terminal. There are two kinds of taxis in the Emirates: the new ones, with guys in uniform and a meter, and the old ones, which are kind of an informal taxi service, with no visual sign that the car is a taxi. (Maybe this was not a taxi, after all!) My driver was a guy from Afghanistan. He asked me where I wanted to go, and we haggled over the price. It is a ninety-minute ride, and I thought the taxi interior would make a good sketch, rich in details. The driver was quite happy with the result and took a picture of the sketch with his cell phone.

8.25" x 5" | 21 x 12.5 cm; Faber-Castell Pitt pen (sanguine), Winsor & Newton pocket watercolor set, waterbrush on Moleskine large watercolor book; about 90 minutes

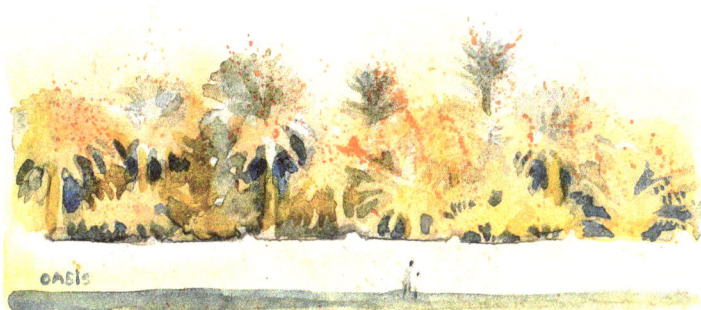

♪ **Urban Oasis** Al Ain is an oasis in the middle of a sea of red sand dunes. High buildings are forbidden, and you see parks and green all around, says Jaramillo. "The view of the palm trees at sunset is quite magic."

Tip "Start with a glaze from bottom to top (invert the paper for doing that) with alizarin crimson, adding a little water on the way. Wait till it dries and repeat the procedure with blue from top to bottom. Work with the negative spaces to create the palms."
— *Omar Jaramillo*

8.25" x 5" | 21 x 12.5 cm; Winsor & Newton pocket watercolor set, waterbrush on Moleskine watercolor book; 40 minutes

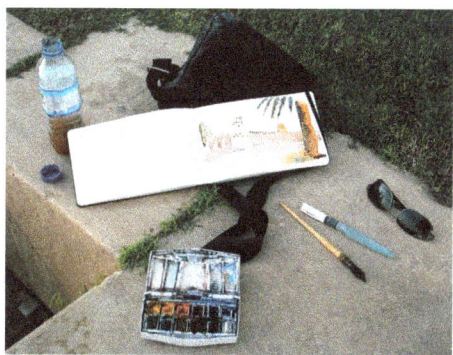

♪ Omar's sketching tools

PUNE

Ancient Hindu temples and British colonial architecture mix it up in Pune, a city in Western India with more than three million residents, located less than three hours from coastal Mumbai. The city has a beautiful mix of old and new, says local architect Sanjeev Joshi, who enjoys making quick watercolor impressions with a calligraphic flair.

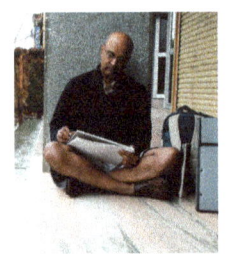

ARTIST PROFILE
Sanjeev Joshi
I am passionate about sketching, as I believe that only when one puts pen to paper does the real observation start. Sketches can be only done on the spot, as the atmosphere, the smells, the sounds, the sunlight, and the whole experience become a part of your memory. When I see my sketch, even after a year, or so, I remember everything that is associated with the experience of that particular sketch.

On tours or outside travels, I don't photograph much but sketch a lot. I do direct watercolor sketches, carrying just two shades of paint and a small palette, and ink pen sketches. I love sharing my sketches online once they are done, but I primarily sketch for my own satisfaction and happiness. If someone else also likes them, then it's an additional bonus for me.

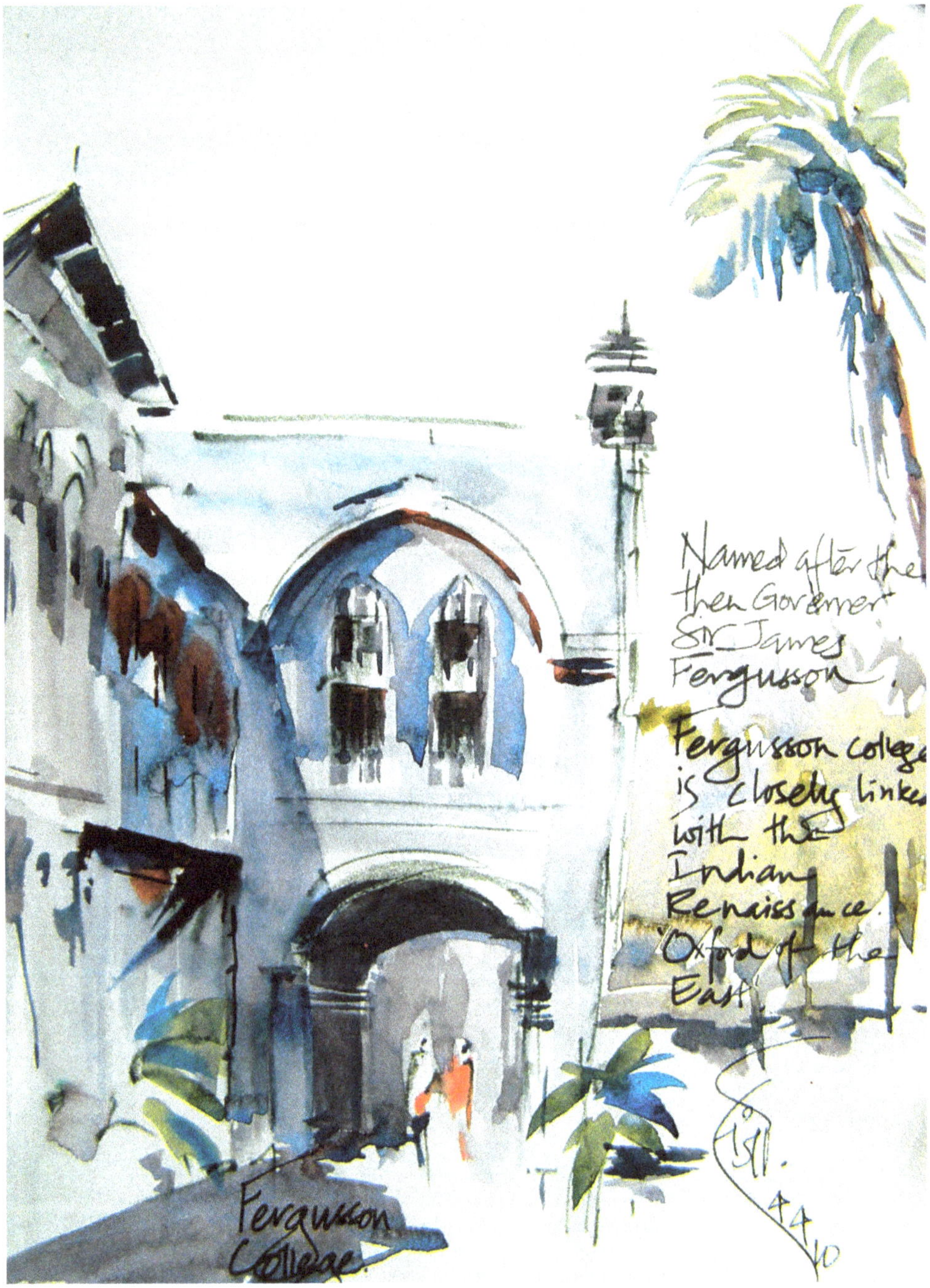

"I am trying to include calligraphy in my sketches as a way of writing the information and by just using my signature to compose the sketch on paper."

Named after the then Governor Sir James Fergusson

Fergusson college is closely linked with the Indian Renaissance. 'Oxford of the East'

Fergusson College.

⌒ Centenarian Institution Fergusson College's neo-Gothic architecture makes it a good sketching location in Pune. The school is more than 125 years old.

Tip "I don't try to show details of the colonial buildings—they are too intricate, but I try to give that feel by putting lines over the watercolor washes with my ink pen. This is an effective and fast way of sketching." — *Sanjeev Joshi*

8" x 11" | 20 x 28 cm; watercolor and ink pen; 15 minutes

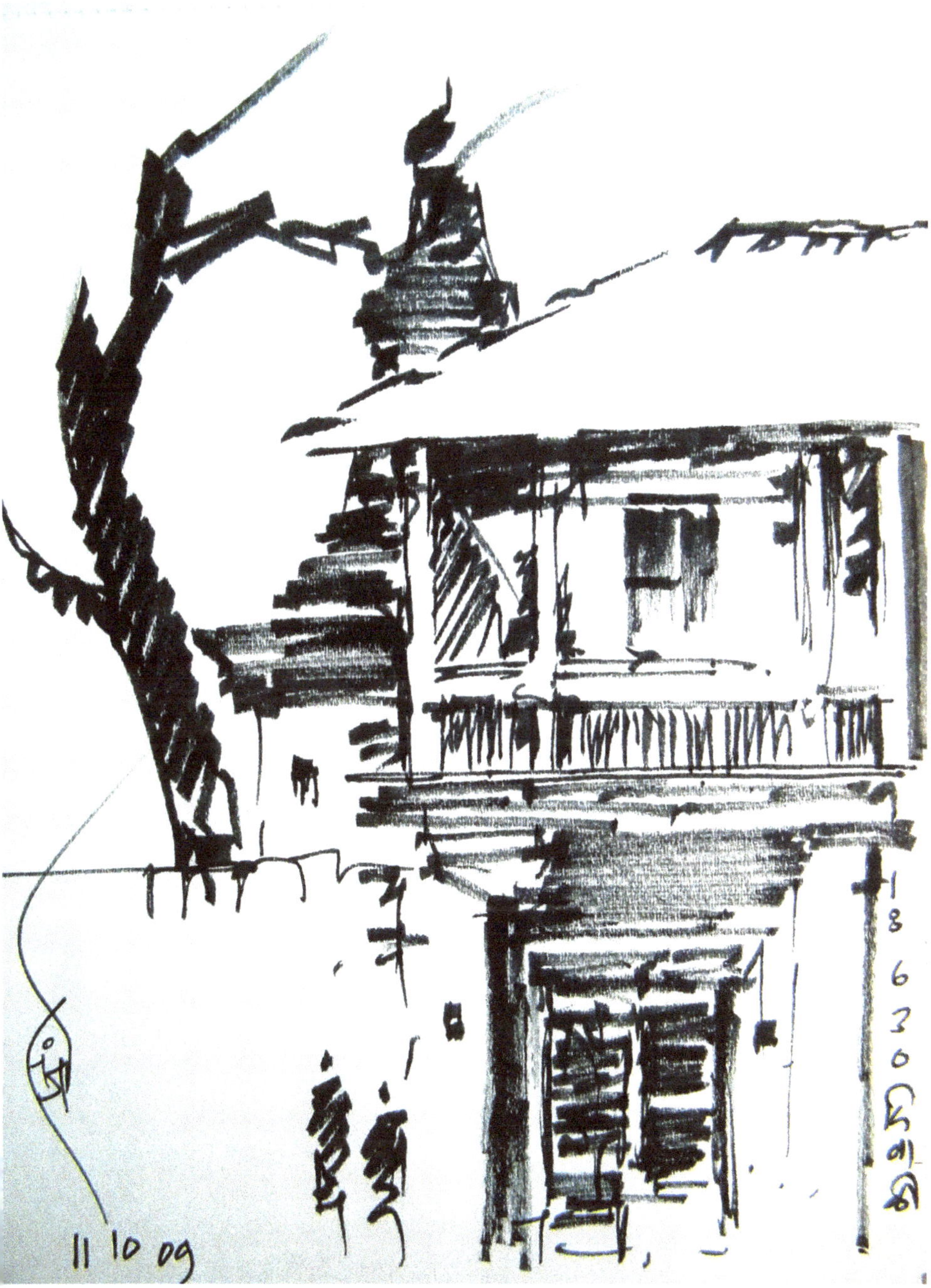

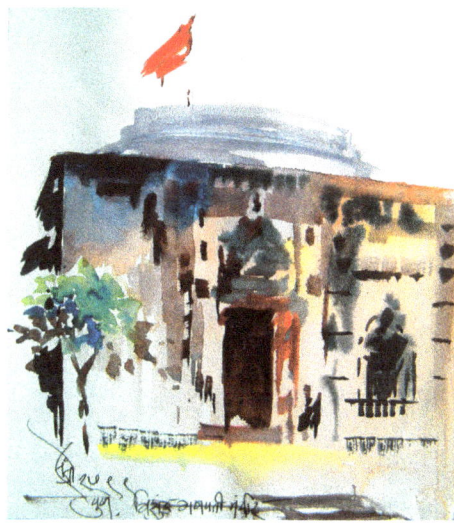

ⴒ **Trishund Ganapati Temple** The carved-stone features of this temple, which dates back to 1754, make it a difficult sketch subject, says Joshi.

Tip "Do it quick—if it takes more time, it becomes painting and not a sketch." — *Sanjeev Joshi*

8" x 8" | 20 x 20 cm; watercolor on 130-gsm artist paper sketchpad; about 10 minutes

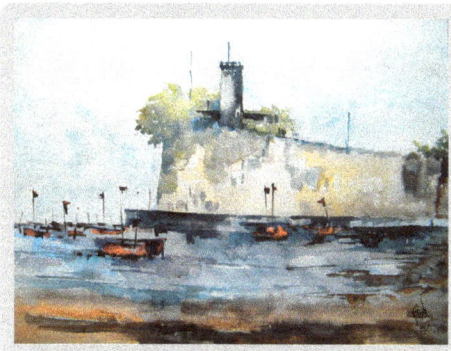

TRAVEL JOURNAL

Sketching Trip to Fishing Village

by Sanjeev Joshi

The Indian Ocean coastline is about five hours' drive from where I live in Pune. I visit it once or twice a year. Last year, I visited a fishing village called Harne, which is a harbor for small fishing trollers. It was fun sketching boats for two days, as I rarely get the opportunity to sketch a seaside scene. This sketch shows the lighthouse and fishing boats.

14" x 10" | 35.6 x 25 cm; watercolor on handmade paper sketchpad; 20 minutes

ⴒ **Gupchup Ganapati Temple** This temple dates back to the seventeenth century. It is dedicated to Lord Ganesha, a Hindu deity.

Tip "The calligraphic chiseled pen is my favorite tool when I draw black-and-white sketches. It's easy to fill masses and also to draw thin lines." — *Sanjeev Joshi*

8" x 11" | 20 x 28 cm; black chiseled marker on sketchpad; 5 minutes

BANGKOK

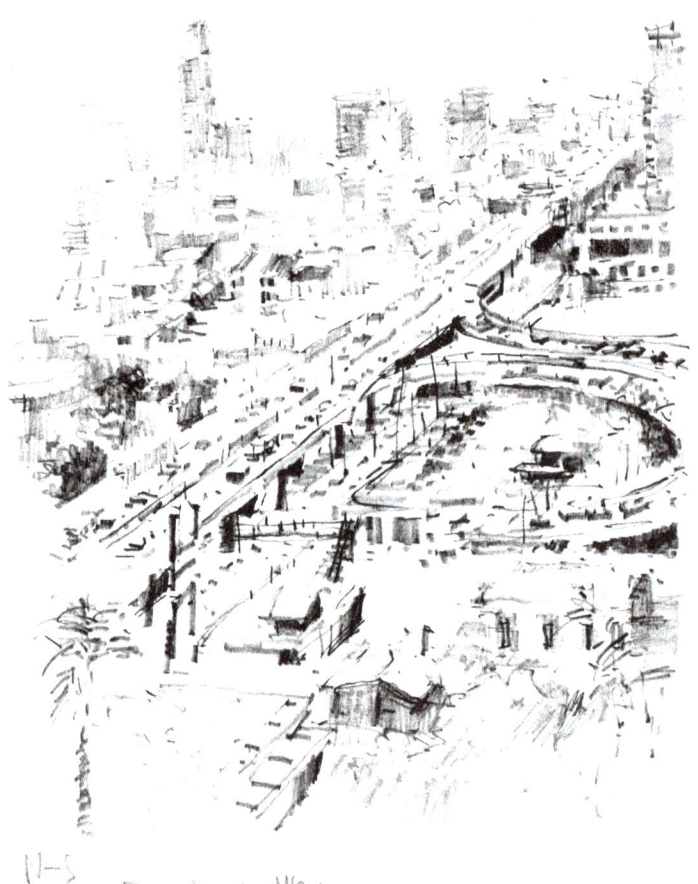

Local artist Asnee Tasna describes Bangkok as a chaotic city—but that makes it more fun to sketch, he says. Behind the wheel of his car or on drawing excursions to its vibrant downtown, Tasna uses a broad range of media to capture suggestive impressions of the Thai capital.

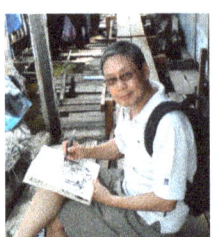

ARTIST PROFILE
Asnee Tasnaruangrong

After living in Singapore for almost thirty years, my wife and I moved back to Bangkok, where I was born, while my son went to study in Western Australia. We started traveling around our homeland, Thailand, and that's how sketching became part of my everyday life. I do lots of drawing and sketching as an architect, but it's totally different from what we call sketching on location. I also reunited with my old love of watercolors.

Sketching helps me discover another side of life. I find happiness in doing something that's devoid of monetary value but gives me meaning no money can buy: walking in unfamiliar places, observing crowds, and talking with total strangers who care to take a break and want to looking at what I am drawing.

♠ Rama VI Road and Skyline A view of one of the many expressways criss-crossing Bangkok, looking south from the Tipco Building along Rama VI Road. The Baiyok Tower II, an eighty-five-floor hotel that is the tallest building in Thailand, can be seen at the top left.

Tip "I stack layers of broad lines to create the building height, a line for each floor. Try to line up rows of short strokes for building windows, short slants on a distant street for the shadows of cars, blocks of dark areas with vertical white gaps for a building's columns in the sun. Just draw a suggestion of the negative space, and you get the positive element, or even the whole building, for free." — *Asnee Tasna*

5.5" x 7.5" | 14 x 19 cm; Derwent Graphic 2B pencil on hardcover sketchbook with 100-gsm blank pages; about 45 minutes

"I lack the patience for details or the desire for realistic accuracy."

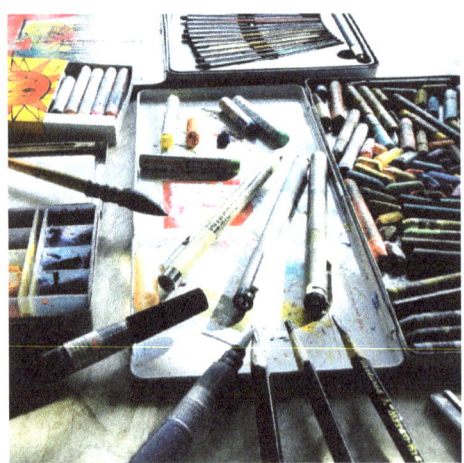

♠ Tasna's sketching tools

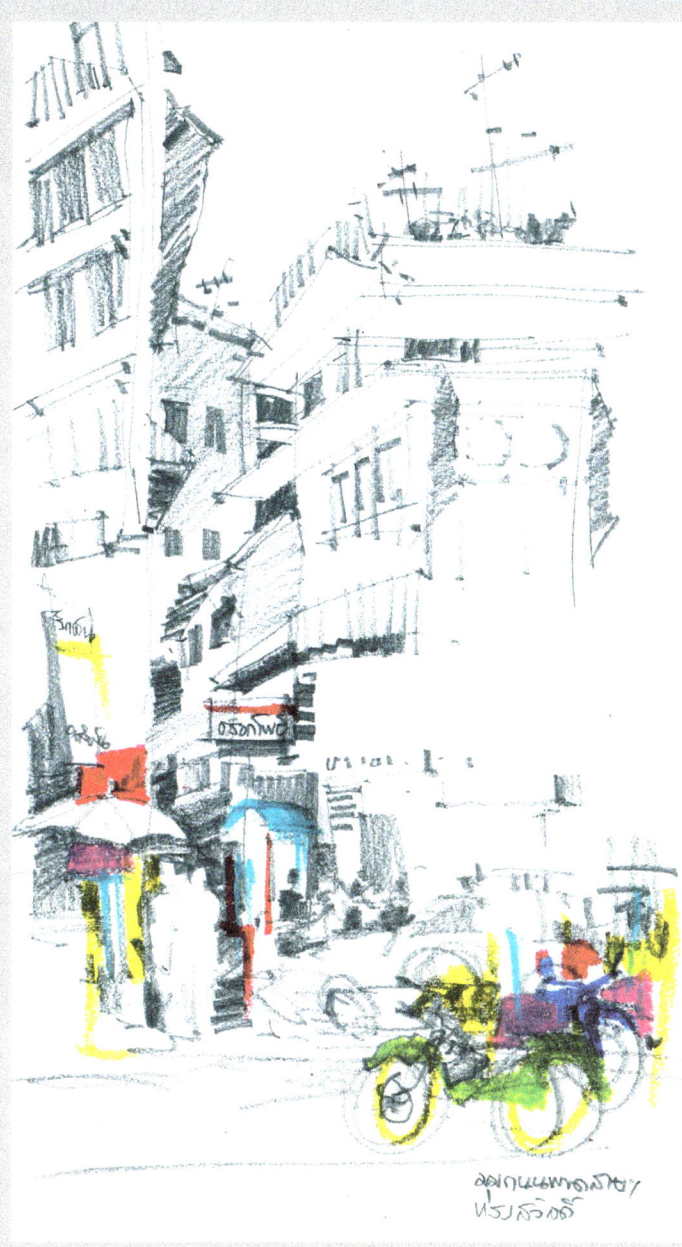

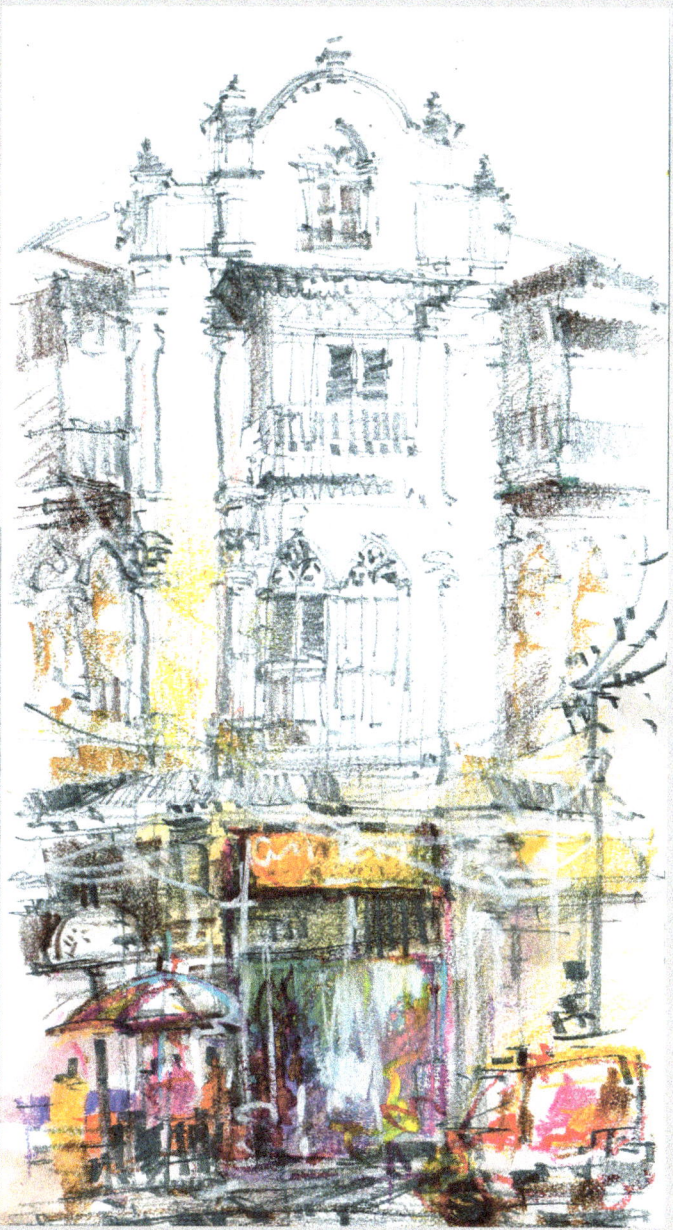

STYLE AND TECHNIQUE

Bangkok's Chinatown

For these drawings, Tasna used a broad-tip pencil on paper. He chose a tall format to express the narrow passages of the streets and also experimented with partial coloring.

🎧 **Trok Poh Road** "The broad-tip pencil offered the most effective result for such architectural elements, and it did not take long at all to translate them onto paper, despite the sketch's reasonably large size. The omission of the nonessentials in a sketch is what excites me most. Since the narrowness of the alley was what I was after, I took down only what I really needed, nothing more." — *Asnee Tasna*

7" x 14.5" | 18 x 37 cm; 4B Derwent Graphic pencil, Caran d'Ache Museum water-soluble wax pastels on 190-gsm, fine generic drawing paper; about 30 minutes for pencil work, 10 minutes for color added later

🎧 **The Songwad Road** "The same broad-tip pencil was used in this sketch to create suggestive lines, shadows, and details to portray the charm and delicate features of this Western-style building. However, the nonessentials omitted in the Trok Poh Road sketch were replaced here with the suggestion of a certain feature or detail. The presence of just a few of them suggests that they are all there.

Notice how I simplified some of the floral motif, railing, roof tiles and window panes? It would take days to draw all of them, not half an hour!" — *Asnee Tasna*

7" x 14.5" | 18 x 37 cm; 4B Derwent Graphic pencil, Caran d'Ache Museum watercolor leads, 190-gsm, fine generic drawing paper; about 30 minutes for pencil work; and 30 minutes at home for color

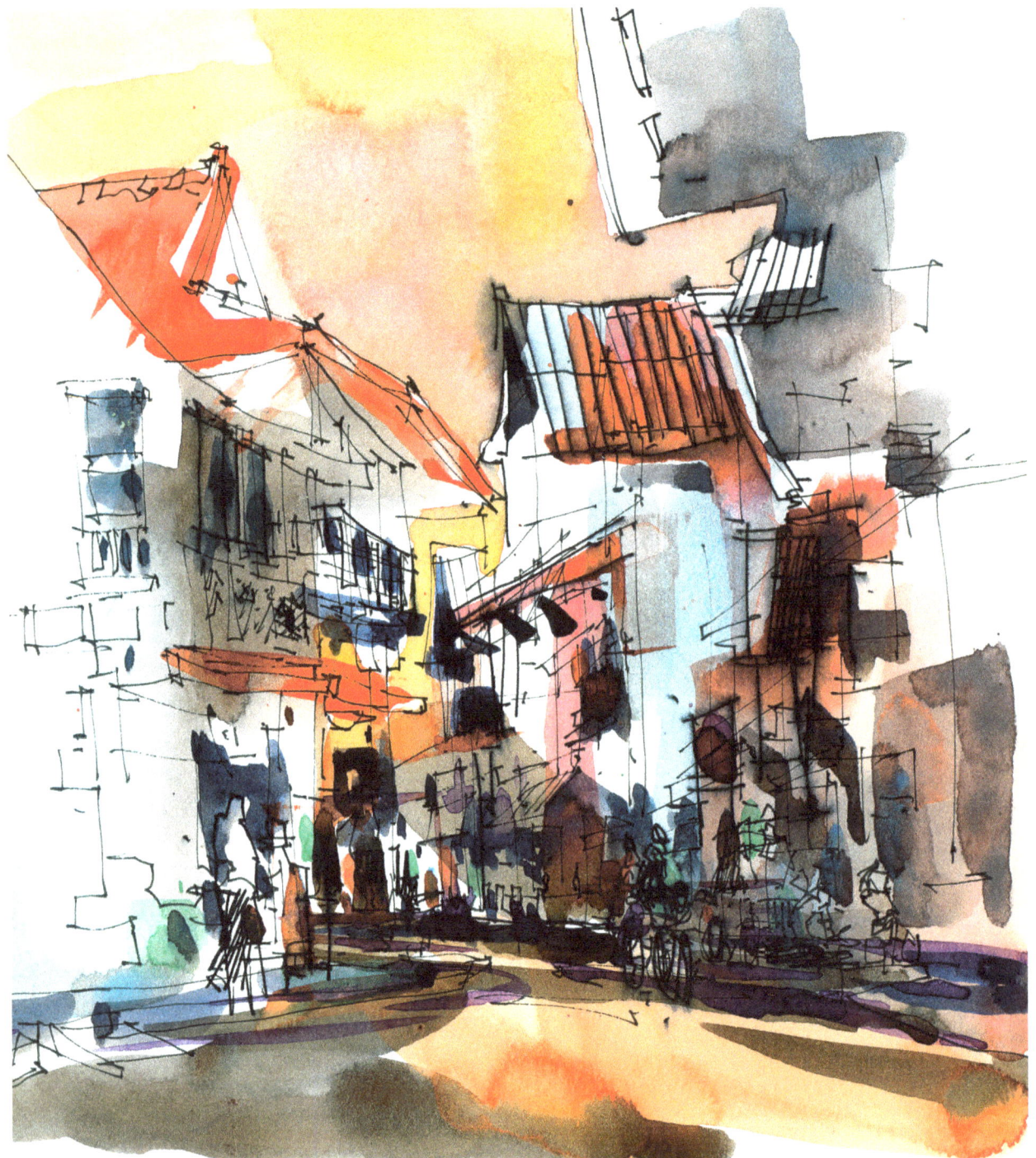

☊ **Street of Hua Hin** Hua Hin is a small seaside resort town some 124 miles (200 km) south of Bangkok. Hua Hin's popularity can be traced back to early 1900, with the building of several summer palaces for the royal family, including the first resort golf course, built in 1924.

Tip "This is basically a line-work sketch. Those strong colors do make the drawing colorful, but it's the unpainted areas that give the sketch a needed punch." — *Asnee Tasna*

7" x 7" | 18 x 18 cm; Micron 02 Micro waterproof pigment ink pen, Royal Talens 24-pan watercolors, # 2 pointed Pébéo squirrel mop brush on custom-made, fine-surface 200-gsm sketchbook; 45 minutes

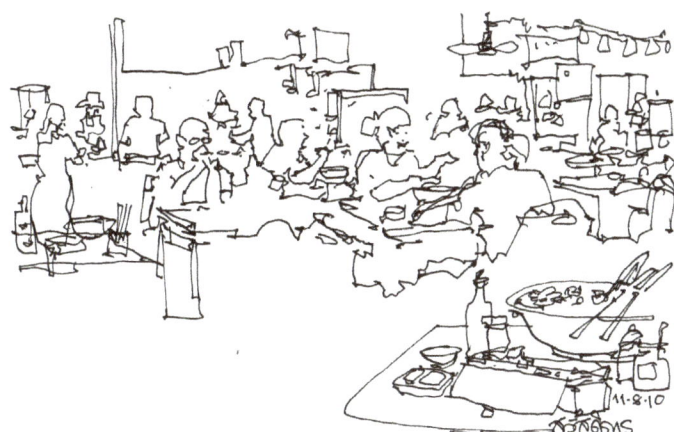

Ω **Egg Noodle Stall** A sign above this popular food stall in a local market loudly proclaims, "The Most Delicious Egg Noodle." For years, the crowd in front of the stall has proved its claim. "Not only does it taste good, at 25 baht a bowl, it is one of the cheapest in town," Tasna says.

Tip "Sketching the noodle stall was great fun as a figure study on human posture. I could never have imagined before how animated eating persons can be, particularly when they are in a group!" — *Asnee Tasna*

4" x 6" | 10 x 15 cm; Micron 03 Micro waterproof pigment ink pen, Daler-Rowney sketchbook; about 30 minutes

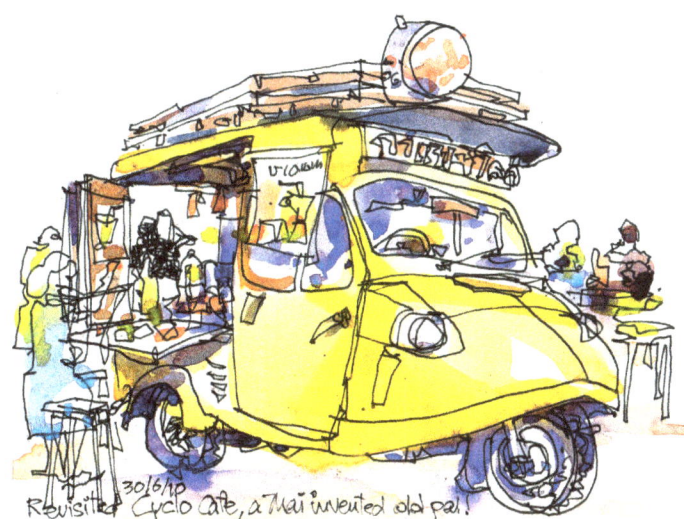

Ω **Tuk Tuk** A motorized three-wheeled taxi in Bangkok, fondly referred to as a Tuk-Tuk, is one of the easiest ways to get acquainted with the city. This restored model serves coffee with Thai-style toast and butter and sugar, says Tasna.

8.25" x 6.25" | 21 x 16 cm; Micron 02 Micro waterproof pigment ink pen on a page from a plain, smooth, common soft-cover school exercise book; 30 minutes

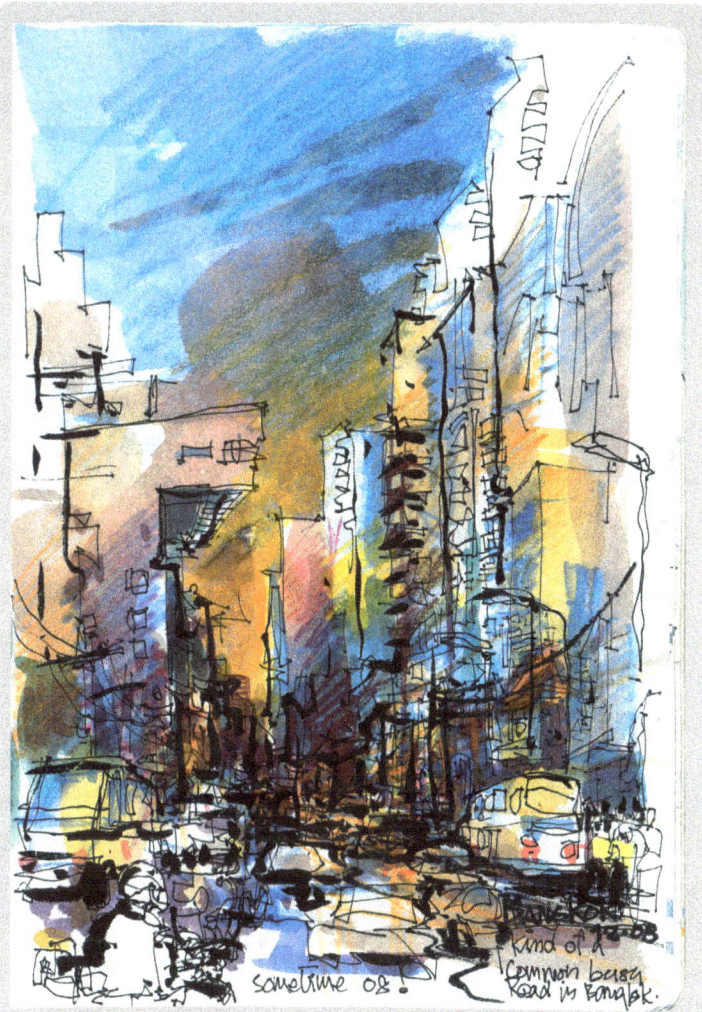

FIRST PERSON

Stuck in Traffic and Late for Holiday Dinner

by Asnee Tasna

Traffic in the city was at its usual maddening peak, and I was already late for an early Christmas dinner. The two-way traffic was virtually at a standstill, giving me time for leisurely sketching of the middle of the road from the high vantage point of my seven-seat Kia.

I had many stops to readjust my bearing. Fortunately, each stop brought me to a new spot not far from the last, so I had no problem capturing and adjusting my sketch to accommodate the new corners of a building that was hidden from view a moment ago.

The sketch was done in the traffic, and, of course, I did the watercolor wash at home, some time later. You don't expect me to give a color wash in the car while driving, do you?

8.25" x 5.75" | 21 x 14.6 cm; Mitsubishi uni PIN fine line pigment ink pen, Pentel Color Brush (black), Van Gogh watercolor travel box set, Caran d'Ache Museum water-soluble color leads on A5 Monologue Soft sketchbook; 15–20 minutes for overall line work; another 20 minutes for color at home

PENANG

From magnificent mosques to houses built on stilts over the water, sketching opportunities abound on the small Malaysian island state of Penang. The island's historic capital of George Town was designated a World Heritage site by UNESCO in 2008 for its unique architectural and cultural townscape, without parallel in Southeast Asia.

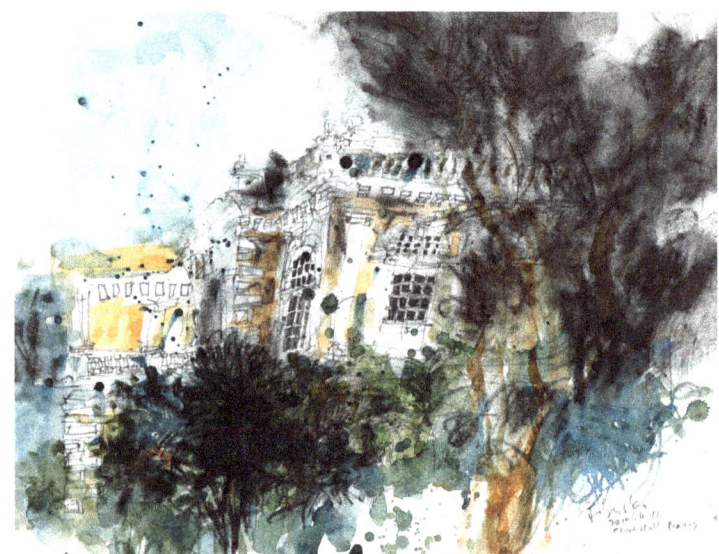

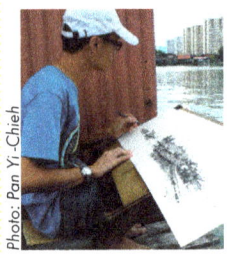

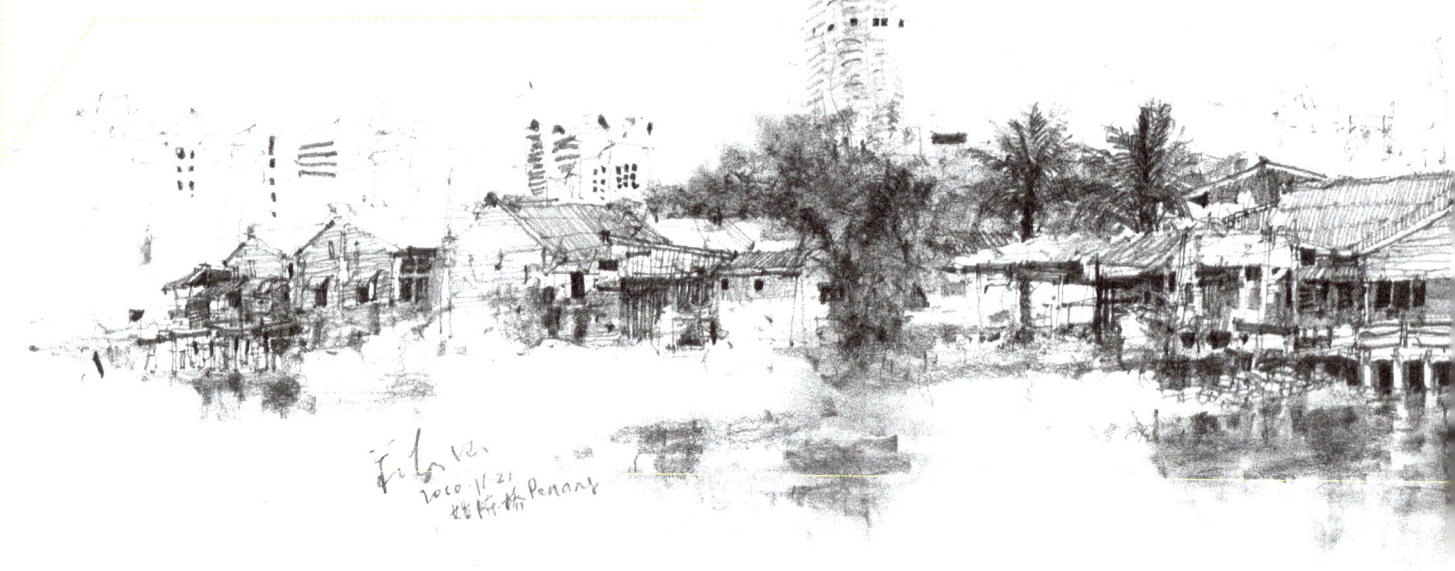

ARTIST PROFILE
Ch'ng Kiah Kiean

I was trained as an architect but currently work as a graphic designer in Penang, where I was born. Most of my jobs are related to the art, culture, and heritage of Penang. Through urban sketching, I have a better understanding of my hometown and feel the sense of space here. I started doing urbanscape sketching in school. At first, my sketches were for recording ideas and as a visual diary for myself. Later, I found that my sketches could be a complete artwork. After trying different formats, I found that the long landscape format best fits the subject of the shop houses and streets of George Town. I love to sketch the details of architecture on the streets, like windows and signage.

⌒ Kiah Kiean sketches row houses perched on stilts in Tan Clan Jetty, a unique settlement linked by planked walkways over the water.

11" x 30" | 28 x 76 cm; 9B and 6B graphite and 4B pencil on paper; about 3.5 hours

Photo: Pan Yi-Chieh

⌒ **A Corner of Town Hall** The back of Penang Town Hall connects to a little park with a water fountain. Ch'ng Kiah Kiean did this sketch at about 12:30 p.m. on a very hot day. Despite the big trees, he says he could feel the tropical heat of George Town.

Tip "I did the quick sketch with some details of the Town Hall building and did the rest with watercolor wash. The bigger tree on the right was done with graphite smudge, followed by some watercolor wash." — *Ch'ng Kiah Kiean*

11" x 15" | 28 x 38 cm; graphite and pencil, Winsor and Newton watercolors on cartridge paper; about 1 hour

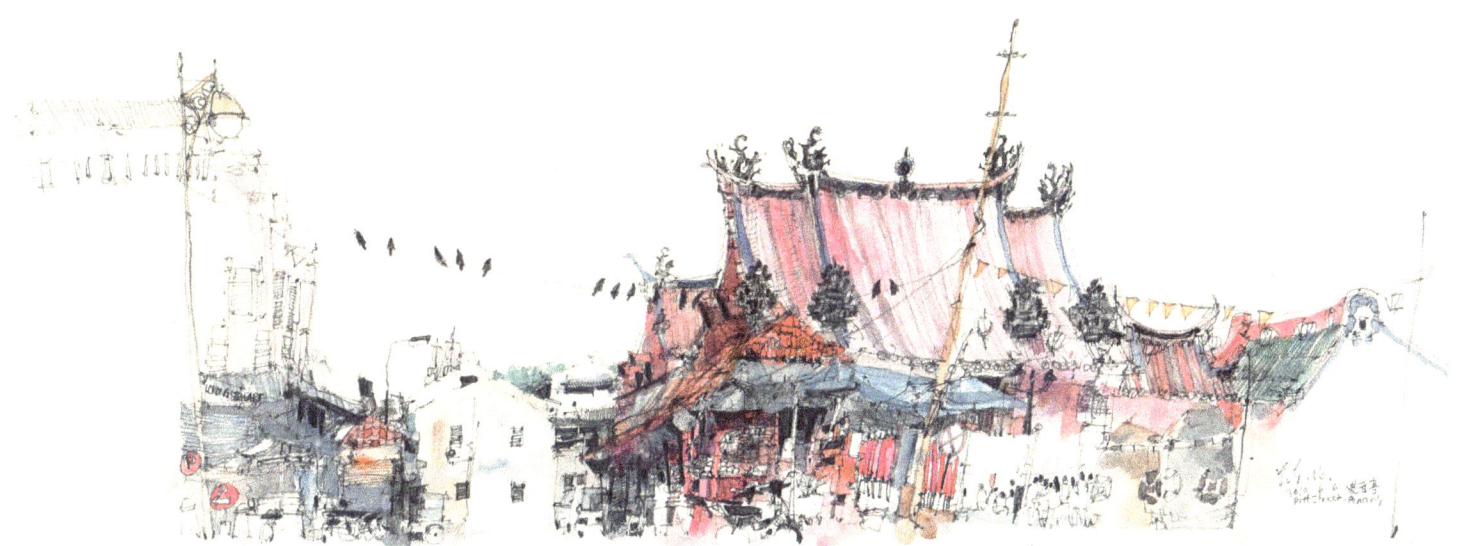

"Art makes life beautiful; this is my belief and practice."

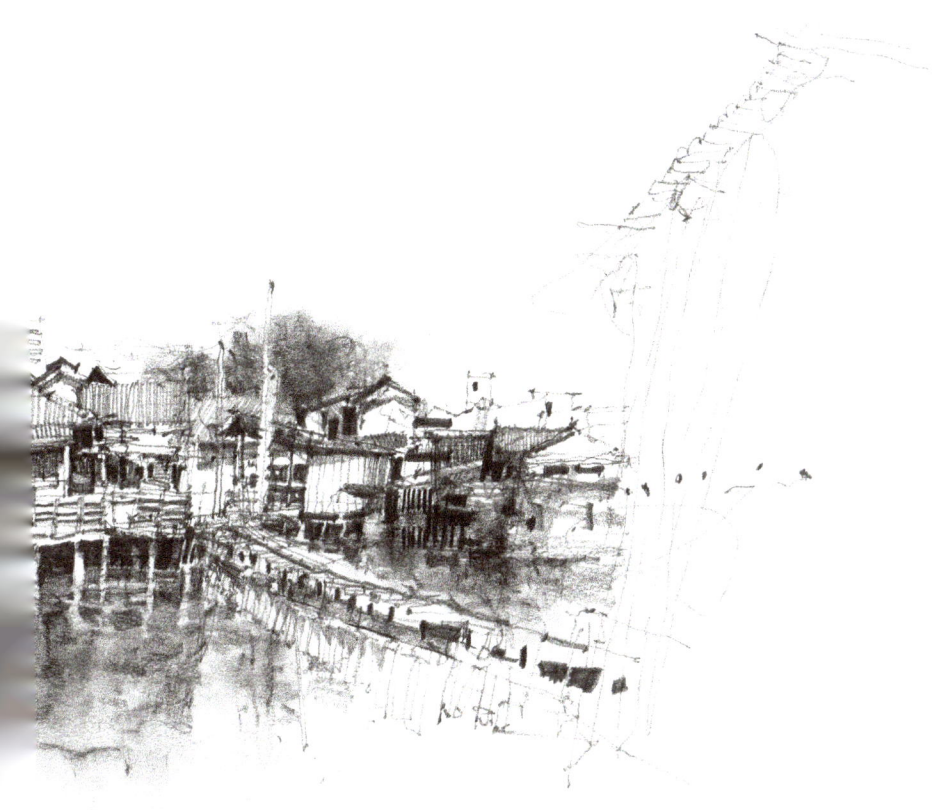

◖ Goddess of Mercy Temple This is one of the oldest Chinese temples in Penang. Ch'ng Kiah Kiean says it is always crowded with tourists and local devotees. In front of the temple are stalls selling joss sticks, flowers, and fruits for prayer purposes.

Tip "I first did the sketch in only black and white graphite lines then later decided to add the reddish tone to the temple building, as it is the favored color scheme for the local Chinese in George Town." — *Ch'ng Kiah Kiean*

11" x 30" | 28 x 76 cm; graphite and pencil, Winsor & Newton watercolors on cartridge paper; about 2.5 hours

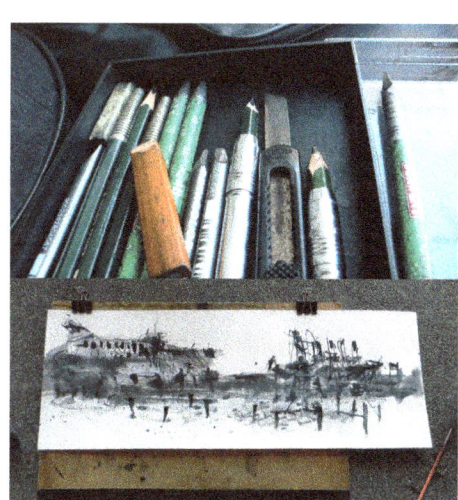

◖ Ch'ng Kiah Kiean's sketching tools

SINGAPORE

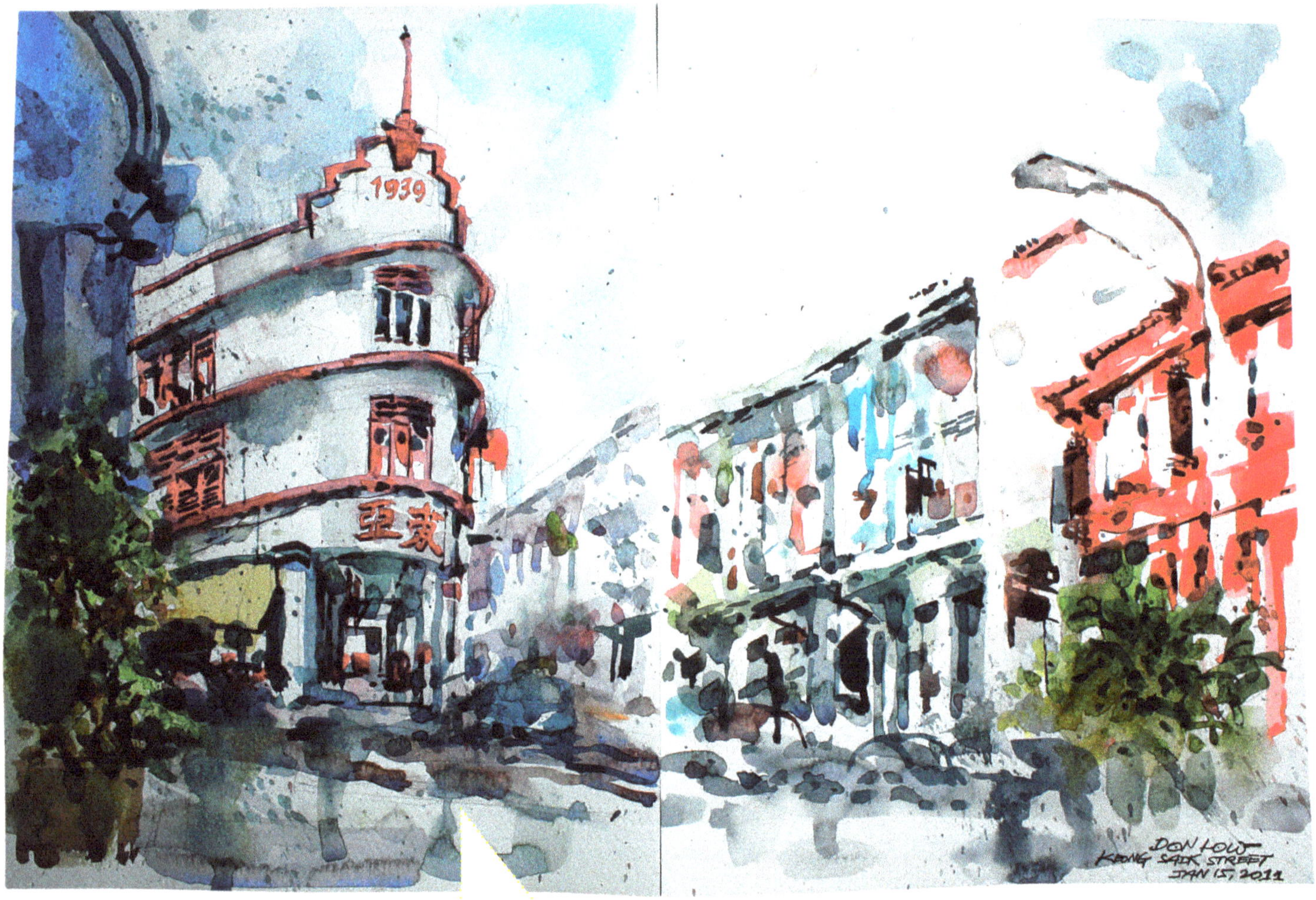

Drawing outdoors in the tropical city–state island of Singapore can be a hot and humid experience, but local sketchers find plenty of subject matter in preserved colonial buildings, traditional shop houses, and food merchants. Illustrator Don Low says everything is manmade or new in the country. "Even the trees are planted in an orderly manner."

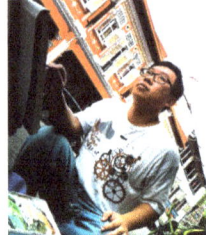

🎧 Don Low sketches at Keong Saik Street, a 1940s-era street that has been "refurbished" with modern pubs, cafés, and offices.

18" x 12" | 45.5 x 30.5 cm (diptych); 2B pencil and Winsor & Newton watercolors; 1.5 hours

ARTIST PROFILE
Don Low

I used to think sketching was a personal and lonely process, but now I enjoy very much going out sketching with like-minded people, who aren't too embarrassed to draw in public and don't mind people looking over their shoulders.

I am always on the lookout for things that represent Singapore, especially buildings from when it was still under British colonial rule, like prewar shop houses and historic Chinese temples. I try not to include too many details in my sketches. I am beginning to sketch more loosely and not be too bogged down by details.

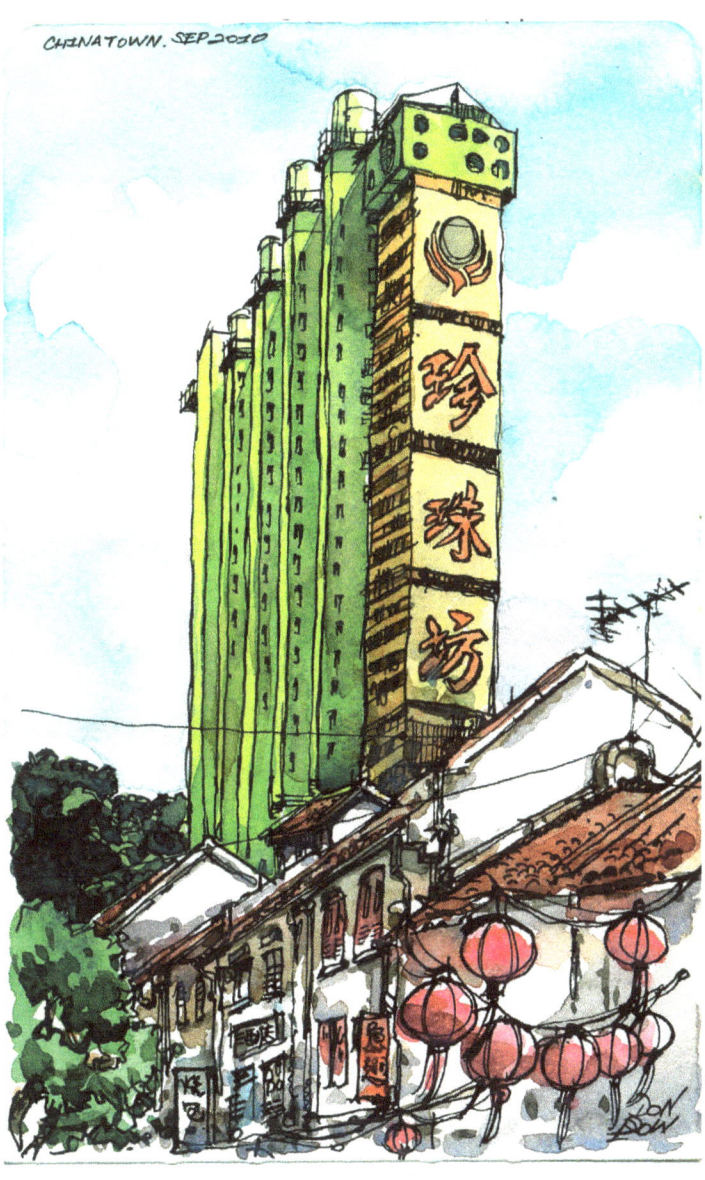

CHINATOWN. SEP 2010

"Urban sketching is like getting to know someone I haven't met before."

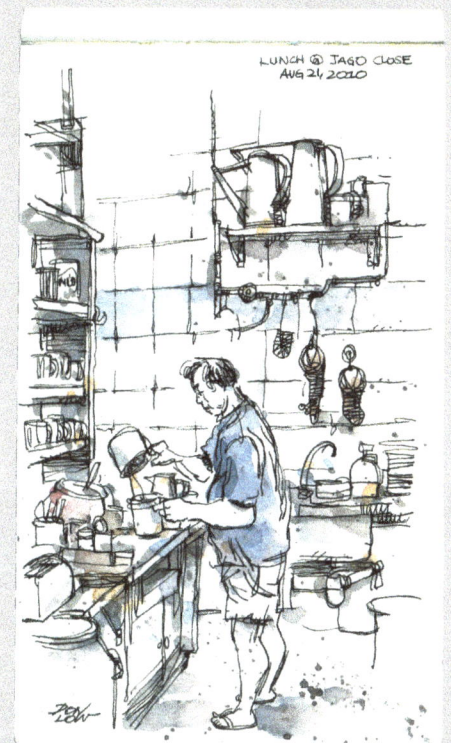

LUNCH @ JAGO CLOSE
AUG 21, 2010

♩ **People's Park Complex** This towering residential and commercial building from the 1970s left a deep impression on Don Low when he was a child. "Through the years, it has undergone very little change, except that, once in a while, it would receive a new coat of paint," Low says.

Tip "I keep my lines as straight as possible when sketching urban buildings like this, to describe more effectively its scale, height, and proportion." — *Don Low*

A5 (8.3" x 5.8" | 21 x 14.8 cm); Hero fountain pen with Noodler's black ink, Winsor & Newton watercolors, on Moleskine watercolor book; 40–60 minutes

FIRST PERSON

Open-Air Coffee Shop

by Don Low

I wanted to capture the gesture and essence of how Nanyang coffee is made in the traditional way. The worker fills up a pot with coffee powder and then pours in boiling hot water to mix and dissolve the coffee. The speed at which the water is poured and its temperature determines the fragrance and taste of the finished coffee. The mixture is then filtered using a socklike fishnet device that can be seen in the sketch. When the worker realized that I sketched him, he came over to pat my shoulder and gave me a very broad and satisfied smile.

A5 (8.3" x 5.8" | 21 x 14.8 cm); Lamy fountain pen with Noodler's ink, Winsor & Newton watercolor wash, Moleskine watercolor book; 30 minutes

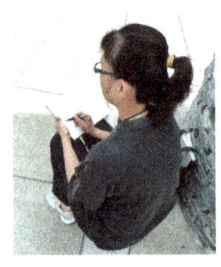

ARTIST PROFILE
Tia Boon Sim

I am an architect by training but chose to be an art and design educator. Sketching became more of a daily activity for me years ago, when I combed through Club Street, drawing rows of shop houses on Saturday mornings, while I waited for my son's art lessons to end.

Today, armed with my favorite Hero M86 fountain pen, pocket color gear, and a small stool, I continue to comb the streets with a group of sketchers. We sketch, walk, rest, eat, and drink—a great way to foster friendship while actively promoting location drawing in Singapore. What's important is not how well you sketch but having the passion, enthusiasm, and courage to respond to your immediate environment by expressing that emotion on a piece of paper.

" I am always intrigued by the shape of shadows and how quickly they move and change on a building façade."

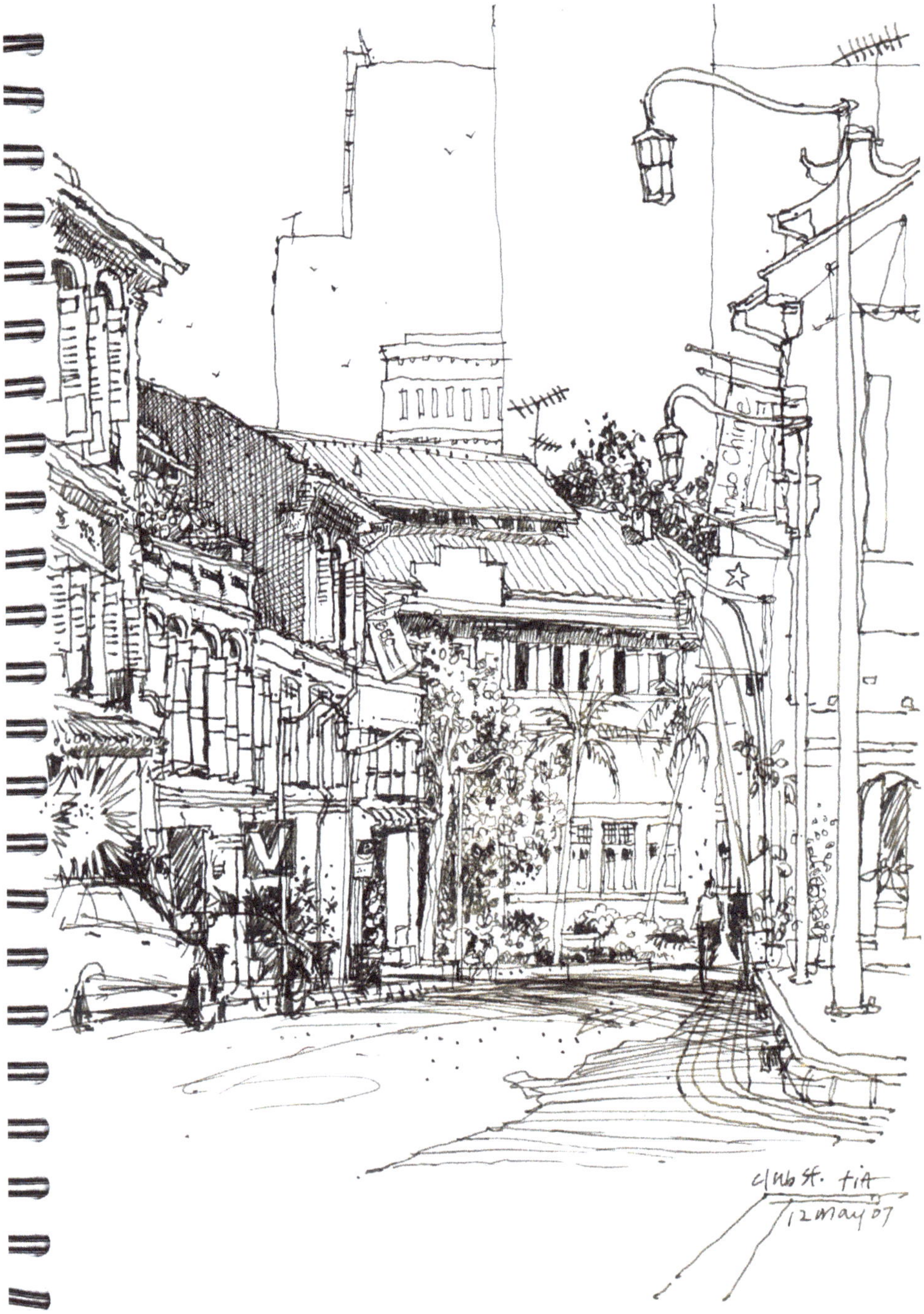

⋒ Uniquely Club Street Singapore's famed Club Street is a popular place for pubs, cafés, restaurants, spas, furniture stores, offices, and boutiques. Because the street is a stone's throw from Chinatown, the street lamps and public signage have an oriental theme.

Tip "Composition is the key for this piece. The layering effect was achieved by using different tones and textures. Vertical, horizontal, and diagonal lines create a visually interesting sketch." — *Tia Boon Sim*

A4 (8.3" x 11.7" | 21 x 29.7 cm); Lamy Safari fountain pen with Parker Quink ink, hardbound ring-binder sketchbook; 1 hour

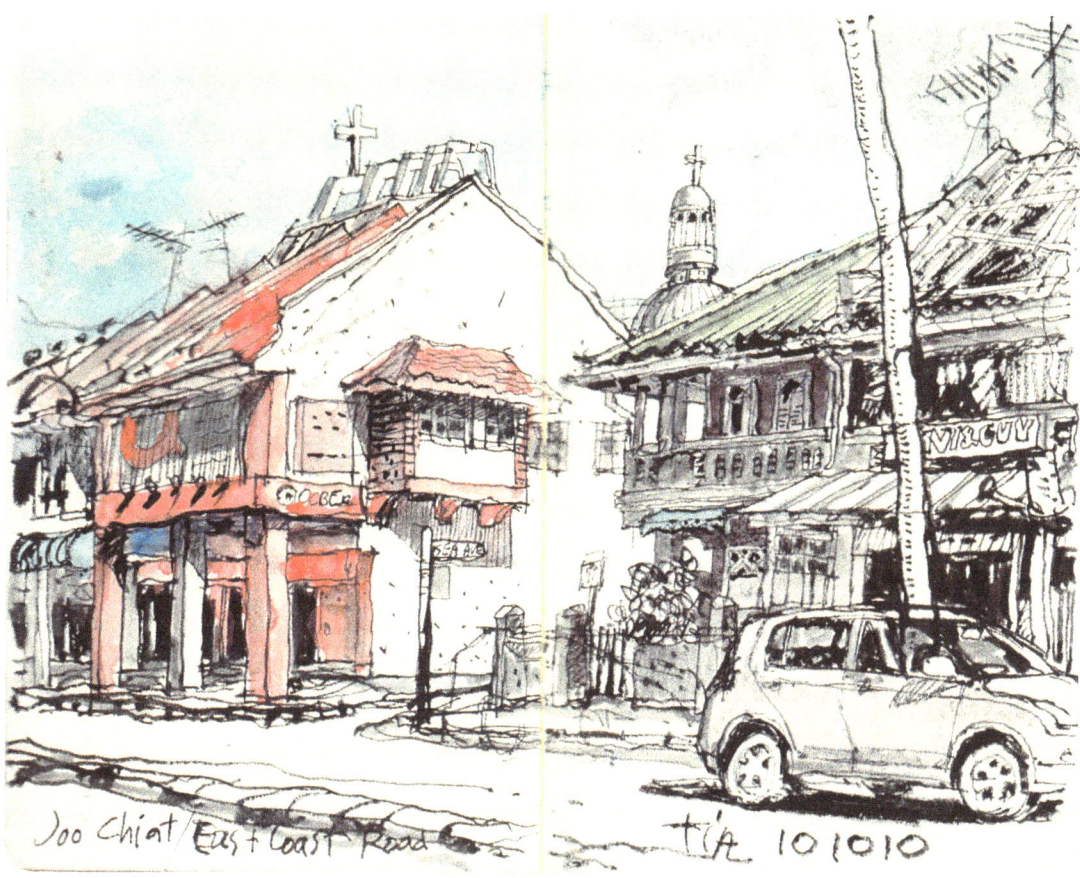

🎧 **Hot Outside** From the comfort of an air-conditioned car, Boon Sim sketched an attractive row of shop houses, with the Church of the Holy Family in the distance.

Tip "I had an imaginary grid in my mind and fixed the side window roughly in the middle of the page. With the understanding of a two-point perspective, I was able to pull all the vertical, horizontal, and oblique lines together very quickly." — *Tia Boon Sim*

3.5" x 5.5" | 9 x 14 cm; Hero M86 fountain pen with black Noodler's ink, Daler-Rowney Aquafine watercolor pocket set, and Holbein waterbrush on Moleskine pocket sketchbook; 45 minutes

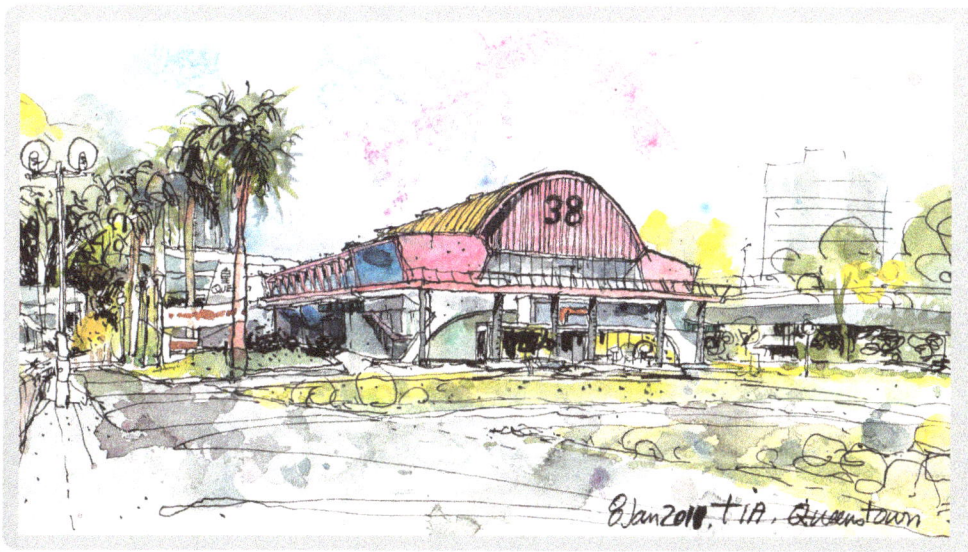

FIRST PERSON

My Childhood Wet Market

by Tia Boon Sim

I have lots of memories of this building, which used to be a wet market—an open food market, where live animals are sold. My mother brought me here almost every day in the 1960s, when our home was just a block away. At that time, ducks and chickens were slaughtered here, and their feathers were dried in the open space outside the market. The complex and a few blocks of old public flats will be demolished to make way for new housing flats. However, block 38, with its parabolic roof, will be preserved.

16" x 8" | 40.6 x 20 cm; Hero M86 fountain pen, Holbein waterbrush, salt, and Daler-Rowney Aquafine watercolor pocket set on Daler-Rowney Aquafine 300-gsm, cold-press watercolor paper; 1 hour

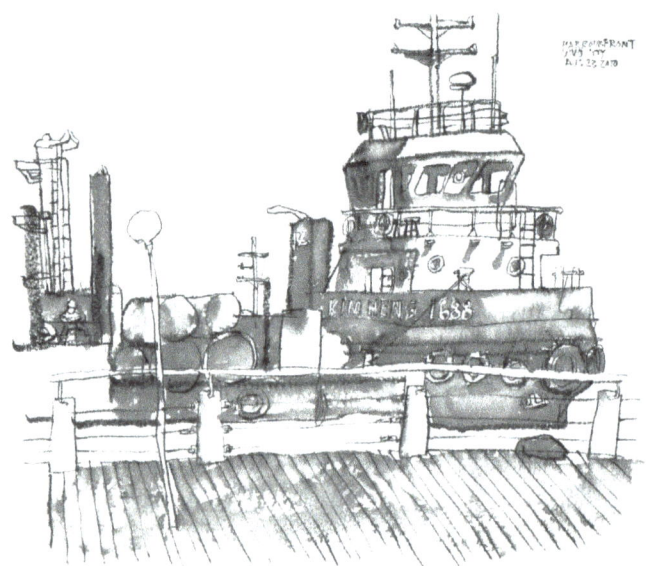

⋂ Tugboat at Sentosa Miel, a Singapore newspaper cartoonist, drew a tugboat under the hot, noontime sun. "Everything was 'solarized,' in the sense that the lines around objects, buildings, and people and the shadows they cast melted into the light." — *Miel*

10" x 8.25" | 25 cm x 21 cm; water-soluble ink, brush, and waterbrush on loose sketching paper; 10–15 minutes

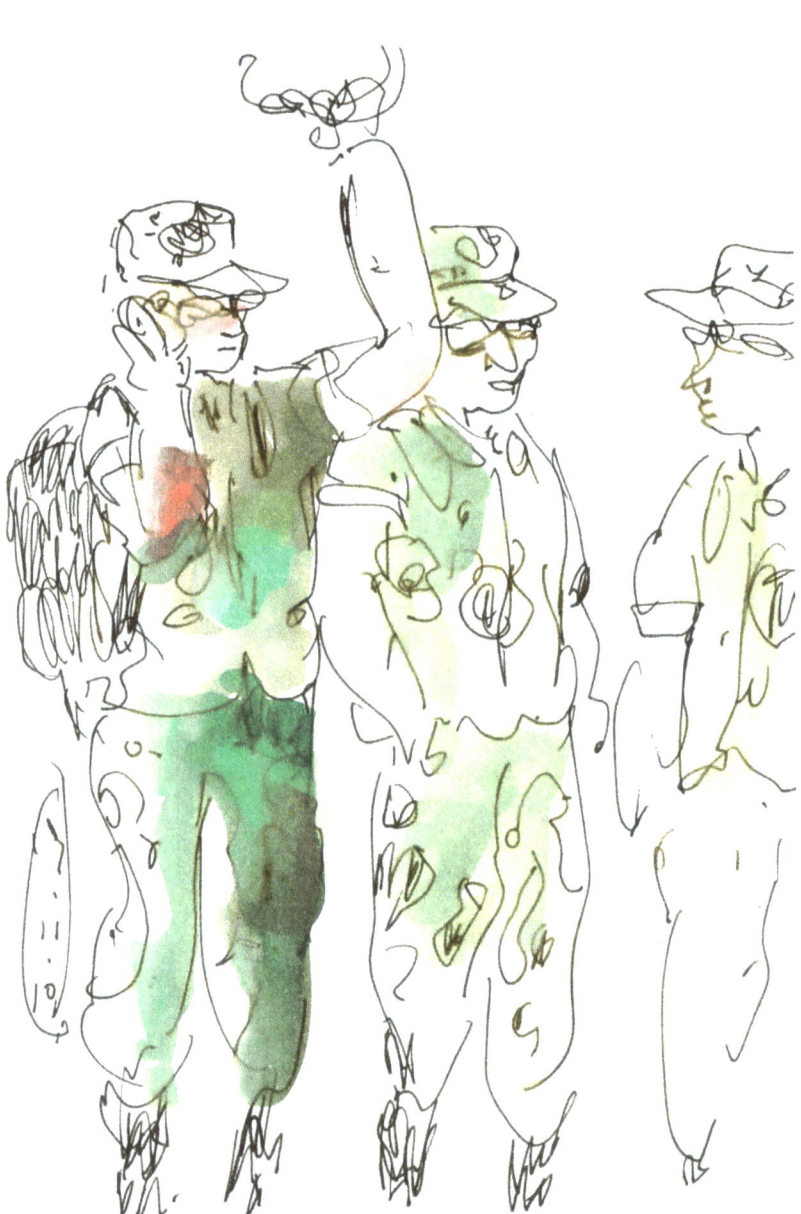

☾ Army Boys James Tan was on the train when three army members boarded. Tan says two years of army service is mandatory in Singapore, and these men, with their fresh crew cuts and tanned skin, seemed newly enlisted.

Tip "I was unsure of when they'd get off the train, so I tried to quickly capture the bare essentials, bearing in mind that, sometimes, 'less is more.'" — *James Tan (a.k.a. Seiji)*

5.5" x 6.75" | 14 x 17 cm; pen and watercolor on cartridge paper; 10–15 minutes

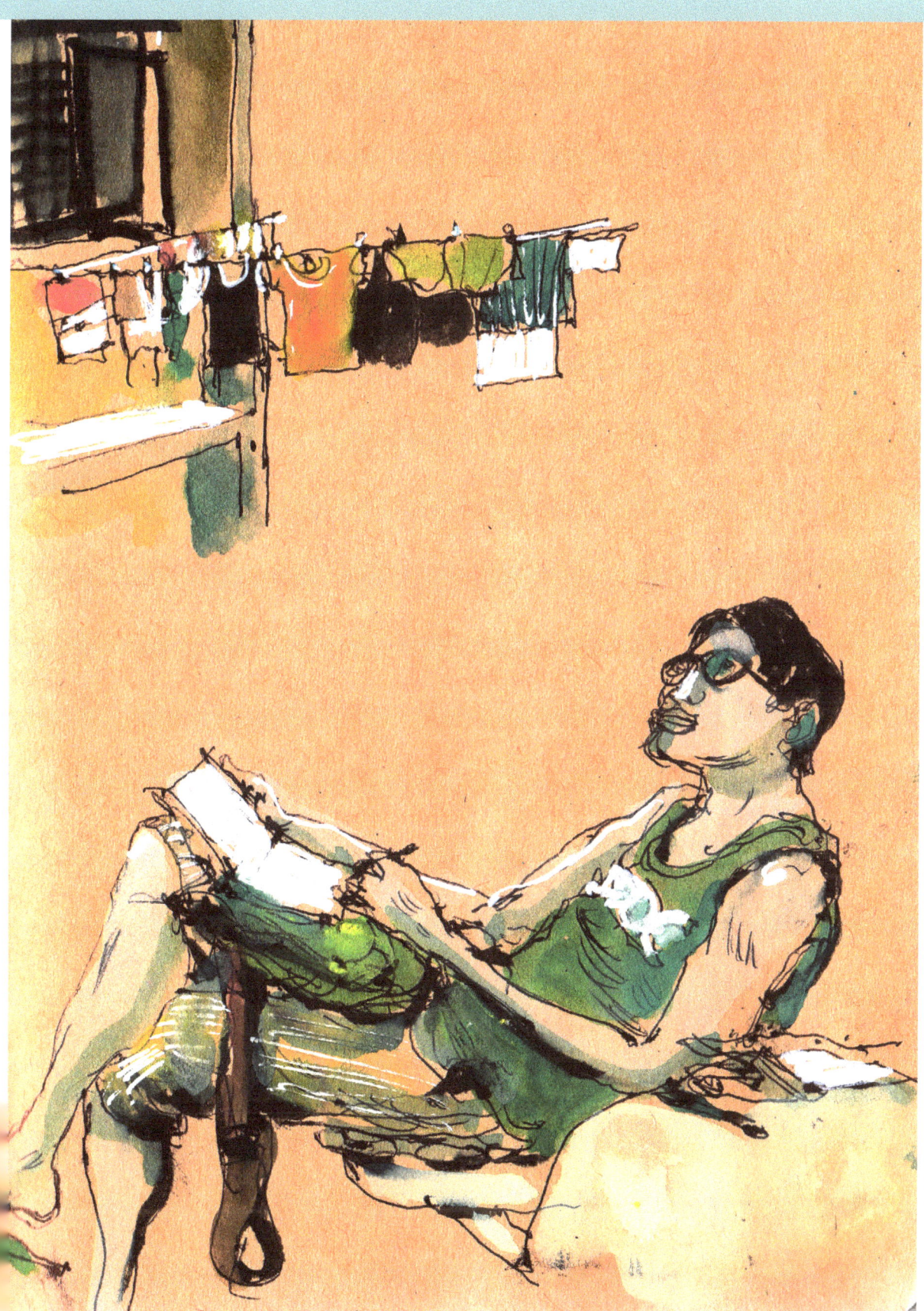

◖ **Sketcher Friend**
Andrew Tan says he likes drawing organic forms during sketchwalks, such as his friend James sketching at an old housing development along Bukit Ho Swee.

Tip "To draw faster, I draw smaller. I use a fine ballpoint so my lines still remain thin. I draw in loose, fast lines to capture things that don't stay still for long, like people. My brown paper provides a nice texture and also an instant midtone to my drawings. For highlights, I simply have to dab some quick white correction fluid as a finishing touch and it's done." —*Andrew Tan*

4.25" x 6" | 11 x 15 cm; ballpoint pen and gouache on brown-paper sketchbook; 5 minutes

JAKARTA

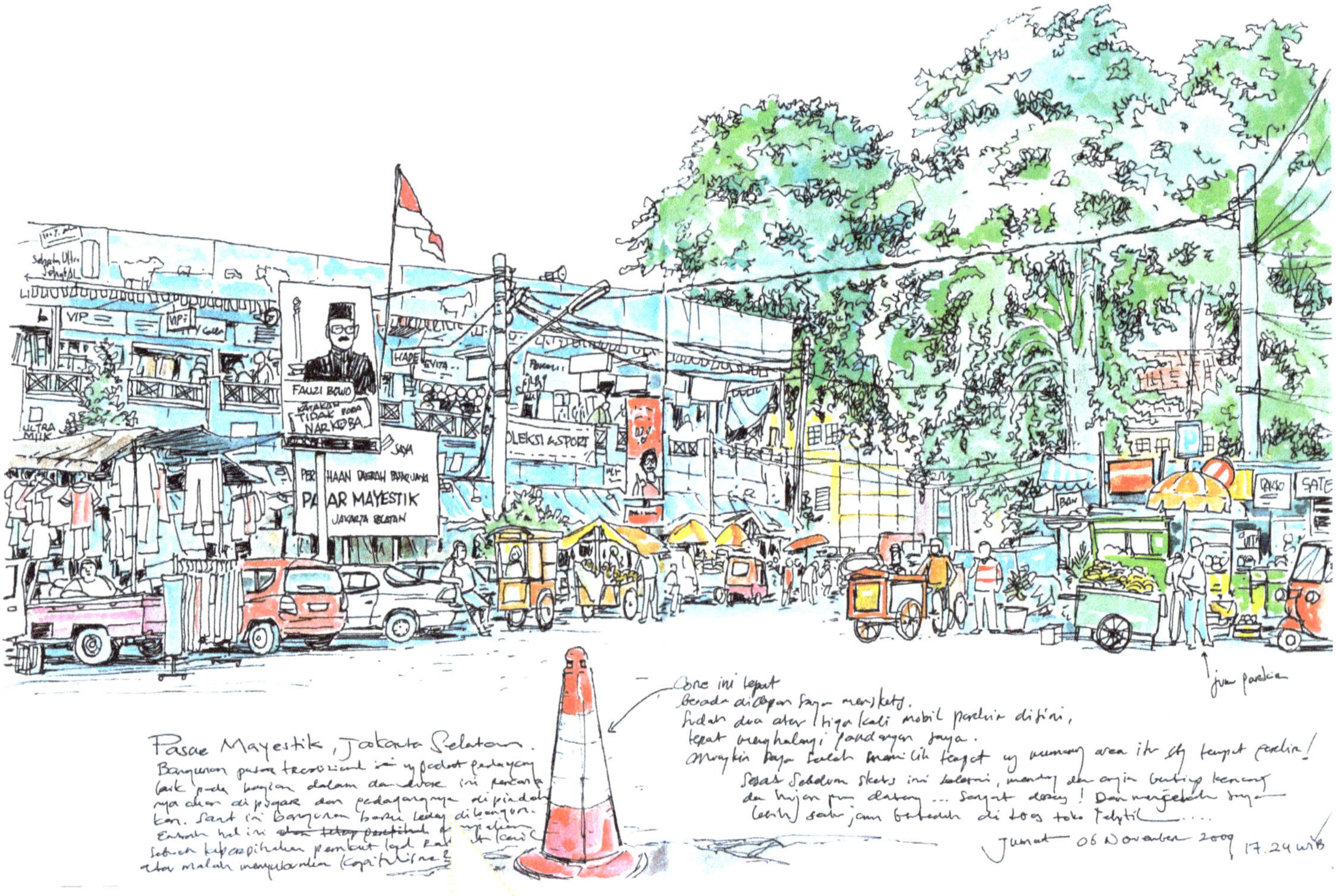

The sketch shows *Pasar Mayestik, Jakarta Selatan* with handwritten Indonesian notes around it and the date *Jumat 06 November 2009 17.24 wib*.

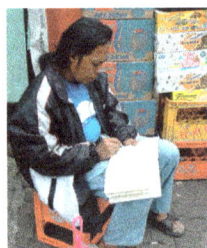

The Indonesian capital of Jakarta is home to almost ten million people, which makes it the 10th-largest city in the world. Its thriving urban sketching community is led by local illustrator and designer Dhar Cedhar. He especially likes to capture colorful crowded markets as well as the people and stories behind all the activity.

"I always try to have conversations with the people I'm sketching and throw in some humor."

Dhar Cedhar sketching at the Mayestik Market in South Jakarta, Indonesia.

ARTIST PROFILE
Dhar Cedhar

In the beginning, I made sketches only as an exercise and to document various objects that served as important visual references. For an illustrator, visual reference is important in supporting the quality of pictures to be made. Recently, sketching has turned from simple visual reference into an art expression as well as a medium of socialization between me and my surroundings.

There are thousands of complex problems on all sides of life in metropolitan Jakarta. Urban society in crowded areas, river banks and railway lines, traditional market merchants, walking merchants, and a community of middle- to high-class people at luxurious cafés and malls are all interesting sketching subjects.

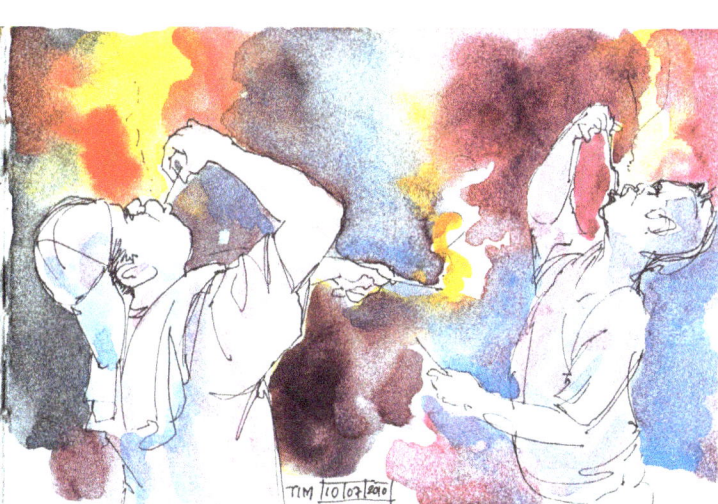

𝕆 Street Artist Cedhar says this beautiful traditional Indonesian art is starting to lose its place in society. The itinerant group members are usually family, and they live off donations from bystanders. They usually perform at bus intersections in the evening, so that people can see the fire better.

Tip "I made small thumbnails sketches first, observing carefully their signature poses, and finally decided on the best composition to capture. Take enough time to make various poses, so that you can switch from pose to pose as the acts progress." — *Dhar Cedhar*

11.75" x 3.75" | 30 x 9.5 cm; Kenko Hi TECH H .28 gel pen (black), Cotman watercolors, Sakura Koi waterbrush, on custom-made sketchbook with 200-gsm Canson watercolor paper; ink sketch 3–5 minutes, coloring 5 minutes per page

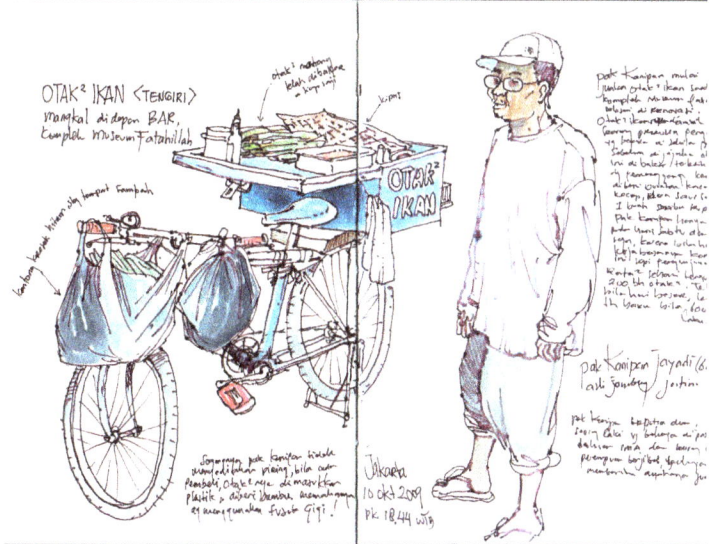

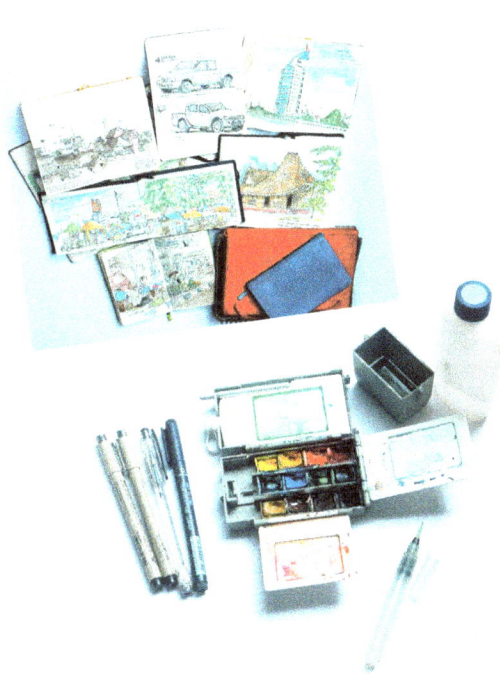

𝕆 Fishcake Street Merchant Cedhar ordered a dish from this street merchant and decided to sketch and have a little chat with him.

Tip "I started with the bicycle, from front to back. Sanipan was added last, as we became familiar with each other and created a mutual trust through conversation. Always create a nice warm atmosphere with your subject so he or she will relax." — *Dhar Cedhar*

11.5" x 8.25" | 29 x 21 cm; Staedtler Triplus fineliner (brown), Winsor & Newton Cotman watercolors on Monologue A5 sketchbook; about 5 minutes

𝕆 Cedhar's sketching tools and sketchbooks

SEMARANG

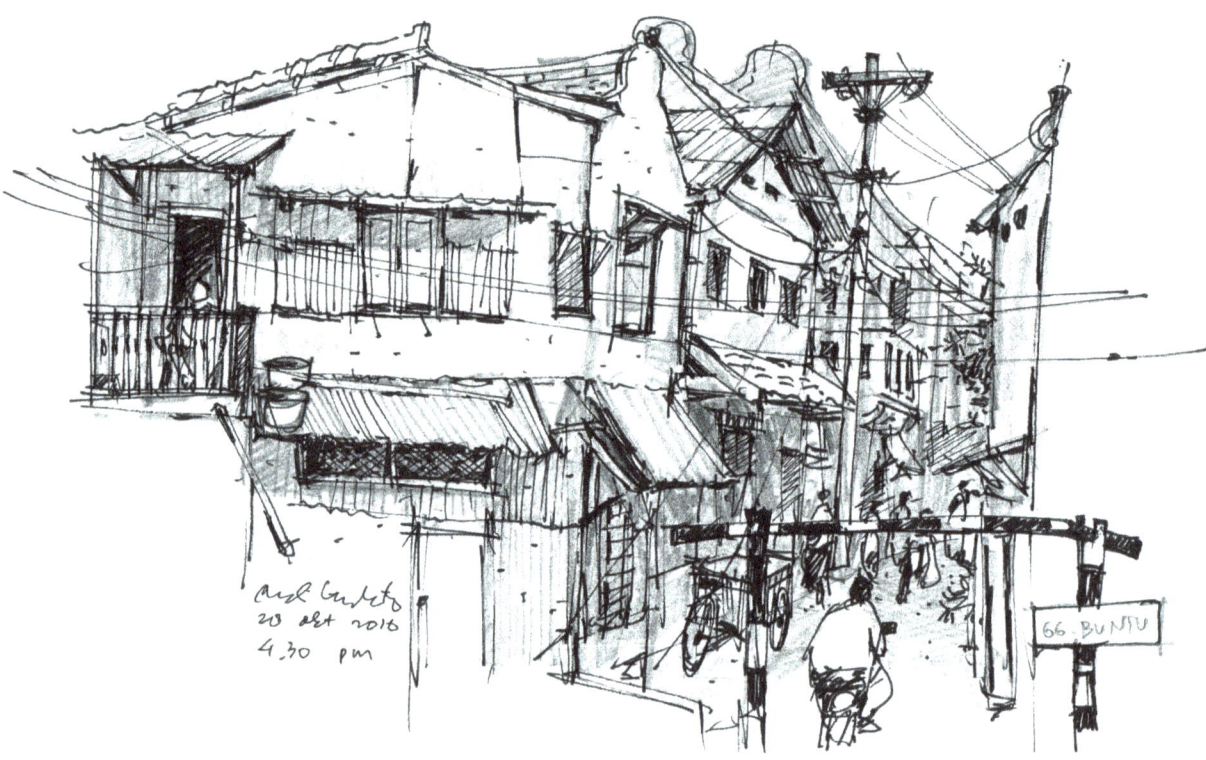

Tropical Semarang is located on the northern coast of the island of Java, Indonesia. Local architect Rudi Hartanto enjoys drawing old buildings, many of which have a Dutch and Chinese influence, and the activity surrounding them. Hartanto also brings his sketchbook along when on spiritual retreats in Sumatra, to capture the village life.

⋒ **The Chinese Houses in Semarang** Although Hartanto originally intended to sketch a Chinese temple across the canal, his eye caught this spot, and he found it attractive. "I like the Chinese roof architecture, which is slowly being removed in the name of modernization," he says.

Tip "First, I sketched the proportions and perspective lines using pencil, then I worked on the detail with a drawing pen and finalized the shadow with a pencil again." — *Rudi Hartanto*

A4 (8.3" x 11.7" | 21 x 29.7 cm); 0.8 and 0.3 Snowman drawing pens, Faber-Castell 2B pencil, on Canson 110-gsm Student Visual Diary; about 30 minutes

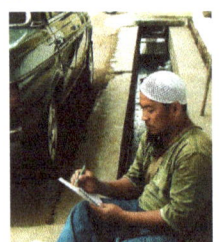

ARTIST PROFILE
Rudi Hartanto

The phrase "urban sketcher" sounded good from the first time I found it. In fact, I have been urban sketching on and off for some years; I just never realized that I was an urban sketcher.

As an architect, I feel that freehand drawing has been and still is an effective way to build good communication with clients. It is quick, expressive, and lively information. Sometimes, I sketch a quick design idea for a client, and it mostly works well. Everybody needs everything quick. They do not only like fast food but also fast design, fast drawing, and fast sketching.

"Market crowds, smells, and conversation are a beautiful drama, in my eyes."

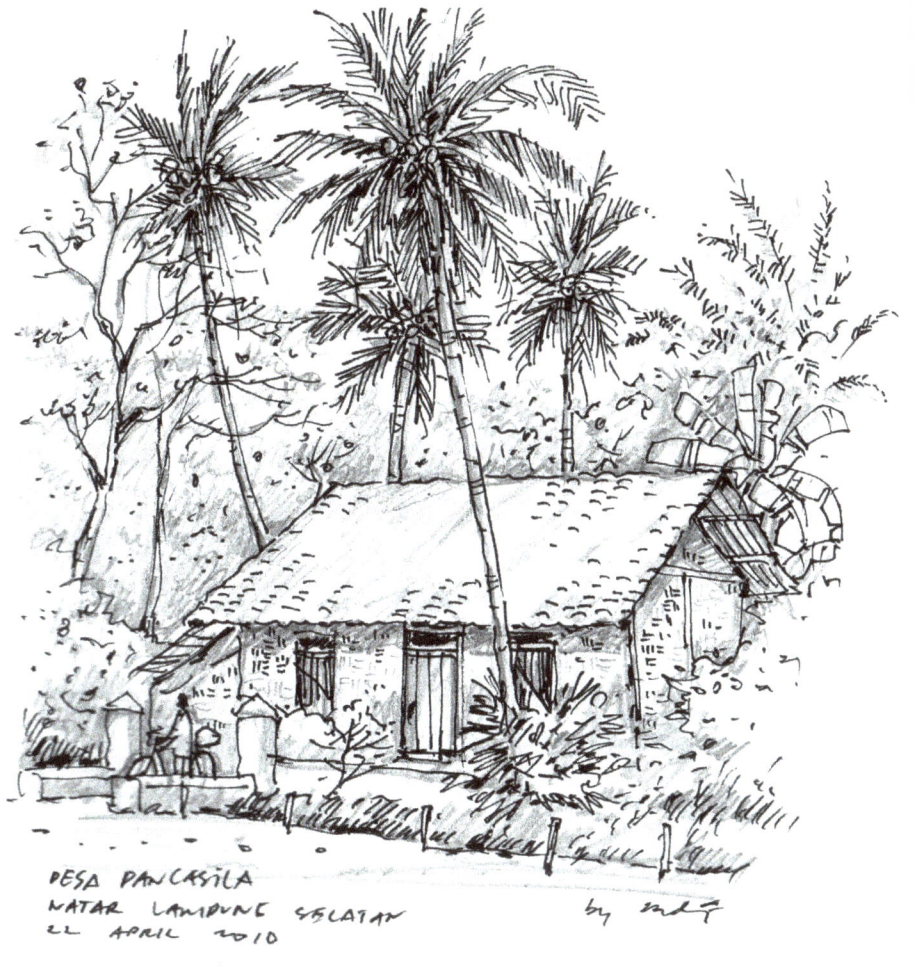

DESA PANCASILA
NATAR LAMPUNE SELATAN
22 APRIL 2010

by mdg

☾ 40 Days Spiritual Retreat in Sumatra
By looking at simple village houses, Hartanto says, we learn that simplicity is one of the roots of happiness. The walls are made of bamboo, the roof is handmade terra-cotta tile, and the floor is mud. "It really brings me back to a natural life."

Tip "After observing the object, I first draw perspectives and outline forms, using pencil, for about five minutes. Then I start detailing with a drawing pen for about fifteen minutes. The last ten minutes are for adding the shadow with pencil and rendering trees. What brings this drawing alive are the different kinds of trees, so I really put attention on the shapes of the leaves." — *Rudi Hartanto*

7.25" x 7.25" | 18.5 x 18.5 cm; Snowman 0.5 drawing pen, Faber-Castell 2B pencil on Canson 120-gsm Carnet de Croquis sketchbook; about 30 minutes

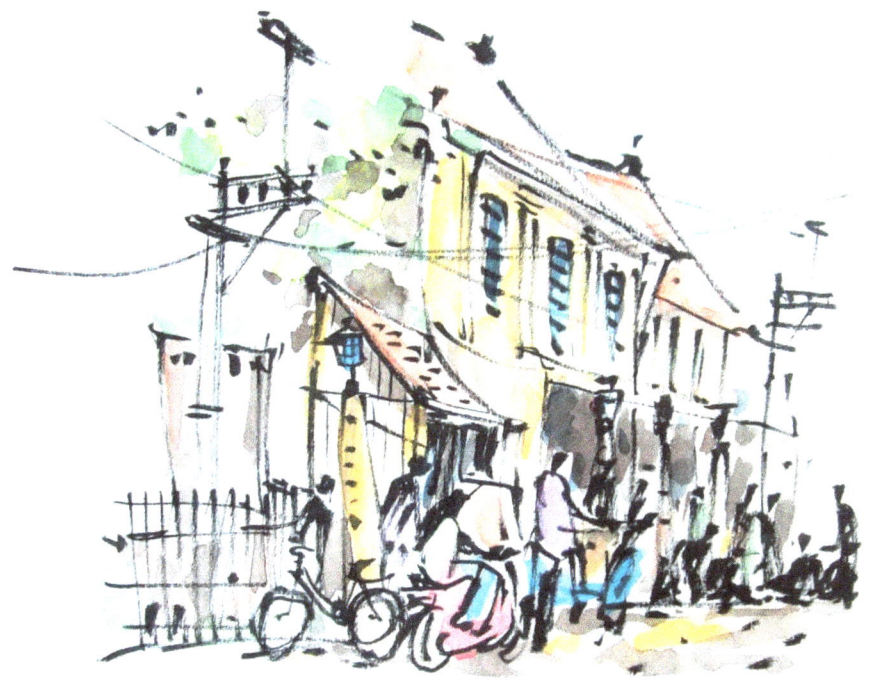

☾ The Street Hartanto says this spot in the old town is the cockfighting area. "I like this spot because of the beauty of the old buildings around," he says. "You can see the building in the background is of Dutch heritage."

Tip "When using a brush pen, you really have to make your arm flow on the paper. Never push too hard on the brush. It is a good tool for making a loose sketch. Pick up the bright color and use lots of water." — *Rudi Hartanto*

A4 (8.3" x 11.7" | 21 x 29.7 cm); Chinese brush pen and Pentel watercolors, Canson all-purpose drawing pad; 10 minutes

HONG KONG

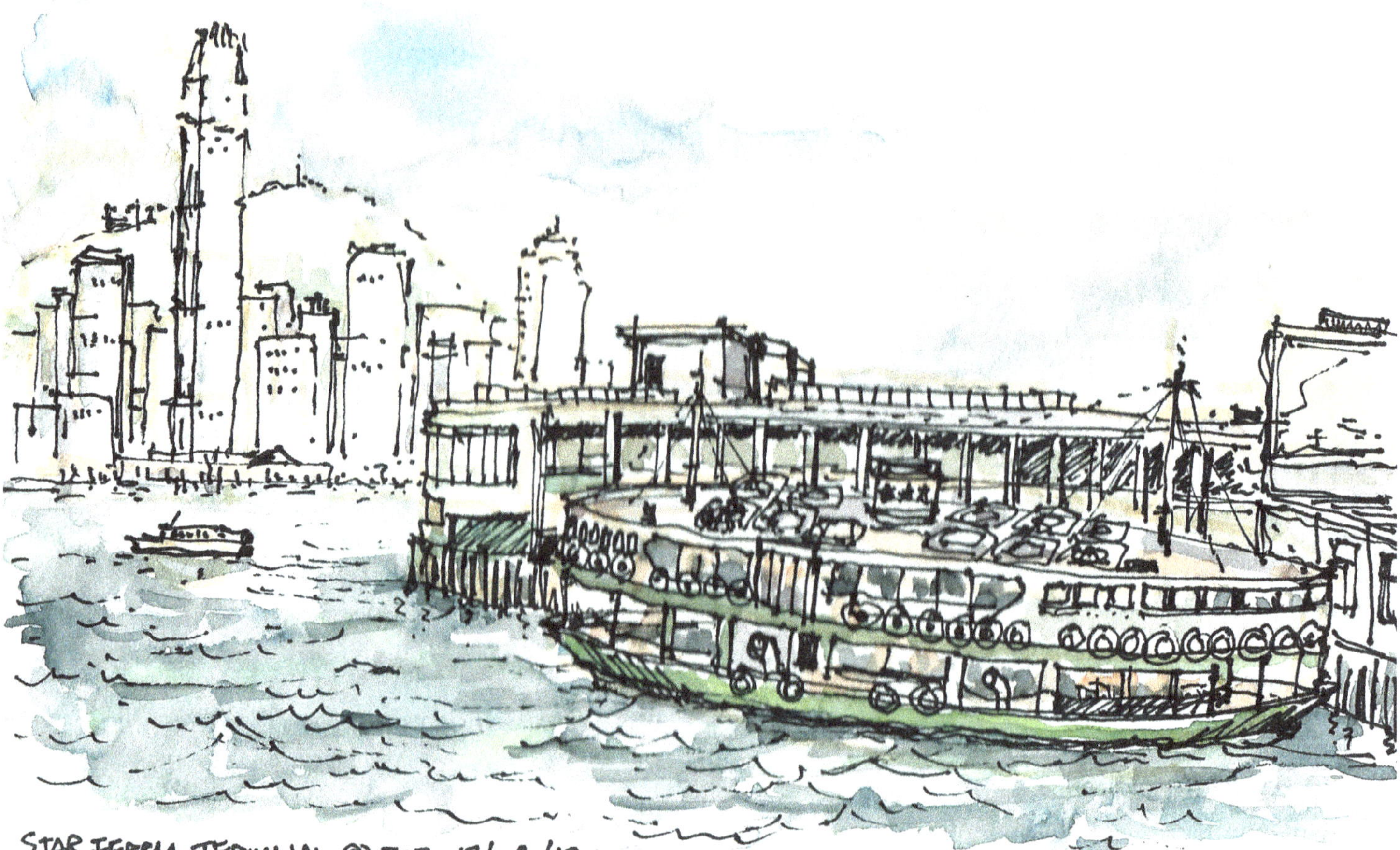

STAR FERRY TERMINAL @ TST 17/04/10

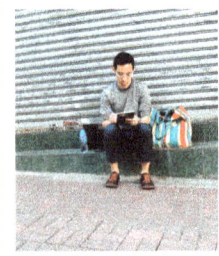

🎧 Paul Wang sketches an old shop in central Hong Kong.

ARTIST PROFILE
Paul Wang

I am an art and design teacher working for an international school in Hong Kong. I often use my sketches to inspire my students and as practical examples during my teaching. My personal mantra is "less is more," and I am still working on reducing the clutter when I sketch.

Sketching is a unique way of telling stories as I discover the world. Urban sketching is about a deeper, deliberate connection with unique spaces and preserving lost memories. Some days, I like to see the big picture; some days, I find joy in the details. My training and background in technical theatre, specializing in set and stage lighting, has helped me add a dramatic touch to my sketching techniques. My sketches are bold and vibrantly colored. The spirit of the place is what I try to capture.

🎧 **Star Ferry Terminal** These ferries have been carrying passengers between Kowloon and Hong Kong island since 1888. The ride is relatively cheap, Wang says, and offers a great view of Hong Kong's many famous skyscrapers.

Tip "Leave lots of free space for the sky, to capture the vastness of the harbor." — *Paul Wang*

8.25" x 5.25" | 21 x 13 cm; Zig black sketching pen, Winsor & Newton and Schmincke pan watercolors

A dramatic skyline of towering skyscrapers, bustling streets, and colorful markets characterize Hong Kong, one of the most densely populated cities in the world. "The key to sketching here is the ability to simplify the often very crowded scenes," says local sketcher Paul Wang.

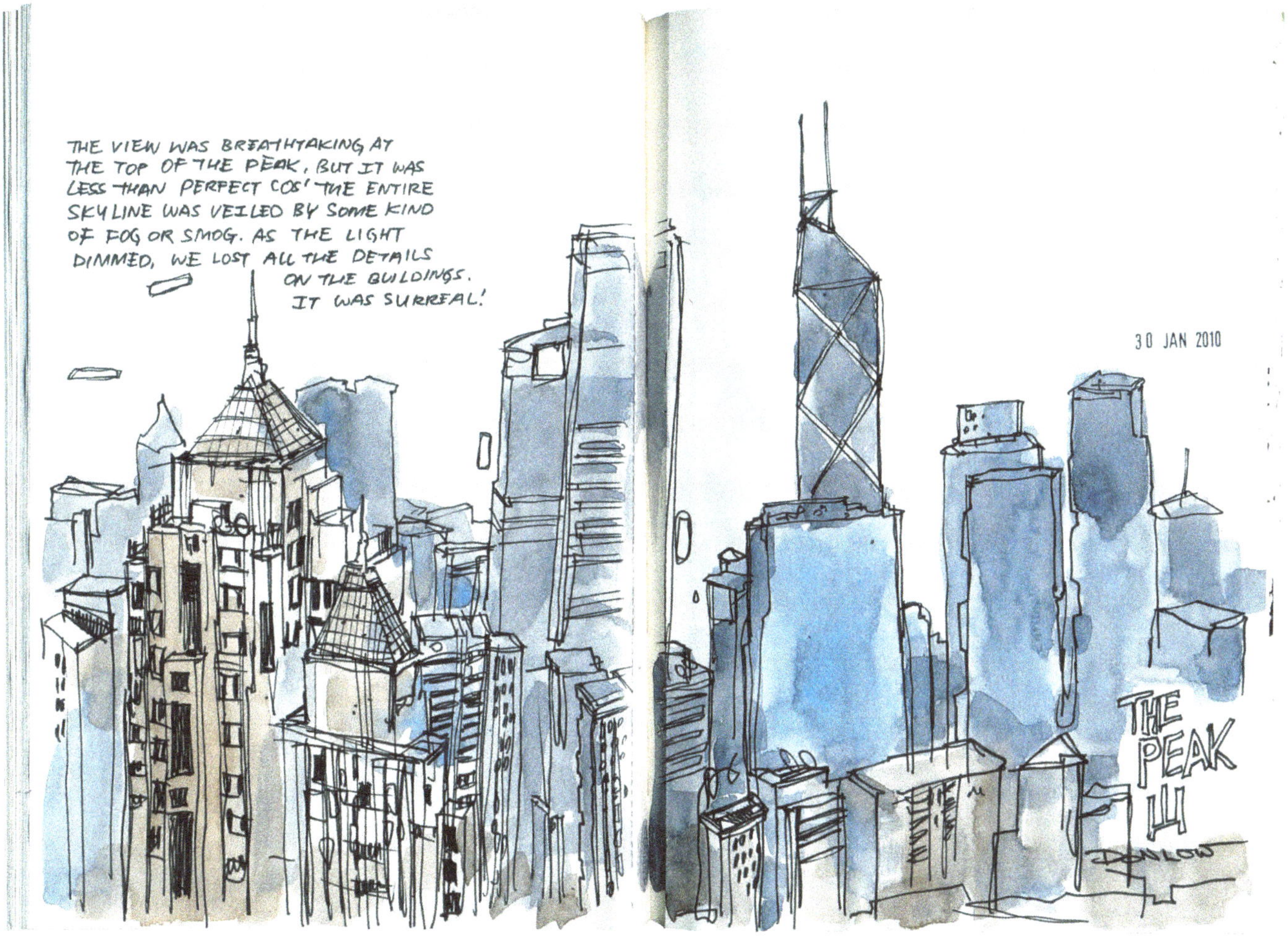

THE VIEW WAS BREATHTAKING AT
THE TOP OF THE PEAK, BUT IT WAS
LESS THAN PERFECT COS' THE ENTIRE
SKYLINE WAS VEILED BY SOME KIND
OF FOG OR SMOG. AS THE LIGHT
DIMMED, WE LOST ALL THE DETAILS
ON THE BUILDINGS.
IT WAS SURREAL!

30 JAN 2010

THE PEAK

∩ Up on the Peak Despite visiting for nine days, Singaporean illustrator Don Low says he managed to get only a glimpse of Hong Kong's fragrant harbor. "There is so much to see and so much to do and too much to eat," Low says. On this day, Low says it was also too hazy to have a clear view of the buildings. "I couldn't really see the details on the skyscrapers, but that helped me a lot in simplifying the forms."

Tip "Don't be too caught up by the details on the buildings. Use simple shapes to suggest windows and other details." — *Don Low*

11.5" x 8.5" | 29 x 21.6 cm; Faber-Castell Pitt markers (black, F), Winsor & Newton Cotman 12-color watercolor box set, watercolor brush pen made in Japan (no brand) on Daler-Rowney sketchbook; 30 minutes

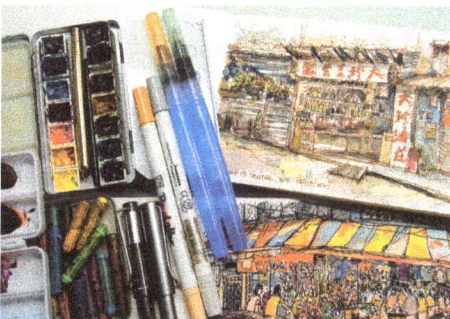

∩ Wang's sketching tools

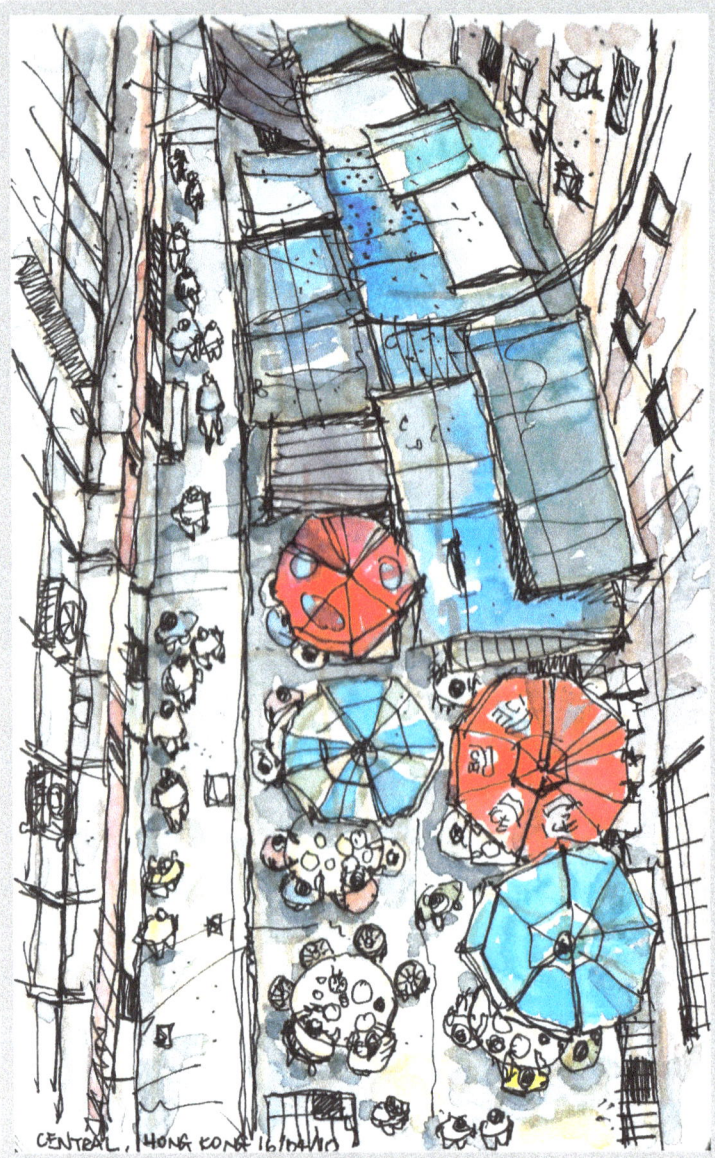

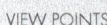

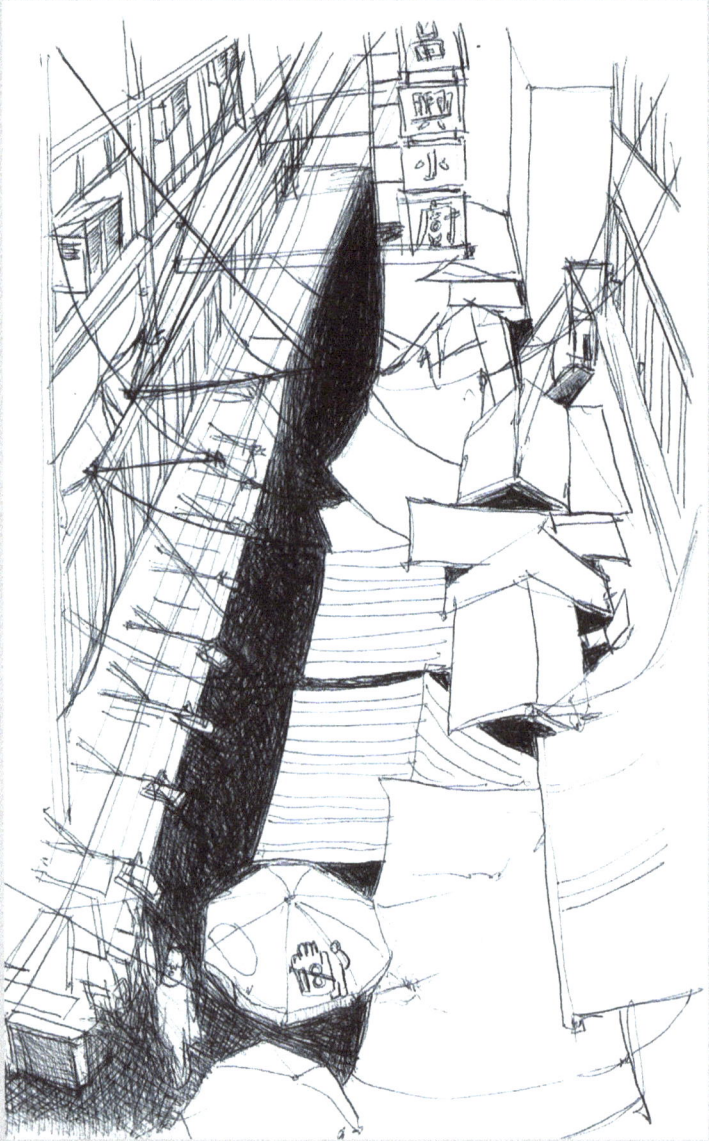

SoHo Escalator

An ultralong, 869-yard (795 m) -long outdoor covered escalator in the SoHo district is a must-see, must-sketch location in Hong Kong.

🎧 "Try sketching from a new vantage point. Looking down from the escalator gave me a new perspective on the busy streetscape." — *Paul Wang*

8.25" x 5.25" | 21 x 13 cm; Zig black sketching pen, Winsor & Newton and Schmincke pan watercolors on Moleskine watercolor book; 1 hour

🎧 "I drew this at a corner of the escalator, where a lot people were squeezing past me, so I decided to use my ballpoint pen, which is smoother and easier for quick sketching." — *Jeremiah Teo Cheng Huat*

6.25" x 8.75" | 16 x 22 cm; uni Laknock fine, 0.5 ballpoint pen on Daler-Rowney 150-gsm, acid-free sketchbook; about 30 minutes

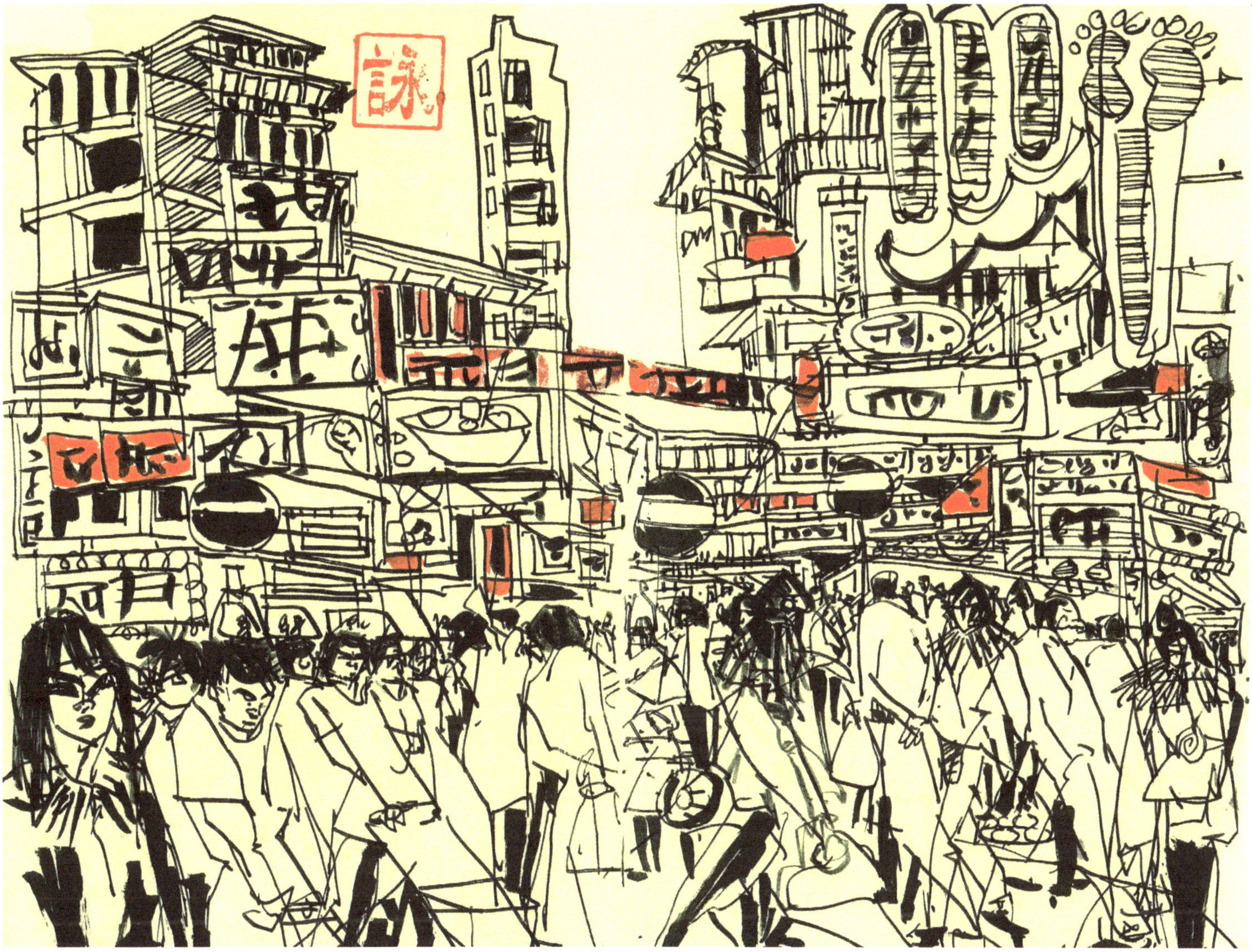

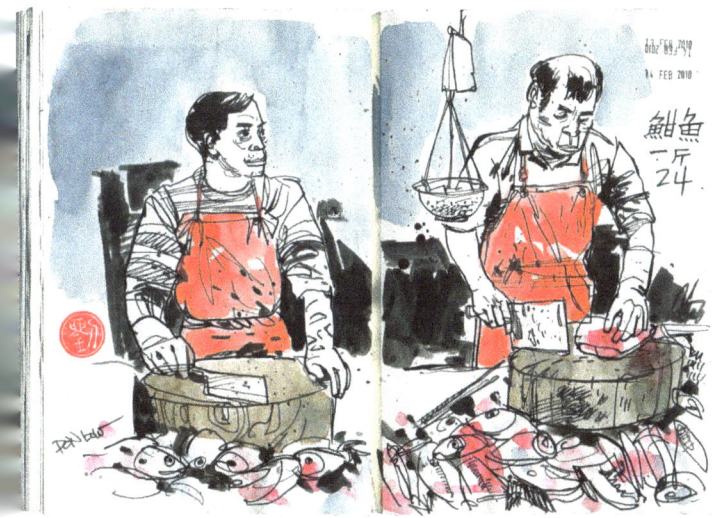

⋂ Hong Kong Krazy! Like many New Yorkers, illustrator Melanie Reim found it hard to imagine a city grander in scale than her hometown. "Boy, did I get that wrong!" Reim says. "Hong Kong is *huge*—and bustling, 24/7! People crossing, biking, wheeling, eating, shopping, and on the move wherever you go.

Tip "I was so excited by all the activity and the endless blinking of neon—and also self-consciousness that, with my streaked, curly locks in this neighborhood of not-too-many tourists, I was an oddity, standing and drawing. I needed to get it all down, fast!" — *Melanie Reim*

10" x 8" | 25 x 20 cm; Pelikan cartridge pen and Pentel brush pens (black and red) on Moleskine sketchbook; about 20 minutes

⊆ Fish Peddlers Fresh-fish sellers are a common sight in Hong Kong's wet markets, such as the one Don Low found along a street at Causeway Bay. "We could see decapitated fishes breathing and their hearts still beating, fighting to survive. This rather gruesome and bloody sight indicates how fresh the fish are in the market," Low says.

11.5" X 8.5" | 29 x 21.6 cm; Japanese G pen (dip pen) and Sumi ink, Winsor & Newton Cotman 12-color watercolor box set, watercolor brush pen made in Japan (no brand) on Daler-Rowney sketchbook; 30 minutes

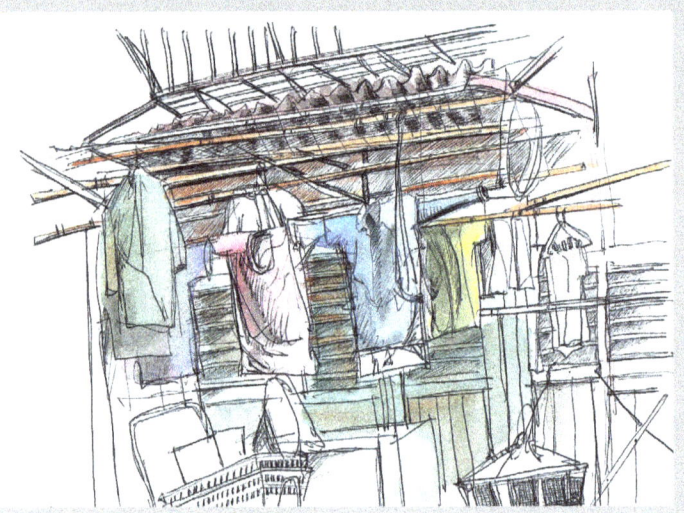

FIRST PERSON

Wing Lee Street

by Jeremiah Teo Cheng Huat

I went down to Wing Lee Street, after reading the news that the site would be demolished to make way for some upmarket development. I realized that I have been around here many times to take photos of old houses and shops but have never sketched in this area. TV antennas and phone lines can be seen all over the buildings. Here, the safest way to dry clothes is to have the bamboo poles going through the clothes and secured by ropes, in case of bad weather.

I hope that these places can be preserved as part of Hong Kong's history and heritage for the younger generation.

6.25" x 8.75" | 16 x 22 cm; Royal Talens watercolor cakes, Holbein waterbrush (medium-tip), uni Laknock fine, 0.5 ballpoint pen, on Daler-Rawney 150-gsm, acid-free sketchbook; about 5.5 hours total for all sketches

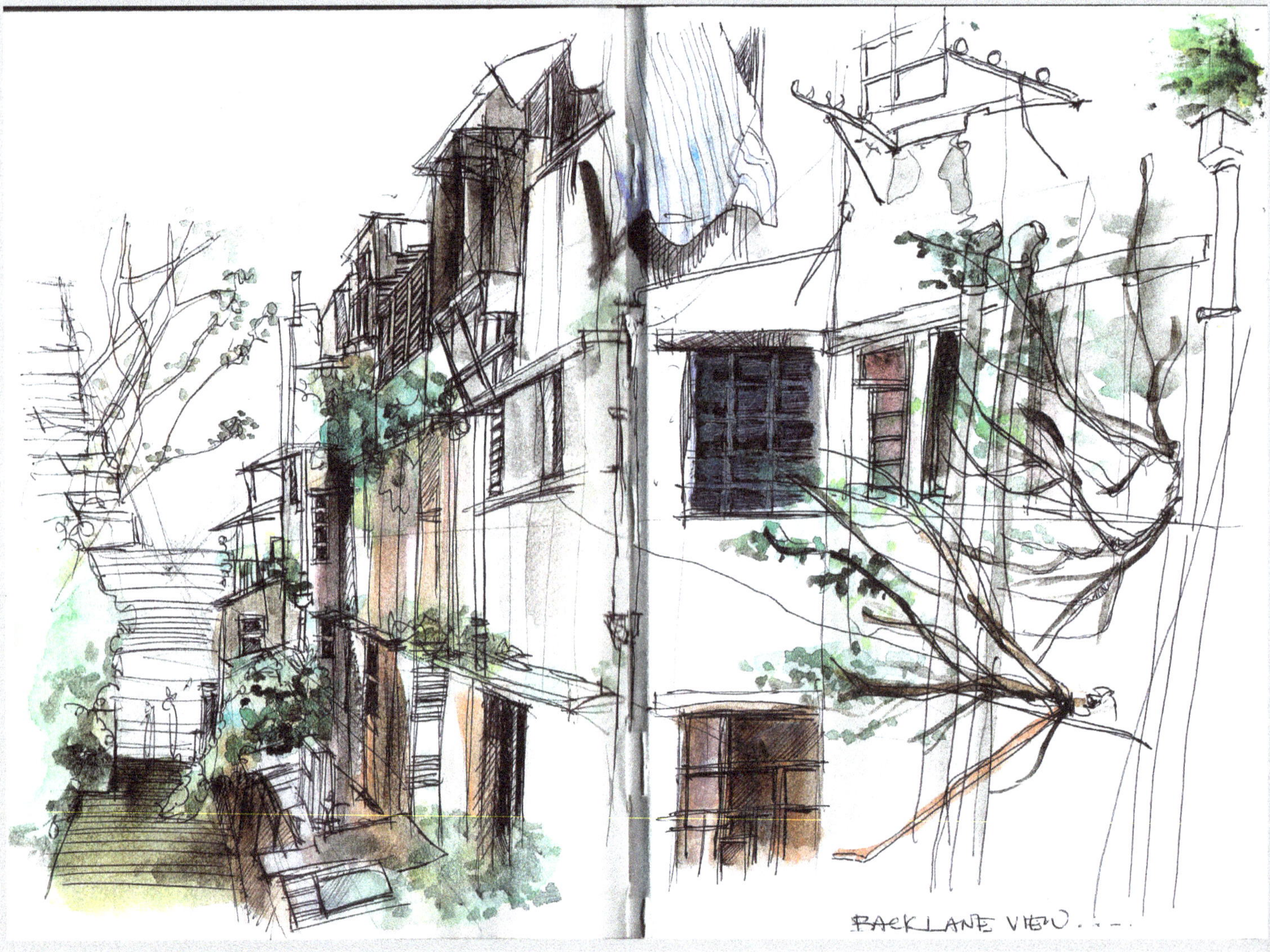

BACKLANE VIEW....

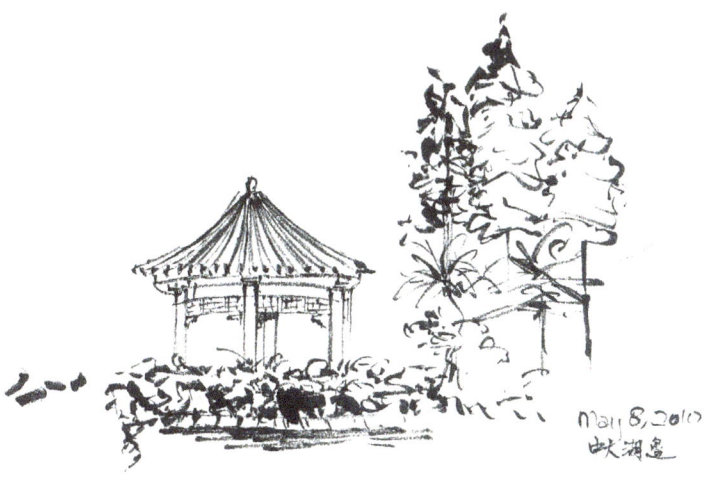

Chinese Pavilion During a break, Chow Yuen Kwan Perry used a Chinese ink brush to draw this pavilion beside a pond near the Chinese University of Hong Kong.

Tip "Because I use a medium-sized brush, I cannot draw very detailed. I was looking at the scene and drawing quickly." — *Chow Yuen Kwan Perry*

4" x 6" | 10 x 15 cm; Chinese ink brush, cream writing paper notebook; 7 minutes

Flower Street, Kowloon During the two hours Beijing-based interior designer Jeremiah Teo Cheng Huat spent putting the main color in this sketch, the potted-plants vendor he was drawing hardly moved. "He is actually listening to the radio for the racing results, one of the favorite pastimes here in Hong Kong on weekends, besides shopping and eating," he says.

Tip "Try to control the amount of color used, so as not to mess up the composition. Leave some pockets of white areas and give some parts really black shade for contrast." — *Jeremiah Teo Cheng Huat*

10.75" x 8" | 27.5 x 20 cm; Royal Talens watercolor cakes, medium-tip Holbein waterbrush on Holbein 120-gsm, 3F multidrawing book; more than 2 hours

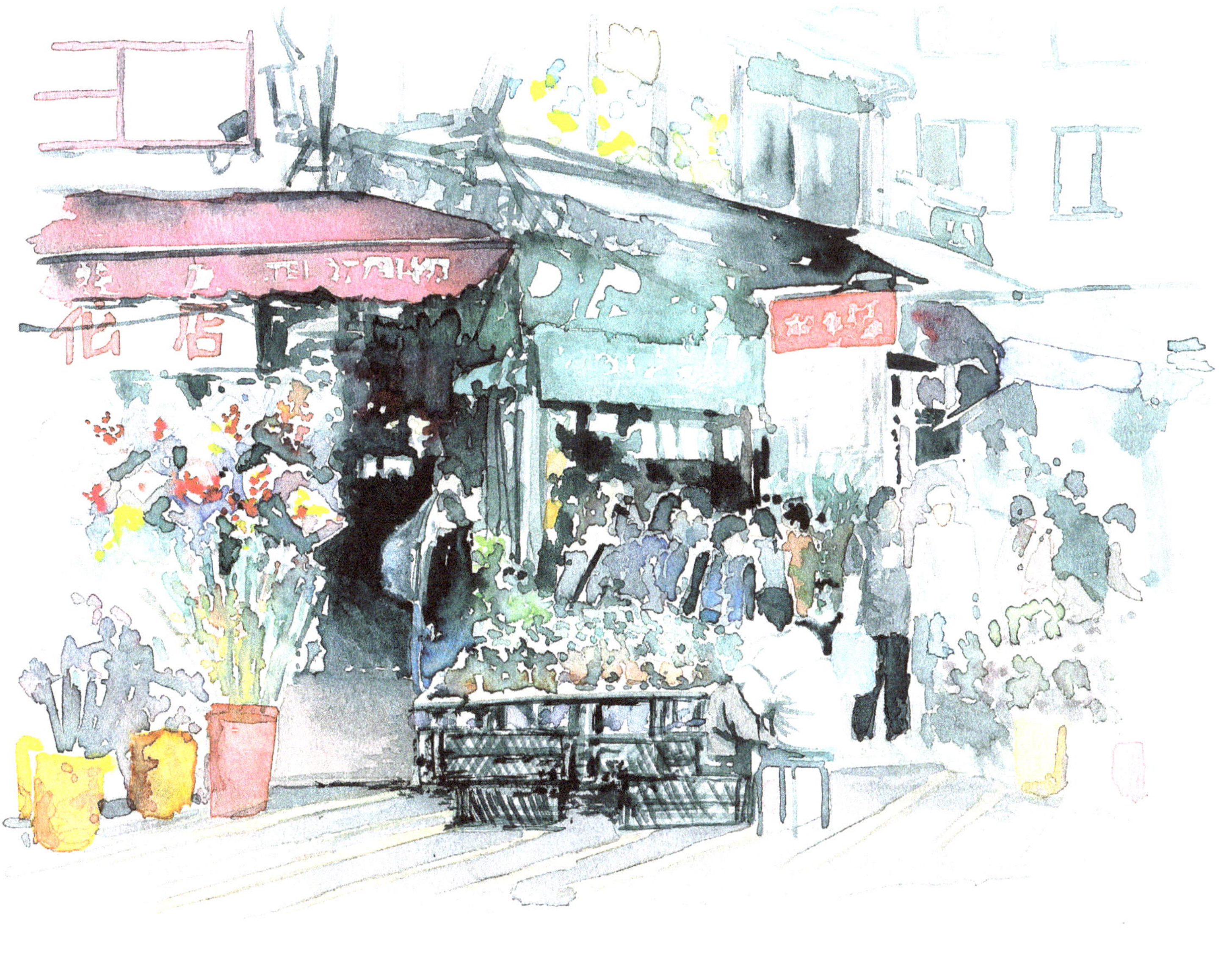

SEOUL

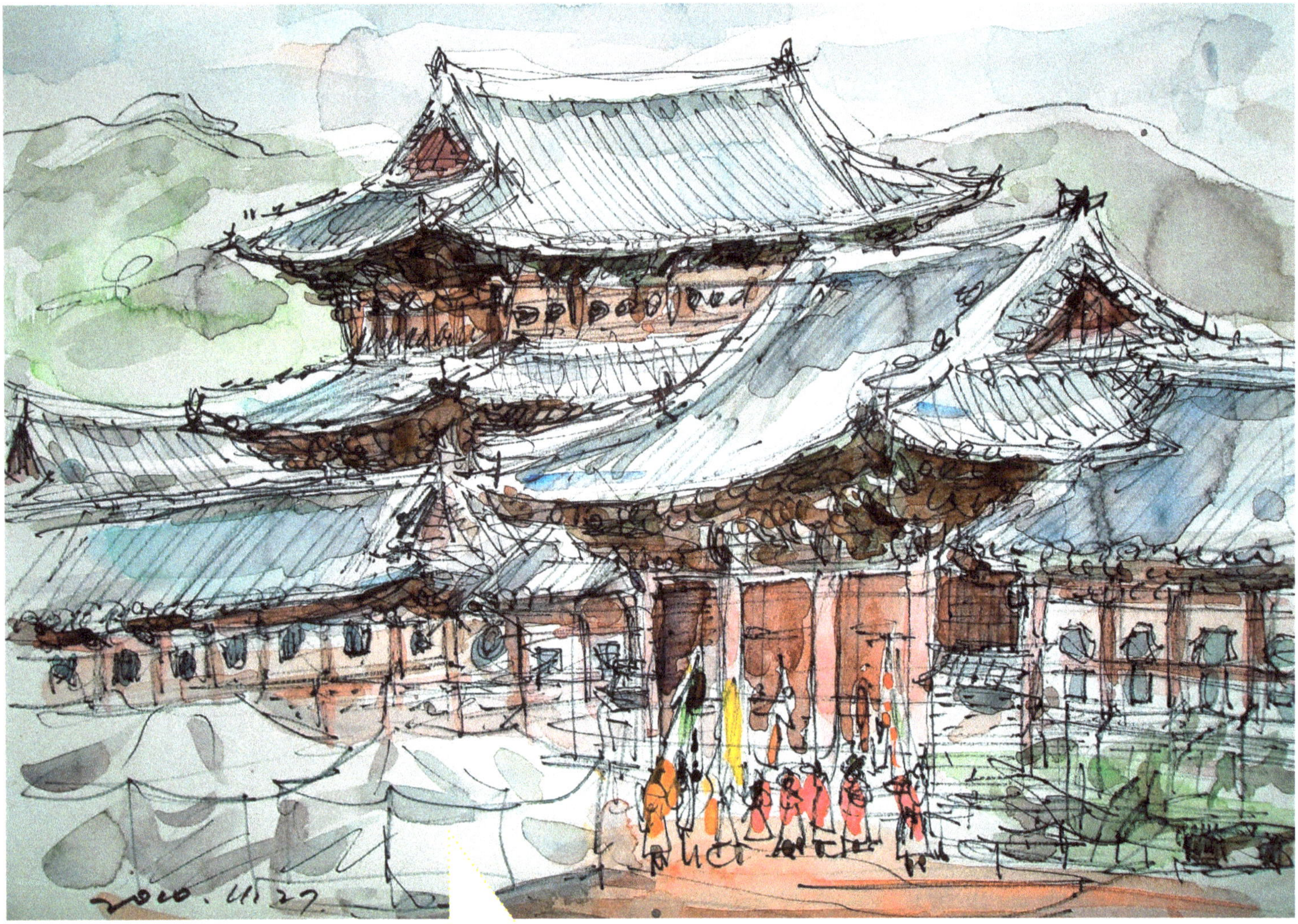

Seoul's mix of palaces, old Korean-style houses, and contemporary high-rise buildings offers a varied sketching experience. Add to that a population of more than ten million, and lively scenes are guaranteed to please the sketcher looking for things to draw in this metropolis surrounded by mountains on the shores of the river Han.

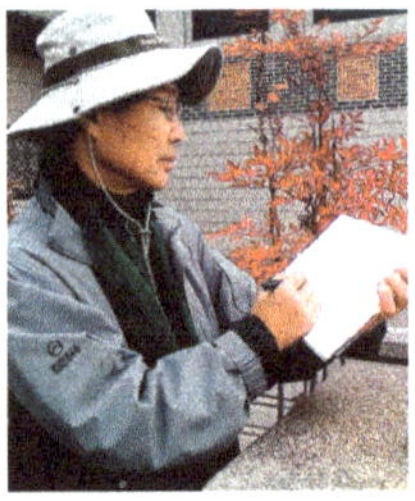

Lee Yong Hwan sketching in the entrance of Kyungbok Palace Museum

ARTIST PROFILE

Lee Yong Hwan

I have lived in Seoul since 1949, when I was born. From childhood, I wanted to become a painter and practiced. But because of the Korean War and the economic development, it was so hard for artists to make a living painting that my parents never agreed to art college. So I chose architecture.

For 30 years, I lived as an architect, but I kept a hope to be a painter. In 1994, I happened to meet several watercolorists, who painted every Sunday outdoors. The next week, I joined them, and I have been painting with them for more than fifteen years. I sketch, paint, and finish on the spot before I come home. That's my motto.

8.25" x 11.75" | 21 x 30 cm; MonAmi pen F, Alpha, ShinHan, and Holbein watercolors on 94-lb. Fabriano Accademia paper pad; 40 minutes

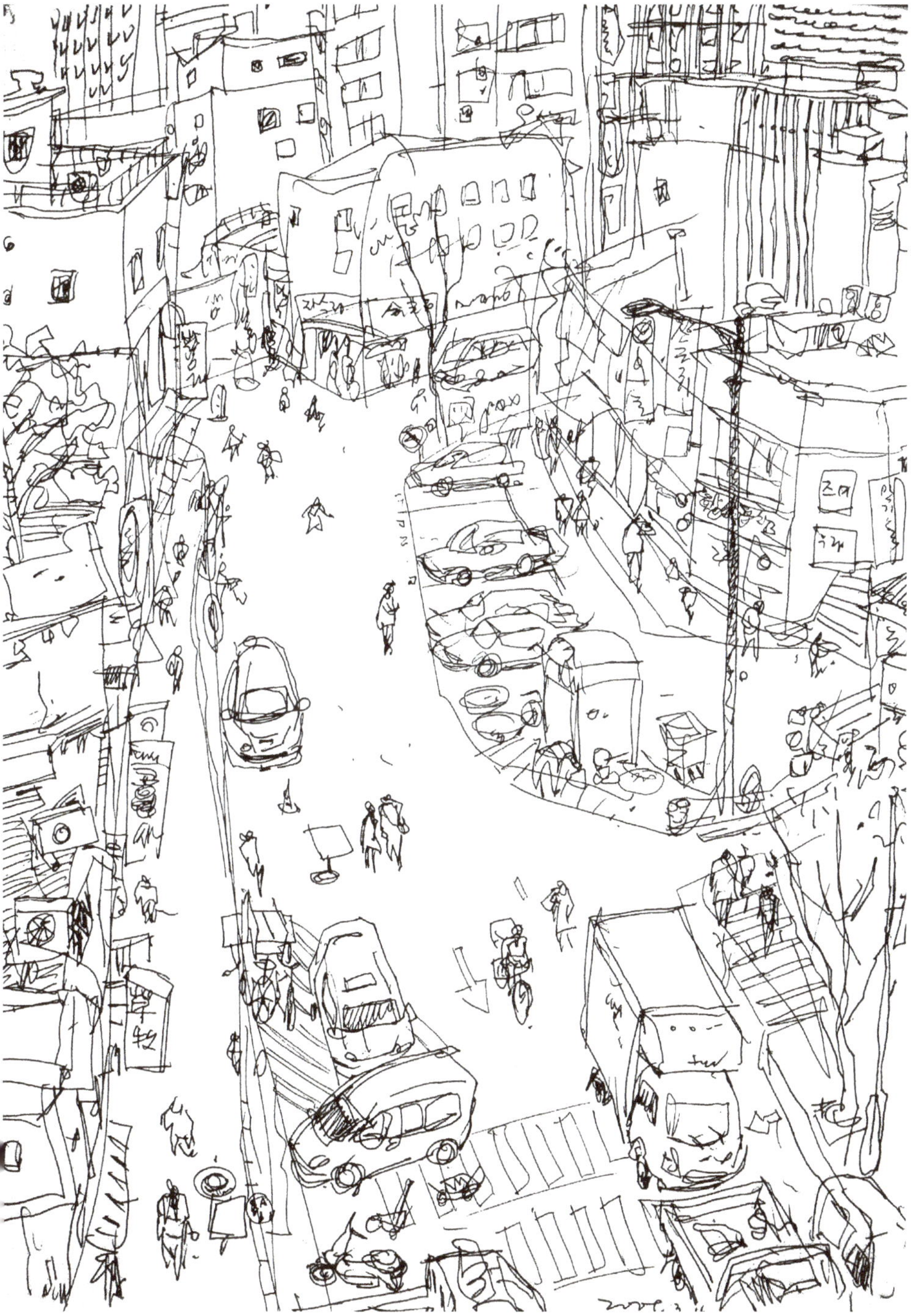

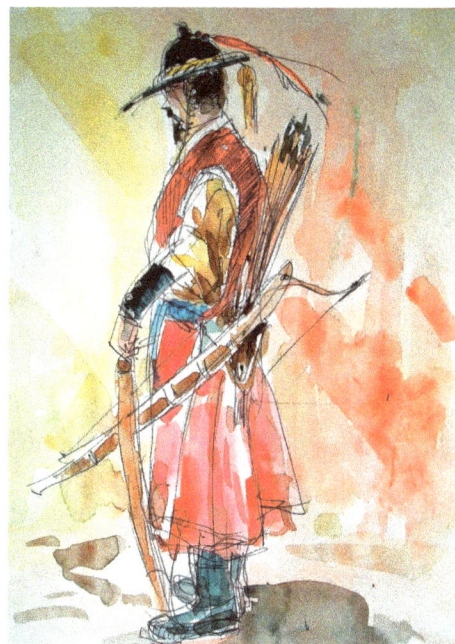

♠ **Gatekeeper at Duck Soo Palace** The changing of the traditional gatekeepers at Duck Soo Palace is popular with foreign tourists and kids from all nations. This gatekeeper wears the traditional clothes of the Chosun dynasty, and, in front of the palace plaza, volunteers provide Korean-style clothes for taking photos."
— *Lee Yong Hwan*

8.25" x 11.75" | 21 x 30 cm; Dong-A U-Knock pen, 0.7, Alpha, ShinHan, and Holbein watercolors, Hwa Hong #12 flat brush, Haio #10 round brush on Daler-Rowney 150-gsm, acid-free cartridge paper; 30 minutes

◖ **Insadong Street** Lee Yong Hwan often sketches from the roof of this shopping center to capture the irregular street scenery crowded with trucks and people below.

Tip "Looking down lets me see the scenery as a united whole. To divide the dense buildings and the street properly should be considered from the start."
— *Lee Yong Hwan*

8.25" x 11.75" | 21 x 30 cm; Dong-A U-Knock pen, 0.7 on Daler-Rowney 150-gsm, acid-free cartridge paper; 30 minutes

" love sketching because it doesn't take a long time to capture the feelings and the essence of a place."

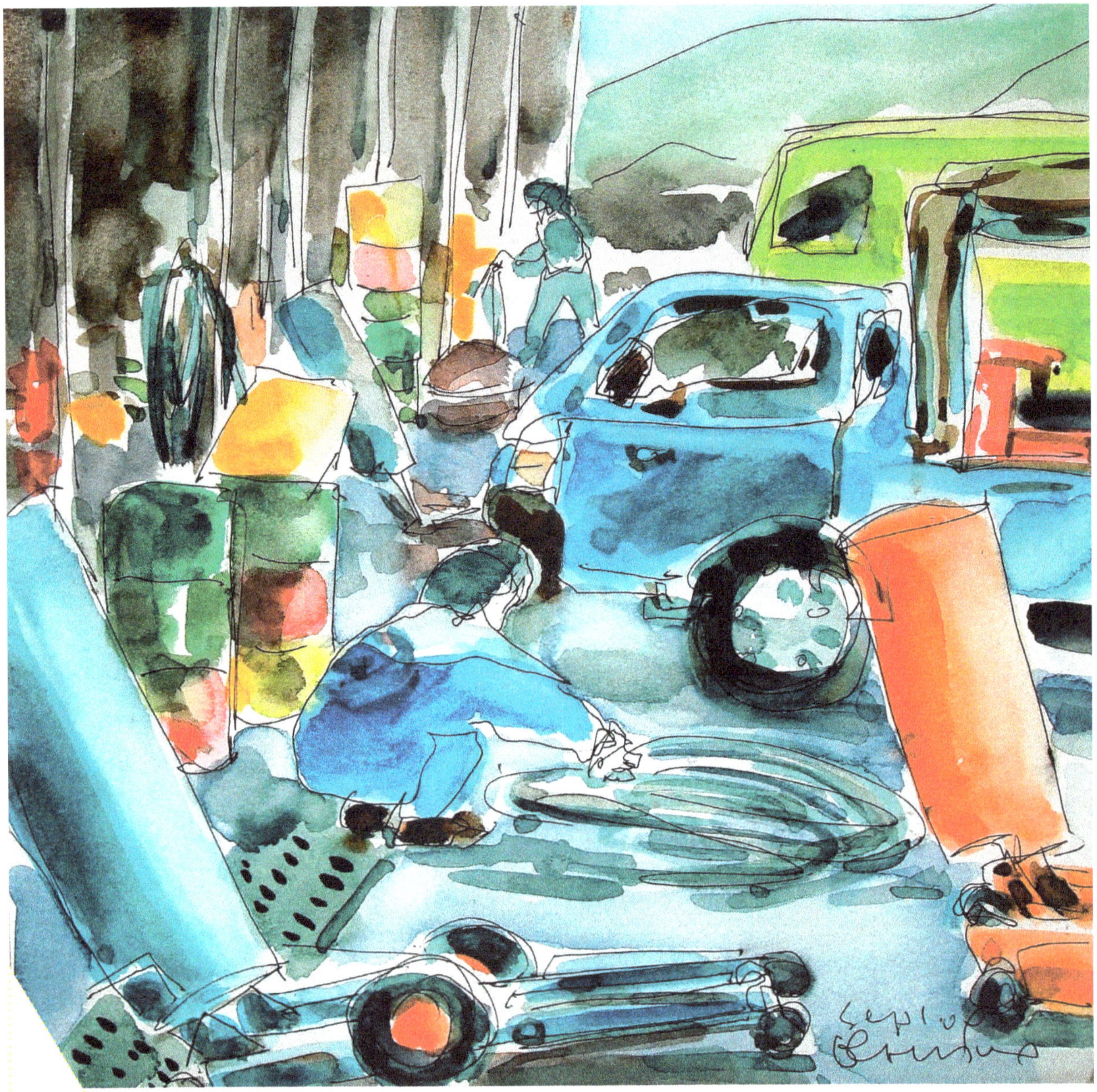

2″ x 10″ | 5 x 25 cm; Bic
Gel Intensity Clic Classic,
0.7, Hwa Hong #10 round
brush, ¾″ Alpha flat brush,
Alpha, ShinHan, and Holbein
watercolors, on 110-lb. Daler-
Rowney sketchpad; 40 minutes

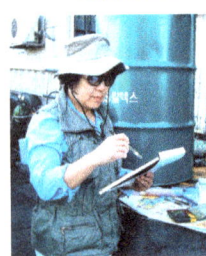

⌂ Yoo Byung Hwa
sketching the engineers
and mechanics' tools at
Eunpyeong Public Bus
Garage

ARTIST PROFILE

Yoo Byung Hwa

I began painting at the age of forty-five, when my daughter chose painting as
her major. Because I had no basic training in art, I studied art books for years.
Drawing on location has been the most important principle to me. Looking
at the scenes through the naked eyes, not using photos, I aim to translate
vivid impressions on paper. Urban sketchers must pay attention to the change
of the light, temperature, shade, and many other factors. Rough and strong
lines drawn urgently on the spot give viewers the same impressions as if
they were there.

*"Urban sketchers must be alert and
fast to capture the situation, like a
jaguar in the jungle."*

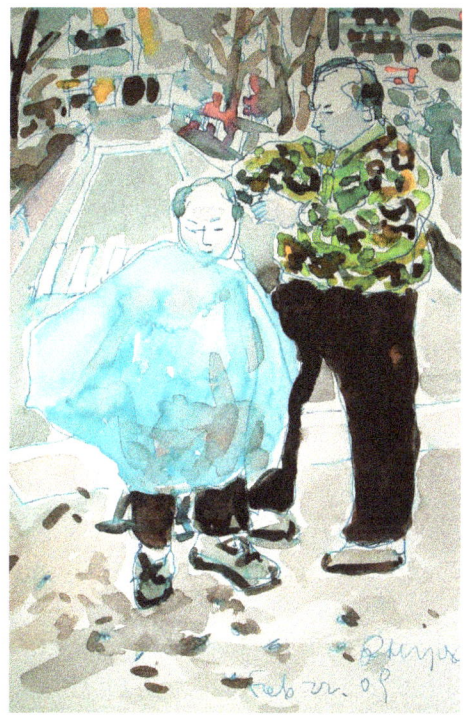

↻ **Street Barbershop** A TV show ran a story about a city alley, where old people gather to reminisce and get cheap meals and haircuts. After watching the show, Yoo Byung Hwa went there several times and had meals at a restaurant, where an old man made food; he was missing his family left in North Korea. "I remember his tears when he was talking about his wife and family on the TV program," she says.

Tip "By drawing my subjects, I can learn and share emotionally with them more than if I just passed by. This scene was unusual, not often seen in big cities like Seoul." — *Yoo Byung Hwa*

7.75" x 10.5" | 19.5 x 26.5 cm; Bic Gel Intensity Clic Classic, 0.7, Hwa Hong #10 round brush, ¾" Alpha flat brush, Alpha, ShinHan, and Holbein watercolors on 120-gsm sketchbook made in Korea; 20 minutes

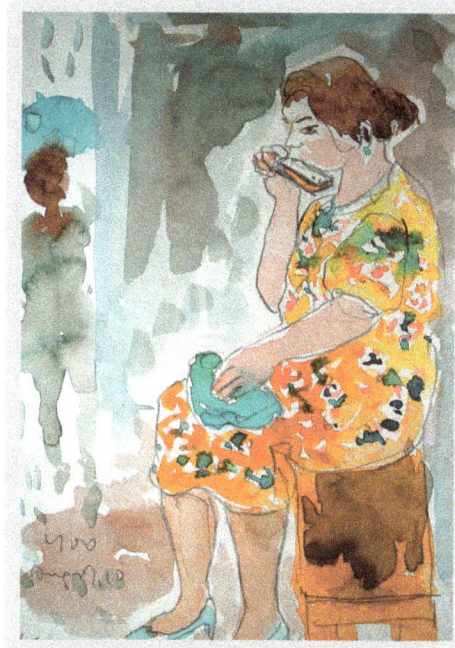

FIRST PERSON

Playing the Harmonica on a Rainy Day

by Yoo Byung Hwa

I was waiting for a bus. It rained heavily. I could hear the sound of a harmonica but couldn't find the source, until I saw this older woman, sitting on a bus stop bench. The music might have touched most of the people there. I pulled my sketchbook out of my sack and began to draw her. She missed her bus, and I did too, but it was such a special experience for me to see a woman enjoying playing her own musical instrument in such a place. The tunes she played still remain in my heart.

8.25" x 11.75" | 21 x 30 cm; Faber-Castell TK 9400 clutch pencil, Hwa Hong #10 round brush, ¾" Alpha flat brush, Alpha, ShinHan, and Holbein watercolors on Canson 43-lb., XL sketchpad; 10 minutes

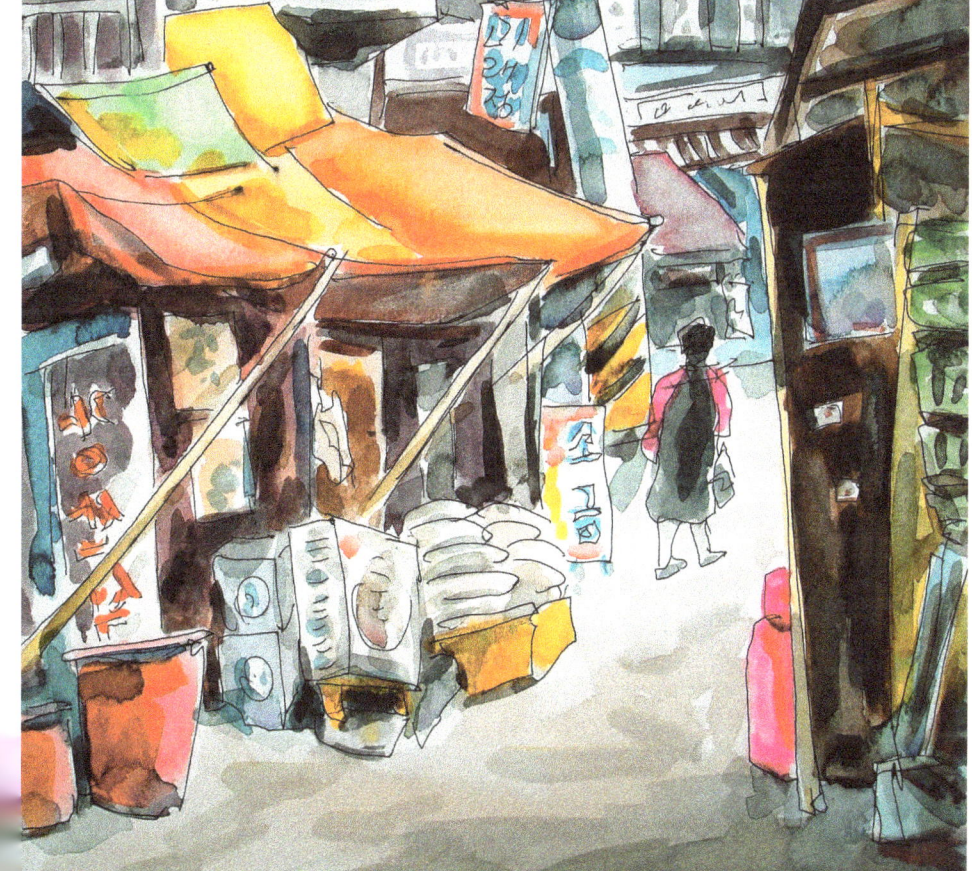

↻ **Shops at Ahyundong** High-rise apartments have been built in this part of Seoul, but an old market remains. The shops sell salt, rice, flour, dried red peppers, and other ingredients needed for traditional Korean food.

Tip "I sketched one woman who passed by, because the drawing would seem lifeless if there was no one in the narrow alley of the market." — *Yoo Byung Hwa*

10" x 10" | 25 x 25 cm; BIC Gel Intensity Clic Classic, 0.7, Hwa Hong #10 round brush, ¾" Alpha flat brush, Alpha, ShinHan, and Holbein watercolors on 110-lb. Daler-Rowney sketchpad; 1 hour

TOKYO

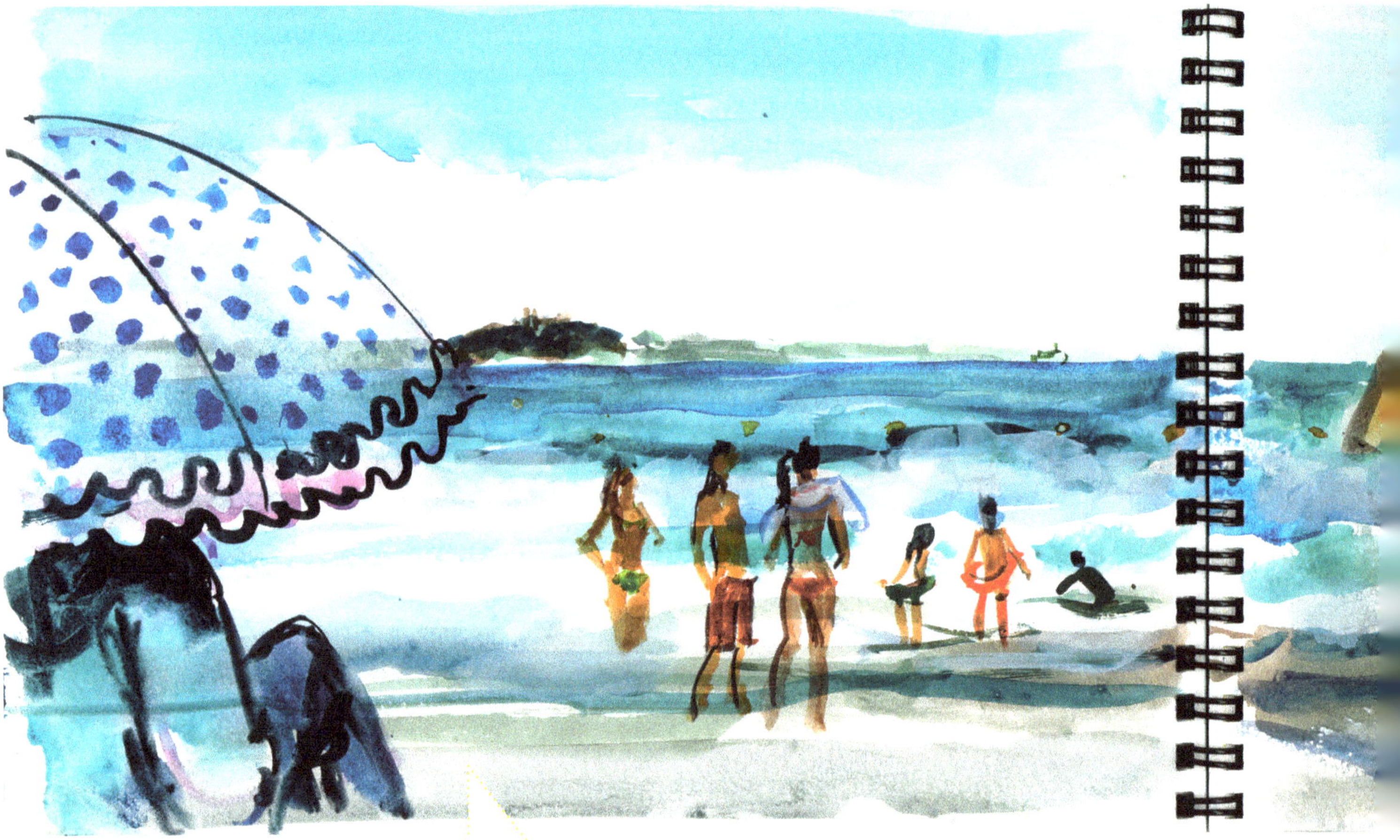

Tokyo's fast-paced environment is no obstacle to practicing urban sketching. Lok Jansen captures the city's anonymous inhabitants in one-minute pen sketches when he rides the subway, and Kumi Matsukawa can re-create a crowded scene with colorful brushwork while standing in a crowded alley.

"Sharing my drawings and stories online really broadens the significance of my sketching."

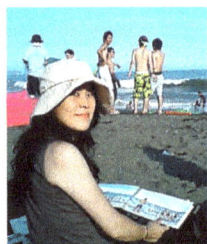

⌒ Kumi Matsukawa enjoys sketching the seaside views in Kanagawa Prefecture.

Talens 24-color watercolor set and Pentel Aquash waterbrush on sketchbook; 1 hour

ARTIST PROFILE
Kumi Matsukawa

I am an illustrator. I draw mainly storyboards for TV commercials, and I also teach watercolor and pastel classes in my neighborhood. Both works entail sketching, and I think sketching is the most essential and fun part of any form of drawing. Sketching trains my insight and facilitates a quick grasp of my surroundings; most important, sketching is free and pure indulgence.

I enjoy sketching landscapes, buildings, people, animals, plants, or whatever. It's like a dialogue with the subject. For example, when I draw an old tree, I feel as if I am listening to its story. An old tree—like an old man—has a long, complicated story, and what I do is transcribe it in the form of a sketch. That's how I understand everything I draw.

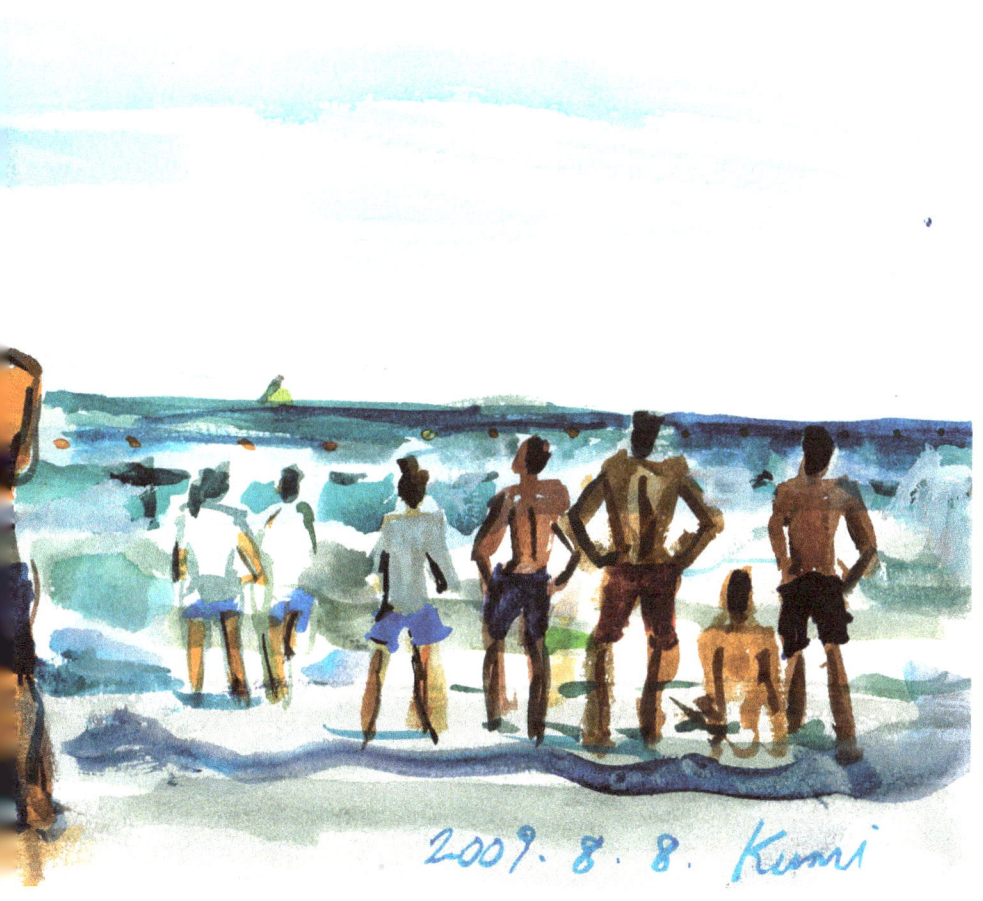

2009. 8. 8. Kumi

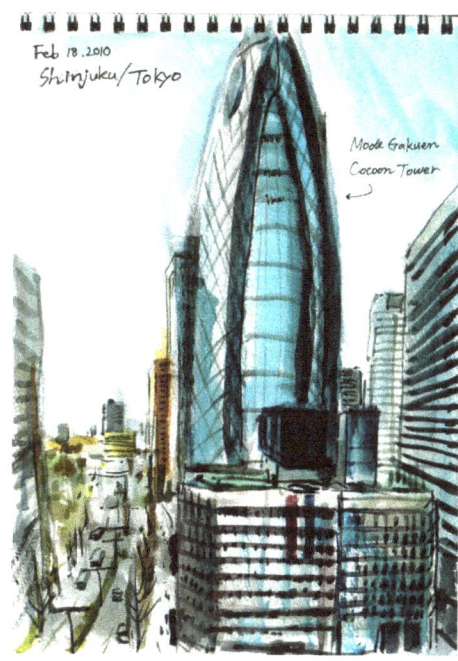

Feb 18, 2010
Shinjuku/Tokyo

Mode Gakuen
Cocoon Tower

∩ Mode Gakuen Cocoon Tower Kumi Matsu-kawa drew this view from the Odakyu department store's 13th floor. Mode Gakuen Cocoon Tower—a 669-foot (204 meter), fifty-story educational facility—is a landmark in the Nishi-Shinjuku district in Shinjuku, Tokyo.

Tip "To capture the correct value in gray scale, squint your eyes to see how bright or dark the windows are against the background sky." — *Kumi Matsukawa*

F1 (6.4" x 8.8" | 16.2 x 22.5 cm); Talens 24-color watercolor set, Pentel Aquash waterbrush on Maruman Art Spiral sketchbook; 1.5 hours

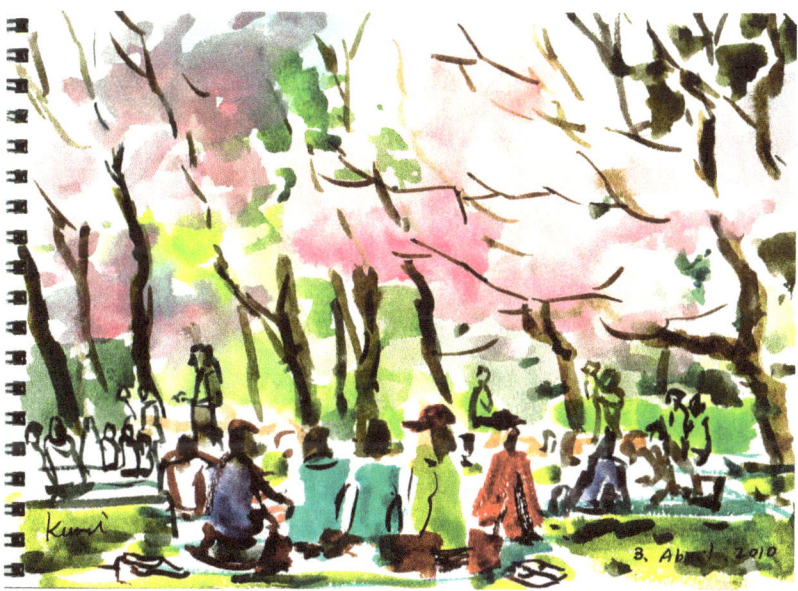

⊂ Cherry Blossom Viewing Groups of people had gathered at Komazawa Park for a cherry-blossom viewing party. Our group had drinks and food. It was a gathering of our Spanish class, so I wrote the date in Spanish.

Tip "I saw the people in the foreground as one unit and figured out that this unit occupies one third of the bottom of the plane. Within this small space, I simplified each figure, with their clothing colors and the length of their hair. The priority was 'quick grasp' then accuracy." — *Kumi Matsukawa*

F1 (6.4" x 8.8" | 16.2 x 22.5 mm); Talens 24-color watercolor set, Pentel Aquash waterbrush on Maruman Art Spiral sketchbook; 30 minutes

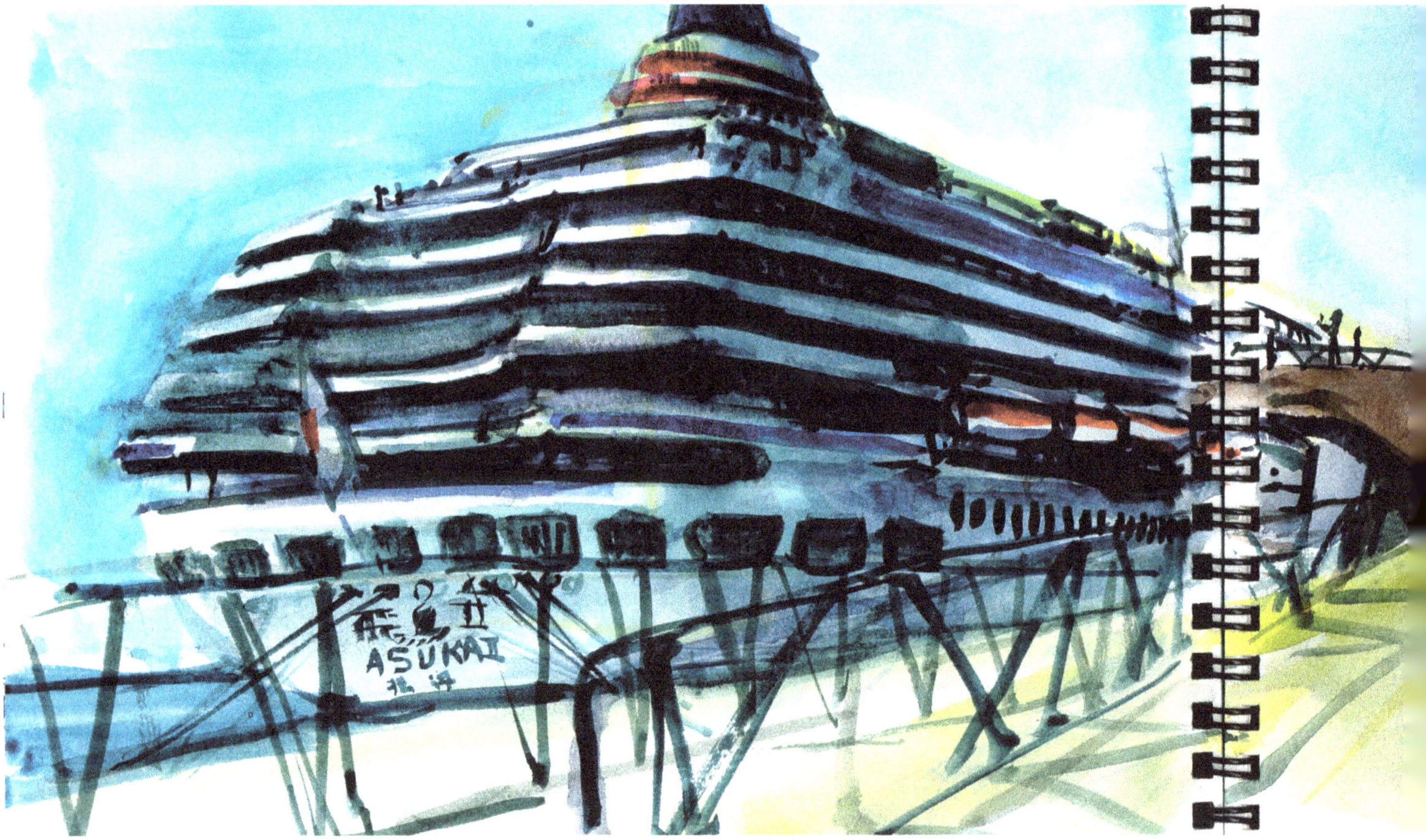

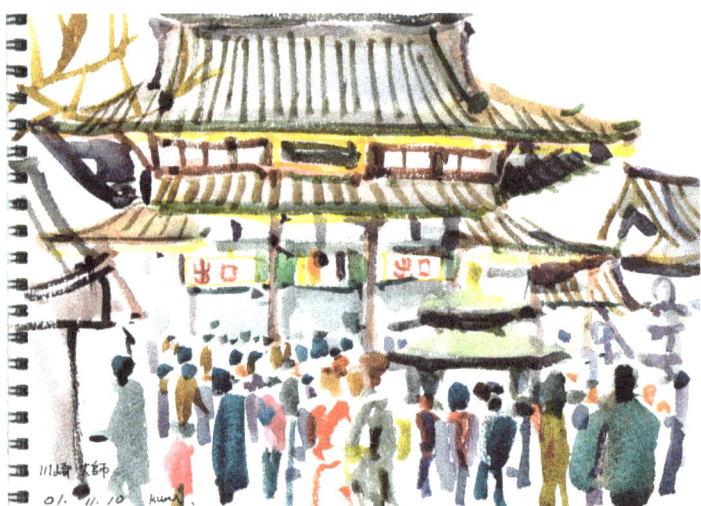

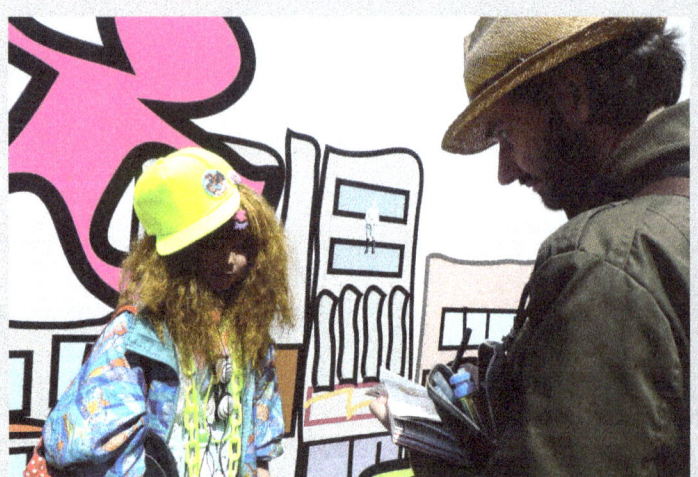

♩ **Left, above: Kawasaki Daishi Cathedral** At the center of the foreground, two kimono-clad girls were having a coming-of-age ceremony, which Matsukawa drew from a crowded alley, standing and conversing with strangers.

F1 (6.4" x 8.8" | 16.2 x 22.5 cm); Talens 24-color watercolor set, Pentel Aquash waterbrush on Maruman Art Spiral sketchbook; 20 minutes

TRAVEL JOURNAL

Cosplay

by Lapin

Harajuku, and, more precisely, Takeshita Street is the famous place in Tokyo where, during the weekend, all the cosplayers (short for costumed play, a type of performance

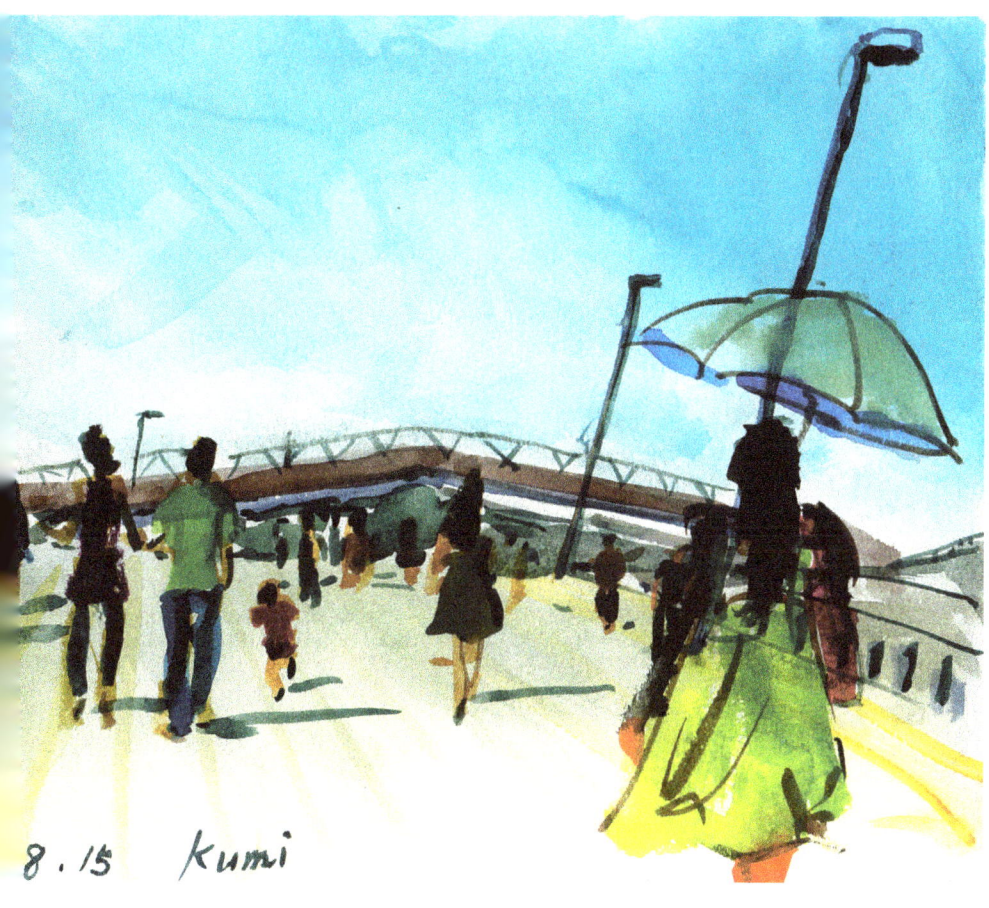

8.15 Kumi

☾ **Asuka Cruise Ship** The Asuka was tied up along-side Yokohama pier; just as Kumi Matsukawa finished sketching her, she sailed off.

Tip "I kept asking myself, 'How dark is the ship's shadow against the background sky? How big are these people in the middle ground, compared to the ship's height?' Here are the answers." — *Kumi Matsukawa*

9.25" x 6.25" | 23.5 x 16 cm (double-page); Talens 24-color watercolor set, Pentel Aquash waterbrush on Holbein sketchbook; 1.5 hours

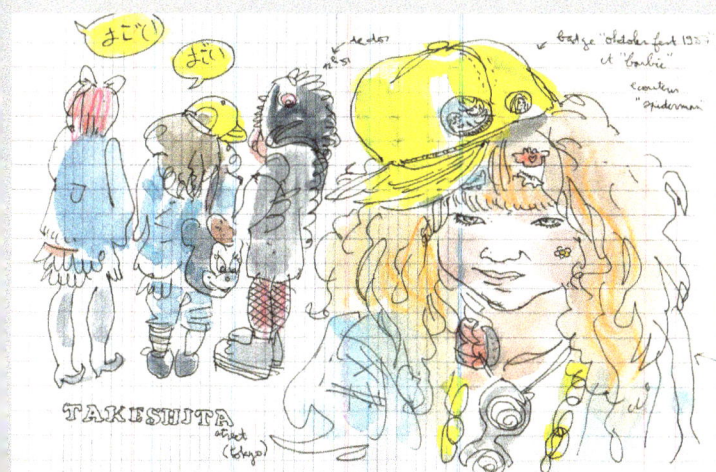

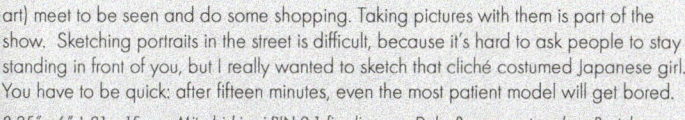

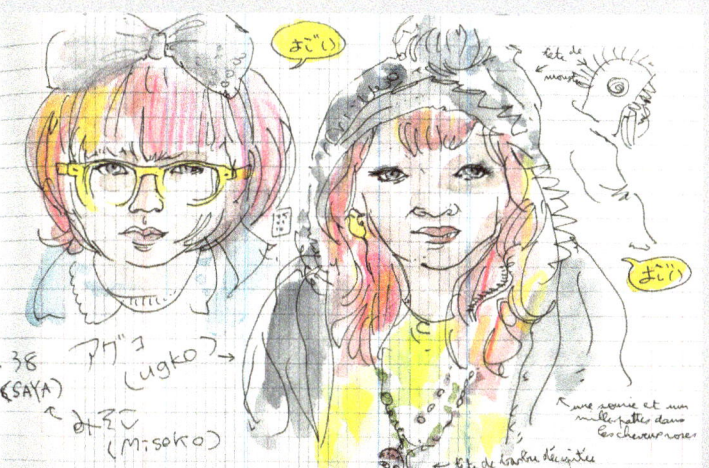

art) meet to be seen and do some shopping. Taking pictures with them is part of the show. Sketching portraits in the street is difficult, because it's hard to ask people to stay standing in front of you, but I really wanted to sketch that cliché costumed Japanese girl. You have to be quick: after fifteen minutes, even the most patient model will get bored.

8.25" x 6" | 21 x 15 cm; Mitsubishi uni PIN 0.1 fine line pen, Daler-Rowney watercolors, Pentel waterbrush, colored pencils, liquid yellow ochre watercolor on handmade sketchbook with a mix of vintage papers inside; fewer than 10 minutes each

ARTIST PROFILE
Lok Jansen

I am an architect-turned-illustrator, living and working in Japan. Most of my sketching happens in the metropolis of Tokyo and deals with urban surroundings and the people who live in them.

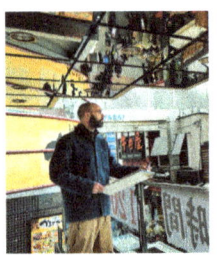

Lok Jansen draws a "roofscape" in Tokyo.

A3 felt-tip pen on paper; 30 minutes

With my city sketches, I'm trying to capture the character of the environments we live in, almost like portraits—but of the metropolis.

When I'm not drawing up on the rooftops, I often ride the subways and trains and watch the flow of people come and go. I do quick, one-minute sketches and try to capture the cities' anonymous inhabitants and the brief chance encounters I have with them on the train.

"I go up on a lot of rooftops and take a lot of walks through the city at night and try to show something of the sensation of living in the sensual, colorful, anonymous embrace of this giant, growing organism."

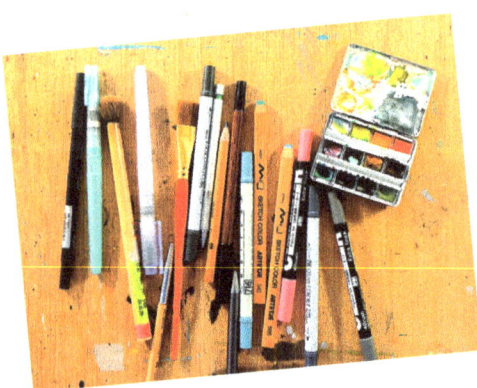

Jansen's sketching tools

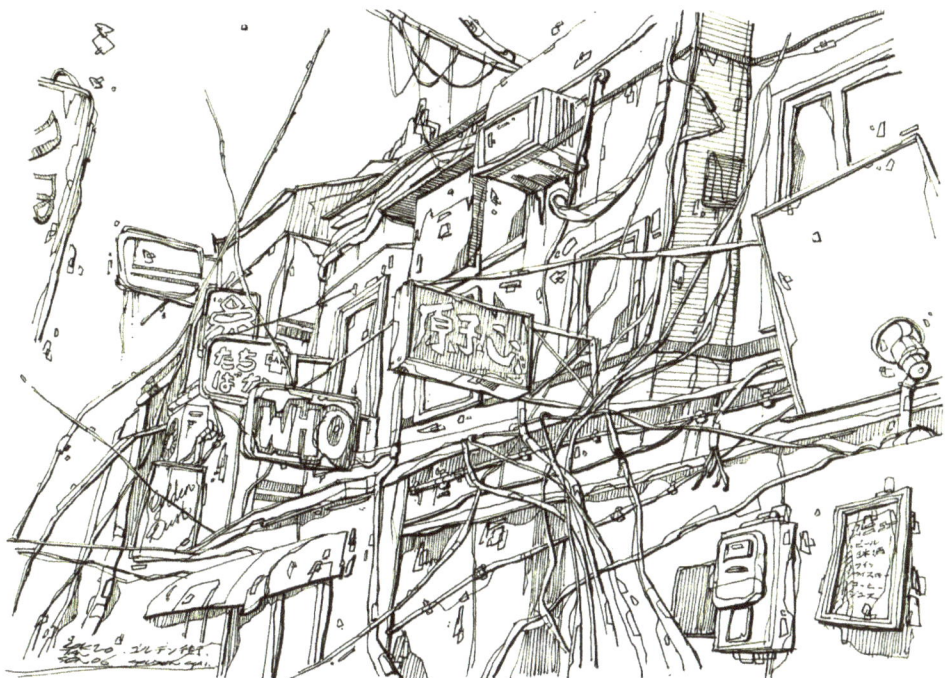

∩ Golden Gai, Tokyo "One of the things I really like to do when sketching is to go into the little side streets and look for the undesigned and unexpected," says Lok Jansen. "Golden Gai, in particular, is a place you can find a wonderful mess of tiny local bars strung together with electrical wires."

Tip "I try to first take in the scene and find what fascinates me about it. I never sketch it out first but try to see the drawing before I put it down on paper." — *Lok Jansen*

B4 (13.9" x 9.8" | 35.3 mm x 25 cm); Mitsubishi brush pen and felt-tip pen; 1 hour

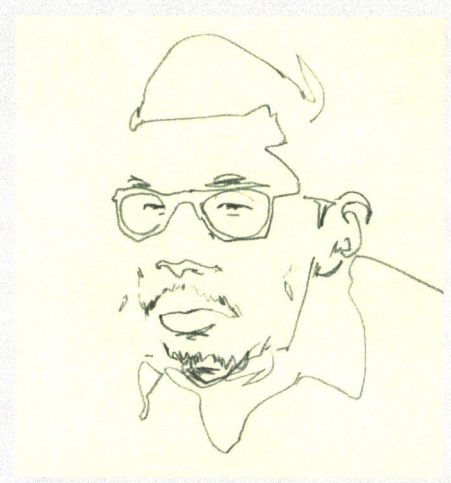

STYLE AND TECHNIQUE

Fleeting Faces on the Subway

by Lok Jansen

I often look first at the people, to see who I'd like to draw and also who is moving around a lot and who is not. I spend some time looking, finding the gesture of the face, and then quickly putting it down on paper. The train moves, people get on and off, block the view, so it's good to be bold and only bother with the essentials. If it's "wrong," you can always start another one. When the drawings start to be too automatic, I'll often switch from pen to pencil. The different medium forces me to refocus on how to translate what I see onto the paper.

A6 (5.8" x 4.1" | 14.8 x 10.5 cm) pocket sketchbook, pen and pencil; 1 minute each

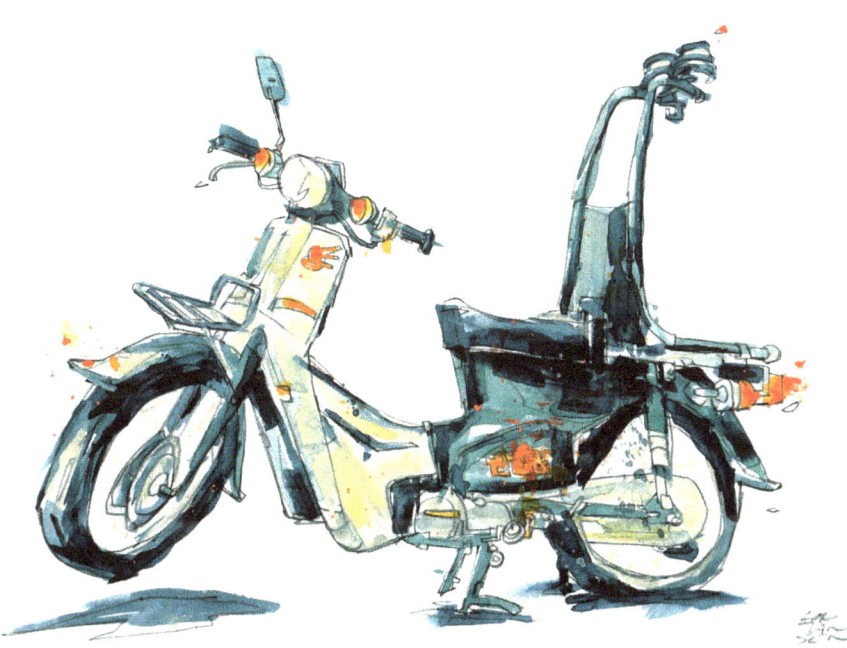

☾ Vroemvroem "This is a typical food delivery bike here in Tokyo, although it's missing some of the springs in the back," Jansen says.

Tip "It helps to have a piece of paper next to you, to test your color and paint/medium balance. Gouache can be unforgiving, but if you spend some time mixing your colors and values till you see it's right, you can put down your strokes boldly." — *Lok Jansen*

A6 5.8" x 4.1" | 14.8 x 10.5 cm; Derwent Drawing colored pencils, Holbein Artists' gouache, on Fabriano Artistico hot-press watercolor paper

AUCKLAND

The New Zealand city of Auckland is built on a dormant volcanic field spread between two harbors. Its population is a cosmopolitan mix of Maoris, Europeans, Polynesians, and Asians. The people and dramatic geography provide excellent vantage points for sketchers.

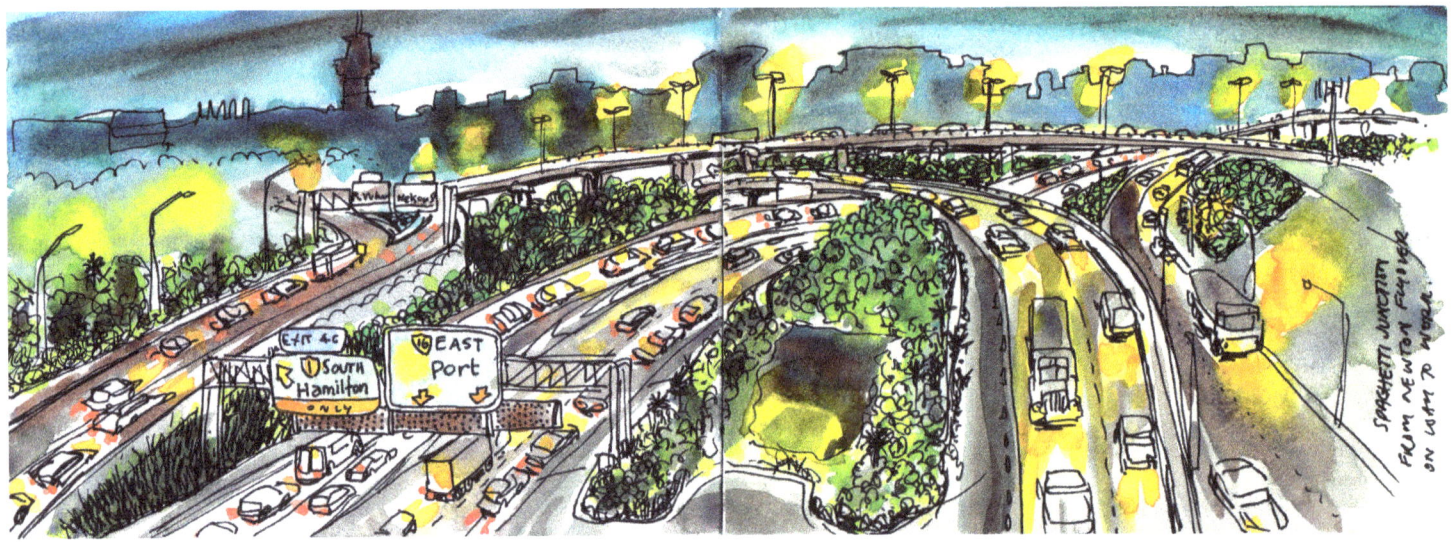

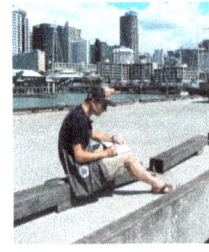

ARTIST PROFILE

Murray Dewhurst

Drawing on location is a refreshing break from the many hours spent on a computer at my graphic design business. It opens my eyes to what's around me and helps me feel more connected to where I live.

New Zealand is known for its clean green alpine, beaches, and bush scenery, but, in reality, something like 85 percent of us live in an urban environment. Wherever the city meets the sea provides excellent sketching opportunities, from the busy shipping port and frequent cruise liners in summer to sailing boats and surfers at the beach.

🎧 Murray Dewhurst sketches at the Viaduct Harbour.

16" x 6" | 40.6 x 15 cm; watercolors and pigment liner; 30 minutes, with some time to apply extra color at home

🎧 **Morning Commute** This is a scene Dewhurst walks past every day on his way to work. "Although not exactly beautiful, I find it a really interesting spectacle," Dewhurst says. "I am constantly amazed that a city this size has such an enormous motorway junction!"

16" x 5.75" | 40.6 x 14.6 cm (spread); Rotring Tikky Graphic 0.5 pen, Winsor & Newton watercolors, Hahnemühle A5 landscape sketchbook; 45 minutes – 1 hour

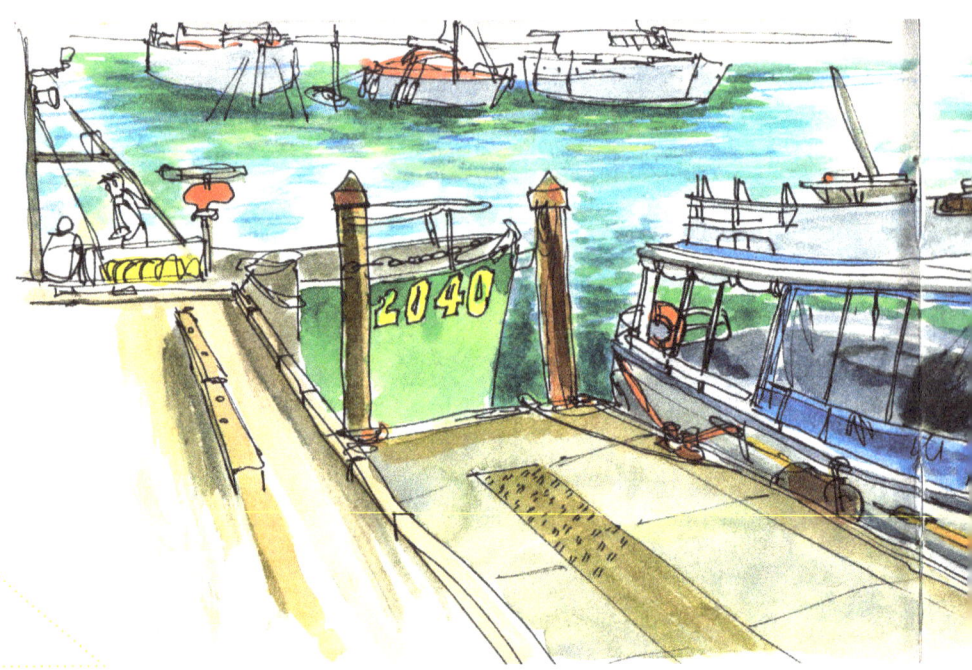

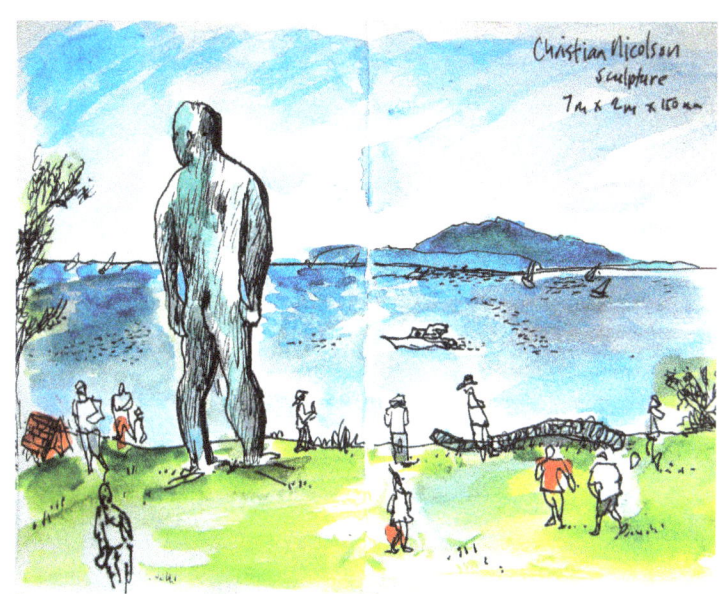

Christian Nicolson
Sculpture
7 m x 2 m x 150 mm

⋒ **Giant Sculpture** This impressive, 23-foot (7 m) -tall, nude wooden figure by Christian Nicolson looks across the Hauraki Gulf to Rakino Island and the Coromandel peninsula.

Tip "I quickly got the scene down, with one eye on my kids, who were so excited by all the unusual and interesting works that they would run furiously to each one, giving me very little time to draw!" — *Murray Dewhurst*

8" x 6" | 20 x 15 cm; Rotring Tikky Graphic 0.5 pen, Winsor & Newton watercolors, Hahnemühle A6 sketchbook; 10 minutes

⊃ **Viaduct Harbour**
This is a classic harbor-meets-city view across the Viaduct Basin toward downtown Auckland.

Tip "Inspired to try a 'tall' sketch, after seeing other urban sketchers work in that format, I discovered it's quite difficult. To hold the sketchbook vertically isn't natural or steady, so it's very easy to make your vertical structures look a bit wayward.
— *Murray Dewhurst*

16" x 5.75" | 40.6 x 14.6 cm (spread); Rotring Tikky Graphic 0.5 pen, Winsor & Newton watercolors, Hahnemühle A5 landscape sketchbook; 1 hour

"A frustrated traveler stuck at the bottom of the world, I couldn't believe my luck when, one day, I stumbled across the work of other urban sketchers online."

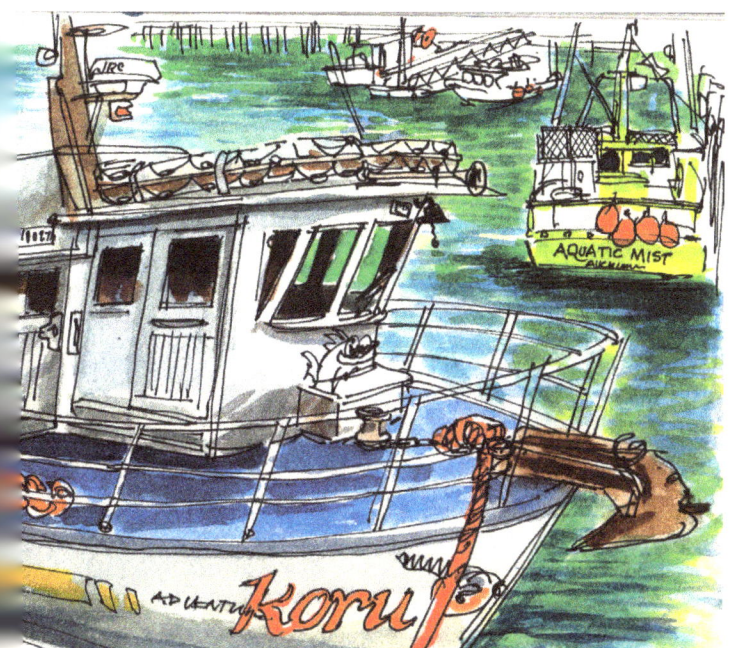

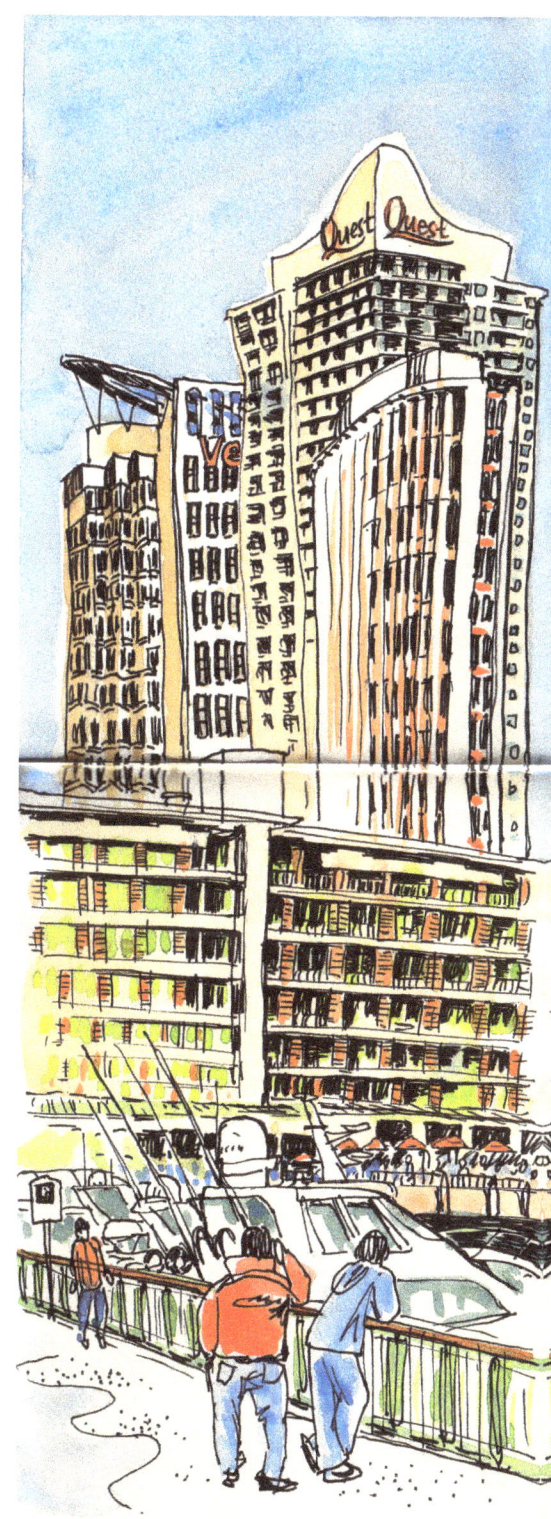

SYDNEY

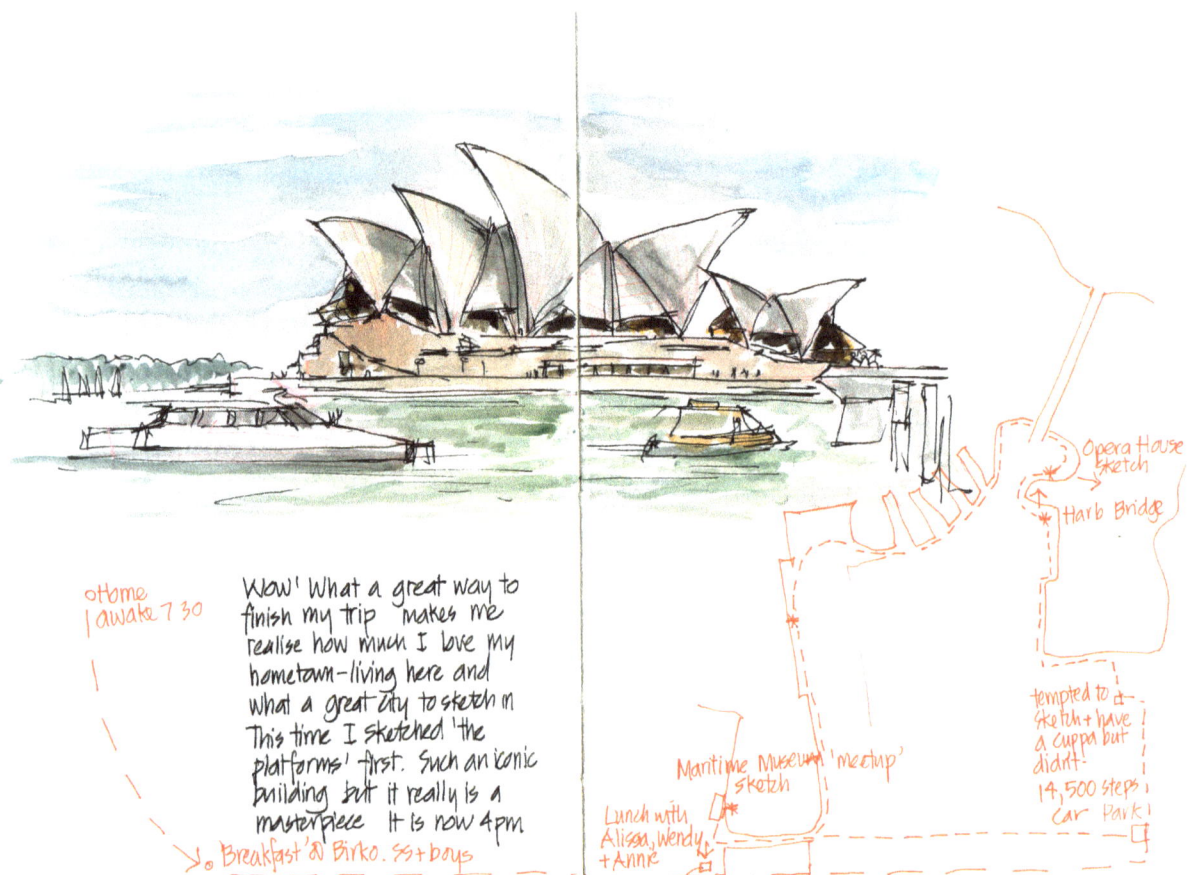

World-famous icons, such as the Opera House and the Harbour Bridge, stunning beaches, a lively downtown, and city parks make Sydney an urban-sketching–friendly city. "Sketching and the outdoor lifestyle of many Sydney-siders go together so well," says local architect Liz Steel.

"Living in such a beautiful city, with great weather all year round, I have no excuse for not getting out to sketch."

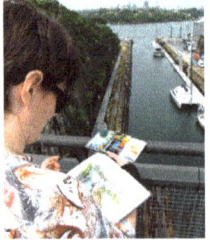

ARTIST PROFILE
Liz Steel

As an architect, I draw all the time, but these are mainly quick working sketches of my own designs and not what I see in front of me. The frustration of numerous failed attempts to keep a sketchbook while traveling finally led me to sketch regularly to get "in training" for a long trip to Europe. But it has turned out that this almost-daily habit has become an end in itself. In addition to filling sketchbooks as a visual record of my day-to-day life, I often go on Saturday excursions specifically to find a new area of Sydney to sketch.

Sketching is the ultimate way of understanding and recording my experience of buildings—it gives me insight into the mind of the original architect. I have a particular interest in European architectural history and love drawing Renaissance or over-the-top baroque architecture, such as the work of Francesco Borromini.

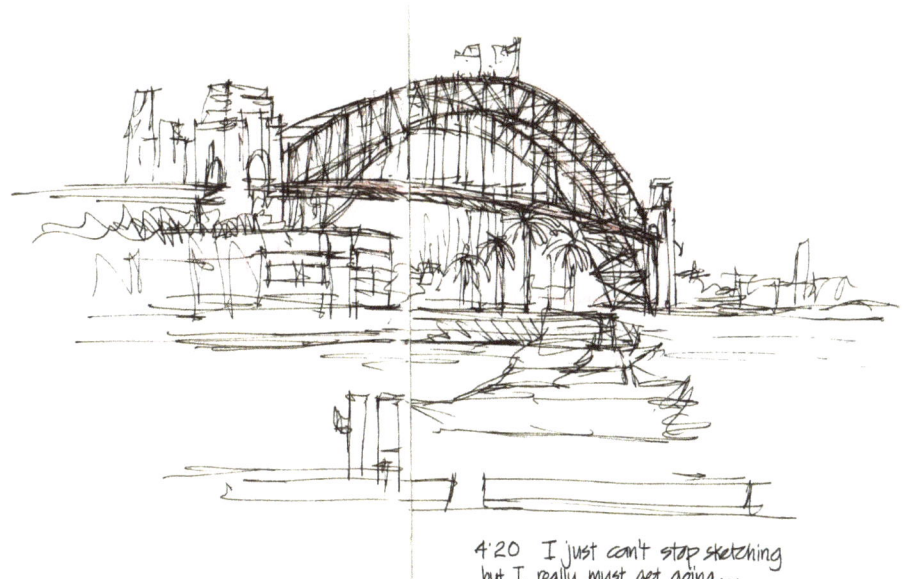

4:20 I just can't stop sketching but I really must get going...

⟳ Sydney Harbour Bridge This 1930s arched steel bridge, anchored by four granite pylons, sits perfectly in the city's harbor and attracts a constant string of people doing "the bridge climb," says Steel.

Tip "When drawing a complicated trussed structure such as a steel bridge, make sure you understand the structure first and draw that, rather than getting lost in all the members you can see." — *Liz Steel*

8" x 8.5" | 20 x 21.6 cm; medium Lamy Safari pen with Noodler's ink on Daler-Rowney 150-gsm Ebony sketchbook; 15 minutes

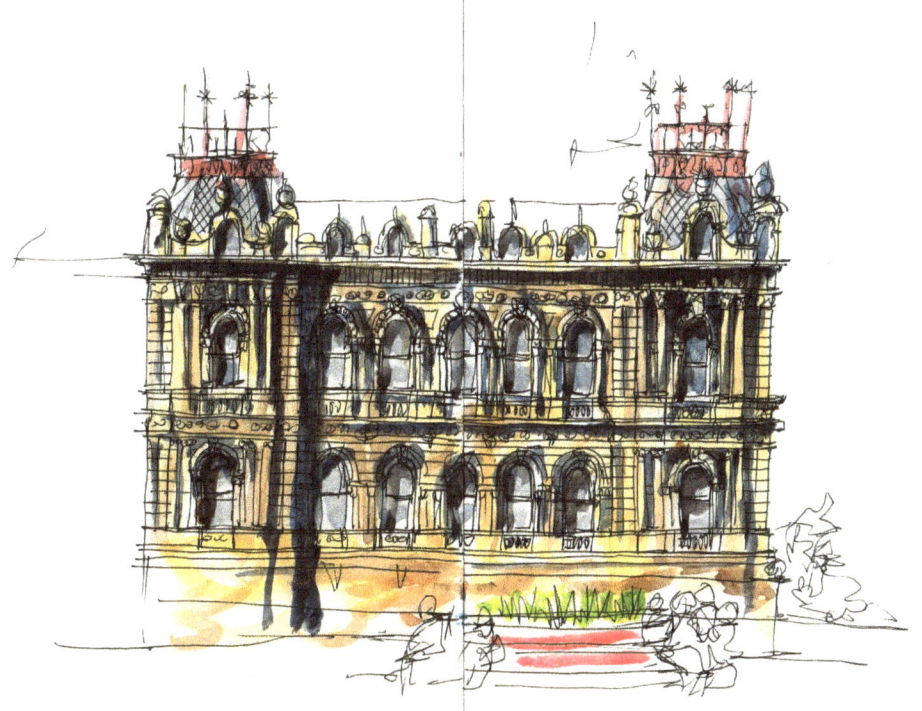

⟳ Sydney Town Hall Steel purposely went into the center of Sydney to find a building that was most like Paris to sketch. "In fact, the town hall proved more complex than any building I had sketched in Paris, and this is only the side view!" Steel says.

Tip "For complicated buildings, I find it helpful to do a diagrammatic 'mud map' of the main rows, the columns, the windows—the bones of the building—to simplify the structure." — *Liz Steel*

8" x 8.5" | 20 x 21.6 cm; medium Lamy Safari pen with Noodler's ink, Daniel Smith and Winsor & Newton Artists watercolors, Pitt artist pen (superfine, color 188) on Daler-Rowney 150-gsm Ebony sketchbook; 1 hour

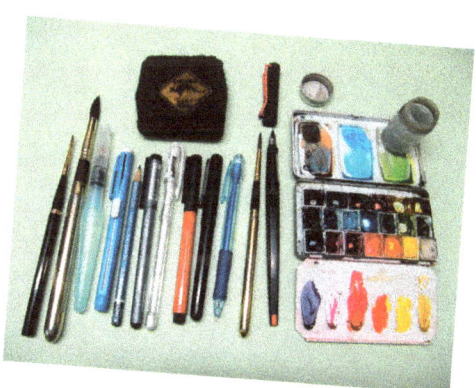

🎧 Steel's sketching tools

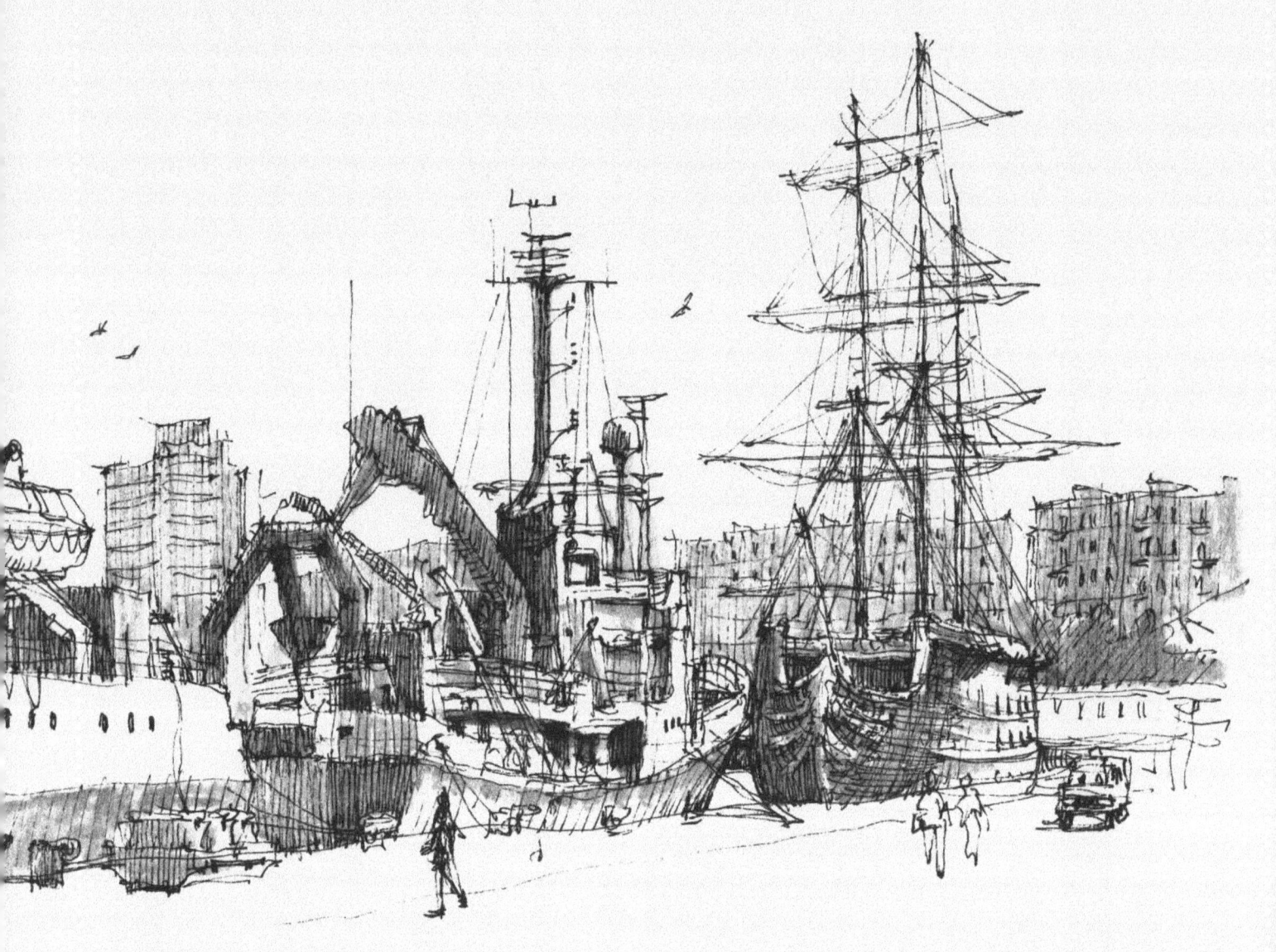

– Luis Ruiz

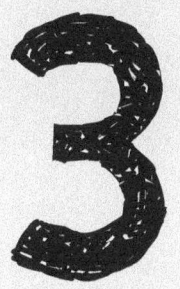

DRAWING INSPIRATION

Sketching opportunities abound, even where you least expect them. You might be drawn to the signage of an old storefront or captivated by that industrial site on the edge of town that everyone considers an eyesore. To get started as an urban sketcher, here are some themes for inspiration.

SKYLINES, CITYSCAPES, AND PANORAMAS

Whether they're drawing from a window, a roof, or a hill, urban sketchers relish the opportunity to draw above ground level. The effort to find an elevated location pays off when you can draw a panoramic view. Belgian architect Gérard Michel spent more than thirty hours perched on a roof to create an arresting 360-degree rendition of the city of Liège. "His tremendous panorama inspired me to forget my vertigo and venture onto my roof," says Brooklyn-based illustrator Stephen Gardner, who saw Michel's work online. The sketches in this chapter might inspire you, too.

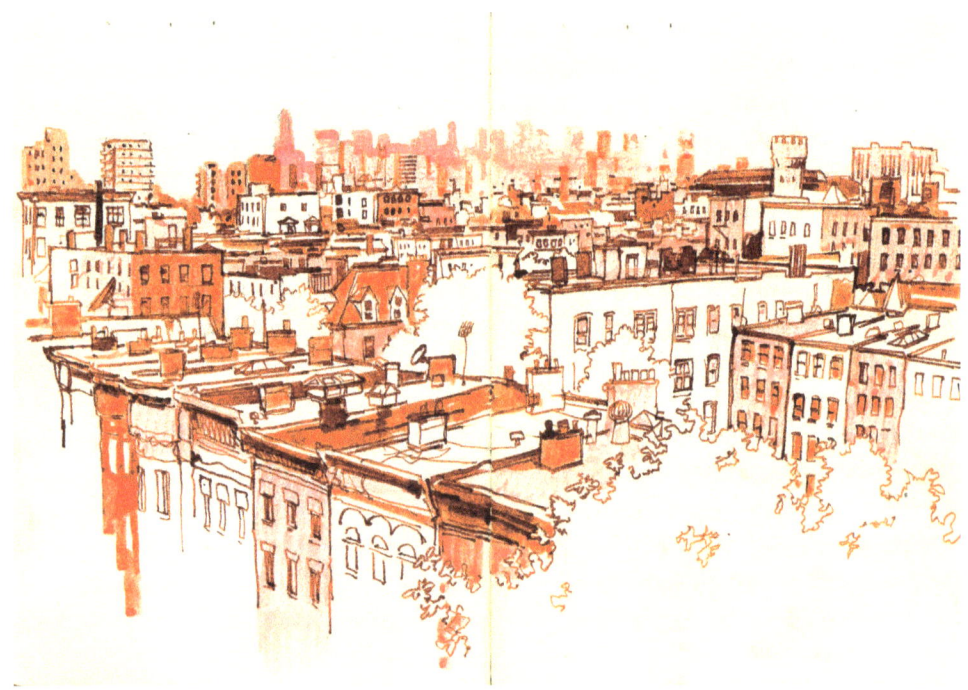

⋒ **Up on the Roof in Brooklyn** "I took a kitchen stool, my radio, and a cup of tea up to the roof with me," says Stephen Gardner. "I loved the peace and quiet I experienced while drawing this one."

Tip "I did a light pencil sketch to block in my composition then started to work over it. Drawing with a ruling pen forces you to consider each mark before you make it; there is no going back." — *Stephen Gardner*

16" x 11.5" | 40.6 x 29 cm; Pelikan brown ink and ruling pen on Moleskine A4 sketchbook; 1 hour

STYLE AND TECHNIQUE

Drawing a 360-degree Panorama

by Gérard Michel

I decided to sketch 45 degrees on each page. I began by putting reference marks on my paper with my pencil to indicate the number of "pencil lengths" for 45 degrees on a horizontal line. Then, I began my drawing with the same standard (my pencil) for the heights. In my panorama, the most important thing for me was the density. To find the relationship between all the things I had to draw—it was important to take measures. Without measures, the mistakes would be numerous.

Eight pages A4 (8.3" x 11.7" | 21 x 29.7 cm); Staedtler pigment liners on Seawhite of Brighton sketchbook, stitched together later in Photoshop; eight sessions, 4 hours each, for a total of 32 hours

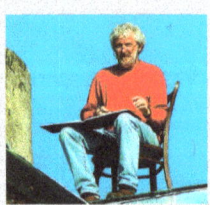

⋒ Belgian architect Gérard Michel had to do some repairs on the roof of his daughter's house and was impressed with the view. When the repairs were done, the sketching job started.

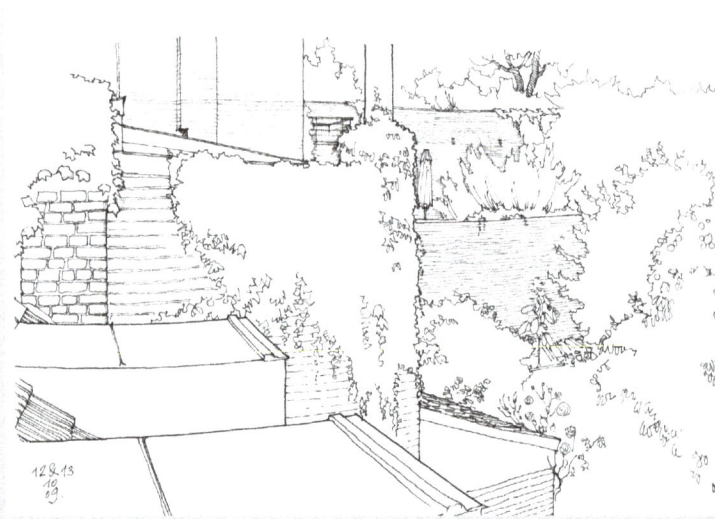

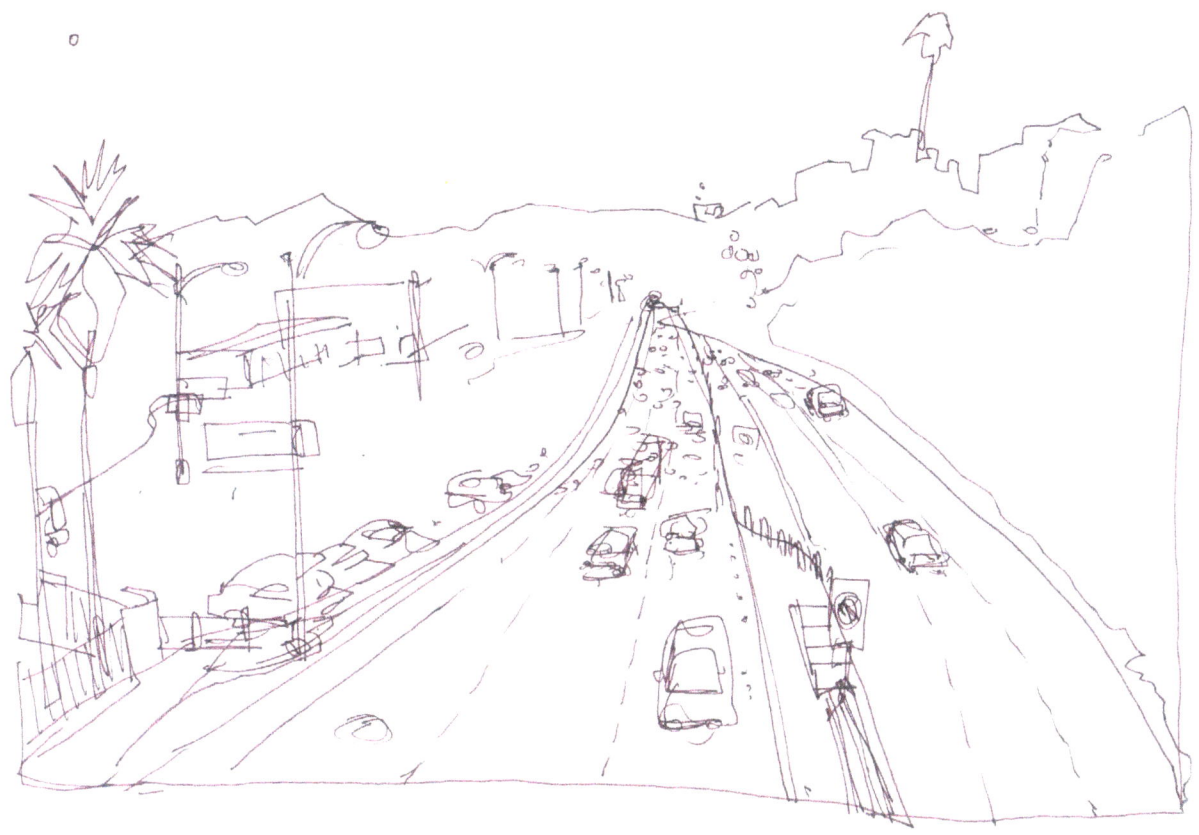

☾ **Pacific Coast Highway in Santa Monica, California**

Santa Monica illustrator Shiho Nakaza drew this sketch standing on a pedestrian bridge that connects a cliffside park with the Santa Monica beaches. "The sun just set minutes before I started drawing—the small dot on the top left corner is Venus, the first 'star' visible at night," she says.

Tip "I drew the road first and the background silhouette of trees and mountains second.
— Shiho Nakaza

7" x 5" | 18 x 12.5 cm; Uni-ball Signo .38 pen (brown-black) on Holbein Multi-drawing Book; about 10 minutes

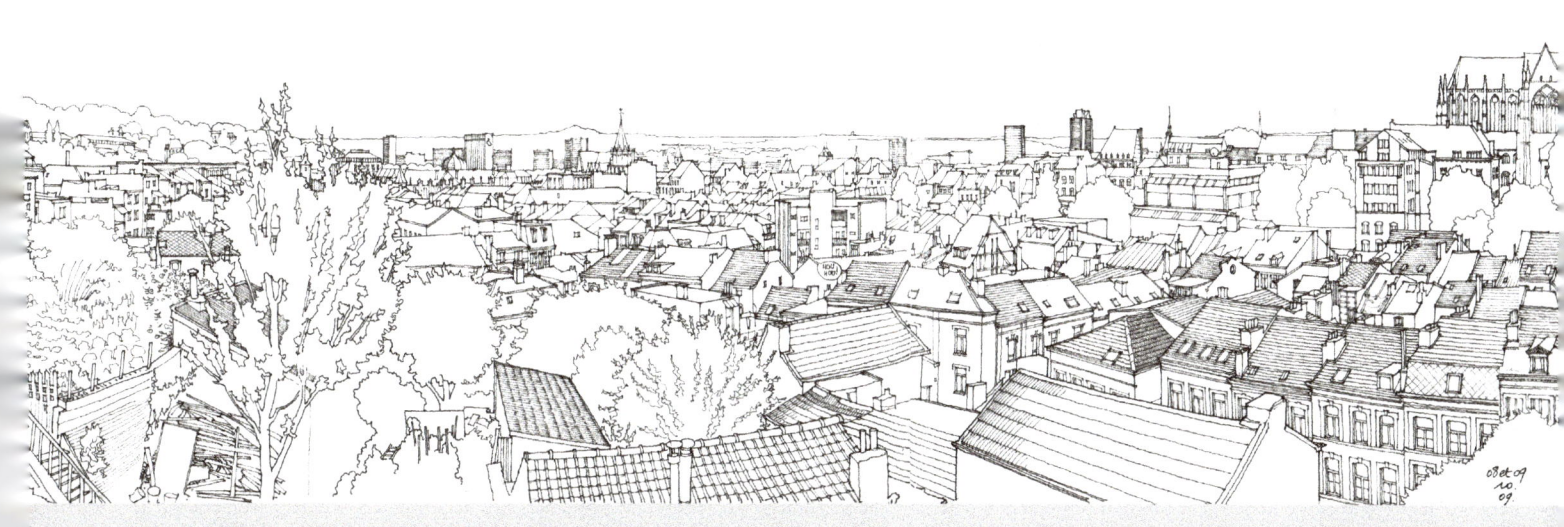

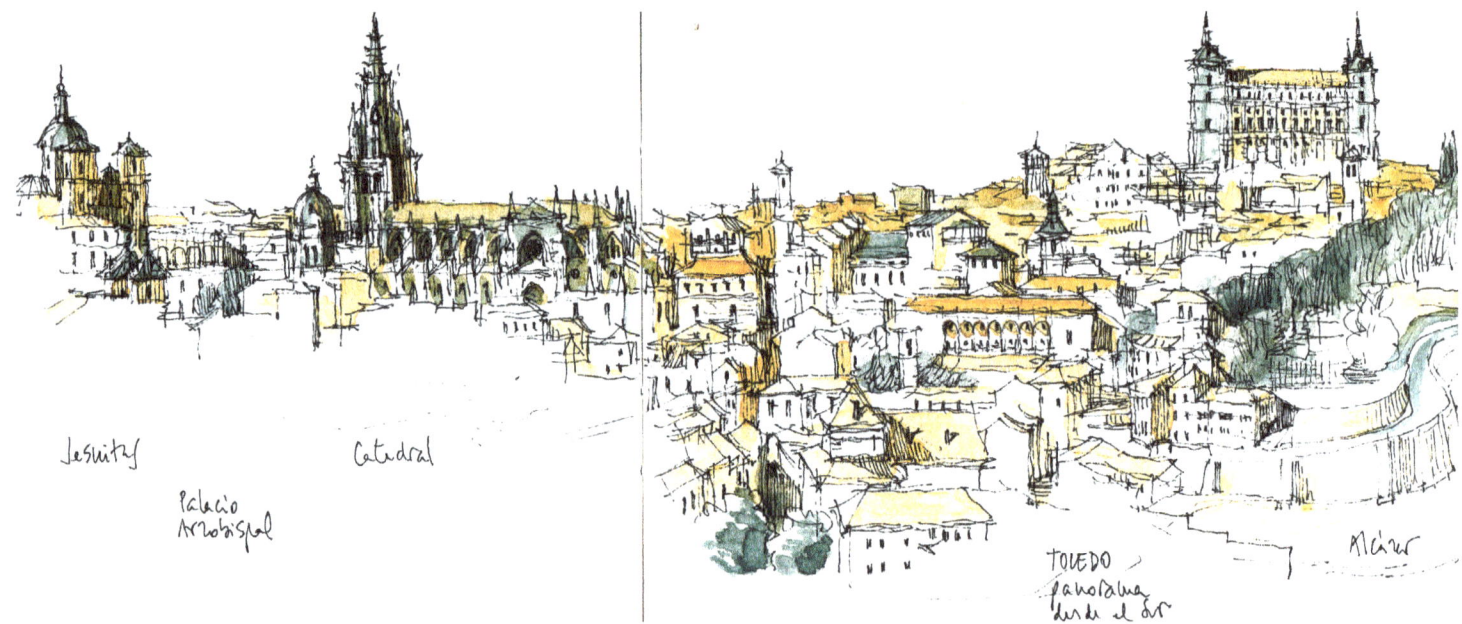

Jesuitas Catedral

Palacio
Arzobispal

TOLEDO
panorama
desde el ar

Alcázar

⌂ Toledo, Spain, Panorama One of Toledo's highlights is the majestic view of the city from the bank of the Tagus River. Málaga sketcher Luis Ruiz says you could sit here for hours under the shade of a mulberry tree and just watch how the light and shadows change and produce magic effects on the city's intricate architecture.

Tip "When facing this kind of view, you get so much information, that being selective becomes necessary. I started drawing the outline and continued drawing the main monuments; only then did I draw the rest." — *Luis Ruiz*

11.75" x 5" | 30 x 12.5 cm; .05 Staedtler pigment liner, Tombow brush pens on Moleskine sketchbook; 75 minutes

⊃ Salzburg before Sunset German architect Florian Afflerbach spent the end of an early spring day on an overview drawing from one of the hills around Salzburg, a city surrounded by mountains.

Tip "When drawing a city silhouette, take care on the proportions of the important landmarks, and don't count all the windows." — *Florian Afflerbach*

19.5" x 8" | 50 x 20 cm; 4B Faber-Castell pencil, Schmincke watercolors, #4 and #6 da Vinci brushes on Boesner 170-gsm sketchbook; 1 hour

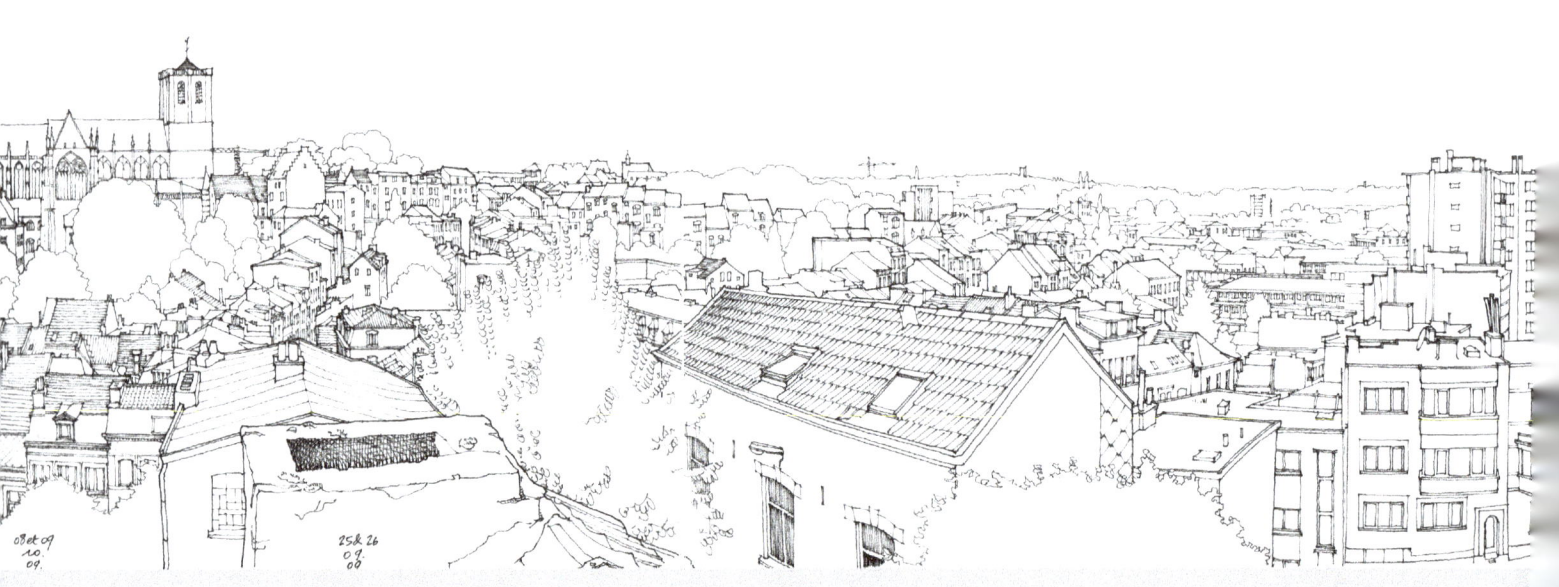

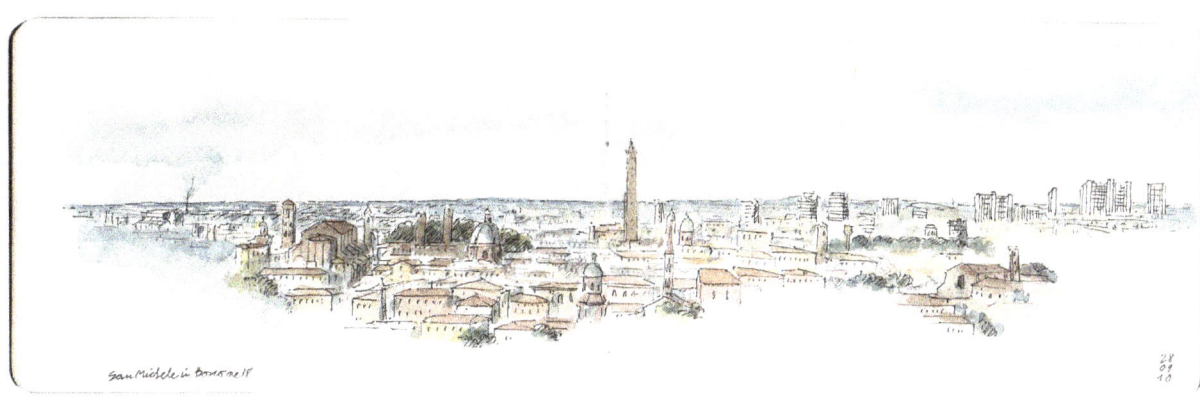

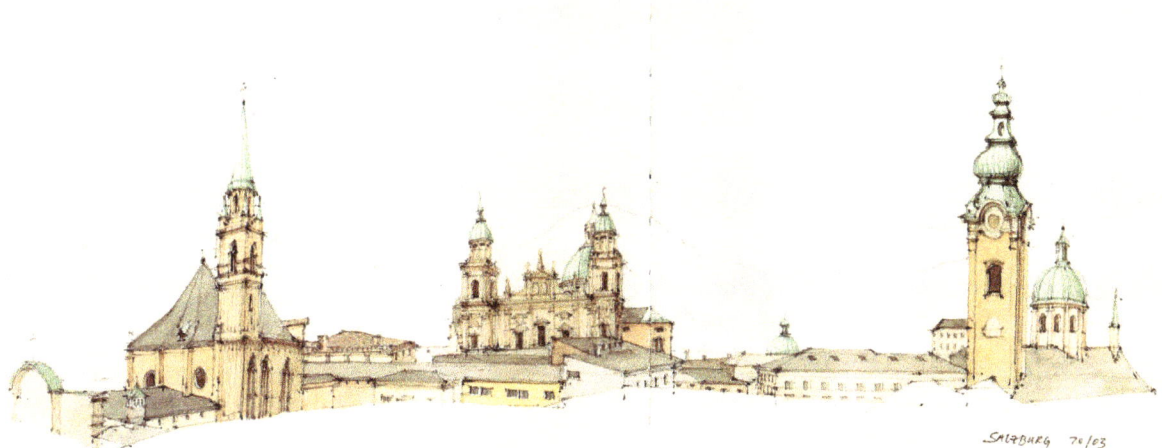

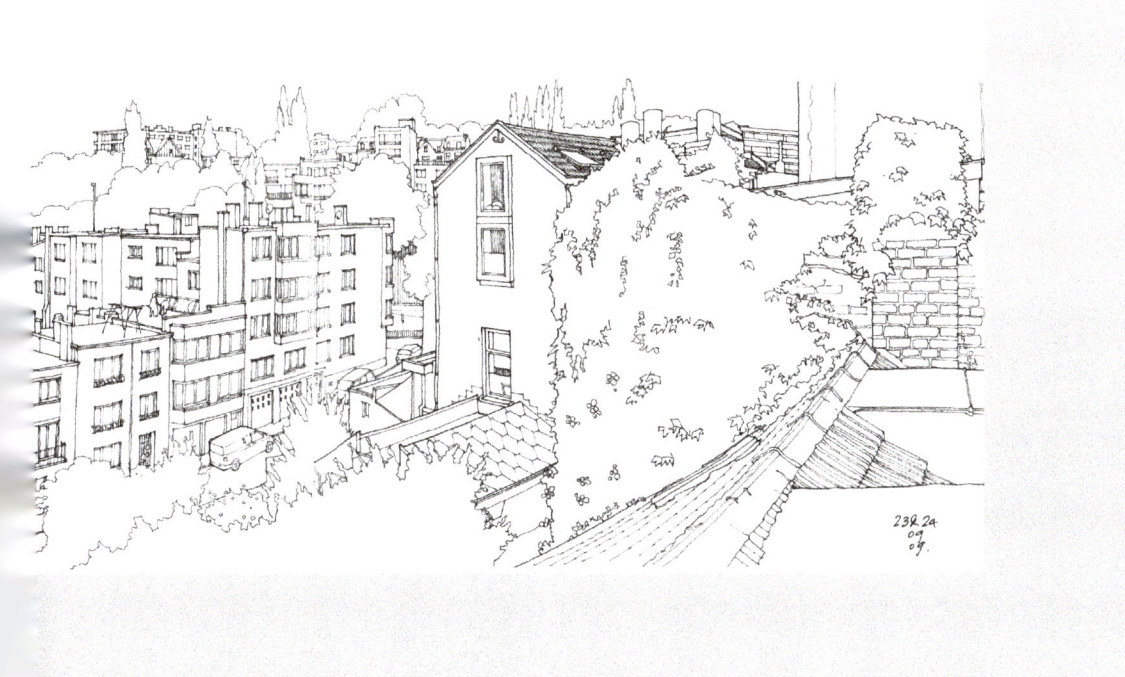

◑ **The Tallest Tower in Bologna** On the right are the towers of the Kenzo Tange fair district, which are shorter than the 318-foot (97 m) Asinelli medieval tower.

Tip "The main problem with sketching a panorama is deciding how much of it will fit on the page. It should not be necessary to turn our head or even the eyes while drawing, meaning that we are trying to include more than our 30-degree (max 60-degree) scope of vision. Being far away from the subject makes it easier to not distort it."
— *Simonetta Capecchi*

8.25" x 5" | 21 x 12.5 cm; Mitsubishi Uni-ball ultra-fine, waterproof pen, Winsor & Newton watercolors, and Pentel waterbrush on Moleskine large watercolor book; about 20 minutes

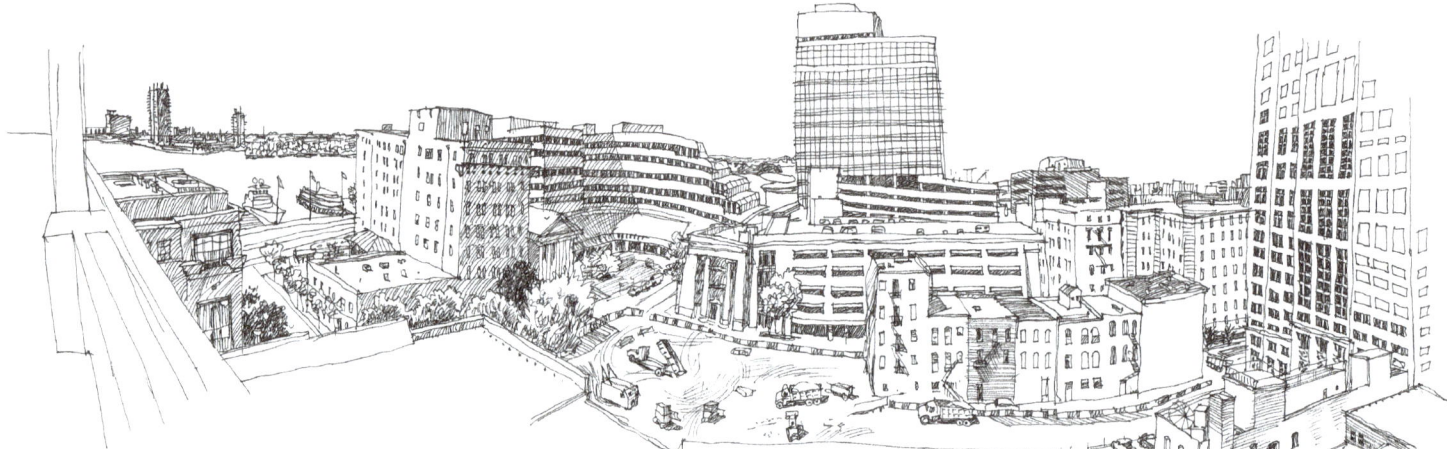

☊ **Norfolk Skyline** Walt Taylor considers sketching a form of self-medication. "If it weren't for the roof of that parking garage, I might have strangled one or more of my coworkers when I worked in downtown Norfolk," he says. "As soon as lunch hour hit, I would bolt for the stairwell. As I drew window after tiny window, my blood pressure would gradually drop to normal levels."

Tip "For this drawing, I literally started at the right side of the page and worked my way leftward, until I reached the other edge, which accounts for the idiosyncratic perspective."
— *Walt Taylor*

About 14" | 35.6 cm; Rotring Artpen on Strathmore Drawing sketchbook; 1 hour

☋ **Market Street, High and Low, San Francisco** The Humboldt Bank Building is one of the first things Marc Taro Holmes drew in San Francisco. Three years later, he discovered a new vantage point from the View lounge, on the 39th floor of the Marriott hotel. "You can see a panoramic view of the city and the Bay Bridge. It's a great spot to watch the sun set and the city lights come up," he says.

Tip "This image is three separate drawings combined. I just overlap the pages and draw right over the seam, knowing I'll combine them later in Adobe Photoshop."
— *Marc Taro Holmes*

Three 8.5" x 11" | 21.6 x 28 cm sheets combined; Uni-Ball disposable writing pen and Pentel GFKP brush pen on 100-lb. cardstock printer paper from the office supply shop

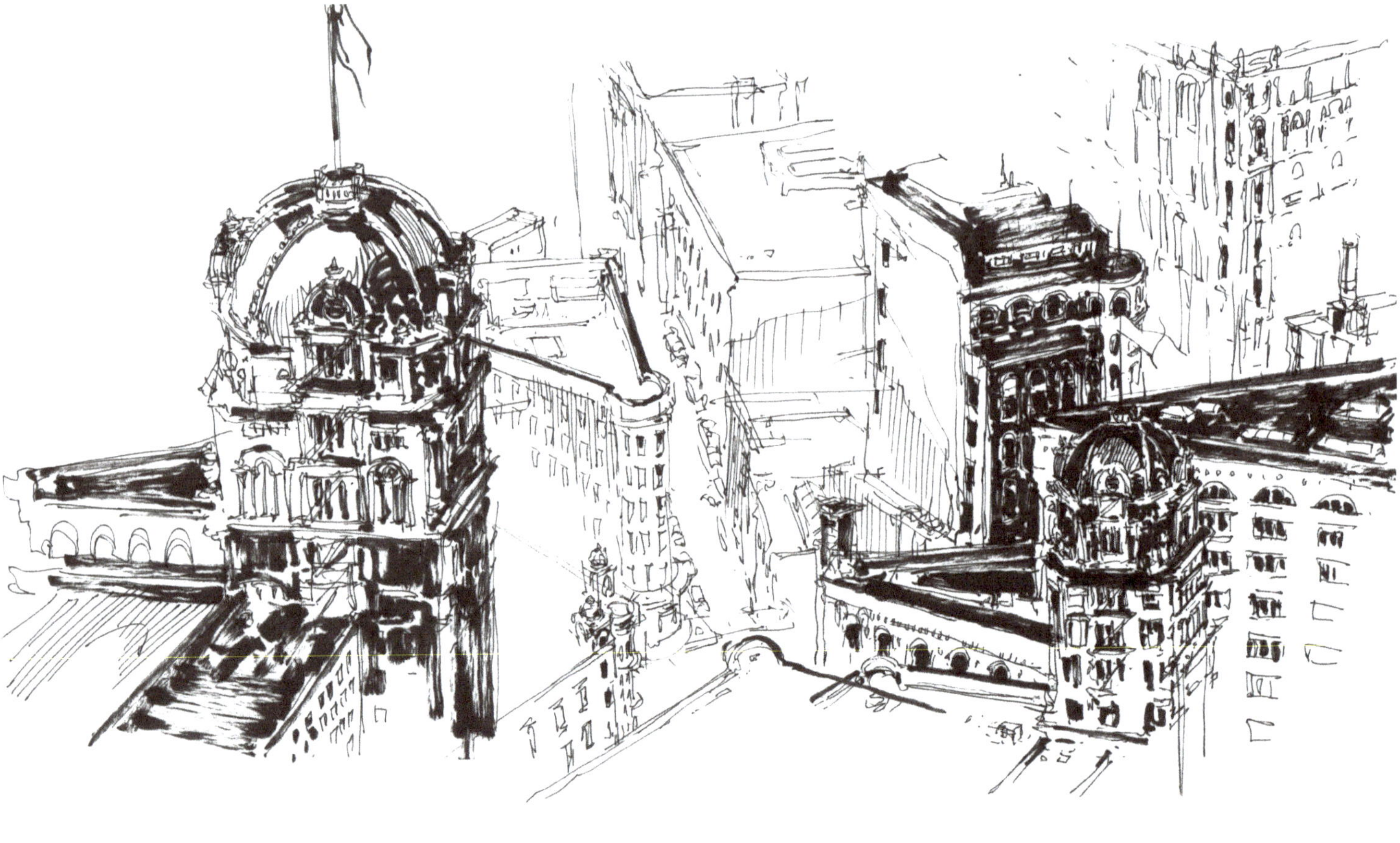

STYLE AND TECHNIQUE

Catania from the Top

by Omar Jaramillo

In a sketch, the line is the main element; with watercolors, shapes are the most important part. I want to catch in my watercolors the spontaneity of the moment—that is why I avoid using a pencil and directly apply the color to the surface. I painted elements in the background and in shadow with cerulean blue and in the foreground with a warm color. I let both colors approach and mix on the paper and used this mixture to create more elements. Don't overwork it, and let it dry before continuing.

Choose a 'king,' or an element in the skyline that is the center of the sketch—not necessarily in the middle of the drawing. Elements close to that center should be more accurate, more colored and detailed.

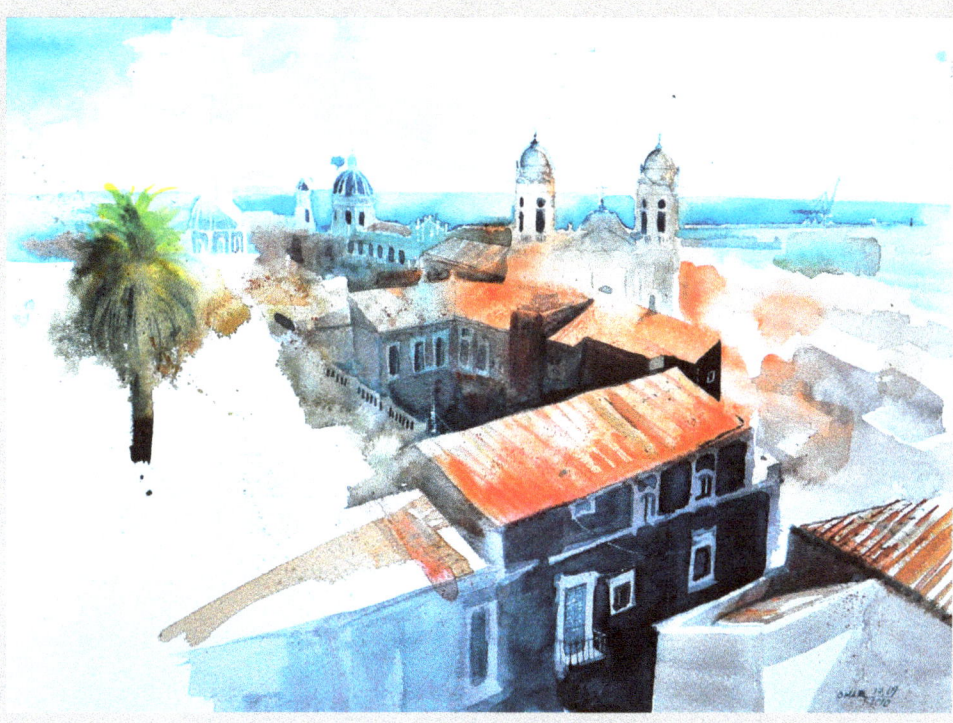

15.75" x 19.5" | 40 x 50 cm; White Nights watercolor set, medium-size French watercolor brush, #22 da Vinci Cosmotop Spin brush, sable brush, flat brushes, and Swiss knife on Daler-Rowney 300-gsm "the Langton" watercolor block; 2 hours

5.25 "x 8.25" | 13 x 21 cm; Faber-Castell Pitt artist pen (sepia), Winsor & Newton pocket watercolor set and waterbrush on Moleskine watercolor book; 20 minutes

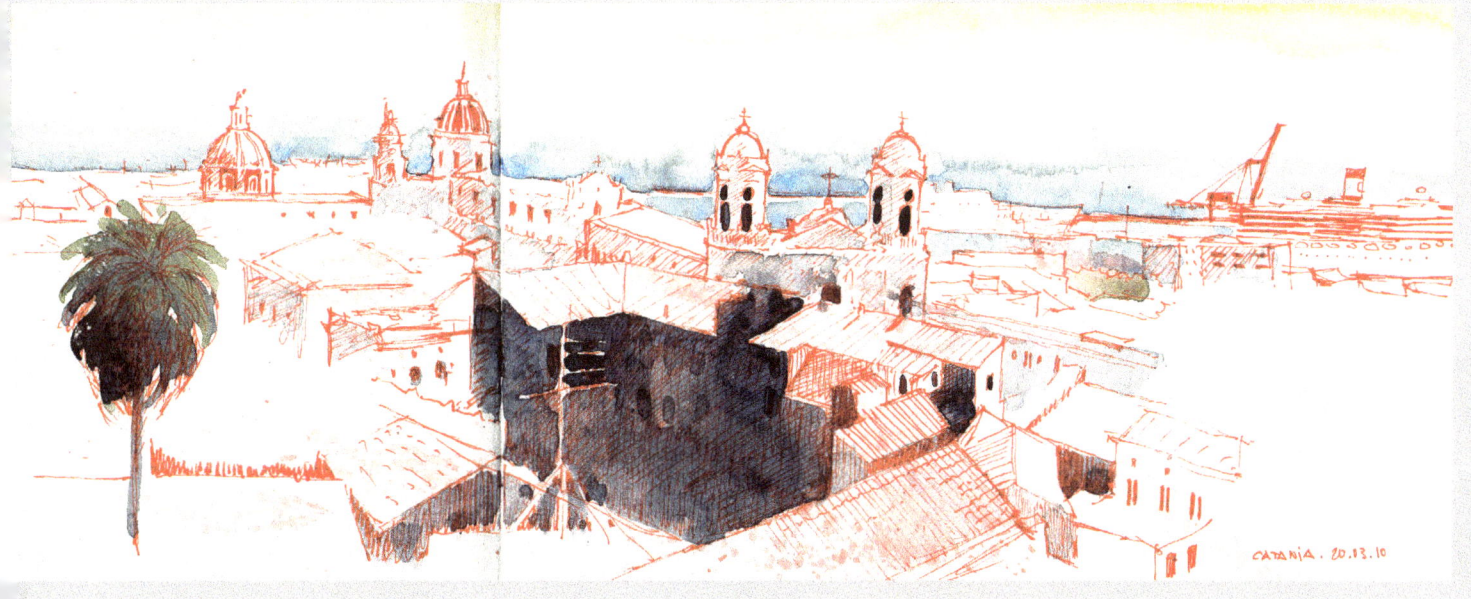

BUILDINGS AND ARCHITECTURE

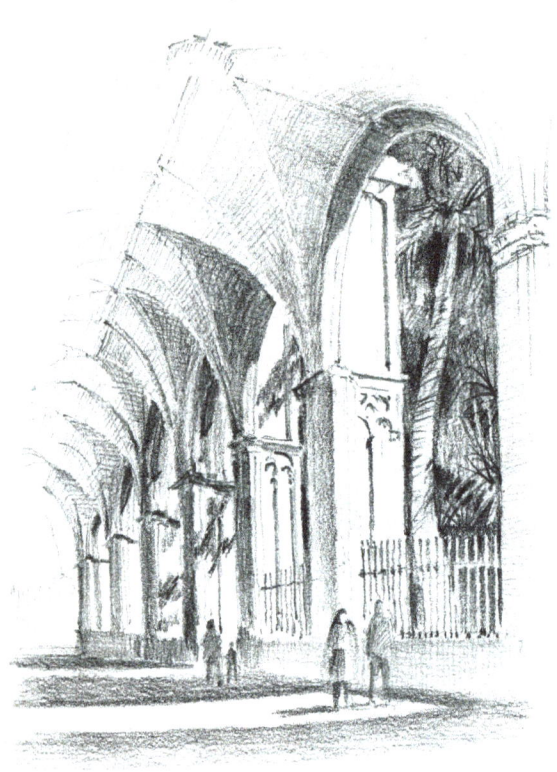

⋒ Barcelona Cathedral Cloister When tackling buildings, Matthew Brehm recommends a patient approach in setting up the perspective and blocking out the entire sketch in light pencil lines. "If the sketch is set up properly, it's relatively easy to indicate detail and value," he says.

5" x 8" | 12.5 x 20 cm; Staedtler Mars Lumograph 2B on Moleskine watercolor book; 20 minutes

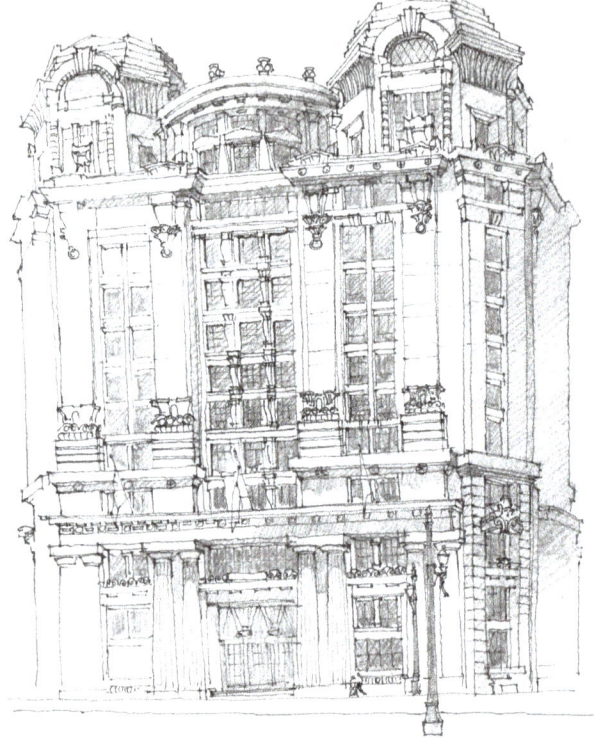

⋒ Ramos de Azevedo The symmetrical domes and stylized owls, of this building in São Paulo's city center caught Eduardo Bajzek's attention.

Tip "I love drawing this type of historic building here in São Paulo, because I keep dreaming about the history of the construction and the time it was made." — *Eduardo Bajzek*

11.5" x 8" | 29 x 20 cm; .005 and .01 Micron pens, KOH-I-NOOR pencils on Hahnemühle 140-gsm sketchbook; 2.5 hours

With buildings, more than with any other urban sketching subject, it pays to really study the subject beforehand, rather than rushing to put pen to paper. While it's easy to fake the shape of a tree, the wrong perspective in a streetscape will be easily noticeable. Most sketchers agree that patience is step number one for drawing architecture.

STYLE AND TECHNIQUE

Drawing Façades

by Alvaro Carnicero

Córdoba's Downtown Plaza de Las Tendillas is considered the center of Córdoba. Its buildings, mostly built in the first half of the twentieth century, with these types of "hats" or tops, are a demonstration of the class and pride of the Córdobans but without any excesses or overly modern, spectacular elements. One of the secrets is to be organized and patient. I think that with a basic technique, in which we go from less to more, you can obtain very good results.

61" (unfolded) x 8.25" | 155 x 21 cm; Pilot G-Tec C4 (black ink) and Pentel Pocket Brush with watered ink, Moleskine large Japanese sketchbook; 10 hours

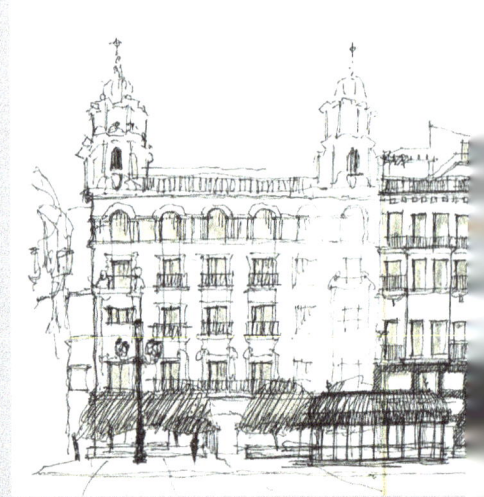

STYLE AND TECHNIQUE

Bangkok's Window Strokes

by Asnee Tasna

A felt-tip pen draws thick, even lines and is most suitable for scenes that require expression of shadow, especially buildings. The thick lines give such an effect of depth that a glass window of a building, with shadows thrown in, can be done with only two lines, instead of four! A single line across the width of a distant building is good enough to express the entire row of window openings for the whole floor.

7" x 7" | 18 x 18 cm; black Pentel Sign Pen, Van Gogh 24-pan, super-fine watercolor set on recycled blank-page book with spiral wire spine; about 20 minutes for line work and 15 minutes on color wash at home

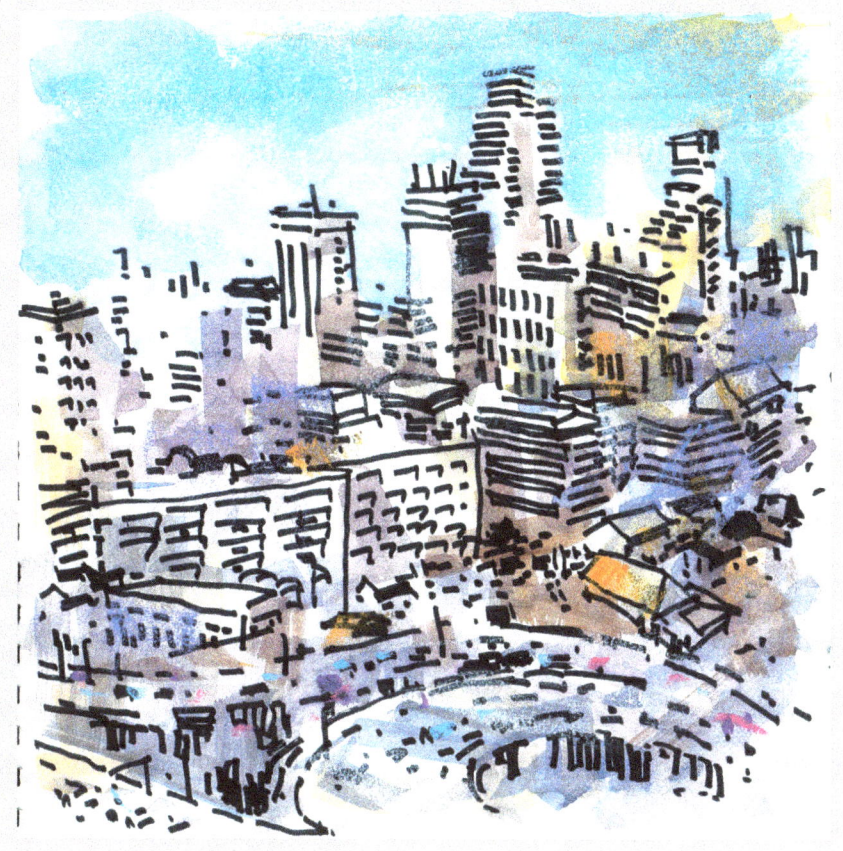

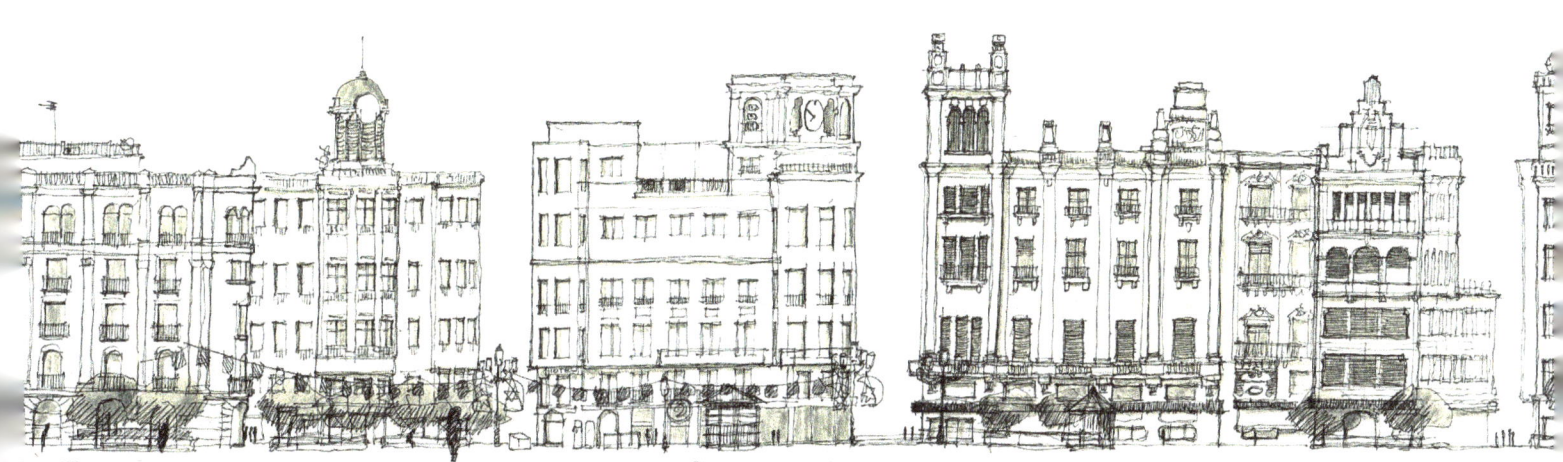

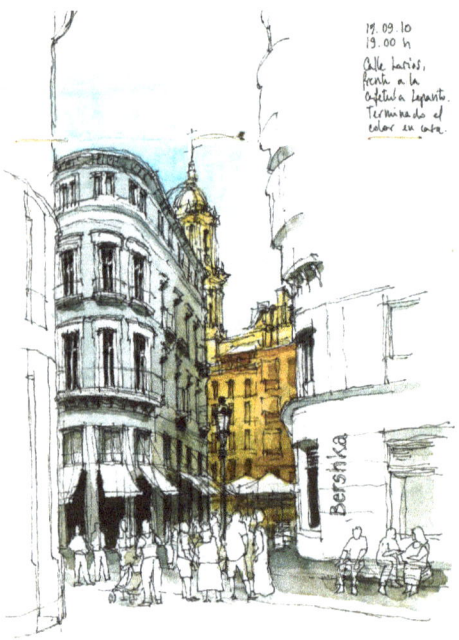

♪ Calle Larios Larios is the main commercial street in the center of Málaga. Ruiz loves how its space flows through perpendicular narrow alleys toward the bulk of the cathedral.

Tip "I like to execute the washes with economy of color—I just highlight the parts I consider important and leave the rest aside." — *Luis Ruiz*

7.75" x 10.25" | 19.5 x 26 cm; .05 Staedtler pigment liner, Rembrandt watercolor set on Hahnemühle sketchbook; 75 minutes

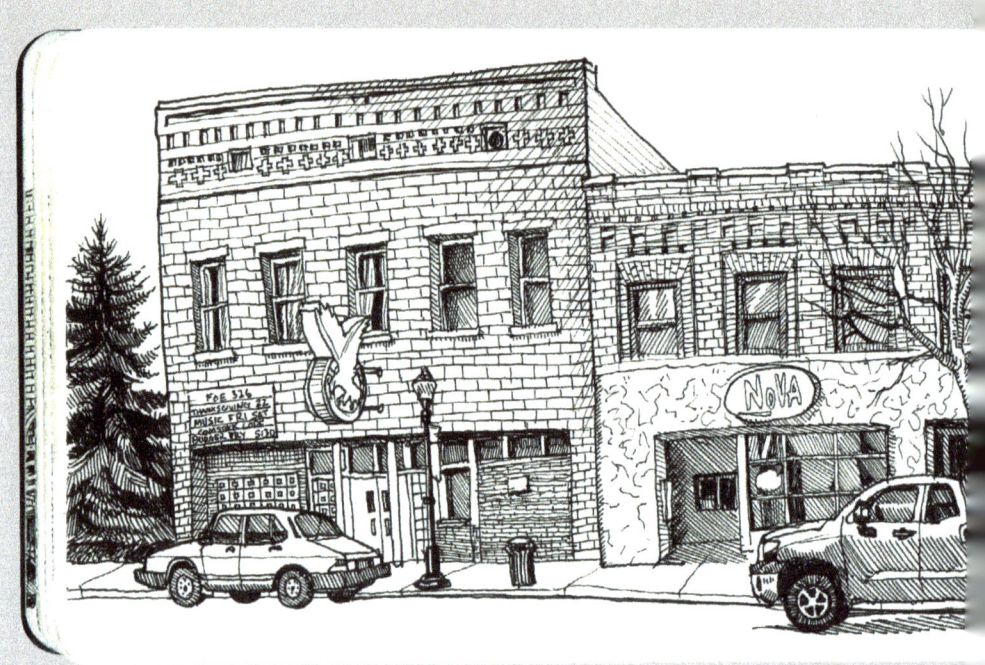

CITY LANDMARK

Bozeman's Main Street

Inspired by the work of Ed Ruscha and Matteo Pericoli, artist Paul Heaston sketched every building on Bozeman's Main Street between Grand and Rouse Avenues, first facing north, then facing south, all in a 3.5" x 5.5" (9 x 28 cm) sketchbook. All the drawings were done onsite, from benches, a portable chair, or while standing.

"For nine months, I worked through rain, snow, and sleet, wasp stings, and sunburns," Heaston says. "I peered between parked cars and curious onlookers." The project includes more than sixty-seven buildings, 109 cars and motorcycles, hundreds of windows, and thousands of individual bricks."

3.5" x 11" | 9 x 28 cm; Staedtler pigment liner pens, "pen-and-ink" brand sketchbook; 9 months

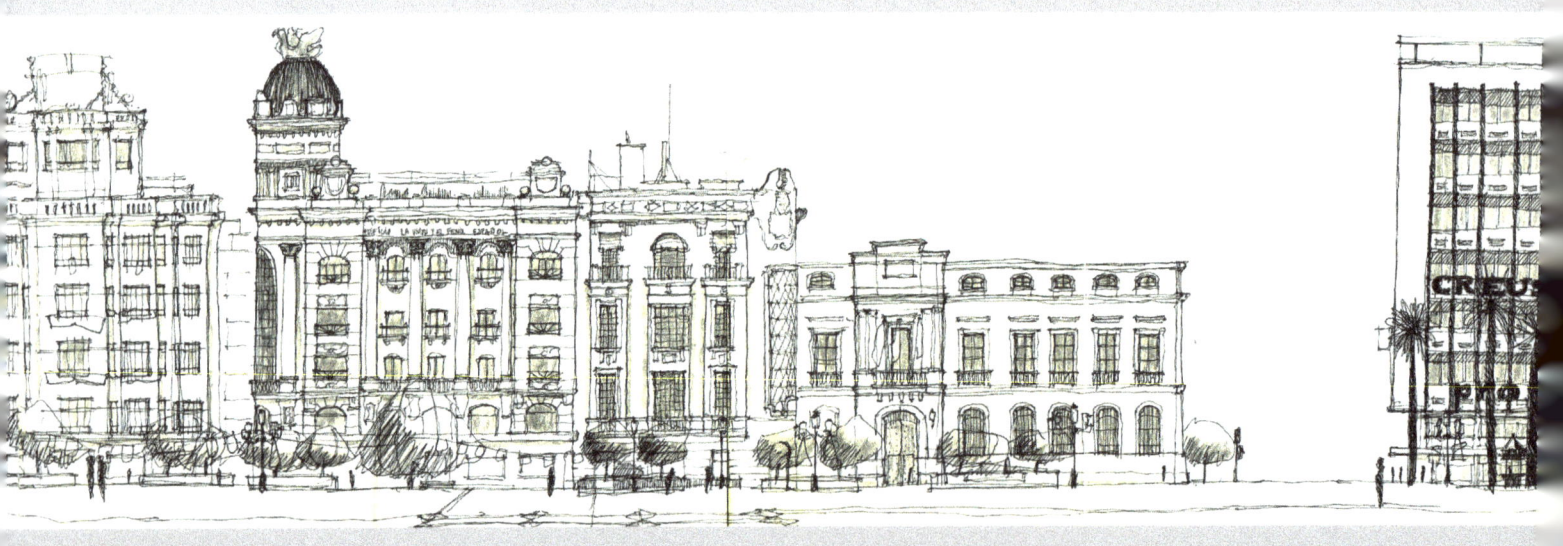

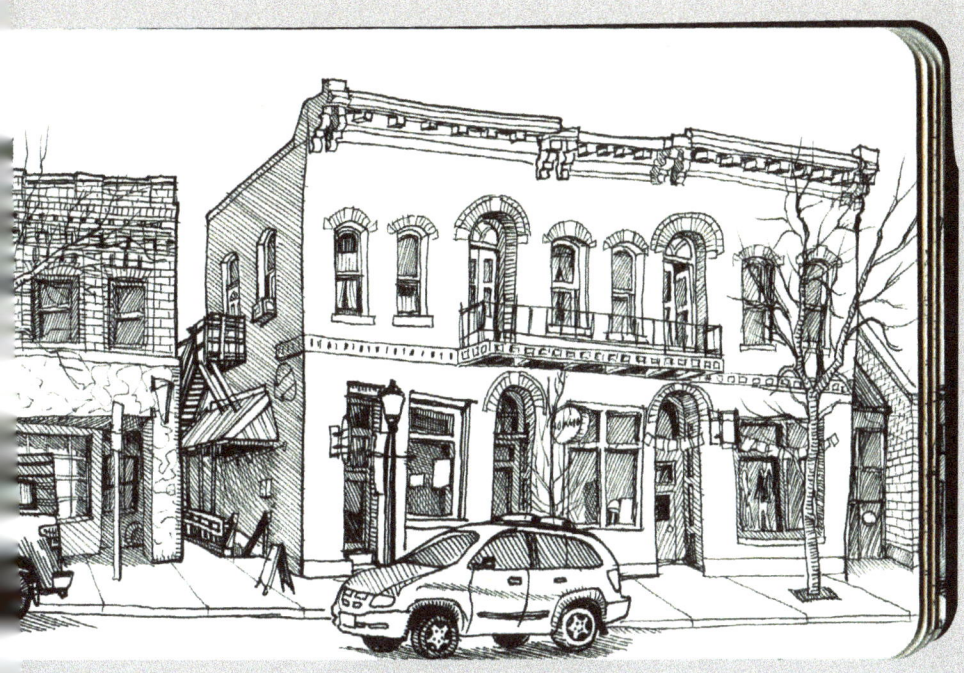

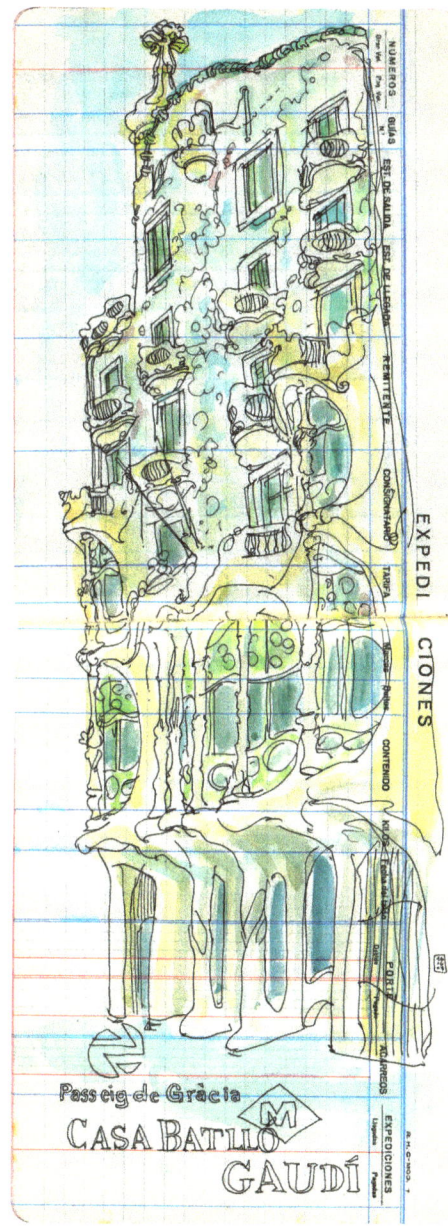

Carnicero's Tips for Drawing Façades

- Observe the fundamental parts of the building: base, central part of the building, and top. Although this is a concept of Greek and neoclassical architecture, it is still a popular way to construct, even today.

- Use dots or auxiliary lines to establish the proportions and outline the basic shapes.

- Continue adding pillars or columns, floors, cornices, and windows and balconies.

- Avoid thick lines until it's time to accentuate shadows, gaps, and differences in materials.

- Last, add antennas, streetlights, dirt stains, and the effect of the passage of time, as well as trees, pedestrians, and shadows.

⌒ Casa Batlló, Barcelona "I always spend a short time watching my subject before sketching, but, for this kind of architecture, I need more time to understand the structure," Lapin says. "I love this modernist architecture; it goes well with my fluid and alive line.

Tip "With such a famous building as Gaudí's—one of the most symbolic of the city—choose your point of view carefully and focus on the feeling you have when in front of it. Forget about what you already know and study it closely." — *Lapin*

6" x 16" | 15 x 40.6 cm; Mitsubishi uni PIN fine line 0.1 pen, Daler-Rowney watercolors on vintage accounting notebook; 30 minutes

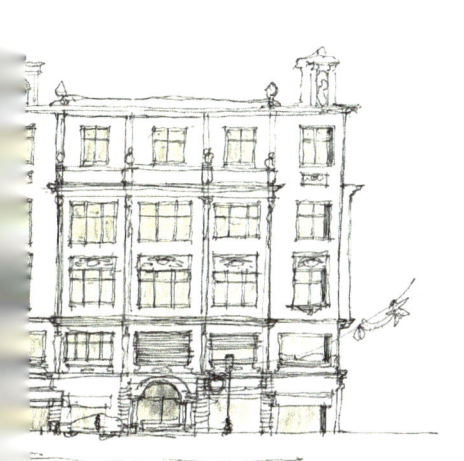

STYLE AND TECHNIQUE

Buildings That Pop Out of the Picture

Stockholm artist Nina Johannson drew this view from her kitchen. To create a sense of distance, she used different pens: a gray brush pen for the buildings farther away and a black ink pen and more detail for the closer ones, "to make them pop" she says.

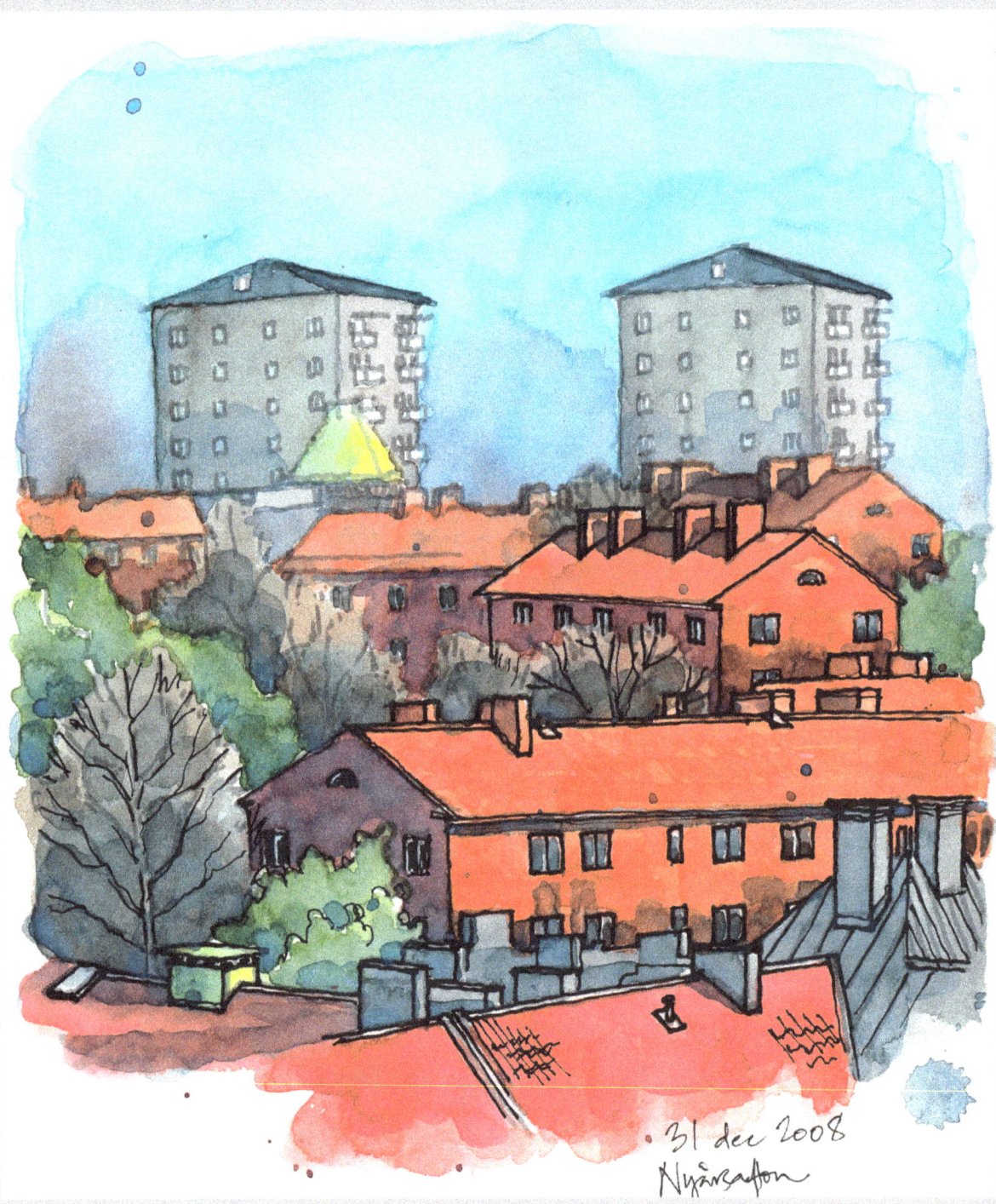

7" x 8.75" | 18 x 22 cm; Faber-Castell Pitt Artist brush pen (gray) and Pitt Artist pen (fine), Winsor & Newton watercolors on Fabriano Artistico hot-press, 200-gsm paper in hand-bound sketchbook; about 1 hour

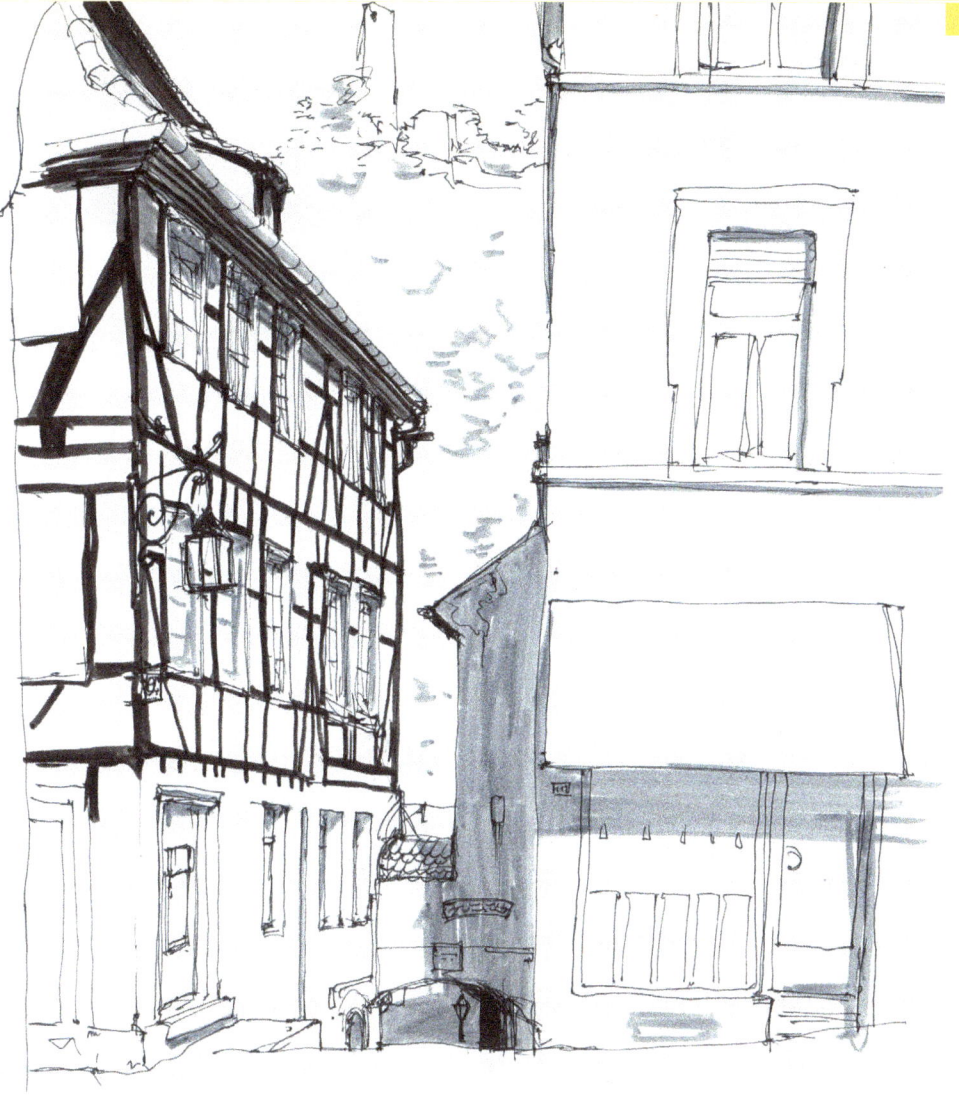

↻ **The Market and Old Castle of Weinheim an der Bergstrasse** Berlin artist Oona Leganovic was drawn to the pattern of the old wooden framework of the house on the left and its contrast to the much cleaner lines of the more recent (but still probably more than a century old) building on the right. "I took great care to give the right spacing and angles to the black beams, but I think I still had to improvise a bit at the end, because not everything fit together the way it should have. Strange angles like this are tricky to draw!" she says.

7.5" x 8" | 19 x 20 cm; Pilot 0.3 ballpoint pen, black and gray brush pens (probably Faber-Castell Pitt artist pens) on leftover blank dummy of a printed book; 45 minutes

↺ **Penang Buildings** Ch'ng Kiah Kiean purposely finished this sketch with some simple outlines of buildings on the far left, so the viewer's eyes are not distracted by too many details.

11" x 30" | 28 x 76 cm; graphite and pencil on cartridge paper; about 2 hours

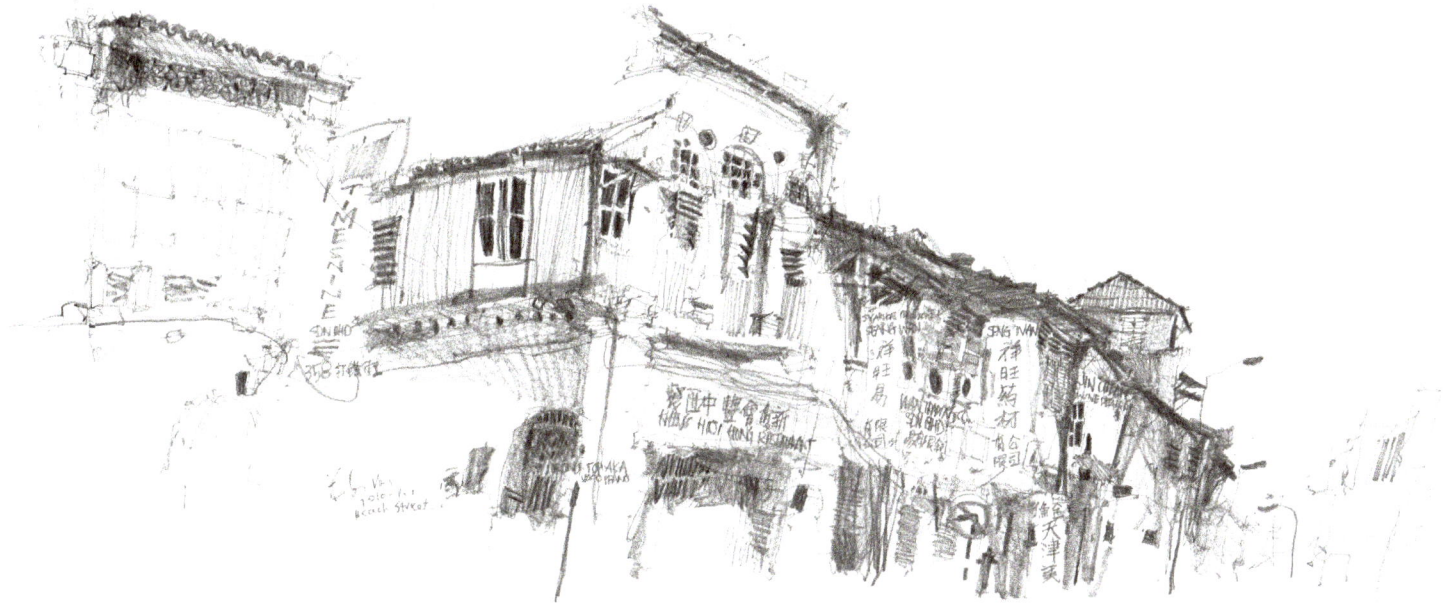

INDUSTRY AND CONSTRUCTION SITES

Industrial sites in the city outskirts might seem ugly to most people. The urban sketcher, however, delights in drawing intricate structures of pipes, chimneys, and conveyor belts. The constantly changing nature of a construction site keeps sketchers coming back to document the progress.

ʘ Construction of the New Giants Stadium
Drawing a construction site has special challenges, says New Jersey illustrator Greg Betza. "I find that there tend to be many restricted areas, which can make it difficult to find a good angle from which to make the drawing. When my views are limited, I choose an important symbol, such as a crane or a construction worker, and I build the concept and design of my drawing from there."

14" x 17" | 35.6 x 43 cm; Aurora fountain pen, Caran d'Ache Neocolor II water-soluble crayons, Staedtler Mars Graphic 3000 duo marker, and Prismacolor Nupastels, on Strathmore smooth drawing paper; 45 minutes

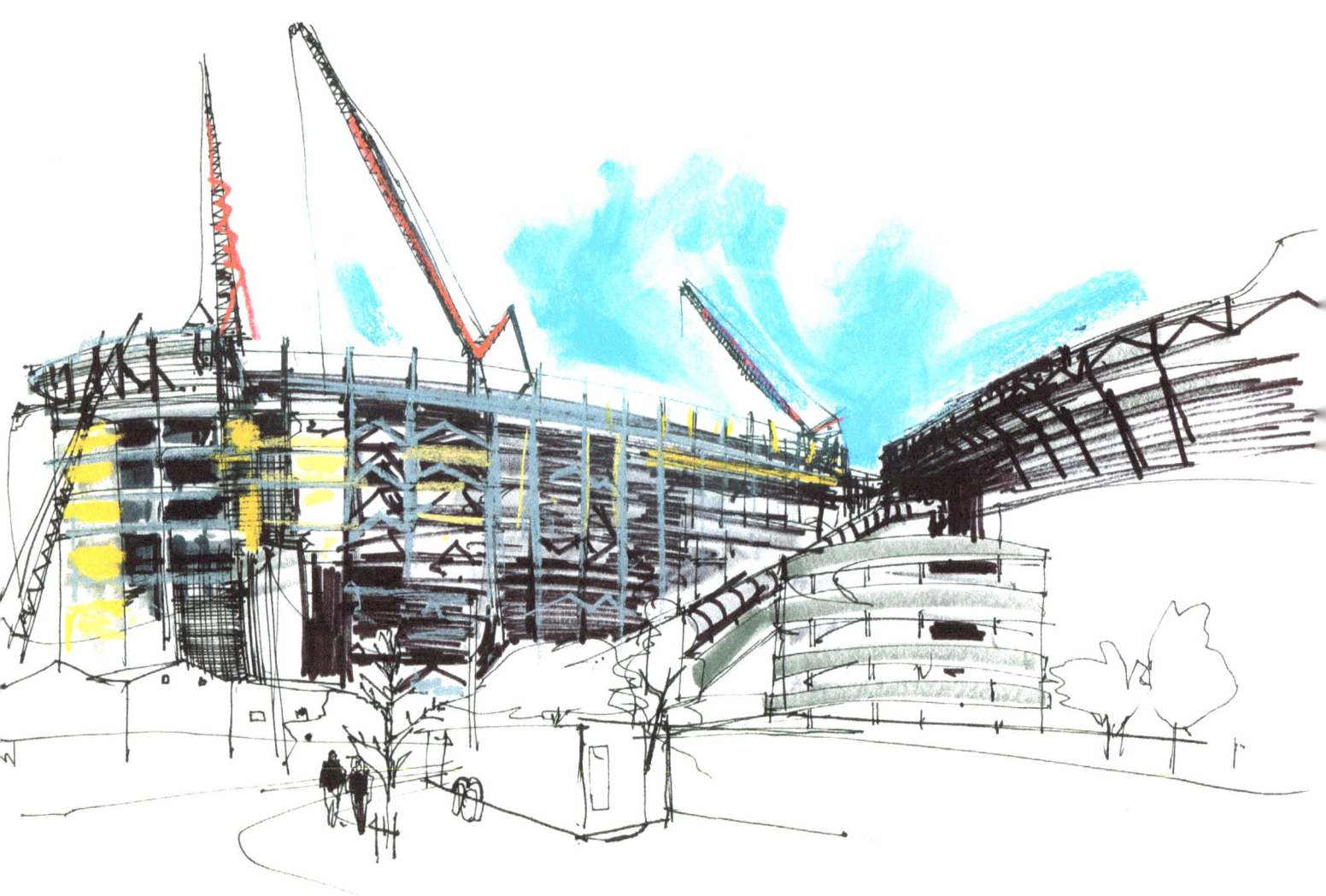

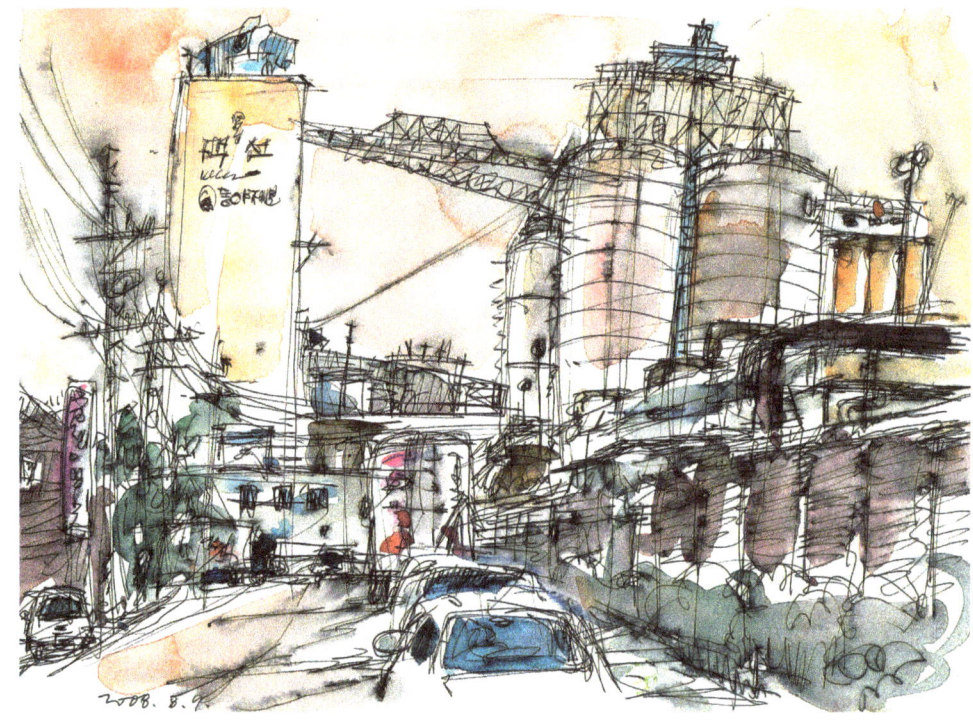

◔ Milling Factory The "great massiveness" of the Dong-A flour-milling factory silos attracted Seoul architect Lee Yong Hwan. He often comes to Inchon city to sketch because of its many factories, timber mills, fishing wharves, and ships.

11.75" x 8.25" | 30 x 21 cm; Dong-A U-Knock gel pen, Hwa-Hong brushes, ShinHan watercolors on Fabriano Accademia 94-lb. drawing paper; 40 minutes

◔ Under Construction Walt Taylor documented the progress of the Trader Building construction over a period of several months during his lunch hours, when he worked in downtown Norfolk.

Tip "I have a tendency to get lost in detail when sketching a scene like this. I have to back off every so often and make sure my proportions have some relationship to reality." — *Walt Taylor*

10.5" x 7.75" | 26.5 x19.5 cm; Micron 02 pen on Cachet Classic ecru sketchbook; 2 hours

◔ Cement Factory Gary Amaro likes to sketch on the outskirts of San Francisco, where he can find interesting subjects, such as the Lone Star Industries cement factory in Oakland.

10.5" x 8.25" | 26.5 x 21 cm; pencils on Moleskine large sketchbook; about 3 hours

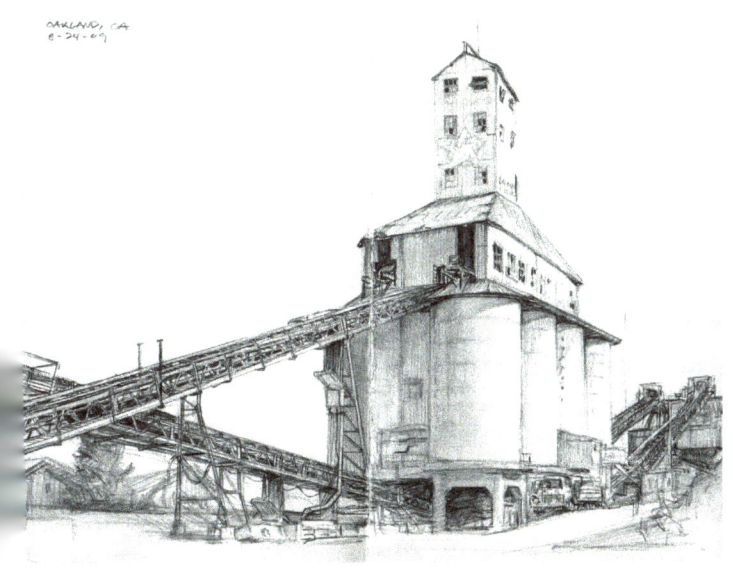

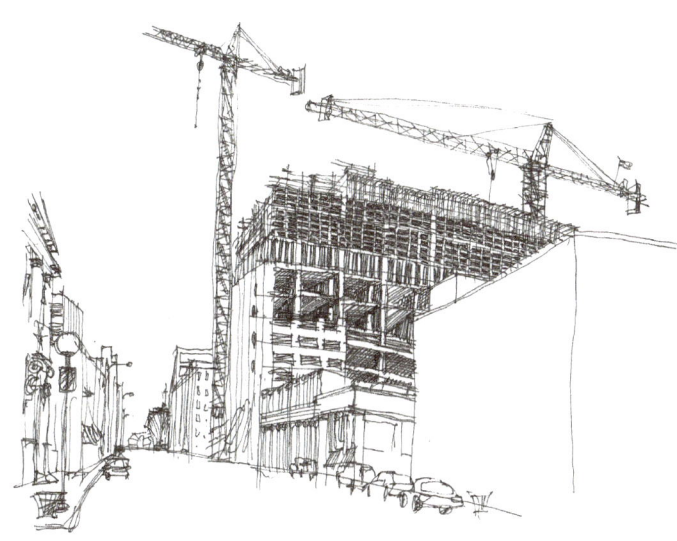

HARBORS AND WATERFRONTS

Tired of sketching buildings and cars? The most picturesque city views can often be found along shorelines and riverfronts, amid the boats and the ships. Maritime activity also presents the added challenge of drawing water and its constantly changing mirror effect.

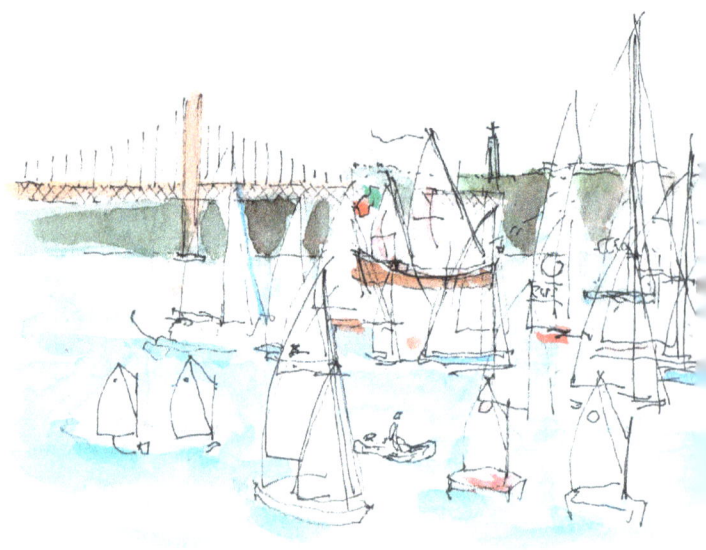

⤷ Foot of Freemason Street In Hampton Roads, you're never very far from water. "Few things are more pleasing than walking to the end of a quiet street and having a great watery vista," says Walt Taylor.

Tip "Since the real world rarely looks like it's made of fine, black-and-white lines, the sketcher is constantly creating visual metaphors for what he's seeing. This process is particularly challenging when drawing water, which stubbornly refuses to have clear outlines and linear patterns. What works most often for me is to let my line drift and flow like a current might."
— Walt Taylor

9" x 6" | 23 x 15 cm; Micron 02 pen on Cachet Classic ecru sketchbook; 45 minutes

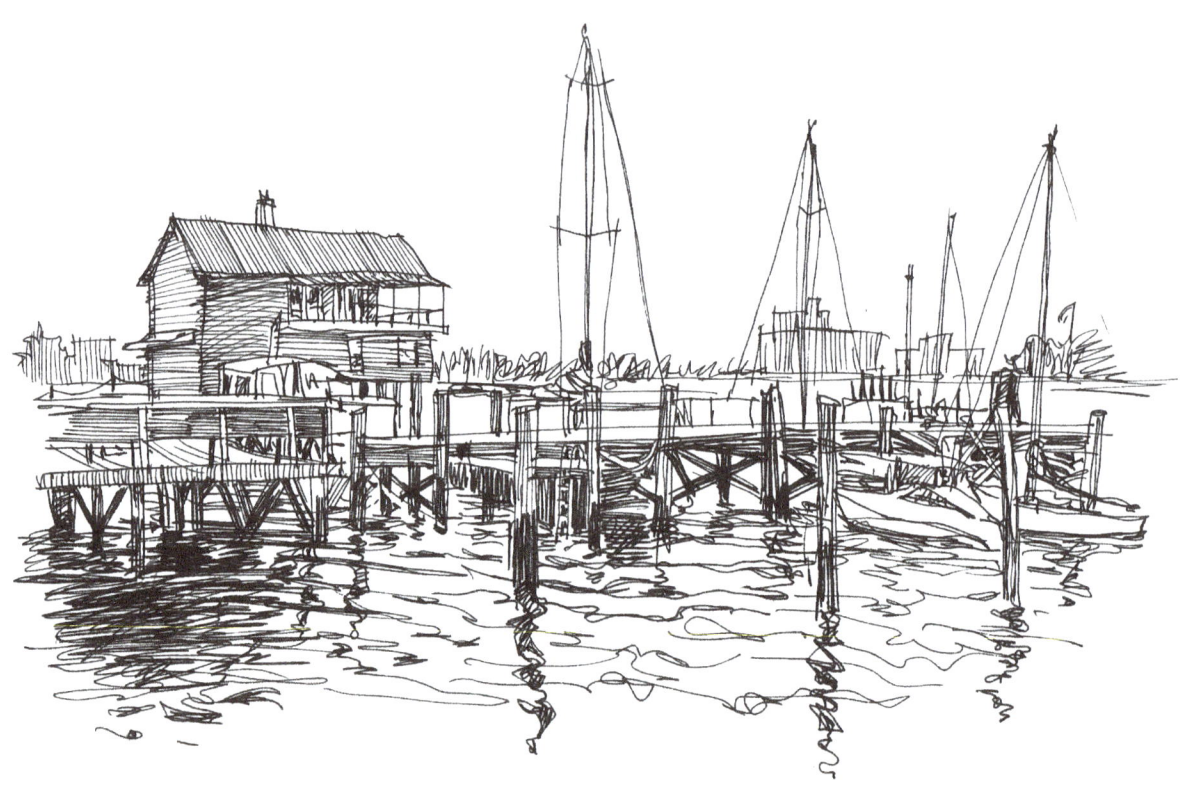

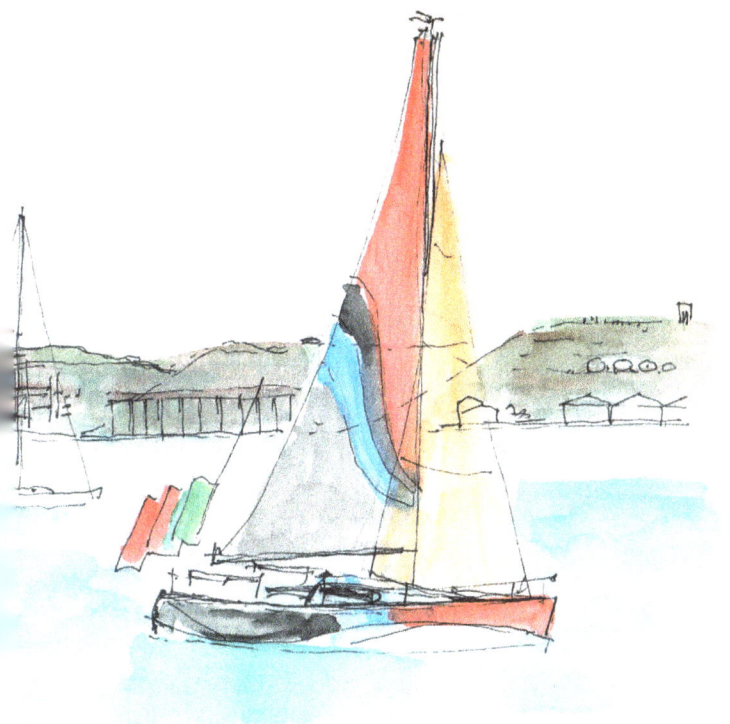

↻ **River Tagus** Francisco Lobato, a Portuguese sailor, won a solo race from France to Brazil. Pedro Cabral sketched Lobato's boat and his surrounding fleet of supporters as Lobato left Lisbon for another race in France.

Tip "I had previously drawn the river and landscape, but the boats are very fast and I could not make a proper measured drawing. I had to take some very fast measures and try to scale the different boats according to their sizes."— *Pedro Cabral*

5.5" x 11" | 14 x 28 cm; pencil, Winsor & Newton watercolors, Pilot DR 0.3 pigment ink pen, Hand•Book Travelogue Journal; 30 minutes

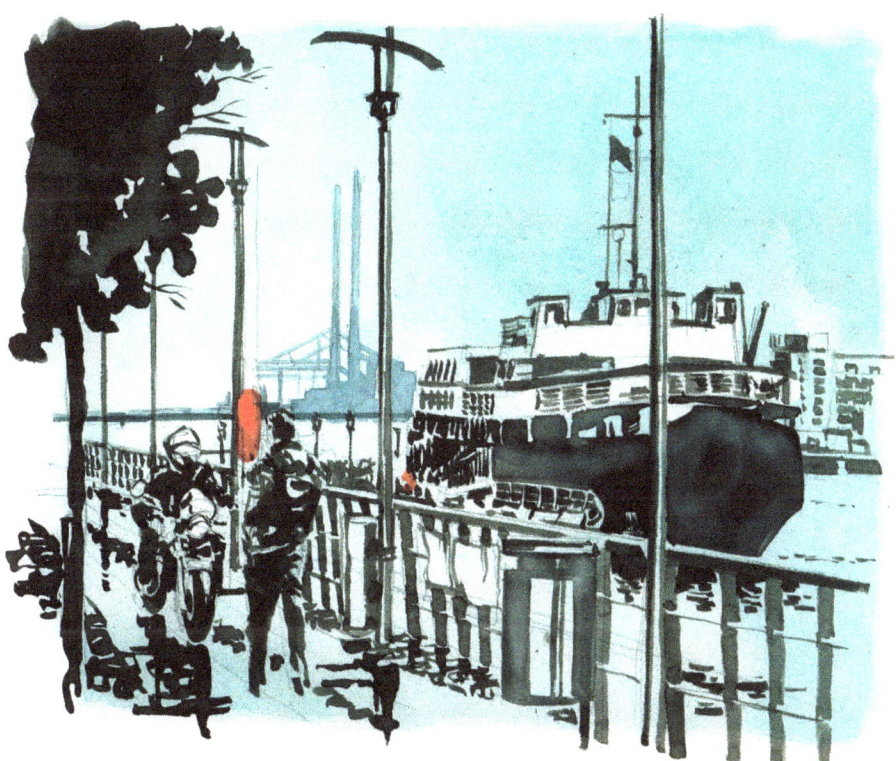

↻ **Dublin Docks** On mornings when the north quays are shrouded in fog and you can taste the sea salt on your face, the docks seem more visceral and real, says Roger O'Reilly.

Tip "This drawing was worked up through three layers of progressively darker washes, applied with a waterbrush pen filled with diluted liquid acrylic ink. I started with an almost invisible line, to get all the objects and people in place, then tightened it up with a mid-gray and finally filled in the blacks. With that done, I washed in the sky and put in the distant power station in gray-blue watercolor." — *Roger O'Reilly*

8" x 6" | 20 x 15 cm; brush pen, acrylic ink, and watercolor on Canson A5 heavy cartridge sketchpad; 45 minutes

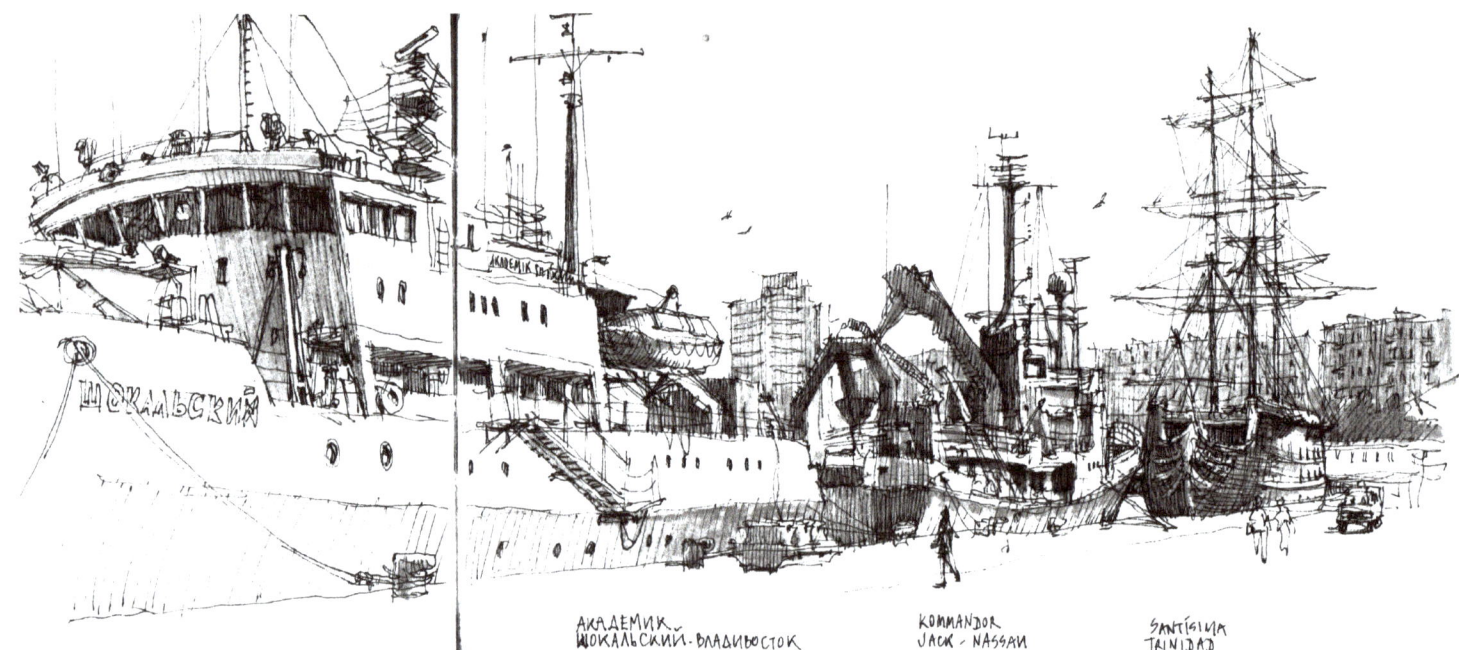

АКАДЕМИК.
ШОКАЛЬСКИЙ-ВЛАДИВОСТОК

KOMMANDOR
JACK - NASSAU

SANTÍSIMA
TRINIDAD

☊ **Gulls and the Smell of the Sea in Málaga** Luis Ruiz enjoys walking by the docks of the old wharf. On this day, he was drawn to the scene of ships from different countries. "What a gift for dreaming minds!" he says, "Hamburg, Odessa, Varna, Nassau, Vladivostok . . ."

12.75" x 5" | 32 x 12.5 cm; Staedtler .05 pigment liner, Tombow brush pen on Moleskine sketchbook; 50 minutes

EYEWITNESS

The Queen Victoria Visits Auckland

by Murray Dewhurst

I enjoy the opportunity to draw events or happenings in Auckland, such as this cruise liner, which only stayed in port for the day. We get lots of visiting cruise ships over summer. I'm always amazed at their immense size—often dwarfing the surrounding waterfront buildings. I tried to capture this scale in my drawing. When you are drawing an event, you have limited time to work with. I find this time pressure adds some excitement and really gets me going. Sketching something unusual also gives you an excuse to be really nosy and take a closer look than you normally would if you were just passing by.

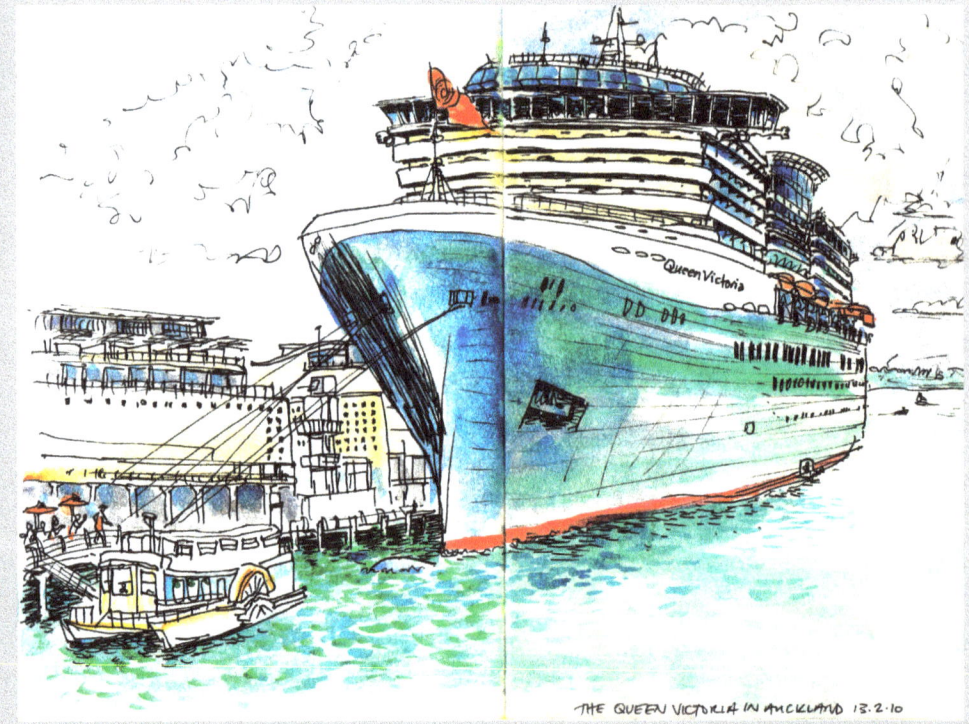

THE QUEEN VICTORIA IN AUCKLAND 13.2.10

13.75" x 9.5" | 35 x 24 cm; Rotring Tikky Graphic 0.5 fineliner, Winsor & Newton watercolors on Nood department-store hardbound sketchbook; 45 minutes

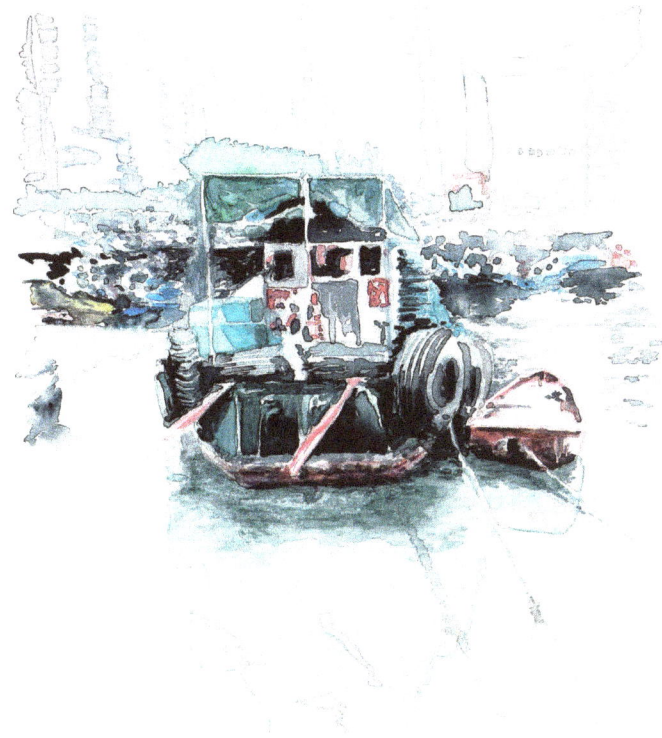

☾ **Hong Kong Boats** Beijing-based interior designer Jeremiah Teo Cheng Huat describes Lei Yun Mun as a fishing village with many tiny houses and fantastic sea views. "Some fishing boats are now used as water taxis for transportation between the Hong Kong island and Kowloon," he says.

Tip "I always remember, when drawing boats, that, even though they are tied up, they tend to change direction and might never come back to the same position. Usually, I will do a quick study outline of the overall shape and start with stuff and details inside the boat." — *Jeremiah Teo Cheng Huat*

10.5" x 8" | 26.5 x 20 cm; medium-tip Holbein waterbrush, Royal Talens watercolors on Holbein 120-gsm, 3F multi-drawing book; 3.5 hours

6.25" x 8.75" | 16 x 22 cm; Chung Hwa 2B pencil on MUJI 90-gsm, F1 recycled-paper sketchbook; 40 minutes

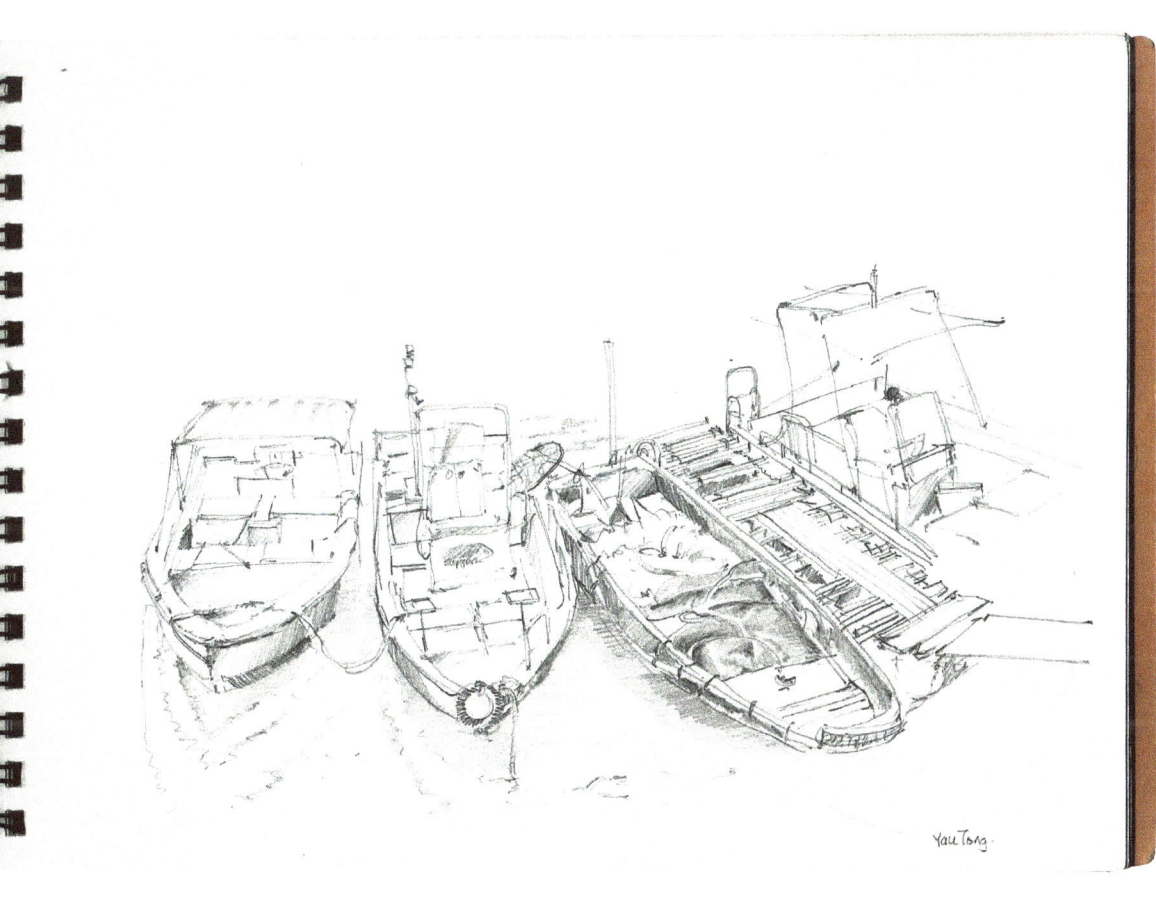

MONUMENTS, CARS, AND URBAN FURNITURE

A streetscape full of buildings and pedestrian activity might sometimes feel intimidating to draw, with multiple vantage points that create lines going in all directions. A good exercise is to attempt to draw smaller elements of the urban landscape, such as monuments, lamp posts, fountains, cars, or even electrical posts. Statues erected to prominent figures also offer an opportunity to learn about the history of the city.

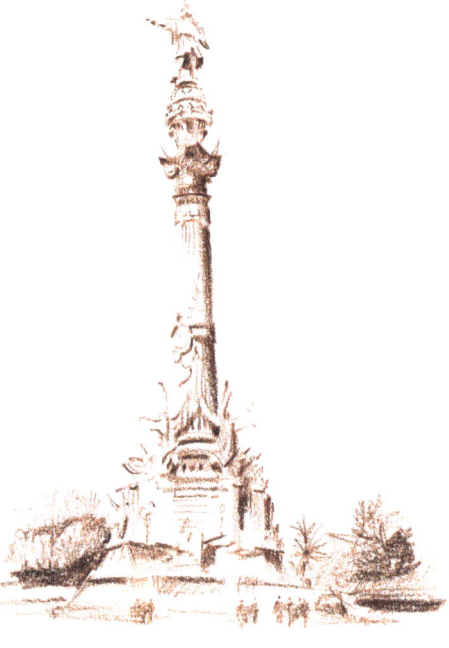

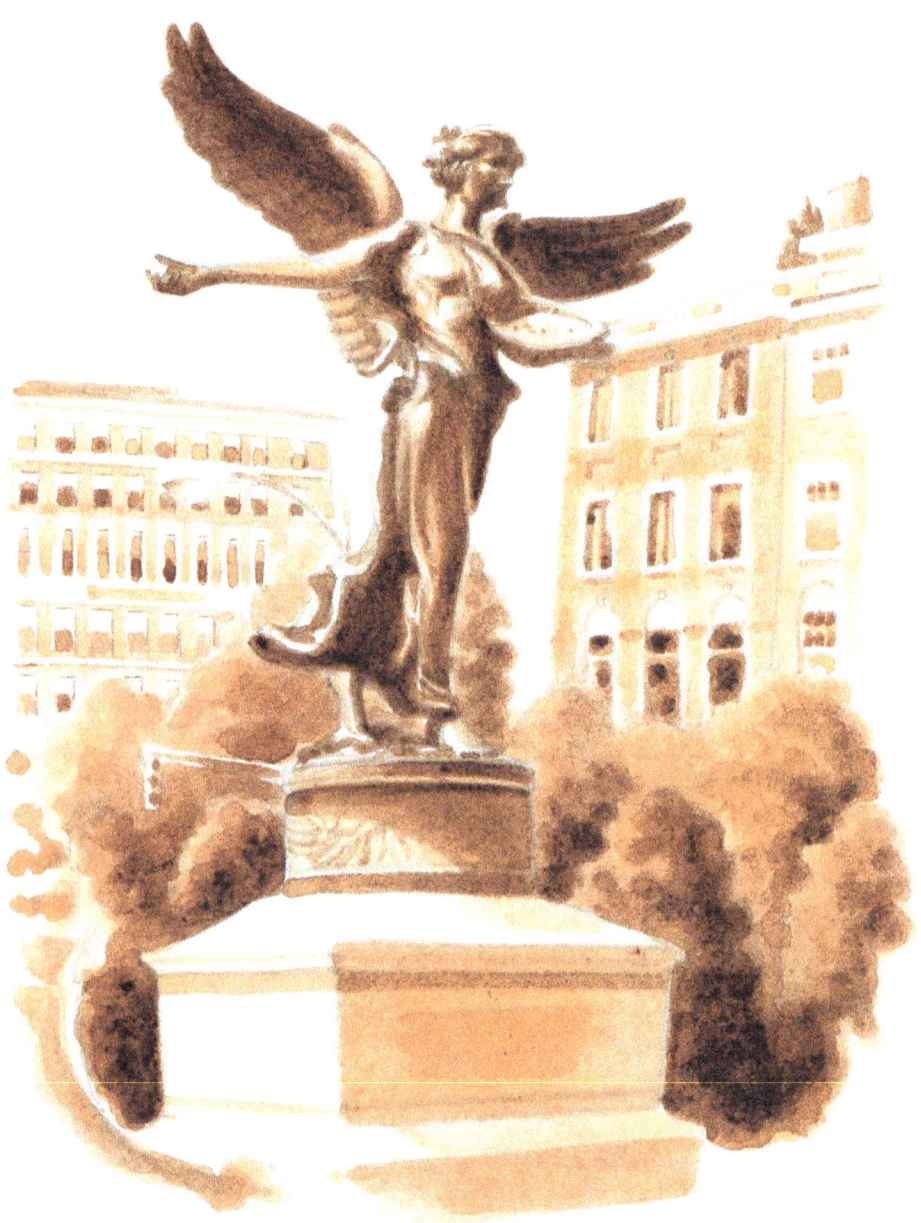

∩ Monument to Christopher Columbus "With a subject like this Barcelona statue, it's important to plan the composition before starting. Give yourself room on the page to sketch the context at the base—it's easy to focus on the column, especially the top, and then run out of space at the bottom." — *Matthew Brehm*

5" x 8" | 12.5 x 20 cm; Derwent Venetian Red pencil on Moleskine watercolor book; 25 minutes

↺ Boston Public Garden Boston artist Fred Lynch sat undisturbed in a corner of this garden to sketch the memorial statue known as "Casting Bread upon the Waters."

Tip "I start all my sketches the same way, with a light gestural drawing in pencil, making every effort to create with a mood, impression, or story in my head. Next come details, again in pencil, with more attention to specifics. Finally, I lay in ink washes, working from broad areas to specific details". — *Fred Lynch*

6" x 4" | 15 x 10 cm; Winsor & Newton nut brown ink and Artists' watercolor (sable) on Arches 140-lb., hot-press watercolor block; 2 hours

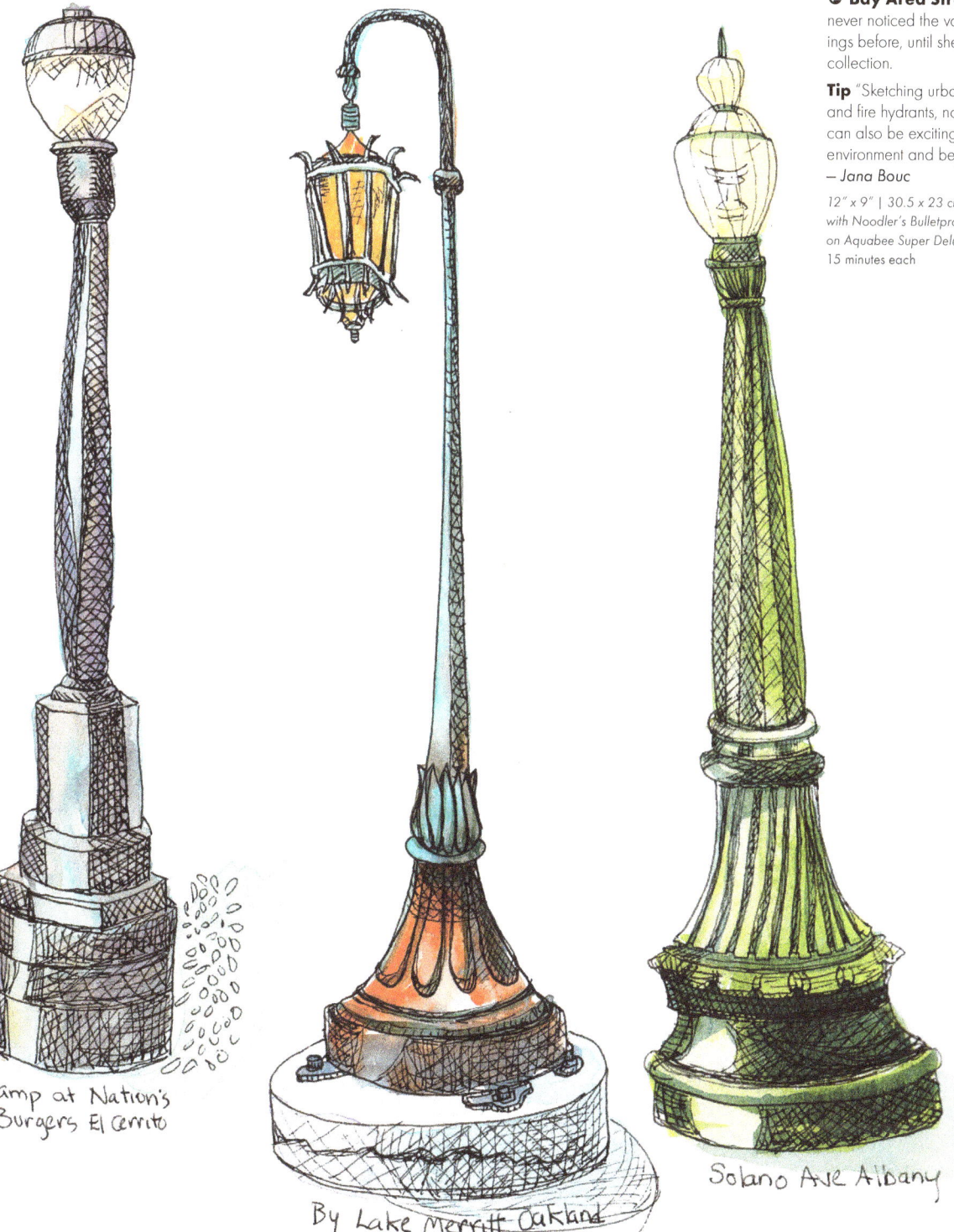

☾ Bay Area Streetlights Jana Bouc says she'd never noticed the variety of street lamps in her surroundings before, until she had fun capturing them for this collection.

Tip "Sketching urban furniture, such as lamp posts and fire hydrants, not only helps hone drawing skills; it can also be exciting to look closely at objects in our environment and begin to notice all the details."
— Jana Bouc

12" x 9" | 30.5 x 23 cm; Lamy Safari fine-point fountain pen, filled with Noodler's Bulletproof Black ink, Winsor & Newton watercolors on Aquabee Super Deluxe spiral-bound sketchbook; about 15 minutes each

Lamp at Nation's Burgers El Cerrito

By Lake Merritt Oakland

Solano Ave Albany

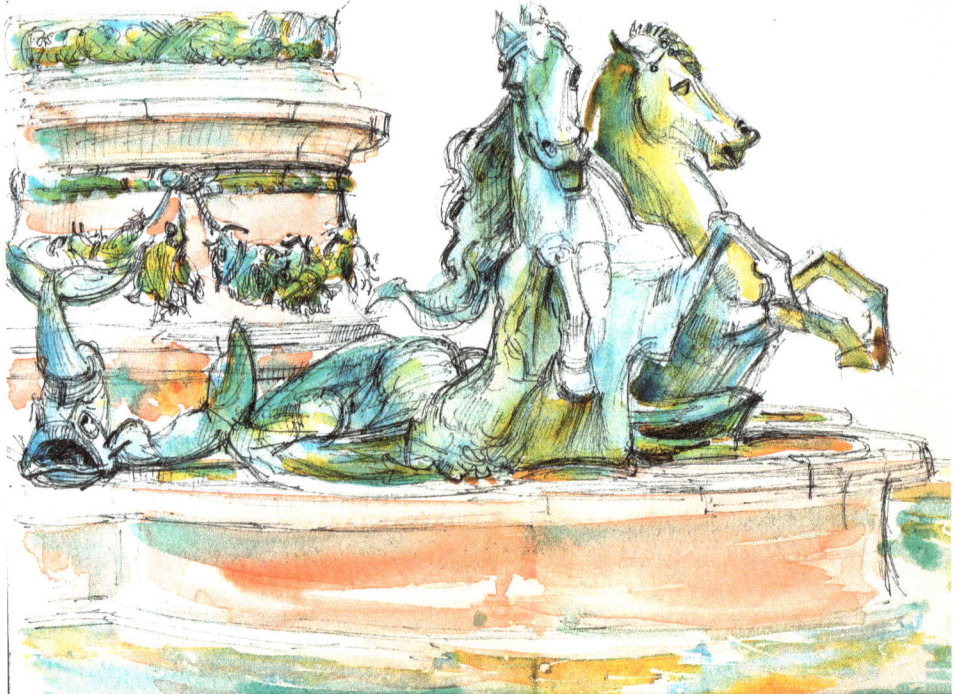

♫ Fontaine de l'Observatoire, Paris Laura Frankstone says she's drawn this particular fountain several times over the past few years. "There's so much going on, in terms of energy and ornamentation, that I find it irresistible!" she says.

Tip "Don't be daunted by the complexity of the shapes. Choose a manageable segment of the subject and then just settle into its intricacies, enjoying every single curve and angle." — *Laura Frankstone*

9" x 13" | 23 x 33 cm; Faber-Castell Ecco Pigment pen with Schmincke watercolor washes on accordion sketchbook custom-made with Fabriano cold-press paper; 1 hour

⊃ Telephone poles
São Paulo illustrator João Pinheiro says he's always looking up at buildings when he walks around. He's also especially fond of telephone and electrical poles and tries to imagine their expression, as if they were people, when he draws them. "They are like sentinels watching over our heads," he says.

8.25" x 11.75" | 21 x 30 cm; ink nankin pen and brush on sulfite paper

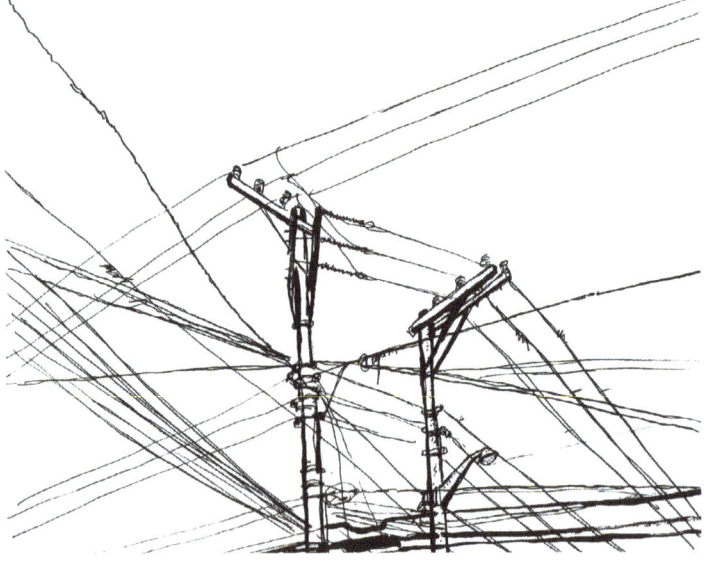

Sketching Parked Cars

⊃ Seat 600 "I have sketched more than fifty of these vintage cars, sitting in the streets along my way. My criteria is quite simple: I like old cars, from a Model T Ford to a Cadillac or Alfa Romeo from the '70s. Years give cars more appeal to me. The funny thing is that I do not have my driving license, so I only focus on the aesthetics of it and don't really care about its performance; it's just a beautiful subject to me. My point of view is always the same: I sketch cars while sitting on the ground, about 1 to 2 meters (3.5 to 6.5 feet) in front of them. It gives a fish-eye sensation." — *Lapin*

11.5" x 8.25" | 29 x 21 cm; Mitsubishi uni PIN fine line 0.1 ink pen, Daler-Rowney watercolors, Pentel waterbrush on vintage notebook with numerated corners; 30 minutes

Florian Afflerbach's Tips

- Pay attention to the basic shape—sedan, van, convertible—and the main axes—window columns and belt line (the line directly underneath the side windows).

- Start by measuring the angles and lengths of the main parts of the car, the windows, wheels, and bumpers.

- Continue with details, such as the interior and the logo or hood ornament.

- Add shadows with hatchings or watercolor, to give the drawing volume.

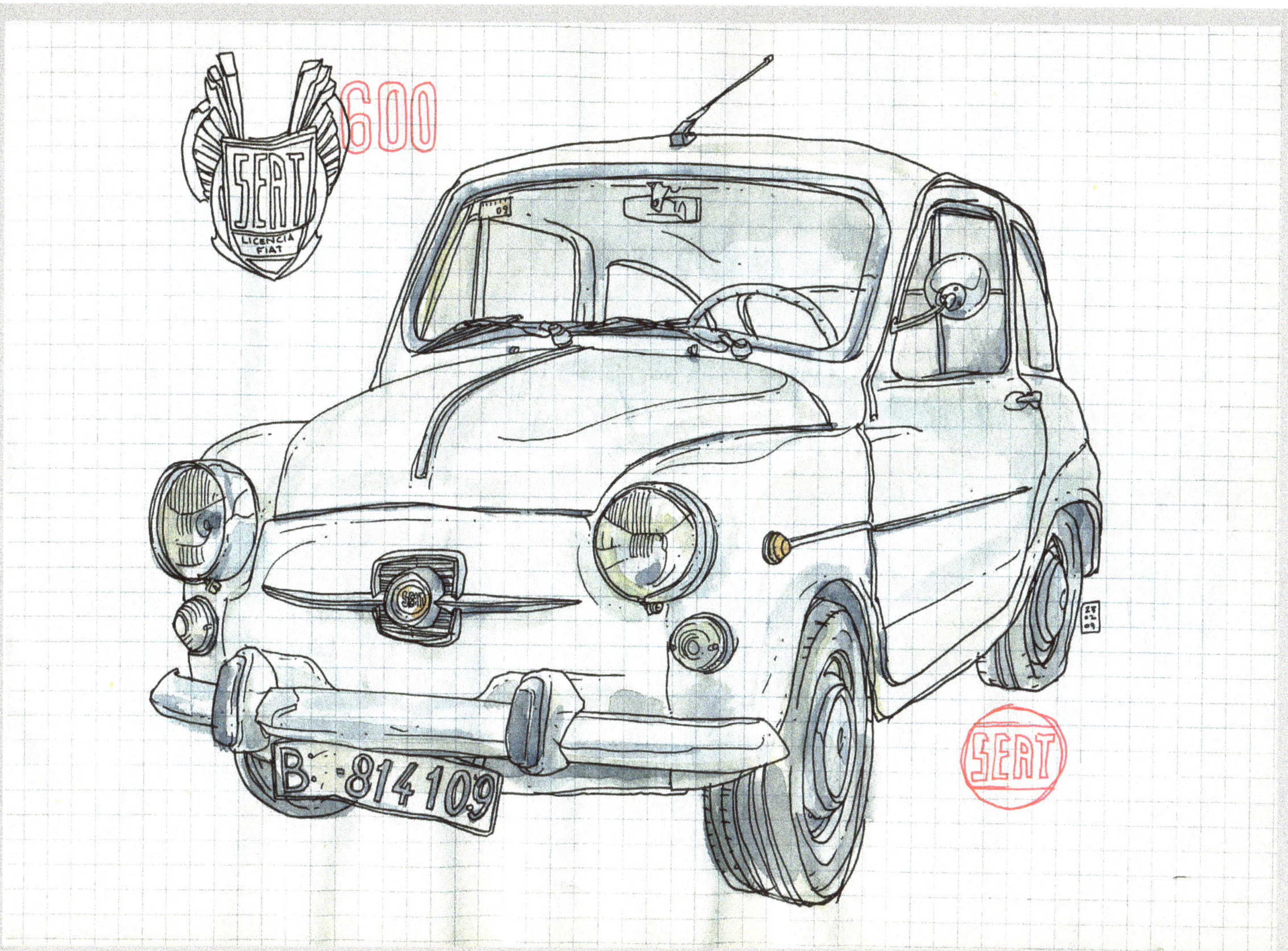

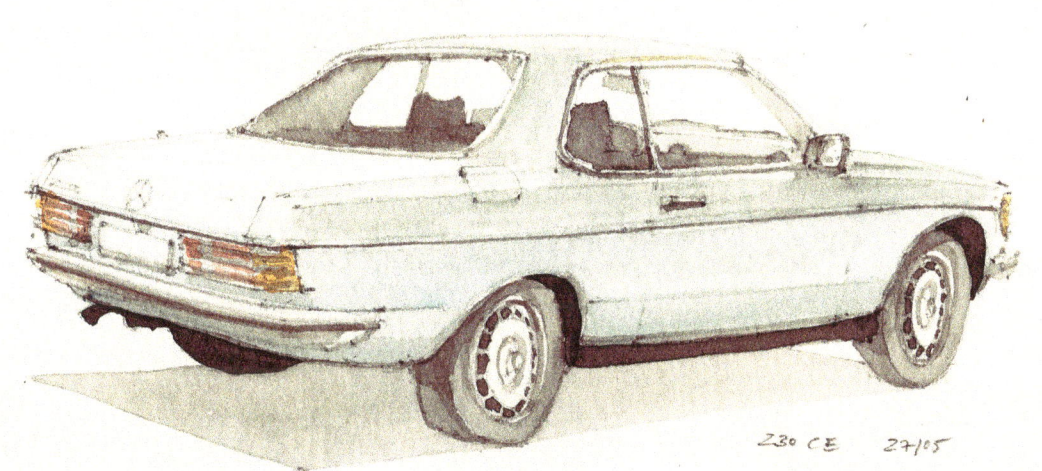

600

SEAT
LICENCIA
FIAT

SEAT

B · 814109

↻ Stuttgart's Mercedes

As Germany's car capital, Stuttgart is full of vintage automobiles. "When you walk around after a hard working day and you crave something to sketch, you'll find one in the streets," says Florian Afflerbach, who enjoys drawing parked cars. He says they are easier to draw than people because they hold still, "unless the owner comes and drives away."

10" x 6" | 25 x 15 cm; 4B Faber-Castell pencil, Schmincke watercolor, #4 and #6 da Vinci brushes on Boesner 170-gsm sketchbook; 45 minutes

230 CE   27/05

THROUGH THE SEASONS

If you think urban sketching is a seasonal activity, think again. Hot or cold, rain or shine—these artists aren't intimidated by freezing New York City winters or hot Mediterranean summers. And when outdoor sketching becomes unbearable, they know how to take refuge in a warm café or shady spot and keep on sketching. Each season also presents an opportunity to shake up their color palette.

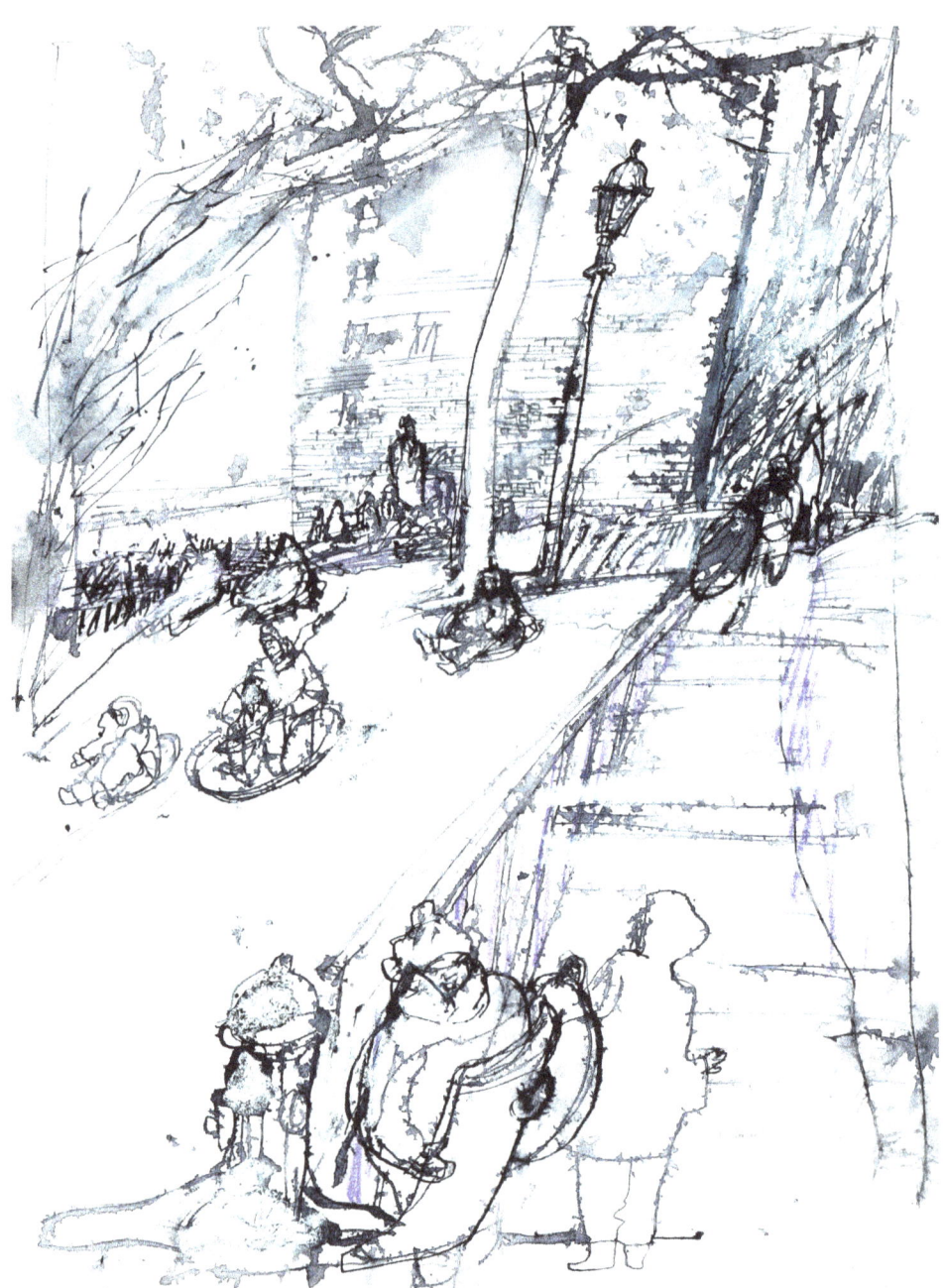

Snow Day! Veronica Lawlor could hear the laughter from the little children sliding down the big hill behind her apartment building. "The snow in New York City is swirling and dancing through the air, and the children are slipping and sliding in their giant snowsuits," Lawlor says. "Moms and dads off from work for the day take their turn down the hill as well, as I sit across the way trying to draw it before my page gets totally soaked!"

Tip "Gloves with the fingertips cut off and many layers to keep warm help in a cold situation such as this. Mainly my recommendation for winter scenes is just draw fast and keep moving for warmth! " — *Veronica Lawlor*

9" x 12" | 23 x 30.5 cm; Higgins water-soluble black ink, Speedball nib pen, purple colored pencil, white pastel, snowflakes on Strathmore sketch paper; about 30 minutes

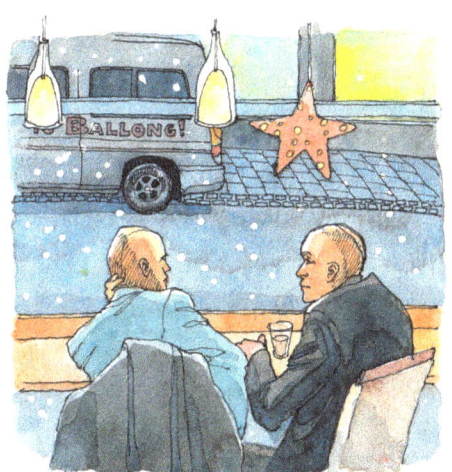

↻ **Snowfall** Nina Johannson remembers the snow on this day in Stockholm staying put on the ground, instead of turning into gray mud in two seconds.

Tip "I used masking fluid on this one, to keep the snowflakes white. I almost never use masking fluid, simply because I don't want to carry so much stuff around in my bag. I found a small plastic bottle of Schmincke masking fluid; it's got a fine nozzle on it, so there was no need to ruin a paintbrush to do this." — *Nina Johannson*

6" x 6.25" | 15 x 16 cm; Copic Multiliner SP and Winsor & Newton watercolors on Fabriano Rosaspina printing paper, in hand-bound sketchbook; 30 minutes

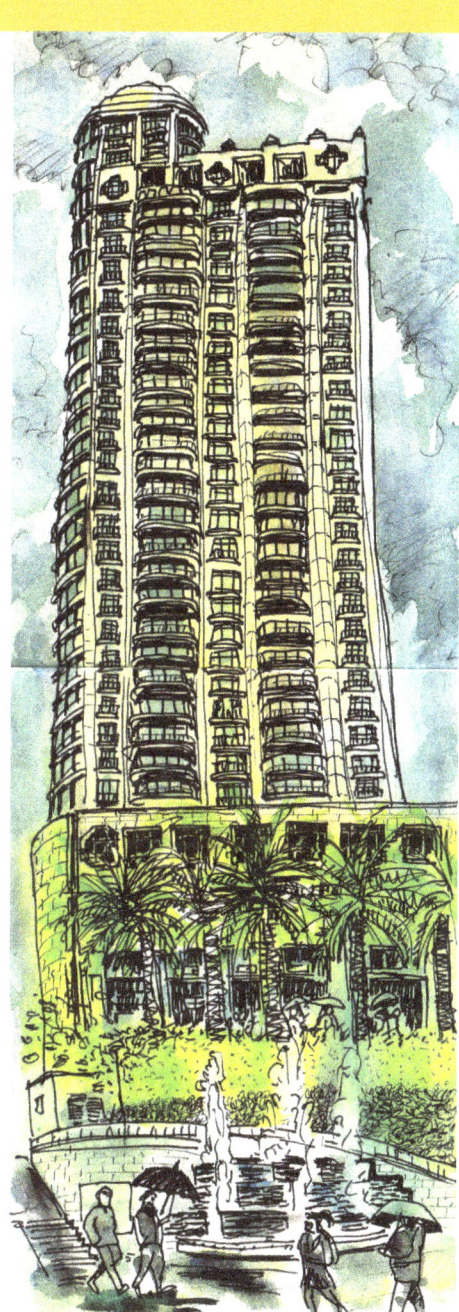

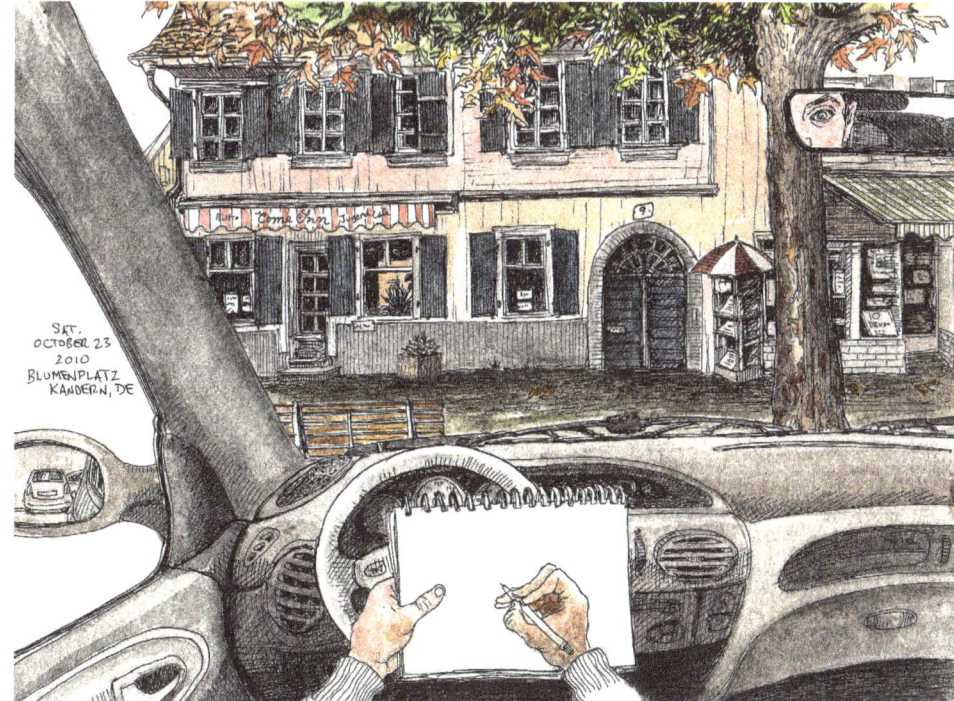
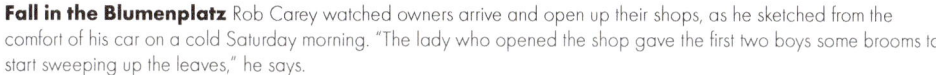

Fall in the Blumenplatz Rob Carey watched owners arrive and open up their shops, as he sketched from the comfort of his car on a cold Saturday morning. "The lady who opened the shop gave the first two boys some brooms to start sweeping up the leaves," he says.

Tip "Because my sketches often take a couple hours to complete, sitting outside in the cold months of the year or in rainy weather is not an option. Therefore, I have found it helpful to sketch from inside my car, occasionally starting up the engine and turning on the heater. In some situations, it's fun to include the interior of the car as well." — *Rob Carey*

8.5" x 11" | 21.6 x 28 cm; standard watercolor set, Faber-Castell fine-point SX permanent pen on Pentalic 130-lb. artists' watercolor paper; 2.5 hours

New Zealand Winter Murray Dewhurst went sketching on "one of our classic wet Auckland winter days. I enjoyed the random effect of raindrops on the page, as the ink and paint bled together."

Tip "I wanted to fit in the people in their raincoats with their umbrellas to accentuate the rainy-day feeling." — *Murray Dewhurst*

5.75" x 16" | 14.6 x 40.6 cm; Rotring Tikky Graphic 0.5 fineliner and Winsor & Newton watercolors on Hahnemühle A5 landscape sketchbook; 1–1.5 hours

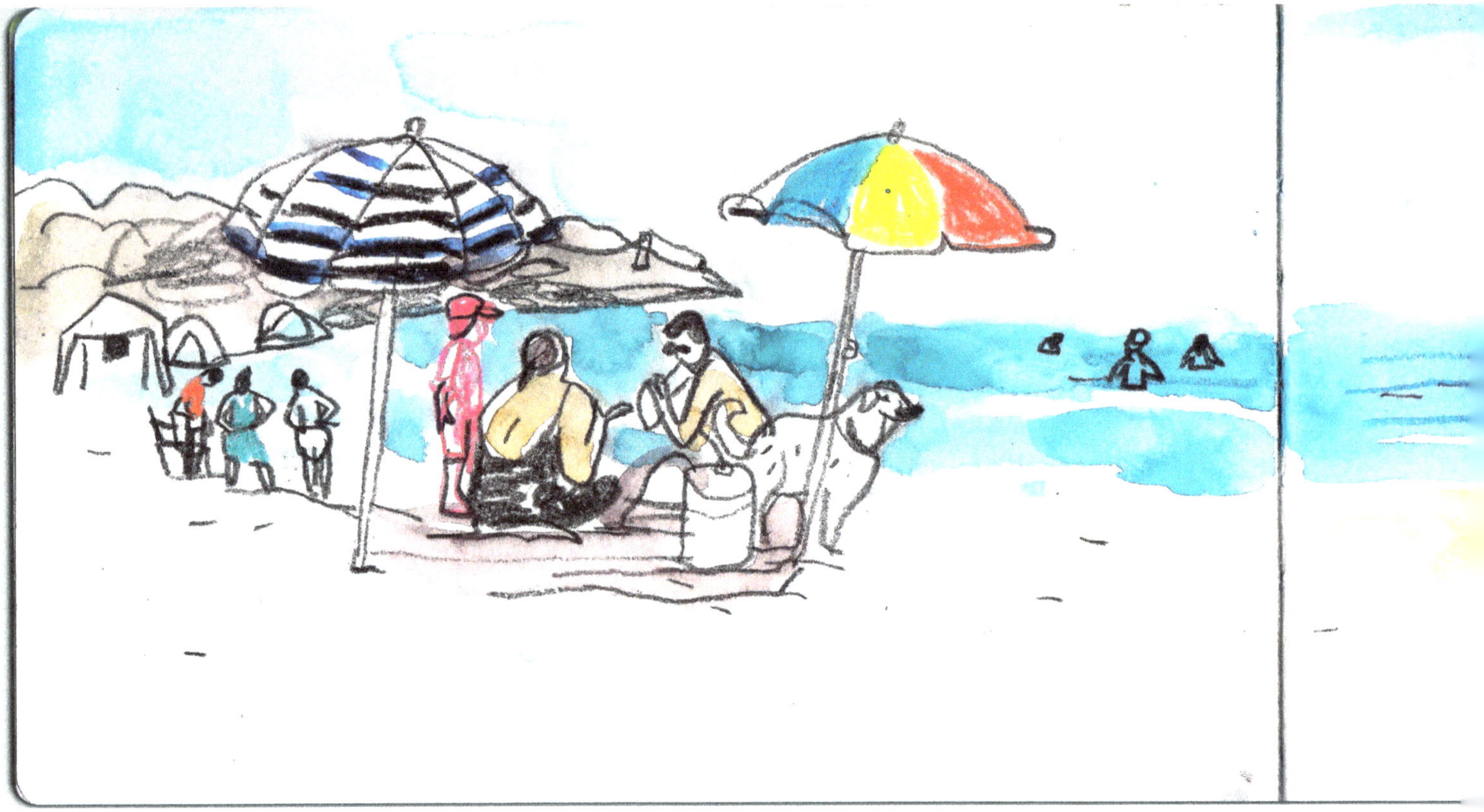

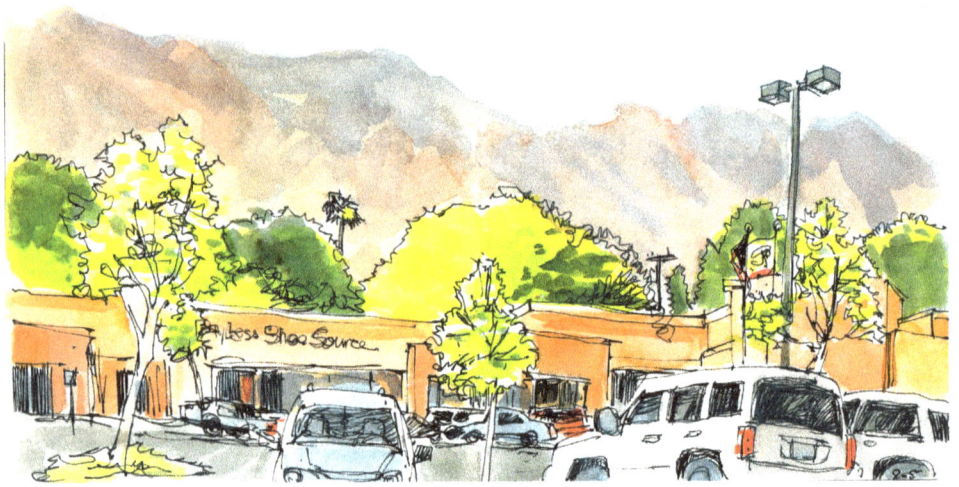

↻ An Ordinary View Summer in the foothills of Los Angeles and eastward to Pasadena. "It was hot and hazy (okay, smoggy), looking north from a Pasadena parking lot," Virginia Hein says.

Tip "This was drawn from the shaded porch of a restaurant, with a cold drink in hand—my advice is to stay in the shade and keep water handy!" — *Virginia Hein*

5.5" x 11" | 14 x 28 cm; Pilot extra-fine V-Ball Grip pen with Winsor & Newton and Holbein colors (Lavender and Verditer Blue) on Hand-Book Travelogue Journal; about 30 minutes

↺ Pedregalejo Beach, Málaga, Spain The previous winter was really hard—cold and rainy, Inma Serrano remembers. "We were living in a little village in the countryside. On a sunny day after work, we drove an hour and a half to spend the afternoon on the beach."

8.25" x 6" | 21 x 15 cm; Pentel brush pen, Schmincke watercolors mixed with white gouache, Winsor & Newton sketchbook; 60 minutes

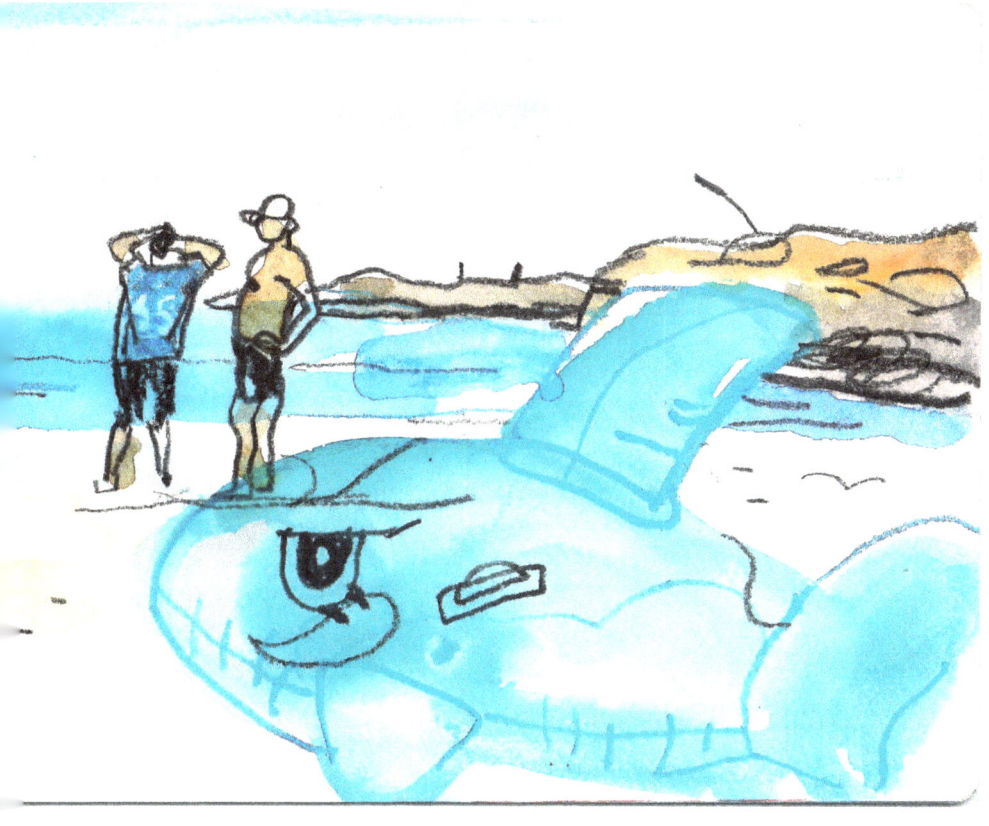

⊆ **Israel Beach** Tel Aviv illustrator Marina Grechanik says she's not a big fan of sleeping in a tent with sand under her cheek, but waking up in the early morning at Habonim Beach and sketching the views "made the experience worth it."

Tip "Bring a box to put your sketching tools and paints into, to avoid getting sand in them. Also, try to find some shade." — *Marina Grechanik*

16" x 5.25" | 40.6 x 13 cm; Van Gogh 12-pan watercolor pocket box, synthetic brushes, Derwent Inktense colored pencils on Moleskine large watercolor book; about 15 minutes

↺ **In the Shade** Davis, California, is really quite hot in summertime, Pete Scully says. "You can almost smell the heat."

Tip "I wanted to convey the coolness of the shade against the blazing summer sun here, so I emphasized the darkness of the shadows and left some areas behind the tree blank." — *Pete Scully*

3.5" x 5.5" | 9 x 14 cm; Micron 01 pen, WH Smith A6 cartridge paper sketchbook; 45 minutes

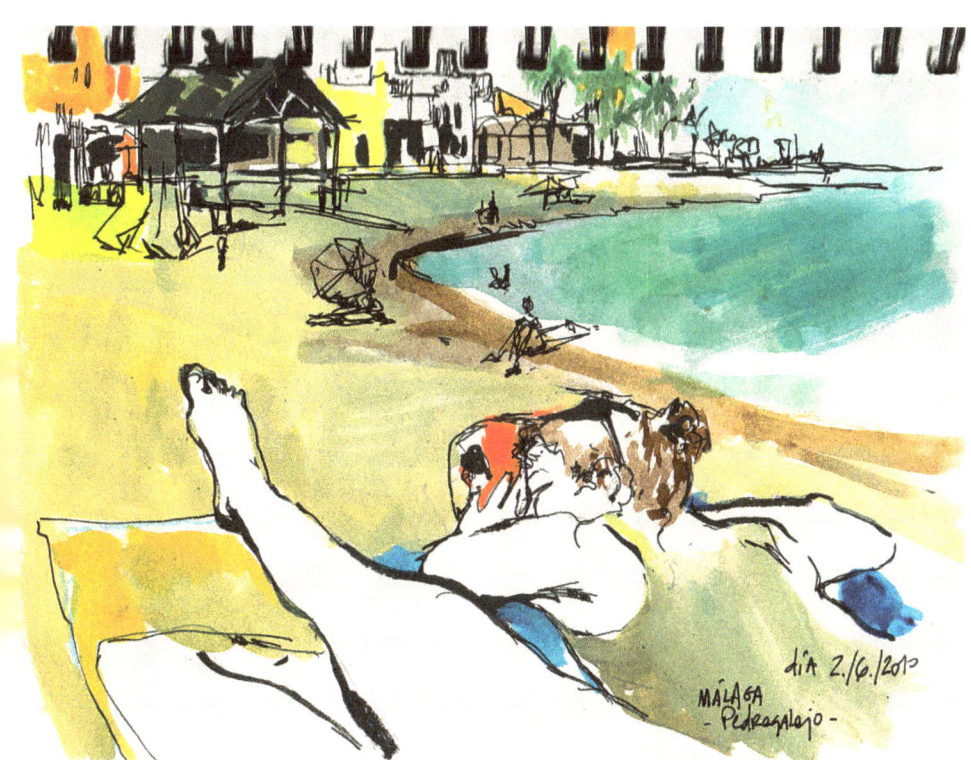

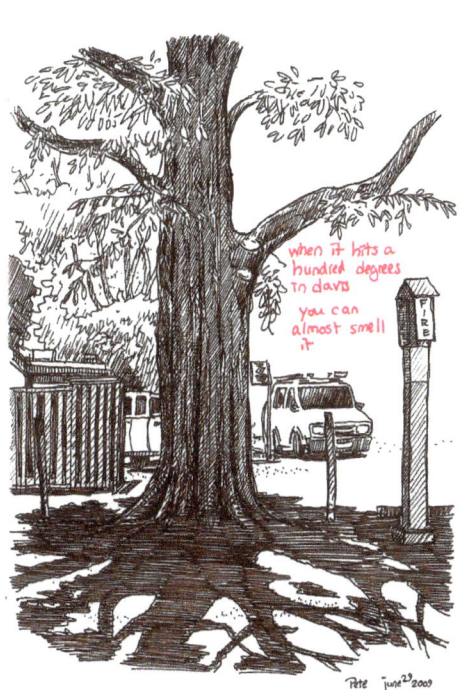

○ **Cherry Blossoms in Kelvingrove, Glasgow** Wil Freeborn was drawing when a gentle breeze blew, scattering the blossom petals. "I sat down and drew the trees and the museum, then a Japanese group sat down for a picnic in almost the perfect place, like serendipity," Freeborn says. For the falling cherry blossoms, he used masking fluid drops, so the leaves could be seen against the dark tree trunks.

10.25" x 8.25" | 26 x 21 cm; pencil and watercolors, on Moleskine large sketchbook; 30–40 minutes, with more time to add watercolor

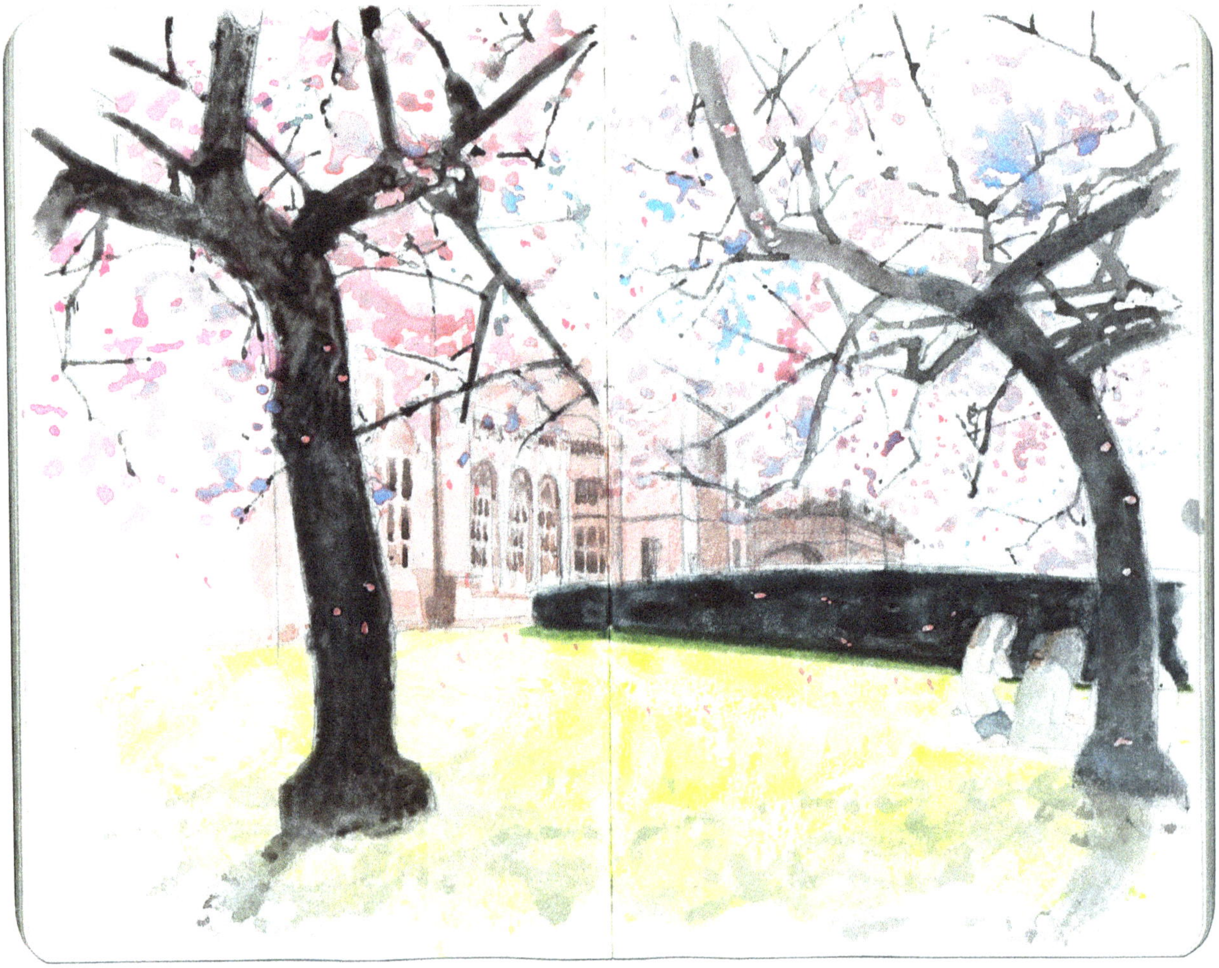

FIRST PERSON

Color Changes from April to October

by Kumi Matsukawa

These cherry blossom trees give this street a unique look and seasonal ambiance. I drew one in October and then thought it might be fun to draw the same place in different seasons. Although I draw the same place, each time the lighting, temperature, and humidity is different.

In October, the leaves of the cherry blossom trees changed color as it got cooler. In April, the blossoms were in full bloom, and I saw many pedestrians enjoying the view, while I was drawing. In May, soon after shedding petals, the trees started to dress in lime green.

13" x 9.5" | 33 x 24 cm; Horadam Aquarell watercolors, Brack Resable 700F Holbein brush, Bonny Bism angular brush #1300, Bumpodo sketchbook; 1–2 hours each

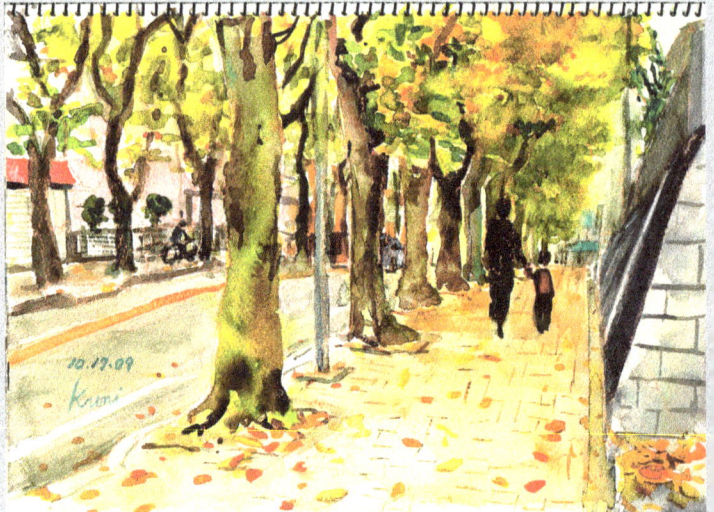

October

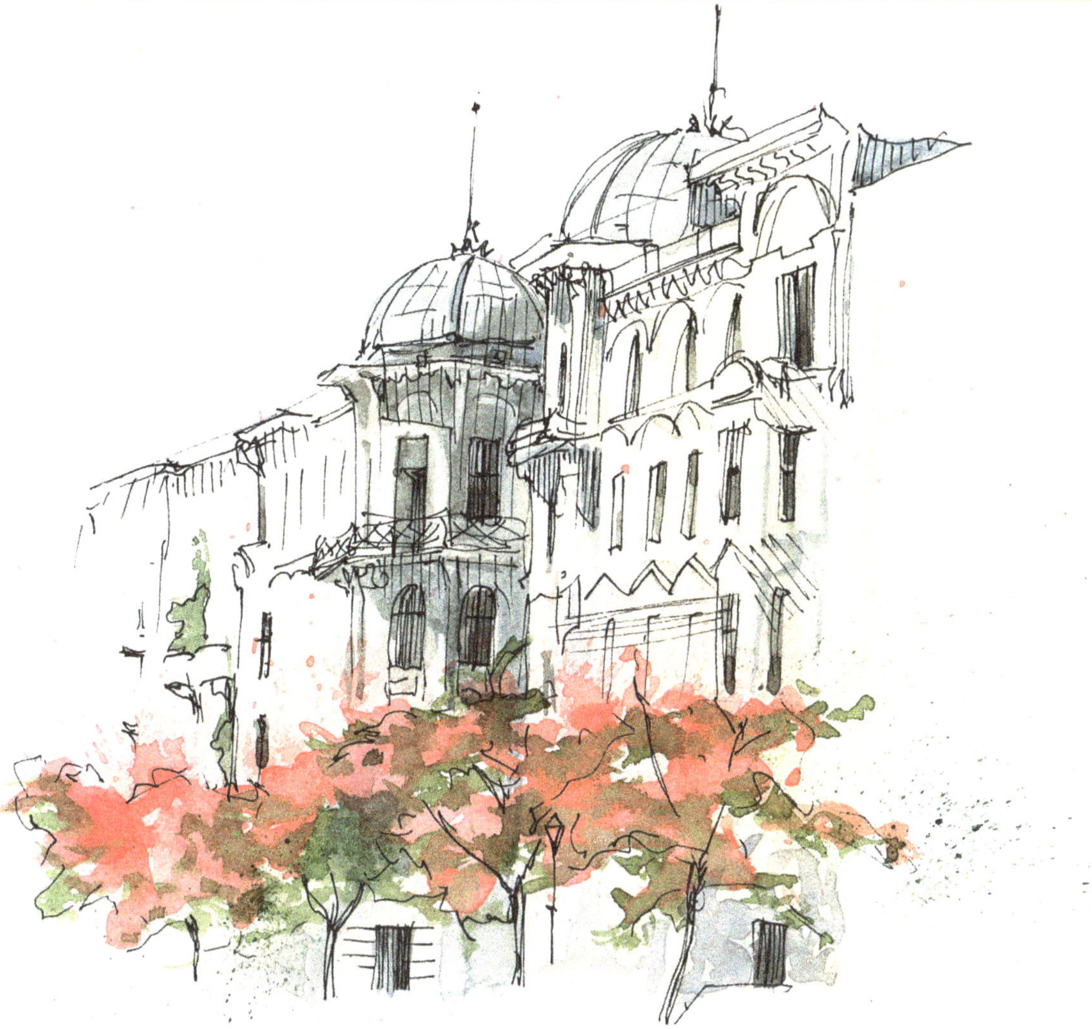

☾ Hagelberger Strasse, Berlin In early April, the trees surrounding the Riehmer's Court residential complex (built at the end of the nineteenth century) begin to bloom.

Tip "I added a color splash with a brush to highlight the blooming of the trees. For this purpose, I sometimes use a simple toothbrush, because it creates a great splash effect." — *Olga Prudnikova*

6" x 8" | 15 x 20 cm; Copic 0.3 liner, St. Petersburg watercolors on Canson paper; about 20 minutes

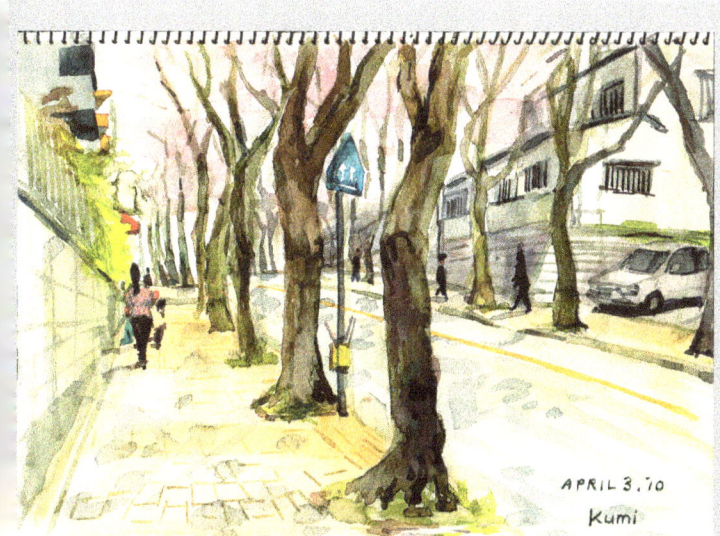

April

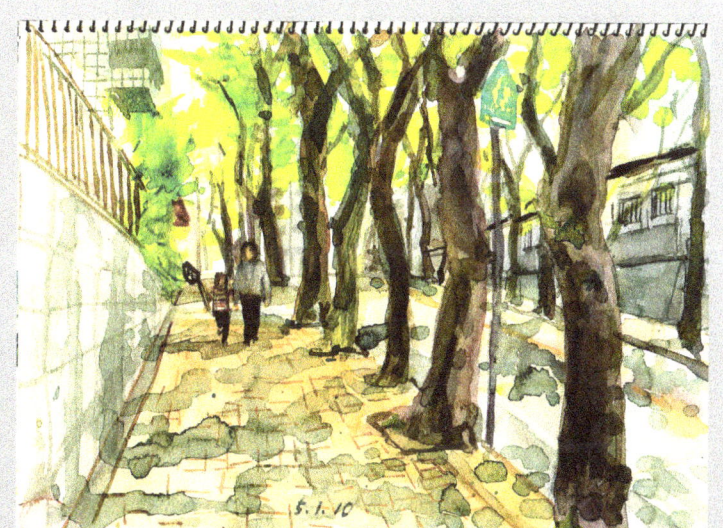

May

EVENTS, NEWS, AND PERFORMANCES

Drawing at events usually requires dealing with crowds and fast-moving performers, but the feeling of being part of history makes the experience worth it. Urban sketchers are always ready to capture the fleeting moments at street markets, sports stadiums, or music halls, creating a record impossible to replicate.

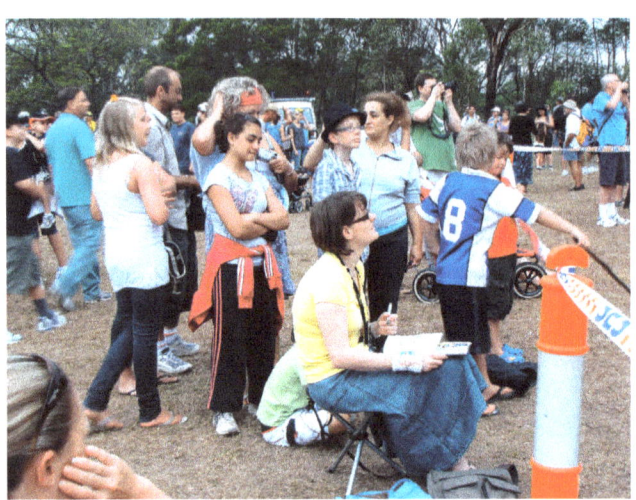

☺ Australia Day Sydney architect Liz Steel had a fun hour sketching hot air balloons at 6 a.m., the earliest she has ever been out sketching, as part of the Australia Day holiday celebrations. "It was really nice to sketch such colorful subjects, and, although they were constantly moving, it was at a gentle pace," she says.

Tip "Don't worry about people looking over your shoulder." — *Liz Steel*

8" x 8.5" | 20 x 21.6 cm; Lamy Safari pen with Noodler's ink, Daniel Smith and Winsor & Newton Artists' watercolors on Daler-Rowney 150-gsm, Ebony cartridge-paper sketchbook; about 30 minutes

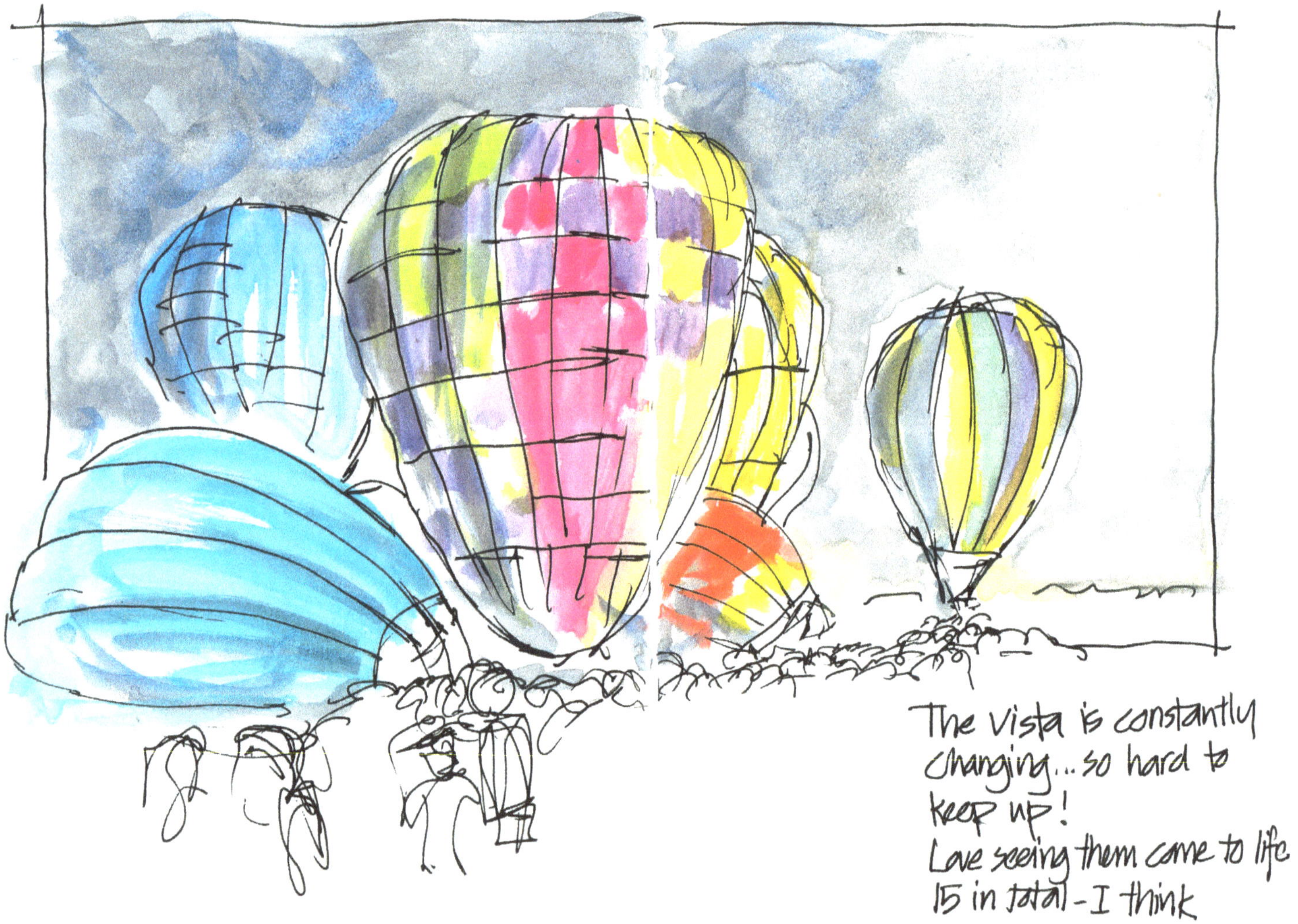

The vista is constantly changing...so hard to keep up!
Love seeing them come to life
15 in total - I think

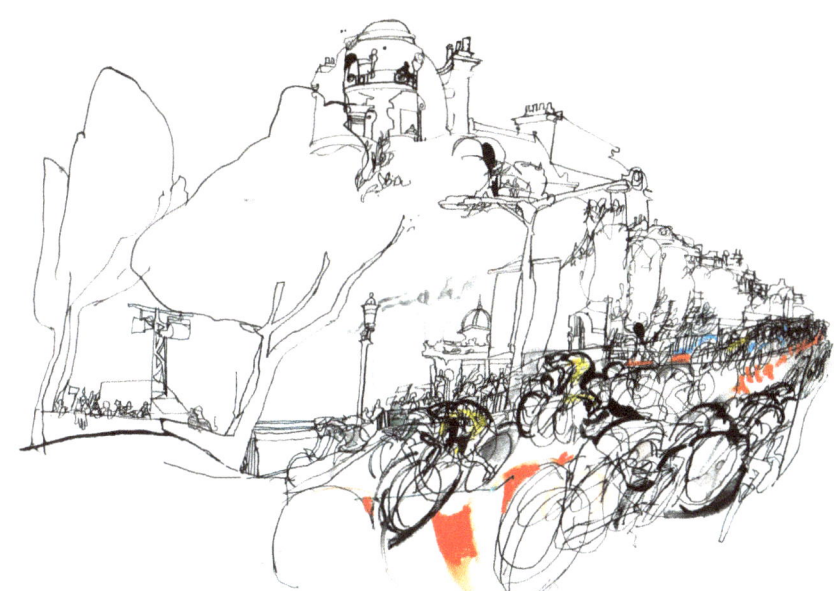

Tour de France at Champs-Elysees New York illustrator Veronica Lawlor waited on the street for hours with the crowd, only to have the bicycles race by in less than a minute. "I felt a part of sports history by recording it. I drew the waiting crowd and also the scene of the street, in preparation for adding the bikers, when they came by."

Tip "When drawing something as fast paced as this bicycle race, trust your instincts and let your hand move wherever your eyes travel. Don't bother looking down at the page to see what you're doing; there isn't time!" — *Veronica Lawlor*

18" x 12" | 45.5 x 30.5 cm; dip pen and brush with ink, Caran d'Ache watercolor crayons, on Bienfang heavyweight drawing paper; 30 minutes of drawing the street, 10 minutes of drawing the bikers (they came around twice)

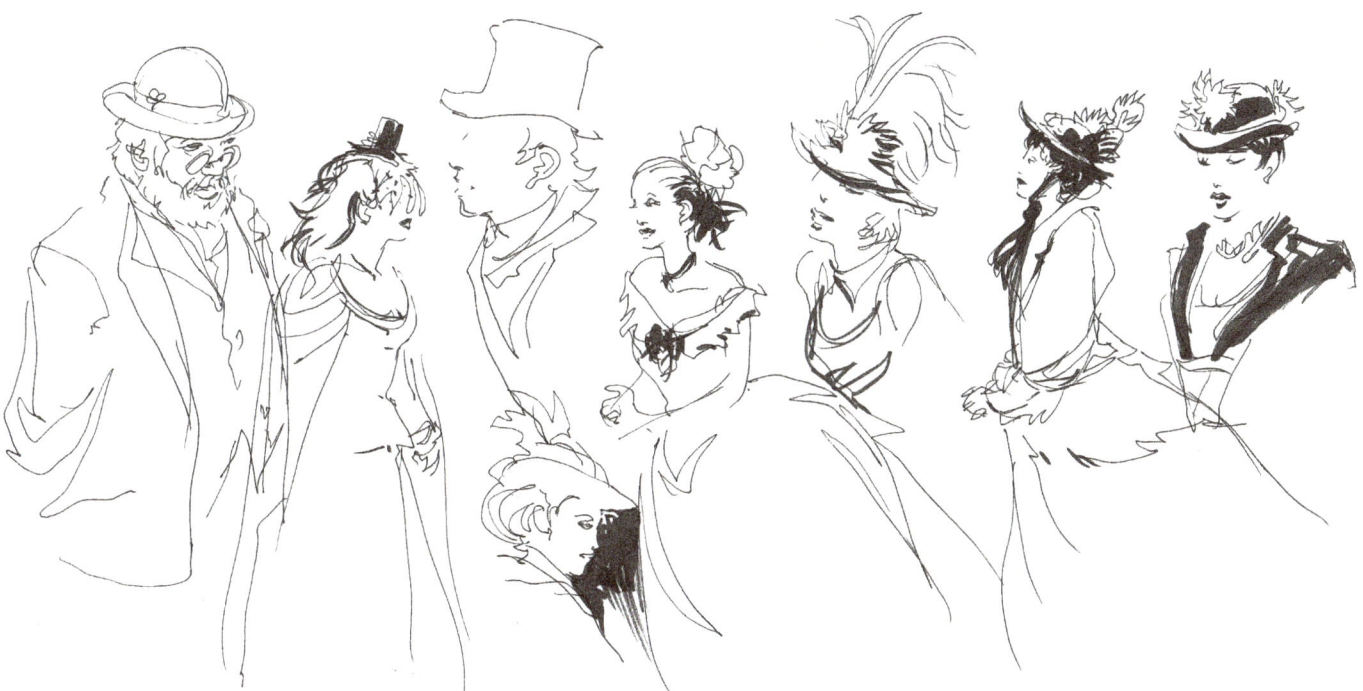

San Francisco's Great Dickens Christmas Fair Hundreds turn out in Victorian-era costume for this event. These quick sketches are just a glimpse of the variety, says Marc Taro Holmes. "There are pirates, rail barons, fortune tellers, carolers, street urchins, admirals, dancing girls, hussars, chimney sweeps, Turkish merchants, deep sea explorers—it just goes on and on."

Tip "People move too quickly to worry much about any one drawing. You have to just keep moving, drawing anything that catches your eye—sometimes even finishing one person with a second person who walks by in a similar outfit." — *Marc Taro Holmes*

11" x 17" | 28 x 43 cm; Uni-ball Signo pen and Pentel GFKP brush pen on 70-lb. photocopy paper; about 1 minute each

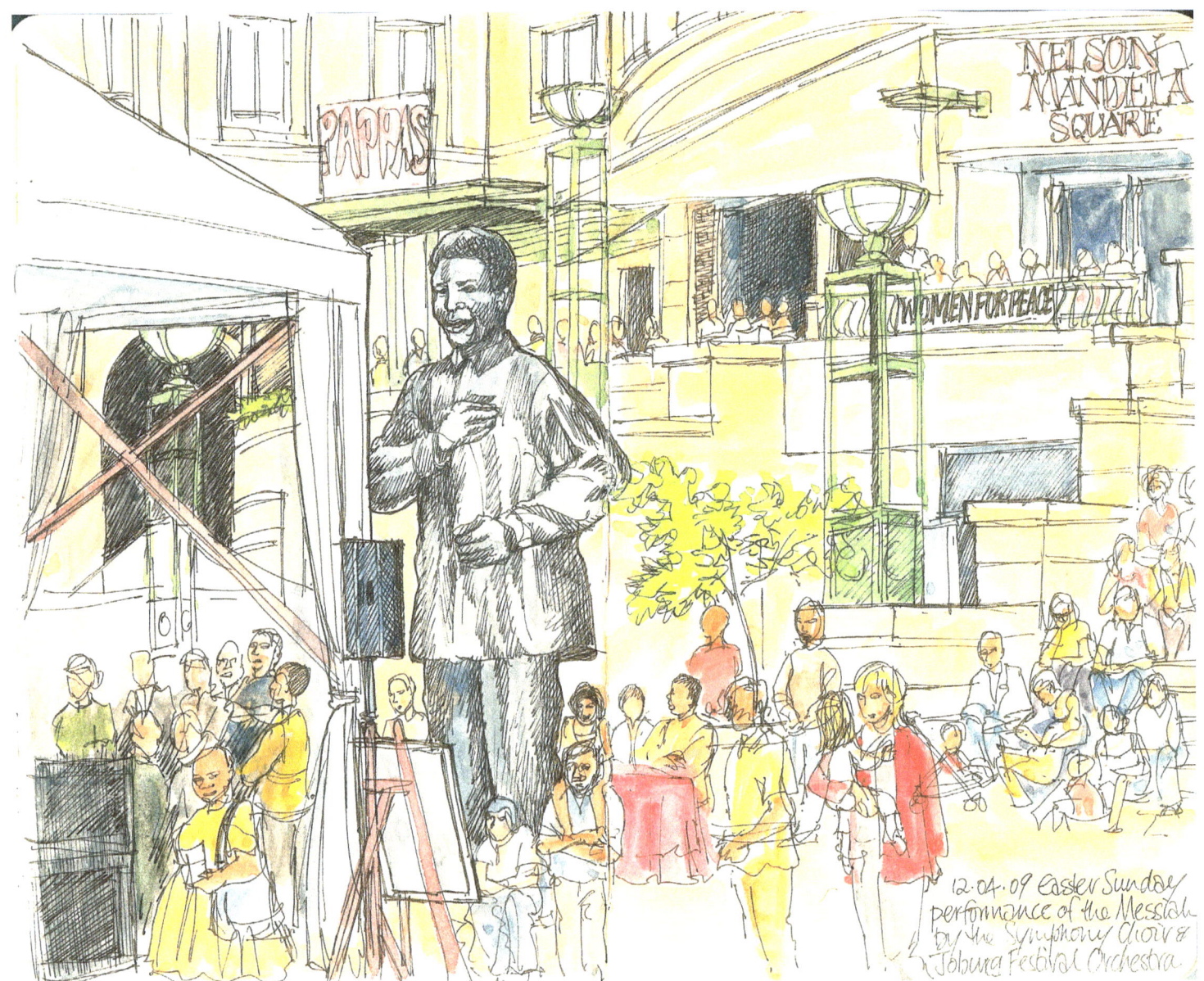

∩ **Nelson Mandela Square** An annual event at Easter time is a free performance of Handel's *Messiah* at Nelson Mandela Square in Johannesburg. Festival Orchestra and the Symphony Choir of Johannesburg. "This was one of my early public sketching attempts," says Cathy Gatland, "and I felt nervous and shaky, but most people ignored, or pretended to, what I was doing.

Tip If there's no room to spread out paints, make light pencil notes about main colors and add them later." — *Cathy Gatland*

10.25" x 8.25" | 26 x 21 cm Mitsubishi uni PIN 0.2 pen, Cotman watercolor travel set, Pentel Aquash waterbrush on Moleskine sketchbook; about 1.5 hours

⊃ **NYC's Fashion Week** As a professor at New York's Fashion Institute of Technology, Melanie Reim might have a lot to say to the reporters covering Fashion Week at Columbus Circle, but she was more interested in recording them in her sketchbook. "They could not be more oblivious of me–and that added to my interest in drawing them," she says. "Fashion Week brings out all the pundits discussing the latest trends in color and length, sleeves or strapless, one shoulder or two, and how our First Lady now has the added responsibility of leading the pack," says Reim.

10.25" x 8" | 26 x 20 cm; Flair marker, Staedtler Mars Brush Marker, on Moleskine pad; 10 minutes

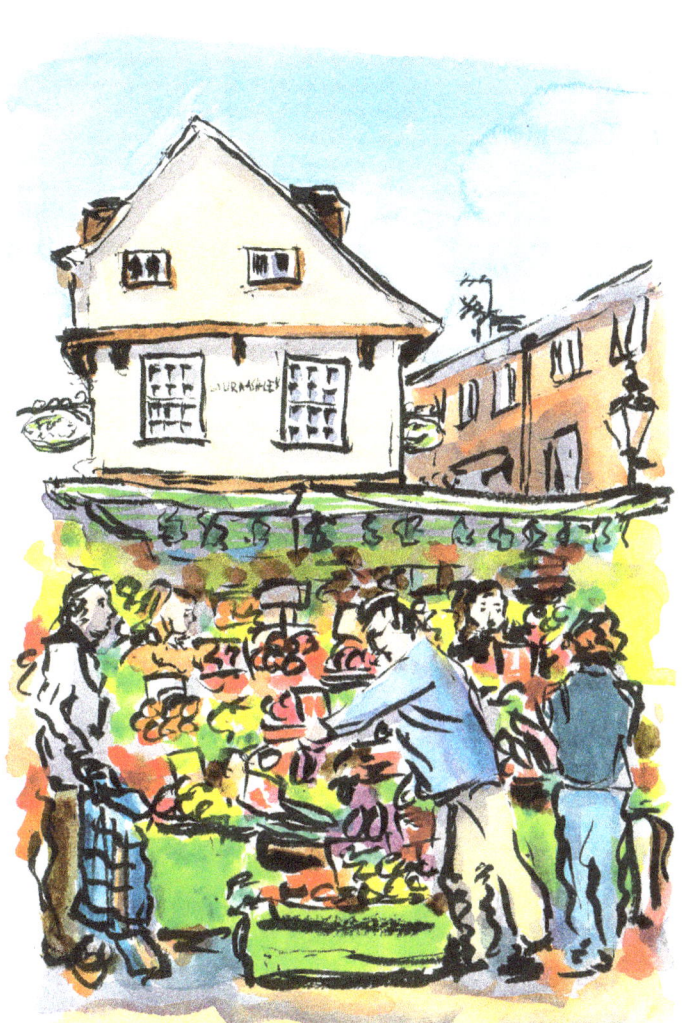

ℭ St. Albans Saturday Market

Illustrator Julie Oakley feels fortunate to live in a town with a monthly farm-ers' market, a lively street market every Wednesday and Saturday, and the occasional French and Italian market days. She says she attracted quite a lot of attention while doing this sketch sitting on a camping stool.

Tip "If you draw in a crowded place, be prepared to chat to lots of people looking over your shoulder, or get there very early, before the crowds arrive."
— *Julie Oakley*

8" x 5.25" | 20 x 13 cm; Pentel brush pen and Winsor & Newton watercolors on Moleskine watercolor book: 30 minutes

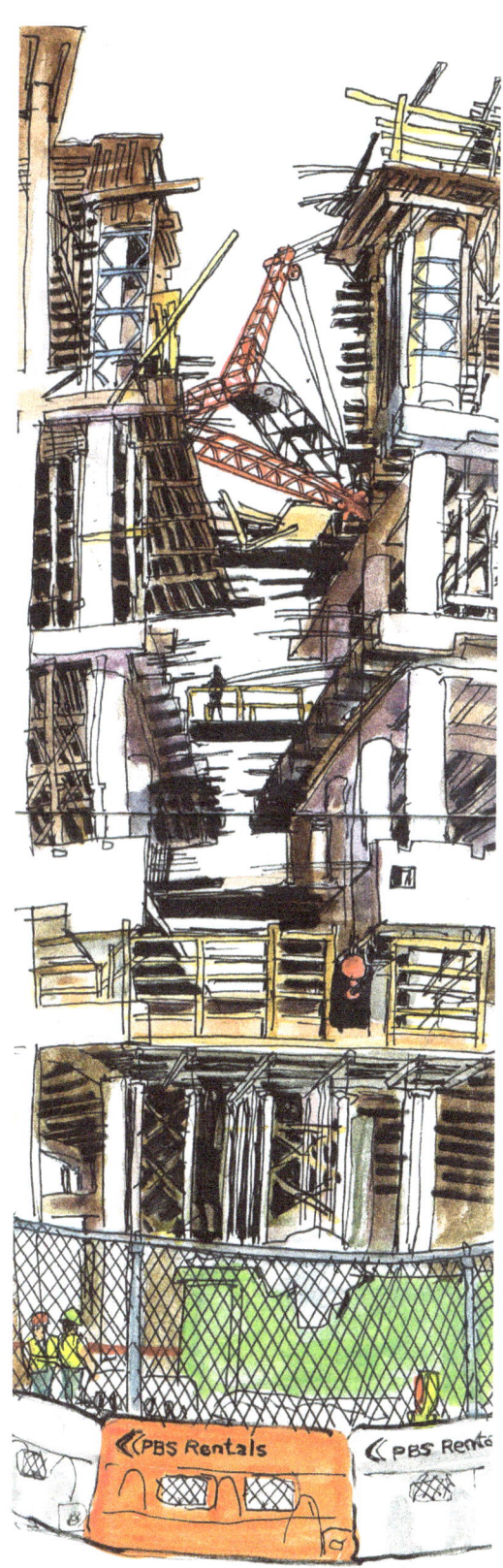

ℭ Crane Collapses

Thomas Thorspecken headed downtown about thirty minutes after this crane collapsed. "The operator was taken to the hospital in shock, but there were no injuries," Thorspecken says.

Tip "I simply sat down between news crews and started sketching. If you look like you belong, you do belong. I don't make it a habit to chase ambulances, but if something big happens, I will be drawn to it like a moth to a flame."
— *Thomas Thorspecken*

16.5" x 5.25" | 42 x 13 cm; Micron pens, Winsor & Newton watercolors on Hand-Book Travelogue Journal; 1.5 hours

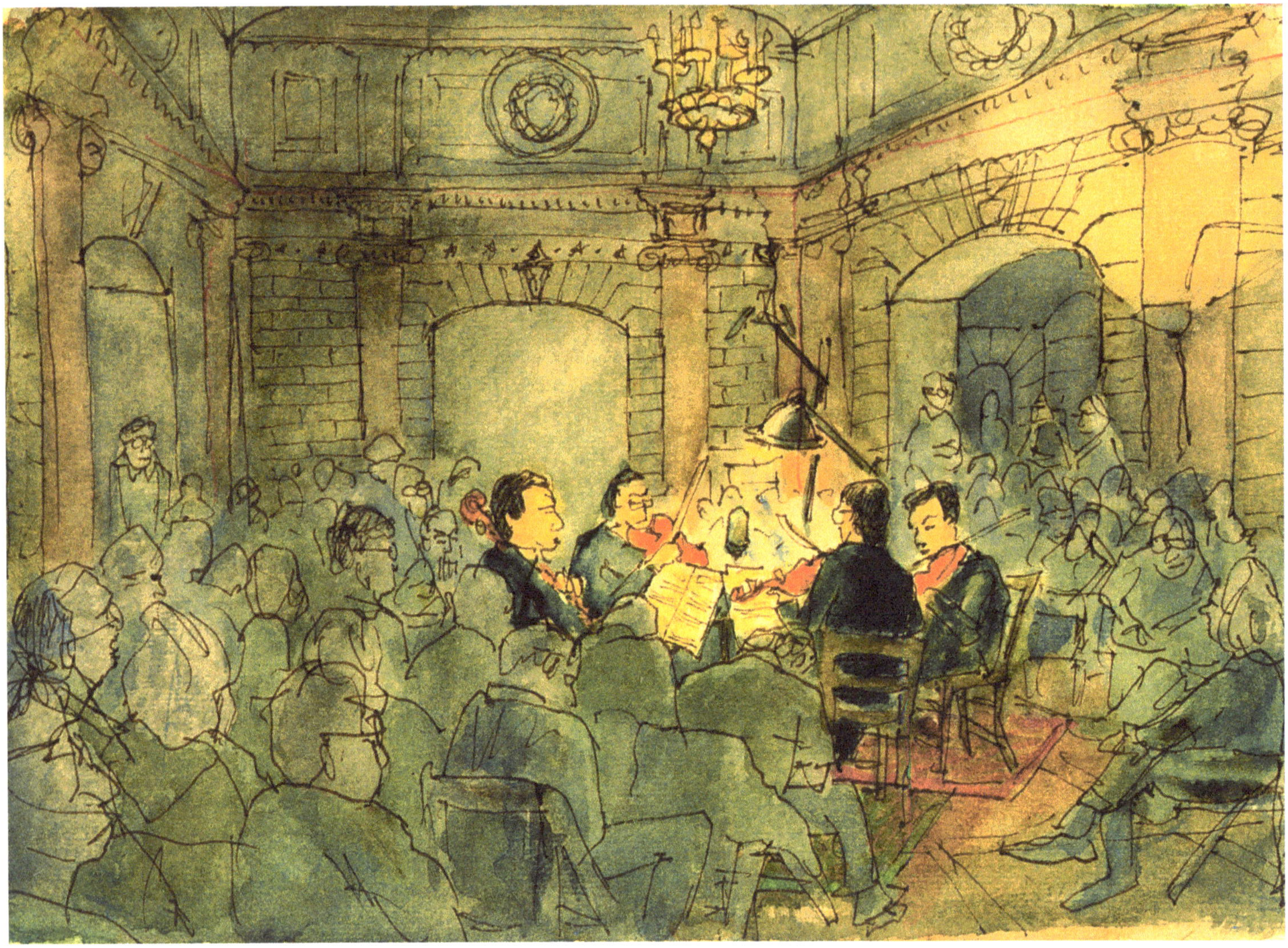

String Quartet Brooklyn artist Jason Das says the success of this sketch is largely due to the perspective and the completeness of the scene. "The whole room is there, and all the people in it. The lighting is very focused, but there are not a lot of shadows. Most elements are simply either lit or not. I kept adding layers of gray paint, until the lit areas popped enough," says Das.

5" x 7" | 12.5 x 18 cm; Pitt Artist pen (sepia) and watercolors (various brands) on a handmade sketchbook bought at a craft fair; about 20 minutes for the sketch, with more time for painting afterward

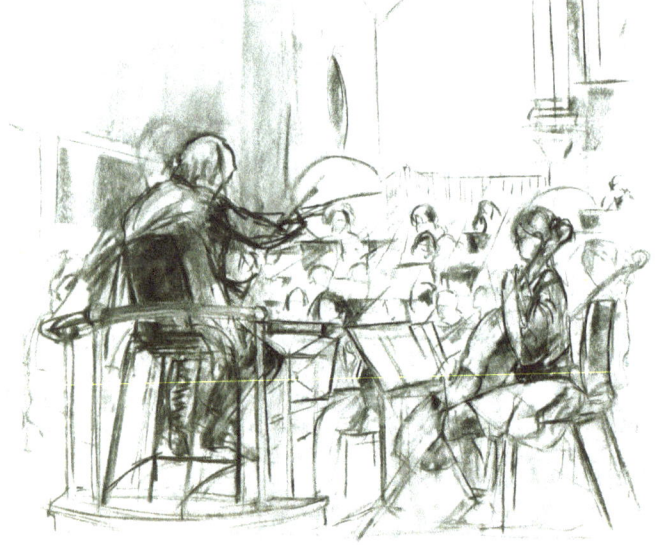

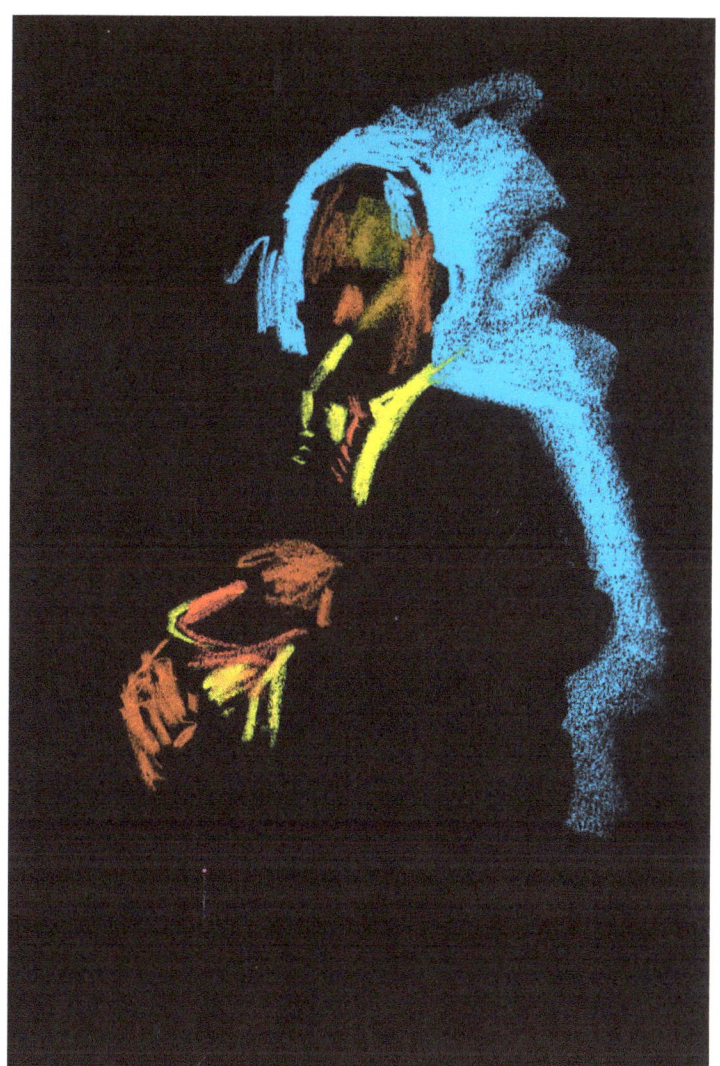

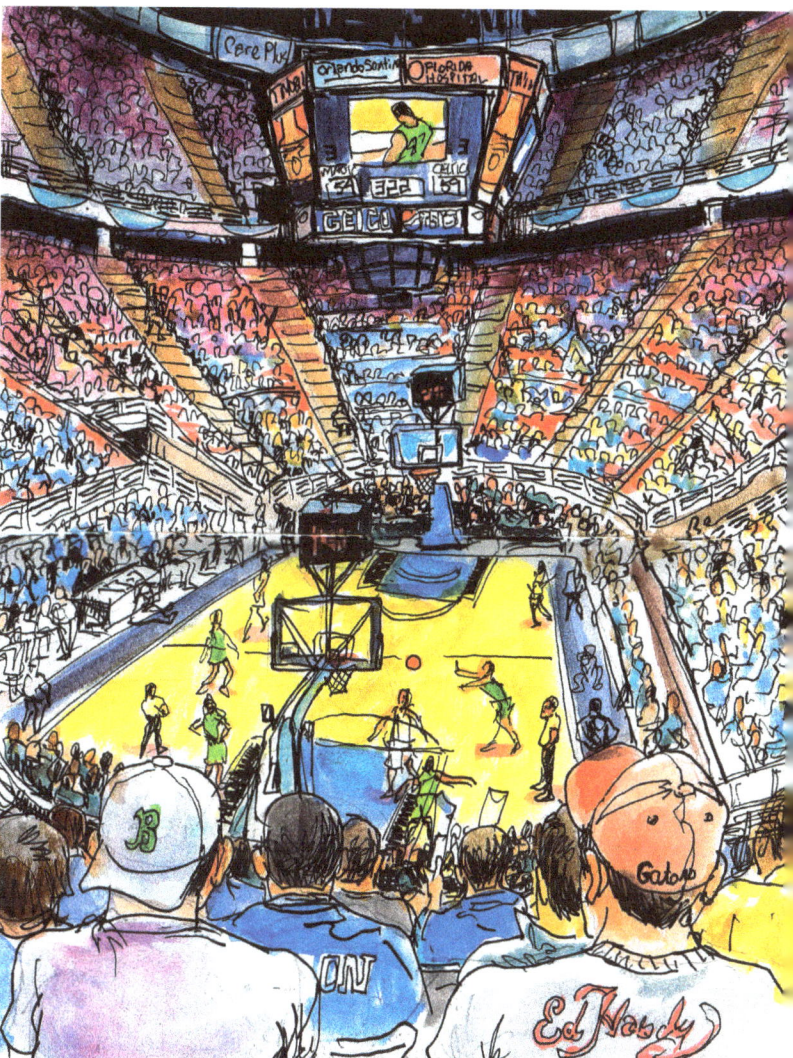

♫ Jazz at Lincoln Center Knowing that he was going to draw jazz musicians in a dark club, New York City illustrator Greg Betza brought materials that would allow for an expressive line as well as visibility. "The crayon popped off of the black paper, making it easy to see my drawing in the dimly lit club," he says.

A4 (8.3" x 11.7" | 21 x 29.7 cm); Caran d'Ache Neocolor II water-soluble crayons on Daler-Rowney Canford black paper; 5 minutes

♫ Orlando Magic and the Boston Celtics "I finished the sketch with only a few minutes to go in the game," Thomas Thorspecken says. "The crowd was standing and going wild.

Tip "I started by trying to figure out how much of the stadium I wanted to fit onto the page. Once I had those big decisions made, lightly in pencil, I focused on details that didn't move. When I felt confident I could finish the sketch in the time I had, I relaxed, throwing in crowd details." — *Thomas Thorspecken*

8.25" x 10.25" | 21.6 x 26 cm; Micron pens, Winsor & Newton watercolor, on Hand-Book Travelogue Journal; the duration of the game

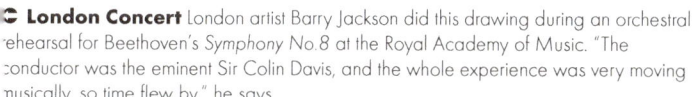

♫ London Concert London artist Barry Jackson did this drawing during an orchestral rehearsal for Beethoven's *Symphony No.8* at the Royal Academy of Music. "The conductor was the eminent Sir Colin Davis, and the whole experience was very moving musically, so time flew by," he says.

Tip "There had been three or four less successful drawings, in different media, before this. I find that, faced with complex subjects, the first drawings are seldom successful, so it's best not to expect them to work until you're at number four." — *Barry Jackson*

17.5" x 13.75" | 44.5 x 35 cm; charcoal on Daler-Rowney 180-gsm cartridge paper

SUBWAYS, BUSES, AND AIRPORTS

Sketching and travel go hand in hand. Whether you are commuting across town or flying across the world, something about being in transit makes you want to keep a record of the journey. Subways, in particular, seem to be sketch incubators, deserving of a category of their own in the art of urban sketching.

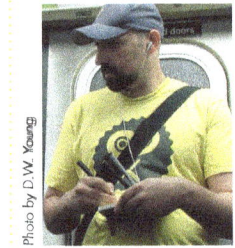

Photo by D.W. Young

ARTIST PROFILE
Ami Plasse

A temporary long commute to Queens years ago inspired me to spend a little more time drawing on the train. The richness of the subject matter was unparalleled. Since then, I have also become addicted to using Moleskine sketchbooks, which fit perfectly in a back pocket and can be easily whipped out, whether I am sitting or standing against a door or pole.

As someone who loves to draw characters, I think there is no greater source of inspiration than the New York City subway system. On any given day, you can find people of multiple races and nationalities. I've drawn thousands of subway sketches, by now, posting them on my blog and exhibiting them in art galleries.

"If you can get rid of the fear of mistakes and creating a bad drawing, then you can get loose enough to start doing really honest, expressive work."

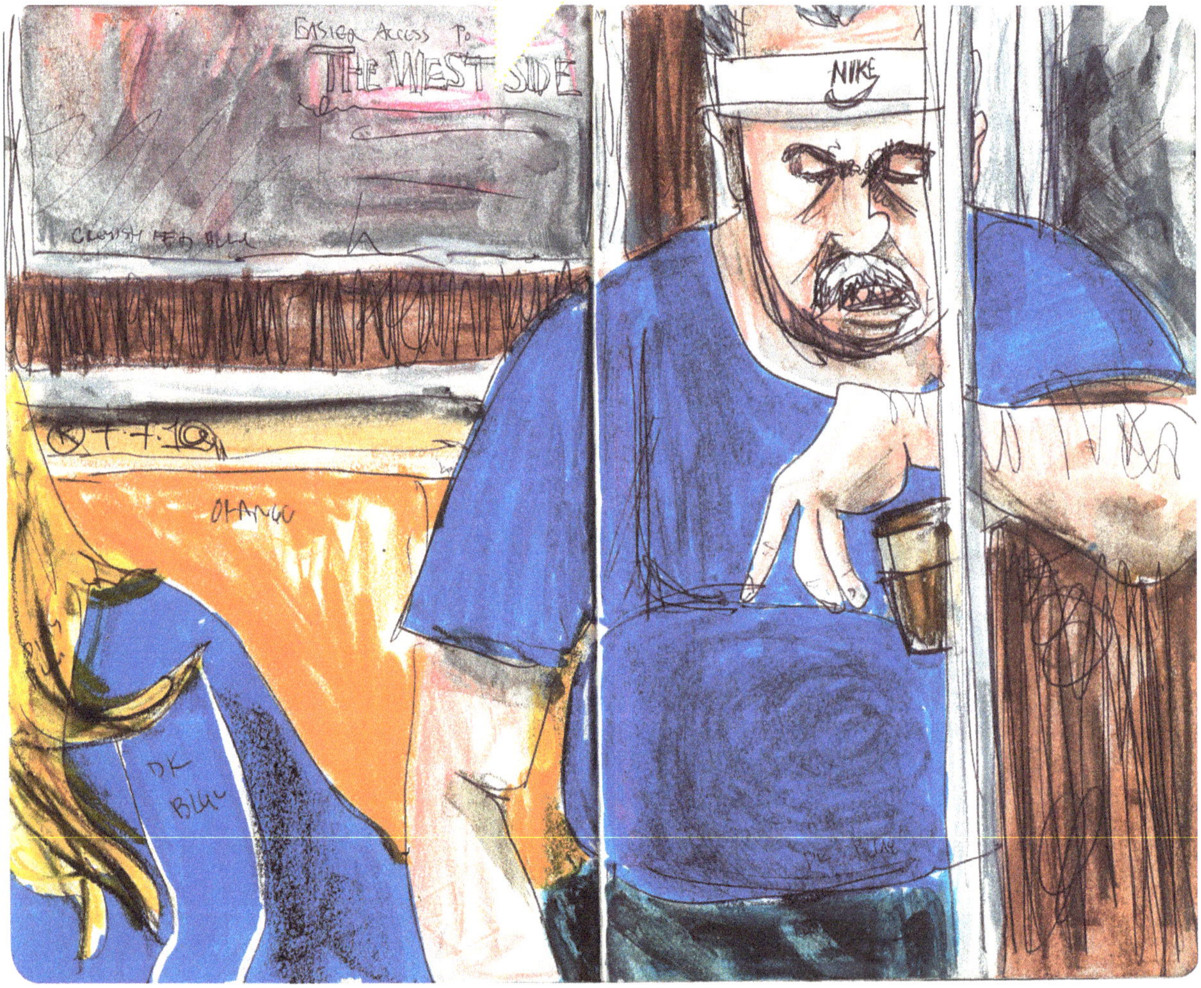

5.5" x 7" | 14 x 18 cm;
Moleskine pocket sketchbook, pen, and markers

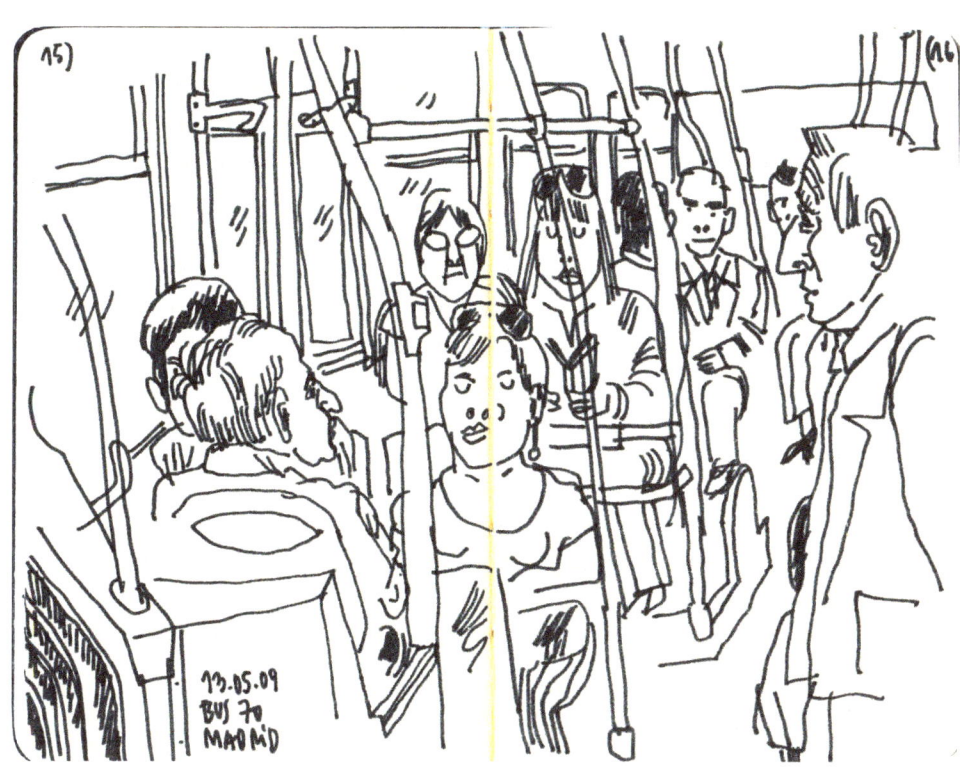

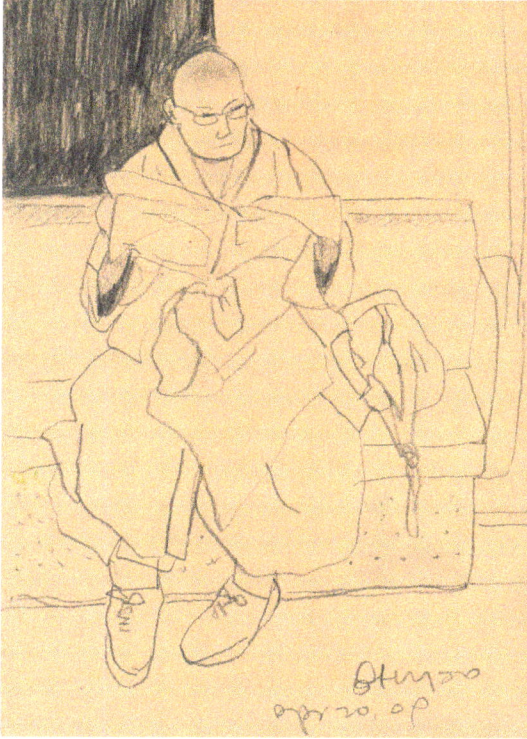

🎧 **The Stage** Madrid-based illustrator Richard Câmara stood up the entire time the bus was moving, but he said this sketch was done quite slowly. "It became a challenge to set all the poles and people in their places, which made me understand more about the inside of the bus—as if it was a theatre," Câmara says. "Suddenly, every commuter seemed an actor in this four-wheeled moving stage."

Tip "Use the poles as a visual reference to place the passengers inside the bus." — *Richard Câmara*

5.5" x 7" | 14 x 18 cm; black Pilot SignPen felt-tip pen on Moleskine pocket sketchbook; 15–20 minutes

🎧 **Seoul Subway Sketch** Yoo Byung Hwa sketched a Buddhist nun reading a free daily newspaper. "There was no wrinkle in her gray robe. I drew her with a feeling of respect for her peaceful feature and mood," he says.

Tip "Sketchers can't guess when their models will get up and leave the train, so you need to draw simply, resolutely, and immediately, without caring about the results." — *Yoo Byung Hwa*

8.25" x 11.75" | 21 x 30 cm; Faber-Castell TK9400 4B clutch pencil on packaging paper; 10 minutes

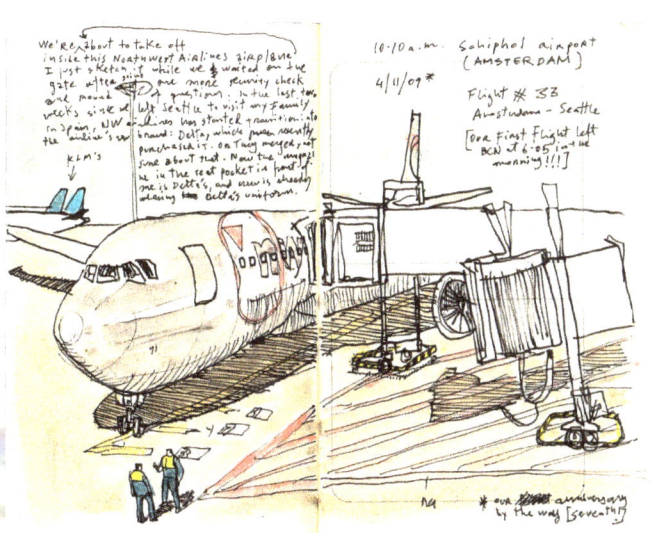

⟲ **Ready for Takeoff** Amsterdam's Schiphol airport is a regular stop for Seattle sketcher Gabriel Campanario almost every time he flies to see family in Spain.

Tip "Wait time at airports is a perfect opportunity to sketch. I always try to draw my airplane before it takes off." — *Gabriel Campanario*

7" x 5.5" | 18 x 14 cm; Micron pen on Moleskine pocket sketchbook; 15 minutes

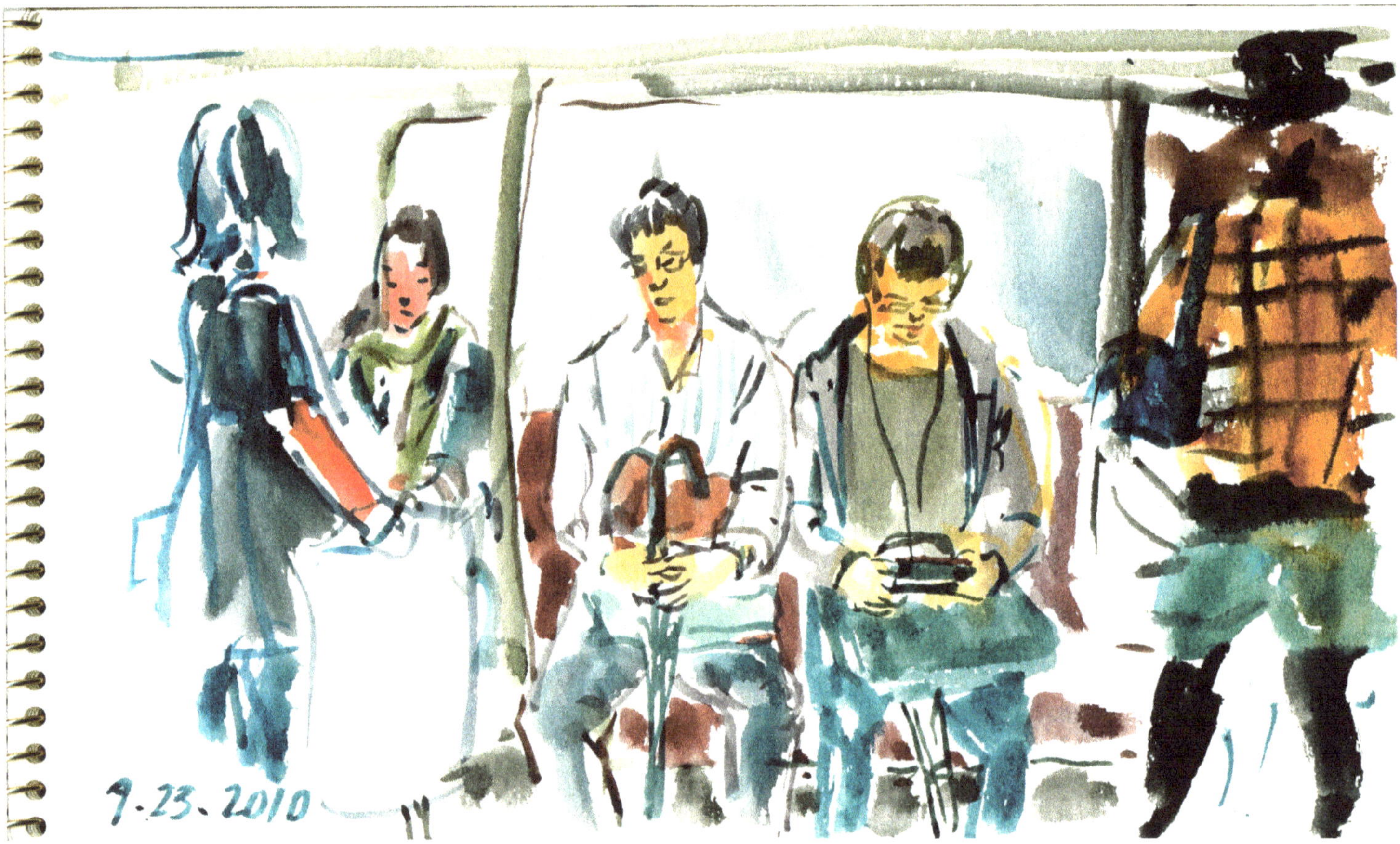

🎧 **In the Train** Kumi Matsukawa says the guy wearing headphones kept playing his game and never noticed her sketching him.

Tip "Keep your tools compact and handy on your lap. Stay relaxed. Don't watch but glance."
— *Kumi Matsukawa*

G1 (5.5" x 8.8" | 14 x 22.6 cm); 12-color pocket field sketch box, Pentel Aquash waterbrush, on Muse landscape sketchbook; 20 minutes

↪ **Train Commuters** On the train, we can draw different models every day, without having to pay them, says João Catarino. "The variety is extraordinary. It's also a challenge to draw surreptitiously, as well as a way to take advantage of the time. People on the train always have different expressions, depending on the day being sunny or rainy or whether they're on the way to work or back home."

23.5" x 8.25" | 60 x 21 cm; Talens Ecolines ink, water brush, Cadernos Flecha sketchbook from Papelaria Fernandes; 15 minutes

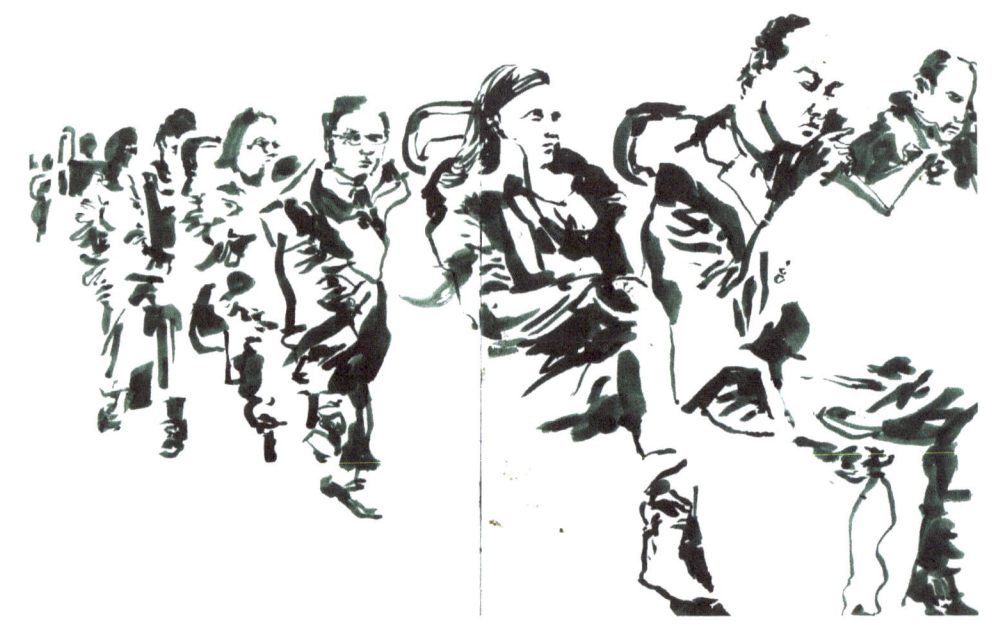

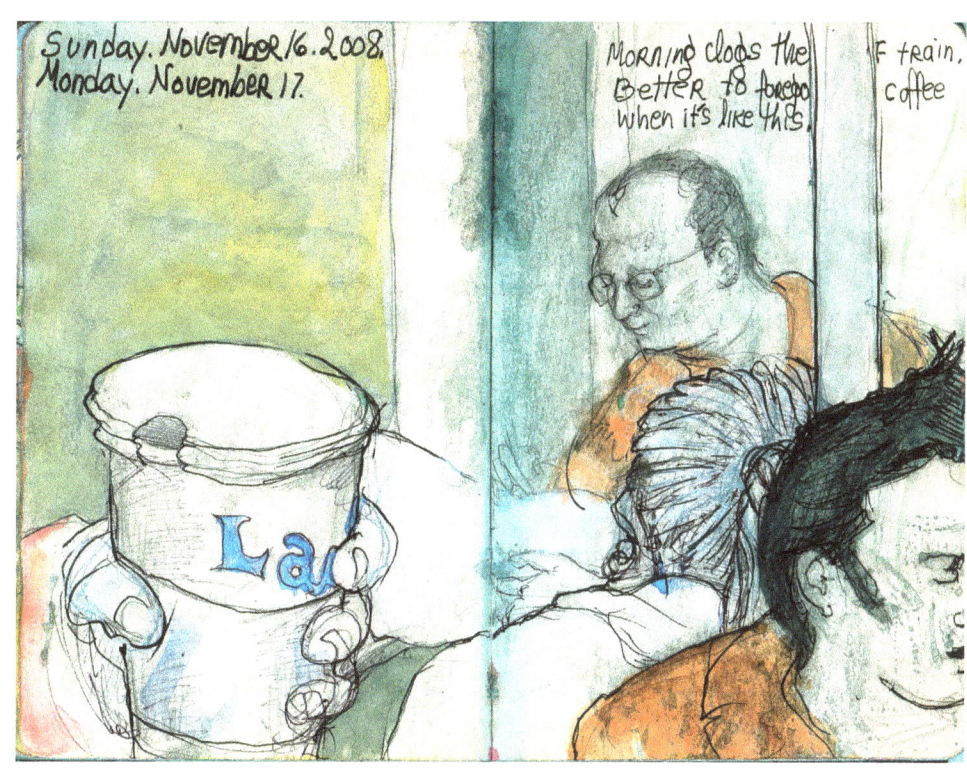

Sunday. November 16. 2008.
Monday. November 17.

Morning clods the! Better to forego when it's like this.

F train, coffee

↺ **Scatter-shot, on the F train** Sharon Frost was standing with one arm hooked around the pole, holding her sketchbook and nervously eyeing the coffee in the hand of her neighbor ("although coffee makes an excellent wash," she says).

Tip "When you're drawing on the subway, you have to learn to go with the flow. If you're standing and swaying, you have to let that happen in your drawing. You have to let go of the urge for control." — *Sharon Frost*

5" x 7" | 12.5 x 18 cm (double-page spread); Pilot Better Retractable ballpoint pen, Staedtler mechanical pencil, Lamy Safari fountain pen, various watercolor pencils, primarily Derwents, various water pens, Dove blender pen; Cotman watercolor field box, on Moleskine plain notebook; about 20 minutes, with some finishing at home

FIRST PERSON

The Young Couple—Greenwich to Belvedere

by Adebanji Alade

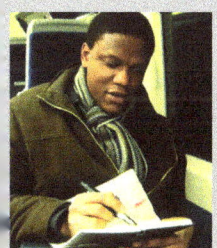

While on the train from London Bridge to Belvedere, I saw this guy and girl sleeping. I quickly started sketching. Then, the models became curious, and, in a not so friendly voice, the guy said, "What do you think you are doing?" That got me alarmed! I said, in a more friendly voice, "sketching"; I showed him some pages from my sketchbook, and he just sighed in disgust. He said, "Why are you doing this?" I simply said, "This is my life, I'm an artist, I do this every day." Then, a few minutes later, as I continued, he said, "Let me see the one you are doing of us." I showed him and watched his mood suddenly change. He shouted, "Wow!" He then apologized for speaking to me aggressively. I promised to send him a scanned copy. He was all smiles at the end! I left the train with a beam of the joy of sketching!

8" x 6" | 20 x 15 cm; Tombow brush pen #75, Bic Biro ballpoint pen on Daler-Rowney A6 sketchbook with 150-gsm, acid-free cartridge paper; 21 minutes

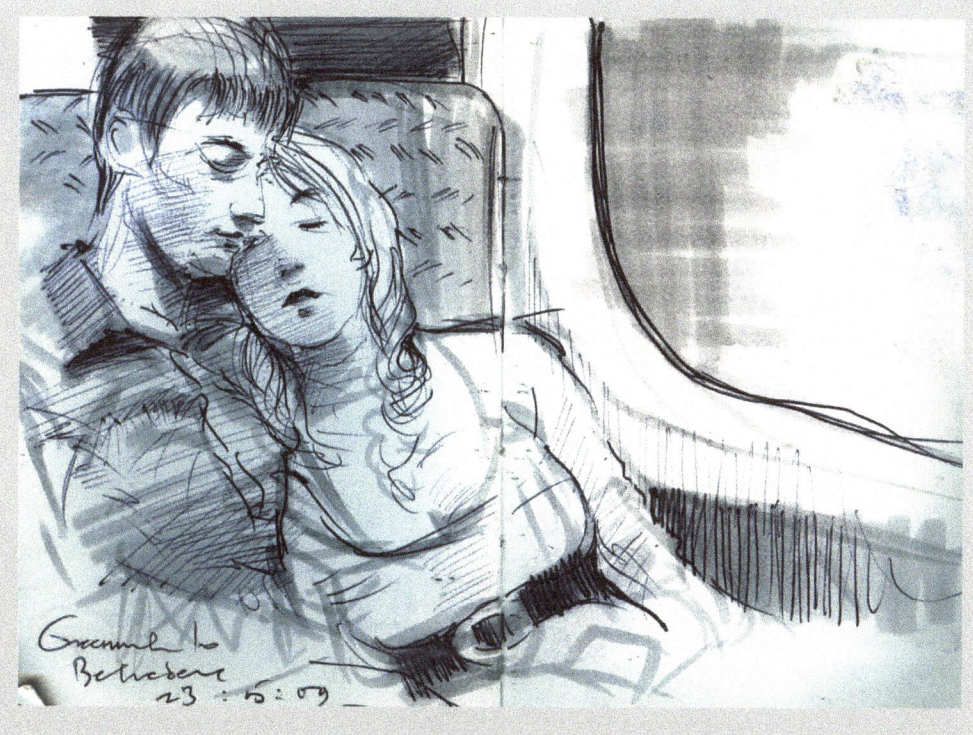

Greenwich to Belvedere 23.05.09

⊃ Bus Runway Bus rides give sketchers an opportunity to draw all sorts of people. Some might be there for the whole bus trip; others make a quick exit, giving an unexpected twist to every sketch. "It's like a free live-model class—especially if you want to focus on certain details, such as faces, hands, feet, legs, and profiles," says Richard Câmara.

Tip "Place each portrait randomly on the spread, to create a more dynamic layout, drawing in different sizes and mixing postures. If this seems complicated at first, don't think too much about it and draw freely." — *Richard Câmara*

11" x 3.5" | 28 x 9 cm; black Bic ballpoint pen, Moleskine plain pocket notebook with 60-gsm paper; about 20 minutes

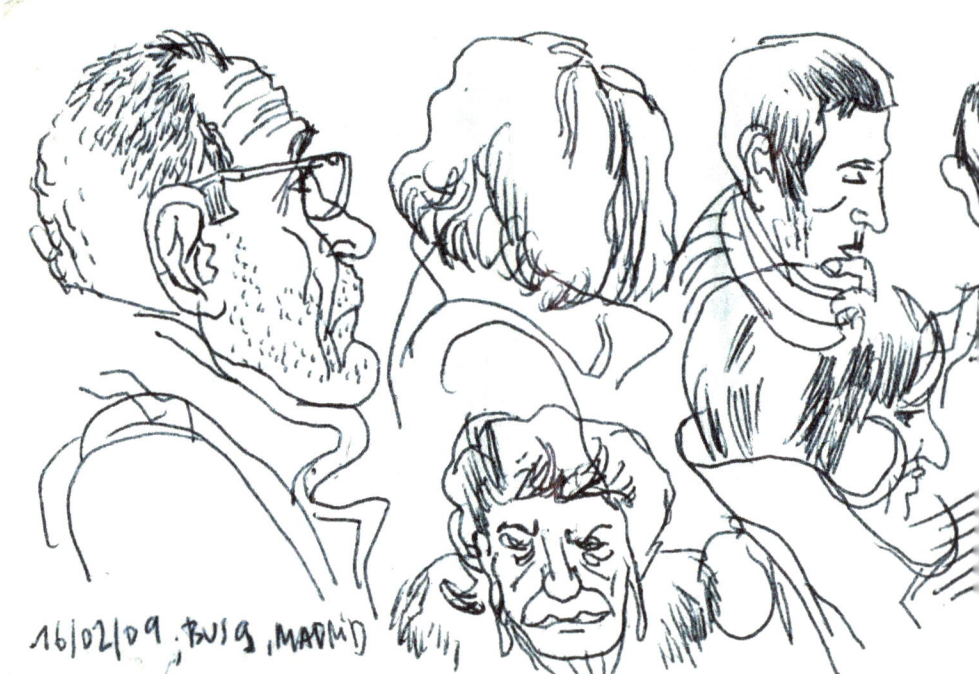

⊃ Life on the 5
Stephen Gardner says he used to read on his subway commute, but now sketching consumes his time instead.

Tip "I always try to draw people who are asleep or reading. I do not want the subjects to know they are being drawn, and, most times, if they spot me, the drawing is over. I used to hate my commute, but now I really enjoy the subways for the drawing opportunities they offer."
— *Stephen Gardner*

3.5" x 5.5" | 9 x 14 cm; .7 mechanical pencil with F or B lead on Moleskine sketchbook; about 20–30 minutes

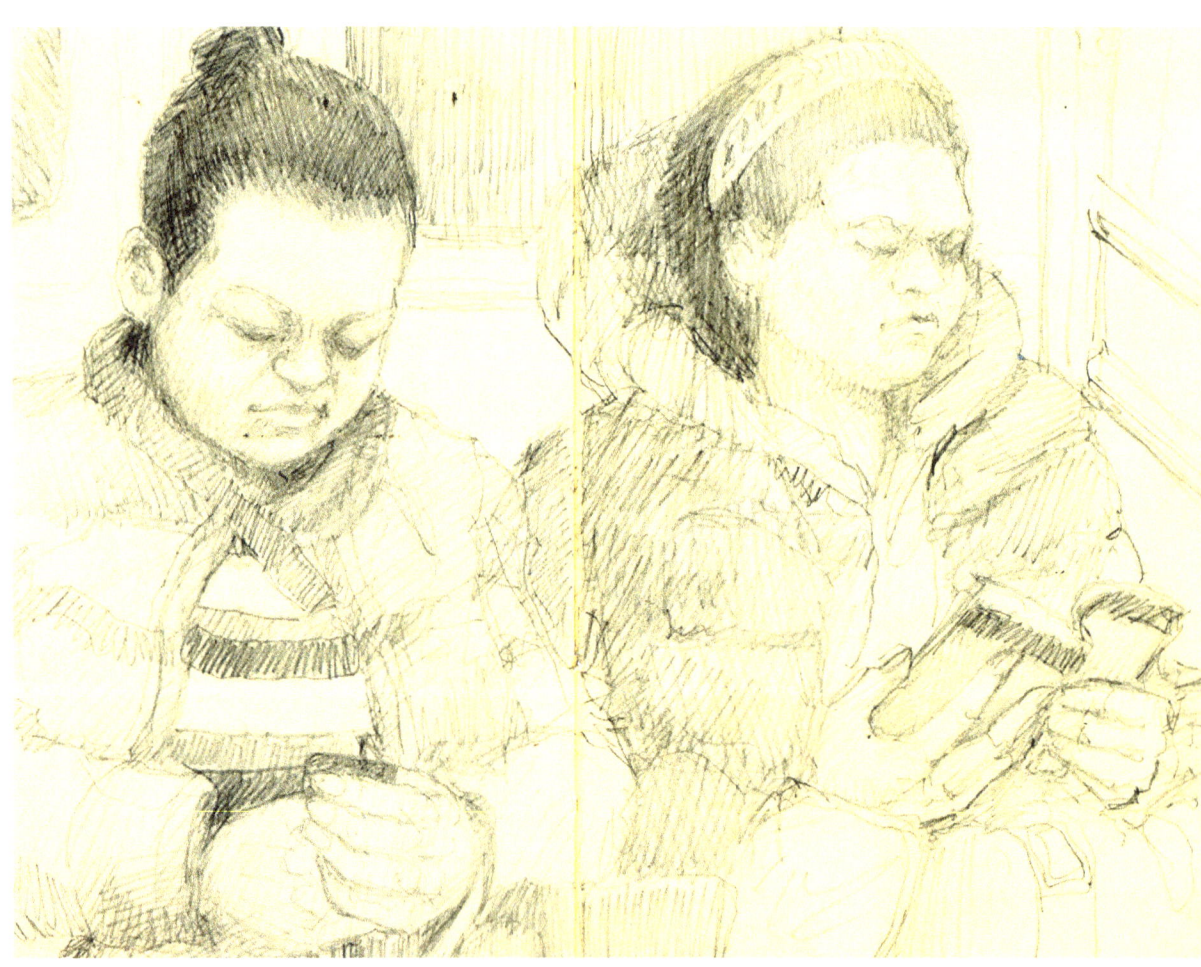

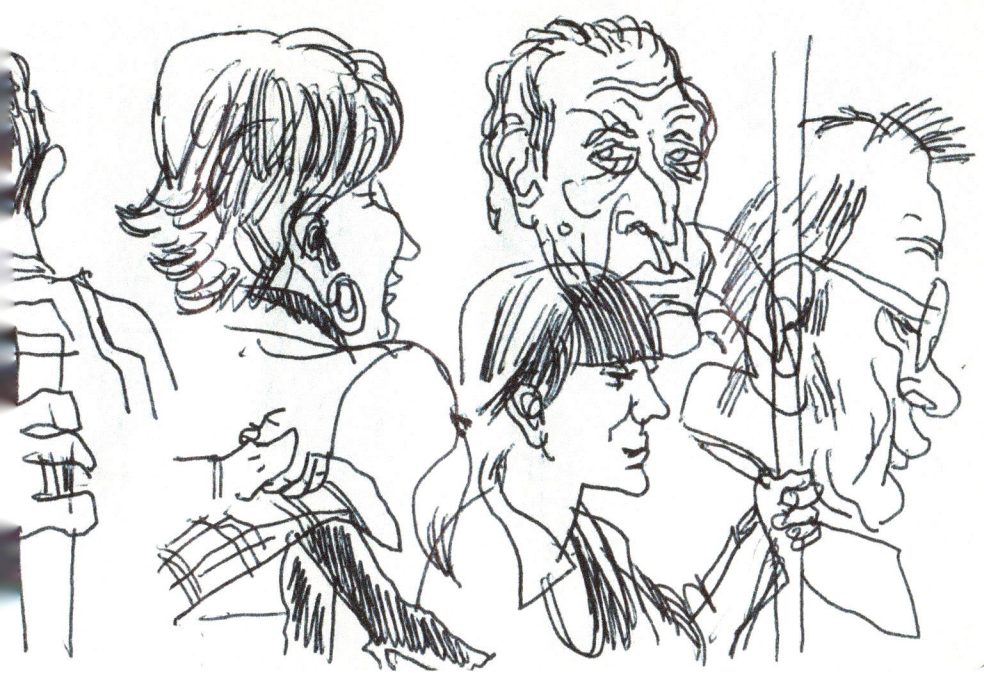

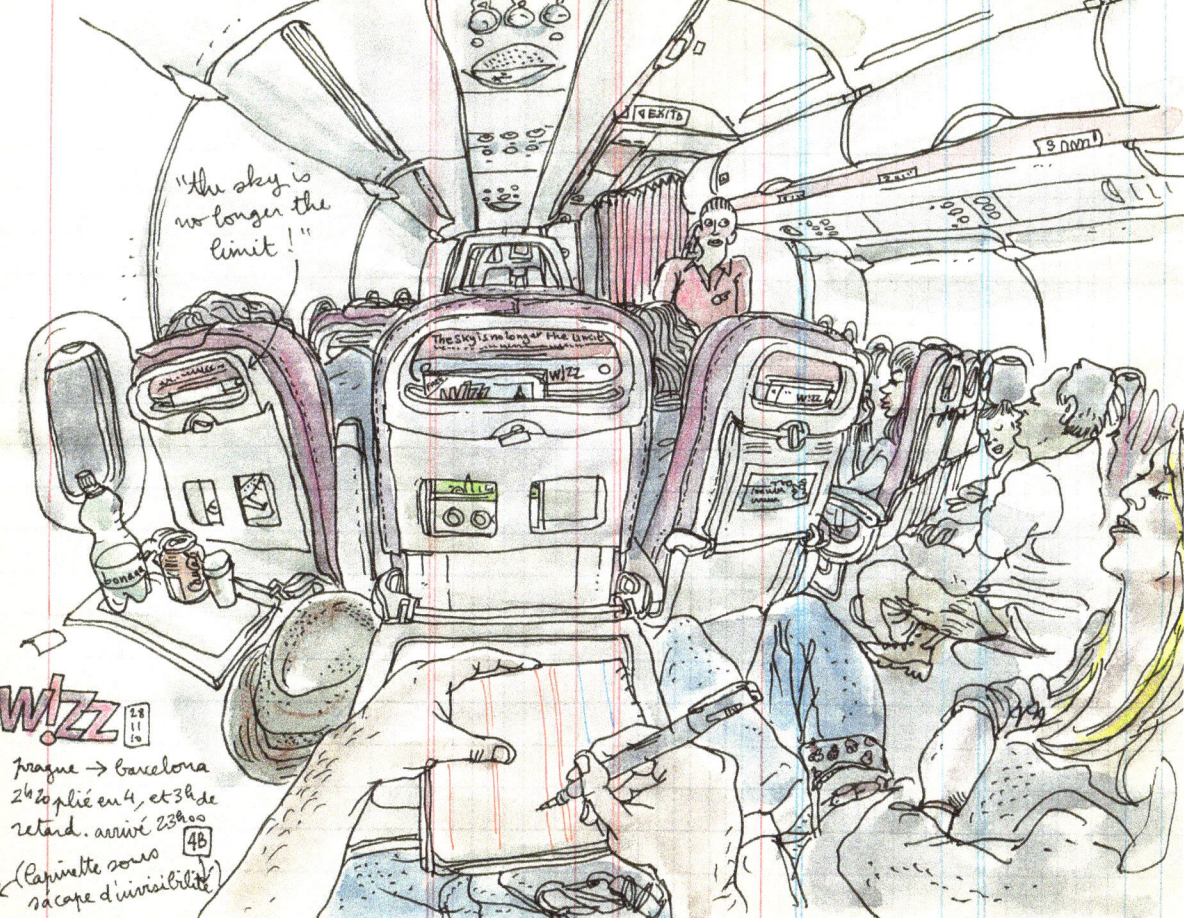

↻ **Wizz Airline** During a burst of frequent travel on short trips around Europe, Lapin started to sketch the view from his seat to pass time. "It makes the flight feel shorter," he says.

Tip "I wish I could explain this fisheye effect, but it's just the way I see the scene and draw it on paper. No tricks."— *Lapin*

8.25" x 6" | 21 x 15 cm; Mitsubishi uni PIN fine line 0.1 inkpen, Daler-Rowney watercolors, Pentel waterbrush, wax crayons on vintage account book; 40 minutes

CAFÉS, RESTAURANTS, AND BARS

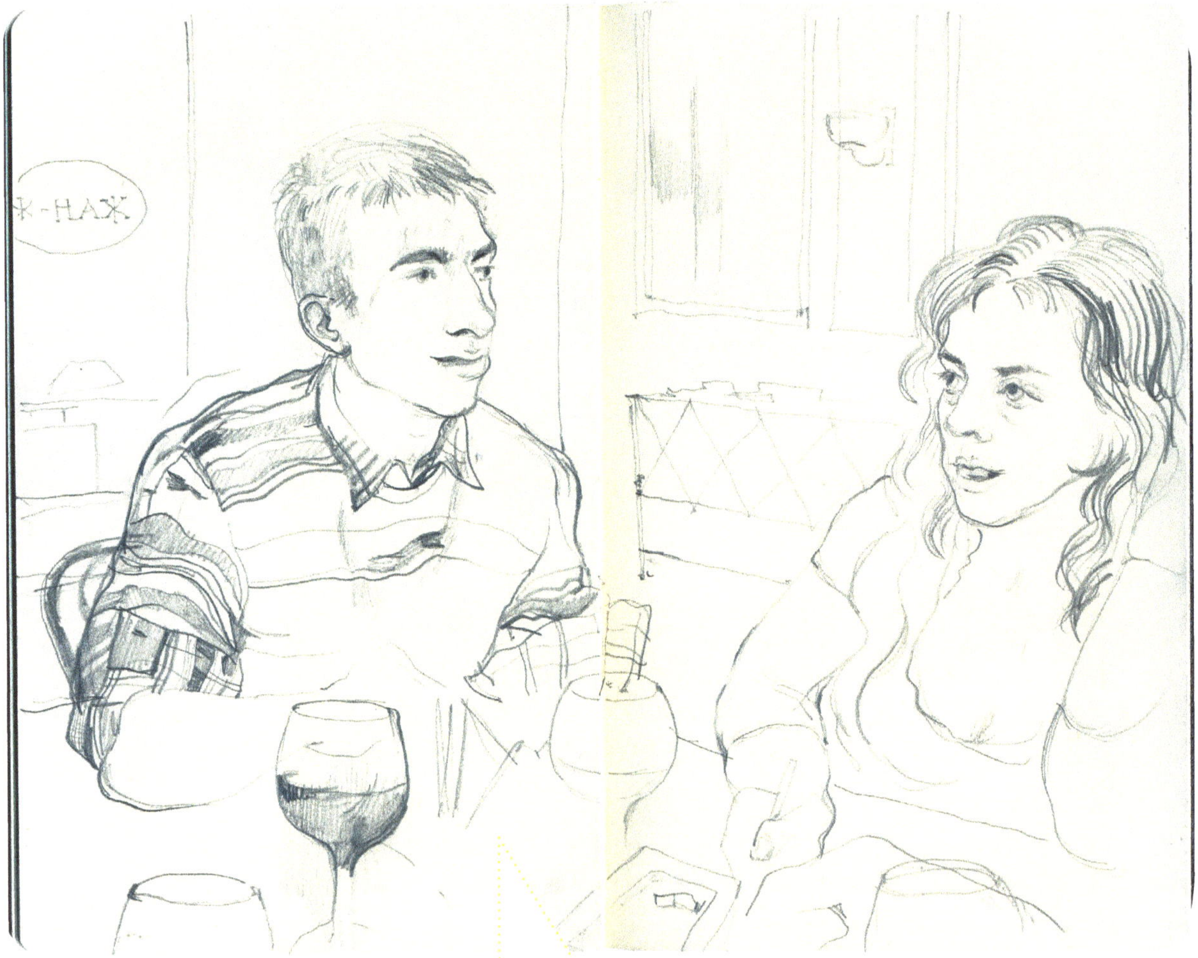

Cafés and restaurants are ideal for sketching people absorbed in reading or conversation, your own cup of coffee, or the food on your plate, if you are fast enough to draw it before it gets cold. Urban sketchers are always ready to pick up their pens as soon as they put down their utensils and vice versa.

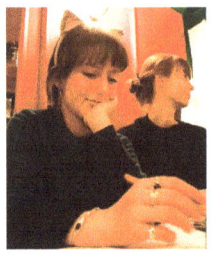

One evening at the Jean Jacques Rousseau café, Ekaterina Khozatskaya drew friends who met for the first time.

5.25" x 8.25" | 13 21 cm; pencil; about 2 hours

ARTIST PROFILE
Ekaterina Khozatskaya

For me, visiting a bar is the same cultural experience as going to the theater or museum or watching a movie. It is architecture, music, literature, and cinema all in one. Drawing in bars helps to get these things altogether—you choose the seat with the best view and start spying. Different people around, how they act in the place, the way they look around, different stories, different voices, and music make the real mood. That's where you can get inspiration, even without alcohol.

You can imagine the ideal evening: dark party bar, Billie Holiday playing, wine shines in the glasses, drops of beer on the table, the smell of cinnamon and somebody's perfume, soft light, beautiful dresses and colors, people laughing. And you can draw it all the way you want!

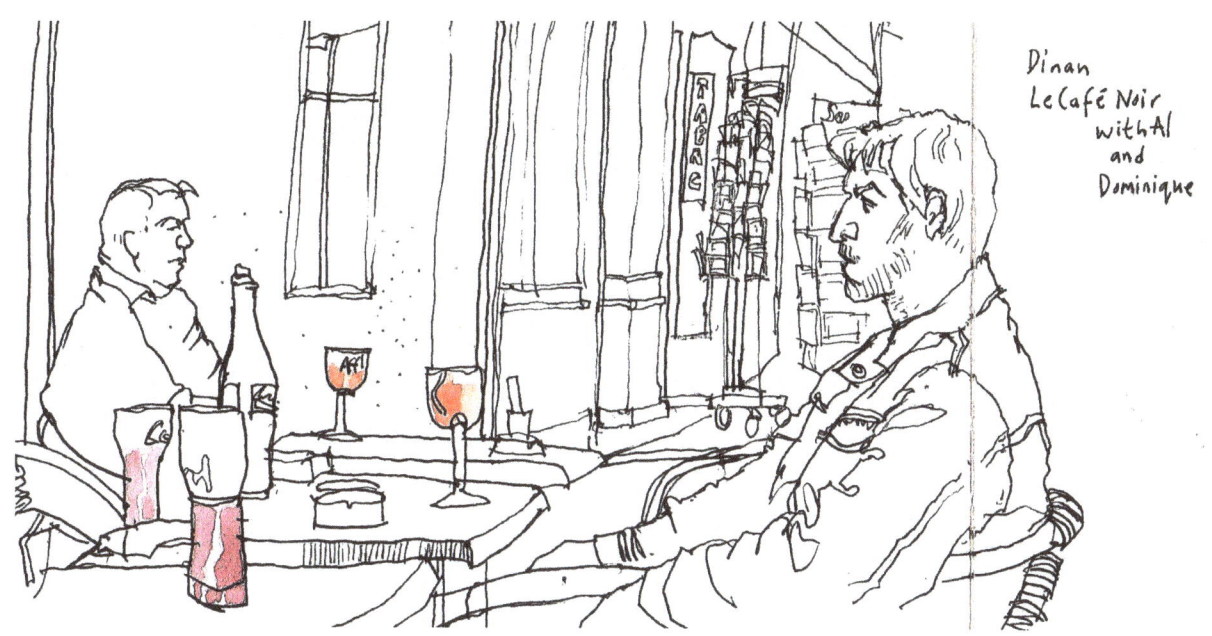

Dinan
Le Café Noir
with Al
and
Dominique

⟲ Le Café Noir, Rennes Caroline Johnson says she draws while the people she's with talk or *discutent* (argue). "They discuss world wars, books, music, art, and film—and how that man who went by was staring so intently at that lady's bottom."

5" x 9" | 12.5 x 23 cm; Parker Junior pen (medium nib), Noodler's Bulletproof ink, Winsor & Newton watercolor sketch set, #2 Raphael petit gris pur brush on Moleskine sketchbook; 40 minutes

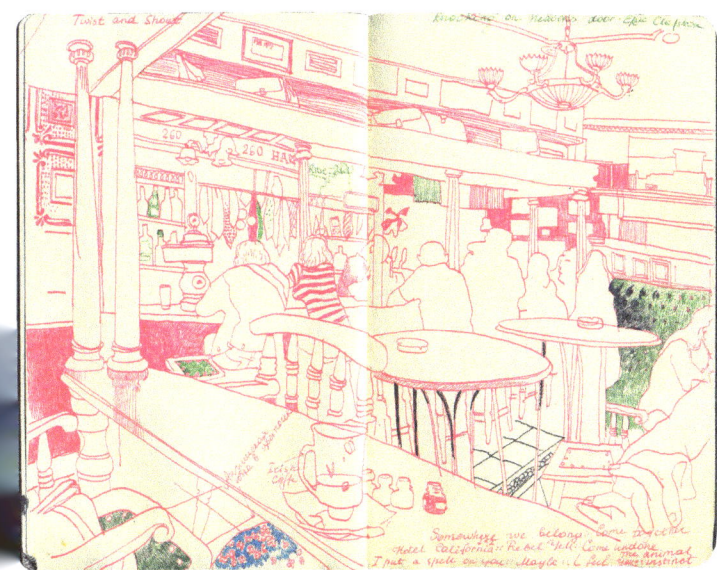

♫ Office Pub Ekaterina Khozatskaya wanted to show the bar from the wide angle, because "pubs are always full of small, interesting details, and I couldn't resist drawing everything I saw."

Tip "It's so delightful to use ink of different colors; it's my obsession." — *Ekaterina Khozatskaya*

6.25" x 8.25" | 13 21 cm; pen, Koh-I-Noor ink on Moleskine sketchbook; 2 hours

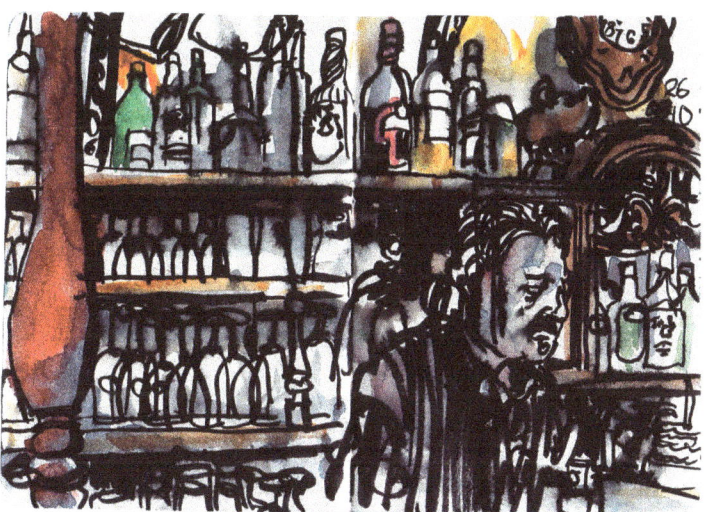

♫ Berlin Pub Rolf Schroeter started sketching while drinking beer in this neighborhood pub, with no plan where the thing might end. "The barman had a look at the result and said he looked too old but otherwise was quite content," Schroeter says.

Tip "Sometimes a concept-free doodle ends in a reasonable sketch, just by continuing to draw what you see, with no consciousness switched on." — *Rolf Schroeter*

5.25" x 7" | 13 x 18 cm; Pentel brush pen, Winsor & Newton watercolors on Brunnen FiLou sketchbook; 20 minutes

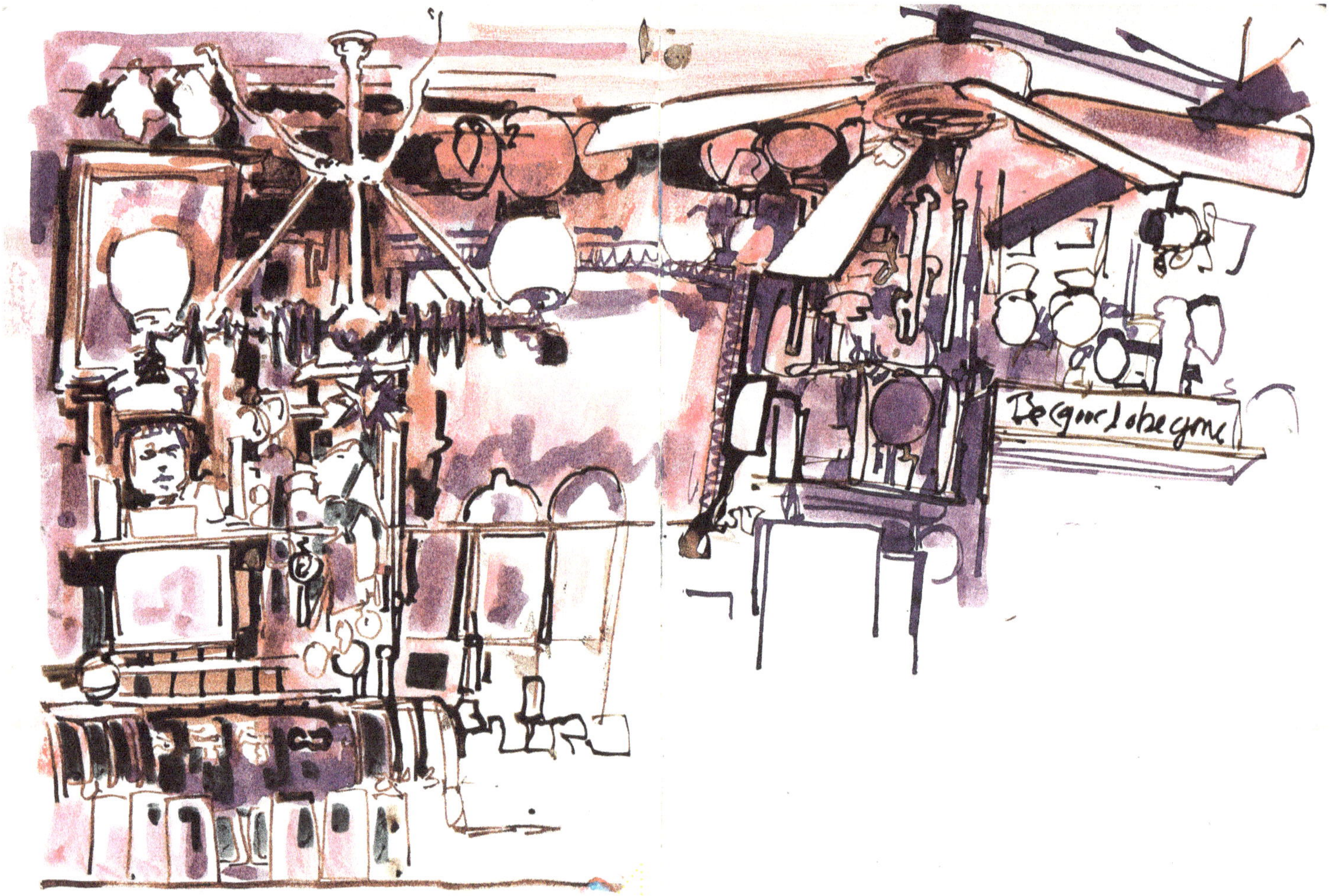

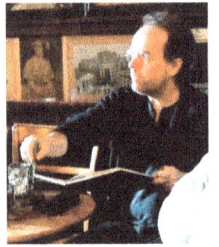

ARTIST PROFILE

Stephen Gardner

McSorley's bar has to be my favorite spot to draw in New York. It tends to get a bit crowded on evenings and weekends, but if you can manage to get there for lunch during the week, you will see the place for what it is, a living museum. The light in this place is magnificent, and with a pot-bellied stove for heat on a cold day, you can't beat it for atmosphere. I wish I was there right now.

"Manhattan has so many great bars,
and I've drawn in most of them.
Drawing and a pint—now you're talking."

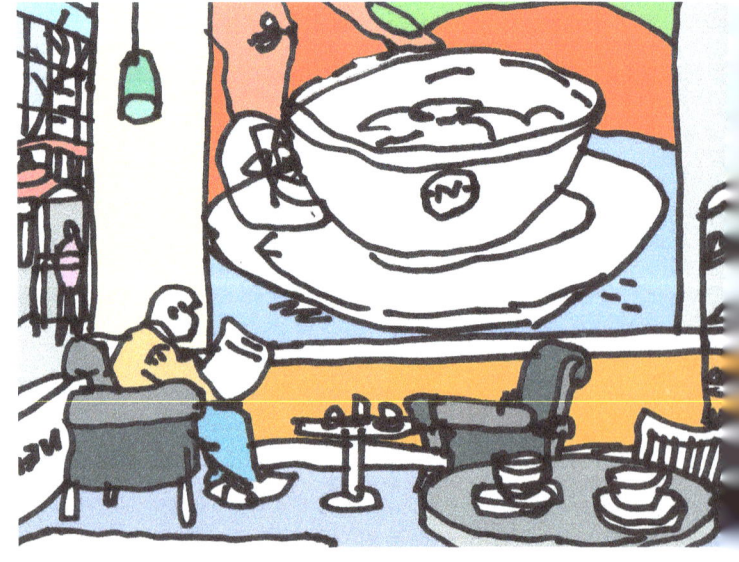

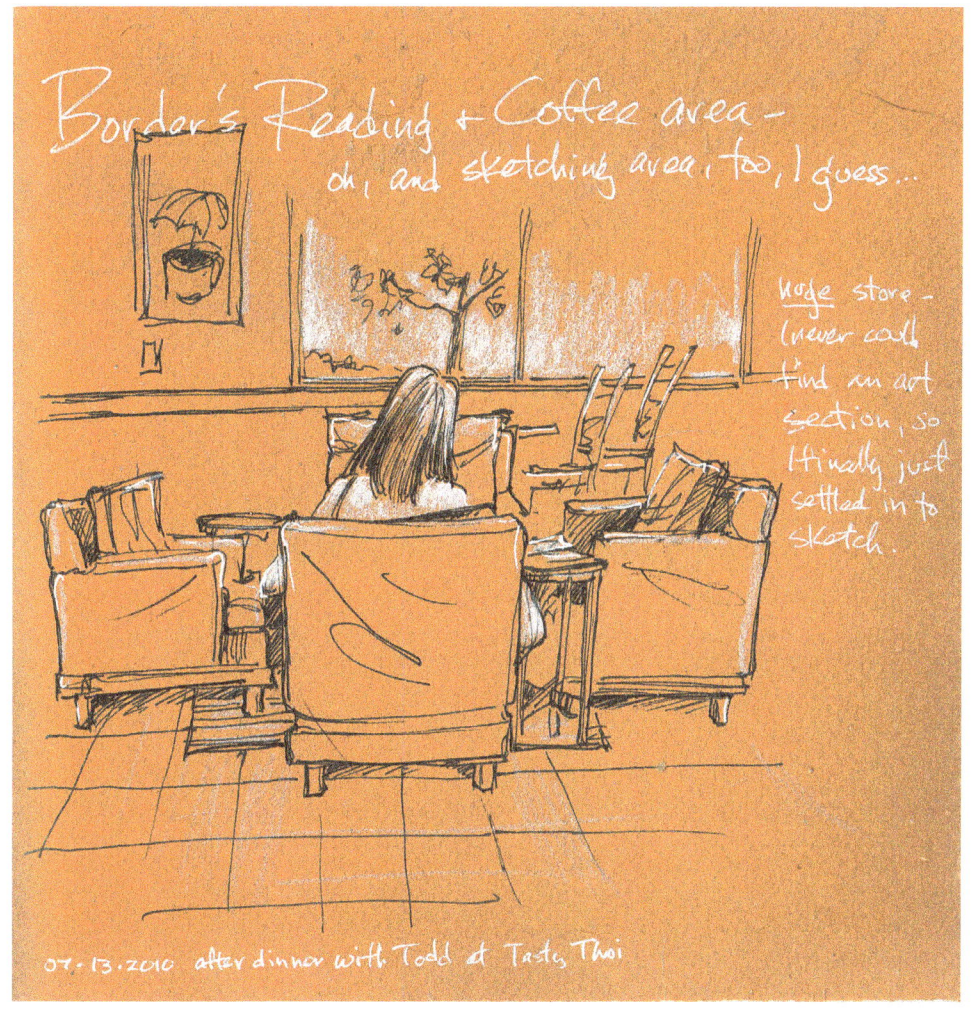

Border's Reading + Coffee area — oh, and sketching area, too, I guess...

huge store — (never could find an art section, so I finally just settled in to sketch.

07-13-2010 after dinner with Todd at Tasty Thai

☾ **Bookstore Café** Cathy Johnson found a quiet spot and sketched, while her husband browsed for books.

Tip "It's usually best to find someplace a bit out of the way, where you can draw unobtrusively. I like a table or booth against the wall, and I often glance around as I sketch, rather than staring. That can make people uncomfortable! Wearing a broad-brimmed hat or wearing sunglasses masks that staring, too."
— *Cathy Johnson*

8" x 9" | 20 x 23 cm; Japanese pocket fountain pen, white Prismacolor pencil, white Gelly Roll pen on brown-toned paper in handmade book; about 30 minutes

☽ **Red Cold Lines** Johannson sat in a café to sketch these two fellows, who sat outside with a coffee when it was 41°F (5°C) and dark.

Tip "Using monochrome colors is fun. In this case, I had one darker red drawing pen and a lighter brush pen to put in some shadows and tones." — *Nina Johansson*

5.25" x 4" | 13 x 10 cm; Neopiko red ink pen and Faber-Castell Pitt Artist brush pen on cheap no-name sketchbook paper in hand-bound sketchbook; 20 minutes

☾ **Tottenham Court Road Café** The large coffee cup on the wall is in stark contrast to what goes on around it, says James Hobbs; it was what made him want to draw this scene in the first place.

Tip "The only way to overcome shyness with drawing in public, I think, is to do it over and over again, preferably in busy places. It's like public speaking. After a while, it becomes second nature." — *James Hobbs*

4" x 6" | 10 x 15 cm; Edding 400 and 404 permanent marker pens, with digital color, on Seawhite sketchbook; 15 minutes

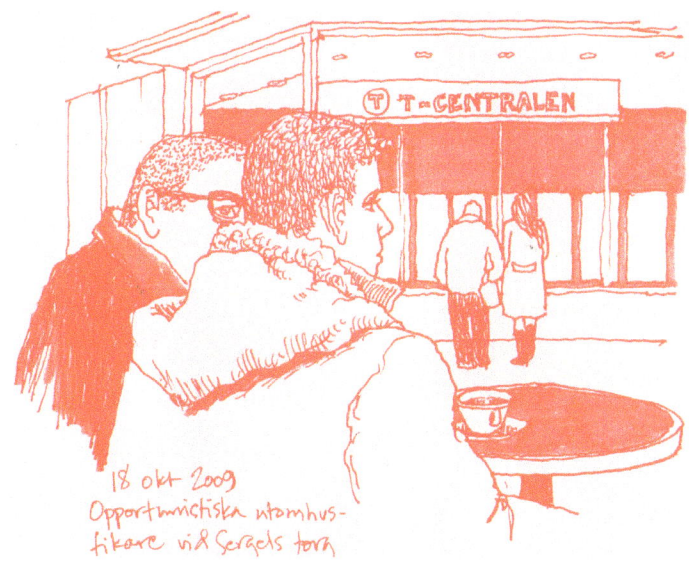

18 okt 2009 Opportunistiska ntomhus-fikare vid Sergels torg

Sketching Your Food

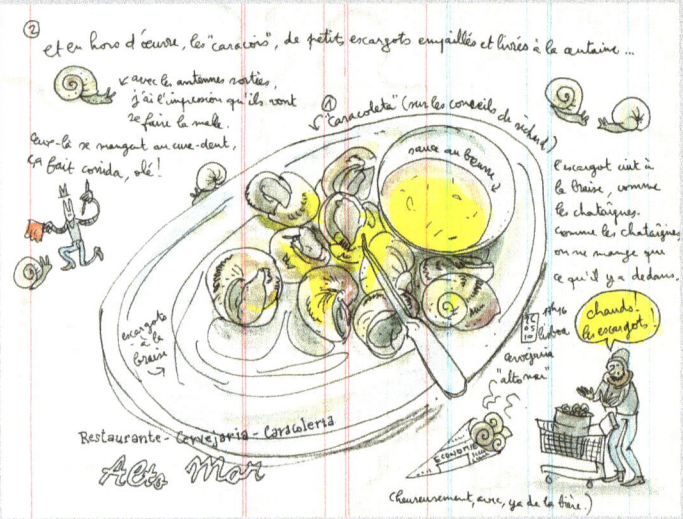

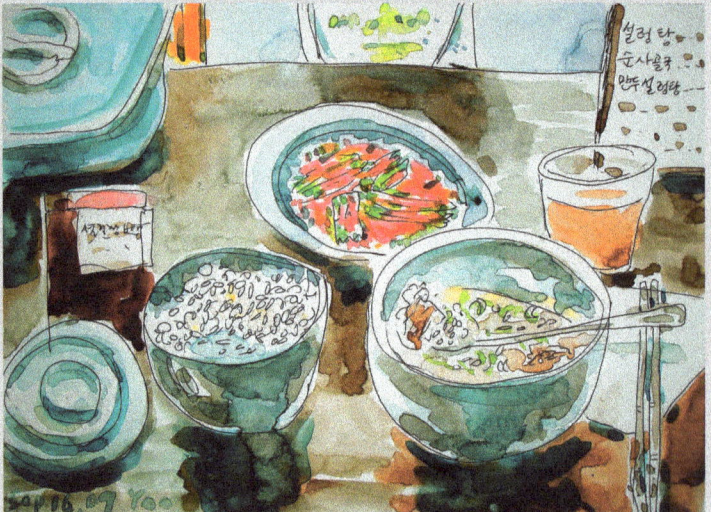

𝇮 Caracoleta It's fun to sketch your food, says Lapin, especially when you're traveling and eating exotic dishes, like this Portuguese dish of snails cooked with chestnuts and served with butter sauce. "I'm French, so snails do not scare me, but I must say that it did not taste good for me. I did that sketch to remember never to order that again," Lapin says.

8.25" x 6" | 21 x 15 cm; Mitsubishi uni PIN 0.1 fine line, Daler-Rowney watercolors, Pentel waterbrush, 6B pencil, liquid yellow watercolor on vintage account book found in a Barcelona flea market; 15 minutes

𝇮 Korean Food *Sulungtang,* a traditional Korean dish, is a soup made by boiling the bones and meat of a cow; it is served with cooked rice and hot kimchi. "Anytime I'm having a delicious or unusual meal, I like to record the experience," says Yoo Byung Hwa.

8.25" x 11.75" | 21 x 30 cm; Faber-Castell TK 9400 clutch pencil, Hwa Hong #10 round brush, 3/4" Alpha flat brush, Alpha, ShinHan, and Holbein watercolors on Canson 43-lb., XL sketchpad; 30 minutes

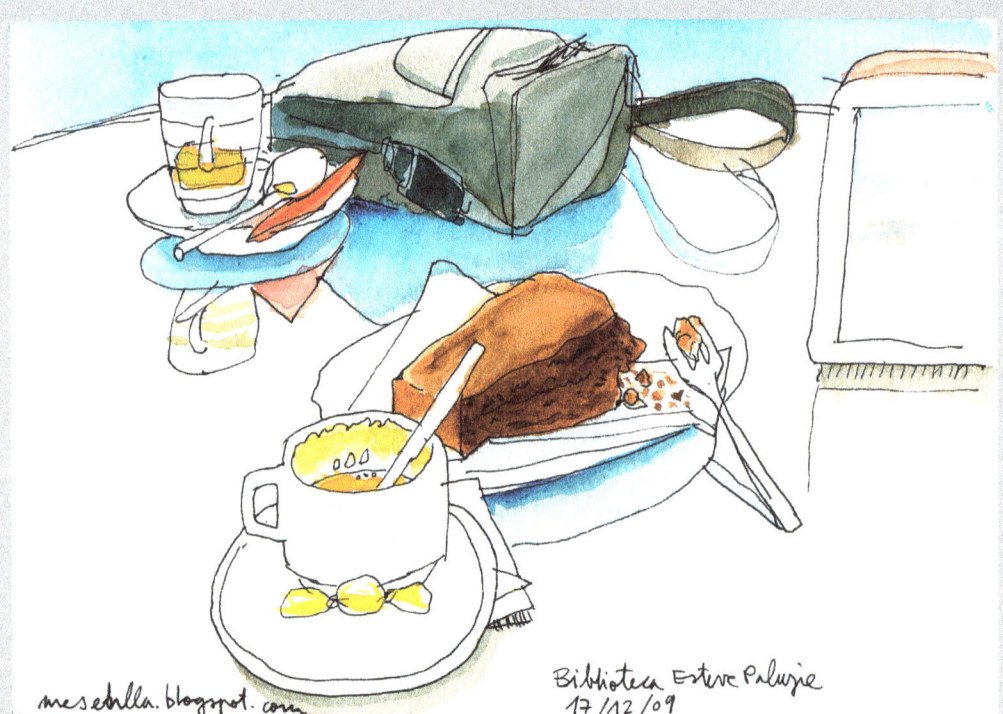

↺ Coffee with Milk and a Chocolate Cake Víctor Martínez Escámez (a.k.a. Swasky) sketched with a colleague at the Public Library Cafeteria in Barcelona. "Before drawing outside, I took a coffee with milk, and my colleague asked for a piece of chocolate cake. And there it was, a spontaneous still life, waiting to being drawn," he says.

5" x 7" | 12.5 x 18 cm; black Uni-ball ballpoint pens and Winsor & Newton Cotman watercolors on Fabriano paper; 15 minutes

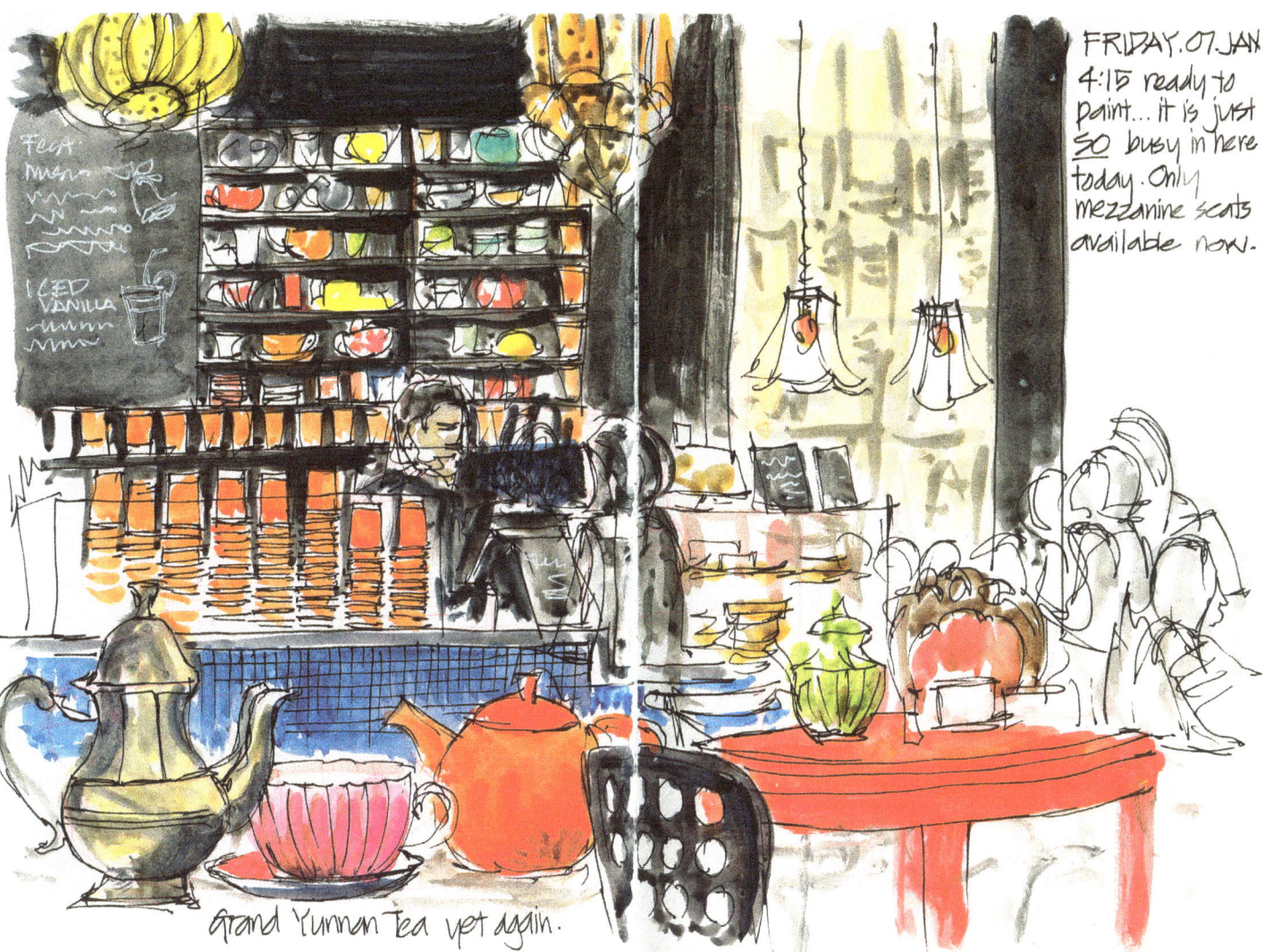

FRIDAY. 07 JAN
4:15 ready to
paint... it is just
SO busy in here
today. Only
mezzanine seats
available now.

Grand Yunnan Tea yet again.

T2 Teahouse Liz Steel's favorite tearoom has an eclectic Chinese and baroque
interior and also serves loose-leaf tea, each time in a different mismatched tea cup,
saucer, and teapot. "After two years of visiting this place once a fortnight, I have not
exhausted all the views that I could sketch in here!" Steel says.

Tip "I started with a basic outline of the counter and the back wall and adjacent table. I
then started sketching the details, working from foreground to background, using a looser
approach in the background."— *Liz Steel*

" x 8.5" | 20 x 21.6 cm; Lamy Safari pen with Noodler's ink, watercolor on Daler-Rowney Ebony
Sketchbook; 45 minutes

PEOPLE IN ACTION

Urban sketching is not about posed portraits or staged figure drawing sessions; it's about capturing people in action as they go about their activities, whether skating in the park or doing their jobs. At close range or from afar, the human figure makes a sketch feel alive.

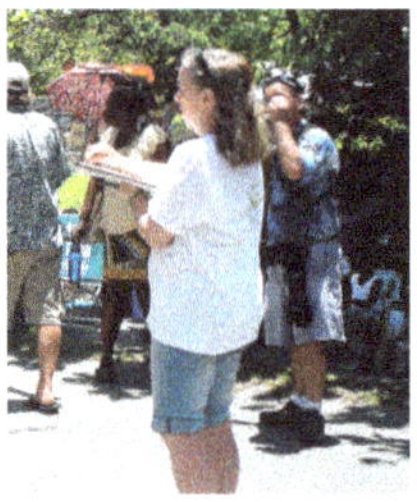

ARTIST PROFILE

Margaret Hurst

I have been drawing on location for as long as I can remember. In fact, it's difficult to work in the studio, because I've been drawing outside for so long. There is nothing like reportage drawing in the midst of swirling humanity or in the calm of a garden. All the sights, sounds, and smells find their way into your drawings.

Drawing on location creates aliveness, animation, and spontaneity in all your art, not just in your reportage drawings. To go somewhere and filter that world through your eyes and hands and create a piece of art that no one else can create is a great feeling. It's an experience I love to live, whenever I get the chance.

"Once you become a reportage artist, everything you do is infused with motion and life."

Central Park Skaters This particular drawing is of one of the newer skaters from the Central Park Dance Skaters Association, Margaret Hurst says. "He was on the ground at this point, kicking, weaving, twisting, and generally having a great time! Amazing dexterity!"

Tip "Observe the person's movements while you are drawing them. And draw directionally into the page, so that you create dimension and movement." *— Margaret Hurst*

8.5" x 11" | 21.6 x 28 cm; charcoal pencil, Xerox paper; about 5–10 minutes

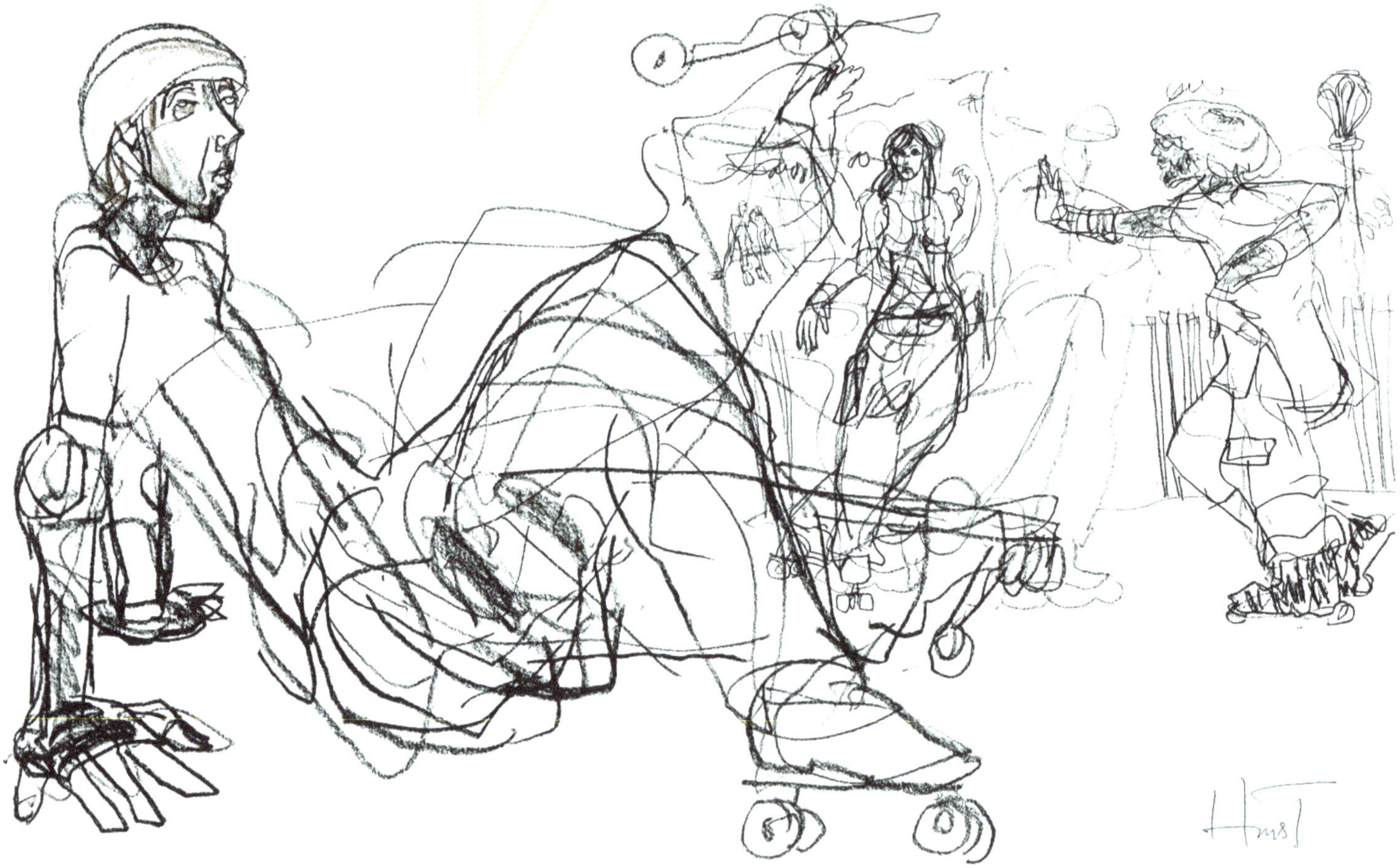

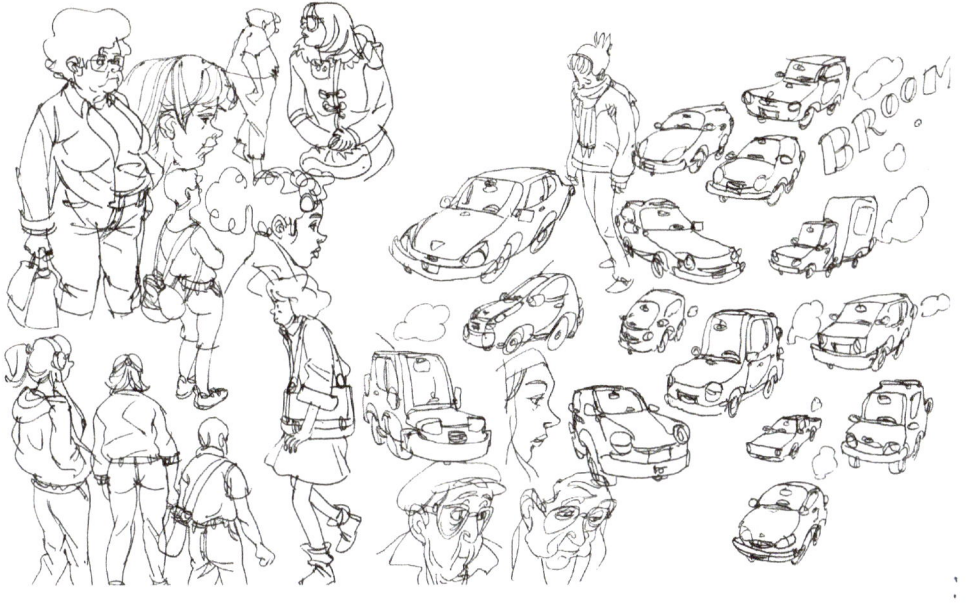

↻ Sketched in Rome Benedetta Dossi offers this tip: While you're watching people walking in the street, try to think of their gestures, how their clothes fit, or how someone's jacket creates folds when his arms move. In the end, when you have created this big database of images, you will be able to look at a person for two seconds and reproduce the essential lines of his figure in your notebook."

11.75" x 7" | 30 x 18 cm; Bic pen, normal white paper; I draw people and cars on my way to work—the travel lasts 40 minutes

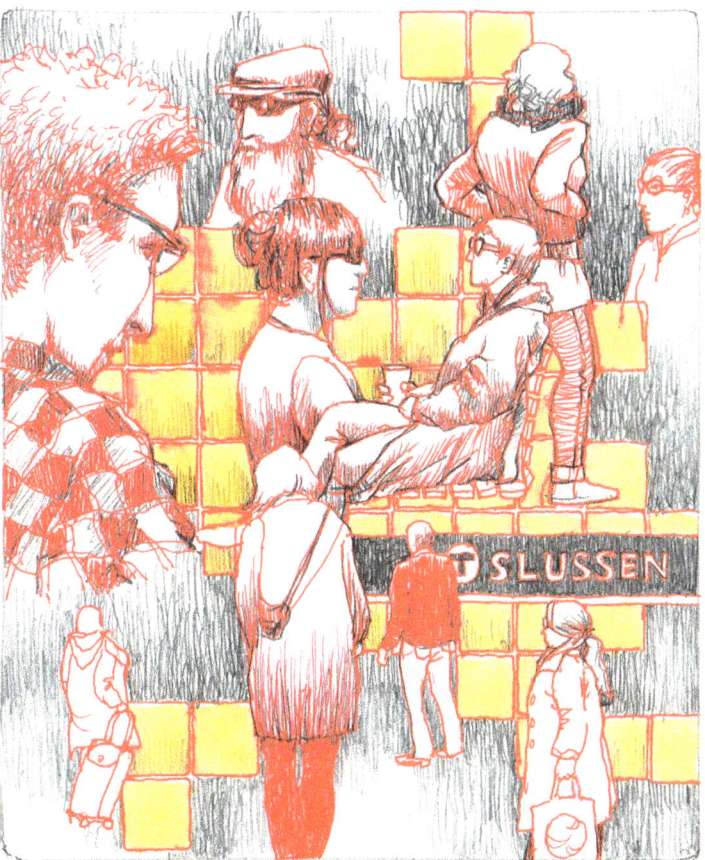

↻ The Beach Danielle C. McManus did this sketch at a beach in Long Island, New York, called Long Beach. "When I saw these two little girls running to fill their buckets up to make a sand castle, I couldn't help but draw them," McManus says. "I really wanted to capture their excitement and innocence."

4" x 6" | 10 x 15 cm; black Varsity fine-point fountain pen on cream color Moleskine paper pad; about 1–2 minutes

↻ Slussen II, Stockholm The tiles are everywhere at Slussen station, at all levels: light blue, yellow, turquoise, and dark blue. Nina Johansson thought it would be nice to pick up that pattern and use it as an element in her drawing.

Tip "Drawing people from life is difficult but fun—everyone is constantly moving, so you have to work fast. I just drew these people anywhere on the paper, sometimes almost on top of each other—I didn't worry about page layout or composition at all. Afterward, I added the yellow tiles and pencil marks, to make the page feel a bit more united." — *Nina Johansson*

6.25" x 7.5" | 16 x 19 cm; orange MUJI gel pen, 2B pencil, and Winsor & Newton watercolor, on Fabriano Rosaspina printing paper, in hand-bound sketchbook; 30–40 minutes, plus time later to add pencil marks and watercolors

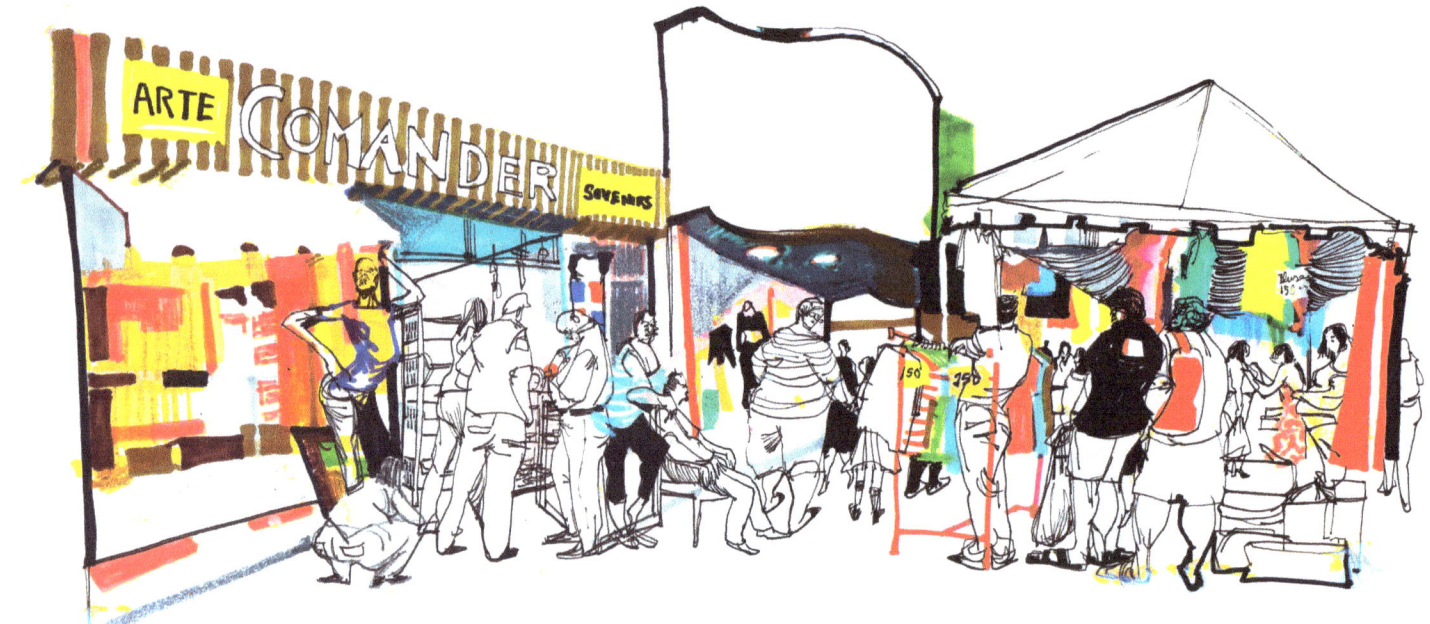

Ⓞ Christmas Shopping in Santo Domingo El Conde is a street in the colonial part of the city, where ladies and gentlemen of yore would stroll sedately or ride in carriages, Nathalie Ramírez says. "Today, it is lined with loud *bachata* (guitar-based music), shouting vendors, and a sour-sweet concoction of smells. Dominicans are never shy about letting you know if you are doing a good job in your drawing or if you drew them a bit too fat."

Tip "It is better for me to work on people and architecture simultaneously; that way, the people feel more connected to their surroundings and vice versa." — *Nathalie Ramírez*

8" x 20" | 20 x 50.8 cm; Sharpie markers, black China ink, Pelikan fountain pen, Caran d'Ache crayons on Daler-Rowney Cachet sketchbook, about 90 minutes

Ɔ St. Valentine's Day Shoppers were swarming around the chocolates section at a department store in Ginza, Tokyo, for St. Valentine's Day. "You are not always welcomed when you're sketching in a department store, but luckily, the staff members were too tied up this day," says Japanese sketcher Kumi Matsukawa.

Tip "I first drew the interior perspective with thin watercolor then gradually added customers and other details in the background." — *Kumi Matsukawa*

F1 (6.4" x 8.8" | 16.2 x 22.5 cm) Talens 24-color watercolor set, Pentel Aquash waterbrush on Maruman Art Spiral sketchbook; 20 minutes

Ⓤ Jardim da Estrela in Lisbon Sitting on a bench and sketching passersby in this park located in the center of Lisbon is a good exercise, says Eduardo Salavisa.

5" x 16.5" | 12.7 x 42 cm (open spread); Rotring pen on Moleskine landscape sketchbook; less than 1 minute per person

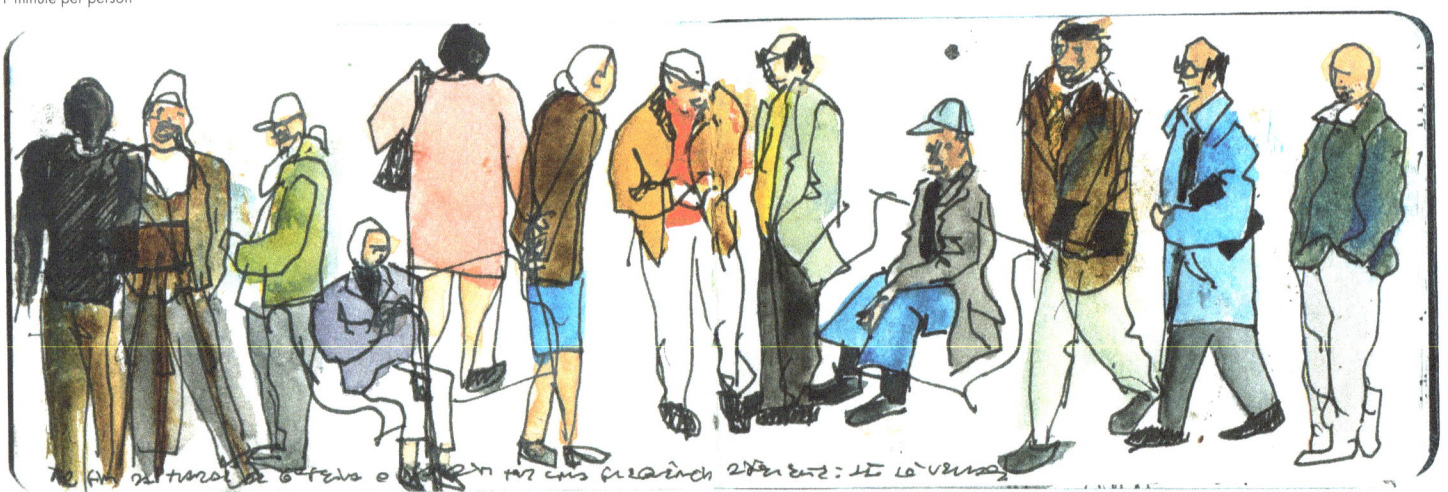

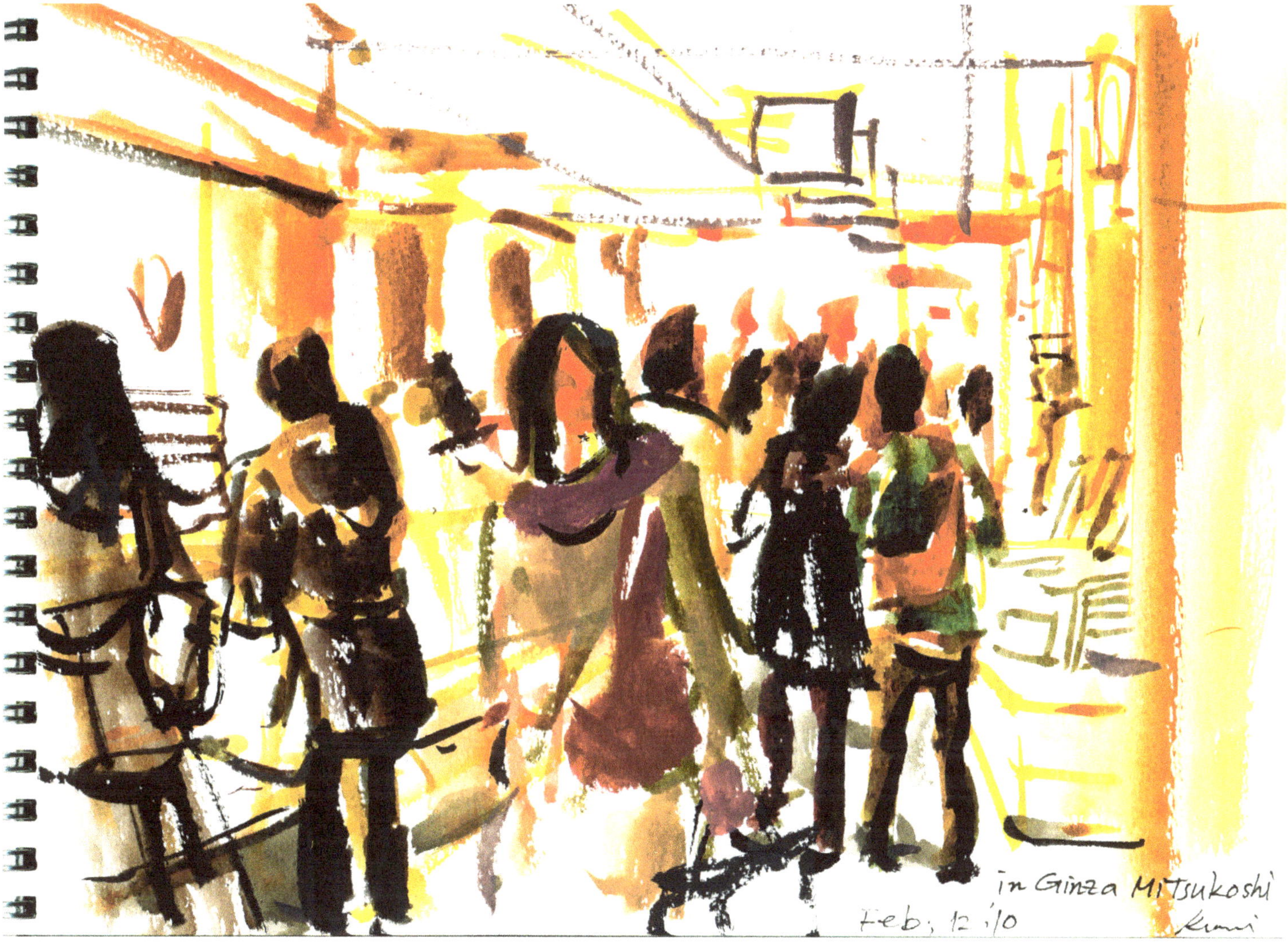

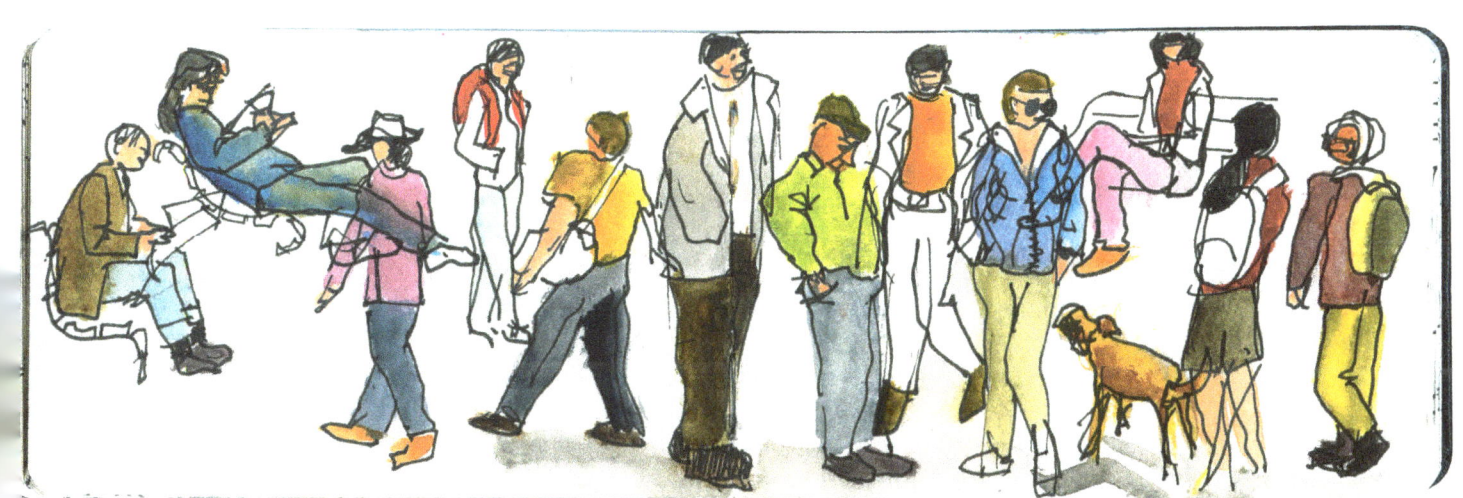

in Ginza Mitsukoshi
Feb. 12. '10

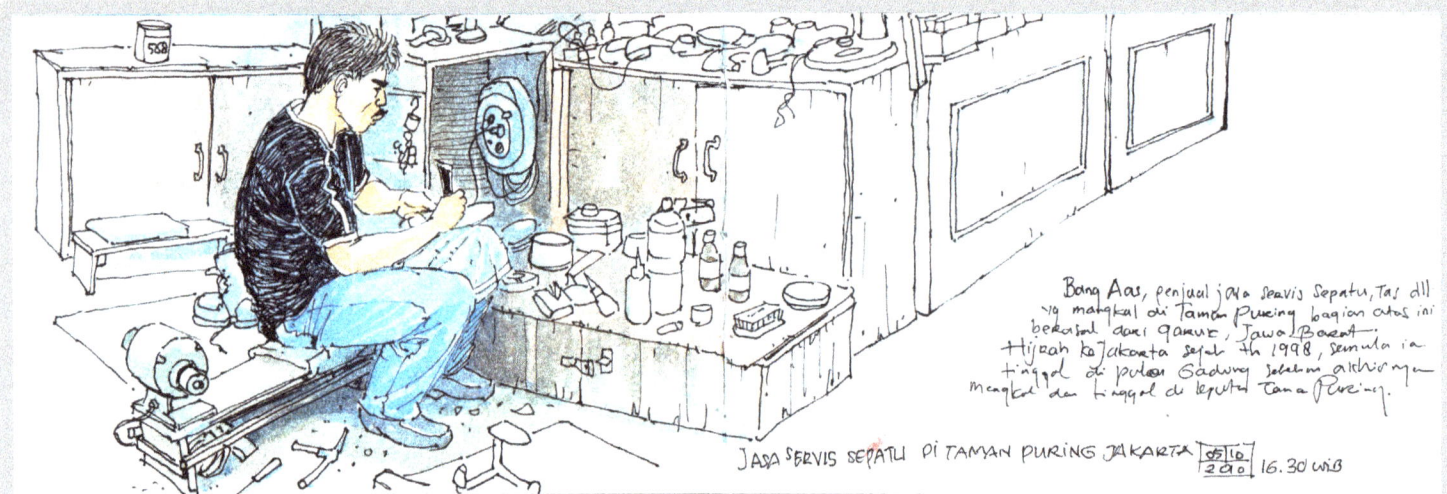

SUBJECT MATTERS

Sketching People at Work

⌂ **Indonesian Shoe Repairman** Jakarta illustrator Dhar Cedhar says Bang Aas is a humble shoe repairman who calls every client of his "boss" because he respects them, despite their gender, age, and social background. Dhar says he started off with figure drawing, concentrating on his subject's most prominent features, such as his Sudanese facial features and personality.

Tip "Since his shoe-fixing action requires him to move his hands a lot, I picked a pose that I thought he would come back to naturally, from time to time. Every time his hands moved back to that signature pose, I would also come back to it and leave the other parts, until he started moving again." — *Dhar Cedhar*

11.75" x 3.75" | 30 x 9.5 cm; Kenko Hi-Tech-H gel pen .28 (black), Cotman watercolors and Sakura Koi waterbrush on custom-made sketchbook using 200-gsm Canson watercolor paper; 20 minutes initial ink sketch, 10 minutes coloring

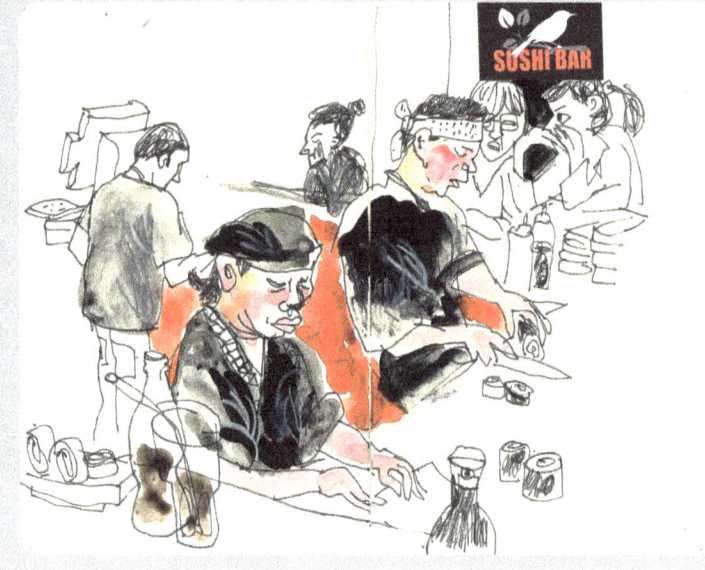

⊃ **At a Restaurant in Tel Aviv** These two Japanese chefs were so into their jobs, they didn't notice Marina Grechanik sketching them from "zero distance." Grechanik says she loves to eat at the bar and watch the skilled chefs preparing colorful plates of sushi and sashimi. "When you're drawing a person at work, like these two guys, whose hands are moving very fast, try to 'photograph' the most interesting postures and put them into your sketch."

5.5" x 7" | 14 x 18 cm; Faber-Castell fiber-tip pen, Van Gogh 12-pan watercolor pocket box, Derwent Inktense colored pencils, collage on Moleskine pocket sketchbook; 20 minutes

⊃ **Barber Shop in Al Ain** Although barber shops are similar all around the world, Omar Jaramillo says there are small differences that make them unique in every country. "Like in Turkey, where they burn the hair inside the ears or here, in the Emirates, where the barber wears a mask—why?" Jaramillo wonders. "He looks like a doctor doing a very skilled operation."

Tip "I usually use the pen when drawing scenes with a lot of movement. I try to catch the head and hands first." — *Omar Jaramillo*

8.25" x 5" | 21 x 12.5cm; Faber-Castell Pitt pen (sanguine), Winsor & Newton pocket watercolor set, waterbrush on Moleskine large watercolor book; 30 minutes each

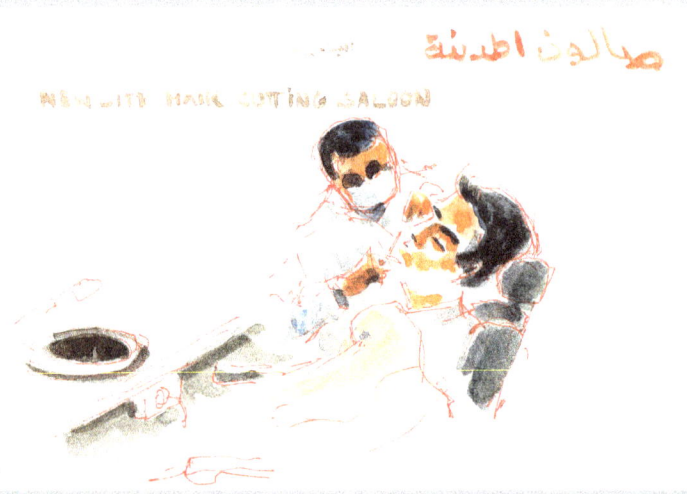

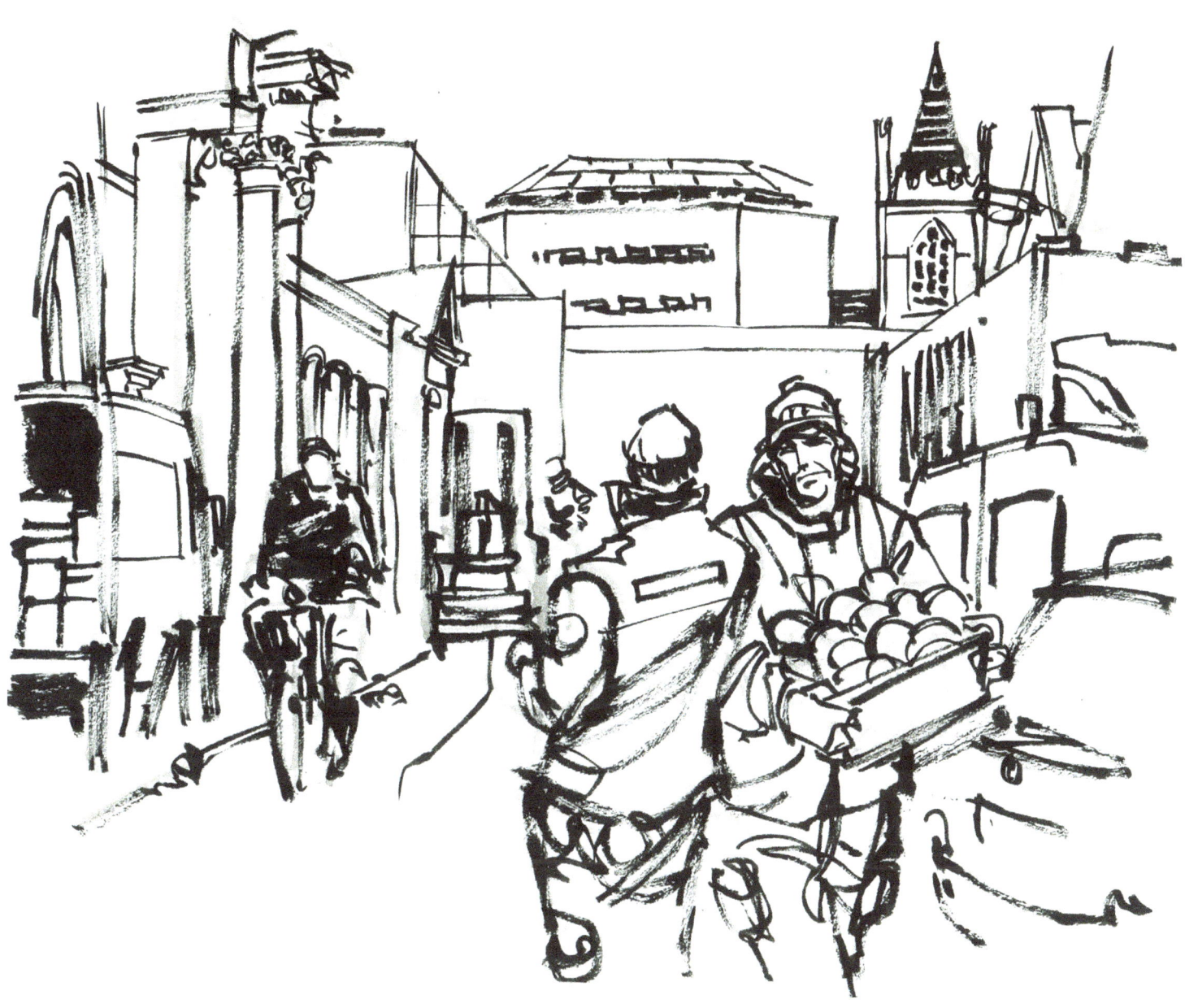

♫ **Smithfield Flower Market** Early on a cold, misty Dublin morning, Roger O'Reilly captured some of the activity around this flower and vegetable market.

Tip "I sketched the two main characters, first. I've deliberately kept the buildings sketchy and sparse, to fit in with the rest of the sketch." — *Roger O'Reilly*

10" x 8" | 25 x 20 cm; Pentel cartridge brush pen on Daler-Rowney heavy cartridge artists' block; 25 minutes

PARKS AND MUSEUMS

Not all urban sketching is about drawing architecture. At parks and green spaces, you can find an escape from the city noise and the opportunity to draw pockets of nature within the urban environment. Another good alternative for peaceful sketching time: museums, which also provide inspiration.

◑ Playtime Tel Aviv's Marina Grechanik often visits the neighborhood park with her youngest daughter. "After we get out our energy running, climbing, and swinging, it's nice to relax and sit on the grass, eating snacks and sketching. I love to sketch in the park—it's always full of small stories. Sometimes, my daughter joins me and we sketch together, which is even nicer!"

Tip "When you're sketching in crowded and full-of-action places, like a park, first try to observe the place and to find your stories. You can start to draw a relatively static group of people, adding landscape that doesn't move. When you see some interesting moving figures, capture them and add them to your story!" — *Marina Grechanik*

8.25" x 10" | 21 x 25 cm; pen, colored pencils, watercolors on Moleskine Cahier notebook; about 20 minutes

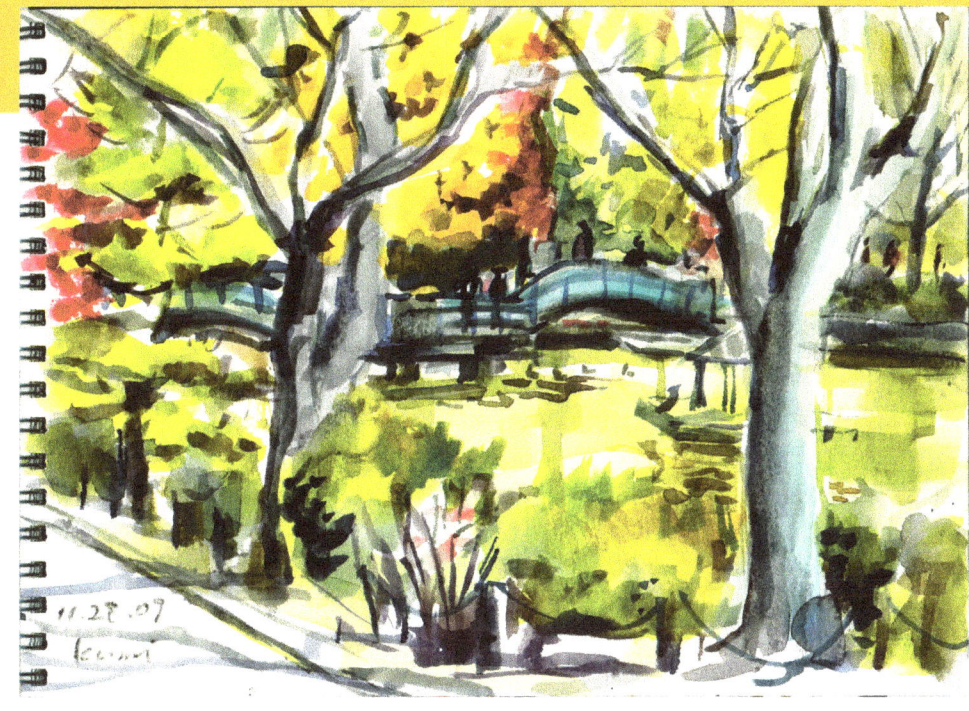

↺ **Yakushi Pond Park** This park in Tokyo features well-preserved, traditional Japanese-style houses, a lovely lotus pond, and an iris garden.

Tip "I wanted to capture the beautiful light and the reflection on the pond. I squinted at the view and measured how bright or dark each part was against the other."
— *Kumi Matsukawa*

F1 (6.4" x 8.8" | 16.2 x 22.5 cm); Talens 24-color watercolor set, Pentel Aquash waterbrush, on Maruman Art Spiral sketchbook

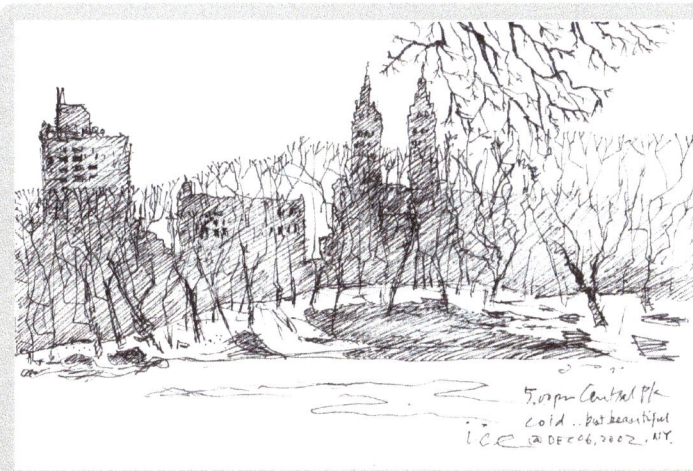

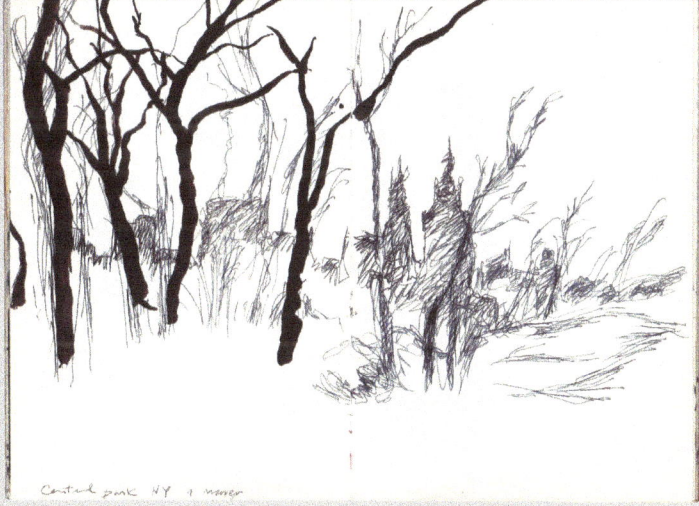

VIEW POINTS

Winter in New York City's Central Park

Singapore's Tia Boon Sim and Lisbon's João Catarino happened to visit New York City's Central Park within months of each other. They each captured a wintry impression of the park in their own way.

❍ "I was told the best time to visit Central Park was one day after a snowfall. I did just that, and the park was so beautiful, just like a postcard. My fingers were all numb when I finished the sketch, but I was happy. It was all gray and white in the winter. I decided to apply the line work in one direction, to achieve some dynamism in an otherwise linear composition." — *Tia Boon Sim*

6" x 8" | 15 x 20 cm; Pilot 08 drawing pen (black) on Lo Scrittoio leather-bound sketchbook from Cavallini & Co; 30 minutes

❍ "For a foreigner, walking through Central Park means reliving all the references from watching movies. Still, there are always surprises behind the noise of the city and its trees without leaves. I only had ten minutes to draw before it started raining." — *João Catarino*

11.5" x 8.25" | 29 x 21 cm; Rotring ArtPen and Pentel brush pen on Papelaria Moderna sketchbook; 10 minutes

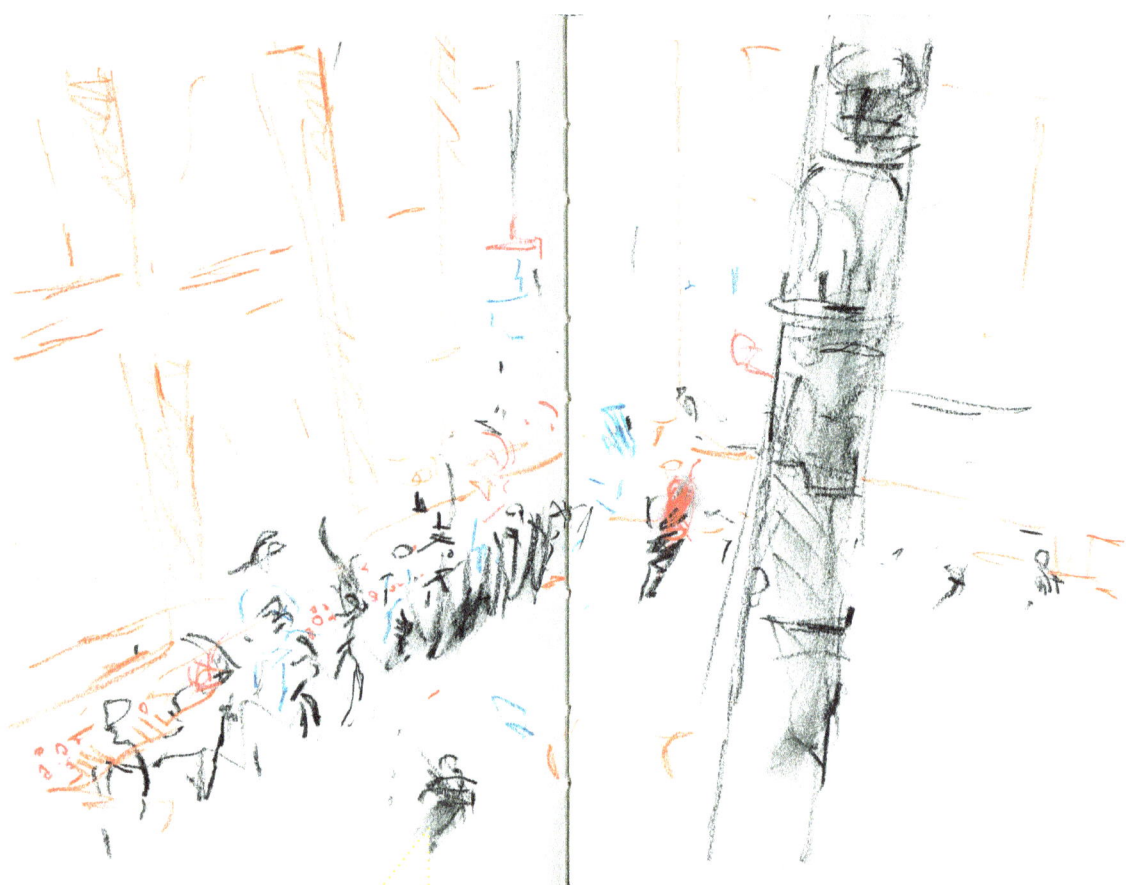

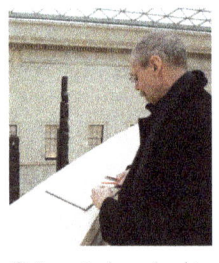

ARTIST PROFILE
Barry Jackson

I generally have a sketchbook, which acts as a kind of journal. However, most of my drawings are the result of deliberate drawing outings, on which I'm often encumbered

⋂ Barry Jackson sketching at the British Museum

with a large variety of materials and a even a drawing board.

I often visit galleries and museums. All London's major galleries and museums encourage drawing, as long as it's dry media, and many of them, including the National Gallery and British Museum, have sketching stools you can borrow for free.

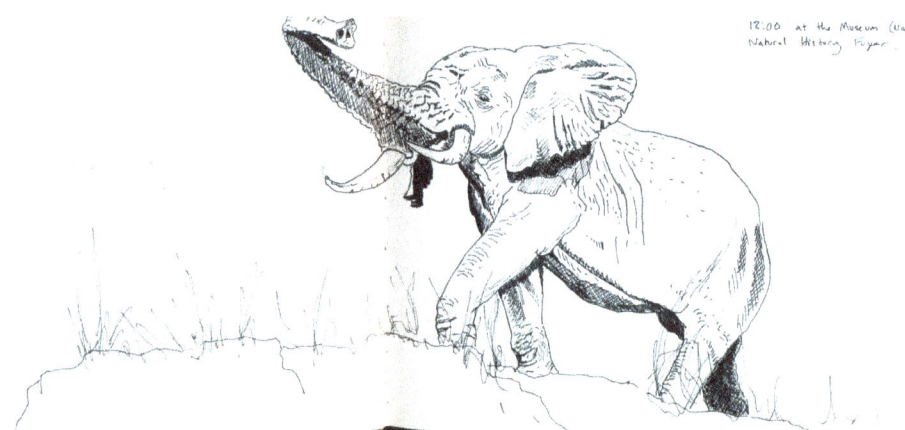

12:00 at the Museum (Nat'l) Natural History Foyer.

⋂ **Museum of Natural History** On a Washington, D.C., sketchcrawl, Christian Tribastone's group decided to stay indoors, because the weather was disagreeable. "We started in the National Museum of Natural History and later moved to the National Arboretum, ending our crawl just before it started hailing outside," Tribastone says.

6" x 16" | 15 x 40.6 cm; pencil and Faber-Castell pens on Cachet sketchbook; about 30 minutes

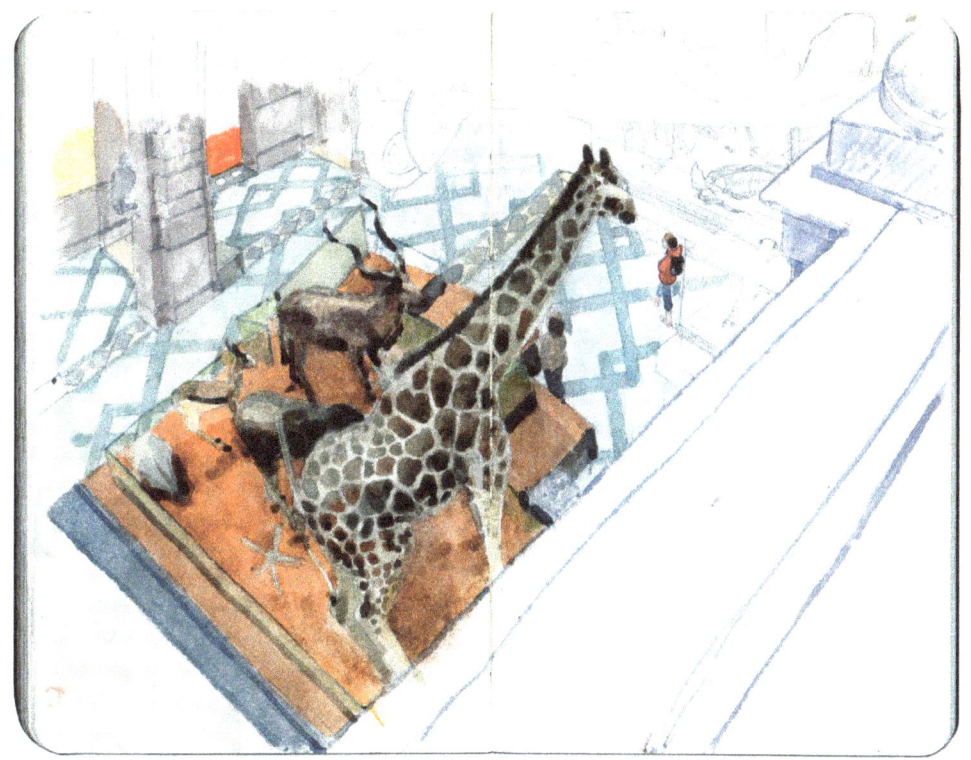

The Giraffe at Kelvingrove Wil Freeborn visits the Kelvingrove Museum for drawing, tea, and cake. "I've drawn the animals quite a few times," he says. "This time, I was looking to get a different view of them; the way the spitfire and edge of the side framed the animals made an interesting composition."

Tip "Museums and art galleries are always good places to draw. There's little of that feeling of vulnerability you can sometimes get from drawing in the streets. So the times you need to recharge your creative batteries and can't quite face drawing outside, it's good to go to your local museum to draw." — *Wil Freeborn*

10.25" x 8.25" | 26 x 21 cm; pencil and watercolors; Moleskine large sketchbook; 30–40 minutes, plus time to watercolor

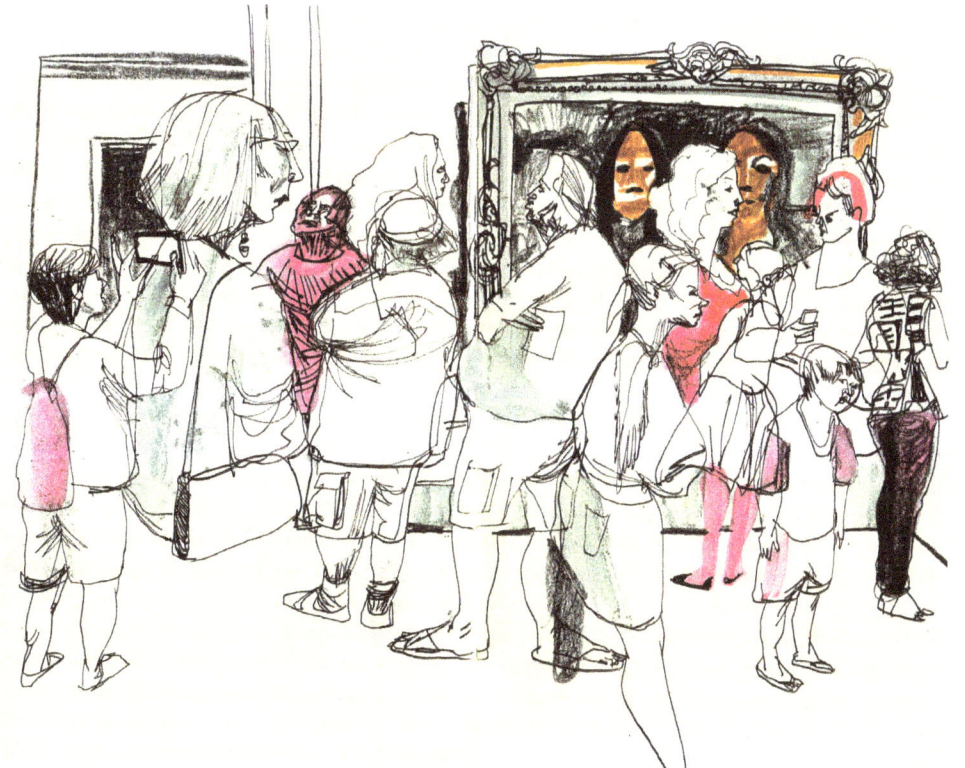

The Met, Inside and Out "There are some places that hold a special connection with you—places that make you feel at home, even if it's your first time there," Nathalie Ramírez says. "The Metropolitan Museum of Art in New York is one such place for me. My heart races like a little kid's, every time I visit. I love looking at the art, I love looking at people looking at the art and somehow getting a sense that the art is secretly looking back at them."

Tip "Be aware of the body language and different personalities of the people you are drawing." — *Nathalie Ramírez*

10.25" x 8" | 26 x 20 cm; black china marker, Pelikan fountain pen with black China ink, Winsor & Newton Vermilion ink, Moleskine sketchbook; about 45 minutes

NIGHT SKETCHING

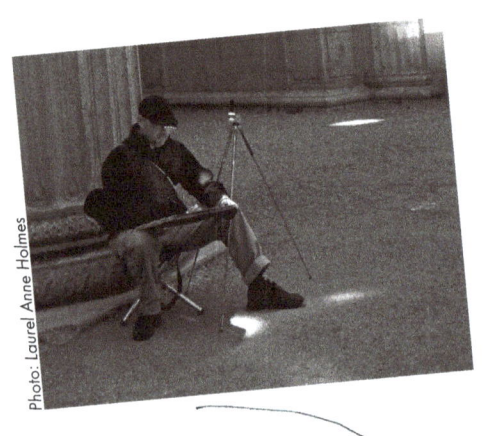

Photo: Laurel Anne Holmes

Sketching at night can be a lonely, slightly creepy, experience, according to Canadian artist Marc Taro Holmes. But it also has advantages, he's found. Artificial lights don't move, for example, so you can enjoy drawing without the worry of losing the light, as often happens when sketching during the day.

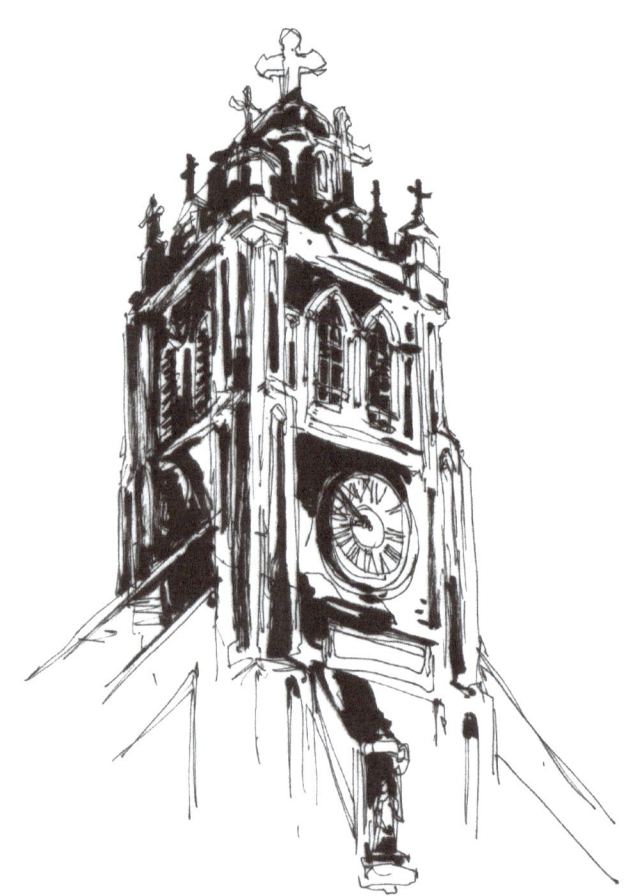

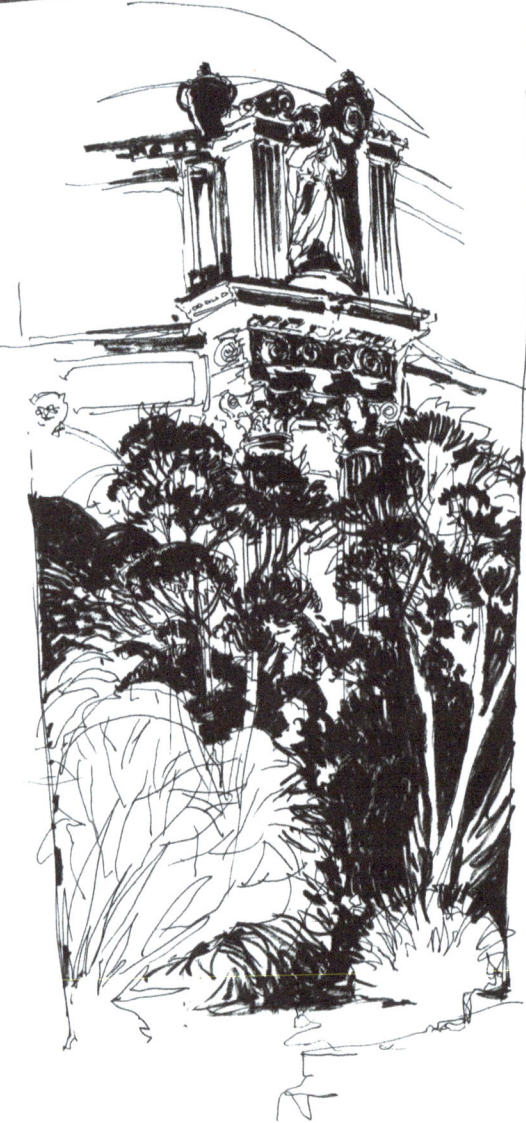

◖ **Old St Mary's Church, Chinatown, San Francisco** Holmes is always on the lookout for public buildings that make good night-sketching subjects. The decorative night lighting of city halls, university buildings, public statues, and old hotels brings out relief carving worth capturing in high, black-and-white contrast.

8.5" x 11" | 21.6 x 28 cm; Uni-ball Signo pen Pentel GFKP brush pen, on 80-lb. cover stock; 20 minutes

◖ **San Francisco Palace of Fine Arts** Holmes drew these brush sketches beneath the sculpted dome at the Palace of Fine Arts in San Francisco. A lit doorway or streetlight often provides enough light to see your drawing board or sketchbook, the Montreal-based illustrator says, but if there's no light around, you can fashion your own. He uses duct tape to mount a bright LED bicycle headlight bought at a sporting goods store to a camera tripod. He also wears a "fisherman's light," a little plastic gadget that clips onto the brim of a standard baseball cap. Its small row of LEDs shine some light wherever he points his face.

11" x 17" | 28 x 43 cm; Uni-ball Signo pen, Pentel GFKP brush pen, on 60-lb. cover stock from the office supply store

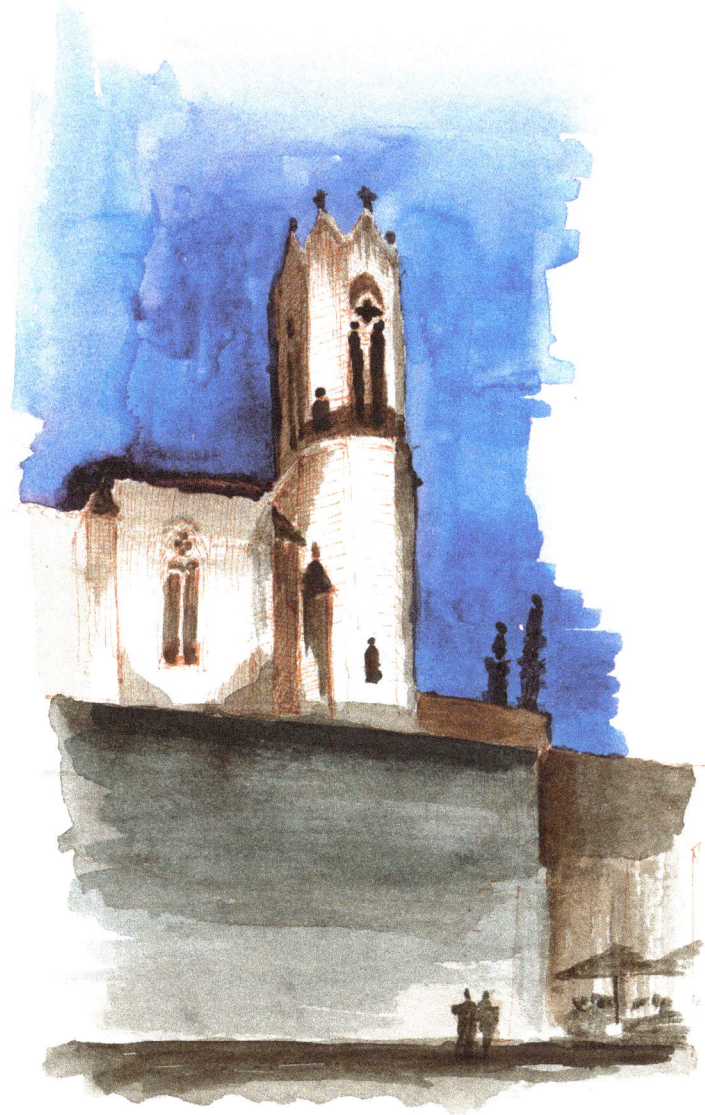

Plaça del Rei, Barcelona 7.3.09

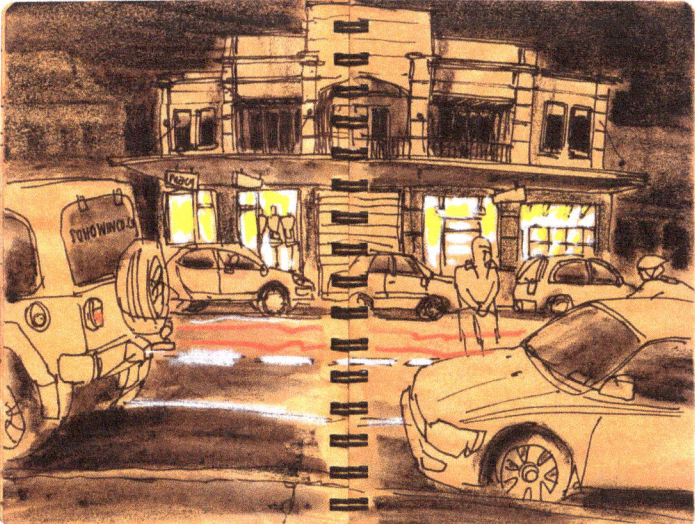

○ **Plaça del Rei, Barcelona** The illuminated tower of a historic building in Barcelona's old town caught the attention of Idaho-based architect Matthew Brehm while he visited the city.

Tip "When trying to sketch a night scene, it's important to reserve areas of white paper, to contrast with the very dark sky and shadows. Also, pay attention to the direction of the lighting." — *Matthew Brehm*

" x 8" | 12.5 x 20 cm; Copic Multiliner (sepia), M. Graham watercolors, #6 round Connoisseur Kolinsky *able brush on Moleskine watercolor book; 30 minutes*

○ **Waiting for Takeaways** While waiting for his food order, New Zealand artist Murray Dewhurst filled his time pleasantly by sketching Ponsonby Road in Auckland.

Tip "To pick out the luminosity of street lights and shop window displays, I like to work on a tinted paper, with Neocolor Aquarelles, which seem to pop off the surface nicely." — *Murray Dewhurst*

8.25" x 6" | 21 x 15 mm; Rotring .5 fineliner, Caran d'Ache Neocolor II Aquarelles on Nood department-store, wire-bound Kraft notebook; 15 minutes

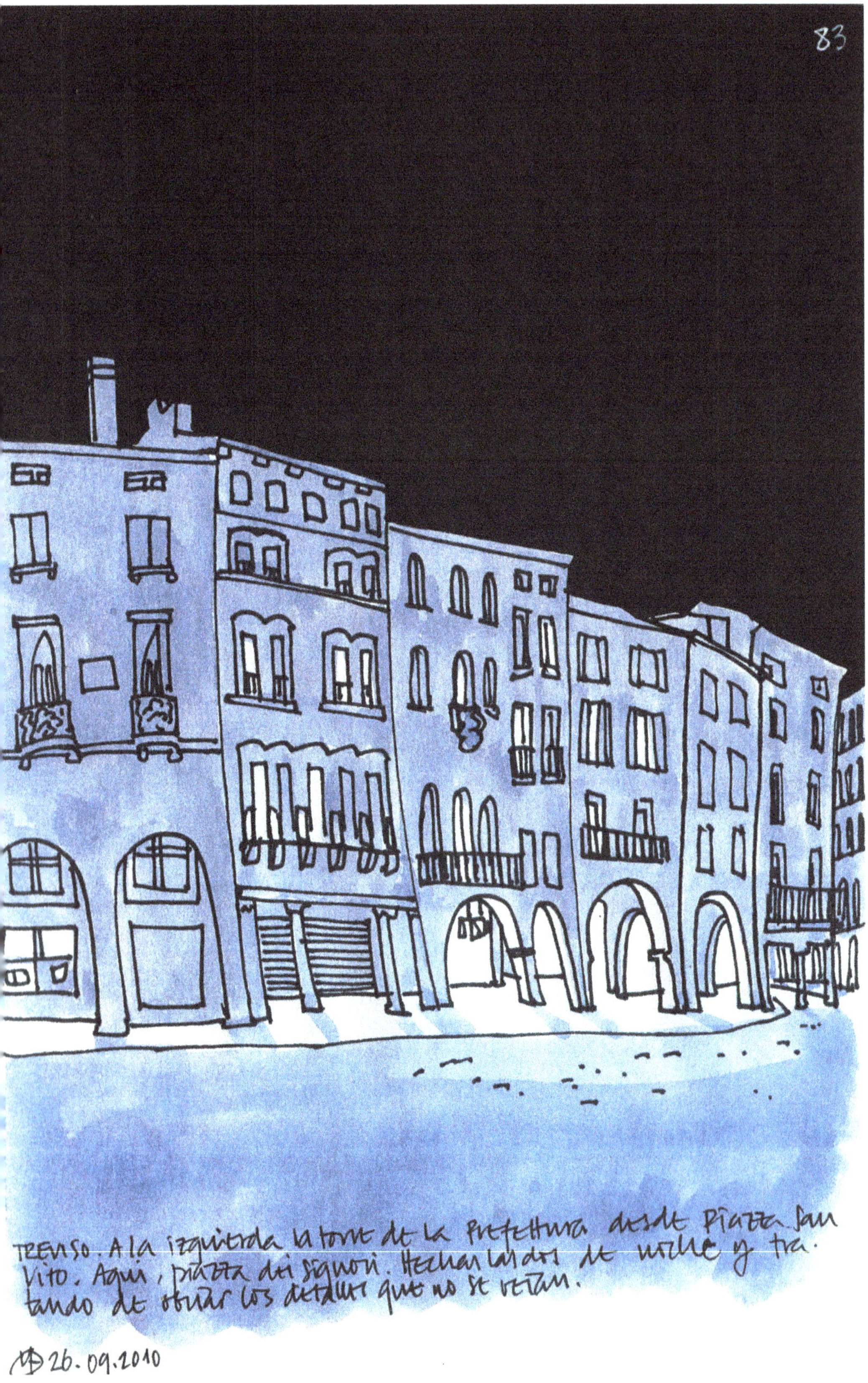

83

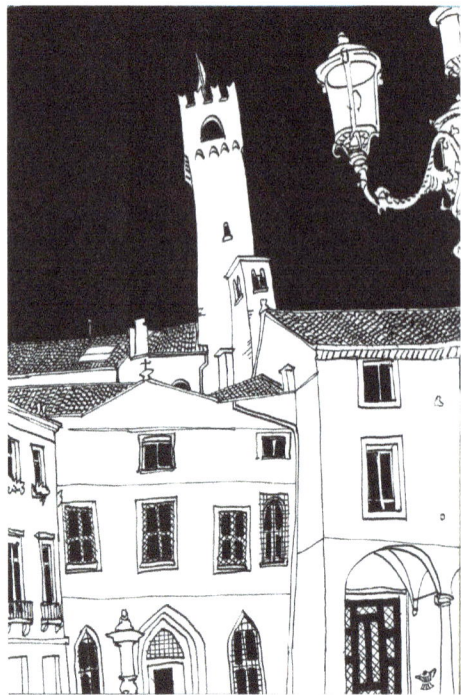

🎧 **Night in Treviso, Italy** Barcelona-based illustrator Miguel Herranz sketched both of these scenes on the same night, an hour apart. On the left is the Prefettura, drawn at 7 p.m.; the second sketch is from Piazza San Vito, drawn about an hour later.

Tip "Because you cannot see the same details as by day, sketching at night is much more creative. You invent what is not clear for the eye and translate it into something suggested by the scene." — *Miguel Herranz*

6" x 8.25" | 15 x 21 cm; fountain pen with a calligraphic nib and Noodler's ink, Micron 0.8 pen, Copic Multiliner brush, watercolors on Ruggeri A5 160-gsm sketchbook; about 45 minutes each

TREVISO. A la izquierda la torre de la Prefettura desde Piazza San Vito. Aqui, piazza dei signori. Hechas las dos de noche y tratando de obviar los detalles que no se vean.

26.09.2010

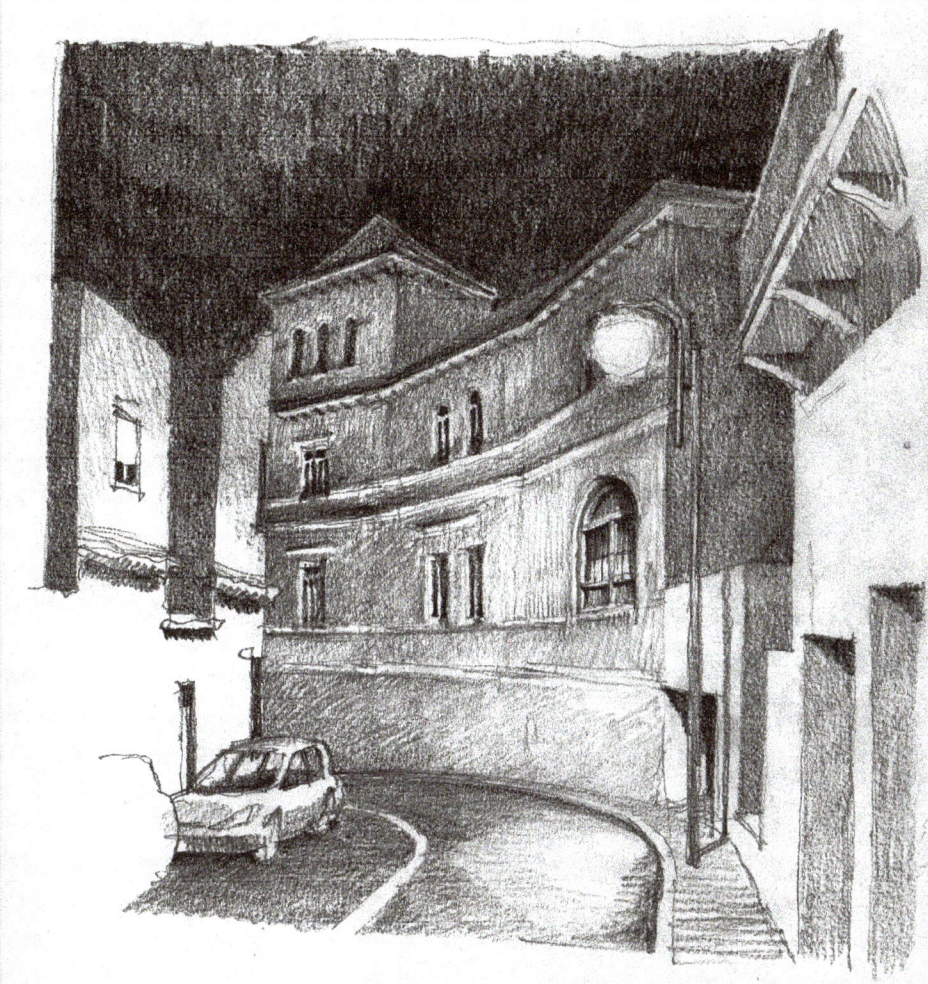

7" x 7" | 18 x 18 cm; 2B pencil on A4 office paper; about 50 minutes

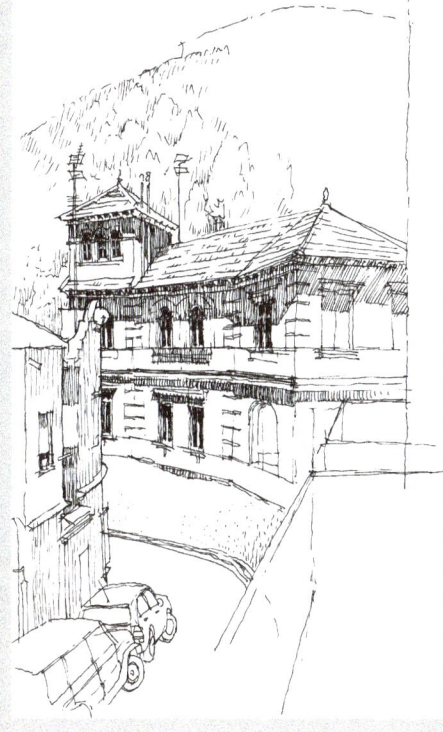

8.25" x 11.5" | 21 x 29 cm; Staedtler 0.5 ink pen on A4 office paper; about 40 minutes

STYLE AND TECHNIQUE

Night and Day in Pencil and Ink

by Luis Ruiz

Although using a thin ink pen was a nice way of capturing the sharp contours of the architecture on a sunny afternoon, soft pencil was a natural choice for me to show the blurry shapes, as seen during the night, when the edges of the details are less clearly perceived.

However, the main point here was also to get a good, well-lit vantage point, which is a must for drawing a night scene. In this case, I was lucky to find a place below one of the neighborhood gateway's lamps.

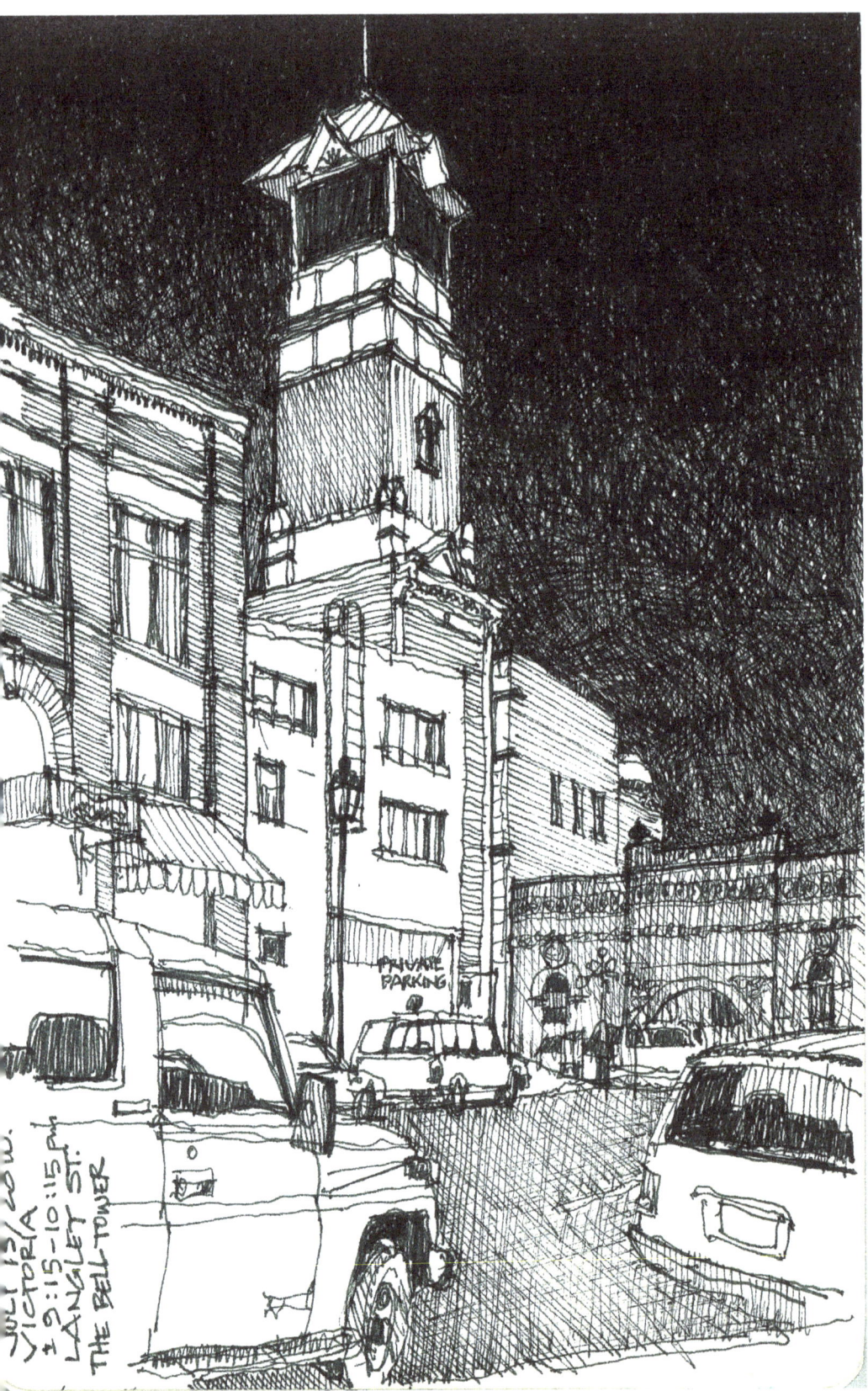

↻ **All Buildings Are Beautiful at Night, Even the Ugly Ones** This drawing shows one of the many buildings Paris sketcher Martin Etienne can see from the seventh floor of his Paris apartment building. "But this one is special, because it is the highest in the district and it is the ugliest, too," Etienne says. "But, when it gets dark and most of its windows are illuminated, its appearance changes. It becomes a fascinating object, like a building with lots of TV screens."

Tip "I love to draw during the night, because darkness forces you to simplify what you see. With the kind of brush pens I used (Pentel), the number of colors is limited and a little bit flashy, so it forced me to make choices that were a bit cartoonish." — *Martin Etienne*

11.5" x 8.25" | 29 x 21 cm; Pentel Color Brush with ink cartridge on typing paper; 30–40 minutes

↻ **Langley Street, Victoria, B.C., at Night**
"Twilight is a beautiful part of the day," says Canadian architect Matthew Cencich. "But it's tricky to draw; it's tough to catch that fading light. But, in one way, it becomes easier when you see less, because it forces you to blur out background detail."

Tip "Bring a new pen with plenty of ink. This image was actually drawn at twilight, which is very difficult to capture because it is so fleeting, but it is a wonderful time to be in drawing mode, because you really observe the beautiful light so much more intently." — *Matthew Cencich*

6" x 9" | 15 cm x 23 cm; Sharpie fine-point felt-tip pen on Hand Book Travelogue Journal; 1 hour

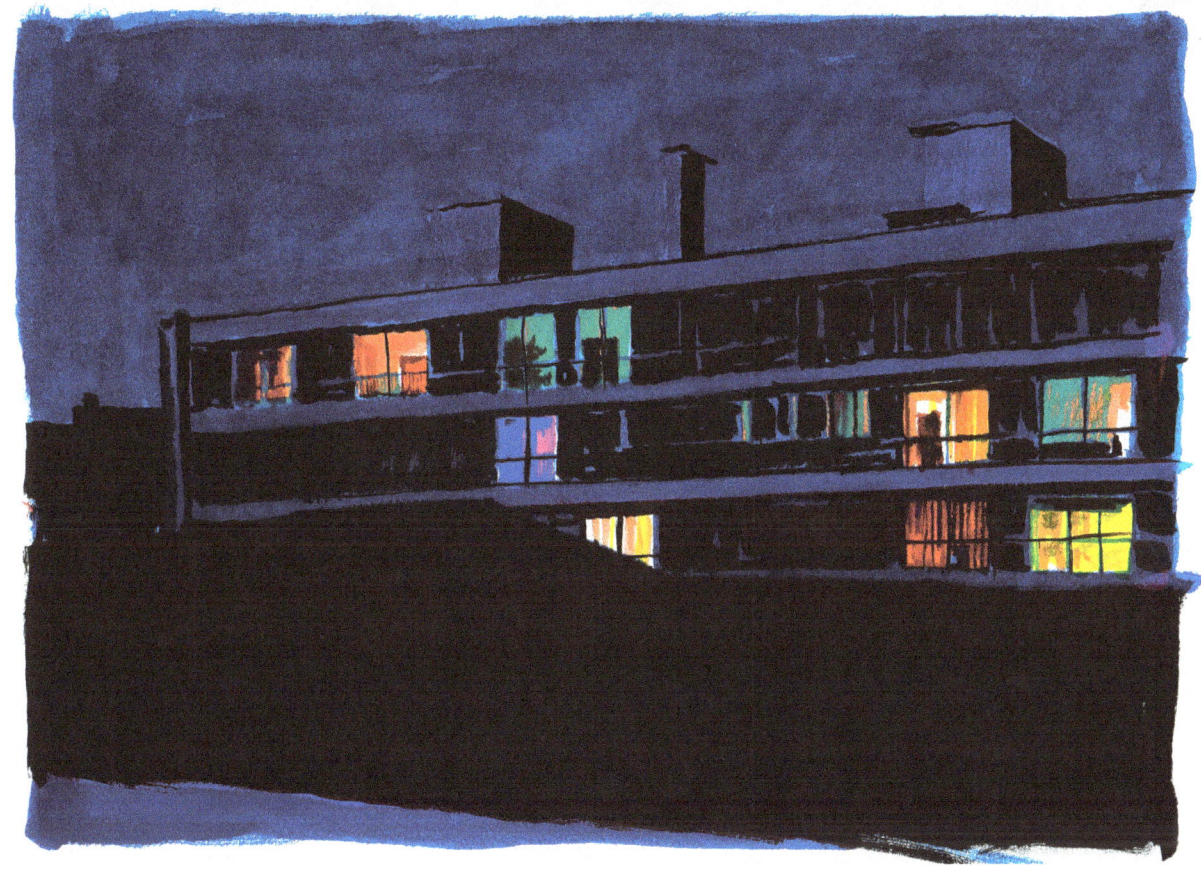

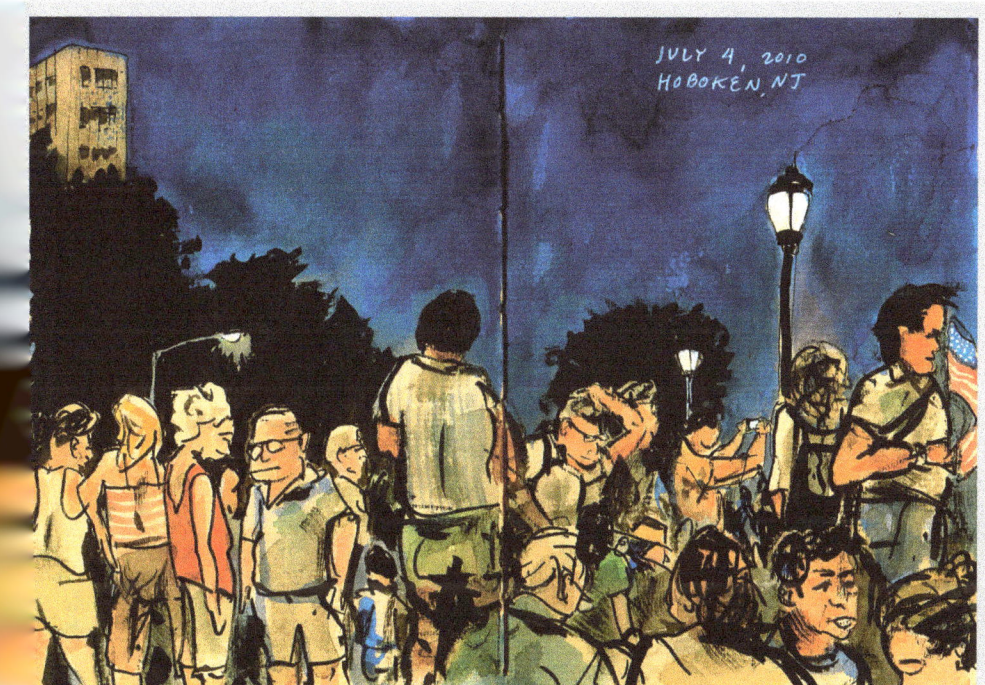

STYLE AND TECHNIQUE

The Night in Color

by Jason Das

At night, colors tend to be desaturated and shadows are often poorly defined. This can leave much of your sketch stuck in middle values. But there are also extremes of light and dark. Large parts of a scene can be completely hidden in shadow, with no discernible detail, so it's helpful to have a way to put down a lot of black at once—a thick marker or brush.

To get a lit area, such as a window, to read correctly, it might be necessary to get rather dark around it. Many of my night sketches—especially if done on the go with a waterbrush—require several layers of gray to get the neutral areas sufficiently dark to contrast with the lit areas. The silhouetted trees and dark sky are really what make this read as taking place at night.

◖ Waiting for Fireworks, Hoboken, New Jersey, 4th of July

10" x 7" | 25 x 18 cm; black Pigma Graphic pens, 01 and 03, watercolors (the sky is Dr. Ph. Martin's Radiant Concentrated), white Sakura Gelly Roll gel pen, Pentel Pocket Brush pen on handmade sketchbook

CONTRIBUTORS

Artist Profiles

Afflerbach, Florian, 182–185, 188, 192, 258, 276
Stuttgart, Germany
www.flickr.com/photos/flaf

Alade, Adebanji, 13, 148, 293
London, England, UK
http://adebanjialade.blogspot.com

Amaro, Gary, 40, 45, 269
San Francisco, California, USA
http://garyamaro.blogspot.com/

Bajzek, Eduardo, 88–90, 262
São Paulo, Brazil
www.ebbilustracoes.blogspot.com

Betza, Greg, 76, 268, 289
New Jersey, USA
www.gregbetza.com

Bonamy, Guillaume, 136
Blois, France
www.gbonamy.blogspot.com

Boon Sim, Tia, 22, 30, 193, 226, 309
Singapore
http://tiastudio.blogspot.com

Brehm, Matthew, 133, 191, 196–199, 274, 313
Moscow, Idaho, USA
http://brehmsketch.blogspot.com

Cabral, Pedro, 125, 271
Lisbon, Portugal
http://bonecosdebolso1.blogspot.com

Câmara, Richard, 124, 291, 294
Madrid, Spain
www.richardcamara.blogspot.com

Campanario, Gabriel, 34, 35, 37, 291
Seattle, Washington, USA
http://gabicampanario.blogspot.com

Capecchi, Simonetta, 202, 205, 259
Naples, Italy
www.inviaggiocoltaccuino.com

Carey, Rob, 186, 279
Kandern, Germany
http://kunst-by-rob.blogspot.com

Carnicero, Álvaro, 116, 262
Córdoba, Spain
http://drawingbookfromspain.com

Catarino, João, 120, 292, 309
Lisbon, Portugal
http://desenhosdodia.blogspot.com

Cedhar, Dhar, 230, 306
Jakarta, Indonesia
http://cedharrsketchbook.blogspot.com

Cencich, Matthew, 38, 145, 316
Victoria, British Columbia, Canada
www.flickr.com/photos/mc_images

Chapman, Lynne, 156, 159
Sheffield, England, UK
http://lynnechapman.blogspot.com

Das, Jason, 72, 288, 317
Brooklyn, New York, USA
http://jasondas.com

Dewhurst, Murray, 211, 250, 272, 279, 313
Auckland, New Zealand
http://mrdewhurst.blogspot.com

Dorantes, Norberto, 96–99
Buenos Aires, Argentina
http://norbertodorantes.blogspot.com

Dossi, Benedetta, 21, 194, 303
Rome, Italy
http://365onroad.blogspot.com

Ejersbo, Ea, 20, 166
Aarhus, Denmark
http://tegneblog.blogspot.com

Etienne, Martin, 140, 316
Paris, France
http://martin-dessin.blogspot.com

Fiadeiro, Isabel, 106–109
Nouakchott, Mauritania
http://mauritania-isabel.blogspot.com

Frankstone, Laura, 19, 142, 144, 276
Chapel Hill, North Carolina, USA
www.laurelines.typepad.com

Freeborn, Wil, 164, 282, 311
Glasgow, Scotland, UK
www.wilfreeborn.co.uk

Frost, Sharon, 74, 293
Brooklyn, New York, USA
http://sharonfrost.typepad.com/day_books

Gardner, Stephen, 295, 298
Brooklyn, New York, USA
http://sketchoftheday.com

Gatland, Cathy, 102–105, 286
Johannesburg, South Africa
http://asketchintime.blogspot.com

Grechanik, Marina, 212, 281, 306, 308
Tel Aviv, Israel
www.flickr.com/photos/marin71

Hartanto, Rudi, 232
Semarang, Indonesia
www.flickr.com/photos/rudi__urbansketcher

Heaston, Paul, 56–59
San Antonio, Texas, USA
http://paulheaston.blogspot.com

Hein, Virginia, 50, 280
Los Angeles, California, USA
www.flickr.com/photos/38539603@N04

Herranz, Miguel, 28, 31, 130, 314
Barcelona, Spain
http://freekhand.com

Lee, Yong Hwan, 240, 269
Seoul, South Korea
http://archiartistlee.blogspot.com

Hobbs, James, 23, 152–155, 299
London, England, UK
www.james-hobbs.blogspot.com

Holmes, Marc Taro, 44, 66, 260, 285, 312
Montreal, Quebec, Canada
http://citizensketcher.wordpress.com

Hurst, Margaret, 302
New York, New York, USA
www.margarethurst.com

Jackson, Barry, 151, 289, 310
London, England, UK
www.flickr.com/photos/barryj

Jansen, Lok, 248
Tokyo, Japan
www.lokjansen.com

Jaramillo, Omar, 189, 214, 261, 306
Al Ain, United Arab Emirates
http://omar-paint.blogspot.com

Johansson, Nina, 28, 168–171, 266, 279, 299, 303
Stockholm, Sweden
www.ninajohansson.se

Johnson, Caroline, 138, 297
Rennes, France
http://artistsmock.blogspot.com

Johnson, Cathy, 60, 299
Kansas City, Missouri, USA
www.cathyjohnson.info

Jones, Matt, 42
San Francisco, California, USA
http://mattjonezanimation.blogspot.com

Joshi, Sanjeev, 216
Pune, India
http://architectpainterjoshi.blogspot.com

Kardos, Stéphane, 52
Los Angeles, California, USA
http://stefsketches.blogspot.com/

Kerr, Stuart, 111, 162
Glasgow, Scotland, UK
www.stupot.com/blog

Khozatskaya, Ekaterina, 296, 297
St. Petersburg, Russia
www.flickr.com/photos/bogema

Kiah Kiean, Ch'ng, 222, 267
Penang, Malaysia
www.kiahkiean.com

Lapin, 15, 126–129, 192, 246, 265, 276, 295, 300
Barcelona, Spain
http://les-calepins-de-lapin.blogspot.com

Lawlor, Veronica, 70, 190, 278, 285
New York, New York, USA
www.veronicalawlor.com

Louro, José, 122
Lisbon, Portugal
www.ajaneladealberti.blogspot.com

Low, Don, 224, 235, 237
Singapore
www.donlowillustration.com/blog

Lynch, Fred, 29, 200, 274
Boston, Massachusetts, USA
www.flickr.com/photos/7821310@N04

Matsukawa, Kumi, 22, 244–247, 282, 292, 304, 309
Tokyo, Japan
www.flickr.com/photos/macchann

McManus, Danielle C., 29, 68, 145, 303
New York, New York, USA
http://aloveofdrawing.blogspot.com

Michel, Gérard, 146, 256
Liège, Belgium
www.flickr.com/photos/31647204@N03

Minond, Edgardo, 100, 133
Bueno Aires, Argentina
www.flickr.com/photos/minond

Nakaza, Shiho, 48, 257
Santa Monica, California, USA
http://shihonakaza.blogspot.com

O'Reilly, Roger, 31, 160, 211, 271, 307
Dublin, Ireland
www.rodgeblog.com

Padron, Luis Ruiz, 112, 258, 264, 272, 315
Málaga, Spain
http://luisrpadron.blogspot.com

Pinheiro, João, 24, 94, 276
São Paulo, Brazil
http://jottapinheiro.blogspot.com

Other Drawings

About the Author

Journalist and illustrator Gabriel Campanario is best known as the founder of Urban Sketchers, an online community and nonprofit organization dedicated to fostering the art of on-location drawing. He's also the author of the *Seattle Times* blog and weekly column "Seattle Sketcher," an illustrated journal of life in the Puget Sound region. Campanario's journalism career has spanned newsrooms in his native Spain, as well as Portugal, Nevada, California, and Virginia. He lives in Mill Creek, Washington, with his wife and two children.

Campanario was sixteen when he drew his first urban sketches in Montemolín, Badajoz, a picturesque Spanish town set amid groves of olive trees, where his parents were born and raised. He didn't know yet that he was an urban sketcher.

Acknowledgments

This book wouldn't exist without the generous contributions of the artists featured. My sincere gratitude goes to every one of them for trusting me with their images and their words, and for meeting the tight deadlines. Eduardo Bajzek, Tia Boon Sim, Simonetta Capecchi, Lynne Chapman, Víctor Martínez Escámez (a.k.a. Swasky), and Luis Ruiz provided invaluable help on the chapters featuring their cities. I shudder to think where I would be, personally and professionally, without Michelle Archer.

Special thanks to my editor, Mary Ann Hall, who helped shape what seemed an overwhelming number of drawings into the book you have in your hands now, copy editor Pat Price, art director Regina Grenier, book designer Luke Herriott, project manager Betsy Gammons and all the team at Quarry Books for this precious gift, which I hope will inspire generations of urban sketchers for years to come.

www.ingramcontent.com/pod-product-compliance
Lightning Source LLC
Chambersburg PA
CBHW041426030126
37280CB00004B/4